Yale Center for British Art, Paul Mellon Collection
THOMAS KING, as Lord Ogleby
by De Wilde

A BIOGRAPHICAL DICTIONARY

OF

ACTORS, ACTRESSES, MUSICIANS, DANCERS, MANAGERS & OTHER STAGE PERSONNEL IN LONDON, 1660–1800

Volume 9: Kickill *to* Machin

by

PHILIP H. HIGHFILL, JR., KALMAN A. BURNIM
and
EDWARD A. LANGHANS

SOUTHERN ILLINOIS UNIVERSITY PRESS
CARBONDALE AND EDWARDSVILLE

Copyright © 1984 by Southern Illinois University Press
All rights reserved
Printed in the United States of America
Edited by Beatrice Moore
Designed by Andor Braun and George Lenox

Publication of this work was made possible in part through a grant from the National Endowment for the Humanities

Library of Congress Cataloging in Publication Data
(Revised for volume 9)

Highfill, Philip H.
   A biographical dictionary of actors, actresses, musicians, dancers, managers & other stage personnel in London, 1660–1800.

   Includes bibliographical references.
   CONTENTS: v. 1. Abaco to Belfille.—v. 2. Belfort to Byzand.—[etc.]—v. 9. Kickill to Machin.
   1. Performing arts—England—London—Biography. I. Burnim, Kalman A., joint author. II. Langhans, Edward A., joint author. III. Title.
PN2597.H5   790.2'092'2 [B]   71–157068
ISBN 0–8093–1129–1 (v. 9)

List of Illustrations

MUSIC AND MUSICIANS

"The Chorus," by Hogarth, 1732	404
"The Music Master," c. 1733	405
A Satire on the English Admiration for Foreign Musicians, c. 1730	406
A Song by Richard Leveridge, 1744	407
Music by Lampe for *The Dragon of Wantley*	408
The 1784 Handel Memorial Concert at Westminster Abbey	409

Previously Published

Volume 1:	ABACO to BELFILLE
Volume 2:	BELFORT to BYZAND
Volume 3:	CABANEL to CORY
Volume 4:	CORYE to DYNION
Volume 5:	EAGAN to GARRETT
Volume 6:	GARRICK to GYNGELL
Volume 7:	HABGOOD to HOUBERT
Volume 8:	HOUGH to KEYSE

Volume 9
Kickill *to* Machin

Kickill, Mr [*fl.* 1762], *actor.*
Mr Kickill was a member of Samuel Foote's troupe at the Haymarket Theatre in the summer of 1762. He was a participant in *The Orators*, which opened on 1 May, but his name was not mentioned in other bills.

"Kiddy." *See* DAVIES, WILLIAM.

Kidman. *See* CADMAN.

Kidwell, William [*fl.* 1671–1675], *violinist.*
A warrant in the Lord Chamberlain's accounts dated 28 October 1671 made William Kidwell (or Kydwell) a musician in ordinary in the King's Musick, but without fee. He had to wait until a salaried post became vacant. The only other mention of Kidwell concerns his playing violin in the court masque *Calisto* on 15 February 1675.

Kilbourn, Master [*fl.* 1733–1734], *actor, singer.*
Master Kilbourn (or Kilburn) made his "first appearance on any stage" on 7 November 1733 at Drury Lane, playing Tom Thumb in *The Opera of Operas*. From 4 February through 2 March 1734 he was Cupid in *Cupid and Psyche*. Perhaps he was the son of the composer James Kilburn, who was active from 1721 to 1749.

Kilby, Miss [*fl.* 1736–1741], *actress, dancer.*
With a company of "Lilliputians," Miss Kilby played Lady Grace in *The Provok'd Husband* at the Haymarket Theatre on 29 June 1736. The bill said she was making her first appearance on any stage. (*The London Stage* lists a Miss Kilby as Kitty in *Flora* at Covent Garden on 27 September 1733 and subsequent dates, but that is clearly an error for Mrs Elizabeth Kilby, who later became the wife of William Havard.) According to Latreille, Miss Kilby's second appearance on any stage was on 26 April 1738, when she danced with Desse at Covent Garden. On 10 March 1739 she danced in the *Grand Ballet* which was a part of *Harlequin Shipwrecked*, then she appeared as one of the Graces and Juno in *Mars and Venus* and Mrs Coaxer in *The Beggar's Opera*. She also danced in *The Harlot's Progress*, performed a minuet with Leviez, and appeared in a solo chaconne. After the 1738–39 season her name dropped from the bills, but she remained one of the corps of dancers at Covent Garden, for the accounts list her in 1740–41 at a salary of 6s. 8d. daily.

Kilby, Elizabeth. *See* HAVARD, MRS WILLIAM.

Killigrew, Charles 1655–1725, *manager.*
Charles Killigrew, the eldest son of Thomas Killigrew and his second wife, Charlotte, was born at Maestricht on 29 December 1655. *The Dictionary of National Biography* has it that Charles was a gentleman of the King's privy chamber in 1670 and continued in that office into the reign of William and Mary in the 1690s. At first he probably held the post in name only, since in 1670 he was only 15 years old. On 27 June 1670 his father set up a trust which involved, among other things, the reversion of the governorship of the King's Company of actors to Charles when he came of age. Charles was not quite 20 when his father turned to him in an effort to settle dissension in the ranks of the players. Some of the sharing actors, finding that they were getting precious little profit from their shares, had threatened to cease acting and to leave the manager Thomas Killigrew with a total loss on his hands. Thomas asked Charles, in 1675 apparently, to serve as mediator and try to work out a new contract with the players. According to Leslie Hotson, who provides a great deal of information on theatrical finances in his *Commonwealth and Restoration Stage*, Charles agreed to give the actors Hart and Kynaston £100 and £60 respectively, and he persuaded them, along with Wintershall, Cartwright, Mohun, Lacy, Burt, and Shatterell, to cancel their former articles with Thomas Killigrew and enter into a new agreement. The new agreement of 1676 was favorable to the actors, and Hotson believes that Charles Killigrew engineered it for his father in return for assurance that Charles would receive the company patent and governorship.

He received nothing. Father and son squabbled, and the Lord Chamberlain settled matters by putting the actors Hart, Mohun, and Kynaston in charge of the company on 9 September 1676. Hart eventually took over as sole manager. On 22 February 1677 the law forced Thomas Killigrew to turn over his power and authority to Charles. Two days later Charles became Master of the Revels, replacing his father, and it is probable that the elder Killigrew gave up that post to his son for some monetary consideration. The younger Killigrew headed the Revels office until his death in 1725.

Charles had little experience in theatrical affairs, and the actors complained of his governorship to the Lord Chamberlain. On 30 July 1677 a warrant was issued allowing the actors to rule themselves, though Charles Killigrew was to continue receiving whatever sum he had been paid as "proprietor," and in the years that followed he was regularly named in official documents. In 1678, for instance, Charles Killigrew's name headed the list of people signing a petition against John Dryden for breaking his agreement with the King's Company to write them three plays yearly. The same year the company treasurer James Gray complained that, because of dissension among Killigrew, his half brother Henry, and other partners, playing was suspended. Gray joined other actors and went to Edinburgh but was lured back by the Killigrews, who offered to pay his traveling expenses; they assured him that the King's Company troubles were over. He returned in February 1680, but his traveling expenses were not reimbursed, and he was not reappointed treasurer until the middle of 1681.

In a Chancery suit that Gray brought against his masters he charged Charles Killigrew and the actor Shatterell (one of the company sharers) with secretly mortgaging the stock of the theatre—the costumes, scenery, and properties—to George Sayer, Thomas Sheppey, and Thomas Morley for £300. Charles Killigrew and Morley replied that they had neither asked Gray to come back from Scotland nor assured him of reimbursement for his expenses on the road, though they admitted mortgaging the company's stock to help pay debts. Henry Killigrew, though presumably on the management side, testified on Gray's behalf. The Lord Chamberlain found for Gray on 8 February 1684. Most of the evidence points to Charles having been a poor manager, and the troupe desperately needed good leadership in the late 1670s.

On 30 July 1680 Charles worked out a new agreement with the troupe, assuring their willingness to serve under his direction. The plan did not include the old actors Hart and Mohun, once the pillars of the company, who by 1680 seldom performed. A new sharing system was also set up, but the troupe was by then in such serious financial trouble that no rearrangements could save it. Killigrew in 1681 and 1682 fought a losing court battle over the Killigrew theatrical property—the shares, the patent, and the governorship of the company. It was finally decreed on 14 December 1682 that it all belonged to Richard Kent's trustees. Indeed, part of the problem was the fact that whatever profits the company made in the late 1670s were going to Kent, to whom old Thomas Killigrew had mortgaged his nine shares in the theatre building. It was found in February 1681 that the company income was less than the outlay, yet the company struggled on for another season, acting intermittently.

About April or May of 1682 negotiations began between London's two acting troupes for the absorption of the faltering Killigrew band by the Duke's Company. William Smith of the Duke's players testified that Charles Killigrew "in great despondency of making any advantage Suitable to the charge of their future acting" saw that the Duke's Company was prospering and "applied himself not only to the said Charles Davenant but likewise to Thomas Betterton Gent . . . and to this Defendant" and proposed a union.

On 4 May, according to Hotson, the following general agreement was reached: the companies would unite, all plays to be given under the joint governorship of Charles Davenant and Charles Killigrew; the King's Company would be dissolved within six days and its stock delivered to Davenant; Charles Killigrew would be paid £3 for each acting day at either Drury Lane or the Duke's Company playhouse in Dorset Garden once Drury Lane was handed over to Davenant; and acting profits would be divided into 20 shares, with Killigrew getting three. Killigrew worked out a favorable situation for himself, but he negotiated without the consent of the King's Company owners (the trustees of Kent) who held legal control of the troupe. Killigrew had virtually no power in his own right, but the Duke's Company must not have known that. Two weeks after Killigrew dissolved the King's Company, the actor Philip Griffin sued him for usurpation of powers. Drury Lane was leased to Charles Davenant for 19 years beginning on 9 November 1682.

Killigrew battled in court to see who actually held control of the King's Company interests. After losing that litigation to Kent's trustees, Killigrew spent the years between 1683 and 1693 wrangling with the Davenants over his share in the new United Company.

Though Charles Killigrew's name appeared frequently in the Lord Chamberlain's accounts in connection with United Company business, his involvement probably lessened with the years, and the Davenants doubtless did most of the decision-making until the wily lawyer Christopher Rich gained control of the troupe. In any case, the participation of Killigrew and of the Davenants was chiefly financial and had little to do with theatrical problems. Decisions concerning casting, scenes and machines, repertory, and the daily business of operating the company devolved upon the leading actors, especially Thomas Betterton.

Killigrew may well have turned more and more of his attention to the office of Master of the Revels, a post which he apparently occupied with some seriousness. He had been especially concerned with the entertainers who turned up at the late summer fairs and performed without licenses. Morley in his *Memoirs of Bartholomew Fair* quotes a typical newspaper notice, in the London *Gazette* of 13–17 April 1682:

Whereas, Mr. John Clarke, of London, bookseller, did rent of Charles Killigrew, Esq., the licensing of all Ballad Singers for five years; which time expired at Lady-day last: these are, therefore, to give notice to all Ballad Singers that they take out Licences at the Office of the Revels at *Whitehall*, for Singing and Selling of Ballads, and small Books, according to an ancient Custom. And all persons concerned, are hereby desired to take notice of, and to suppress all Mountebanks, Rope-Dancers, Prize-Players, Ballad-Singers, and such as make shew of Motions and strange Sights, that have not a Licence in Red and Black Letters, under the Hand and Seal of the said Charles Killigrew, Esq., Master of the Revels to His Majesty; and, in particular, to suppress one Mr. Irish, Mr. Thomas Varley, and Mr. Thomas Yates, Mountebank, who have no Licence, that they may be proceeded against, according to Law.

In the preface to her play *The Lucky Chance* (1687) Aphra Behn wrote that Killigrew's censorship was "more severe than any, from the strict Order he had, [and he] perus'd it with great Circumspection."

Killigrew lived at Somerset House; with the accession of William and Mary his post as Master of the Revels was renewed and so, too, was it necessary for all the "stageplayers, Mountebanks, Rope-Dancers" and other entertainers of any kind whatsoever to renew their licenses with him, their previous licenses "being void," as a printed notice of 1688 announced. At the same time, the Lord Chamberlain's accounts show that Killigrew, at least in name, was regularly involved in United Company cases— payments for plays acted before royalty, a ruling to deduct from the actor Freeman's salary a sum to pay one of his creditors, an order to receive Mrs Corey back into the company.

As early as 1692 some of the actors had sought redress from Charles Killigrew and Thomas Davenant for reductions in their salaries caused by low company income. But that familiar-sounding complaint was nothing compared to the series of charges and countercharges that came in 1693 and 1694 and led to the split in the United Company. In December 1693 Rich and his partner Skipwith told Charles Killigrew, Betterton, and others that they had allowed Alexander Davenant to farm out their shares. Rich pretended to divide the direction of the company with Killigrew, though in fact he arrogated all the power to himself, very likely because Killigrew was not on the spot to prevent him. The list of complaints presented by Betterton and his rebel actors of necessity named Killigrew at many points, but usually in connection with agreements made when the United Company was formed in 1682 and not with problems that had developed since then. The villains of the piece were clearly Christopher Rich and the slippery Alexander Davenant.

With the split in the United Company Charles Killigrew appears to have lost his interest, financial and otherwise, in the theatrical companies, though he continued to exercise his authority as Master of the Revels and censor of plays. On 9 November 1701 the lease on Drury Lane expired, and Charles joined an attempt to gain control from Christopher Rich. He went to Betterton and his rebel troupe at the rival Lincoln's Inn Fields playhouse and sought the support of the building investors of

Drury Lane. Rich held firm, possession being nine-tenths of the law, and his rivals were not able to persuade the building investors to come to a new agreement that would exclude Rich. Killigrew seems then to have given up any attempts at theatre management.

As Master of the Revels Killigrew rode roughshod over some of the plays he read. Colley Cibber gave an instance in connection with his 1699 version of *Richard III*. Killigrew, said Cibber, "assisted this Reformation with a more zealous Severity than ever. He would strike out whole Scenes of a vicious or immoral Character, tho' it were visibly shewn to be reform'd or punish'd." Killigrew "expung'd the whole first Act without sparing a Line of it." When Cibber begged Killigrew to leave a few lines so that the other four acts might make better sense, "no! he had not leisure to consider what might be separately inoffensive." Even years later, in 1714–15, when Cibber was a patentee at Drury Lane and the managers did the censoring, Killigrew, by "custom," still claimed his 40*s*. fee for every new play, whether he read it or not. That practice was then abandoned, and Killigrew received no fees for plays that had been censored by Cibber and others. It is difficult to understand how over so many years Killigrew was permitted, as his father had been before him, to serve as Master of the Revels and continue to hold an interest in a particular theatre, but he did. He was cited as a shareholder in Drury Lane at least as late as 1709.

Charles Killigrew had married Jemima (surname not known) the niece of Richard Bokenham, mercer, of London, according to *The Dictionary of National Biography*. The registers of St Mary-le-Strand reveal some family history. Elizabeth Killigrew, daughter of Charles (no wife mentioned), was born at Somerset House on 26 February 1689 and christened at St Mary's on 1 March; Jemina (*sic*) Killigrew, daughter of Charles and Jemina (*sic*) was christened on 3 August 1692. George "Killeegrew" from Somerset House was buried on 21 April 1690; he must have been related in some way, judging by the address, and so, too, must have been "Elasabeth" Killigrew, who was buried on 23 May 1690. She perhaps was Charles Killigrew's sister. Thomas Killigrew, son of Charles and Jemima, was christened on 23 February 1694; he, we would guess, was the Thomas Killigrew who wrote the play *Chit-Chat* in 1719. Jemima Killigrew (the first child Jemima having died, evidently), daughter of Charles and Jemima, was christened on 25 December 1696, and "Gillford" Killigrew, son of Charles and Jemima, was christened on 31 March 1701. The registers of St Mary-le-Strand also contain the records of the burial of Ann Killigrew on 23 January 1699 and of Dr Henry Killigrew on 19 March 1700, as well as the burial of Charles Killigrew's mother Charlotte on 22 April 1715. Further, a Henry Killigrew had been buried there on 28 January 1660.

Charles Killigrew was buried in the Savoy on 8 January 1725. He had written his will on 30 May 1723. He left £10 to the poor of his parish. To his wife Jemima he bequeathed his plate and household goods at Thornham Hall, Suffolk, until her death or remarriage. He left her £20 for mourning. The residuary legatee was his son Charles. Young Charles was also to receive the lease of his father's houses in Scotland Yard (which indicates that those houses, originally owned by Thomas Killigrew the elder and bequeathed at his death in 1683 to his son Henry, had in time reverted to Charles Killigrew), his rights and interest in Drury Lane Theatre (Charles must still have held some building shares), and his goods and chattels at Somerset House except his "Study of books," which he desired to be sold. (The *DNB* states that Killigrew's library was sold in December 1725). To his son Guilford and his heirs Killigrew left property in Landersville and Bray in South Morton, Berkshire. To Guilford and Charles he left £20 each for mourning and his stock in the South Sea Company, share and share alike. Guilford was to receive Killigrew's stock in the African Company and his two houses in Bell Inn Court. To his cousin Brigadier General Sayer, who was in 1723 at the Hague, Killigrew left whatever right and title he held "to any Estate more." He left £200 to Mrs Catherine de la Froce of Gerard Street, St Ann, Westminster (now Soho), and discharged all her debts to him. The residue of the estate was to go to Killigrew's sons Charles and Guilford. The will was proved on 4 January 1725, four days before his burial.

Jemima Killigrew made her will on 19 January 1727(8?) at Thornham Hall, where she evidently retired after her husband's death. She bequeathed to her son Charles not only Thornham Hall but Stoke Hall, Swats Hall nearby, and other property in Thornham. The condition on which she left Charles those properties was that he should rear and educate Jemima Frost, daughter of William Frost of Thornham Magna to the age of 21, and then give her £400 in cash. Her son Guilford was to receive £5. She left other bequests to godchildren, servants, the poor of various parishes near her, and Ann Warn, a poor child, the daughter of Robert Warn, to whom she left £100. Her will was proved on 4 July 1731.

Killigrew, Henry *1637–1705, proprietor.*

Henry Killigrew was born on 9 April 1637, the son of Thomas Killigrew and his first wife, Cecilia, née Crofts. He was christened at St Martin-in-the-Fields on the sixteenth. Little is known of his early years, but he seems to have been brought up in England during the Commonwealth; his mother died on 1 January 1638, and his father spent most of the 1640s and 1650s on the Continent. In the late 1650s Henry went to the Continent; by that time his father had remarried, and Harbage in his biography of the elder Killigrew guesses that Thomas may have procured Henry a post as groom of the bedchamber to the Duke of York in 1656. In July 1660, according to John Harold Wilson's *Court Wits*, young Harry Killigrew fought a duel in Heidelberg. By 1661 he was back in England, serving as page of honor to Charles II, and the following year he was appointed (or reappointed) groom of the bedchamber to the Duke of York and married Lady Mary Savage, sister-in-law of Sir Charles Sedley.

A romanticized and disorganized version of Henry's escapades can be found in Anthony Hamilton's *Memoires du Comte de Grammont*, but a clearer and more accurate account was told, bit by bit, by Samuel Pepys in his diary and Charles II in his letters to his sister. Pepys went to Moorfield to see a puppet show on 1 September 1666 and was "there horribly frighted to see Young Killigrew come in with a great many more young sparks; but we hid ourselves, so as we think they did not see us. By and by they went away, and then we were at rest again." A month and a half later, on 21 October 1666, Pepys picked up the latest court gossip from Sir Hugh Cholmley: "how Harry Killigrew is banished the Court lately, for saying that my Lady Castlemayne was a little lecherous girl when she was young, and used to rub her thing with her fingers or against the end of forms, and that she must be rubbed with something else. This she complained to the King of, and he sent to the Duke of York, whose servant he is, to turn him away. The Duke of York hath done it."

On 20 July 1667 at the Lincoln's Inn Fields playhouse there was a scuffle involving our hero:

[Creed] tells me [wrote Pepys on 22 July] of the Fray between the Duke of Buckingham at the Duke's playhouse last Saturday . . . and Henry Killigrew; whom the Duke of Buckingham did soundly beat and take away his sword and make a fool of, till the fellow prayed him to spare his life. And I am glad of it, for it seems in this business the Duke of Buckingham did carry himself very innocently and well.

Pepys was not alone in his disgust for Killigrew's behavior; the King wrote to his sister, the Duchess of Orleans, on 10 March 1668:

My L^d of Buckingham is as affraide, that you should thinke that he is the cause that Killigrew does not return hither [i.e. to court] since you have desired him to forgive what is past, as he has again desired me to tell you, there is nothing of what relates to him in the case; as in truth there is not, but he has offended so many of the Ladyes relations in what concerns her, as it would not be convenient for him to shew his face heere. The truth is, both for his owne sake and oure quiett heere, it will be no inconvenience for him to have a little pacience in other countries.

The King noted in a letter to his sister on 17 October 1668:

For Harry Killigrew, you may see him as you please, and though I cannot commende my Lady Shrewbury's conduct in many things, yett Mr. Killigrew's carriage towards her has been worse than I will repeate, and for his *demelé* with my Lord of Buckingham he ought not to brag of, for it was in all sorts most abominable. I am glad the poor wrech has gott a meanes of subsistence, but have one caution of him, that you beleeve not one word he sayes of us heere, for he is a most notorious lyar and does not want witt to sett forth storyes plesantly enough.

On 30 May 1668 Pepys, his friend Rolt, and the actor Henry Harris went up the river to the pleasure garden at Vauxhall, or, as Pepys spelled it, "Fox Hall":

and there fell into the company of Harry Killigrew, a rogue newly come back out of France, but still in disgrace at our Court, and young Newport and others, as very rogues as any in the town, who were ready to take hold of every woman that come by them. And so to supper in an arbour: but Lord! their mad bawdy talk did make my heart ake! And here I first understood by their talk the meaning of the company that lately were called Ballers; Harris telling how it was by a meeting of some young blades, where he was among them, and my Lady Bennet [the procuress] and her ladies and their dancing naked, and all the roguish things in the world. But, Lord! what loose cursed company was this, that I was in to-night, though full of wit; and worth a man's being in for once, to know the nature of it, and their manner of talk, and lives.

Killigrew bounced back and forth between France and England a number of times in 1667 and 1668. The Fleming manuscripts in the Historical Manuscript Commission reports reveal that Henry was sent to the Tower on 20 July 1667 for his quarrel with the Duke of Buckingham and then fled to France; by 30 May 1668 he was back in England, but by the following October he was again in France. In April 1669, in London, Christopher Chapman sued him for a debt.

His most notorious escapade came in 1669 and involved Lady Shrewsbury, his mistress. On 19 May Pepys wrote:

Here the news was first talked of Harry Killigrew's being wounded in nine places last night, by footmen, in the highway, going from the Park in a hackney-coach towards Hammersmith, to his house at Turnham Greene: they being supposed to be my Lady Shrewsbury's men, she being by, in her coach with six horses; upon an old grudge of his saying openly that he had lain with her.

On the afternoon of 19 May, the day after Killigrew had been skewered by Lady Shrewsbury's footmen, Pepys wrote,

In discourse this afternoon, the Duke of York did tell me that he was the most amazed at one thing just now, that ever he was in his life, which was, that the Duke of Buckingham did just now come into the Queen's bed-chamber, where the King was, and much mixed company, and among others, Tom Killigrew, the father of Harry, who was last night wounded so as to be in danger of death, and his man is quite dead; and [Buckingham] there in discourse did say that he had spoke with some one that was by (which all in the world must know that it must be his whore, my Lady Shrewsbury), who says that they did not mean to hurt, but to beat him, and that he did run first at them with his sword; so that he do hereby clearly discover that he knows who did it, and is of conspiracy with them, being of known conspiracy with her, which the Duke of York did seem to be pleased with.

By 30 September 1669 Killigrew had made his peace with Buckingham and Lady Shrewsbury and was again in favor at court, though the Lord Chamberlain's accounts show that he had not made peace with some creditors in 1672 and 1674. Just as he bounced back and forth between England and France, so he bounced back and forth between service with the King and service with the Duke of York. By 22 October 1674 he was again groom of the bedchamber to the King. On 8 February 1677 Killigrew's servant was stabbed in a room next to the King's chamber, and Harry was suspected of the crime. The following 29 October Killigrew's wife died. On 1 November 1677, in a letter to the Earl of Rochester, Savile said "Harry Killegrew has been a widdower these two dayes and laments his condition that fortune has made it possible for him to play the fool again, considering what use hee is wont to make of the power of committing errours, besides human frailty in generall." On 11 December he was again banished from the court for insulting Nell Gwynn.

After that contemporary sources do not mention Killigrew's misdeeds so frequently, perhaps because he turned his attention to the Killigrew theatrical properties, which at that time had devolved upon his half-brother Charles. Their father Thomas had by 1678 mortgaged most of what he had once held—the patent for the King's Company and his shares in the building and the acting company—so that when Charles Killigrew became governor of the King's players in his father's place, the Killigrew holdings did not lie in Killigrew hands, and the general health of the King's Company was precarious. What the troupe needed was a good leader, and Charles Killigrew turned out to be a poor one. It certainly could not have helped much to have the bright, witty, ne'er-do-well Henry participating in company affairs as well.

Harry was Thomas Killigrew's eldest son and heir, so his name had begun figuring in the history of the King's Company quite early. On 4 July 1662 Thomas Killigrew granted £4 weekly to Henry for life, the sum to come from the elder Killigrew's two shares in the acting company. For some unknown consideration, shortly after that, says Hotson, Henry made over his £4 weekly to Thomas Porter for life, and Porter sold it to Sir John Sayer and his wife for £600. Years later, on 27 June 1670, Thomas Killigrew set up a trust for Dame Sayer (by that time a widow); in the process of doing so he arranged for the £4 weekly which the Sayer family then enjoyed to remain theirs during Henry Killigrew's life, after which it was to go to Henry's son and heir, James Killigrew.

When Charles Killigrew came into the governorship of the King's Company in 1677 he mismanaged things by himself for a while and in 1678 was joined (willingly or unwillingly we do not know) by Harry Killigrew. That year the two Killigrews plus five others, mostly actors, were listed as "Master Partners or sharers" in the troupe. The situation within the King's Company deteriorated steadily in the late 1670s. There was dissension, said the treasurer James Gray in a court case later, between Henry and Charles Killigrew and other partners; playing ceased temporarily and a few of the members of the company (including Gray) went off to Edinburgh. Some of the company stock of costumes and properties was mortgaged to pay bills, and the rival Duke's Company began making overtures to two King's Company actors to help bring about the dissolution of the King's troupe and the formation of a joint company. In one of the court cases which developed out of the King's Company troubles, involving the mortgaging of the company stock, Henry Killigrew sided against his half-brother. In another case the actor Edward Kynaston in 1696, long after the event, charged Henry Killigrew with having joined with the actor William Wintershall in absconding with the company stock of books, costumes, and apparel.

In 1682 the Duke's Company and the King's Company were united, or, more accurately, the former absorbed the latter. The Killigrew family interests in the theatre by that time were in the hands of Richard Kent and his trustees, to whom Thomas Killigrew had mortgaged them for ready money. After Thomas died in 1683 Henry Killigrew, his heir, sued his half brother Charles along with Richard Kent, accusing the two of having connived to gain control over the Killigrew theatrical interests. Harry Killigrew seems not to have gotten very far with that case, though not all the details of the outcome have come to light. He remained at least partly involved with the affairs of the new United Company, however, and in 1689 made an apparently unsuccessful attempt to lure some of the players—Mrs Corey (who was hired by Harry in the first place), Leigh, Nokes, and Mountfort—away from the company to act under his governorship. The last notice of Harry Killigrew in connection with the theatre dates from 30 January 1693, when, according to Luttrell, a Mr Chamberlain fought a duel with "Mr. Killigrew of the playhouse."

How long Henry was supported by the crown is not certain, but payments to him of gifts and bounties amounting to sometimes £400 annually, are recorded regularly from as early as 22 October 1679, in the reign of Charles II, to 2 October 1688, under James II. Under William III, Killigrew in July 1694 was made a member of the Commission to regulate hackney coaches, and the following November he was appointed jester to the King, a post his father had held under Charles II. But he was still a difficult person to get along with, apparently, for he has turned out of the hackney commission in May 1695. Yet Henry Savile in a letter to Killigrew had addressed him, according to Wilson's *Court Wits*, as "sweet namesake of mine, happy-humoured Killigrew soul of mirth and all delight." Harbage indicates that Henry Killigrew died in 1705. He was, perhaps, the Henry Killigrew who was buried at St Martin-in-the-Fields on 16 December that year. Thomas Killigrew had been a member of that parish for some time, though after his death most of the Killigrews belonged to St Mary-le-Strand, because Charles lived in Somerset House.

Killigrew, Thomas *1612–1683, proprietor, playwright, actor.*

Thomas Killigrew was born in Lothbury, London, on 7 February 1612 and was christened at St Margaret, Lothbury, on the twentieth. His parents were Sir Robert Killigrew and his wife, the former Mary Woodhouse, daughter of Sir Henry Woodhouse of Waxham, Suffolk. Thomas was Sir Robert and Lady Mary's fourth son; the couple had a total of 12 chil-

KILLIGREW

National Portrait Gallery

THOMAS KILLIGREW
after Van Dyck

dren, of whom five sons and four daughters lived to maturity. A son Charles died before he was 23 and a son Robert matriculated at Oxford—but little more is known of either of them. The other seven all developed connections at court: Anne waited on Queen Henrietta Maria, Katherine was a maid of honor to the Princess Royal of Orange, Mary became the wife of the courtier Sir John James, Elizabeth was a maid of honor to Queen Henrietta Maria and bore the second natural child of Charles II (Charlotte Jemima Henrietta Maria) while married to Francis Boyle (later Lord Shannon), William was knighted by Charles I and helped guard the King during the civil wars, Henry received a doctor of divinity degree from Oxford and accompanied the Duke of York in exile, and Thomas, our subject, became the manager of the King's Company of players and served as jester to Charles II.

The family spent much of their time at Hanworth, an estate near Hampton Court which Queen Elizabeth had given to Thomas's grandfather, Sir William Killigrew. By Sir Robert Killigrew's time Hanworth had become a luxurious but expensive place to live, and the family had some difficulty in maintaining it. The Killigrews from time to time resided in their rented house in London, where Thomas was born. Samuel Pepys many years later heard from Sir John Mennis that as a boy Tom Killigrew "would go to the Red Bull [Theatre], and when the man cried to the boys, 'Who will go and be a devil, and he shall see the play for nothing?' then would he go in and be a devil upon the stage, and so get to see plays." The playhouse was about a half-hour walk from the Killigrew town house.

Tom should have been getting a proper education, but his father tended to neglect him, and as a result, as Anthony à Wood wrote, Killigrew was "not educated at any university (and therefore wanted some learning to poise his excellent natural parts) but in the royal court, where he was page of honour to king Charles I." Others commented on his lack of formal education, but William Cartwright the playwright thought it rather a good thing:

*You have not what diverts some Men from sense,
Those two Mysterious things, Greeke and Pretence.*

Later, Tom did not mind calling himself an "illiterate Courtier" in the epilogue to one of his plays, *The Parson's Wedding*. His jottings in his family Bible, as Alfred Harbage points out in his helpful biography of Killigrew, reveal an orthography erratic well beyond what was typical in his day.

But Tom probably received a grammar school education, and his plays show that he read not widely but well. He learned some French, stumbled along in Italian, and liked music without being able to practice it. Harbage quotes a delicious example of Killigrew's orthography, courtly style, in a letter written in 1636 to Lord Feilding:

I will not be faltey of so much vanetey as to belief I chan desserfe such a sevilletey as your lettar brought . . . but though it be not in my powr to desserfe, yet grattitude is myne as freiley to bestoe as obligastianes yourres, and with that coyne, if it be currant in Vennis, I dare hope to pay sum of your sevilletes backe.

He probably learned that elegant style, if not the wayward spelling, at the court of Charles I, where he was employed perhaps as early as 1625 as a page at £100 annually, and there he received an apprenticeship as a courtier that stood him in good stead in later years.

Thomas's father died in 1633, just when Tom came of age. Sir Robert left him 100 acres of land in Lincolnshire and a part interest in a Cornish manor which probably was not very valuable. One of the ways a young courtier in those days could increase his income was by petitioning the King for a benefit from a confiscated estate. In September 1633 Killigrew and David Ramsey begged the estate of Francis Smith, who had recently been convicted as a dangerous Jesuit. In 1636 Tom and another courtier were given the property of Francis Lockwood, who had died a Catholic priest. In that manner Killigrew managed to bolster his income in order to live a more courtly life, and Charles I seems to have been willing to grant most of his petitions. Killigrew also gained some favor with Queen Henrietta Maria, who shared his interest in plays.

Killigrew's first play, *The Prisoners*, was written by 1635. That year Walter Montague, author of *The Shepherd's Paradise*, in which the Queen had performed at court in 1632, returned from the Continent, and when he went back he took Thomas Killigrew with him. Montague's destination was Rome, but he and his entourage made something of a grand tour. They went to Calais, then on to Paris, Tours, Orleans, and Loudon, spending in all about two months in France. Then they journeyed to Basle and on to Vercelli by 17 January 1636. Finally they arrived in Rome, and there and in Naples Killigrew spent most of the winter. By the summer of 1636 Tom was again in England, where on 26 June he married Cecilia Crofts, a maid of honor to Queen Henrietta Maria, at whose house at Oatland the wedding took place.

Cecilia was the daughter of Sir John Crofts of Saxham, Suffolk, and his wife Mary, the daughter of Sir Thomas Shirley. The marriage was a happy but short one. Killigrew's own entries in his family Bible tell the bare facts:

I was maried to my First wife Ms Cissillia Croftes of Saxsame in Suffolke at Otlands apone Sant Peiteres day being the 29 of Juene 1636. Tho Killigrew

My Sueene Harrey Killigrew was borrn apoen Esterday following being the 9 of Aprill and Sunday 1637. Tho. Killigrew

My wife died apoen Nue Yeares day after being the 1 of Januarey and apone a Monday 16$^{37}/_{38}$ nue stiell in London and lies berried in Westminster Abbey. Tho. Killigrew [The burial was on 5 January.]

His marriage and the blessing put upon it by the Queen set Killigrew firmly in favor at court. Sometime after his return to England *The Prisoners* and *Claricilla* were produced at the Phoenix Theatre, and even though he made no pretensions to a poet's rank, his prose plays established him as a successful author and he was accepted in literary as well as courtly circles. Those two works were published in 1641.

Sometime after his wife's death Tom Killigrew became more rakish in his behavior, as evidenced, perhaps, by *The Parson's Wedding* (c. 1637–1642), which was much lower in tone than his previous works and clearly written for a popular rather than courtly audience. He lived beyond his means, though his annual stipend in 1637 had risen only to £150. Whitehall had been his home until 1636, after which he had lodgings with his wife and then lived as a widower at No 8, the Great Piazza of Covent Garden, until at least 1640, though in 1639 and 1640 he traveled to France and Switzerland. When the civil war broke out he remained loyal to the King, of course, and in late 1641 served as something like a courier. The Commons summoned him before the house on 26 February 1642 for his royalist activity, and within a few months Killigrew was kept from serving the King. Creditors were after him, for on 16 May 1643 he asked Parliament for protection against them; the House of Lords voided suits against him as long as he remained a prisoner, though not incarcerated. On 27 July he was exchanged for another prisoner and allowed to join his royalist friends. After that he seems to have left England. Harbage believes that he may have gone with Queen Henrietta Maria to France in 1644, though there is no certain evidence of his whereabouts until 1647.

Prince Charles, later Charles II, sent Killigrew to Italy by an order dated 20 April 1647, to borrow money for the Prince and the royalist cause. By March 1648 Tom was again in France, having been successful in procuring funds in Italy. He went into the service of the Duke of York and by May 1648 was at the Hague. After Prince Charles was proclaimed King of England, on 5 January 1649, following his father's death, Killigrew changed his service from the Duke of York to the King's household in Paris. Killigrew was sent to Italy as envoy to the Savoy and Florence and as Resident at Venice, by an order dated 1 May 1649. He had arrived in Turin by 12 November, received a favorable reception, and then went on to Genoa, Leghorn, Pisa, and Florence. In Florence he was to borrow, if he could, 10,000 pistoles for Charles II, but the Medicis were not receptive, for they were reluctant to antagonize the Cromwell government by taking sides.

Killigrew was in Venice by 14 February 1650 and settled there for over two years, accomplishing very little in the way of gaining support for Charles II. Though he busied himself with testimonials and pleas, he was seldom answered by the Venetian Senate, and he had the time to write two two-part plays, *Cicilia and Clorinda* and *Bellamira Her Dream*, romances not suited for or even intended for stage production.

His enemies accused Killigrew of vicious behavior while he was in Venice, though Harbage feels that the evidence shows Killigrew to have behaved well enough and certainly less viciously than some of the Venetians of the time. He ran into trouble with the Senate in June 1651 when he countenanced smuggling on the part of some of his servants. When in September 1651 the royalist army in England was routed at Worcester the cause of Charles II looked very weak to the Venetians, and accordingly, on 20 June 1652, the Senate moved to have Killigrew dismissed as Resident because of his customs evasions. Killigrew was recalled by the King at that point, so he would have left Venice anyway, but it was a blow to him to leave under a cloud, and an embarrassment to see the English representative in Venice appointed from the Commonwealth rather than from King Charles.

He went to the Hague, to be greeted by a lampoon by John Denham:

> Our Resident Tom,
> From Venice is come,
>   And hath left the Statesman behind him:
> Talks at the same pitch
> Is as wise, is as rich,
>   And just where you left him you find him.
>
> But who says he was not
> A man of much Plot

> May repent that false Accusation;
> Having plotted and penn'd
> Six Plays to attend
>   The Farce of his Negotiation.

A reconciliation with the King was effected by 1653, perhaps indicating that Killigrew's dismissal from Venice had been at least partly trumped up and that Killigrew's behavior had not been unduly bad.

Tom entered the service of the Duke of Gloucester and by May 1653 was in Paris, where the Duke joined Queen Henrietta Maria. There, about 1654 (or possibly in Madrid, where he may have been sent to raise money), he wrote his last play, *Thomaso, or the Wanderer*, a two-part comedy laced with autobiographical references, but not a work for the stage. By September 1654 Killigrew had become a part of the King's household once more, an indication that despite having alienated some royalists, especially Chancellor Hyde, Killigrew was favored by the King—and that was all that mattered. In 1654 he courted Charlotte de Hesse, a Dutch woman who was heiress to £10,000. The couple were married on 28 January 1655 at the Hague. She was 17 years younger than Killigrew, and in *Thomaso* the author has the hero say,

A gray Wanderer is but a bad Tragedy to himself, though an old Beggar may be a comedy to others: These thoughts, and the noble nature of this vertuous Maid, have made me resolve to abjure this humour; and having bid farewel to all the follies of my youth vow my whole thoughts to the friendship of the fair Serulina, a maid, whose Dower and Beauty may satisfie.

Through the offices of the Queen of Bohemia (the aunt of Charles II), Killigrew received a command appointment, though his work was not as a military man but as a courtier. Killigrew settled in Maestricht and was given, apparently, the rights of Dutch citizenship. In December 1655 his son Charles was born.

By the time Charles II returned to England in 1660 Killigrew was firmly established in the King's circle of courtiers and was considered, as Pepys wrote on 24 May, "a merry droll, but a gentleman of great esteem with the King." Most of the courtiers who came back with the King petitioned for favors; Killigrew, as Harbage points out, asked to be keeper of the armory at Greenwich, to be allowed to appoint officers of excise in Munster, to be given £1200 worth of white plate that had belonged to Oliver Cromwell, and so on. Being in favor with the King, Killigrew was awarded £500 annually as a groom of the bedchamber, another £400 for having served Charles I, and later was given the Mastership of the Revels, worth £200 yearly. What with other stipends and gifts and his old practice of begging estates, Harbage estimates, Killigrew must have had a yearly income of £2000. Nevertheless, he was almost constantly in debt, and the theatrical company that he headed during the Restoration period ended up in similar financial difficulties, partly if not mostly due to Killigrew's financial mismanagement.

With the return of the monarchy, theatrical activity in London, which had been officially banned for 18 years (though there were a number of surreptitious performances), began again. Two courtiers, Thomas Killigrew and Sir William Davenant, were granted patents by Charles II that gave them a virtual theatrical monopoly. Davenant had received a patent from Charles I in 1639 but had never used it. On 9 July 1660 Killigrew received a similar one. Under their patents Davenant and Killigrew were given permission to form two companies of players, build theatres, produce "tragydies, comedyes, playes, operas, and all other entertainments of that nature," set their own admission fees and employee salaries, serve as licensers of the plays they presented, and put down anyone else who tried to perform in London. By 21 July 1660 the monopoly was official, though the Master of the Revels Sir Henry Herbert (whose post Killigrew had been promised) kept up a running battle with the new patent holders to retrieve some of the powers they were usurping.

Killigrew was evidently given both first choice of patrons and first choice of actors. He chose the King on the one hand and mostly older players with pre-Commonwealth experience on the other; Davenant had the Duke of York as his company's patron and mostly younger performers who had to be trained from scratch. As things turned out, Davenant had the stronger company, and with his greater knowledge of the inner workings of repertory companies the Duke's players ultimately proved to be superior to the King's, and by 1682 the former absorbed the latter.

Before the two new troupes were established and had begun performing under their patents in November 1660, there was a fluid period of several months, during which there was theatrical activity taking place at the Red Bull, at the Cockpit in Drury Lane, and at Salisbury Court, all relics of earlier days. It is significant that neither Killigrew nor Davenant chose to remain in one of the old playhouses; each ultimately chose a tiny tennis court and converted it. Killigrew took Gibbons's tennis court in Vere Street, Clare Market, and fixed it up in something like the Elizabethan manner, that is, without the changeable wings, shutters, and borders that had been features of the earlier English court theatre but not of the public playhouses. Davenant chose Lisle's tennis court in Lincoln's Inn Fields and fitted his little playhouse with scenes and machines. Within three years Killigrew and the King's Company had a new theatre, the first one built on the site of the present Drury Lane Theatre, complete with scenes and machines. There was a period of three years, however, when Killigrew was following something like the public theatre staging tradition of earlier days. But it was Davenant's scenes and machines that pleased the elite patrons, as might be expected. We have no way of knowing if Killigrew actually hoped to revive a staging tradition similar to that of the public theatres of Shakespeare's day; he may simply have chosen a sceneryless theatre in order to save money and provide for the early erection of a new playhouse.

The King's Company began acting on 5 November 1600 at the old Red Bull; by the eighth Killigrew had moved to his converted tennis court in Vere Street. If Davenant was able to organize his company and begin operations by 5 November, the records do not show it; the Duke's Company may have begun performing at Salisbury Court by 15 November, but not until early 1661 do the existing records show a real competition between the two companies, and not until 28 June 1661 did Davenant have his theatre in Lincoln's Inn Fields ready for productions featuring scenery. For virtually one full season Killigrew and the King's Company had the best of it and performed much of the time against little competition. Given that, and the fact that Killigrew had a nucleus of experienced players—Charles Hart, Michael Mohun, John Lacy, Nicholas Burt, Walter Clun, and others—and what should have been a strong repertory of old plays—a number of pieces by Beaumont, Fletcher, Shirley, Jonson, and Shakespeare—one would expect to hear that the King's troupe acted their rivals off the boards and forced them out of business. It did not work that way, and Killigrew and his company must have blundered badly during their first season to have lost such a golden opportunity.

Surely part of the problem was Killigrew himself. Though he had written some plays, he was really a closet dramatist; he had been interested in theatre, but he had spent precious little time putting on plays. His rival Davenant, on the other hand, had by 1660 a considerable professional background in theatre, and that may have made the difference.

Sir Henry Herbert tried everything in his power to gain more control over the activities of Killigrew and Davenant, suing them jointly in Trinity term 1661 for performances in October 1660 and suing Davenant alone in 1662 for performances in 1660 and 1661. What Herbert wanted, as much as control, was money; he was due fees from the two managers for their performances; otherwise, in his view, they were performing illegally. On 4 June 1662 Killigrew agreed to pay Herbert his arrears in fees since 11 August 1660, plus legal expenses, and £50. Killigrew, rather underhandedly, agreed to help Herbert reestablish the power of the Revels Office (which Killigrew hoped to inherit)—a blow against Davenant.

Killigrew had already busied himself (or his company had) with plans for a new playhouse, the first to be built from the ground up after the Restoration. A lease was signed on 20 December 1661 with the Duke of Bedford for a plot of ground in Bridges Street. Signing with Killigrew were the actors Hart, Burt, Lacy, Mohun, Robert Shatterall, Clun, Cartwright, and Wintershall, as well as Sir Robert Howard. The party of the third part consisted of William Hewett and Robert Clayton. Those two were given the lease in trust for the others for a period of 41 years. On the site the King's Company agreed to build a playhouse for £1500 before Christmas 1662 and to pay an annual ground rent of £50.

On 28 January 1662, a month after the original lease was made, Hewett and Clayton made over the property to the building sharers. There were 36 shares in the building, of which Howard had nine, Killigrew nine, Lacy four, and the other actors two each. By the time the new theatre was completed it had cost £2400, and it did not open until 7 May 1663. The rival Duke's Company did not try to erect a new theatre until 1671.

While all that was going on, Killigrew and Davenant got together, on 30 December 1662, and worked out a surreptitious plan to use a performing license that had been issued to George Jolly. Jolly had been an irritation to the two patent-holders, and they were at some pains to force him out of business in London. They posted a £2000 bond and agreed to pay Jolly £4 weekly, that money to come from the profits of a London company which Killigrew and Davenant would form while Jolly pursued his career in the provinces. As soon as Jolly left town, Killigrew and Davenant represented to King Charles that they owned Jolly's London license outright; they asked for a new license

National Portrait Gallery

THOMAS KILLIGREW
by Sheppperd

giving them complete control of theatres in London and permission to erect a third one—a "nursery" for young actors. Persuaded, the King revoked Jolly's license, and a new license was issued on 30 March 1664 in the name of William Legge, a sleeping partner of the two patentees, who gave them full control. When Jolly reappeared in London and demanded the money Killigrew and Davenant owed him, they refused to pay him, gave him back his license, and then tried to have him apprehended for acting illegally. Jolly had right on his side, and despite the efforts of Killigrew and Davenant he managed to perform at the Cockpit in 1664–65.

Much of our information on the machinations of Killigrew and Davenant comes from the research of Leslie Hotson, whose *Restoration and Commonwealth Stage* is an invaluable source. What Killigrew did with his King's Company shares was incredibly complex. On 4 July 1662 he granted £4 weekly for life to his son and heir Henry, wastrel though he was. That £4 was to be paid from Killigrew's two acting shares in the King's Company. Henry soon made over the £4 to Thomas Porter for life, and Porter sold it for £600 to Sir John Sayer and his wife by deeding it back to the Killigrews and having them assign it to the Sayers. Thomas Killigrew also had nine building shares. On 1 May 1663, just before the new Bridges Street playhouse opened, Tom made over his nine shares to Sir John Sayer, apparently to be held by Sayer in trust for Killigrew. Later, on 27 June 1670, Sir John having died, Killigrew set up a trust in the names of Dame Sayer and Thomas Elliott, granting them his patent and all of his interest in the Bridges Theatre, except for a £4 annuity, in trust for Killigrew during his life. After Tom's death the Sayers (mother and son) were to have the £4 weekly during Henry Killigrew's life, after which it was to go to Henry's heir, James. The remainder of Thomas Killigrew's theatrical estate was to be divided five ways, two to be held in trust for his wife Charlotte during her life and three in trust for their children—except that their eldest, Charles Killigrew, was to have a double share when he reached his majority and was to become governor of the theatre. One wonders how anyone could have made sense out of all that, and the court cases that ensued in later years suggest that they could not.

But that was not the end of Killigrew's manipulation of his theatrical holdings. On 21 June 1673 he made over his nine building shares (then not actually in his hands but in trust for widow Sayer, if we have interpreted the data correctly) as security for a loan from Sir Lawrence Debusty of £950. That was evidently done with the agreement of Dame Sayer. A month later, on 22 July 1673, Killigrew borrowed £1600 from Richard Kent, using as security his theatrical patent. Kent's loan to Killigrew kept gaining interest, and on 22 March 1676 Killigrew made over his patent, building shares, and acting shares to Kent through Kent's trustees. Kent, as mortgage holder of all of Killigrew's interests, then tried to pay himself back out of the theatre profits, to the ultimate ruin of the company.

In 1663–64 Killigrew perhaps tried to manipulate an acting share that did not belong to him. After the death of the elder Theophilus Bird, Killigrew appropriated his acting share, which may or may not have been legal, for we do not know what Bird's wishes may have been. The litigation that developed over the matter revealed other information about the operating of the King's Company. Killigrew had at some point delegated the actual direction of the company to the actors Hart, Mohun, and Lacy. They paid themselves for their services by taking an acting share (not Bird's, apparently) and dividing three quarters of it among themselves; their dealings were evidently not legal, for the delegated power was withdrawn and the share was returned to the troupe. That may have meant that Killigrew had to take a more active part in the company management, but we have found little information about the day-by-day operation of the company and Killigrew's part in it.

The Lord Chamberlain's accounts contain many warrants naming Killigrew, however, so whether he was only nominally manager or really worked at theatre management, his name was attached to many of the orders concerning the company operation. For example, on 25 January 1663 money was given to him for clothes for the musicians in *The Indian Queen;* the following 4 April, and many times before and after, he was paid for plays performed by the King's Company before royalty; and later, on 22 July 1667, he was granted livery as master of the troupe.

KILLIGREW

On 2 August 1664 Samuel Pepys went to see *Bartholomew Fair* at the Bridges Street playhouse:

I chanced to sit by Tom Killigrew, who tells me that he is setting up a Nursery; that is, is going to build a house in Moorefields, wherein he will have common plays acted. But four operas it shall have in the year, to act six weeks at a time; where we shall have the best scenes and machines, the best musique, and every thing as magnificent as is in Christendome; and to that end hath sent for voices and painters and other persons from Italy.

The Nursery was indeed set up, in Hatton Garden, and was in operation from 1667 to 1669 under various leaders—Edward Bedford, Jolly, and John Perin. The operation moved to Gibbons's tennis court by April 1669.

And on 12 February 1667 Killigrew boasted to Pepys of his theatrical achievements:

That the stage is now by his [Killigrew's] pains a thousand times better and more glorious than ever heretofore. Now, wax-candles, and many of them; then, not above 3 lbs. of tallow: Now, all things civil, no rudeness anywhere; then, as in a bear-garden: then, two or three fiddlers; now, nine or ten of the best: then, nothing but rushes upon the ground, and every thing else mean; and now, all otherwise: then, the Queen seldom and the King never would come; now, not the King only for state, but all civil people do think they may come as well as any. He tells me that he hath gone several times, eight or ten times, he tells me, hence to Rome to hear good musique; so much he loves it, though he never did sing or play a note. That he hath ever endeavoured in the late King's time, and in this, to introduce good musique, but he never could do it, there never having been any musique here better than ballads. Nay, says, "Hermit poore" and "Chevy Chese" was all the musique we had; and yet no ordinary fiddlers get so much money as ours do here, which speaks our rudenesse still. He do intend to have some times of the year these operas to be performed [such as by Draghi] at the two present theatres, since he is defeated in what he intended in Moorefields [at the Nursery] on purpose for it; and he tells me plainly that the City audience was as good as the Court, but now they are most gone [due to the plague].

The following 9 September Killigrew chatted again with Pepys about music and musicians:

he tells me that he will bring me to the best musick in England (of which, indeed, he is master), and that is two Italians and Mrs Yates, who, he says, is come to sing the Italian manner as well as ever he heard any: says that Knepp [one of his actresses] won't take pains enough, but that she understands her part so well upon the stage, that no man or woman in the House do the like!

Pepys learned from Killigrew on 24 January 1669 that the theatre manager "is fain to keep a woman on purpose at 20s. a week to satisfy 8 or 10 of the young men of his house, whom till he did so he could never keep to their business, and now he do." From all that one would gain the impression that, especially in connection with music at the theatre, Killigrew was rather fully involved with the King's Company affairs.

Though he had not continued writing plays, Killigrew had his comedies and tragedies published in folio in 1664. His own copy, now at Worcester College, Oxford, contains a number of manuscript emendations made at his direction, apparently by a secretary. Some plays he left untouched, but he made a number of cuts and emendations in *Bellamira*, *The Parson's Wedding*, *The Pilgrim*, and *Thomaso*. He suggested possible casting of the last play, which he evidently considered for production in November 1664. But his playwrighting drew the scorn of some of the wits about town. Denham wrote:

Had Cowley ne're spoke, Killigrew ne'er writ,
Combin'd in one, they'd made a matchless wit.

And in *The Session of the Poets* (1668) the tenth stanza has Killigrew hoping for the laurel:

Tom Killigrew boldly came up to the bar,
   Thinking his gibing would get him the bays,
But Apollo was angry and bid him beware
That he caught him no more a-printing his plays.

He probably realized some income from the publication of his works, but his frequent manipulation of his theatrical holdings indicates clearly that he was regularly in financial difficulty. So, too, does other evidence. Aphra Behn pleaded with him for financial aid in 1666 (three desperate letters from Antwerp) but Killigrew did not oblige. In November 1668 Tom and another groom of the King's bedchamber, James Hamilton, were granted the property of a convicted Irish papist, so Killigrew was still in the business of begging estates, even, in that case, where the annual income came to only £10. On 13 February 1668 Pepys heard that Killigrew "hath a fee out of the Wardrobe for cap and bells, under the title of the King's Foole or Jester and may with privilege revile or jeere any body, the greatest person, without offence, by the privilege of his place."

Killigrew was not able to get away with everything, however. On 17 February 1669 Pepys told his diary of an occurrence the day before:

[A]mong the rest of the King's company, there was that worthy fellow my lord of Rochester, and Tom Killigrew, whose mirth and raillery offended the former so much, that he did give Tom Killigrew a box on the ear in the King's presence, which do much give offence to the people here at Court, to see how cheap the King makes himself, and the more, for that the King hath not only passed by the thing, and pardoned it to Rochester already, but this very morning the King did publickly walk up and down, and Rochester I saw with him as free as ever, to the King's everlasting shame, to have so idle a rogue his companion. How Tom Killigrew takes it, I do not hear.

The playhouse in Bridges Street burned in 1672, and the King's Company had to act temporarily in the Lincoln's Inn Fields Theatre, which the Duke's Company had abandoned in 1671. Plans were immediately made to build a new theatre on the site of the Bridges Street house, and in 1674 the first Drury Lane Theatre opened. Articles had been entered into on 17 December 1673 by the sharers in the King's Company on the one hand, and a group of building investors on the other. The company sharers agreed to act at the new playhouse and pay the investors £3 10s. per acting day if the cost of the new building was £2400, and proportionally more if the cost was more. Hotson tells us that Drury Lane eventually cost £3908 11s. 5d., and the rent to the investors came to £5 4s. per acting day. But by the time Killigrew was entering into those articles in 1673 he was already in the process of leasing out his theatrical holdings. And after the death of Sir Henry Herbert, Killigrew had on 1 May 1673 become Master of the Revels, a post he had wanted for years and which doubtless brought him a fair income. But by February 1677 he had resigned the post to his son Charles (for a sum of money, probably).

By 1675 the sharing actors in the King's Company were gaining so little from their work that they threatened to stop performing unless given by Killigrew several sums of money due them according to articles entered into on 20 March 1674. Killigrew had by that time pawned so much of his interest in the building and the company that a cessation of acting would have left him with a total loss. Hotson says that Killigrew asked his son Charles to mediate and persuade the players to enter into new articles. In return for his services Charles was to receive from his father the patent and the governorship of the King's Company. Charles agreed, says Hotson, and persuaded the sharing actors to enter into new articles on 1 May 1676 that assured each sharer 5s. each acting day for life and £100 to his executors upon his death instead of the previous arrangement, which paid each sharer £1 13s. 4d. each acting day until his £160 investment in the company was repaid. (Charles Killigrew was only 21 at that time, and the arrangements were probably made by lawyers in his name.)

The hitch was that Thomas Killigrew then refused to give his son the promised patent and governorship; indeed, if we have interpreted his earlier manipulations correctly, the patent was not his to give. The Lord Chamberlain stepped in and placed the actors Hart, Mohun, and Kynaston in charge of the company on 9 September 1676; eventually Hart was given sole control. Thomas Killigrew was forced by law to turn over his power and authority to his son Charles on 22 February 1677. Poor Charles, however, was not much liked by the company, and the players were successful in getting the King to allow them to govern themselves beginning on 30 July 1677. Charles was in an equivocal situation in any case. It took the court until 14 December 1682 to figure out just who owned Thomas Killigrew's theatrical property. The decision was that the trustees of Richard Kent controlled the property, and the Killigrews were locked out. By that time, however, it could not have mattered much to the aging Thomas Killigrew, for after 1676 he seems to have had little to do with the King's Company, and references to him in the Lord Chamberlain's accounts ceased.

The records tell us only a little about Killigrew's home life. He arranged in April 1662 for the naturalization of his Dutch wife Charlotte and their sons Charles, Thomas, and Robert; the act was passed by the House of Lords, Harbage notes, but dropped by the

Commons. Thomas borrowed money from his wife for two houses he caused to be built in Old Scotland Yard, and he had a countryplace at Isleworth. In May 1662 Mrs Killigrew was appointed keeper of the sweet coffer to the Queen and in June she became first Lady of her Majesty's privy chamber. She became, Harbage says, by courtesy "Lady Killigrew," and received an annuity of about £300 for life.

Of Thomas Killigrew's children, only Henry, his son by his first wife, turned out badly. He and his brother Charles, since they became involved in theatrical affairs, have notices in this dictionary. Thomas's son Robert became a page at court, entered the army, and died a brigadier general on 14 April 1707 at the battle of Almanza. Thomas the younger went to New College, Oxford, but died on 3 June 1674. Harbage points out that the Thomas Killigrew who wrote the play *Chit-Chat* in 1719 was probably a grandson or grandnephew of our subject. (As set forth in Charles Killigrew's entry, we would suggest that Thomas was, indeed, our subject's grandson, born in 1694.) Roger Killigrew was Thomas's fourth son, and we have found his baptismal records in the registers of St Martin-in-the-Fields: Roger was born on 17 September 1663 and christened the following 2 October. He became water-bailiff of the Thames and died shortly before July 1694. Harbage stated that despite early references to Thomas Killigrew having had daughters, there were no records of a daughter in the Killigrew family; but the registers at St Martin's show that Elizabeth Killigrew, daughter of Thomas and Charlotte, was born on 3 July 1666 and christened four days later. Perhaps she was the "Elasabeth" Killigrew who was buried at St Mary-le-Strand on 21 April 1690.

On 15 March 1683, four days before his death, Thomas Killigrew made his will, describing himself as one of the grooms of the King's bedchamber and "weake and indisposed in body." To the embarrassment of his second wife, he requested burial in a vault in Westminster Abbey "where my dear deceased wife and my sister Shannon doe lye interred." He gave his servant Elizabeth Bryan an annuity of £20 from the income of his two houses in Scotland Yard, lately in the possession of Sir Richard Mason and Sir James Sheane. He stated that on 30 and 31 May 1682 he had leased to Thomas Balderston, citizen and grocer of London, his Scotland Yard houses and all his other estate in Whitehall; what remained he now gave to his son and heir Henry for life, with Henry's son James the residuary legatee. All of his arrears from the crown he left to Henry, "excepting only such part thereof as I have heretofore made Assignments off." That doubtless meant that he had mortgaged most of his arrears. Harbage notes that in 1680 the King had granted Killigrew £231 and recommended payment of £850 arrears in pension money due Killigrew, but the arrears kept increasing. Thomas did not mention Mrs Killigrew and his other children in the will.

Thomas Killigrew died on 19 March 1683, and King Charles contributed £50 toward his interment, which took place in Westminster Abbey. (*The Dictionary of National Biography* has it that he was buried on 18 March.) Charlotte Killigrew received a pension of £200 annually, according to the *Calendar of Treasury Books*.

"Charlotta Kiligrew" was buried on 22 April 1715 at St Mary-le-Strand. Administration of her estate was granted on 15 May 1716 to her son Charles; she was then described as Charlotte Killigrew of St Mary Le Savoy, widow. The estate was again administered on 5 June 1725 to Guilford Killigrew, son and executor of Charles Killigrew.

Anthony à Wood said that Thomas Killigrew "was much respected by all for the generosity and good acts he did for several poor cavaliers, that had in woeful manner suffered for his Majesty's cause." Harbage was able to establish that as a fair statement, and though Killigrew's financial difficulties came partly from his penchant for high living and his inability to manage money sensibly, they stemmed also from his generosity. In an age full of courtiers who sometimes behaved most reprehensibly (as Tom's son Henry certainly did), Thomas Killigrew seems to have been no worse than most of his fellows. Harbage takes great pains to show that much of the dishonor which has fallen on Tom Killigrew's head actually belonged to his rascally son Henry. But Thomas should not be whitewashed; there is evidence enough of his slippery practices in connection with his theatrical life and finances.

There are several versions of William Sheppard's painting of Thomas Killigrew seated at a table, in fur cap, with a dog at his knee, but the original is not certainly known. The magnificent canvas in the Blathwayt Collection at Dyrham House was noted by James Vertue as "perhaps the original." The version in the National Portrait Gallery (No 3795), dated 1650, was acquired from the Duke of Bedford's collection at Woburn Abbey in the Bedford sale at Christie's on 19 January 1951 (lot 136). A version is in the collection of Michael Berine at Sotherley Hall. Another belongs to Sir James B. East. Others are recorded as being in Marlborough House in 1732 and later in the Durant Collection at Tong Castle; in the Portland Collection, Welbeck; in the collection of the Earl of Kimberley, offered at Christie's on 28 February 1947 (lot 7); in the collection of G. Watson Taylor and then owned by Mrs James Heald, before it was destroyed by enemy action in World War II. A version was offered in the Bounton House sale on 2 December 1952 (lot 467). A black chalk drawing heightened with white on buff was reproduced in the *Burlington Magazine*, March 1969.

Engravings of the Sheppard portrait were done by: W. Faithorne for the frontispiece to Killigrew's *Comedies and Tragedies*, 1664; J. J. van der Berghe (actually after S. Harding) as a plate to *Memoirs of Count Grammont*; E. Scriven for another edition of the *Memoirs of Count Grammont*, 1810; and P. Tempest.

There are also several versions of a portrait of Killigrew by Anthony Van Dyck, c. 1635. The original, once belonging to Lely, is in the Devonshire Collection at Chatsworth. Another, perhaps the finest version, is owned by the Earl of Bradford at Weston Park. Copies after Van Dyck are in the National Portrait Gallery (No 892), bought in the Tyrell of Plashwood sale at Christie's on 12 March 1892 (lot 130); owned by the Duke of Richmond at Goodwood House; at Lumley Castle. A version was formerly owned by the Duke of St Albans at Bestwood, and one was in the Berkeley Sheffield Collection, offered at Christie's on 16 July 1943 (lot 74). These last two may be the pictures now at St Michael's Mount, Cornwall (copy by William Dobson) and at Belfield House, Poltimore, Essex. A copy by Greenhill is noted in Vertue's *Notebooks*. No engravings of this Van Dyck are known.

Another portrait by Van Dyck of Killigrew seated with Thomas Carew is at Windsor Castle. It has been reproduced in Cust's *Paintings at Buckingham Palace and Windsor Castle*, 1905, and in his *Van Dyck*, 1900.

A portrait of Killigrew engraved by J. vr. Vaart, after W. Wissing (but marked "E. Cooper exc."), shows him with a large beard, in a furred mantle, with his hand on the hilt of a sword. A copy, also by vr. Vaart, has J. Smith's name substituted for Cooper's.

Killigrew was also shown in pilgrim's dress, holding a staff, by an anonymous engraver, who perhaps was Faithorne. Another anonymous engraving shows Killigrew and Henry Hare, second baron of Coleraine, as "The Princely Shepherds," apparently in a masque. A satirical print by Hollar in 1664 shows Killigrew seated sadly at a table, wrapped in a large cloak and wearing a crown-like cap. The lining of the cloak contains pictures of women of various ages and conditions. An ape is seated on a cushion in a similar attitude. The verses beneath the print castigate Killigrew for his lechery:

Foole that I was, who had so faire a State,
    Fower or five thousand by the yeare at least.
And wast it so as I have done of late,
    On W———s and Bawds, and like a filthie beast
Caught fowle diseases which consume mee sore,
And all proceedes from loving every w———e.

Killing, Mr [fl. 1726], *musician.*
On 23 September 1726 a Mr Killing was entered on the Lincoln's Inn Fields Theatre's pay list as a musician, at a salary of £1 5s. per week.

King, Mr [fl. 1783], *hairdresser.*
A Mr King was a hairdresser at the King's Theatre in 1783, according to a document among the Lord Chamberlain's papers in the Public Record Office.

King, Mr [fl. 1784], *singer.*
A tenor singer named King was among the vocal performers at the Handel Memorial Concerts in Westminster Abbey and the Pantheon in May and June 1784, according to Charles Burney's list. He was said to be of Stilton, Huntingdonshire.

KING

King, Mr [*fl. c.* 1775?–1815], *dancer, equestrian, actor, singer.*

"In his infancy, Mr. King belonged to the [Royal] Circus, where he was instructed in dancing, riding, &c.," declared the *Authentic Memoirs of the Green Room* (1804), adding, "He became afterwards an Harlequin at the [Sadler's] Wells, Royalty [Theatre], &c. and at length his attention and industry procured him an engagement at" Covent Garden Theatre.

We find the King of that memoir advertised as in his first appearance at Sadler's Wells on 22 April 1794, when he danced with others in the brief ballets *Irish Courtship* and *Penmaenmawr*. On 12 July 1794, he was Harlequin in the pantomime *Pandora's Box* and danced in *William Tell* and *Penmaenmawr*. Surviving Sadler's Wells bills show him in the following characters in pantomime and ballets in the following decade: the Shepherd in *Momus's Gift* in April 1795; Abudah Harlequin in *The Talisman* on 29 March 1796; Dubour in *Sadak and Kalasrade*, Harlequin Tormentor in *The Mountain of Miseries*, and Watkin Morgan in *Britain's Defenders* in 1797; Harlequin Skipper in *Blue Beard, Black Beard, Red Beard, and Grey Beard* in 1798; and Cheatall in *Edward and Susan*, Labour in *Fire and Spirit*, Sandy in *Red Riding Hood*, Richard Coeur de Lion in *The Old Man of the Mountains*, the English Lieutenant in *Philip Quarll*, and the Serjeant in *British Amazons* in 1803. In addition, King did specialty dances—like *The Strawberry Pickers* and *The Apple Stealers*—and at least once was named among the "Vocal Characters," in 1797, when he played Mercury in *The Mountain of Miseries*.

Meanwhile, King was also employed in the winter season at Covent Garden, his first appearance there being with Mrs Watts and Blurton, dancing *The Wapping Landlady*, on 1 April 1788. In 1801 he "commenced a regular actor . . . having, we believe, never opened his mouth before on the stage but in recitative and songs." But he remained in the dance corps there, it seems, every season through 1814–15. (In 1800–1801 his salary was averaging £3 per week; by 1813–14 it had risen to £5 but in 1814–15 had receded to £4.)

A Birmingham bill of 29 June 1800 shows a Mr King "of the Theatre Royal, Covent Garden," dancing a hornpipe.

The *Authentic Memoirs* reported that King was "serviceable," a "good dancer, and much approved of in Welch songs." He even had a "chief character" for which he was admired: "little Dickey, in Mr. Holman's comic opera of Abroad and at Home." He was, at least in 1804, "a married man, and more domesticated and industrious than the generality of his profession."

King, Mrs [*fl.* 1736–1749], *actress, singer.*

Mrs King received a benefit at Lincoln's Inn Fields Theatre on 29 April 1736, when she advertised that tickets could be obtained of her at her house at the corner of Playhouse Passage in Bridges Street. She played Lady Dunce in *The Soldier's Fortune* on that occasion. Mrs King was not cited in London bills again until 6 October 1741, when she appeared as Dorcas in *The Mock Doctor* at the James Street playhouse. She may have been in the Drury Lane troupe in 1741–42, taking parts too small to be noticed in the bills most of the season; there on 13 May 1742 she shared a benefit with four others, and on 14 May she played Jenny Diver in *The Beggar's Opera*.

From 1742–43 through 1745–46 Mrs King acted and sang at Drury Lane. (She may also have served at Richmond in the summers. A bill of that house dated 30 July 1743 shows she played Lucy in *The Beggar's Opera*.) At Drury Lane she was seen as Peggy and Kate in *The King and the Miller of Mansfield*, Jenny in *The Tender Husband*, Mrs Chat in *The Committee*, Mrs Trippet in *The Lying Valet*, Betty in *The Old Bachelor*, Situp in *The Double Gallant*, Peg in *The Way of the World*, a Countrywoman in *The Stratagem*, the Second Colombine in *Robin Goodfellow*, Mrs Topknot in *The Gamester*, the Second Lady in *Chrononhotonthologos*, Trusty in *The Provok'd Husband*, Lady Squeamish in *The Country Wife*, Sukey Tawdry in *The Beggar's Opera*, Mrs Japan in *The She Gallant*, Betty in *Sir Courtly Nice*, and Beatrice in *The Anatomist*. Then, after an absence from the London stage, she played Mrs Chat in *The Committee* on 27 February 1749 at the New Wells, Goodman's Fields.

King, Mrs [*fl.* 1794], *singer.*

Mrs King sang in some of the Handelian performances in Westminster Abbey, according to Doane's *Musical Directory* (1794), which does not specify which ones. She lived at Clapham, Surrey, like the singers George and John King. She was probably the wife of one of them. Maybe she was the Mrs King the *Monthly Mirror* reported singing at Liverpool's Theatre Royal in the winter of 1799.

King, Mrs, née Pero [fl. 1800], *actress*.

Miss Pero acted with her father Walter (or William) Pero and her stepmother (who had been "the Widow Villars," according to W. J. Lawrence) in Atkins's company at the Mill Gate Theatre in Belfast in 1778. A playbill of 20 April 1778 cited "Mr., Mrs. and Miss Pero." Miss Pero was still acting with her father during his management of "the theatres in Stamford, Nottinghamshire, Derby, &c.," according to the *Bristol Journal* of 7 November 1789, which also reported that Miss Pero had recently married an actor named King. The *Stamford Mercury* of 16 April 1790—giving no dates or first names—said that the ceremony had been at St Martin's, Stamford-Baron.

Mrs King appeared in London for the first time on 27 June 1800 when she played Florella in *My Grandmother* at the Haymarket Theatre. So far as we know, she never acted in London again.

King, Miss [fl. 1743], *dancer*.

Miss King participated in a dance called *Les Amant volages* at Drury Lane Theatre on 4 February 1743 and subsequent dates that season.

King, Miss [fl. 1782], *actress*.

Miss King made her London debut as Lavinia in *The Fair Penitent* on 30 December 1782 in a performance at the Haymarket Theatre.

King, Charles 1687–1748, *singer, organist, composer*.

Charles King was born at Bury St Edmunds in 1687. He became a chorister at St Paul's under John Blow and Jeremiah Clarke and then a supernumerary in the choir at £14 yearly. The *Daily Courant* of 5 July 1707 reported that "This Morning Mr Charles King (one of the Choire of St Paul's Church) sets out from hence to Oxford, to take the Degree of Batcheler of Musick; which Degree has not been taken in that University for many years past." He received the degree on 12 July.

At the death of Clarke, whose sister King had married, King became almoner and master of the choristers at St Paul's, and in 1708 he was appointed organist of St Benet Fink, Royal Exchange. With John Young and John Hare he published at his own shop (apparently) in London House Yard, near St Paul's, the works of his late brother-in-law Clarke. King's pupils among the choristers at St Paul's included William Boyce, John Alcock, and Maurice Greene. About 1716 Greene married Mary Dillingham of Hampton, Middlesex, who was related to King's wife and to Jeremiah Clarke.

King in 1720 applied for but did not win the post of music master at Christ's Hospital, London. In 1722 he sang at the Duke of Marlborough's funeral, and on 7 January 1726 he became one of the 13 original members of the Academy of Vocal Music, which met at the Crown Tavern in the Strand. He sang in a concert at the Inner Temple on 2 February 1726, and on 31 October 1730 he was made vicar-choral of St Paul's. King composed a number of anthems and services, some of which, despite their lack of musical merit, were frequently used. Hawkins attributed King's inferiority in composition to indolence and not lack of talent.

At some point King married a second time, his first wife presumably having died. Bumpus in *The Organists and Composers of St. Paul's Cathedral* said the second Mrs King appears to have brought King a fortune of £7000, left her by the widow of Humphrey Primatt, a druggist of Smithfield, and the villa at Hampton which later became the country home of David Garrick.

Charles King died in London on 17 March 1748. He had drawn up his will the previous 20 December, describing himself as of Hampton. To his three daughters he left the money due him from the sale of leasehold property in Bumstead and a house in Fish Street, lately occupied by John Moor, barber and perukemaker. King had already deeded to his daughters the rest of his property in London and Hampton. Two of King's creditors—Mr Forist, a pastry cook at Temple Bar, and Thomas Odr, a staymaker—were owed £100 and £150 respectively. King asked his daughters to see that they were paid. Anna King, spinster, daughter of the musician, proved the will on 18 March 1748, the day after her father's death.

King, Daniel *d. 1731, boxkeeper.*

On 14 June 1703 the boxkeeper King received a shared benefit at Drury Lane Theatre. Judging by the benefit bills over the years, he served at Drury Lane at least through 1708 and was at the Queen's Theatre in 1710 but back at Drury Lane by 1713. There he remained, at least through 1724, if not until his death in 1731. His Christian name was Daniel, and for some reason he was occasionally styled Captain. The *Daily Post* on 27 September 1731 reported that King had died on the twenty-fourth at Hammersmith; he had "formerly belong'd to the old Playhouse."

Possibly King's wife was Melior Clayton, the daughter of John Clayton and a descendant of a Restoration musical family; in John Clayton's will in 1713 Melior Clayton was described as married to one Daniel King, but there is no way of determining whether or not that person was the boxkeeper.

King, Erasmus [*fl. c. 1750*], *lecturer and exhibitor.*

According to Warwick Wroth in *The London Pleasure Gardens of the Eighteenth Century*, Erasmus King read lectures at the Great Room at Lambeth Wells in Three Coney Walk (Lambeth Walk) "and exhibited experiments in natural philosophy (admission sixpence)" about 1750. In the exhibition King was evidently emulating and extending into paid public performance in a pleasure garden the practice of Dr John Theophilus Desaguliers (1683–1744) whose coachman King had been. Desaguliers was a natural philosopher and inventor, said to have been the first man to deliver learned lectures to general audiences.

King, George *d. 1805, actor, singer.*

When the Dublin *General Evening Post* of 29 May 1783 reported the marriage "lately" of Miss Frances Cadell to George King the singer, he was said to be of the "Theatre Royal," Dublin. He was probably the King who sang James Hook's songs at Ranelagh Gardens in London in 1783 and 1785. He was said to be from Smock Alley when he came to Covent Garden on 14 November 1786. At his debut he sang the leading part of Young Meadows in *Love in a Village*. During the season he added only Rimines in *Artaxerxes*, one of the Bacchanals in *Comus*, and Balthazar in *Much Ado about Nothing*, so far as the bills show. He must have been the King who advertised himself as "from Covent Garden" when he sang Macheath in *The Beggar's Opera* at Derby on 21 December 1786. Later in the season of 1786–87 he was at Smock Alley Theatre in Dublin. The W. J. Lawrence transcripts at the University of Cincinnati reveal that he was still there in 1787–88. Perhaps he was the King in Pero's company at Derby in late August 1788. From October through 12 June 1789 "G. King" was playing sailors, messengers, and other minor parts at Manchester. Was he the King who at Bristol on 19 October 1791 played William in the comic opera *No Song No Supper* and on the same bill Charles in *Know Your Own Mind*?

George King continued active in London from time to time through about 1794 at least. In that year Doane's *Musical Directory*, calling him an "alto" (i.e., countertenor), said he was a member of the Handelian Society who had sung in some of the Handel Memorial Concerts at Westminster Abbey and in the spring oratorios at Covent Garden. He lived, when Doane wrote, at Clapham, Surrey. Perhaps he was the Mr King who acted under Ward at Manchester in 1796 and who appeared as a Servant in *The Dramatist* and the Landlord in *The Son-in-Law* for Young's benefit at Manchester on 24 March 1800. He was probably related to the singer John King and the Mrs King who also lived at Clapham about 1794.

King, Henry [*fl. 1784–1823?*], *bassoonist.*

In 1794 Doane's *Musical Directory* listed Henry King of No 358, Oxford Street, as a bassoonist attached to the band at Vauxhall Gardens. Doane also noted that King belonged to the Academy of Ancient Music and participated in some of the Handelian concerts at Westminster Abbey. That year, in the list of subscribers, he was named as Secretary of the New Musical Fund.

Probably Henry King was the Mr King who was listed by Charles Burney as a bassoonist in the Handel Memorial Concerts at the Abbey and the Pantheon in May and June 1784. He may have been the King who was elected to membership in the Irish Musical Fund and the H. King who was a member of its professional committee in 1822 and 1823.

King, Mrs Henry, Mary [*fl.* 1769–1787], *actress, teacher.*

Mr and Mrs Henry King were evidently apprentice actors when Tate Wilkinson hired them at Hull in 1769. They—and especially she—were to gain a considerable following at York and Hull and other places on Wilkinson's Yorkshire circuit in years following. Wilkinson several times amiably rehired them after they had left him for adventures elsewhere and he has much to say about them in his *Wandering Patentee* (1795). When they first came to Hull, Henry King "was very attentive, and played some fops well. Mrs. King gave tokens of a promising improvement: She was much approved in Lady Townley and Jenny in Lionel." But "they could not prolong their engagement, as they were under agreement with David Ross" at Edinburgh.

The Kings were at Edinburgh in 1769–70 and Norwich in 1770–71 but no record of their roles at either place survives. The only known criticism of Henry King at Edinburgh, that of the anonymous author of *A New Rosciad* (1770), was devastating:

> *In him, the emperor you see*
> *Of high strain'd sharp monotony:*
> *With hems—and haws—he clears his throat,*
> *And chatt'ring parrot-like by rote,*
> *Unfelt, unfeelingly goes on,*
> *An universal unison!*

The critic's comment on Mary King was just as mischievous, if slyer. After praising her teeth and her figure he concluded:

> *. . . where such rare perfections grow,*
> *No matter, if she act or no.*

The Committee Books of the Norwich Theatre bear the notation for 17 August 1770: "Mr. and Mrs. King if approved on their trial at Norwich £3.3 p week. Agreed if they sign an Article penalty 300 £." Wilkinson received them again at York in July 1771. Mrs King had a "voice not musical nor very powerful, but [had] a great deal of spirit, [and was] always perfect, well dressed and of good private behaviour. . . ." She "took the lead in every principal character in tragedy and comedy." When the northern circuit actors opened their new season at York in January 1772 their "tragedy queen, Mrs. King . . . led the van." She was flattered "by several persons of distinction as promising rapidly to be one of the first London actresses." Wilkinson described the consequences: A deputation led by "Sir William Anderson, a gentleman of great benevolence," waited upon Wilkinson and offered to support a second benefit each year for Mrs King and to pay her 50 guineas over and above her salary each year for three years if she would remain with the York company. But, says Wilkinson, though Mrs King had all the best roles and she and her husband "were paid my first salaries, fifty-four weeks in the year, that is double for three public race-weeks; and had three benefits, one at York, one at Hull, and the third at Leeds," the flattery only persuaded her that she might do even better elsewhere. Mrs Barry had left Dublin for London, and Mrs King determined to step into her roles in Ireland. Seeing the uselessness of exhortation, Wilkinson, who was himself engaged for a few nights at Crow Street that spring, "undertook

Harvard Theatre Collection
MARY KING
engraving by Smith, after Hamilton

to be her negotiator with the Dublin managers. . . ." The Kings opened at Crow Street in October 1772. By the fall of 1773 they had rejoined Wilkinson: "Mrs. King had not succeeded as she expected; her benefit in Dublin was but very indifferent, and her payment of salary I fancy not the most punctual."

Mary King was still restive, and London was on her mind through the next two seasons on the York circuit. She had, moreover, lost favor with her patrons and audiences at York and Hull because of what they saw as her ingratitude. In her absences Mrs Horatio Thomas M'George had taken over her best roles and now resisted relinquishing them. In July 1775 a daughter, Maria, was born to the Kings and baptized at Lancaster Priory Church while they were on tour. The child died a few days later and was buried at St Mary's in Lancaster. The Kings moved on to Austin and Whitlock's company at Chester. Henry King began negotiating with Drury Lane.

Two letters from Henry King at Chester, one to George Garrick and one to David Garrick, survive. The second, dated 30 August 1775, shows not only the fervent desire of the Kings to be under Garrick's management and star-making tutelage but King's recognition of his wife's professional superiority:

Our wish is to be settled in the capital, and nothing can afford us more satisfaction than to be thought worthy the notice of so great a man as you; our study will be to merit your kindness and friendship, nor will I on any occasion appear unreasonable or impatient. I well know it is in your power to bring Mrs. King into fame, and she is willing to be in all respects guided by you, whom every one allows to be the most capital actor in the world. As to terms, I in a letter to Mr. George Garrick mentioned my desire of leaving them to you; but since you press me to demand, I must. I beg leave to observe, Sir, that the stage requires expensive decorations, when supported with proper dignity; nor can performers of any rank in the theatre reflect a credit on their situation, without some little regard to appearances in private, however frugal and economical their desires may be. We have ever supported some degree of gentility, though always steered exceeding wide from prodigality. Our income in York would have made three hundred a-year. This in the country, Sir, is considerable, and I cannot but hope you will not think me unreasonable, if I request for Mrs. King's service, five pounds a week, and according as you find her abilities and utility, shall be willing for the future to submit entirely to your judgment, candour, and friendship. I have by your desire sent a list of Mrs. King's parts, and have marked a few of those she esteems favourite ones.

With respect to myself, my usual way of performing has been in genteel comedy, and some of the coxcomical and smart characters; but if there should be any doubt of my being worthy employment in that way, or should you not be in any want of my assistance, I shall with the utmost cheerfulness resign my pretensions to an engagement; nor shall a declaration of that nature in any degree retard Mrs. King's acceptance of the present or future connection.

King appended to the letter a list of some 60 roles ("a few may have escaped my recollection") which his wife had studied. He placed asterisks beside 27 of her favorites: Lady Townly in *The Provok'd Husband*, Lady Betty Modish in *The Careless Husband*, Clarinda (he specifies "*Suspicious Husband*"), Belinda (he specifies "*All in the Wrong*"), Araminta in either *The Old Bachelor* or *The School for Lovers*, Lady Brampton (i.e., Lady Brumpton in *The Funeral*?), Widow Belmour (Lady Bellmour in *The Way to Keep Him*), Mrs. Sullen in *The Beaux' Stratagem*, Rossetta (Rosetta; he specifies "*The Foundling*"), Violante in *The Wonder*, Beatrice (presumably in *Much Ado about Nothing*), Sylvia (he specifies "*Recruiting Officer*"), Portia (he specifies "*Merchant of Venice*"), Rosalind in *As You Like It*, Euphrasia in *The Grecian Daughter*, Hermione in either *The Distrest Mother* or *The Winter's Tale*, Mandane (he specifies "in *Cyrus*"), Horatia (he specifies "*Roman Father*"), Zaphia in *Barbarossa*, Arpasia in *Tamerlane*, Lady Macbeth, Monimia in *The Orphan*, Juliet (in *Romeo and Juliet*?), Athenais in *Theodosius*, Belvidera in *Venice Preserv'd*, Calista in *The Fair Penitent*, and Rutland in *The Earl of Essex*.

In addition, she knew Millamant in *The Way of the World*, Mrs. Harley in *False Delicacy*, Charlotte in *The Refusal*, Miss Charlotte Rusport in *The West Indian*, Miranda in *The Tempest*, Lady Sadlife in *The Double Gallant*, both Indiana and Phillis in *The Conscious Lovers*, both Oriana and Bisarre in *The Inconstant*, Miss Walsingham in *The School for Wives*, Miss Hardcastle in *She Stoops to Conquer*, Miss Sterling in *The Clandestine Marriage*, Ann Lovely in *A Bold Stroke for a Wife*, Estifania in *Rule a Wife and Have a Wife*, Amanda in *Love's Last Shift*, the

Second Constantia in *The Chances*, Hippolita (Hypolita in *She Wou'd and She Wou'd Not*), Cleopatra (in *All for Love?*, *Antony and Cleopatra?*), Almeria in *The Mourning Bride*, Rosamond in *Henry II*, Imogen in *Cymbeline*, Imoinda in *Oroonoko*, Emmeline in *King Arthur*, Eleonora (Eleanor in *King John?* or Leonora in *The Mourning Bride?*), Matilda in *Matilda*, and Statira in *The Rival Queens*.

Henry King's own hope of signing articles at Drury Lane was dashed. He never acted in London, so far as we know. But Garrick decided to try out Mary King's abilities. She lasted one season at Drury Lane. Her debut was as Rosalind in *As You Like It* on 13 October 1775 and it was fairly auspicious. Hopkins the prompter wrote in his diary: "Mrs. King from the York Theatre made her first appearance on this stage in Rosalind. She is very Tall and would look well enough if she did not paint her face so much with white and Red. She has a course [*sic*] Voice—and does not speak very Naturally. She was received with great applause." Her second appearance, again as Rosalind, on 18 October occasioned some dismay. Hopkins wrote: "Mrs. King was put in the Bills in the following manner: Rosalind By Command by Mrs. King. A Circumstance I never knew before, nor do I know by what accident it happened. I'm Sure its a particular Honour, which her acting cannot deserve." In copying the statement onto his copy of the playbill, John Philip Kemble added an explanatory note: "This circumstance was a contrivance of Mr. Garrick's in order to mortify Mrs. Yates, Mrs. Abington, and Miss Younge." During the rest of the season, in some 55 performance nights, Mrs King was the original Elmira in the farce *The Sultan*, and the original Laetitia in the new farce *The Spleen* (and spoke its epilogue); she added to her repertoire Lady Minikin in *Bon Ton*, Milwood in *The London Merchant*, Lady Fanciful in *The Provok'd Wife*, Dorcas Zeal in *The Fair Quaker*, Ruth in *The Committee*, Emily in *The Deuce Is in Him*, Mrs Knightly in *The Discovery*, and Lady Elizabeth in *The Earl of Warwick*; she also played Arpasia in *Tamerlane*, Lady Macbeth, and Araminta in *The School for Lovers*.

Mrs King was not to be rehired at Drury Lane. Garrick was retiring at the end of the 1775–76 season and a new management was taking over. Besides, she had not really been given a fair chance, according to Tate Wilkinson. She

did not please as a first-rate, though of great utility. I saw her play Lady Macbeth on the sudden indisposition of Mrs. Yates, and Lady Fanciful, on the illness of Mrs. Abington, and that to Mr. Garrick's matchless performance of Sir John Brute. But still she only played principal characters, when necessity brought her before the audience, at a few hours notice, and was obliged to trust her memory for what she had acted in the country the year before that of her unexpected exaltation at Drury Lane.

Evidently her eager generosity in stepping forward at short notice and ill-prepared was a principal cause of difficulty for Mrs King. Hopkins noted on 4 November 1775: "Miss Younge being ill, Mrs. King play'd Arpasia *very bad* much hiss'd."

Wilkinson thought that her implication as a principal in "a bad farce," *The Spleen*, late in the season, a farce "pushed by the Manager, against the will of the audience," had further damaged her reputation. For the audience yawned over it and trickled out,

and the remaining few were all up, and solemnly departing, while Mrs. King was speaking a bad epilogue to [their] backs. . . . This brought her into disrepute and neglect, and of course she was much chagrined and disappointed, and at the end of the season was not retained at Drury-Lane, nor I believe wished to be. But her not being received in a principal light . . . of course lowered her fame in the country. Our theatrical barometer is much guided by London criticisms and decisions. . . . Mrs. King retired . . . into a country company.

From December 1776 through April 1777 Mrs King was acting a large selection of her line of characters at the Theatre Royal, Shakespeare Square, Edinburgh. On 7 October 1778 the indulgent Wilkinson (who had a real esteem for the couple) welcomed them once more, at Wakefield. "He acted Dashwould, and she Lady Bell, in Mr. Murphy's *Know Your Own Mind*,—But the loss of fashion . . . wofully hurt her consequence. . . ." In fact, when the company opened at York "caprice and fashion had sounded the *tocsin*, for retreat, and she was neither attended, admired, or done common justice to."

At the end of the Doncaster season on the York circuit tour, in October 1779, the Kings left Wilkinson's management for the last time. They enlisted in the Lincoln company, where for a short space she flourished; but, on repetition, the benefits began to fail; the company was neither good, fashionable, nor well attended. By playing at Lynn, several inhabitants noticed and admired their private worth, punctuality, and integrity; and the principal families there proposed to Mr. and Mrs. King, (what was much wanted there) an established boarding-school for young ladies.

In 1781 the school came into being, "the new scheme succeeded beyond expectation," and in 1787, when Wilkinson was acting at Lynn, the Kings paid him "great civilities and attention."

King, James [*fl.* 1798–1838?], double-bass player.

James King of No 2, Chapel Street, Soho, was listed in Doane's *Musical Directory* (1794) as a player on the double bass (viol), a member of the New Musical Fund, and a participant in the Professional Concerts. He was probably the Mr King whom Burney had listed among the double basses in the Handel Memorial Concerts at Westminster Abbey and the Pantheon in May and June 1784. He was probably also the King who played double bass in the band of the opera at the Pantheon in the season of 17 February–19 July 1791.

He was certainly the J. King who was double-bass player at the Haymarket in 1797–98. James King was on the Court of Assistants of the New Musical Fund in 1794 and Secretary of the Fund in 1805 (when his address was No 14, Little Chapel Street, Soho) and 1815. A J. King was elected to the Royal Society of Musicians on 4 January 1824, appeared on the minute books from time to time through 1838, was a Governor of the Society in 1827, and was a Member of the Court of Assistants in 1835 and 1838. That J. King may have been James King, the subject of this entry, but in view of the date of his election, it was probably another, possibly his son.

"King John." *See* KEMBLE, JOHN PHILIP.

King, John [*fl.* 1765–1771], dancer.

John King's first appearance was on 29 April 1765 at Covent Garden Theatre. He performed a "Scotch dance" with Miss Pitt, a minuet with Miss Valois, and a solo hornpipe. It was benefit night for his teacher, the veteran harlequin Francis Miles, and for Mrs Green and Mrs Baker, the sort of occasion when juvenile and other novelties were employed. He danced at the benefit a year later, on 21 April 1766, for the same trio.

Despite the designation "Master," King was in 1766 nearing the end of his nonage apparently, for he was placed among the adult dancers on Arthur Murphy's salary list of the Covent Garden company for the season of 1767–68. That year he was earning £1 5s. per six-day week. His given name first appeared among a number of signatures of Covent Garden performers on a letter addressed to the manager George Colman in *The Theatrical Monitor* on 5 November 1768. How long he remained with the theatre is not known. But he was probably not the dancer named King who was there in the late 1790s, though he is so identified in *The London Stage*, for the *Authentic Memoirs of the Green Room* says of that later dancer, "In his infancy Mr. King belonged to the Circus, where he was instructed in riding and dancing," and the Royal Circus did not open until 1782. John King, however, may have been related to the later dancer.

John King had married Ann Miles, the daughter of Francis and Mary Miles, by the time Miles made his will on 1 April 1771. Ann was made residuary legatee of income from a trust fund worth £700 and inherited various items of household furniture.

King, John [*fl.* 1794–1795?], singer.

A John King, "Bass," was listed in Doane's *Musical Directory* (1794) as a member of the Handelian Society, a participant in several of the Handel Memorial Concerts in Westminster Abbey, and a singer in the spring oratorios in Covent Garden Theatre. He lived in Clapham, Surrey. Very likely he was related to the singer, George King, his contemporary, who also lived at Clapham. (A John King began subscribing to the Irish Musical Fund on 1 April 1795.)

King, Matthew Peter 1773–1823, pianist, composer.

On 16 May 1793 a young pianist named King played "a concerto of his own composition, on the Grand Piano Forte" at Covent

Garden Theatre at the close of the mainpiece. It was said to be his first appearance in public. A notation by John Philip Kemble on a manuscript in the Folger Shakespeare Library and one jotted on the bill for that evening, now in the Enthoven Collection, identify the performer as Matthew Peter King, who was 20 years old in 1793. He had already furnished a number of songs to popular singers and on 10 August 1787 had heard his song "In vain do idle vi'lets blow" sung by Miss George at her benefit at the Haymarket Theatre. Probably King performed again, but no record survives. He did, however, maintain a close relationship with the theatre. On 15 April 1800 "an entire new Glee, composed by King, *The Witches*, the Words selected from the First Scene of Shakespeare's MACBETH" was sung by Incledon, Townsend, Linton, and the Chorus at Covent Garden. It became a popular attraction.

For 15 years after 1803 King busied himself supplying the music for melodramas, operatic farces, and comic operas, for which there was a growing vogue at Covent Garden, Drury Lane, the Sans Souci, and then the Lyceum. In 1804 he wrote the music for James Kenney's *Matrimony*, in 1805 for John Tillallingham's *The Weathercocks* and Kenney's *Too Many Cooks*, in 1806 for Theodore Edward Hook's *The Invisible Girl*, and in 1807 for three by Keaney— *Ella Rosenberg*, *False Alarms* (with John Braham), and *The Blind Boy*. In 1809 King wrote the music for Samuel James Arnold's *Up All Night*, in 1810 for Kenney's *Oh, This Love* and Arnold's *Plots*. In 1811, his most productive year, he composed the score (with Michael Kelly) for Matthew G. Lewis's *One O'Clock; or The Wood Demon*, *The Americans* by Arnold and the anonymous *The Magicians* (both with Braham), and Lewis's *Timour the Tartar*. In 1812 King composed the score for Kenney's *Love, Law, and Physic* and *Turn Him Out*, and in 1819 (with John Davy) for J. Tobin's *The Fisherman's Hut*. Some fifteen of King's songs, glees, minuets, and sonatas, for voices, violin, harpsichord or piano, and several marches are listed in the *Catalogue of Printed Music in the British Museum*.

Matthew Peter King died in London in January 1823, leaving his widow Mary Petronia King "of Chenies Street Bedford Square" an estate valued at under £100, according to the records of the administration of his property.

King, Robert [*fl.* 1680–1728?], *violinist, flutist, impresario, composer.*

The violinist Robert King was admitted to the private music of Charles II, replacing John Banister, on 6 February 1680. In March and June 1697 King, identified as a member of the royal band, went to the home of James Brydges (later the Duke of Chandos) to rehearse flute scores. The Lord Chamberlain's accounts refer to King regularly during the 1680s and 1690s, revealing that he received at first an annual salary of £30 under William III, was appointed a court composer, had his salary raised to £40 by 1697, and on occasion accompanied the King on trips to Windsor. King composed music for St Cecilia Day and other court works.

But much of King's career was outside the court. On Christmas Day 1689 he was granted permission by the King to present public concerts. The royal order stated that no one was "rudely or by force to enter in or abide there during the time of performing ye sd Musick without observing such Rules & paying such prices as shall be by [King] sett down." At first King seems to have been in competition with Johann Wolfgang Franck, who in 1690 was supervising concerts at a music room in Bow Street, though even then King may have been in partnership with Franck. The London *Gazette* on 15 January 1691 carried an advertisement stating that the concerts sponsored by King and Franck (as partners) were held on alternate Thursdays at a music room next to Bedford Gate in Charles Street (now Wellington Street), Covent Garden. To attract a larger gathering, King and Franck either operated an art gallery or joined with the operator of one, for the advertisement said that there would be "speedily a Sale of Valuable Paintings which may be seen on the Musick nights." On 17 September 1691 the partners announced that they were enlarging their establishment, and by March 1692 they had named their room the "Vendu." King occasionally participated in the concerts. *The London Stage* erroneously calls him Mr Knight on 2 April 1691 when he and Franck performed. Their concerts attracted a very elegant audience, once, indeed, on 5 December 1691, drawing the Ambassador from Morocco and his entourage.

That partnership of King and Franck seems not to have continued beyond 1692. In 1692 King received a bachelor of music degree from

Cambridge. The *Post Man* of 6–8 January 1698 carried an advertisement for a benefit concert for King and Banister at York Buildings on 10 January. A second benefit was held a week later. At York Buildings King had, with Banister, a music-selling business. The pair were, from 1700 to 1702, agents for music published in Rome and Amsterdam. Wood said that King taught music and "playes on the Harpsicon in the Kinges Play-House, and playes on the Violin—in Salisbury Court."

King also had a considerable career as a composer of popular songs and music for the theatre. Many of his songs were included in the popular collections of the 1680s and 1690s. His theatre songs were for *The Disappointment* and *A Duke and No Duke* in 1684, *Sir Courtly Nice* in 1689, *The English Friar* and *The Amorous Bigotte* in 1690, and *The Rape* in 1692. His instrumental music for *The Spanish Fryar* (1680) is at the British Library. His songs were still popular in later years, a number of them being in *Wit and Mirth* in 1719. The *Catalogue of Printed Music in the British Museum* contains a fair list of his individual songs to compare with the list in Grove.

Grove states that Robert King was still a member of the royal band in 1728; Willard Thorp in *Songs from the Restoration Theatre* thinks he may have died about 1711. But the Lord Chamberlain's accounts show King to have been in the royal musical establishment until 6 November 1727, when he was replaced by John Barnard.

King, Samuel [fl. 1739], musician.

Samuel King was one of the original subscribers to the Royal Society of Musicians when it was founded on 28 August 1739.

King, Thomas 1730–1805, actor, singer, dancer, manager, proprietor, playwright.

Thomas King was born on 20 August 1730 in the parish of St George, Hanover Square, where, early sketches of his life agree, his father was a prosperous tradesman. The *Monthly Mirror* of May 1800 asserted further that he was "descended, on the father's side, from a respectable family in Hampshire; and from the mother's side, as we believe, from the Blisses in Gloucestershire." The Reverend John Genest in *Some Account of the English Stage* (1832) reported that "A gentleman told me that King's

Harvard Theatre collection

THOMAS KING
engraving by Smith, after Hamilton

father kept a coffee house, and that King, when a boy, had often brought him a dish of coffee." That is possible, but it sounds more like a fictional attempt to connect the actor with the Tom King (d. 1737) who kept the disreputable coffee house beneath the portico of St Paul, Covent Garden. That Tom King was indeed an Etonian and a gentleman. Harwood's *Alumni Etonienses*, in an account of students elected from Eton to King's College in 1713, says: "Thomas King, born at West Ashton, in Wiltshire, went away scholar in apprehension that his fellowship would be denied him; and afterwards kept that Coffee-house in Covent Garden, which was called by his own name." But though the insistence of the actor's father upon a public school education for his son might tempt us to accept a relationship to the Tom King of the coffee house, no such connection was ever mentioned during the lifetime of the well-publicized actor.

James Winston's narrative of King's career

in No VI of "The Manager's Notebook" in the *New Monthly Magazine* (1837) states that "the early part of his education was at a grammar school in Yorkshire; he was afterwards at Westminster school." But he cannot have been long in Yorkshire, for Westminster school records show that he was in the second form in 1736, when he was only six years of age. Young Tom was articled at 14 to a London solicitor. But, wrote Winston,

a fellow clerk introduced him to a private theatre, and he had scarcely attained his seventeenth year (in October 1747) when he ran away with his friend and joined a strolling company at Tunbridge upon a sharing principle, where he remained but a short time, but during that period he played Hamlet, Sharp, spoke a prologue and an epilogue, and by way of result, shared *fourpence*. After that he rambled from barn to barn till the summer of 1748, when he was engaged by [Richard] Yates, who had fitted up a sort of booth at Windsor.

An account of King's life and career published in the *European Magazine* in 1783 adds details not found elsewhere and (since apparently not contradicted by King) perhaps authentic: that his father, also named Thomas, was then still "living in Berkshire on a small but independent fortune," that his first theatrical appearance was at Yarmouth, as Osric in *Hamlet*, and that after that experience he went to sea—but for two days only—before joining another company in Kent. The *Monthly Mirror* remarked many years later that King, to the end of his career, was fond of relating the adventures of those apprentice days and commenting on them "with great point and humour."

Garrick saw King at Windsor, "tried him in a few lines (the Herald in 'King Lear') unannounced [on 8 October 1748] and, approving of his execution of the little he had to do in that brief part, advertised him by name on the 19th of October, 1748, in the part of Allworth, in Massinger's 'New Way to Pay Old Debts.'" Though King played some two dozen times that season at Drury Lane Theatre, he was entrusted with smaller supporting roles only—one of the Shepherds in the new masque *The Triumph of Peace*, Truman in *The Squire of Alsatia*, Solanio in *The Merchant of Venice*, Cinthio in *The Emperor of the Moon*, Tattoo in *Lethe*, and Clerimont in *The Miser*. He was also said to have been the original Murza in Dr Johnson's *Mahomet and Irene* on 6 February 1749, but the bill does not name the actor who took that role. He ended his season rather disappointingly with an unnamed role in *The Hen-Peck'd Husband*, by the prompter Richard Cross, who noted sadly in his stage diary that the piece was "damn'd before half over."

In the summer of 1749 King joined other London players at the Jacob's Wells Theatre in Bristol where on 3 August he took a benefit. Winston says that "Mrs. [Hannah] Pritchard was also in the company, and at her particular request, he played Ranger to her Clarinda, and Benedick to her Beatrice . . . he also played Romeo and George Barnwell."

Returning to Drury Lane in the fall of 1749, King was cast in a variety of roles, few of which suited his style or were in the comic "lines" which he would later develop. The parts were (in addition to several performed the season before) the younger brother in *Comus*, Claudio in *Much Ado about Nothing*, Young Fashion in *The Relapse*, Axalla in *Tamerlane*, Ferdinand in *The Tempest*, Prince Brunetto in *A Duke and No Duke*, Saunter in *Friendship in Fashion*, Carlos in *The Fatal Marriage*, Dollabella in *All for Love*, Fribble in *Miss in Her Teens*, the Fine Gentleman in *Lethe*, and the Duke of Athens in William Shirley's new tragedy, *The Black Prince*. In addition, William Whitehead, who had been impressed by his acting at Bristol, insisted that King act the role of Valerius in Whitehead's poor but extravagantly applauded tragedy *The Roman Father*, which opened on 24 February 1750.

Why a 20-year-old actor, performing an expanding repertoire under David Garrick's direction at London's foremost theatre, should have found his situation so displeasing as to cause him to leave after two seasons cannot now be known. Perhaps Garrick suggested to him the desirability of provincial "seasoning," as he often did to youngsters. Maybe King simply received a larger offer from Thomas Sheridan, to whose management at Dublin's Smock Alley Theatre he went in the fall of 1750, accompanied by the young dancer and soubrette, Miss Cole, after spending the summer at Bristol. He opened at Smock Alley as Ranger in *The Suspicious Husband* on 28 September. He remained in Dublin for the next four winter seasons, during the "golden age"

(1750–1754) of Thomas Sheridan's enlightened management. In the season of 1755–56 he left for the Orchard Street Theatre in Bath where he acted and also served as manager. He then returned to the Dublin company, again under Sheridan, through 1758–59. In August 1757 and in August 1758 he played at Cork.

During his Irish sojourn King narrowed but deepened his line in the direction of comic eccentricity and in doing so attracted a devoted following among Dubliners. At Smock Alley he discovered one of his most valuable talents—prologue and epilogue delivery—and after a benefit performance of *The Suspicious Husband* he introduced the famous epilogue "Bucks Have at Ye All" (probably written by James Love, possibly by Thomas Mozeen, but sometimes attributed to King) which he used as an applause catcher as long as he played Ranger. Thomas Wilkes, in *A General View of the Stage*, published on 29 March 1759, as King was preparing to leave Ireland, summed up his achievement to that point in his career:

> Mr. King, a sprightly and useful Comedian, in some parts reminds us of Woodward. He has not as yet attained elegance sufficient for the Foppingtons, or Fine Gentlemen: however, there are several characters which hit his humour and genius; among which are Sir Joseph Wittol [in *The Old Bachelor*], Tom in The Conscious Lovers, Brass [in *The Confederacy*], Scrub [in *The Beaux' Stratagem*], the Lying Valet [i.e., Sharp in the play of that title], Pedlar in Florizel and Perdita, &c. in all which his performance must ever appear pleasing.

Probably Thomas was the Mr King reported by Boswell and Gentleman in their pamphlet *A View of the Edinburgh Theatre During the Summer Season, 1759* as playing (and miscuing) the Beggar in *The Beggar's Opera*. On 2 October 1759 Tom King reappeared at Drury Lane Theatre, as the winningly pert servant Tom in *The Conscious Lovers*. On 6 October, when he repeated that role, Mary Baker, a hornpipe dancer and actress whom he had brought with him from Ireland (and whom he would marry in the summer of 1766), made her first Drury Lane appearance, dancing with Grimaldi and others. (*The Secret History of the Green Room* [1792] asserted that he had lived with Miss Baker at Bath in 1755 and that Fanny Abington had then inspired "something more than stage affection" in King "greatly to the mortification of Miss Baker.")

In 1760 King took lodgings in Broad Court, Bow Street, Covent Garden, his London address for the next 10 years. He was reported by the newspapers to have signed an agreement with Mossop to appear at Smock Alley for eight nights from 21 May 1762, but he was either long delayed or did not go at all, for he acted at Drury Lane on 21 May. His *Love at First Sight: A Ballad Farce* was produced as an afterpiece on 17 October 1763 but achieved only the author's third and sixth nights before disappearing. By the season of 1764–65 King was—at £8 per week—abreast of Holland on the salary list and behind only the Yateses and Garrick. King was now regarded as Drury Lane's chief comedian and principal attraction after Garrick. His eminence was confirmed after 20 February 1766, when he came on as Lord Ogleby in Garrick and Colman's triumphant comedy *The Clandestine Marriage*, a role he had accepted with the utmost reluctance. In July 1766 King fell from his horse and fractured his thigh bone. He was unable to return to the stage until the following November. In 1766–67 he and his bride Mary were receiving jointly £12 per week. In the summer of 1767 he performed at the Liverpool Theatre. On 14 April 1768 King's second and final attempt at dramatic composition, *Wit's Last Stake*, was staged at Drury Lane for Cautherley's benefit. King took the lead role, Martin. The farce had a mild success and was repeated several times in subsequent seasons.

In 1769 King was Garrick's indispensable foil at the Stratford Jubilee. In a carefully planned sequence before the assembly in the Rotunda, Garrick challenged Shakespeare's detractors, and King rose, dressed in the costume he habitually assumed for his Frenchified fops, and lisped out an attack on Shakespeare which skillfully combined Voltaire's strictures with the jibes Garrick's enemies had leveled at the celebration. It was the cue for Garrick to answer with his masterful and wildly applauded Jubilee Oration. (James Boswell, who had met the Kings at tea in the Amphitheatre and found King "a genteel, agreeable man," deplored the "smart, ironical attack upon Shakespeare in the Character of a modern refined Man of Taste. This might have been done well on some other Occasion; but in my Opinion, it had better have been omitted at this noble Festival: It detracted from it's Dignity. . . . I must however do justice to Tom King, and allow that he played his Part exceedingly well.")

In the following season, when Garrick brought his Jubilee entertainment to the Drury Lane stage in a successful attempt to recoup his losses at Stratford, King was again prominent. He was loudly applauded and encored speaking Garrick's prologue, he played the bumpkin Ralph in the spoken sequence of *The Jubilee*, and he marched in the splendid procession of Shakespeare's characters as Touchstone.

After the death of William Powell in July 1769 and of Charles Holland the following December, Tom King entered into partnership with the surviving co-manager of Bristol's King Street Theatre, Matthew Clarke, and with Samuel Reddish, to direct summer performances of a company which included Lee Lewes, John Moody the elder, Charles Bannister, and Jane Barry. King also took a principal share in

Courtesy of the Garrick Club

THOMAS KING, as Touchstone
by Zoffany

performance. On the way from London to Bristol on 3 June 1771 his post chaise overturned near Marlborough. Mrs King broke her left arm and King was severely bruised. Lee Lewes fell ill and there were defections from the company. In December 1771, having lost some £80, King sold his share at Bristol to James William Dodd.

Also, alternately with his performance at Drury Lane in the winter season, the energetic King had been acting clowns and harlequins at Sadler's Wells. By the summer of 1769 he had also assumed direction of that enterprise under the proprietorship of Thomas Rosoman, for the British Library holds signed articles of agreement between Thomas King, "manager," and the dancer Peter "Daigueville" (D'Egville) of Drury Lane, on behalf of himself and some pupils, dated September 1769 and witnessed by Rosoman. In October 1771, having in prospect the sale of his Bristol lease, King purchased three-fourths of Sadler's Wells from Rosoman, his partners in the new enterprise being a Mr Serjeant, a musician of the Royal Band, and Thomas Arnold, a goldsmith. King kept his share in Sadler's Wells until 1785 when Arnold and the actor Richard Wroughton bought out his and Serjeant's interests for £12,000. During King's tenure of Sadler's Wells, which he at first rented for £100 annually, and later for £150, King secured the services of three young composers—John Abraham Fisher, James Hook, and Charles Dibdin—who turned the fare more decidedly in a musical direction. But pantomimes, rope dancing, and tumbling still had their place. In 1771 King had the house redecorated, and before the 1778–79 season he raised the ceiling of the auditorium and increased the rake of the pit floor. He also introduced to the increasingly patrician audiences at the Wells Joe Grimaldi, the great clown, destined in time to become the theatre's greatest attraction.

During those years King's popularity with audiences and his fellow actors made his position at Drury Lane secure. King did not particularly care for either of the Lacys, but David Garrick became his very close friend. Only one brief gale ruffled the surface of their relationship. In 1772 King, perhaps egged on by his wife and other performers and upset by what he considered slights to himself and his wife, engaged in an emotional exchange of letters with Garrick. King was piqued because he had learned that the comedian Woodward and the tragedian Smith, leading lights at the rival Covent Garden, drew more pay than he did, he had "long thought there was too great a disproportion between the [salary of the] Barrys and my own" at Drury Lane, and his wife complained of the quality of her dancing partners and of overwork. Garrick, a master at displaying hurt feelings, returned stately and sorrowful replies which played upon King's sensibilities, and so the crisis passed. By the time Garrick retired in the spring of 1776 King had become Garrick's closest and most trusted professional friend. Garrick sent King his stage rapier, accompanied by a graceful note:

Dear King.
Accept a small token of our long & constant attachment to Each other—I flatter Myself that this Sword, as it is a theatrical one, will not cut Love between us, and that it will not be less valuable to You for having dangled at my side some part of the last Winter—

to which King replied:

Your retiring from the Stage being justly consider'd as a severe stroke to every Performer on it, and regretted by every admirer of the Drama, how must I feel, who not only suffer in each of those capacities, but lament at the same time the absence of a worthy Patron and most affectionate Friend?

Garrick died in January 1779 and on 14 February was succeeded as Master of the Drury Lane Theatrical Fund by Tom King, who held the office until he thought it proper to resign in September 1782, on taking over the Drury Lane's stage management for R. B. Sheridan. King did not like the vexation of managing "these cursed disorderly people," and he soon found that he was losing money, too. Winston points out that "In 1780–1–2, he received £700 *each year* as his salary and compensation in lieu of a benefit," and that in 1782–83, the first season of his management, he received only £564 13s. 10d.—the one-eighth share of Drury Lane profits, £4517 10s. 10d., which sum he had agreed to as his compensation for acting and managing. In June 1783 he declined signing management and acting articles for the following season and, leaving the direction of Sadler's Wells in Wroughton's hands, departed his house in Gerrard Street for engagements in Edinburgh, Glasgow, Dublin, and elsewhere in Scotland and Ireland. King returned to London in the summer of 1784. Early in September two highwaymen stopped his carriage near his villa at Hampton and robbed him of six guineas and a silver watch.

On 30 September 1784 King played Lord Ogleby at Drury Lane, incorrectly billed as making his first appearance there in two years. Winston said that

In the following October it was announced in the daily papers, by the authority of Mr. King, that he was not the manager of Drury Lane Theatre: his abilities and long service induced the proprietors to offer him a very liberal salary, and certain distinctions for his performance, advice, and attention, which Mr. King accepted conditionally that he should not be deemed manager, or be active in accepting or rejecting either dramatic pieces or performers.

Nevertheless, responding to the wheedling of the charming and exasperating Sheridan, King continued as acting manager of the increasingly debt-ridden Drury Lane Theatre through the season of 1787–88, receiving each year a thousand guineas for his services. He also brought out with James Cobb, the successful pantomime, *Hurly Burly; or the Fairy of the Well*, on 26 December 1785. But the multiple vexations of management again proved too trying for his amiable temperament. He did not reappear at Drury Lane in the fall of 1788. On 9 October the *Public Advertiser* carried his statement, penned "At a very considerable distance from the metropolis," promising an explanation of his "sudden retreat" in a few days. He assured his adherents that John Philip Kemble, "the gentleman who succeeds to my unenviable office . . . has, ever since we have been known to each other, lived with me in habits of friendship . . . nor was he appointed till I had most peremptorily renounced the situation. . . ." King pursued the matter in a longer letter, denying that the course of his defection had been a salary dispute. His argument throws much light on the uncomfortable situation of the patent-house stage manager in general and, in particular, that of Tom King, working with no clear commission or certain authority, under a mercurial genius like the new co-patentee, Sheridan:

There has been for some few years something undefined, if not undefinable, in my situation; the consequences of which have been, that I have sustained many inconveniences, and have been liable to very disagreeable attacks, I have been called to account by ladies and gentlemen, authors of various dramatic pieces, for breach of promise, in the non-performance of works I never before heard of; arraigned for rejecting performers with whom I had no power to treat, and censured for the very limited number of pieces produced, which it was not any part of my province to provide. Should any one ask me what was my part at Drury Lane Theatre—and add the further question—if I was not manager, who was? I should be forced to answer, like my friend Atall, in the comedy, to the first—*I don't know*; and to the last—*I can't tell*. I can only once more positively assert—I was not manager; for I had not the power by my agreement—nor indeed had I the wish—to approve or reject any dramatic work; the liberty of engaging, encouraging, or discharging any one performer—no sufficient authority to demand the cleaning of a coat, or adding, by way of decoration, a yard of copper lace—both which, it must be allowed were often much wanted, &c. &c. In a very serious though most friendly way, I urged my desire and expectation of having some written instrument between us; I was not solicitous about parchment stamps or legal forms; that any memorandum would satisfy me; but that I might have something to refer to, in case there should be any failure or misunderstanding. The theatre was opened without any reply respecting dresses, which, though greatly wanted, I could not venture to order. I saw my danger, and determined not to appear, either as manager or actor, until I was properly warranted so to do. I hope it will at least appear that, in quitting the theatre, I was not actuated by avarice or caprice; but I feared, from the various attacks and disappointments I had formerly experienced, my doubtful station would at some future period produce unlucky misconstructions, that might deprive me of the countenance and protection of a generous Public, which, however little I have merited, I have for many years enjoyed, &c. &c. &c.

Thomas Davies thought that

no man ever exerted his abilities to greater satisfaction of the publick, or consulted the interest of his employees with more cordiality or assiduity—as a manager, his judgment was solid and his attention unwearied—when he thought proper to quit his post, those of his own profession, regretted the loss of a friend and companion, whose humanity and candour they had experienced, and on whose impartiality and justice they knew they could firmly rely.

Once again, King set forth on tour. "Got into the Mail Coach for Bath at Kensington about eight in the Evening" of Sunday 14 September 1788, he jotted in a diary (now at the British Library) which he was to keep for the next nine months. In it he briefly but vividly registered his progress to Birmingham, Bristol, Dublin, Belfast, Glasgow, Edinburgh, York, Leeds, and way points, and back again to London on 23 June 1789. At each place he was enthusiastically received, socially and professionally, but he endured some hardships traveling because of the unusually heavy snowfalls in the spring of 1789. He also suffered long sieges of the gout, to which he was increasingly susceptible, attacks brought on perhaps by the late hours and conviviality which he could not resist and which he ruefully recorded. Despite sentimental ties to the Drury Lane house and its company, King, still smarting from his managerial experiences, was in no hurry to return to Sheridan and Linley. The profits from his successful tour gave him leisure to search for alternatives, and the notices of those successes gave him greater bargaining power. He began a correspondence with Thomas Harris of Covent Garden Theatre which culminated in an agreement of 11 November 1789 now in the Harvard Theatre Collection, one of the most interesting documents of its kind still surviving:

Messieurs Harris and King.
To commence as soon as may be thought advantageous to both Parties. K. to find his own Dresses. To finish the first part of the Agreement on the 9th of February unless Mr. Harris should choose to fix the Benefit Night on Thursday the 11th,—of which night it is to be understood K expects to be allow'd to give the Publick a fortnight Notice. The Reward five hundred Pounds and a Benefit free of all Expence—three hundred of said five hundred pounds to be paid in manner following—the first on the 9th of December 1789, the second on the 9th of January 1790, and the third on the 9th of February 1790.

The second Part of the Agreement to commence on or about the 10th of April and to continue till the 10th of June 1790. The fourth hundred to be paid on the 10th of May, the last on finishing the Contract—the which K will perform with attention and the heartiest of good-will, still having it understood, that, (as he is known to be neither capricious nor indolent) *real* Illness shall not be considered as a breach: and hoping that should any un-avoidable delay happen, in travelling to fulfill the last part of the Engagement, no Advantage will be taken in such case by Mr. Harris, who seems inclined to deal liberally in every other.

In other letters, leading up to that agreement, King looked forward to a renewal of the engagement in a second and then a third season. But the attractions of the elder patent house would prove too strong.

On 20 November 1789 King made his first appearance at Covent Garden Theatre, playing Touchstone in *As You Like It* and Sir John Trotley in *Bon Ton*. He acted there some two dozen times, choosing to play for his benefit on 2 February 1790 Sancho in *Lovers' Quarrels*, his own alteration of Vanbrugh's comedy *The Mistake*. But he rejoined the Drury Lane Company in 1790–91 and during the rebuilding of the theatre in 1791–92 went with the Drury Lane company to the King's Theatre in the Haymarket. Michael Atkins brought King to Belfast's Rosemary Lane Theatre for six nights and engaged him at Derry for six more in July and August 1791. In the summer of 1792 he played for a while at Richmond, Surrey, and at Birmingham in the summer of 1793, missing his benefit there on some undisclosed date because of a badly sprained ankle incurred in performance, according to a Folger manuscript. At 63 he was still dancing. In April 1794 King performed in the new Drury Lane house. He remained there until the end of his career, though with increasing vexation, not only because of arrears in his own pay but also because of the general decline of Drury Lane under the listless and irresponsible direction of Sheridan.

King was perpetually anxious about money and was frequently near want or in danger of jail for debt, despite his large earnings. His gregarious nature led him to frequent gambling clubs and he lost heavily. The story goes that one night, when he had recovered £2000 of his losses David and Eva Maria Garrick induced him to take an oath that he would never again touch cards or dice. The resolution was kept until the death of Garrick. But in 1785 he entered his name at Miles's Club in St James's Street, and soon he was gambling again. He lost his savings and an opportunity to purchase a share in Drury Lane. He sold his Hampton villa and moved to the modest house at No 56, New Store Street, Bedford Square, in which he lived until his death.

A signed salary receipt in the Harvard Theatre Collection shows King to have been receiving £700 "for Salary and in lieu of Benefit" in the 1780–81 season, a sum which James Winston asserts he also enjoyed in 1781–82 and 1782–83. Evidently the privilege was then withdrawn. A manuscript in the British Library states that in 1790–91 "He acted exactly fifty nights, which made his Engagement 500 Pounds, besides his Benefit." The account book for the season shows his benefit receipts that year to have been £296 17*s*. which, after house charges of £114 3*s*. 3*d*. were subtracted, left him £182 13*s*. 9*d*. In a rapidly inflating economy he was far worse off in 1791 than he had been in 1781. Despite his great popularity, bad weather, a competing public spectacle, or some other occurrence could diminish his benefit takings. It was a chance all actors took. A clipping in the Enthoven Collection chides the public roundly for neglecting him on 24 May 1797: "Mr. King's night. —A very indifferent house indeed!!! Such is the gratitude of the public, and thus is merit rewarded. It deserves to be recorded, that one of the best, the oldest, and most favorite performers in the kingdom, had, on the night of his benefit, little more than expenses in the house." The account book confirms it: receipts £290 9*s*. 6*d*., charges £211 18*s*., profit: £79 11*s*. 6*d*. The salary was constant—£500, but, with inflation, worth less each year. The benefit profits fluctuated: in 1797 £79, but the next year £462, principally because King inveigled his old friend William "Gentleman" Smith back to the stage after eight years of retirement, to play his original Charles Surface. But a year later King gained only £206 7*s*.

Still, King was over the years an extremely well-paid actor, and even though he had unwieldy debts and expensive habits, he could have been comfortable if he had been able to receive from the evasive Sheridan even the larger proportion of what he earned. In the British Library and the Folger and Huntington libraries, letters survive from King to his embarrassed friend Richard Peake, the theatre's treasurer, reflecting King's frustration at the fact that his salary was perpetually in arrears. A few excerpts will convey his anguish. In 1791 he wrote Peake:

Courtesy of the Garrick Club

THOMAS KING as Sir Peter Teazle, FRANCES ABINGTON as Lady Teazle, WILLIAM SMITH as Charles Surface, and JOHN PALMER as Joseph Surface.

by James Roberts

The salary, which was to have been *regularly* sent me every Monday, is not only defer'd till the middle of the week, but when two are due one is sent. Of the six guineas a week, which you said shou'd be sent faithfully in the course of each week, . . . not *one single* payment has been offer'd, nor even mentioned, though there are . . . *six* now due . . . I suffer extremely. I was . . . very hardly run by Mr Sheridan's breach of promise in last year's payments—of which I have since only received twenty pounds. Of this year's salary, which if regularly paid, wou'd have amounted to more than £240—I have received, on much importunity, only £110. 13. 4.

And in 1799:

I will not *in imitation of certain great examples* [i.e., Mrs Siddons] say I will not play till I have my money—but in a tone of kindness and sincerity I must tell you, that if I do not get my future money in a style of regularity . . . I shall be oblig'd *in spite of myself*, either to shut myself up, or run away—

And in 1800:

I thank you for your very kind note. I think I am safe for to night—but "the snake is scotch'd, but not kill'd"—What have I suffer'd for a few days last past! It is a most dreadful thing to have business with a man, whose talents one must admire, to whose interest one is sincerely devoted—*but* on whose word one cannot with safety rely!

But though King found that "All this wailing and bickering is dreadful—nay 'tis damnable," he had to keep up those tactics to the end of his Drury Lane days.

On 24 May 1802, on the occasion of his

final benefit at Drury Lane, King played Sir Peter Teazle and spoke to a tearful audience a farewell address composed for him by Richard Cumberland the popular writer of sentimental comedy:

> *Whilst in my heart these feelings yet survive,*
> *That keep respect and gratitude alive—*
> *Feelings which, tho' all others should decay,*
> *Will be the last that time can bear away,*
> *The fate that none can fly from, I invite,*
> *And do my own dramatic death this night.*
>
> *Patrons, farewel!——*
> *Tho' you still kindly my defects would spare,*
> *Constant indulgence who would wish to bear?*
> *Who that retains the scenes of brighter days,*
> *Can sue for pardon, while he pants for praise?*
> *On well-earn'd fame, the mind with pride reflects,*
> *But pity sinks the man whom it protects.*
> *Your fathers had my strength, my only claim*
> *Was zeal, their favour was my only fame;*
> *Of late, too often, when the whole was due,*
> *I've paid half service to the Muse and you.*
> *Not what I was, I now decline the field,*
> *And ground those arms which I but feebly wield,*
> *The poet nearly breathless, lame, or blind,*
> *Whilst the Muse visits his creative mind,*
> *Continues waving his immortal wreath,*
> *Lives in his fame, and triumphs over death!*
> *Whilst every chance that deals the passing blow,*
> *Lays the poor actor's short-liv'd trophies low.*
> *That chance has come to me, and comes to all,*
> *My drama's done, I let the curtain fall.*

King then retired to the green room, where the comedienne, Dorothy Jordan, on behalf of the Drury Lane company, presented him "with a silver cup, cover, and salver of the value of one hundred guineas," according to Winston. The salver was "richly decorated with his arms splendidly engraved in the centre." On the cup were engraved the names of all the performers of the house, and these lines from *Henry V*: "If he be not fellow with the best King,/Thou shalt find him the King of good fellows." He had been 55 years on the stage.

Few players in the history of the London stage have come anywhere near playing so many excellent "original" parts in comedy as Tom King did. Foremost among them were, in 1766, Lord Ogleby in *The Clandestine Marriage* and, in 1777, Sir Peter Teazle in *The School for Scandal*. Lord Ogleby, which Garrick had written with himself in mind, King gradually molded to his own personality. But Sir Peter—like Frances Abington's Lady Teazle, William Smith's Charles Surface, John Palmer's Joseph, and all the other parts—was tailored by Sheridan closely to fit the personality of the performer. It became the finest example of King's comic proficiency.

Other characters introduced to the stage by King, in order chronological, by season, were: in 1759–60, Sir Harry's Servant in James Townley's *High Life below Stairs*, Squire Groom in Charles Macklin's *Love à-la-Mode*, Harlequin in David Garrick's *Harlequin's Invasion*, and William in Arthur Murphy's *The Way to Keep Him*; in 1760–61, Scribble in George Colman's *Polly Honeycomb*, Florimond in John Hawkesworth's *Edgar and Emmeline*, Sir Harry Beagle in Colman's *The Jealous Wife*, and Captain LeBrush in Joseph Reed's *The Register Office*; in 1761–62, Mask in Colman's *The Musical Lady*; in 1763–64, Smatter in King's own *Love at First Sight*; in 1766–67, Linco in Garrick's *Cymon* and Spatter in Colman's *The English Merchant*; in 1767–68, Glib in Garrick's *A Peep behind the Curtain*, Syllogism in William Kenrick's *The Widow'd Wife*, Cecil in Hugh Kelly's *False Delicacy*, Shatterbrain in Isaac Bickerstaffe's *The Absent Man*, and Martin in his own *Wit's Last Stake*; in 1768–69, Dr Cantwell in Bickerstaffe's alteration of *The Non-Juror* called *The Hypocrite*, Pistol in William Kenrick's *Falstaff's Wedding*, and Captain Lloyd in Elizabeth Griffith's *The School for Rakes*; in 1769–70, Ralph in Garrick's *The Jubilee* and Sir George Hastings in Kelly's *A Word to the Wise*; and in 1770–71, Muskato in Bickerstaffe's *'Tis Well It's No Worse* and Belcour in Richard Cumberland's *The West Indian*.

King introduced also, in 1771–72, Sir Dingle in Garrick's *The Institution of the Garter* and Mortimer in Cumberland's *The Fashionable Lover*; in 1772–73, Hargrave in William O'Brien's *The Duel*; in 1773–74, General Savage in Kelly's *The School for Wives*; in 1774–75, Bayes in Garrick's *The Meeting of the Company*, Old Groveby in John Burgoyne's *The Maid of the Oaks*, Nightshade in Richard Cumberland's *The Choleric Man*, and Sir John Trotley in Garrick's *Bon Ton*; in 1775–76, Jerry in Henry Bate's *The Blackamoor Wash'd White*, and Young Dormer in Thomas Vaughan's *Love's Metamorphoses*; in 1776–77, Trimwell in Robert Jephson's *The Hotel* and Sprightly in George Colman's *New Brooms*; in 1778–79, Sir George Boncour in

Henry Fielding's *The Fathers* and Lord Jehu in *Jehu* (author unknown); in 1779–80, Puff in R. B. Sheridan's *The Critic*, and Sir William Woodley in Mrs Elizabeth Griffith's *The Times*; in 1780–81, Sir Andrew Acorn in M. R. Andrews's *Dissipation*; in 1781–82, Commodore Broadside in Richard Griffith's *Variety*; in 1782–83, Sir Hercules Caustic in Samuel J. Pratt's *The School for Vanity*; in 1784–85, Jack Hustings in Cumberland's *The Natural Son*; and in 1785–86, Aldobrand in James Cobb's *The Strangers at Home* and Sir Clement Flint in Burgoyne's *The Heiress*.

King's zest for learning new parts hardly diminished with the years. He added, in 1786–87, Mr Wilmot in Thomas Holcroft's *Seduction* and Don Alexis in Hannah Cowley's *A School for Greybeards*; in 1787–88, Mr Vandercrab in Henry Lee's *The New Peerage* and Mushroom in Cobb's *Love in the East*; in 1789–90, Sancho in King's own *Lover's Quarrels*; in 1791–92, Admiral Cleveland in Joseph Richardson's *The Fugitive*; in 1794–95, Sir Adam Contest in Elizabeth Inchbald's *The Wedding Day*, Sir Miles Mowbray in Cumberland's *First Love*, and Tempest in Cumberland's *The Wheel of Fortune*; in 1795–96, Lord Leverington in Cumberland's *The Dependent*, Sir Marmaduke Maxim in Prince Hoare's *Indiscretion*, and the Fool in Samuel Ireland's "Shakespeare" forgery *Vortigern*; and in 1796–97, Sir Solomon Cynic in Frederick Reynolds's *The Will*.

In addition, King played original parts unspecified in Kitty Clive's *A Fine Lady's Returning from a Rout*, in 1762–63; in Colman's *The Deuce Is in Him* and Mrs Frances Sheridan's *The Dupe* in 1763–64; in Mrs Clive's *The Faithful Irishwoman* and James Townley's *The Tutor*, in 1764–65; and in Edward Thompson's *The Hobby Horse*, in 1765–66.

Besides those "creations" Tom King gave interpretations, more often than not the best of his time, to dozens of the characters large and small which populated the comic repertoire. On rare occasions, usually on his benefit nights (when by custom the beneficiary was allowed to choose his role) he tried a tragedy part but he was seldom so successful. The list of his other roles as he accumulated them includes: in 1759–60, Sosia in *Amphitryon*, Dick in *The Apprentice*, Flash in *Miss in Her Teens*, Sancho in *The Mistake*, Scrub in *The Beaux' Stratagem*, Petruchio in *Catherine and Petruchio*, Tattle in *Love for Love*, and Sir Amorous Vainwit in *Woman Is a Riddle*; in 1760–61, Stephano in *The Tempest*, Feignwell in *A Bold Stroke for a Wife*, and the Gentleman Usher in *King Lear*; in 1761–62, Osric in *Hamlet*, Smirk, Shift, and Mrs Cole in *The Minor* (all in an evening), Cloten in *Cymbeline*, the Clown in *Florizel and Perdita*, Archer in *The Beaux' Stratagem*, and Clincher Junior in *The Constant Couple*; in 1762–63, Parolles in *All's Well that Ends Well*, Pistol in *2 Henry IV*, Trappolin in *A Duke and No Duke*, the Frenchman in *Lethe*, Kastril in *The Alchemist*, Speed in *The Two Gentlemen of Verona*, Wellbred in *Every Man in His Humour*, Buck in *The Englishman in Paris*, Gibby in *The Wonder*, and Lord Trinket in *The Jealous Wife*; in 1763–64, Jeremy in *Love for Love*, Sir Harry in *The Jealous Wife*, Tom in *The Conscious Lovers*, Count Basset in *The Provk'd Husband*, Squib in *Tunbridge Walks*, and Lovel in *High Life below Stairs*; and in 1764–65, Ranger in *The Suspicious Husband*, Prattle in *The Deuce Is in Him*, Roderigo in *Othello*, Sir John in *All in the Wrong*, Sparkish in *The Country Wife*, and Marplot in *The Busy Body*.

He added to his repertoire in 1765–66, Coupée in *The Virgin Unmask'd*, Young Philpot in *The Citizen*, and Abel in *The Committee*; in 1767–68, Linco in *Cymon*, Apollo in *The Royal Chace*, Captain LeBrush in *The Register Office*, Novel in *The Plain Dealer*, Sir John Restless in *All in the Wrong*, and Witwoud in *The Way of the World*; in 1768–69, Cecil in *False Delicacy*, Lord Lace in *The Lottery*, Sir Bashful Constant in *The Way to Keep Him*, Hodge in *Love in a Village*, Ralph in *The Maid of the Mill*, Aesop and Lord Chalkstone in *Lethe*, Touchstone in *As You Like It*, and Dr Cantwell in *The Hypocrite*; in 1769–70, Sir John Restless in *All in the Wrong*, Shylock in *The Merchant of Venice*, Lissardo in *The Wonder*, the Copper Captain in *Rule a Wife and Have a Wife*, and the title role in *Richard III*; in 1770–71, Leander in *Harlequin's Jubilee*, Cadwallader in *The Author*, and Trim in *The Funeral*; in 1771–72, the title role in *The Miser*, Malvolio in *Twelfth Night*, Moody in *The Country Girl*, Brilliant in *The Ladies' Last Stake*, and Mizen in *The Fair Quaker of Deal*; in 1772–73, Wilding in *The Gamesters*, Hargrave in *The Duel*, Sir Paul Plyant in *The Double Dealer*, the Drunken Colonel in *The Intriguing Chambermaid*, and Minuet in *The Englishman in Paris*; in 1773–74, Martin in *Neck* or *Nothing*, Bayes in *The Rehearsal*, and Mortimer in *The Fashionable Lover*; in 1774–75, Lucio in *Measure for Measure*; and in 1775–76, Sir Amorous in *Epicoene*.

King added, in 1776–77, Sir Joseph Wittol in *The Old Bachelor* and Sir Anthony Absolute in *The Rivals*; in 1777–78, Sir John Brute in *The Provok'd Wife*; in 1778–79, Sir Anthony Branville in *The Discovery*; in 1782–83, Mr Plenty in *The City Madam*; in 1785–86, Stanza in *The Widow Bewitch'd* and Sir Clement Flint in *The Heiress*; in 1786–87, Benedick in *Much Ado about Nothing*; in 1787–88, Ben in *Love for Love*; in 1792–93, Governor Harcourt in *The Chapter of Accidents*; in 1793–94, Sir Archy Macsarcasm in *Love à-la-Mode*; in 1794–95, Duke Murcia in *The Child of Nature*; in 1796–97, Cimberton in *The Conscious Lovers* and Don Manuel in *She Wou'd and She Wou'd Not*; and in 1798–99, Linger in *A Will and No Will*.

> *The lively King, so sprightly and alert,*
> *Seems formed by nature for the smart and pert;*
> *Nothing his progress in this cast can stop,*
> *A jaunty clown, a valet, or a fop;*
> *In other walks of humour he can please,*
> *And excellently hides his native ease,*
> *And rises pleasing to the candid eye,*
> *But truth declares not eminently high.*

So declared the anonymous author of *The Rational Rosciad* early in 1767, when King had been some 20 years on the stage. Yet though he continued to the end of his career to play the "smart and pert," the valet and the fop, he had begun in 1766, with his Lord Ogleby in *The Clandestine Marriage*, to exploit with great skill a sub-specialty of aristocratic eccentrics, usually elderly, which would especially endear him to his public.

In *The Dramatic Censor* of 1770 Francis Gentleman, his constant partisan but nevertheless his most revealing critic, described King's conception of the character:

> Lord Ogleby . . . is most certainly as much an original, and as much a child of laughter, as any character on the stage—harmlessly vain, pleasantly odd, commendably generous; a coxcomb not void of sense, a master full of whim, a lover full of false fire, yet a valuable friend; possessed of delicate feelings and nice honour: the peculiarities of this difficult part are supported with eminent abilities by that most excellent comedian Mr. KING, who notwithstanding his chief praise derives from being a chaste delineator of nature, here strikes out in the water colour painting of life, a most beautiful and striking caricature, conceived with some degree of poetical extravagance, yet so meliorated by his execution, that thousands who have never seen such a human being as Lord Ogleby, must, amidst involuntary bursts of laughter, allow, nay wish there may be such a man, whose foibles are so inoffensive.

Gentleman—a critic notoriously swayed by "sensibility"—made it plain that in his estimation King's special excellence in the character derived from the amiability of King's own personality:

> If Mr. KING shews more merit in any one passage than another, it is where Sterling says to the young couple "Lovewell, you shall leave my house; and madam, you shall follow him"; to which the peer with infinite good nature replies, "and if they do, I shall receive them into mine." Though it does not always follow that what an actor feels most he can express best; yet we may venture to say a kind of sympathetic unison gives this short sentence peculiar force and beauty in Mr. KING's utterance.

Gentleman had effusive praise for King as Touchstone ("in respect of pointedness and spirit properly mixed, a forceable yet free articulation, Mr. KING stands foremost in our estimation"), as Tom in *The Conscious Lovers* ("for the author's meaning, and nature without any trick, we must appeal to the animated critical execution of Mr. KING"), as Roderigo in *Othello* ("if the reptile can be made sufferable, it is . . . by his performance"), as Linco in *Cymon* ("we don't recollect a more disengaged, chaste piece of acting"). Several actors Gentleman commended in Dr. Cantwell in *The Hypocrite*, but they all want "that essential ease and plausibility which makes us give Mr. KING the preference." He was not seen often enough as Hodge in *Love in a Village*; he was an inimitable Sir John Restless in *All in the Wrong*; he was better than Macklin or Theophilus Cibber as Marplot in *The Busy Body* and as good as Garrick (though second to Woodward).

Gentleman's criticisms were written before King's triumph in his second most favored—and second most favorite—character, Sir Peter Teazle—one that was not only shaped by King's own informing spirit after its creation but tai-

Harvard Theatre Collection

THOMAS KING, as Puff

engraving by Young, after Zoffany

lored to the actor's capabilities by Sheridan. Indeed, one tradition asserts that King assisted in writing the character. The *European Magazine* in 1791 gave him, at any rate, equal credit for the success of that most spirited comedy of the century:

> *The wayward testiness of ancient life,*
> *The froward jealousy and peevish strife,*
> *How well he marks his Teazle shall proclaim*
> *Where bard and actor share a mingled fame.*

One of the most intelligent actors of his century, King usually sensibly confined a talent which could have succeeded to some degree in any walk of performance to those few lines of comedy where he was supreme. There were exceptions. Shylock had a great attraction for him, and he did the part passably well. But though, as Francis Gentleman wrote, "his Shylock is by no means so deficient as many principal parts which might be pointed out at both houses," it added nothing to his fame.

However we admire Mr. KING in a great variety of his undertakings, we cannot so far warp opinion as to think him capital in the Jew; weight, design, and extent of powers, are wanting; the cruelty does not sit easy on his features, nor the violent passions on his voice; which though agreeably distinct, and happily voluble in comic dialogue, cannot trace nature through any violent transitions; to this we may attribute his estrangement from the tragic walk; had he utterance equal to his judgment, easy figure and marking countenance, he could be as conspicuous a favorite with the queen of tears, as he now most justly is with the queen of smiles. . . .

An anonymous critic in *Felix Farley's Bristol Journal* on 18 May 1771 spoke in the highest terms of his acting but singled out his delivery of prologues for special praise:

> As a Prologue Speaker in the comic Style, he is undoubtedly unapproachable (but by Mr. Garrick). There is a happy Distinction in his Ease, Manner, Familiarity, and acting those dramatic Exordiums, so as to render them, in his Possession, Entertainments of the first Kind; indeed, the Audience are so sensible of this, that they never omit calling for them on those Nights the Pieces are represented, with an Avidity and Impatience that strongly indicate their pleasure.

After 1760 Garrick, himself a formidable speaker of prologues, turned most of the important ones over to King. His excellencies in the art saved many a play, for he had so great a fund of approval in the audience that much of it could be transferred even to an inferior play, and dramatists quickly learned that fact. William Hawkins asked, in *Miscellanies in Prose and Verse* (1775):

> And as a prologue speaker in the comic style, I would ask where is his equal? (Garrick . . . excepted); he possesses in an eminent degree, that lively, spirited, and quick sensation in his manner, which is so admirably adapted for speaking this kind of writing. But above all, is that sly knowledge of the world which is so excellently blended in Mr. King's features, and in his action, that it oft-times sends home effects to the furthermost . . . seats of the galleries. . . .

King drew praise, even from the sharp-quilled "Anthony Pasquin" (John Williams) in *The Children of Thespis* in 1786:

> *'Tis long since this veteran led the gay train*
> *Of laugh-loving mortals of poor* DRURY-LANE:
> *Tho' 'tis plain in his acting to trace the old school,*
> *He waits not with Nature, but makes her his rule.*
> *And so aptly his sallies accord with the sense,*
> *We can laugh, yet without giving Judgment offence:*

> *To fasten on sense, and seize on the heart.*
> ....
> In Touchstone *he's perfect,* Malvolio *great,*
> *To thought he gives strength, and to sentiment weight.*

Yet Williams was by then forced to observe that "his characters fade as his spirits decay."

> *And trembling he grasps to support his high station,*
> *In spite of the gout, and its damn'd flagellation.*

But Williams's hint of the imminence of King's professional demise was premature. After 1786, King went on introducing new characters and also, evidently, fresh conceptions during most of the following 16 years. At least one of the conceptions was controversial, critics apparently dividing according to whether or not they approved his stepping out of his long-established stage personality. When he played Falstaff for the first time, at the Haymarket on 6 August 1792, the *Morning Herald* approved: "Falstaff is rather more *satirical* than *facetious*. . . . This idea of the part, King adopted; and he gave the text with such correctness and force, that so far from lessening his reputation by attempting so arduous a character, he had in reality afforded new proof of his critical taste and versatility of genius." But King was rapped sharply in the *European Magazine*:

> Had this performance been a mere trial of his abilities in a new line of acting, the failure might have passed unnoticed, but as it was repeated a second time we are compelled to say that the Theatre hardly ever exhibited an instance of an excellent actor so entirely mistaking his talents. Falstaff in the hands of Mr. King lost all his jocularity. He was cold, sententious, tame and declamatory, and communicated to a very patient and candid audience nothing but surprise at the attempt and dissatisfaction at the execution.

By 1795 his fellow actor Francis Godolphin Waldron, in *Candid and Impartial Strictures on the Performers*, thought his "comic powers" were "considerably impaired by the great length of years since they were first called into action," though they had been "of the very first order." "His features have an archness that peculiarly fitted him for all the sprightly parts of comedy. His person is, or rather *was* a good one. . . . We always thought his action to have been considerably injured by an awkward stiffness, or an apparent *deadness* in his hands." Waldron thought King so far "advanced into the vale of years, as no doubt, ere long to compell him to quit the mimic world for ever." But Waldron had also miscalculated King's professional demise by seven years.

During that final period of King's life the young William Hazlitt saw him act. Hazlitt, unlike Williams and Waldron, had no memories of King's brilliance when he was at his zenith. He could, however, compare him to the aging "Gentleman" Lewis, Jack Bannister, Dicky Suett, J. W. Dodd, and John Quick, and to the more recent John Liston, Samuel Simmons, and Andrew Cherry. Hazlitt's memoirs of King among the others, in the *London Magazine* of January 1820, is famous:

> there was King, whose acting left a taste on the palate, sharp and sweet like a quince; with an old, hard, withered face, like a John-apple, puckered up into a thousand wrinkles; with shrewd hints and tart replies; "with nods and becks and wreathed smiles"; who was the real amorous, wheedling, or hasty, choleric, peremptory old gentleman in Sir Peter Teazle and Sir Anthony Absolute; and the true, that is, the pretended, clown in Touchstone, with wit sprouting from his head like a pair of ass's ears, and folly perched on his cap like the horned owl.

Every surviving piece of evidence about King points to a man intensely professional, a quick study, prompt in attendance at rehearsals, never feigning illness or throwing a tantrum to avoid a part, and, except for the one instance we have cited (which appears to have been at least partly the fault of his wife and partly that of Garrick), never difficult about contract terms. On 10 June 1800 he played Sir Peter Teazle for the two hundred and fifty-fourth time, and it was then noted that since its first night, 8 May 1777, he had missed only two announced performances, both because of illness. Gentleman underlined his sense of responsibility and his willingness "when occasion calls" to

> condescend agreeably and make trifles interesting: this is no small point of praise; for many capital actors, thinking a character beneath their dignity, throw contempt on the audience; but Mr. KING's great good sense and respect for the public, prevents him from so ridiculous a start of vanity—I wish every theatrical gentleman would follow the excellent example, and comparatively speaking, take

Courtesy of the Garrick Club
THOMAS KING
by Wilson

as much pains with two or three lengths, as two or three and twenty.

King's concern for his fellow actors extended beyond his fostering the Drury Lane Fund and fighting for their rights at that house. When, in February 1800, Johnstone, Holman, Pope, Incledon, Munden and other leading members of the Covent Garden company published a pamphlet accusing their proprietor Thomas Harris of unjustly curtailing their free tickets, advancing house charges for benefits, and increasing fines for rules infractions, they invited King to their council of war at the Garrick's Head Tavern. He prudently demurred but sent them a warm letter of encouragement:

. . . I beg leave not only to say, but *most publicly to avow*, that I do not merely and luke-warmly *approve* the conduct of the gentlemen of the Covent-Garden Committee, but consider it as *highly meritorious*; challenging the thanks of the whole body of actors, of which body I have now the honour to boast myself the father.

King's amiable, clubbable personality earned him many friends outside the profession. In his younger and middle years he kept company with the sporting beaus and bloods of England's upper middle class. The rake William Hickey in his *Memoirs* recalled that, about 1768,

In the summer we had another club, which met at the Red House in Battersea fields, nearly opposite Ranelagh, a retired and pretty spot. . . . This club consisted of some very respectable persons, amongst them were Mr. Powell of the Pay Office; Mr. Jupp, the East India Company's architect; Mr. Whitehead, a gentleman of independent fortune; King, the celebrated actor; Major Sturt of the Engineers; and others. The game we played was an invention of our own and called field tennis, which afforded noble exercise.

On 22 February 1783 King was elected to the Sublime Society of Beefsteaks, which contained representatives of the professions and elevated members of London society as well as prominent players. In later years he seems to have been on the outer edge of the glamorous Garrick circle. He knew and was entertained by prominent persons all over the three Kingdoms. (Curiously, Charles Dibdin in his first *Musical Tour* [1788], put forth the opinion that "there was no man whom Mr. Garrick openly caressed and secretly hated as much as Mr. King. I know this as fact, or I would not assert it." Dibdin attributed the "fact" to King's independent spirit joined to his great ability. Dibdin even believed that Garrick assigned King the objections to Shakespeare in the dialogue the two spoke at the Jubilee of 1769 in order to arouse subconscious animosity to King, there "in the place where about twelve hundred people were in enthusiastic admiration of SHAKESPEARE." The opinion would be troublesome to Garrick's reputation if not to King's, were it not for the fact that Dibdin's own highly suspicious and quarrelsome nature robs his testimony of force.)

King's devotion to his wife was absolute, as, apparently, was hers to him. They lived together in conspicuous amity for 40 years. On his acting tour to Ireland and Scotland of 1788–89, when he was away for over nine months, he wrote Mrs King four or five times a week and recorded in his diary the reception of above 110 letters from her.

Harvard Theatre Collection
THOMAS KING
engraving by Daniell, after G. Dance

He was a man of culture, if not of deep learning, and his Westminster schooling shows in the stylistic grace and easy classical quotation of some of his letters to his friend the Etonian and Cantabrigian William Smith, as well as in the dramatic efforts we have mentioned.

King's health had not been good since before 1790, for he was not willing to forego the pleasures of the table. He had grown heavy, and gout, which had plagued him for years, laid longer and more serious sieges. He wrote in his memorandum book on 14 December 1800: "Awoke with the gout in both feet—lay in bed," and he remained in bed through 25 December, and was confined to his room until January. It is likely that he died of complications from the disease.

King died at his house in New Store Street, Bedford Square, on 11 December 1805. He was buried in the churchyard of St Paul, Covent Garden, on 20 December, attended by the entire company of Drury Lane. On 12 February 1806 his widow was given a benefit. Winston reported that "The produce of this night, together with a handsome contribution amongst the principal performers of both theatres, procured her a respectable addition to what would otherwise have been but a scanty income." A feature of the evening was the recitation, with music and action of "Thalia's Tears! A Tributary Sketch inscribed to the Memory of the late, *Thomas King*, Comedian," written by the comic actor Andrew Cherry. It was not published but the manuscript is among the Larpent papers in the Huntington Library, along with the prompter Richard Wroughton's application for a license to perform it. The directions are revealing. The scene is a "Gothic Aisle" and "In the Centre a Monumental Urn of King encircled with his Characters. Thalia, weeping at his Tomb, wearing a wreath of Willow. . . ." Apparently a great many of King's characters surround the urn, but only four—Sir Peter Teazle, Sir John Trotley, Lord Ogleby, and Touchstone—are given speaking parts.

The catalogue of the British Library lists Thomas King's *Droll Collection of Oddities*, London, 1810(?), a production with which the actor certainly had nothing to do.

Portraits of Thomas King include:

1. By Richard Crosse, deaf and dumb miniaturist of Henrietta Street, Covent Garden. Present location unknown. Crosse's ledgers record that King sat on 31 December 1784.

2. By George Dance, 1797. Pencil drawing, sold from the estate of the Rev George Dance, grandson of the artist, at Christie's on 1 July 1898. Present location unknown. Engraving by W. Daniell, published by the engraver, 1809.

3. By Thomas Gainsborough. A portrait by Gainsborough supposedly of Thomas King was in the Carroll Gallery, Hanover Square, London, about 1930, and reputedly now is in a collection in Dublin. The identification of the subject is questionable.

4. By Valentine Green, 1769. At the Courtauld Institute, No 4344.

5. By H. D. Hamilton. Present location unknown. Engraving by J. R. Smith, published by Hooper, 1772.

6. By Alexander Pope, the actor. Miniature in crayons, 1791. Bought for £1 15s. by Webster at the Winston sale at Puttick & Simpson on 13 December 1849. In the collection of E. Donner. An anonymous engraving was published by Read, 1799, and an engraving by Ridley was published as a plate to the *Monthly Mirror*, May 1800.

7. By Benjamin Wilson. Full-length, standing among tall trees, looking at a bust of Shakespeare. In the Garrick Club, No 28.

8. By Benjamin Wilson. Full-length, standing, profile to right, hat in right hand, stick in left. In the Garrick Club, No 391.

9. Engraved portrait by R. Stanier. In the British Museum.

10. By unknown engraver. Speaking the prologue to *Dissipation*. Published by Alexander Hogg, 1781.

11. By unknown engraver. Published as a plate to *Hibernian Magazine*, March 1771.

12. By unknown engraver. Oval frame on pedestal.

13. As Sir Clement Flint, with Elizabeth Farren as Lady Emily, in *The Heiress*. Engraving by J. Jones, after J. Downman. Published by Jones, 1787; reissued by Tayleure, 1823.

14. As Brass in *The Confederacy*. Engraving by Audinet, after De Wilde. Published as a plate to *Bell's British Library*, 1792. The same picture, by an anonymous engraver, was printed by Cooke, in 1806, but undated.

15. As Brass. By unknown engraver. Standing, legs apart, hand in trouser pocket.

16. As Captain Bobadil in *Every Man in His*

KING

Humour. Engraving by Terry. Published by Harrison as a plate to an edition of the play, 1780.

17. As Fame speaking the prologue to *The Maid of the Oaks.* Engraving by Cook. Published 1779.

18. As Lissardo in *The Wonder.* Engraving by J. Roberts. Published as a plate to *Bell's British Theatre,* 1776. The portrait appears on a Delftware wall tile; an example is in the City of Manchester Art Gallery.

19. As Lucio in *Measure for Measure.* By unknown engraver. Published by Harrison as a plate to an edition of the play, 1779.

20. As Marplot in *The Busy Body.* By J. Roberts. Head and shoulders version. Offered at Christie's on 6 November 1973.

21. As Marplot. Engraving by Thornthwaite, after J. Roberts. Whole length. Published as a plate to *Bell's British Theatre,* 1776.

22. As Marplot. By unknown engraver. Published by Wenman as a plate to an edition of the play, 1777.

23. As Lord Ogleby in *The Clandestine Marriage.* Drawing by Jean Louis De Fesch. When an engraving by an unknown engraver was published by Smith and Sayer in 1769, the drawing belonged to the Duchess of Northumberland. Bought by Stone for 2s. in the Winston sale at Puttick & Simpson on 13 December 1849. Present location unknown. An engraving by J. Basire was published by Jeffrey & Faden, 1773.

24. As Lord Ogleby. By S. De Wilde. Canvas in the Garrick Club. Different from No 25.

25. As Lord Ogleby. By S. De Wilde. Location unknown. Engraving by Thornthwaite, published as a plate to *Bell's British Library,* 1792. An engraving by Clayton was published as a plate to Jones's *British Theatre,* 1792; and an anonymous engraving was published as a plate to *British Drama,* 1794.

26. As Lord Ogleby. By S. Drummond. Location unknown. Engraving by W. Bromley, published as a plate to the *European Magazine,* 1791.

27. As Lord Ogleby. By Lemoine. Sold at Christie's on 22 July 1871. The canvas is now in the Players' Club, New York.

28. As Lord Ogleby, with Sophia Baddeley as Fanny Sterling and Robert Baddeley as Canton. By Johann Zoffany. The painting was commanded by George III after seeing a performance on 12 October 1769. In the Garrick Club, acquired with the Matthews Collection in 1835. Engraving by R. Earlom, 1772.

29. As Lord Ogleby. By Johann Zoffany. Once owned by Sir Henry Irving. Sold at Christie's on 16 December 1905. Present location unknown.

30. As Lord Ogleby. By unknown engraver. Standing, flowers in right hand, left hand inside waistcoat.

31. As Parolles in *All's Well that End's Well.* By unknown artist. Pen, ink, and wash drawing in the British Museum. An anonymous engraving was published by Wenman as a plate to an edition of the play, 1778. This engraving was published again, by Laurie and Whittle in 1802, when it was incorrectly called Garrick as Leon in *Rule a Wife and Have a Wife.*

32. As Sir Paul Plyant in *The Double Dealer.* Watercolor by S. De Wilde. In the Harvard Theatre Collection.

33. As Perez in *Rule a Wife and Have a Wife.* Engraving by J. Collyer, after D. Dodd. Published as a plate to *New English Theatre,* 1776.

34. As Sir Peter Teazle, with William Smith as Charles Surface, John Palmer as Joseph Surface, and Mrs Abington as Lady Teazle, in the screen scene in *The School for Scandal.* Canvas by James Roberts, 1777. In the Garrick Club.

35. As Sir Peter Teazle. With title "The Original Sir Peter Teazle." By unknown engraver. Another impression titled "Sir Peter! The King of the Old School" was published as a plate to *Attic Miscellany,* 1792.

36. As Puff in *The Critic.* By Johann Zoffany, about 1780. In the collection of Brymer about 1900. Engraving by J. Young, published by King, 1803. A small engraving of the head by J. Goldar was published by Bellamy & Roberts, 1789.

37. As Rimenes, with an unknown performer as Mandane, in *Artaxerxes.* Engraving by Angus, after C. R. Ryley. Published by Lowndes, 1788.

38. As Sosia in *Amphitryon.* Engraving by Terry. Published by Harrison as a plate to an edition of the play, 1780.

39. As Touchstone in *As You Like It,* in a group of 17 Drury Lane performers in Shakespearean characters, in the "Immortality of Garrick." Canvas by G. Carter, 1782. In the

Gallery of the Royal Shakespeare Theatre, Stratford-upon-Avon. Engraving by Smith and Caldwell, published with key-plate, 1783.

40. As Touchstone. Engraving by Grignion, after Parkinson. Published as a plate to *Bell's Shakespeare*, 1775.

41. As Touchstone. By Johann Zoffany. In the Garrick Club.

42. As Touchstone. By unknown engraver. Published as a plate to *Hibernian Magazine*, 1789.

43. As Touchstone. By unknown artist. India ink and wash drawing in the British Museum. Anonymous engraving published by Wenman as a plate to an edition of the play, 1777.

44. As Mr Vandercrab, with Elizabeth Farren as Lady Charlotte Courtley and other actors in *The New Peerage*. By unknown engraver. Published as a plate to *Lady's Magazine*, 1787?

King, Mrs Thomas, Mary, née Baker
1730–1813, dancer, actress.

The juvenile Miss Baker whose first recorded appearance was in a *Peasant Dance* with Master Morgan at Goodman's Fields Theatre on 27 October 1746 was probably related, as sister or daughter, to the journeyman dancer and actor Thomas Baker, who was that year of the same company. She remained in the company for the season. The next season Goodman's Fields closed its doors and she was not listed anywhere. In 1748–49 she and her relative were dancing for Rich at Covent Garden. Miss Baker and Mrs Baker, also a dancer (and her mother?), joined Garrick at Drury Lane in 1749–50.

On 21 September 1750 Miss Baker, advertised as from Drury Lane, danced for the first time at the Smock Alley Theatre, Dublin. After she appeared as Juliet in *Romeo and Juliet*, advertised as making her debut in a speaking part, on 29 March 1751, she was apparently allowed occasional dramatic roles. The scattered notices show her repeating Juliet, for her benefit on 29 January 1751, to West Digges's Romeo and on 17 April 1752 playing Flora in *She Wou'd and She Wou'd Not*, "being the first time of her appearing in Boys Cloaths." She remained at Smock Alley, dancing and acting, through at least 1757–58 and was also seen at Cork in the summers of 1757 and 1758.

By 1750 Mary Baker (for the girl we have been following was certainly she) had met the masterful comedian, Thomas King, who that year came to Ireland and stayed for four consecutive winter seasons. It is not known when a serious relationship began with King, but when, after a season at Bath and several more at Dublin, he returned to Drury Lane in 1759, he brought Mary Baker with him. That season she seems to have been employed exclusively as a dancer, usually with many others, as in *The Flemish Feast*, in the afterpiece *Fortunatus*, with Grimaldi, Giorgi, Noverre, and Mrs Baker. She was both a Fantastic Spirit and a Pastoral Person in a musical version of *The Tempest*, figured in an unnamed dance following *The Enchanter*, and participated in a *Dance of the Millers* in *Harlequin Ranger*. Miss Baker's line was unvaried, in fact, for the next two seasons, except that on 22 October 1761 she was allowed Columbine in *Queen Mab* opposite Rooker's Harlequin, was given the speaking part of Lucy in *The Minor* on 9 November, and played Lucinda in *The Englishman in Paris* on 19 February 1762 and following. She opened the season of 1762–63 as Lucinda, but it was not an omen for her future, for besides a few minor named comedy parts—Phillis in *The Spring*, Mindora in *Daphne and Amintor*—and the retention of some columbine leads, she did not distinguish herself acting at Drury Lane under her maiden name. (On 13 November 1765, for some reason unknown, she played Lucinda in *The Conscious Lovers* at Covent Garden.) She was principally a chorus dancer.

Mary Baker's marriage in the summer of 1766 to the excellent Tom King, a power at Drury Lane since his great success on 20 February 1766 as Lord Ogleby in Garrick and Colman's *The Clandestine Marriage*, did not change her status at the theatre. She first appeared under her new name dancing a hornpipe in *The Beggar's Opera* on 25 September 1766. For the next six seasons she went on dancing in groups, playing columbines in a succession of pantomimes—*Queen Mab*, *The Hermit*, *The Elopement*, *The Witches*—and doing solo hornpipes incidental to the principal pieces. In fact her treatment (or fancied mistreatment) by the Drury Lane management from about the 1768–69 season was cited by King in a letter to Garrick of 3 November 1772 which alarmed Garrick and caused a momentary breach in his close friendship with King. King's principal complaint was the fact that he was paid less than Henry Woodward, the Covent Garden comedian. But he also had been "hurt . . . greatly" by the fact that his wife "seemed to be considered by the managers, though she never was by me, or I believe by the town, as an appendage to your humble servant." King added:

In her private capacity I allow she received, as her behaviour always merited, marks of attention; but in her public, I think she was in the latter period of her time, very indifferently treated. These motives partly (I cannot say wholly) induced me to take her from the theatre, before the time should come that I expected to treat with you again, that she might not be subjected to another slight, and that I might claim an addition to my own income, after having removed what seemed to be looked on as an incumbrance brought on you by me.

There was a flurry of expostulation and reply in which King detailed his charges of Mrs King's hard work and exploitation and Garrick vehemently declared "My Conscience cannot upbraid Me with One single Act of Injustice, or Neglect toward You or your Wife." King's salary was raised, Garrick's ruffled feelings were smoothed, and the friendship was resumed and continued to the end of Garrick's life. But Mrs King, "withdrawn" from the stage by her husband at the end of the 1771–72 season, never returned to it. Garrick, incidentally, had played for Mary King's final benefit, on 1 May 1772, netting her £223 2s. She had danced also at Bristol in the summers of 1771 and 1772.

Mary King may or may not have been valued at her worth by Drury Lane, and her ambitions as a dramatic performer were unfulfilled. But the judgment Sylas Neville set down in his diary after seeing her shine in *The Irish Lilt*— "certainly a very fine dancer and has the best set of legs I ever saw"—seems confirmed by the surviving performance record. Her private life seems also to have been exemplary, her marriage to the amiable Tom King quiet and devoted.

Mrs King had subscribed the usual £2 2s. to the Drury Lane Fund in 1766, but a disconnected series of entries in the Drury Lane Fund Book, beginning in March 1806, seem to reflect her difficulty in collecting aid when she applied for it. Perhaps that was because she was thought to be in better circumstances than she then was. Her husband had died on 11 December 1805. On 12 February 1806 she was granted a benefit which was supposed to have secured for her £610. But because of the disordered state of Drury Lane's finances under Sheridan in 1806, it may have been that not all of the money found its way into her hands. Moreover, Thomas King had spent expansively the large salaries he had earned, and his final years were straitened because of gambling losses. Mrs King had made some representation to the Fund, which her husband had so carefully fostered, by 18 March 1806. For on that date the Fund Book carried the notation "Mrs King was ans[were]^d. and agreed to make available a schedule of her affairs." By the meeting of 3 May Mrs King had "made no ans^r." On 6 June 1806 the theatre (presumably in behalf of the Fund) paid "Widow King for cloaths [£]35——." On 23 June the actor John Moody addressed her petition, asserting that she had not "a Shadow of Claim" from the Fund, inasmuch as she had admitted an income of £60 per annum, and on 10 August 1806: "Mrs King has withdrawn her application." There are no more entries concerning her in the Fund Book until 23 June 1810: "a L[ette]r from Mr [Richard] Wroughton [the old actor and former prompter] on Mrs Kings business." On 23 March 1811 "Mrs King pray'd relief" again; and on 21 July 1811 there is a note (not in the Fund Book, but in the miscellanea relating to the Fund, in the Garrick Club) signed by William Maddocks the Secretary: "Rec^d of Mr Moody [the treasurer?] the Sum of Ten Pounds for the use of Mrs King."

Mary Baker King died on 30 November 1813, according to the *Gentleman's Magazine*. The registers of St Paul, Covent Garden, show that she was buried there, "aged 83," on 8 December 1813.

Mary King's portrait was engraved by J. R. Smith, after H. Hamilton, and published by S. Hooper, 1772. An anonymous engraver pictured her as Ulla in an unnamed play; the print may not, however, be of Mrs King.

King, Thomas [*fl. 1794*], *violinist*.
Thomas King, of No 17, Union Row, Walworth, a violinist who played in the concerts

King, William [fl. 1750], *musician*.

A William King was bound apprentice to John Ward of the Worshipful Company of Musicians on 24 April 1750, according to the company's records at the London Guildhall. There is no record of his becoming a freeman.

King, William [fl. 1793–1809], *dancer, singer, actor*.

A W. King was at the Crow Street Theatre, Dublin, in the 1793–94 season, advertised as being on his first Irish adventure. When W. King came back to Crow Street in 1794–95, the bills hailed him as "from Sadler's Wells."

King made his debut at Covent Garden on 25 March 1799 as one of the more than 40 "principal characters" in the new pantomime *The Magic Oak*. He was paid £2 a week the first season to repeat several times whatever he did in that harlequinade and to go through similar motions (surely involving singing and dancing) as one of a crowd of Europeans in *Ramah Droog* and a Peasant in *The Old Cloathsman*. But he also achieved two named parts—Claud in *Raymond and Agnes* and Kildare in *The Round Tower*.

In 1799–1800 he added Harlequin Blacksword in *The Volcano; or, The Rival Harlequins* and Ulrick in *Joanna* but was also one of numerous Islanders in *Captain Cook*. That season he was raised to £3, a figure which was constant through 1804–5, which is as far as the Folger Library's Covent Garden accounts carry him. He was, however, on the roster until 1809, when he signed "William King" to a Covent Garden receipt for pay. He seldom served in anything but pantomime.

"King John." See KEMBLE, JOHN PHILIP.

"King of Clowns." See GRIMALDI, JOSEPH.

"King of Grief, The." See LEWIS, PHILIP.

Kingeston. See HINGESTON.

Kingham, Mrs [fl. 1780–1781], *actress, singer*.

Mrs Kingham played Louisa Dudley in *The West Indian* and Miss Tittup in *Bon Ton* at the Crown Inn, Islington, on 29 February 1780. She performed through 19 April, appearing as Miss Biddy in *Miss in Her Teens*, Lady Anne in *Richard III*, Colombine in *The Death and Restoration of Harlequin*, Juliet in *Romeo and Juliet*, Isabinda in *The Busy Body*, Bell in *The Deuce is in Him*, Nancy Grainger in *The Camp*, Maria in *The London Merchant*, Widow Brady in *The Irish Widow*, Cherry in *The Beaux' Stratagem*, and Jacintha in *The Suspicious Husband*. A year later, on 26 March 1781 at the Haymarket Theatre, she acted Ursula in *The Padlock*. Mrs Kingham was also a singer; on 5 April 1780, for instance, she introduced an epilogue song into *The Irish Widow* and sang "Tally O" after the fourth act of *The Beaux' Stratagem*.

Kingiston. See KYNASTON.

Kingshorne, Mr [fl. c.1705], *singer*.

The *Catalogue of Printed Music in the British Museum* lists a song entitled *As Oyster Nan stood by her Tub*, published about 1705 and described as sung by Mr Kingshorne.

Kingston, Mr [fl. 1671], *musician*.

On 4 August 1671 a Mr Kingston and several other musicians were ordered arrested by the Corporation of Music for having attempted "to teach practice and exercise musick in companeys or otherwise, to play at publique meetings without the approbation or lycence of the Marshall and Corporation of musick and in contempt of his Majesty's authority."

Kinnaston. See KYNASTON.

Kinnear. See MELLON.

Kipling, John [fl. 1719–1737], *treasurer*.

The *London Gazette* on 8 December 1719 cited John Kipling as the deputy treasurer of the Royal Academy of Music through whom subscriptions were available. He was also, either then or later, a deputy governor of the Academy. From time to time throughout the 1720s Kipling was mentioned in advertisements for Handel's opera house (the King's Theatre), which he served as cashier. When Handel's opera productions moved to Covent Garden in the spring of 1737, Kipling moved with them.

He was last mentioned on 5 July 1737 on the Prince of Wales's Register of Warrants.

Fortunately a personal note has survived about John Kipling in the *Craftsman* of 27 February 1727:

> He is, in short, a Man of undoubted *Integrity*, of consummate *Wisdom*, and of exemplary *Gravity*. He is compos'd and sedate in his Conduct, rigid in his Morals, and tall in his Person; slow in his Speech, yet using many words; and, to conclude all, a TREASURER *with* clean *and* empty Hands!
>
> I am persuaded, that every Reader must, by this Time, perceive that I can mean no body, in my description of the fore-going character, but that very worthy and excellent man Mr. KIPLIN, *Treasurer to that Honourable Corporation, the Royal Academy* of MUSICK.

Kipling, John *d. 1811, actor.*

At the Haymarket Theatre on 5 June 1784 John Kipling made his first London appearance, as Abel Drugger in *The Tobacconist*. He acted Simkin in *The Deserter* on 24 August and Simon in *The Apprentice* on 17 September.

On 8 January 1785 Kipling played Old Philpot in *The Citizen* at the Theatre Royal in Edinburgh. He acted there through July, appearing as Crabtree in *The School for Scandal*, Darby in *The Poor Soldier*, Davy in *Bon Ton*, Dr Freelove in *More Ways Than One*, D'Oyley in *Who's the Dupe?*, Filch in *The Beggar's Opera*, the Gravedigger in *Hamlet*, Grumio in *Catherine and Petruchio*, Hardy in *The Belle's Stratagem*, Inis in *The Wonder*, Jacob in *The Chapter of Accidents*, the Old Woman in *Rule a Wife and Have a Wife*, Probe in *A Trip to Scarborough*, Sir Fretful Plagiary in *The Critic*, Sir Harry Beagle in *The Jealous Wife*, Sir Shenkin in *Fontainebleau*, Spy in *The Rival Candidates*, Squire Thomas in *The What D'Ye Call It*, and Toby in *The Walking Statue*.

He performed again in Edinburgh in the spring of 1786 in such roles as Acres in *The Rivals*, Lord Grizzle in *Tom Thumb*, Master Stephen in *Every Man in His Humour*, Simpkin in *The Deserter*, Appletree in *The Recruiting Officer*, Tony Lumpkin in *She Stoops to Conquer*, and Ventoso in *The Tempest*. In 1787 Kipling acted at Brighton and at the Royalty Theatre in London, and in 1787–88 he played at Manchester and then Hanley. The 1788–89 and 1789–90 seasons found "Kippling" in Pero's troupe at Derby; in the winter of 1790–91 he acted again at the Theatre Royal in Edinburgh; and he was probably the Kipling at Richmond in 1796. Mrs Kipling, who seems not to have acted in London, appeared with her husband in the summer of 1784 at Brighton and was with him in Edinburgh in 1785. John Kipling died on 26 October 1811.

Kirby, Mr [*fl. 1748*], *actor.*

Mr Kirby played Worcester in *1 Henry IV* at Covent Garden Theatre on 6 December 1748.

Kirby, Mrs [*fl. 1767–1771*], *actress.*

Mrs Kirby was a member of Samuel Foote's summer company at the Haymarket Theatre in 1767. She played Jenny in *The Commissary* on 4 June and followed that with Lucia in *The Cheats of Scapin*, an Attendant in *The Taylors*, Delia in *Theodosius*, Myrtilla in *The Provok'd Husband*, Dolly Trull in *The Beggar's Opera*, Scentwell in *The Busy Body*, and Kitty in *The Lyar* (on 16 September, evidently her final appearance of the summer). She performed at the Orchard Street Theatre, Bath, from 1767–68 through 1769–70, and on 2 March 1771 Mrs Kirby played Ophelia in *Hamlet* at the theatre in Hall's Croft, Stratford.

Kirby, [Susannah?], [*fl. 1770?–1784?*], *actress, singer.*

Susannah Kirby was reported by John A. Langford in *A Century of Birmingham Life* (1870) as performing in Birmingham in 1770. Perhaps she was the Miss Kirby who acted for Joseph Fox at Brighton in 1777 and again in 1779, and perhaps also she was the Miss Kirby who from 1 January 1778 was on the Drury Lane pay list at a salary of (apparently) 5*s.* daily. She did not attract much attention that spring, though the bills named her as a member of the singing chorus for *Romeo and Juliet*. In the fall she began a full-season engagement at 6*s.* 8*d.* daily and was named in the playbills as Phoebe in *As You Like It*, the Niece in *The Chances*, Ariel in *The Tempest*, Teresa in *The Spanish Fryar*, an unspecified character in *The Wonders of Derbyshire* (which proved very popular), Arante in *King Lear*, the Milliner in *The Suspicious Husband*, Mrs Bruin in *The Mayor of Garratt*, Narcissa in *The Rival Candidates*, and the Masked Lady in *A Bold Stroke for a Wife*.

She remained at Drury Lane until December 1781, adding a number of new characters: Gipsy in *The Stratagem*, Lesbia in *Selima and Azor*, Mrs Henpeck in *The Times*, Myrtilla in *The Provok'd Husband*, Corinna in *The Citizen*, Ruth in *The Committee*, Lady Bab in *High Life below Stairs*, Jenny Diver in *The Beggar's Opera*, Wheedle in *The Miser*, Gymp in *Bon Ton*, Bianca in *Catherine and Petruchio*, Inis in *The Wonder*, Charmion in *All for Love*, Kitty in *The Lyar*, Margery in *Love in a Village*, Sukey Chitterlin in *Harlequin's Invasion*, Charlotte in *The Apprentice*, Mincing in *The Way of the World*, Clara in *Rule a Wife and Have a Wife*, Madam Florival in *The Deuce is in Him*, Theodosia in *The Maid of the Mill*, Miss Labradore in *Dissipation*, Arabella Zeal in *The Fair Quaker*, Charlotte Weldon in *Oroonoko*, Bridget in *Every Man in His Humour*, Maria in *The Register Office*, and Nancy in *The Camp*. In addition she participated in a number of works in generalized or unnamed characters, and she regularly sang in such spectacles as *The Maid of the Oaks* and in the choruses of *Macbeth* and *Romeo and Juliet*. The benefit bill at Drury Lane for 6 May 1780 indicated that tickets were available from Miss Kirby at Andrews's, No 70, Longacre.

After 14 December 1781 Miss Kirby left Drury Lane for Edinburgh, where she appeared at the Theatre Royal on 29 December as Lucy in *The Beggar's Opera*. During the rest of the season at Edinburgh she was seen in such parts as Macheath in *The Beggar's Opera Reversed*, Celia in *As You Like It*, Charlotte in *The Apprentice*, Charlotte in *Man and Wife*, Columbine in *Robinson Crusoe*, Diana in *Lionel and Clarissa*, Harriet in *The Guardian*, Louisa in *The Deserter*, Louisa in *The Duenna*, Louisa Dudley in *The West Indian*, Lucy in *William and Lucy*, Lydia Languish in *The Rivals*, Madge in *Love in a Village*, Maria in *The Maid of the Oaks*, Miranda in *The Busy Body*, Miss Biddy in *Miss in Her Teens*, Miss Walsingham in *The School for Wives*, Nancy in *The Camp*, Rose in *The Recruiting Officer*, and Sally in *Thomas and Sally*.

Miss Kirby returned to London to appear on 27 July 1782 as Macheath at the Haymarket Theatre. During the first two weeks in July she acted Sally in *The Candidate*, Charlotte in *Who's the Dupe?*, and Maria in *Twelfth Night*. She then returned to Edinburgh, where, apparently, she was in Jackson's company in 1782–83 and probably 1783–84.

Kirk, Mr [*fl.* 1776–1781], *housekeeper.*

Mr Kirk served Drury Lane Theatre as housekeeper at £40 annually from as early as 1776. The accounts mentioned him frequently over the years, as did the benefit bills, through 1781. Among his duties, according to a letter of Richard Brinsley Sheridan in 1777, were the supervision of the dressing rooms and dressers and the dressing room assignments of performers. The benefit bills show that Kirk was replaced as housekeeper by Fosbrook in 1781–82.

Kirk, Mr [*fl.* 1787–1792], *dancer.*

The dancer Kirk was added to the Drury Lane paylist on 13 October 1787 at 3s. 4d. daily. His first mention in the playbills did not come until 6 June 1788, when he danced with Miss J. Stageldoir a minuet de la cour and an allemande. Kirk's benefit tickets were accepted that evening. He did not perform in London in 1788–89. On 17 August 1789 he danced Peerua in a ballet entitled *The Death of Captain Cook* at the Theatre Royal in Plymouth, and perhaps he had been appearing at that theatre throughout the season. Kirk was at Drury Lane again in 1789–90 and 1790–91, obscured in the dancing chorus most of the time. He was in *Harlequin's Frolicks*, appeared as Pero in *The Fairy Favour*, and danced in *Don Juan*.

The Drury Lane accounts show regular payments to Kirk of £1 10s. weekly in the spring of 1792, though he was not cited in the bills, and *The London Stage* does not list him in the company roster for the 1791–92 season. In 1792 he performed in a company managed by Johnson at Barking, Essex, and the *Thespian Magazine* of May that year said "Kirk has merit as a dancer." Not merit enough for London, it seems, for Kirk was not mentioned again in the bills or accounts there.

Kirk, Mrs [*fl.* 1729–30], *actress.*

Mrs Kirk appeared for the first time at the Goodman's Fields playhouse on 1 December 1729 as Mrs Day in *The Committee*. The bill implied that she had acted elsewhere before that, but no record of her previous activity has been found. During the rest of the 1729–30 season Mrs Kirk played Mrs Sealand in *The Conscious Lovers*, Abigail in *The Drummer*, Lady Darling in *The Constant Couple*, Lucy in *The Recruiting Officer*, Mrs Motherly in *The Provok'd Husband*, Edging in *The Careless Husband*, Mrs Quickly in *The Merry Wives of Windsor*, Advocate in *The Fair Quaker of Deal*, Lucetta in *The Rover*, and Mrs Frail in *Love for Love*. In midseason, on 11 March 1730, she had gone over to the Haymarket Theatre to go into breeches as Mat in *The Metamorphosis of the Beggar's Opera*.

Kirkham, [Daniel?] [*fl.* 1681?–1691], actor.

A Mr Kirkham played Traffique in *Sir Anthony Love* with the United Company at Drury Lane Theatre in November 1690 (according to Robert Hume; not late September, as *The London Stage* states). During the rest of the season he was seen as an Attendant in *Alphonso*, the Singing Master in *Love for Money*, and Brisac in *Bussy D'Ambois*. Perhaps he was Daniel Kirkham, who with George Powell was indicted for robbing the Dorset Garden playhouse nine years earlier, 9–12 September 1681.

Kirkham, Mary [*fl.* c.1715], house servant?

Mary Kirkham is named occasionally in the Drury Lane accounts at the Folger Shakespeare Library, but it is not clear what her position was in the theatre or, indeed, if she was actually on the theatre staff. But she seems to have been a house servant about 1715.

Kirkman, Abraham 1737–1794, singer, harpsichord maker?

Doane's *Musical Directory* of 1794 listed a Mr Kirkman, of No 50, Old Gravel Lane, as an alto (singer, presumably) who participated in the oratorio performances at Covent Garden Theatre and Westminster Abbey. He was very likely the A. Kirkman who was an honorary subscriber to the New Musical Fund that year, who was also very likely Abraham Kirkman (or Kirckman) the nephew of the Alsatian harpsichord maker Jacob Kirckman (1710–1792). Abraham was born in Bischweiler in 1737, according to the *New Grove*, and died in Hammersmith in 1794. He was buried on 16 April. Abraham left a son, Joseph, with whom he had been in partnership.

Kirkman, Jacob *d. 1812?, organist.*

When Jacob Kirkman was recommended for membership in the Royal Society of Musicians on 5 May 1781, he was described as having served his apprenticeship under John Keeble of the parish of St George, Hanover Square. Kirkman was said to be single and to hold the post of organist at Audley Chapel, Grosvenor Square. He was admitted to the Society, but the minutes contain hardly any further references to him. Doane's *Musical Directory* of 1794 listed Kirkman as organist of St George, Hanover Square. The Royal Society of Musicians Minutes on 6 September 1807 stated that Kirkman was over two years in arrears in his subscription and was expelled from the organization.

The *New Grove* suggests that our subject may have been a nephew of the harpsichord maker Jacob Kirckman; the nephew died in 1812. The elder Jacob Kirckman (1710–1792) had a shop in Broad Street near Golden Square in 1763, when *Mortimer's London Directory* came out; when Doane's *Directory* was published in 1794, the address had changed to No 19, Broad Street, Carnaby Market. The elder Kirckman was regularly hired by Drury Lane Theatre to tune harpsichords; the accounts cite payments to him from 1783 to 1791. We do not know if our subject was associated with the harpsichord making business, as was Abraham, another nephew of Jacob Kirckman.

Kirkpatrick, Mr [*fl.* 1775–1777], actor.

On 7 November 1777 "A Gentleman" played Richard III at Covent Garden Theatre. The *Morning Chronicle* the following day identified him as Mr Kirkpatrick, who had acted twice the previous summer at Richmond and had played Richard once at the Crow Street Theatre in Dublin. The Dublin records examined by the late W. S. Clark show that Kirkpatrick had made his debut at the Smock Alley playhouse in Dublin in 1775–76, had played at Crow Street from May 1776 on and during the 1776–77 season. He was perhaps related to the Kirkpatrick who performed in Dublin in 1744–45 and in 1755–56; but that Kirkpatrick seems not to have appeared in London.

Kirth, Mr [*fl.* 1778], house servant?

A Mr Kirth (if the name has been transcribed correctly) was cited in the Drury Lane accounts on 8 January 1778 as receiving an annual salary of £20. He was probably one of the house servants.

Kirton, Mr [*fl.* 1784], *double-bass player.*
Mr Kirton played double bass in the Handel Memorial Concerts at Westminster Abbey and the Pantheon in May and June 1784.

Kirton, Miss [*fl.* 1791–1796], *actress, singer.*
In the fourth volume of this dictionary Miss Curten was noticed; further information makes it possible for us to identify her as Miss Kirton, an actress and singer. Her name appeared in the account books variously as Curten, Curteen, Curtin, Kertin, or Kerton; in the bills she was almost invariably cited as Miss Kirton. On 15 October 1791, with the Drury Lane company at the King's Theatre, she was a Priestess in *The Cave of Trophonius*; other named roles she had that season (at the King's Theatre with the Drury Lane troupe) were Madalon in *The Surrender of Calais* and Anna in *Dido Queen of Carthage*. She also sang in the choruses of *Macbeth* and *Dido*. Her weekly salary was 15s. In 1792–93 she again labored obscurely in the choruses of *Macbeth*, *The Pirates*, and probably other lavish productions.

Miss Kirton moved to Covent Garden in 1793–94, where she was paid £1 5s. weekly and given occasional named roles. She was a Bacchante in *Comus* for her first notice there on 29 October 1792; then on 28 November she was given the title part in *Nina*. That season she also sang in *The Woodman*, *Harlequin and Faustus*, *Harlequin's Chaplet*, *Hamlet*, *The Ward of the Castle*, *Macbeth*, and *Romeo and Juliet*. She continued at Covent Garden through 1795–96, singing regularly in the choruses of such works as *Oscar and Malvina*, *The Mysteries of the Castle*, *Lord Mayor's Day*, *The Battle of Hexham*, and *Lock and Key*. She was named for a solo part: Mrs Vixen in *The Beggar's Opera* beginning 24 October 1795. Miss Kirton continued to receive £1 5s. weekly to the end of her engagement.

Doane's *Musical Directory* of 1794 listed Miss Kirton as a singer in the oratorios at Westminster Abbey and gave her address as No 24, Plough Court, Fetter Lane.

Kisheir, Mr [*fl.* 1743–1744], *house servant?*
Mr Kisheir (or Keisher) shared benefits with several others on 24 May 1743 and 21 May 1744 at Drury Lane Theatre. Possibly the following entry in the registers of St George, Hanover Square, concern the Drury Lane employee: on 5 October 1738 Benjamin Kishere, bachelor, married Rachel Benefold, spinster. Both were from the parish of St James, Westminster (now St James, Piccadilly).

Kitch. *See* KYTCH.

Kitchen, Mr [*fl.* 1735–1740], *property man.*
Mr Kitchen, the Drury Lane property man, was present at the theatre in 1735 when Charles Macklin killed Thomas Hallam in a dispute over a property wig. In the murder trial that ensued Kitchen was twice cited. Though *The London Stage* does not list him, he was, according to Latreille, one of those whose benefit tickets were given out for 14 May 1740.

Possibly the property man was the Samuel Kitchen from the parish of St James, Westminster, who was buried at St Paul, Covent Garden, on 18 July 1744. There was a Thomas Kitchin who was active as an engraver of music from about 1743 to 1761, according to Humphries and Smith's *Music Publishing in the British Isles*. Our subject may have been related to him, or, indeed, may have been the same person.

Kites. *See* KYTCH.

Klanert, Charles Moritz *d.* 1843, *actor, dancer.*
Charles Moritz Klanert made his debut at Covent Garden on 8 October 1798 as Paris in *Romeo and Juliet*. His father was Steward to Lord Egremont and had articled his son to an attorney in Marsden Lane, Covent Garden, according to a clipping preserved in the Richmond Library. The *Authentic Memoirs of the Green Room* in 1800 said Klanert had declined a lucrative situation in the legal profession to follow a theatrical career. He had acted at Cheltenham before his first appearance at Covent Garden.

During the rest of the 1798–99 season Kla-

London Borough of Richmond upon Thames, Libraries Department

CHARLES M. KLANERT
artist unknown

nert played what the *Authentic Memoirs* called "the very inferior walk of valets, waiters, &c." Some of his roles were not named in the bills, but among those that were we find the Valet in *Secrets Worth Knowing*, an Officer in *Macbeth*, a Dutch Lover in *The Magic Oak*, Thessalus in *Alexander the Great*, Ratcliff in *Richard III*, a Sportsman in *Harlequin's Chaplet*, and Salanio in *The Merchant of Venice*. In 1799–1800 he was given similar roles, such as Buckle in *The Suspicious Husband*, Scarlet in *Robin Hood*, an Islander in *The Death of Captain Cook*, a Gentleman in *King Lear*, Frank in *Management*, a Sailor in *The Turnpike Gate*, the first Spirit in *Comus*, Colombine in *The Volcano*, Jeffery in *Barnaby Brittle*, Henry in *Speed the Plough* (the *Authentic Memoirs* noted that he undertook the role on short notice because of Johnson's illness and acquitted himself respectably), Mervin in *A Peep behind the Curtain*, Vickery in *Speculation*, and a Musician in *Don Juan*.

Klanert spent the summer of 1800 at the Haymarket Theatre, making his initial appearance there on 13 June as Charles in *The Jew and the Doctor*. He then had such parts as Mirtillo in *'Tis All a Farce*, a Planter in *Inkle and Yarico*, Naclo in *Zorinski*, Frank in *Fortune's Frolick*, Count Lewis in *Peeping Tom*, a Negro Robber in *Obi*, Zenger in *The Point of Honour*, William in *The Deaf Lover*, Mortimer in *Cambro-Britons*, and other forgettable roles in forgotten works. He also danced in such pieces as *St David's Day* and *Raymond and Agnes*.

He returned to Covent Garden in 1800–1801 and to the Haymarket in the summer of 1801, and the Covent Garden accounts show that he remained affiliated there during the winters through 1805–6. He was receiving £2 weekly in 1800–1801 but was raised 10s. the following season and by April 1805 was earning £3 weekly. In the summer of 1805 he was one of the chief dancers at Brighton.

On 28 June 1813 at the Royal Circus a benefit was given Mr and Mrs Klanert; he played Tar Star in *The Wife of Padua*, altered from Shakespeare. The following 7 September he was advertised as starring that night only in the burletta *Matrimony* and was hailed as from the Theatre Royal, Richmond. Indeed, it was at Richmond that Klanert finally found his niche. He served as manager there from 1817 to 1829. In Richmond he lived in a house in the Vineyard and gave a wherry as a prize at the annual rowing match. His melodrama *Elisina*, published in 1824, was apparently staged at Richmond.

Charles Moritz Klanert died at Richmond on 1 February 1843. He had written his will there on 16 July 1842. He asked to be buried in the same vault as his late wife, at the south entrance of the church at Petworth, Sussex, where his son Charles was the parish curate. Klanert left his estate to his son, noting that it included stocks, moneys, a freehold house in North Street, Petworth, and leaseholds in Blackfriar's Road, Surrey, that included a public house. The will was proved on 20 May 1843.

A pen, pencil, and watercolor portrait of Klanert by an unknown artist is at the Richmond Central Reference Library. It was shown in the exhibition "Garrick to Kean" at the Orleans House Gallery, Twickenham, May–September 1974.

Klein, Mons [*fl.* 1706], *dancer.*

At Drury Lane Theatre on 20 June 1706 "a Master lately arrived, new to England" entertained with some dancing. Five days later the same gentleman, still unidentified, offered two *Grotesque Dances*, *The Swiss Dance*, and *Dutch Skipper*. On 28 June the advertisement identified the visitor as Monsieur Klein and said he would offer the *Grotesque Dances* once more plus a *Scaramouch*. He performed again on 5 July and danced at the little-used Dorset Garden Theatre on 9 July.

Kleyser, J. [*fl.* 1718], *oddity.*

In the British Library is an engraving by an unknown artist of J. Kleyser, born without arms, who was exhibited in London in 1718.

Klose, Francis Joseph [*fl.* 1794–1823], *violinist, violoncellist, violist.*

Francis Joseph Klose provided his autobiography to Sainsbury for his biographical dictionary, writing him on 23 October 1823 from No 39, Beaumont Street. Klose studied music under his father and under Francesco Tomich. Klose said he had been a member of most of the orchestras in London, including that at the King's Theatre and that of the Concerts of the Academy of Ancient Music. He was a teacher of pianoforte and a composer of sentimental ballads.

By permission of the Trustees of the British Museum

J. KLEYSER
unknown artist

Doane's *Musical Directory* in 1794 listed Klose as a member of the New Musical Fund who lived in Silver Street, Golden Square. In 1805 he was a member of the Committee of the New Musical Fund. The accounts of Drury Lane show that he played there in 1807–8 for £1 10s. weekly. Not until 3 December 1809 was he elected a member of the Royal Society of Musicians. For that organization in May 1811, 1812, 1813, and perhaps other years, he played violin in the St Paul's Concerts. Klose was a Governor of the Society in 1813 and 1814. He played viola in the opera orchestra at the King's Theatre in 1817 and 1818. A Klose "Junior," presumably his son, played violin in the opera orchestra in 1817 and 1818.

KNAPP

Knapp, Mr [*fl.* 1694–1720], *actor, singer.*

The London Stage lists Mr Knapp (or Knap, Napp) as a member of the United Company in 1694–95 before Thomas Betterton led a group of dissenters away to form a new troupe and play at the Lincoln's Inn Fields playhouse. Knapp joined Betterton and his company, though the first mention of him in the bills was not until June 1697, when he played Mezzetin in "Natural Magick," a part of *The Novelty*. Before the end of the century he was seen as Searchwell in *The Innocent Mistress*, and Heardouble in *The Deceiver Deceived*, and heard as a singer, according to songs published about 1700: *A Swain long slighted and disdain'd* from *Hamlet* and *Love is a God* from *Women Will Have their Way*.

Knapp played Zaporjus in *The Czar of Muscovy* at Lincoln's Inn Fields about March 1701 and Memnon in *Altemira* about December of that year. On 31 December 1702 he played Alphonso in *The Heiress*. About November 1703 he was cited as Draul in *The Different Widows* at Lincoln's Inn Fields. There he remained through 1704–5 playing Timothy in *Love at First Sight*, Bandileer in *The Biter*, and the second Gentleman in *The Gamester*. In 1705–6 he was at the Queen's Theatre, playing "Yhoon" in *Ulysses* and Macario in *The Faithful General*. He appeared at the Queen's again in 1707, acting Fountain in *Wit Without Money* in January and taking a benefit in May. In the spring of 1710 at Drury Lane, Knapp was Indent in *The Fair Quaker* and shared a benefit when *The Woman Captain* was performed in March.

When John Rich recruited a company to play at the new Lincoln's Inn Fields playhouse in 1714–15, Knapp was one of the actors attracted to the venture. There beginning on 7 January 1715 he played such parts as a Sailor in *The Fair Quaker*, Companion in *The Slip*, Lolpoop in *The Squire of Alsatia*, Sancho in *Love Makes a Man*, some comic part unspecified in *Valentinian*, Mordecai in *The City Ramble*, Wilful in *The Doating Lovers*, Baltzar in *The False Count*, Sir Tristram Cash in *The Wife's Relief*, Appletree in *The Recruiting Officer*, Sancho in *2 Don Quixote*, Andrew in *The Lucky Prodigal*, Lord Plausible in *The Plain Dealer*, Doodle in *The London Cuckolds*, a Beggar in *The Royal Merchant*, Cardus in *The Humours of Purgatory*, Semibreve in *Pyramus and Thisbe*, Sancho in *The Pilgrim*, Richard in *The Woman Captain*, La Roche in *Bury Fair*, a comic role in *1 Henry IV*, Teague in *The Twin Rivals*, a comic part in *Oedipus*, Ned in *The Artful Husband*, a Companion in *The Younger Brother*, and Ferret in *The Royal Merchant*. The last mention of him at Lincoln's Inn Fields was on 17 June 1719, when he had a benefit at *The Devil of a Wife*. Knapp was in *Friar Bacon* at Southwark Fair on 5 September 1720.

Knapp, Mr [*fl.* 1782–1792?], *actor.*

Mr Knapp played Sir T. Loveland in *Don Quixote in England* and Buckingham in *Richard III* at the Haymarket Theatre on 4 March 1782. Perhaps he was the Knapp who acted Sir Clement Flint in *The Heiress and Poor Soldier* on 28 May 1792 at Barnstaple, Devonshire, when the theatre there opened for the summer season.

Knapp, Mrs *d. 1734, actress.*

Mrs Knapp began appearing at Lincoln's Inn Fields Theatre at about the time that Mr Knapp (her father?) dropped from the company. She was first noticed on 13 November 1719 as Jenny in *Love for Love*; that season she also played Florella in *Sir Walter Raleigh* (for her shared benefit with Mrs Gulick). At Bartholomew Fair in August 1720 Mrs Knapp acted the title role in *Maudlin*, a droll, and at Southwark Fair in September she had a part in another droll, *Friar Bacon*. She was again at Lincoln's Inn Fields at 1720–21, playing Constance in *The Twin Rivals*, Maria in *Whig and Tory*, Lavinia in *Titus Andronicus*, Cordelia in *King Lear* (which she played for her benefit on 15 May 1721; it brought in £147 5s. before house charges—but she had to share that with two others), and Beatrice in *The Cheats*. At the fairs in August and September 1721 Mrs Knapp played Ardelia in *The Injur'd General*.

She then went to Dublin, where she acted through 1726–27 at Smock Alley such roles as Angelica in *Love for Love*, Eloisa in *The Rival Generals*, Leonora in *The Spanish Fryar*, Isabella in *The Fatal Marriage*, Belvidera in *Venice Preserv'd*, Mrs Brittle in *The Amorous Widow*, Lady Dainty in *The Double Gallant*, Hypolita in *She Wou'd If She Cou'd*, Cleopatra in *All for Love*, and Anna Bullen in *Vertue Betray'd*. Mrs Knapp played at the theatre on St Augustine's Back in Bristol about 1728 or 1729 (just after her last notices in the Dublin bills studied by the

Knapper, Mrs [fl. c. 1674–1677], actress, singer.

The prompter Downes said that Mrs Knapper (or Napier, Napper) joined the Duke's Company at the Dorset Garden Theatre about 1674. Her first recorded part, however, was Betty, a breeches role, in *Tom Essence* in late August 1676. During the 1676–77 season she was cast in a few small roles: Silvia in *Madam Fickle*, Celia in *Pastor Fido*, and Betty in *A Fond Husband*. In *All the King's Ladies* J. H. Wilson states that she was also a singer. Perhaps she was related to the Napper who held a share in the Drury Lane ground rent in the early eighteenth century.

Knapton, Mr [fl. 1713], numberer.

W. J. Lawrence in *Old Theatre Days and Ways*, citing a theatrical lawsuit of 1713, says that Mr Knapton, a relative (by marriage) to Robert Wilks, served Drury Lane Theatre as a numberer at 18s. weekly. Wilks's first wife was Elizabeth Knapton; "Jubilee Dicky" Norris married Elizabeth's sister Sarah; and Anne Knapton served Drury Lane as a dresser.

Knapton, Anne [fl. 1733], dresser.

The Life of Mr. Wilks (1733) states that Anne Knapton, "a Maiden," was a dresser at Drury Lane Theatre. Anne's sister Sarah married "Jubilee Dicky" Norris, and her sister Elizabeth was the wife of Drury Lane co-manager Robert Wilks. The *Life* stated that the Knapton family was originally from Yorkshire, where they had a manor and an estate worth £2000 annually. During the reign of Queen Elizabeth they had moved to Brockenhurst in Hampshire. The father of the three girls was Ferdinand Knapton, Town Clerk of Southampton and Steward of the New Forest. The *Life* speaks of Anne Knapton as alive and working at the theatre in 1733. We can find no corroboration for that statement, but Anne's sister Sarah was named frequently in the Drury Lane accounts in 1714 and 1715.

Knapton, Sarah. *See* NORRIS, MRS HENRY, SARAH, neé KNAPTON.

Knellar. *See* KELLNER.

Kneller, Mr [fl. 1784], bassoonist. *See* KNELLER, MR [fl. 1784], oboist.

Kneller, Mr [fl. 1784], oboist.

Three musicians named Kneller participated in the Handel Memorial Concerts at Westminster Abbey and the Pantheon in May and June 1784. One played oboe, one bassoon, and the third trombone or sackbut.

Kneller, Mr [fl. 1784], trombonist. *See* KNELLER, MR [fl. 1784], oboist.

Knepp, Mrs [Christopher? Elizabeth? Mary?] d. 1681, actress, singer, dancer.

Considering how frequently Samuel Pepys spoke of Mrs Knepp (or Knipp, Kneap, Nepp, etc.) it is remarkable how uncertain we are about a number of basic questions, such as when and where she was born and what her Christian name was. Cunningham in his *Nell Gwyn* stated that Mrs Knepp was the wife of a Smithfield horse-dealer. Her husband's name seems to have been Christopher. On 6 July 1666 Mrs Knepp, using a nickname Pepys liked, "Bab Allen," asked Pepys to be godfather to the child she was then carrying; Pepys accepted, but on 8 July he had heard nothing further. On 6 August he indicated that the child had died. The parish registers of St Paul, Covent Garden, show that "Samuell Son of Christopher Nepp" had been buried on 16 July. Those registers contain no other references to Knepp (under any spelling).

But at St Clement Danes on 26 December 1663 Ursula, the daughter of Christopher and Elizabeth "Knepps," was christened, and on 7 June 1672 their daughter Mary "Knepp" was christened. And the registers of St Giles in the Fields show the burial of Catharine, daughter of Christopher Knepp, on 20 July 1667. There is no proof, of course, that any of those three citations concern our subject. But Mrs Knepp's Christian name may have been Elizabeth; at least she was so named in a Lord Chamberlain's warrant dated 30 April 1672 when she was listed as a member of the King's Company of players. On the other hand, de Sola Pinto found a poem by Sedley addressed to "Mrs. Mary

KNEPP

Napp" and scholars have tended to accept that as her name. J. H. Wilson in *All the King's Ladies* suggests that perhaps she was born Mary Man and married Christopher Knepp, who was described by Pepys in December 1665 as "an ill, melancholy, jealous-looking fellow . . . that spoke not a word to us all the night" at a party at Greenwich. In January 1666 he was with "Knipp and her surly husband" and Pepys thought Mrs Knepp lived a "sad life with that ill-natured fellow . . ." Since Mrs Knepp was not mentioned in connection with the King's Company until 1664 at the earliest, perhaps she married Knepp about 1663 as Wilson suggests. But *The London Stage* lists Mary Man as a member of the King's troupe not only before we find references to Mrs Knepp but after, in 1666–67.

The earliest theatrical reference to Mrs Knepp dates about November 1664; Thomas Killigrew jotted down his intended cast for *Thomaso* and noted Mrs Knepp for the part of Lusetta. That would certainly suggest that she was in his troupe at that time, though not until 1666 was she named in livery warrants and other play casts. It seems likely that she served in 1664–65 as a minor actress, after which season the plague closed the playhouses until the fall of 1666, when Mrs Knepp's name began to be cited with regularity.

The King's players performed either *The Silent Woman* or *The Scornful Lady* at court on 10 December 1666; Mrs Knepp played Epicoene in the first work and the Widow in the second. Until the King's troupe began encountering organizational and financial difficulties in the late 1670s Mrs Knepp was seen as Guiomar in *The Custom of the Country*, Alibech in *The Indian Emperor*, Otrante in *Flora's Vagaries*, Asteria in *Secret Love*, Sevina in *The Black Prince*, Aminta in *The Sea Voyage*, possibly Elspeth in *The English Monsieur*, Emilia in *The Surprisal*, probably Victoria in *The Mulberry Garden*, Beatrix in *An Evening's Love*, Paulina in *The Sisters*, Felicia in *Tyrannick Love* (and either at the premiere or at a revival, or both, she was Nakar in the spirit scene in Act IV), Antonia in *The Roman Empress*, Lady Flippant in *Love in a Wood*, Hippolita in *The Assignation*, Leonella in *The Spanish Rogue*, Lady Fidget in *The Country Wife*, Aglave in *Sophonisba*, Nicholas in *Psyche Debauch'd*, Phorba in *Lucina's Rape*, Eliza in *The Plain Dealer*, Barbara in *The Country Innocence*, and Mrs Dorothy in *Trick for Trick*.

Mrs Knepp also played a number of unnamed characters, participated occasionally in prologues and epilogues, and often danced and sang within or between the acts of plays.

Samuel Pepys seems first to have encountered Mrs Knepp on 6 December 1665 at Mrs Pierce's. Among others there were

Mrs. Knipp, Mr. [Edward] Coleman and his wife . . . the best company for musique I ever was in, in my life, and wish I could live and die in it, both for musique and the face of Mrs. Pierce, and my wife and Knipp, who is pretty enough; but the most excellent, mad-humoured thing, and sings the noblest that ever I heard in my life. . . .

It was two days later at Greenwich that Pepys met, perhaps for the first time, Mrs Knepp's nasty husband. During the supper which Pepys provided, there was "a pleasant scene of Mrs. Knipp's rising sicke from table, but whispered me it was for some hard word or other her husband gave her just now when she laughed and was more merry than ordinary. But we got her in humour again, and mighty merry. . . ."

On 2 January 1666 Pepys was at Lord Bruncker's, where he found "above all, my dear Mrs. Knipp, with whom I sang, and in perfect pleasure I was to hear her sing, and especially her little Scotch song of 'Barbary Allen'. . . ." Pepys on the way home "got into the coach where Mrs. Knipp was and got her upon my knee (the coach being full) and played with her breasts and sung, and at last set her at her house and so good night." It was after that little interlude that Mrs Knepp began signing herself "Bab Allen" in her notes to the diarist. He signed his return letters "Dapper Dicky"— from a song.

In mid-January 1666 Pepys was invited to Greenwich to dance, the group to include Mrs Knepp; "but all blank," the disappointed Pepys told his diary,

through the waywardnesse of Mrs. Knipp, who, though she had appointed the night, could not be got to come. Not so much as her husband could get her to come; but, which was a pleasant thing in all my anger, I asking him, while we were in expectation what answer one of our many messengers would bring, what he thought, whether she would come or no, he answered that, for his part, he could not so much as thinke.

A few weeks later, on 23 February, Mrs Knepp was at Pepys's house:

I spent all the night talking with this baggage, and teaching her my song of "Beauty retire," which she sings and makes go most rarely, and a very fine song it seems to be. She also entertained me with repeating many of her own and others' parts of the play-house, which she do most excellently; and tells me the whole practices of the play-house and players, and is in every respect most excellent company.

One should have expected Mrs Pepys to have spurned Mrs Knepp, but on 28 February the actress dined with Samuel and his wife at their home, "she the pleasantest company in the world. After dinner I did give my wife money to lay out on Knipp, 20s." Mrs Pepys bought Mrs Knepp six pairs of gloves.

The diary is full of other references to Mrs Knepp during the early months of 1666—she was frequently out in company with Mr and Mrs Pepys, or Samuel was with Mrs Knepp and his "Valentine" Mrs Pierce. And though his friends liked Mrs Knepp, by 11 May Mrs Pepys was complaining that when Samuel was in the company of Mrs Pierce, Mrs Knepp, or other women he liked, he did not value his wife and mind her as he should. But Mrs Knepp was pregnant, as was Mrs Pierce, their babies being due about the same time, in July, so perhaps Mrs Pepys felt that for the time Samuel's friendship with the two women was safe enough. On 25 May Pepys reported that Mrs Knepp was within a fortnight of "lying down," but a month later "poor Knipp" was "so big she can tumble and looks every day to lie down. . . ."

Then came the child, evidently named after Pepys. It apparently lived only a few days. On 6 August 1666 Mrs Knepp dropped by to see the Pepyses after dinner (that is, lunch), and Samuel came home from the office and "there I sat and talked with her, it being the first time of her being here since her being brought to bed. I very pleasant with her; but perceive my wife hath no great pleasure in her being here, she not being pleased with my kindnesse to to her." Later that day Mr Pierce and his wife dropped by; she too had had a son who had died in infancy. Samuel took the visitors home, his wife refusing to join them, and on the way Pepys took the ladies to supper in Old Fish Street, "to the very house and woman where I kept my wedding dinner, where I never was since."

Perhaps Pepys steered clear of Mrs Knepp for a while after that, for he did not tell his diary about her again until late October, when once more she began to occupy much of his time and thought. On 14 November 1666 Samuel went to Mrs Knepp's house (unfortunately he did not give its location) to pick her up to take her to his home. She was not ready, so Pepys "staid reading of Waller's verses, while she finished dressing, her husband being by. I had no other pastime. Her lodgings very mean, and the conditions she lives in; yet makes a shew without doors, God bless us!"

On 27 December Pepys finally commented on Mrs Knepp's acting. He saw *The Scornful Lady*, and she played "the widow very well, and will be an excellent actor, I think." A few days later the diarist saw her as the Widow in *The Custom of the Country*, liked her performance, and noted that she "sings a little song admirably." On 15 January 1667 Pepys learned that Mrs Knepp "acts Mrs Weaver's great part [of Alibech] in 'The Indian Emperour,' and [Lord Bruncker] says she is coming on to be a great actor."

Gradually Pepys was drawn into Mrs Knepp's theatrical circle. After seeing a performance of *The Humourous Lieutenant*, in which "Knipp's singing, did please us," Mrs Knepp took Pepys and his friends backstage at the Bridges Street playhouse to meet Nell Gwynn and Elizabeth Hall. Then Pepys stayed on to watch a dance rehearsal for *The Goblins*, which was to be presented the following day. And the next day, 24 January, Pepys's friend Henry Harris, the Duke's Company actor, came to visit the Pepys family in the evening, bringing with him Mrs Pierce "and also one dressed like a country-mayde with a straw hat on; which, at first I could not tell who it was, though I expected Knipp: but it was she coming off the stage just as she acted this day in 'The Goblins'; a merry jade." The evening was filled with merriment, and the party moved to Pepys's office, where it continued until three in the morning. ". . . Knipp felt a little ill, and so my wife home with her to put her to bed." Later Pepys himself arrived home and with Mrs Pierce went up to see Mrs Knepp, "and we waked her, and there I handled her breasts and did baiser la, and sing a song, lying by her on the bed, and then left my wife to see Mrs. Pierce in bed to her, in our best chamber, and so to bed myself."

In *The Chances* in early February Pepys found it "pretty to hear Knipp sing in the play very properly, 'All night I weepe'; and sung it admirably." A week later the manager of the King's players, Thomas Killigrew, told Pepys that "Knipp is like to make the best actor that ever come upon the stage, she understanding so well: that they are going to give her £30 a-year more." But Pepys did not say more than what. On 12 February 1667 Pepys accompanied the composer Giovanni Battista Draghi to Mrs Knepp's "chamber" where Draghi was to teach her a song, presumably in some opera he had just composed. "And so we all thither, and there she did sing an Italian song or two very fine, while he played the bass upon the harpsicon there; and exceedingly taken I am with her singing, and believe that she will do miracles at that and acting. Her little girl is mighty pretty and witty." The little girl may have been a daughter of Mrs Knepp's but was more likely her servant.

By 6 March Mrs Knepp had replaced Mrs Pierce as Pepys's Valentine, so he bought her 32*s*. worth of "things." Clever Samuel: it "is pretty to see how my wife is come to convention with me, that, whatever I do give to anybody else, I shall give her as much, which I am not displeased with." A month later Pepys tried to

enquire out Mrs. Knipp's new lodging, but could not, but do hear of her at the Playhouse, where she was practising [during the morning hours] and I sent for her out by a porter, and the jade come to me all undressed, so cannot go home to my house to dinner, as I had invited her, which I was much troubled at, because I think there is a distance between her and Mrs. Pierce, and so our company would not be so pleasant.

A few days later, on 12 May, Mrs Pepys finally felt she had to put her foot down. She wanted Samuel to swear he would never see Mrs Knepp again.

On 22 May 1667 Samuel stole a moment with Mrs Knepp at the playhouse, but then he told his diary nothing of her until 1 August. After a performance that day Mr and Mrs Pepys took Mrs Knepp to the Neat Houses near where Vauxhall Bridge was later built, "in the way to Chelsey; and there, in a box in a tree, we sat and sang, and talked and eat; my wife out of humour, as she always is, when this woman is by." But at least Pepys was able to see his friend again. When he went alone to the playhouse to see *Brenoralt* on 12 August, he sat in front of Mrs Pierce and Mrs Knepp (their enmity had been forgotten), "who pulled me by the hair; and so I addressed myself to them, and talked to them all the intervals of the play, and did give them fruit. . . ." Afterwards he took the ladies to Mrs Manuel's to hear some singing. When he saw *The Indian Emperor* on 22 August Mrs Knepp sent Orange Moll (Mary Meggs, the fruit seller) to tell him that Mrs Knepp wanted to see him after the play, and Mrs Knepp "beckoned me at the end of the play, and I promised to come; but it was so late."

Pepys still had to be careful, and sometimes if he spied Mrs Knepp at the playhouse, he could not let his wife know of it. In talking to Thomas Killigrew he was pleased that that expert on music thought highly of Mrs Knepp's talent, but the manager complained that she "won't take pains enough" to be as good as she was capable of being.

On 5 October 1667 Pepys went to see *Flora's Vagaries*:

going in, met with Knepp, and she took us up into the tireing-rooms: and to the women's shift, where Nell was dressing herself, and was all unready, and is very pretty, prettier than I thought. And so walked all up and down the house above, and then below into the scene-room, and there sat down, and she gave us fruit: and here I read the questions to Knepp, while she answered me, through all her part of "Flora's Figary's" which is acted to-day. But Lord! to see how they were both painted would make a man mad, and did make me loath them; and what base company of men comes among them, and how lewdly they talk! and how poor the men are in clothes, and yet what a shew they make on the stage by candle-light, is very observable. But to see how Nell cursed, for having so few people in the pit, was pretty. . . .

He seems not to have seen much of Mrs Knepp during the rest of 1667, but early the following year he mentioned her frequently in his diary. In January he took her to see *The Tempest* at the Duke's Theatre, and afterwards Henry Harris and Mrs Knepp went to Pepys's home; in mid-January at *The Wild Goose Chase* at the King's theatre he sat and picked up gossip from Mrs Knepp; in February he enjoyed a prologue Mrs Knepp performed with Nell Gwynn when *The Great Favorite* was performed; in March ". . . Knepp did act her part of grief very well" in *The Sea Voyage*. On 7 April 1668,

After [*The English Monsieur*] done, I down to Knipp, and did stay her undressing herself; and there saw the several players, men and women go by; and pretty to see how strange they are all, one to another, after the play is done. Here I saw a wonderful pretty maid of her own, that come to undress her, and one so pretty that she says she intends not to keep her, for fear of her being undone in her service, by coming to the playhouse.

On 21 April, after a performance of *The Indian Emperor*, Pepys took

Knepp out, and to Kensington; and there walked in the garden, and then supped, and mighty merry, there being also in the house Sir Philip Howard, and some company, and had a dear reckoning, but merry, and away, it being quite night, home, and dark, about 9 o'clock or more, and in my coming had the opportunity the first time in my life to be bold with Knepp . . .

Despite the presence, evidently, of Mrs Turner. Two days later he entertained the actress and others at the Cock Tavern in Fleet Street and then up the river with Mrs Knepp only, "it being darking, and to Fox Hall." On 6 May he was at Mrs Pierce's where he found Mrs Knepp (?) "on a pallet in the dark . . ." and the following night he carried on with Mrs Knepp again, "and so home by moonshine."

After a performance of *The Virgin Martyr* on 7 May 1668 Pepys

took up Knepp into our coach, and all of us with her to her lodgings, and thither comes Bannister with a song of her's, that he hath set in Sir Charles Sidly's [*The Mulberry Garden*] for her, which is, I think, but very meanly set; but this he did, before us, teach her, and it being but a slight, silly, short ayre, she learnt it presently. But I did get him to prick me down the notes of the Echo in "The Tempest," which pleases me mightily.

On 16 May he went to Mrs Knepp's house but found her not at home, so the rascal "did kiss her ancilla [maid], which is so mighty belle. . . ." At the end of the month at Mrs Pierce's he saw Mrs Knepp and was merry, and he "was freed from a fear that Knepp was angry or might take advantage to declare the essay that je did the other day, quand je was con her."

Then Samuel apparently stayed away from her for a while, but he was worried on 17 September for fear one of his friends might have seen him dining with the actress that day. He was giving her occasional amounts of money—five guineas that day; "I having given her nothing a great while, and her coming hither sometimes having been matter of cost to her . . ." By the winter poor Pepys was in torment, trying to avoid Mrs Knepp yet not wanting to. He was out shopping for horses on 11 December 1668 and met Mr Knepp, "who, it seems, is a kind of a jockey, and would fain have been doing something for me, but I avoided him, and the more for fear of being troubled thereby with his wife, whom I desire but dare not see, for my vow to my wife." At the theatre on 1 January 1669 at a performance of *Secret Love*, "Knepp looked upon us from on stage, but I durst not shew her any countenance; and, as well as I could carry myself, I found my wife uneasy there, poor wretch; therefore I shall avoid that house as much as I can."

At *The Heiress* on 2 February 1669 Pepys was enthralled by

the first song that Knepp sings, she singing three or four; and, indeed, it was very finely sung, so as to make the whole house clap her. . . . My wife being in mighty ill humour all night, and in the morning I found it to be from her observing Knepp to wink and smile on me, and she says I smiled on her. . . .

There the tale ends, for Pepys closed his diary. But it is likely that his flirtation with Mrs Knepp was finished.

About the spring of 1679 Mrs Knepp joined some other players from the King's troupe and went to Edinburgh to perform under Thomas Sydserf. There she became mistress to the actor Joe Haines, and late in 1681 she died giving birth to his stillborn child. In 1682 Joe wrote *A Rhymeing Supplication to Nell Gwynn*, hoping that she would intercede for him with King Charles:

*And Pray let His Matie: too understand
How sad I have been in merry Scotland
To loose Mrs: Nep that inchanting Dear Lump
That Fountaine of Love so juicy so Plump
That delicate Compound of Spiritt & Rump*
....

*In Child birth from mee to 'Lizeum departted
Since when Spight of Clarret I've been broken hearted*
....

*I fasted on ffrydayes I drank nought but water
To signifie griefe from my Unborn Daughter.*

Knerber. *See* **KNERLER.**

Knerler, Mr [*fl.* 1743–1748], *violinist.*

A St Cecilia's Day concert was advertised in the Bristol papers for 22 November 1743, though, oddly, the place of the concert was not stated. "Knerler w. Knerler" was to play first violin. He was the violinist Knerler who played at Marylebone Gardens in 1744, according to Wroth's *London Pleasure Gardens*. "Knerber" played violin on 5 September 1744 at the Haymarket Theatre. On 22 April 1748 he performed several concertos on the violin for his benefit at the Smock Alley Theatre in Dublin.

Knight, Mr [*fl.* 1691], *See* **KING, ROBERT.**

Knight, Mrs [*fl.* 1749–1750], *actress, singer.*

When the Frenchified *Beggar's Opera* called *L'Opéra du gueux* opened at the Haymarket Theatre on 29 April 1749, a Mrs Knight played both Mme Delature and Janneton du Plongeon. Beginning on 2 May she added a third role, Diane de la Friperie. On 9 February 1750 the same group turned Farquhar into French in *L'Officier en recrue*, with Mrs Knight playing Silvia. When *L'Opéra du gueux* was revived on 16 February, she again played her three parts, and on 26 February she was Elise in *L'Avare*.

Knight, Frances Maria [*fl.* 1682?–1724], *actress, dancer, singer.*

Was Frances Maria Knight the "Mally" referred to in the epilogue to *The Duke of Guise*?

*When Fortune favours, none but Fools will dally:
Wou'd any of you Sparks, if Nan or Mally
Tipt you th' inviting Wink, stand shall I, shall I?*

The play was performed for the first time on 28 November 1682 by the United Company at Drury Lane. There is a possibility that "Nan" referred to young Anne Bracegirdle, and Frances Maria Knight, a young girl at that time and new to the troupe, seems to be the most likely candidate for "Mally." But the first certain part we have for her is the virtuous young Angelline in *The Disappointment* in April 1684. The Mrs Knight who acted in the 1670s and has sometimes been taken for Frances Maria was Ursula Knight, as warrants in the Lord Chamberlain's accounts show.

Between 1684 and the division of the United Company in 1695 Frances Maria Knight is known to have played Aglaura in *The Commonwealth of Women*, Leonora in *The Libertine*, Flirt in *The Virtuoso*, Teresia in *The Squire of Alsatia*, Mrs Spruce in *The Fortune Hunters*, Ergasto in *Pastor Fido*, the Queen of Navarre in *The Massacre of Paris*, Madame Surelove in *The Widow Ranter*, Dorothea in *The Successful Strangers*, Constantia in *Madam Fickle*, Queen Margaret in *Richard III*, Volante in *Sir Anthony Love*, Miss Jenny in *Love for Money*, Mrs Raison in *Greenwich Park*, Teresia in *The Volunteers*, Madame Squeamish in *The Richmond Heiress*, Widow Lacy in *A Very Good Wife*, Lovewit in *The Female Vertuosos*, Julia in *The Fatal Marriage*, Herminia (Hermione?) in *The Ambitious Slave*, Dorothea in the first part and the Duchess in the second part of *Don Quixote*, and Arabella in *The Canterbury Guests*.

Mrs Knight also danced on occasion, as in *The Rape of Europa* in the winter of 1693–94, and she was a popular speaker of prologues and epilogues. Her assumption from time to time of breeches parts suggests a good figure. By 1691 she may have established a reputation as a loose woman—she certainly had that later—for the epilogue to *Greenwich Park*, spoken to the men in the audience by Mrs Verbruggen, with Frances Maria standing with her, goes:

*If you're displeas'd with what you've seen to night,
Behind Southampton House we'll do you right,
Who is't dares draw 'gainst me and Mrs. Knight?*

Frances Maria figured in the murder of the actor William Mountfort by Captain Hill and Lord Mohun in December 1692. At the trial that followed, Mrs Knight was called to testify:

Mrs. *Knight*. I have nothing to say to my Lord Mohun; but what I have to say, is to Mr. *Hill*. About 4 days before Mr. *Mountford* was Killed, Mr. *Hill* came to me, and spoke to me about *Mrs. Bracegirdle*: He told me he was satisfied she hated him, I told him I did not believe she hated any body, or loved any Body: Yes, he said, she did love some body, but he had thought of a way to be even with that Body. Upon the *Wednesday* Night before Mr. *Mountford* was killed, he came to me as I was coming out of the Dressing Room; sayeth he, Mrs. *Knight* let me speak a Word with you, says he, you are very great with Mrs. *Bracegirdle*, and I desire you to be so kind, as to speak to her for me, and I would beg of you if you would give me leave to give her this Letter from me: No, said I, Mr. *Hill*, I beg your Pardon; you say she hateth you, and if she hateth you, she will not love any body that speaketh for you; and I am not fond of creating my self Enemies in the House, knowing I have some already. What enemies, saith Mr. *Hill*, *Mountford* do you mean? And then repeating a great Oath, I shall find a way with him speedily.

L. H. Steward. A way, with what?

Mrs. *Knight*. A way with him speedily, Hill said it of *Mountford*.

Hill and Mohun dispatched Mountfort, whom Hill thought a rival for his love for Anne Bracegirdle. Both got their comeuppance in the fullness of time.

In 1695 Thomas Betterton and other dissatisfied players in the United Company broke away to form their own troupe and act at Lincoln's Inn Fields. Frances Maria Knight, perhaps because she saw the possibility of better roles for herself, remained with the wily manager Christopher Rich at Drury Lane and, indeed, became one of the company's leading tragediennes.

Her first part (at Dorset Garden) was probably Zempoalla in *The Indian Queen* in mid-April 1695, after which, through the end of 1714 at Drury Lane or Dorset Garden (and briefly in 1710 at the Queen's Theatre), she added to her considerable repertoire such new roles as Bonduca, Cataline in *The Rival Sisters*, Widow Lackit in *Oroonoko*, Elvira in *Agnes de Castro*, Arethusa in *Philaster*, Mirtilla in *The Younger Brother*, Thermusa in *Neglected Virtue*, Belira in *The Lost Lover*, Pandora in *Pausanias*, Sheker Para in Pix's *Ibrahim*, Lady Loveall in *The Female Wits*, Leonora in *Woman's Wit*, Olympia in *The Sham Lawyer*, Beringaria in *The Fatal Discovery*, Cesonia in *Caligula*, Alithea in *Phaeton*, Angellica in *The Campaigners*, Clytemnestra in *Achilles*, Elizabeth in *Richard III*, Astrea in *The Reform'd Wife*, Lesbia in *Love at a Loss*, Elvira in *Love Makes a Man*, Lydia in *The Bath*, Viletta in *She Wou'd and She Wou'd Not*, Florinda in *The Fair Example*, Mrs Haughty in *Vice Reclaimed*, Abenede in *The Faithful Bride*, Lady Easy in *The Careless Husband*, Mrs Fitchow in *The Northern Lass*, Melinda in *The Recruiting Officer*, Hollaris in *Tunbridge Walks*, Jocasta in *Oedipus*, Gertrude in *Hamlet*, Lady Subtle in *The Marriage-Hater Match'd*, Epicoene in *The Silent Woman*, Mrs Termagent in *The Squire of Alsatia*, Lady Lurewell in *The Constant Couple*, Lady Fancy in *The Maid the Mistress*, Lady Macbeth, Alcmena in *Amphitryon*, Margarita in *Rule a Wife and Have a Wife*, Queen Elizabeth in *The Unhappy Favorite*, Roxana in *The Rival Queens*, Almeria in *The Indian Emperor*, Leonora in *The Spanish Fryar*, Angelica in *The Rover*, Berinthia in *The Relapse*, Mrs Woodly in *Epsom Wells*, Laetitia in *The Old Bachelor*, the title role in *The Scornful Lady*, Lady Dunce in *The Soldier's Fortune*, Queen Katherine in *Henry VIII*, Cornelia in *Appius and Virginia*, Maria in *The Fond Husband*, Lyndaraxa in *The Conquest of Granada*, Clara in *The Emperor of the Moon*, Almeyda in *Don Sebastian*, Widow Rich in *The Comical Revenge*, Nourmahal in *Aureng-Zebe*, Mrs Frail in *Love for Love*, Evandra in *Timon of Athens*, Clarissa in *The Confederacy*, Zara in *The Mourning Bride*, Camillo in *The Mistake*, Isabella in *The Lancashire Witches*, Calphurnia in *Julius Caesar*, the Widow in *The Gamester*, Lady Wouldbe in *Volpone*, Lady Cockwood in *She Wou'd If She Cou'd*, Queen Elizabeth in *The Albion Queens*, Leonora in *The Libertine Destroyed*, Cephisa in *The Distrest Mother*, Clytemnestra in *The Victim*, Lady Laycock in *The Amorous Widow*, and Mrs Day in *The Committee*.

Though Mrs Knight was not regularly used as a singer, she is known to have sung Purcell's "O how you protest" in *The Mock Marriage* in December 1695, and she may have done some singing in *The Indian Queen* whenever it was performed. In *The Female Wits* in October 1696 Mrs Knight played a role satirizing the character of Homais in *The Royal Mischief* (April— or more likely May— 1696 at the rival theatre) as well as the acting style of Elizabeth Barry,

KNIGHT

who played the role. The part required of Mrs Knight much ranting and stomping, and when Mrs Knight was stabbed, the authoress-director Marsilia (a satire on Mrs Manley) said, "D'ye hear, Property Man, be sure some red Ink is handsomely convey'd to Mrs. Knight."

A *Letter to A. H. Esq.* in 1698 hinted at Mrs Knight's unsavory offstage reputation: "If we should see Mr. Powel acting a Brave, Generous and Honest Part; or Mrs. Knight, a very Modest and Chaste one, it ought not to give us Offence; because we are not to consider what they are off the Stage, but whom they represent." Tom Brown in his *Letters from the Dead to the Living* in the early eighteenth century indicated that Mrs Knight was one of the Drury Lane players who sold her favors for gain.

Frances Maria evidently had some share in the governing of the company at Drury Lane in 1699, for she was one of six players who signed for the troupe a contract with the scene painter Robert Robinson. No other evidence has been found, however, to show how involved she may have been in company business. When there was a move to unite the Drury Lane and Queen's Theatre troupes in the winter of 1707–8 "Fran. M. Knight" was one of the signers of the protest by the Drury Lane players. She so signed herself, too, in a plea to the Queen in 1709 for redress for the silencing of the company in June.

Among those who defected to John Rich's troupe was Mrs Knight. At the new theatre she continued playing many of her old parts and tried such new ones as Lady Woodvil in *The Man of Mode*, Eugenia in *The London Cuckolds*, Lady Brute in *The Provok'd Wife*, Lady Ample in *The Northern Heiress*, Widow Blackacre in *The Plain Dealer*, Pulcheria in *Theodosius*, Lady Plyant in *The Double Dealer*, Wishit in *'Tis Well If It Takes*, and then, after a gap in her records from the spring of 1719 to the fall of 1723 when she may have retired temporarily or performed in the provinces, several of her old roles plus the Duchess of York in *Richard III*, Andromache in *Troilus and Cressida*, Arane in *A King and No King*, Tamora in *Titus Andronicus*, and Eugenia in *The London Cuckolds*. That return to the stage at Lincoln's Inn Fields for the 1723–24 season constituted Mrs Knight's last work in the theatre. Latreille reports that she retired that season, and of her later life nothing is known.

Knight, John. *See* STERNE, EVERARD.

Knight, Mary, alias Mrs Henry Geery *b. 1631, singer.*

Mary Knight, according to the research of Roger Powell of Debrett's *Peerage*, was the daughter of Stephen and Margaret Knight and was christened at St Gregory by St Paul on 7 April 1631. Her mother, Margaret Birkhead, had married Stephen Knight in 1627 at St Gregory's. Mary married Henry Geery on 30 July 1649 at St Peter, Paul's Wharf, though she appears to have been estranged from him at an early date, and all references to her during the Restoration period are to Mrs Knight. Mary's father died in 1655 and was buried on 30 October of that year at St Benet, Paul's Wharf.

Mary Knight was "the famous singer" who dined with John Evelyn on 19 May 1659. By about 1667 Mary (or Moll) was a mistress of Charles II and helped procure Nell Gwynn for him. On 27 September 1667 Samuel Pepys

Harvard Theatre Collection
MARY KNIGHT
engraving by Faber, after Kneller

went to Gray's Inn Fields hoping to hear Mrs Knight sing, but he was too late and noted in his diary that he would have to "try another time"—which observation suggests that she was singing there regularly, perhaps in a subscription series. A year later Pepys heard that a Spanish woman had just arrived in London and was reputed to be as able a singer as Mrs Knight.

On 2 December 1674 Evelyn heard her at a concert at Mr Slingsby's: ". . . Mrs Knight, who sung incomparably, & doubtlesse has the greatest reach of any English woman; she had lately ben roming in Italy: & was much improv'd in that quality." In the court masque *Calisto* on 15 February 1675 Mary sang Peace and Daphne.

At the Houghton Library at Harvard, among some scurrilous and obscene poems by Rochester and others, is an anonymous work dating about 1678 entitled "Mrs Knights Advice to the Dutchess of Cleavland, in Distress for A Prick."

> *Quoth the Dutchess of Cleavland to Councillor Knight*
> *I'de faine have a P—— knew I how to come by't*
> *But you must be secret and give your advice*
> *Though Cunt be not Coy, reputation is Nice.*
> Knight. *To some Cellar in London your Grace must retire*
> *Where Porters with {Potts?} sett round the Cold Fire*
> *There open your Case, and your Grace cannot faile*
> *Of a dozen of Pricks for a dozen of Ale*
> Dutchess. *Say you soe quoth the Dutchess.*
> Knight. *Ay by God quoth the whore*
> Dutch. *Thou give me the key that Unlocks the back doore*
> *Ide rather be Fuct by Porters and Carman*
> *Then thus be abus'd by Churchill and German.*

Nell Gwynn in a letter (penned by an amanuensis) to her friend Mr Hyde in 1678 referred to a Mrs Knight, though one cannot be certain that Mary was intended: "Mrs. Knight's lady mother[is] dead, and she has put up a scutchin no biger then my Lady Grin's sounchis." Pepys in a letter to Viscount Bruncker on 13 March 1682 said, "I hear Mrs Knight is better, and the King takes his repose there [at Nell Gwynn's?] once or twice daily."

Another scurrilous poem, "Madam Nelley's Complaint: A Satyr," printed in Buckingham's *Works* as by Sir George Etherege but probably not by him, dates from about 1680:

> *Pity poor* Nell *that's haunted by* Moll Knight*:*
> *You that have seen me in my Youthful Age,*
> *Preferred from Stall of Turnips to the Stage,*
> *Those sympathetick Griefs you did bestow,*
> *And Tears to* Scenic *Sufferings once allow,*
> *Employ 'em on my real Torments now.*
> *Knight, cruel Knight, that once lay in my Breast,*
> *My Constant Crony and eternal Guest,*
> *Th'Applauder of my Beauty and my Jest;*
> *She, She, that cruel She to France is fled,*
> *Yet lets me not enjoy my quiet Bed;*
> *When e'er I lay me down to love, or Sleep,*
> *She thro' the opening Curtains seems to peep,*
> *Dreadful as* Gorgon*, turning all to Stone,*
> *Unpainted, and without her Plumpers on;*
> *Her Eyes and Cheeks all hollow, so her Voice,*
> *And this she utters with a dreadful Noise;*
> *Pug, cruel Pug, with whom so long I liv'd,*
> *For whom so well I faithfully contriv'd;*
> *Wherein have I deserv'd so ill of thee,*
> *That thou should'st part my dearest C{olt} and me?*
> *Of Brawny Blockheads hadst thou not before,*
> *By my Industrious Care, a numerous Store,*
> *C{levelan}d her self was never cram'd with more?*
> *By her when first of* W{ycherley} *bereft,*
> *My Charming C{olt} was still a Treasure left,*
> *Nor to my Wishes did he disagree,*
> *I ogled him, and he would Squint at me;*
> *But when his charming Limbs the first time prest*
> *My Heitick {sic} Body, ne'er was Bawd so blest;*
> *Lan{s}d{owne} himself for C{olt} I did despise,*
> *Lan{s}d{owne} the Gay, the Sprightly, and the Wise,*
> *Big with my Joys, to thee I must still run,*
> *Declar'd how oft the Sacred Act was done:*
> *While as the melting History I told,*
> *My twinkling Eyes in their old Sockets roll'd*
> *All this by faithless thee, with Craft was heard,*
> *No blushing sign of kindling Lust appear'd;*
> *Blushing! a thing thou'st conquer'd long agoe,*
> *And Modesty has always been thy Foe;*
> *If e'er thou affect it, 'tis with awkward Grace,*
> *For Bawd is always open'd in they Face;*
> *Bawd is thy Art, Accomplishment and Trade,*
> *For that, not Love, thou were a Mistress made;*
> *No Hero ever to thy Arms was won,*
> *But in some drunken hour when love was done*
> *To wallow, Fumble, Grunt, and Spew upon,*
> *'Till my false Squinter thou did'st lead astray,*
> *And her, that too much trusted thee, betray.*

And so on. The Colt referred to was William Dutton Colt, Prince Rupert's Master of the Horse.

KNIGHT

Mary Knight was the sister (or sister-in-law?) of the poet Henry Birkhead (1617?–1696) and studied music under Henry Lawes. Birkhead died on 28 September 1696, at Mary Knight's house in Birdcage Walk. In his will Birkhead called his sister Mary Knight, alias Geery. Mary was granted a pension by Charles II of £200 annually in 1672; she was still receiving it about 1683 and may have continued receiving it after Charles died.

A portrait of Mary Knight was painted by Kneller, but its present location is unknown to us; it was engraved by J. Faber, Jr.

Knight, Thomas *d. 1820, actor, playwright, manager.*

Thomas Knight was born in Dorsetshire to a family that according to "The Manager's Notebook" was not rich yet "ranked very high in the estimation of their neighbours." He was intended for the law, and in preparation for that profession he was placed in London with the actor Charles Macklin for training in elocution. Knight quickly became enamored of the theatre. He suffered conflict between his inclination for the stage and what he considered his duty to his family, but when family misfortune brought the immediate necessity to make a living he fixed upon the stage.

Early memoirs state that Knight made his first—and an inauspicious—attempt at acting on some unrecorded date at Richmond, as Charles Surface in *The School for Scandal*. He is supposed then to have joined Joseph Austin's company at Lancaster. Austin, however, did not establish his management at Lancaster until 1780, yet a Knight was acting at Edinburgh in 1771 and 1772 and is known to have played Frankly in *The Suspicious Husband* on 30 March of the latter year. The Mr Knight who acted at Edinburgh in 1781 and 1782 was Thomas, and it was there that he was seen by Tate Wilkinson, who, judging him to have talent for tragedy, engaged him for the York circuit.

Knight's first appearance at York in August 1782 as Lothario to Mrs Jordan's Calista in *The Fair Penitent* was, however, unsuccessful, causing Wilkinson to believe that "all his life was to be a *continued rain*" if he followed the stage. But the persevering Knight soon won Wilkinson's admiration in such roles as Charles in *The Jealous Wife*, Spatterdash in *The Young Quaker*, Carbine in *The Fair American*, Touchstone in *As You Like It*, and Claudio in *Measure for Measure*. Wilkinson later wrote in his *Wandering Patentee* that Knight "has to my great satisfaction, as to my auguring so ill, proved and set me down an ass." Knight remained with Wilkinson for five seasons, through 1786–87, gaining the most valuable kind of experience. Through assiduous application he developed into a first-rate actor in comedy. His only dispute with the manager occurred near the end of his engagement over third billing as Twineall on the cast list of *Such Things Are*. At Sheffield on 18 October 1782, while playing in *The Fair American*, Knight and Mrs Jordan narrowly escaped death or serious injury when a heavy roller fell from the top of the stage at their feet. A satire by Knight, *Thelyphthora; or, The Blessings of Two Wives at Once*, was produced at Hull in 1783 but was never printed.

In October 1787 Knight began an engagement with Dimond and Keasberry at Bath that extended for eight seasons and included regular appearances at the Bristol Theatre under the same management. He played numerous roles in comedy, especially in country parts, a

Harvard Theatre Collection
THOMAS KNIGHT
engraving by Bond

line he refined by regularly supping at an inn on the road between Bristol and Bath in order to observe the ostler, who provided an excellent model. Among the roles were Ramilie in *The Miser*, the Marquis in *The Midnight Hour*, Trim in *The Funeral*, Dabble in *The Humourist*, Blunder in *The Honest Yorkshireman*, Mercutio in *Romeo and Juliet*, Random in *Ways and Means*, Billy Bristle in *Hunt the Slipper*, Pistol in *Henry V*, Jack Hastings in *The Natural Son*, and many others listed by Genest. His best role was Jacob Gawkey in *The Chapter of Accidents*, which he acted during his first Bath season. While playing Mercutio in the spring of 1792, he received a severe wound in his thigh from West, who was acting Tybalt. At Bristol in 1790 his prelude *Trudge and Wowski* (taken from *Inkle and Yarico*) was acted for his benefit but was not published.

Also at Bath during these years was Knight's wife, the former Margaret Farren (sister of the more famous Elizabeth Farren) who also had been a member of Wilkinson's York company. The Knights had married on 20 March 1788 at St George, Hanover Square, according to that marriage register, and not at Bath as stated in some early memoirs. By May 1795 they had completed arrangements to join Covent Garden Theatre the ensuing season; the engagement evidently was negotiated through the influence of the Earl of Derby, then Elizabeth Farren's warm patron who was soon to become her husband. The extent of Derby's assistance is reflected in the London press report on 1 August 1795 that Mr and Mrs Knight were said to have been engaged "by Desire of their Majesties." The salaries agreed upon were £5 per week for each.

Knight made his London debut at Covent Garden as Jacob Gawkey in *The Chapter of Accidents* and Skirmish in *The Deserter* on 25 September 1795. That night his wife also made her Covent Garden debut as Bridget in the first piece. (In 1777, before her marriage, Peggy Farren had acted at the Haymarket.) Next day the *Morning Chronicle* reported enthusiastically on Knight's appearance, finding his simplicity untainted with buffoonery and his attention "so wholly engrossed by the business of the scene as to make him appear unconscious of being before an audience." His rustic simplicity charmed the audience, which applauded him vigorously when as Jacob he said "London is a fine place," and that he had "come up to live and die in it." For his second appearance, on 30 September, he performed Sim in *Wild Oats*, with Mrs Knight as Jane, and Watt Cockney in *The Romp*, with his wife as Priscilla Tomboy.

During his debut season in London, Knight was kept busy in such roles as Hodge in *Love in a Village*, Modely in *The Farm House*, Squire Richard in *The Provok'd Husband*, Farmer Harrow in *The Ghost*, Acres in *The Rivals*, Whalebone in *Lord Mayor's Day*, Francis in *1 Henry IV*, Natly Maggs in *The London Hermit*, Chapeau in *Cross Purposes*, Captain Vain in *Lock and Key*, and Slender in *The Merry Wives of Windsor*. He shared with his wife on 6 May 1796, when tickets could be had of them at No 47, Rathbone Place, and they received £331 5s. (less house charges). Knight acted Squire Turnbull and Mrs Knight acted Mrs Turnbull in *The Mask'd Friend*, a piece never published but which survives in manuscript (Larpent 1129) at the Huntington Library. According to *The London Stage* that three-act comedy had been altered by Holcroft from his own *Duplicity*, but "The Manager's Notebook" credited Knight with the adaptation. That evening Knight also delivered a recitation which he had written called *A Ramble to Bath*, with a "descriptive song" in the character of Jacob Gawkey. Fawcett offered a monologue called *The Barber's Petition* with a song "Wigs," both of which according to "The Manager's Notebook" Knight had written.

In the summer of 1796 the Knights played at Plymouth, Cheltenham, Gloucester, and Tewkesbury. Then they returned for their second season at Covent Garden, where Knight acted regularly through 1803–4, becoming a great favorite in flippant coxcombs and rustics. In 1796–97 his roles included Jabal in *The Jew*, Young Testy in the premiere of Holman's *Abroad and at Home* on 19 November 1796, Young Clackit in *The Guardian*, Roderigo in *Othello*, and Crazy in *Peeping Tom*. On 9 May 1797 Knight's two-act farce *The Honest Thieves* (altered from Sir Robert Howard's *The Committee*), with incidental music by William Reeve, was performed for Johnstone's benefit, with Knight creating the role of Abel and his wife playing Ruth. The farce was published that year. *The Honest Thieves* had seven performances that season, including one on 19 May 1797, when the Knights, still living at No 47, Rathbone Place, had their benefit. Total receipts that evening were £221 9s. 6d., but according to a Covent Garden pay sheet for that season Knight received only £35 12s. in benefit proceeds in addition to a total salary of £201.

In 1797–98 Knight added to his repertoire Jack Meggot in *The Suspicious Husband*, Sir Charles Racket in *Three Weeks after Marriage*, Ralph in *The Maid of the Mill*, Colonel Careless in his *Honest Thieves*, Petulant in *The Way of the World*, Dick Dowlas in *The Heir at Law*, and Hillary in *The Italian Villagers*, among other roles. On 11 January 1798 he was Plethora in the premiere of Morton's *Secrets Worth Knowing*. For his benefit with his wife on 15 May 1798, he played Master Stephen, accounted one of his best pieces of acting, in *Every Man in His Humour*. In the afterpiece *High Life below Stairs*, Knight played Sir Harry and danced a "Mock Minuet" with Mrs Knight who played Kitty. Gross receipts that evening were £270 11s. 6d. In the next season, 1798–99, Knight added to his repertoire Tony Lumpkin in *She Stoops to Conquer*, Tag in *The Spoil'd Child*, the Drunken Colonel in *The Intriguing Chambermaid*, Surrey in *Henry VIII*; his original roles were Count Cassel in Mrs Inchbald's *Lovers' Vows* on 11 October 1798, Changeable in Thomas Dibdin's *The Jew and the Doctor* on 23 November. He was Tagg in Dibdin's *Tagg in Tribulation!* on 7 May 1799, for the Knights' benefit, when the gross receipts totaled £392 3s. That evening Knight also acted Goldfinch in *The Road to Ruin*. He had now moved his lodgings to No 38, King Street, Covent Garden.

Knight was a visitor to the Liverpool theatre in June 1799, taking £200 at his benefit. He also played at Weymouth. In July he returned, after some years' absence, to Edinburgh, where the critic Timothy Plain scolded the manager Stephen Kemble for the extraordinary puffing preceding Knight's appearance. But he was well received there as Sir Harry Beagle in *The Jealous Wife*: "His figure, if not perfectly genteel, is manly, his countenance expressive, his voice is clear, and his action in character, avoiding every thing like stage trick, or out of nature," thought Timothy Plain, who had not "seen an actor more improved than this performer since his last engagement here" (in 1782). His Tom in *The Conscious Lovers* was also praised, as was his Jacob Gawkey in *The Chapter of Accidents*—"I certainly have not heard the Somerset dialect so naturally pronounced," asserted the critic, since Dick Johnson, "to whom, in this line, I have not yet found an equal."

Soon after his return to Covent Garden for the 1799–1800 season, in which his salary was £10 per week, Knight brought on his most successful theatrical effort, *The Turnpike Gate*, a two-act comedy afterpiece with music by Mazzinghi and Reeve which opened on 14 November 1799 and enjoyed a total of 27 performances that season. In it Knight acted Robert Maythorn. Published that year, the piece had six editions by 1806. Knight also created the roles of Timothy Starch in Mrs Inchbald's *The Wise Man of the East* on 30 November and Farmer Ashfield in Morton's landmark comedy *Speed the Plough* on 8 February 1800 and played Gingham in *Rage* and Puff in *The Critic*, the

Harvard Theatre Collection

called THOMAS KNIGHT
(private plate, never published)

artist unknown

last for his benefit on 30 April 1800, when receipts were £433 2s. The benefit bill showed that Knight still lived in King Street.

In 1800 Knight was one of the "glorious eight" principal actors (the others being Fawcett, Holman, Johnstone, H. Johnstone, Pope, Munden, and Incledon) who signed the manifesto of the *Differences subsisting between the Proprietors and Performers of Covent Garden*, a protest against what they considered the tyranny of the management for increasing benefit charges by £20, restricting the number of free "orders," and perpetrating other infringements. In his *Dramatic Censor*, defending the proprietors, Dutton claimed Knight had made £566 16s. that season in salary and benefit receipts after charges.

Knight remained at Covent Garden for another four seasons, earning a constant £11 per week beginning in 1800–1801, a season in which he created the role of Corporal Foss in *The Poor Gentleman*. The following year, for his benefit, he produced his one-act *What Would the Man Be At?*, in which he played three brothers of differing personalities; the piece was not repeated. For his 1803 benefit he offered his new two-act farce *Hints to Painters*; it too was not repeated but it brought him a reported £379 that night. During that period he lived at No 10, Tavistock Street. Knight took his farewell benefit at Covent Garden on 15 May 1804, acting Farmer Ashfield in *Speed the Plough* and Lenitive in *The Prize* and speaking a long farewell address which began:

> Twenty-three times hath Phoebus' car gone round
> Since first I ventured on theatric ground. . . .

In explanation of his withdrawal from London, Knight claimed that failing health prevented the adequate discharge of his winter duties. But he had no intention of retiring from the theatrical scene altogether, for by then he was already most busily involved as a provincial entrepreneur. Knight had acted at Liverpool in the summers of 1801 and 1802. During the latter summer Knight and his Covent Garden colleague William Thomas Lewis negotiated the lease of the Liverpool theatre for 14 years. The rental fee of £1500 per year was considerably higher than the £360 paid by the previous lessee Francis Aickin, who closed his Liverpool season on 24 September 1802. Although Aickin's lease did not expire officially until January 1803, the new managers set about having the house extensively remodeled while they were playing the winter season at Covent Garden. Apologizing for slightly raised prices, they opened the Liverpool theatre on 6 June 1803 with *Speed the Plough* and *No Song No Supper* and an address by Knight in the character of a sailor.

After 1803–4, his last season at Covent Garden, Knight devoted his full energies to the Liverpool enterprise for the next 16 years. Despite bad weather in October 1804, the great attraction of Master Betty drew houses close to £300. Lewis and Knight hoped to obtain the lease of the Theatre Royal, Manchester (which also included circuit theatres in Shrewsbury, Chester, and Lichfield), but failed. In 1817, however, when the lease for Liverpool was renewed by Knight and Thomas Drew Lewis, son of his late partner, they admitted into the

Courtesy of the Garrick Club

THOMAS KNIGHT, as Jacob Gawkey
by De Wilde

partnership Samuel Banks, the Manchester manager, and thereby secured a part interest in that theatre.

While managing at Liverpool, Knight had a home at Norton Hall, Lichfield, some 87 miles away, and subsequently at Woore in Shropshire, 65 miles from Liverpool. The last few years of his life he spent in semiretirement, enjoying the life of a country gentleman on a fortune which had been left to him by an uncle. He died suddenly at Woore on 4 February 1820. His wife Margaret had died many years earlier at Bath, on 28 July 1804, and no issue of their marriage is known.

In his will, signed on 2 May 1819, Knight left all his manuscripts to his nephew Paul Slade Knight (a surgeon) and his grandnephew William Wills, Jr, the son of William Wills (a distiller, late of Oxford Street, London), "in strict confidence to be used as they shall upon mature consideration think." To Captain George Knight (son of his late brother George Knight) he gave his gold chain, seals, and gold watch "which was left to me by my late friend Mr David Grant of the Theatres Royal Liverpool and Manchester on the condition that it should be returned to his daughter Miss Jane Grant upon my demise." Nephew George also received £500, which, in case of his decease, was to pass to his son George "lately sent from India to England for his education." His shares in the Olympic Circus and Tavern and stables at Liverpool he left to his niece Charlotte Knight (daughter of his late brother George Knight) and his nephews Paul Slade Knight and William Wills. Other bequests from his substantial estate included £500 each to other daughters of his late brother George Knight: Eliza Croft of Dorset, Lydia Stanton, Martha Kittor, Amelia Knight, Matilda Knight, and Mary Ann Knight, as well as £400 each to the children of his late sister Mary Allen: Eliza Macartney, James Allen, John Allen, and Harriet Allen, all residing in the United States. To Margaret Wills, also the daughter of his sister Mary Allen he left £100 for mourning, books, and his earnest hope "that she and her husband and their son William will use their best endeavours in aid of my executors to render my intentions hereafter expressed efficient towards her brothers & sisters in North America." All of his theatrical interests, effects, and personal and real estate, including a freehold of 160 acres, were placed in trust with his executors for paying all his debts, bonds, and contracts; the residue of his estate was then to be given to Paul Slade Knight, Charlotte Knight, and William Wills, Jr, to be divided equally. The will was proved at London on 4 August 1820 by Paul Slade Knight and again on 16 June 1821 by Charlotte Knight Ireland, wife of William Ireland.

Most testimony agrees that Thomas Knight was "an admirable actor, and a worthy man." In a *Pin Basket to The Children of Thespis* (1797), John Williams wrote of him in lukewarm verses:

His provincial idiom colours his speech:
Not quite purified yet by his vomits and throes,
He's too graceful for clowns, and too clownish for beaus.
....
His SLENDER's *a morceau that honors his skill,*
It offends not sweet Truth—it does Nature no ill.

Apparently Knight had all the requisites of a fine comedian and he worked diligently to improve his craft. Count Cassell, Farmer Ash-

Courtesy of the Garrick Club

THOMAS KNIGHT, as Roger
by Zoffany

croft, Master Stephen, Plethora, and especially Jacob Gawkey, were his superior parts. His repertoire was very similar to that of Edward Knight (1774–1826), who was no relation but with whom he has often been confused. Edward Knight, sometimes called "Little Knight," did not appear in London until 1809.

In addition to the six theatrical pieces and the several recitations cited above, Knight wrote an *Ode on the late Naval War and the Siege of Gibraltar* (Hull, 1784) and some comic songs.

Portraits of Thomas Knight include:

1. Pencil drawing by T. Wageman. In the Garrick Club (No 491D).
2. Engraved portrait by W. Bond. Published by Longman, Hurst, Rees & Orme, 1809.
3. By unknown engraver. In the Harvard Theatre Collection; catalogued as "Private plate, never published."
4. As Farmer Harrow in *The Ghost*. In the Garrick Club (No 116); in the catalogue the character is given as Roger.
5. As Jacob Gawkey in *The Chapter of Accidents*. By Samuel De Wilde. In the Garrick Club (No 205).
6. As Jacob Gawkey. An engraving by J. Fitler, inscribed "Roberts del," but similar to De Wilde's painting (No 5 above). Published as a plate to *Bell's British Theatre*, 1796.
7. As Timothy Quaint in *The Soldier's Daughter*. Drawn and etched by Sam Woolley, published at York, June 1804. In the Harvard Theatre Collection but not in the Hall catalogue.

Knight, Mrs Thomas, Margaret, née Farren *d. 1804, actress, singer.*

Margaret Farren, called Peggy, was the youngest daughter of the strolling players George Farren (d. c. 1770) and Margaret Farren (c. 1732–1803) and the sister of Catherine Farren (d. 1777) and Elizabeth Farren, later the Countess of Derby (1762–1829). Another sister, who may have become a Mrs Hughs, remains obscure. Information on Peggy's family background may be found in the notice, in volume V of this dictionary, of her more famous sister Elizabeth Farren.

Peggy acted with her family in the 1770s at various provincial theatres. Probably her earliest appearance was as Rosetta in *Love in a Village* with Carleton's company playing at the County Hall in Derby on 12 February 1773. In the latter half of that year the family joined the company of James Whitley, the eccentric and influential manager of a circuit in the Midlands, who had rented a theatre in Marsden Street, Manchester. While at Manchester, the Farren family lived successively in Bootle Street, Yates Street, and Jackson's Row, all in the humble area of Deansgate. With Whitley's company in the summer of 1774, Peggy acted at Wakefield—playing Hymen in *Old Mother Red-Cap*—and at Derby and probably at Chester and other places on the manager's circuit. She played at Birmingham with her sisters in the summers of 1775 and 1776 and at Manchester and Liverpool in the winter seasons of 1775–76 and 1776–77.

On 15 May 1777, Peggy made her London debut as one of the Lilliputians in Garrick's *Lilliput* at the Haymarket Theatre under the management of the elder George Colman. After eight more appearances in that piece, she was brought on as Titania in *The Fairy Tale*, Colman's adaptation of *A Midsummer Night's Dream*, that was produced with a cast of young performers on 18 July 1777 and was repeated six times during the summer.

Returning to the provinces after her brief summer in London, Peggy continued her circuit playing and on 30 April 1782 joined Tate Wilkinson's company at York. But in the autumn of that year she left Wilkinson for Ireland and then went to Scotland. She made her debut at the Theatre Royal, Edinburgh, as Desdemona on 11 January 1783. Two nights later she played Ophelia and then performed an impressive repertoire there, one which included, among other roles, Angelica in *Love for Love*, Annette in *The Lord of the Manor*, Caroline in *The Dead Alive*, Cecilia in *The Chapter of Accidents*, Cherry in *The Beaux' Stratagem*, Diana Oldboy in *Lionel and Clarissa*, Lady Anne in *Richard III*, Laura in *The Agreeable Surprise*, Leonora in *The Padlock*, Louisa Dudley in *The West Indian*, Lucy in *The Beggar's Opera*, Miss Hardcastle in *She Stoops to Conquer*, and Patty in *The Maid of the Mill*.

After another stint in Ireland, she rejoined the York company in 1786, "greatly improved indeed," in the judgment of Wilkinson, with whom she remained until 1788. Wilkinson later called her "Mrs Utility." At York she met and acted with Thomas Knight, who in October 1787 left there to take up an engagement at Bath. Peggy married Knight at St George, Hanover Square, London, on 20 March 1788. She joined him at Bath, where on 22 April she played Miss Peggy to his Sparkish in *The Country Girl*. Over the next seven years Mrs Knight was a popular favorite at Bath and Bristol. On 4 May 1788 John Colls (later the husband of the actress Sarah Titter) wrote to Edward Jerningham from Bath: "There is a Mrs. Knight (Sister to the elegant Farren), who is the Jordan of this Stage—and really she is very great. There is in her an awkward simplicity bordering on cunning—that spreads the sunshine of laughter." Colls was obviously charmed by her; in the Huntington Library is his letter to Jerningham of 27 January 1789, in which he sent some lines he had written on "a very wise little woman," Mrs Knight:

> *When Knight, Thalia's fav'rite fair,*
>   *Comes tripping on the Stage,*
> *Pleasure unbends the brow of care,*
>   *And warms the heart of Age.*
> *'Tis her's with nature's torch illum'd*
>   *To win unbounded praise,*
> *For each conceives it unassum'd,*
>   *Whatever part she plays.*
> *Then sure this mirth inspiring Child,*
>   *(who charms in ev'ry Scene),*
> *Of pleasure, may be aptly stiled,*
>   *The little Fairy Queen.*

In 1790 Mrs Knight went to play the summer at Edinburgh, where she was seen as Anne Lovely in *A Bold Stroke for a Wife*, Beatrice in *Much Ado about Nothing*, Belinda in *All in the Wrong*, Clarinda in *The Suspicious Husband*, Fanny in *The Clandestine Marriage*, Lady Teazle in *The School for Scandal*, Miss Tittup in *Bon Ton*, and Widow Belmour in *The Way to Keep Him*, among other roles. She returned to Edinburgh in the summer of 1794 and that autumn went to London with her husband to take up an engagement at Covent Garden Theatre at £5 per week each. The press reported that Lord Derby, lover of Peggy's sister Elizabeth, had persuaded the management to article the Knights.

On 25 September 1795 the Knights made their Covent Garden debuts as Bridget and Jacob Gawkey in *The Chapter of Accidents*. Next she acted Jane in *Wild Oats* and Priscilla Tomboy in *The Romp* on 30 September, Aura in *The Farm House* on 9 October, and Miss Jenny in *The Provok'd Husband* on 15 October. Her other roles that season included Julia in *The Irish Mimick*, Betty Blackberry in *The Farmer*, Sophia in *The Lie of the Day*, Nancy in *The Positive Man*, and Rose in *The Recruiting Officer*. For a benefit with her husband on 6 May 1796 she acted Mrs Turnbull to his Squire Turnbull in *The Mask'd Friend*, a comedy that may have been adapted by Knight from Holcroft's *Duplicity*. The Knights received £331 5s. in benefit proceeds (less house charges), and were living at No 47, Rathbone Place, an address they retained through 1797–98.

In her second season at Covent Garden Mrs Knight acted Lady Flourish in *Abroad and at Home*, Lydia Languish in *The Rivals*, and Lady Dainty in *The Double Gallant*. On 9 May 1797 she played Ruth in the premiere of her husband's *The Honest Thieves* for Johnstone's benefit. In 1797–98 she added to her repertoire Maria in *The Citizen*, Jenny Scud in *False Impressions*, and Kitty in *High Life below Stairs*.

After three seasons in London, Mrs Knight was not reengaged at Covent Garden, despite Harral's claim in his *Monody on the Death of Palmer* that she was that year "of essential service to the theatre." She may have become temporarily separated from her husband, who continued to play at Covent Garden until 1804. In August 1798 the *Monthly Mirror* announced that Mrs Knight "does not quit the stage immediately, but is engaged for the winter season at Edinburgh." Her husband joined her for the summer of 1799 at Edinburgh, where she acted Aura in *The Farm House* on 2 July. In September 1799 the *Monthly Mirror* reported that in the northern capital she had shown herself to be "a very sprightly actress."

Afterwards Mrs Knight performed at Newcastle and other places. She did not again play at Bath, as is sometimes said, but she died there on 28 July 1804 after a lingering illness.

Her husband left Covent Garden in 1804 to become a very successful manager at Liverpool until his death in 1820. No issue of their marriage is known.

Knight, Ursula [*fl.* 1676–1677], *actress*.

On 12 March 1677 Ursula Knight was sworn a comedian in the King's Company at the Drury Lane Theatre. By that time she had served her three-month probationary and unsalaried period and had already been seen as Lettice in

The Plain Dealer on 11 December 1676 and, presumably, other roles not large enough to warrant appearing in cast lists. The only other part known for her was the Queen in *King Edgar and Alfreda* in October 1677. The will of an Ursula Knight, alias Ware, late of the parish of St Botolph, Aldgate, was proved on 15 May 1711 by Elizabeth Percivall and Dorothy Lewis, widows. That Ursula Knight's husband had been Robert Ware. There is not sufficient evidence to identify her with the actress of the 1670s.

Knights, Mr [*fl. 1784–1801*], *actor, singer.*

Mr Knights played Sir Jacob Jollup in *The Mayor of Garratt* at the Haymarket Theatre on 8 March 1784 and Alphonso in *The Spanish Fryar* the following 30 April. He returned to the Haymarket on 26 December 1793 as the Blacksmith in *Harlequin Peasant*; then from 31 October 1794 on he was in the singing chorus of Guards in *The Mountaineers* that season and the next. Back at the Haymarket on 2 July 1800 he was one of the Officers of Government in *Obi*, which ran into early September. Knights was at the Haymarket again in 1801.

Knipp. *See* KNEPP.

Kniveton, Thomas *d. 1775, actor, manager.*

Thomas Kniveton, who spent most of his 16 years on the stage as a provincial actor, made his first known appearance at the New Concert Hall, Edinburgh, as Bagshot in *The Beaux' Stratagem* on 30 June 1757. That summer in Edinburgh he also acted Rosencrantz in *Hamlet* on 11 July, Prince Volscius in *The Rehearsal* on 13 July, Lord Rake in *The Provok'd Wife* on 16 July, Mr Artamon in *The Siege of Damascus* on 9 August, and Serapion in *All for Love* on 20 August. He played with a small company of strollers, probably under Dawson's direction, at Ballymena Market, near Belfast, in September 1759 and at the Town Hall in Coleraine in that December. The performance of 27 December 1759 at Coleraine, in which Kniveton acted Valentine in *Love for Love*, was sponsored by the Masons. In 1760–61 and 1761–62, Kniveton played at Smock Alley Theatre, Dublin, and with members of that company was at Belfast for a month beginning on 29 June 1761.

His peregrinations in the 1760s brought him to Birmingham in the summer of 1762, to Manchester in 1766 as a member of Whitley's company, with whom he remained for some time, and to York in 1769, where he first appeared on 4 February as Tancred in *Tancred and Sigismunda*. Through May of that year at York he also played Hastings in *Jane Shore*, Richard in *Richard III*, Macduff, Townly in *The Provok'd Husband*, Jaffeir in *Venice Preserv'd*, the Ghost in *Hamlet*, Ronan in *The Fatal Discovery*, Achmet in *Barbarossa*, Squire Western in *Tom Jones*, Cantwell in *The Hypocrite*, Cromwell in *Henry VIII*, and Ford in *The Merry Wives of Windsor*. For his benefit on 7 March 1769, when he advertised himself as an "Entire stranger to York," Kniveton played Shylock. According to his York manager, Tate Wilkinson, Kniveton performed "several characters with merit and deserved success; but did not please in the lovers," a line in which it was hoped he would compensate for the loss of Frodsham. After playing the winter season at York, Kniveton continued in Wilkinson's company at Newcastle in the summer, and then returned to Manchester.

Late in the 1769–70 season Kniveton was engaged for a few performances at Covent Garden, making his first appearance as Essex in *The Unhappy Favorite* on 24 April 1770 for the benefit of Mrs Ward, his future mother-in-law. In the farce that night, *The Cheats of Scapin*, he performed the title role. On 22 May 1770 he acted Petruchio in *Catherine and Petruchio* for his second Covent Garden appearance. In the next Covent Garden season he appeared on 30 November 1770 as Ogleby in *The Clandestine Marriage*, a performance which the *Town and Country Magazine* of December 1770 reported was received with "great applause." The writer expressed the hope that Kniveton would be able to supply several other comic characters recently left absent by Woodward's excursion to Ireland. After playing Ogleby again on 22 December, Kniveton appeared as Spatter in *The English Merchant* on 4 and 10 January 1771 and Lofty in *The Good Natur'd Man* on 26 January. His other performances during the remainder of the season included Pamphlet in *The Upholsterer*, Petruchio, the Old Shepherd in *The Winter's Tale*, and an unspecified role in *The Modern Wife*.

Kniveton began the next season at Covent

Garden by acting Ogleby on 23 September 1771. Playing the Chambermaid that night was Margaretta Priscilla Ward, the daughter of the performers Henry and Sarah Ward (née Achurch). Five days later on 28 September Kniveton married Miss Ward at St Martin-in-the-Fields. That season Kniveton was also a busier actor, adding to his repertoire King Henry in *Richard III*, Capulet in *Romeo and Juliet*, Sir Gregory in *The Knights*, Sir P. Wou'dbe in *The Fox*, the title role in *Chrononhotonthologos*, Sir Archy in *Love à-la-Mode*, Gibby in *The Wonder*, and Scapin in *The Cheats of Scapin*. On 11 May 1772 when he acted Cato and his wife played Lucia in *Cato*, they received a joint benefit profit of £83 16s. and tickets could be had from them at Martlet Court, Bow Street. That year in *The Theatres*, Francis Gentleman judged him a good comic—though hardly comparable to King—but "vain" in all his attempts at tragedy.

Kniveton remained at Covent Garden through 1773–74. Then he and his wife joined the company at the Theatre Royal, Liverpool, where he had some share in the management. But by August 1775, Kniveton developed a "white swelling" in one of his legs which necessitated amputation of the limb. The *Public Advertiser* of 25 August 1775 announced that Kniveton had died "last week" at Liverpool. Wilkinson, who characterized Kniveton as "a foe to none, a friend to *all*," lamented that he had died in "the prime of life, after excruciating agonies, of a swelled knee."

Kniveton had a son Thomas who was baptized at St Paul, Covent Garden, on 24 December 1772 but was buried there on 21 March 1773. A Mr Kniveton, who was a scene painter at Manchester about 1798 and whose wife played in that city and in Dublin and then in London in the early 1800s, was probably also the son of Thomas and Margaretta Kniveton. Thomas Kniveton's widow married the provincial actor-manager John Banks (d. 1831). She died at Chester on 27 December 1793.

Kniveton, Mrs Thomas, Margaretta Priscilla, née Ward, later Mrs John Banks *d. 1793, actress, dancer.*

Margaretta Priscilla Ward was one of the daughters of the provincial performers Henry and Sarah Ward. Her father was a playwright and actor who had been at Covent Garden Theatre in 1748. Her mother was one of the daughters of Thomas Achurch (d. 1771), an occasional performer in London and a mainstay in the York company for 30 years. Thomas Achurch had at least three other daughters (the aunts of Margaretta Priscilla Ward): Henrietta and Anne Achurch—the former acted at York in 1763 and both subscribed to Henry Ward's *Works*, published in 1763—and another, first name unknown, who married the actor Robert Mahon. Margaretta Priscilla's elder brother Thomas Achurch Ward (1747–1835), an actor and Manchester manager, in 1775 married the actress Sarah Hoare (1756–1838).

Our subject, announced as Miss Ward, made her stage debut as Juliet in *Romeo and Juliet* at Covent Garden Theatre on 2 April 1764. (This debut would argue against her being the daughter that had been born to Henry and Sarah Ward on 25 October 1752, for it is most unlikely that an 11-year-old would have been ready to act Juliet and the roles soon to follow.) Miss Ward's second appearance was in the following month on 7 May 1764 as Cordelia in *King Lear*. She was not seen again at Covent Garden for another year, until on 26 March 1765 she played Statira in *The Rival Queens* (a precocious role for her age) and Cynthia in *The Oracle*, for her mother's benefit. A year later, on 25 April 1766, she acted Imoinda in *Oroonoko*.

In 1767–68 Miss Ward began a regular engagement at Covent Garden. Earning £1 per week, the same salary as her mother's, Miss Ward played her first character of the season, Amelia in *The English Merchant*, on 5 October 1767. Sylas Neville, who was present, told his diary that she performed "pretty well, but has a stiffness and an indifferent voice." That season she also acted Harriet in *The Jealous Wife*, Rose in *The Recruiting Officer*, Cherry in *The Stratagem*, Miss Biddy in *Miss in Her Teens*, Jenny in *The Provok'd Husband*, and the title role in *The Country Wife*. After playing at Bristol in the summer of 1768, she returned to Covent Garden, where over the next three seasons she maintained her ingénue line, adding to it such roles as Maria in *George Barnwell*, Bridget in *Every Man in His Humour*, the Chambermaid in *The Clandestine Marriage*, and Fanny Goodwin in *The Brothers*, a comedy by Cumberland, which was first performed on 2 December 1769. On 15 April 1771, when

Miss Ward had a benefit (but seems not to have performed), her address was given in the bills as No 5, Broad Court, Bow Street.

Miss Ward began the 1771–72 season by playing the Chambermaid in *The Clandestine Marriage* on 23 September and Cherry in *The Stratagem* on 27 September. On Saturday 28 September 1771 she married the actor Thomas Kniveton at St Martin-in-the-Fields. There was no performance scheduled at Covent Garden that evening, but on Monday 30 September, when she played Maria in *George Barnwell*, her name was still given in the bills as Miss Ward. When she acted Miss Jenny in *The Provok'd Husband* on 4 October, she was advertised as Mrs Kniveton, the name under which she performed at Covent Garden for another three seasons, through 1773–74. Among her new roles during that period were Lettice in *Man and Wife* and Lucia in *Cato* in 1771–72; Jenny the Maid in *Cross Purposes*, an afterpiece by the actor William O'Brien, which was premiered on 5 December 1772; and Mrs Goodwill in *The Duellist* in 1773–74. On 15 March 1773 she played Miss Neville in the first performance of Goldsmith's *She Stoops to Conquer*. (Though the characters were not named in the initial bills of that play that season, she was listed as Miss Neville on 22 October 1773.)

After the 1773–74 season Mrs Kniveton and her husband either resigned or were discharged from Covent Garden and then went to play at the Theatre Royal, Liverpool. Thomas Kniveton, who had some interest in the Liverpool house, died in that city in August 1775. Mrs Kniveton remained at Liverpool, performing winter and summer, at a salary of about £2 per week, until 1778 and probably beyond, for on 23 August 1786 she took £56 at a benefit there. Between January and May 1782 she acted with the company at the Theatre Royal in Shakespeare Square, Edinburgh, playing such roles as Beatrice in *Love Makes a Man*, Emily in *The Deuce Is in Him*, Lady Miniken in *Bon Ton*, Lucy in *The London Merchant*, Mrs Candour in *The School for Wives*, Phillis in *The Conscious Lovers*, and Tilburnia in *The Critic*. From February to April 1783 she was at Manchester, receiving a benefit on 7 April, when tickets could be had of her at Miss Heathcote's, Fountain Street.

Sometime in the late 1780s or early 1790s Mrs Kniveton married the provincial actor John Banks (d. 1831), who had acted with her at Edinburgh in 1782 and was co-manager at Liverpool and Manchester with her brother Thomas A. Ward in the 1790s. She seems not to have acted in London as Mrs Banks. The *European Magazine* of January 1794 reported the death of Mrs Banks at Chester on 27 December 1793. In his *Wandering Patentee*, Tate Wilkinson described her as "a very handsome woman, and a good actress."

By her first marriage, to Thomas Kniveton, she had a son Thomas who was baptized at St Paul, Covent Garden, on 24 December 1772 but died in infancy and was buried there on 21 March 1773. The Mr Kniveton, first name unknown, who was a scene painter at Manchester about 1798, was probably also their son. His wife, acting as Mrs Kniveton, performed in Manchester from about 1798 to 1801, in Dublin between 1801 and 1804, and at Covent Garden in 1810–11 and 1811–12.

Knollys. See KNOWLES.

Knott, Mr [fl. 1729–1732], actor, dancer.

Mr Knott (or Nott) played Harlequin in *The Humours of Harlequin* on 26 May, 14 June, and 23 July 1729 at the Haymarket Theatre and then again at Reynolds's booth at Southwark Fair on 8 September. He repeated the role on 29 November, and a month later there he offered an entr'acte dance. He was again Harlequin in *The Humours of Harlequin* at the Haymarket on 12 February 1730, after which he acted Monsieur Pantomime in *The Author's Farce*. At Tottenham Court on 11 August he was Harlequin in *The Miller's Holiday*, and at Bartholomew Fair on 22 August and 4 September he played the title role in *Harlequin's Contrivance*. On 4 August 1732 at Tottenham Court he was Harlequin in *The Metamorphosis of Harlequin*.

Knowland. See NOWLAND.

Knowles, Mr [fl. 1770–1771], actor.

Mr Knowles, a member of the Edinburgh theatre in 1770 and 1771, also appeared in London at the Haymarket Theatre during those years. In London he played Burgundy in *King Lear* on 18 June 1770 and then Woodford in *The Lame Lover*, Prince Henry in *King John*, and

Dick in *The Minor*. In Edinburgh during the winter season of 1770–71 Knowles was seen at the Theatre Royal as Brush in *The Reprisal*, the Poet in *The Author*, Ross in *Macbeth*, Sanchio in *Rule a Wife and Have a Wife*, a Servant in *The Old Bachelor*, Thomas in *The Virgin Unmask'd*, Trusty in *The Intriguing Chambermaid*, Woodford in *The Lame Lover*, and an unspecified character in *The Devil upon Two Sticks*.

He returned with Samuel Foote from Edinburgh to appear at the Haymarket again, beginning on 15 May 1771. During the summer he tried such new characters as Cruel in *The Commissary* and Whisper in *The Busy Body*. He also acted in *The Oratory* and *Madrigal and Truletta*. His last appearance in London was on 18 September 1771.

Knowles, Mr [*fl.* 1796], *house servant?*

On 22 February 1796 a Mr Knowles was entered in the Drury Lane accounts at a salary of 7s. daily. He may have been a house servant.

Knowles, Thomas *d. 1664, trumpeter.*

On 22 September 1661 Thomas Knowles (or Knollys) was named as one of the trumpeters in the King's Musick at £60 yearly. On 1 February 1664 Joseph Walker was appointed in Knowles's place. The registers of St Margaret, Westminster, indicate that Knowles died in the plague and that he was not buried until 8 October 1665. Knowles left a nuncupative will dated 31 January 1664. In the memorandum he was described as a trumpeter in ordinary to Charles II declaring his will to his fellow trumpeter Thomas Soulthorpe and to Richard Farmer, musician of London. The friends were to receive all debts due to Knowles for the use of Knowles's son Edward, until he "grow to better yeares."

Knox, Mrs [*fl.* 1785], *actress.*

Mrs Knox played Leonardo in *'Tis Well It's No Worse* at the Haymarket on 25 April 1785.

Knyvett, Charles *1752–1822, singer, instrumentalist, impresario.*

The elder Charles Knyvett was born on 22 February 1752, probably in London. *The Dictionary of National Biography* says that he was descended from the Knyvetts of Fundenhall, Norfolk, and Grove adds that his father was

Harvard Theatre Collection
CHARLES KNYVETT
engraving by Daniell, after G. Dance

the Reverend Charles Knyvett. Charles studied under Benjamin Cooke and by 27 May 1775 was playing harpsichord in the Drury Lane Theatre band. On that date he was paid £5 5s. for 14 nights. On 6 July 1777 he was recommended for membership in the Royal Society of Musicians by one of the Ashleys. Ashley said Knyvett was "a sober Industrious Man, & has a Wife & two Children." The children would have been Charles, who was born in 1773, and Henry (later in the army), whose birth date is not known. A third son, William, was born in 1779. Knyvett was admitted to the Society on 4 January 1778.

In September 1783 Knyvett directed the musical portion of the second Chester Music Festival, and in May and June 1784 he was one of the countertenors in the Handel Memorial Concerts at Westminster Abbey and the Pantheon. Knyvett was appointed a Gentleman of the Chapel Royal on 6 November 1786.

On 27 February 1789 he played the organ in a performance of the *Messiah* at Covent Garden Theatre, and a year later he shared with Greatorex the organ chores in the oratorios at the same house. On 2 June 1790 he accompanied Mrs Billington (probably on the harpsichord) in "Mad Bess," a Purcell song introduced into *Hamlet*. He participated again in the oratorios at Covent Garden in 1791 and 1792.

In 1791 Knyvett and Samuel Harrison established the Vocal Concerts at Willis's Rooms. They were carried on until 1794. In the latter year he was living in Stratton Street, Piccadilly, according to Doane's *Musical Directory*. By the 1790s Knyvett's sons Charles and William were also active in London musical circles; therefore distinguishing the careers of the three Knyvetts is not always possible. It seems certain, though, that the "Knyvet" who played violin at the St Paul's Concert in May 1796 was the elder Charles. On the following 25 July he was made organist of the Chapel Royal. Knyvett served as a Governor of the Royal Society of Musicians in 1800 and played in the St Paul's Concerts in 1800 and 1802. In 1801 he had joined with his sons and his friends Greatorex and Bartleman and revived the Vocal Concerts, this time in the Hanover Square Rooms. He relinquished his share in the management in 1802, and in 1808 he gave up his position in the Chapel Royal. After that, unless we have incorrectly assigned some of the activity in the early nineteenth century to the younger Charles Knyvett or to his brother William, the elder Knyvett seems to have retired.

The account of Knyvett in *The Dictionary of National Biography* says that the musician was for some years secretary of the Noblemen's and Gentlemen's Catch Club, which met at the Thatched House Tavern, St James's Street, and that Knyvett also attended the meetings of the Madrigal Society. For a season he replaced Joah Bates as conductor of the Concerts of the Academy of Ancient Music. The *DNB* also states that Knyvett purchased an estate at Sonning in Berkshire. But that account of Knyvett's life incorrectly calls William Knyvett the brother of the elder Charles, and states that Charles married in his twenty-first year—which would have been in 1773, but the younger Charles Knyvett was born in March of that year, and it is likely that the elder Knyvett married earlier than the *DNB* states.

Charles Knyvett died in Blandford Place, Pall Mall, on 19 January 1822. His will, signed on 9 April 1821 and proved twice, in February and again in May 1822, left his second son, Henry Knyvett, of the Depot, Isle of Wight, £14,000, part of two sums (£25,000 and £8,000) due the elder Knyvett on two mortgages. Charles's son William, of Edgeware Road, Portman Square, was also left £14,000 from the same source. Henry's son Henry was given £500. The Reverend Charles William Kynvett of Brinfield, Berkshire, Charles Knyvett's eldest grandson, was given £3000. Whose son he was the will did not state. The grandson William, the eldest son of William Knyvett, was left £1000. Charles Knyvett left £200 to the Royal Society of Musicians, a total of £550 to William Allerway and his family, of Sonning, Berkshire, and £50 to a Mary Jones, apparently Knyvett's servant. No mention was made in the will of Knyvett's wife, who had probably died before 1821, nor did the will cite Knyvett's eldest son, Charles, who may have been provided for in some other way. Charles, William, and Henry Knyvett were named executors.

Attached to the will was an affidavit which declared that the elder Charles Knyvett had formerly lived in Park Lane, in the parish of St George, Hanover Square. The will was proved on 4 February 1822 by Charles Knyvett the younger and on 7 May 1822 by his brothers Henry and William. The double probate is odd, but perhaps it was impossible for all three sons to prove the will together.

A portrait by George Dance of the elder Charles Knyvett was drawn in pencil and colors in March 1799. That drawing was sold at Christie's on 1 July 1898 (No 81), but its present location is unknown. An engraving by W. Daniell of Dance's portrait of Knyvett was published in 1812. Knyvett was also pictured in George Henry Harlow's painting, "The Court for the Trial of Queen Katharine" in *Henry VIII*, which is described at length in our entry for Stephen George Kemble, picture No 15.

Knyvett, Charles 1773–1859?, *singer, instrumentalist, composer*.

The younger Charles Knyvett was born in the parish of St George, Hanover Square, on 23 March 1773, the son of Charles and Rose Knyvett. He was christened at the parish church

By permission of the Trustees of the British Museum
CHARLES KNYVETT, the younger
engraving by Daniell, after G. Dance

on 10 April 1773. In May and June 1784 he was one of the "Treebles" who sang in the Handel Memorial Concerts at Westminster Abbey and the Pantheon. He studied singing under William Parsons and organ and pianoforte under Samuel Webbe. When Doane's *Musical Directory* came out in 1794 Knyvett was living in Stratton Street, Piccadilly, with his parents. He sang tenor with the Academy of Ancient Music. On 1 June 1794 he was recommended for membership in the Royal Society of Musicians. He was described as having served his musical apprenticeship under his father. He was at the time engaged at the Vocal Concerts (which his father helped organize), and he served as a deputy at the Chapel Royal. In addition, he taught singing and pianoforte. Knyvett was elected unanimously on 7 September 1794.

He played violin in the annual St Paul's Concerts in 1795, 1797, and 1798, and in 1800 he published a collection of glees, catches, and rounds composed by several musicians, including his brother William. In 1801 Charles assisted his father in the revival of the Vocal Concerts at the Hanover Square Rooms, and the following year he was appointed organist of St George, Hanover Square. He was probably the C. Knyvett who was a trumpeter in the St Paul's Concert in 1803; what instrument he played at that concert in 1804 is not known. He was probably the Knyvett who served on the Committee for the Concert in 1815 and 1816 (he had served on it in 1798). Knyvett was mentioned in the Society Minute Books in 1822 and 1829, and in 1823 he published a *Selection of Psalm Tunes*, but after the 1820s he seems to have retired. He was named in the will of the musician Thomas Greatorex in August 1830 (proved in July 1831) as trustee and co-executor. Knyvett was described as of Sonning Hill, Berkshire.

According to *The Dictionary of National Biography*, Charles Knyvett died after a long retirement on 2 November 1852; *Grove's Dictionary of Music and Musicians*, on the other hand, gives his death date as 2 November 1859 in London.

A portrait of the younger Charles Knyvett was drawn in pencil and colors by George Dance in June 1800. It was sold at Christie's on 1 July 1898 (No 83), but its present location is unknown. An engraving by W. Daniell of the Dance portrait was published in 1803. An engraved portrait of Knyvett by J. Thomson, after A. Wivell, undated proof before title, is in the British Museum.

Knyvett, William *1779–1856, singer, violinist, conductor, composer.*

William Knyvett was born on 21 April 1779, the third son of Charles and Rose Knyvett of the parish of St George, Hanover Square. William was christened on 9 August. He received his musical training from his father and from Samuel Webbe and Signor Cimador. He was presumably the Master "Knyvetts" who was one of the "Treebles" in the Handel Memorial Concerts at Westminster Abbey and the Pantheon in May and June 1784. His father and his brother Charles also sang in those concerts. In 1788 William sang in the treble chorus at the Concerts of the Academy of Ancient Music, and as early as 1793 his name began to

Harvard Theatre Collection
WILLIAM KNYVETT
engraving by Illman, after Behnes

appear in published songs as a singer at the Vocal Concerts at Willis's Rooms, where William's father was one of the managers. Doane's *Musical Directory* of 1794 listed William Knyvett as a performer in the oratorios at Westminster Abbey and as resident in Stratton Street, Piccadilly, his father's address.

In 1795 Kynvett was principal alto in the Concerts of Ancient Music, and that year, according to the *Catalogue of Printed Music in the British Museum*, he also sang in the Ladies' Catch and Glee Concert. He became one of the Gentlemen of the Chapel Royal in 1797, and shortly thereafter he was appointed a lay vicar. He was recommended for membership in the Royal Society of Musicians on 2 March 1800 and was elected unanimously the following June. At that time he was still unmarried. In 1802 he succeeded Dr Samuel Arnold as one of the composers of the Chapel Royal.

For the Society he played violin in the St Paul's Concert in May 1803, and the Minute Books show that he participated again in 1804 and 1806. He was presumably the "W. Knyvett" who played trumpet in the St Paul's Concert in 1811. The Mrs Knyvett who, with Vaughan, was granted a license by the Lord Chamberlain to present eight concerts at Willis's Rooms beginning on 25 February 1811 was presumably William's first wife.

According to *The Dictionary of National Biography*, William Knyvett sang at the best of the London and provincial concerts for upwards of 40 years. He was a natural bass, but he used his falsetto extensively and usually took alto or countertenor parts. Callcott's glee, "With sighs, sweet rose," was composed for Knyvett. In 1832 Knyvett succeeded Greatorex as conductor of the Concerts of the Academy of Ancient Music, and he conducted the Birmingham Festival from 1834 to 1843 and the York Festival in 1835. He had in 1826 married his second wife, the former Deborah Travis, of Shaw, near Oldham, Lancashire, who had a distinguished career as a singer. Grove suggests that her splendid singing of Handel derived in part from her husband's instruction, for he excelled in the interpretation of Handel's oratorios.

Knyvett was also a popular composer. His glee "When the fair rose" won a prize at the Harmonic Society in 1800, and he composed a number of other songs between 1800 and 1812. Among his unpublished works were coronation anthems for George IV and Queen Victoria.

By 16 July 1828 Knyvett, though he was still active in musical life around England, was living in Ryde, on the Isle of Wight (where his brother Henry was posted). On that date Thomas Vaughan drew up his will, naming Knyvett one of his two executors and trustees. The will was proved on 23 February 1843 by Knyvett alone. *The Dictionary of National Biography* states that Knyvett impoverished himself by unsuccessful speculations and died at Clarges House, Ryde, on the Isle of Wight, on 17 November 1856. His wife survived him by 20 years.

A portrait of William Knyvett by George Dance was sold at Christie's on 1 July 1898 (No 82), but its present location is unknown. An engraving by W. Daniell of the Dance portrait was published in 1803. Knyvett was also pictured in George Henry Harlow's painting, "The Court for the Trial of Queen Katharine" in *Henry VIII*, which is described at length in our entry for Stephen George Kemble, picture No 15. Knyvett's portrait by W. Behnes was engraved by T. Illman and published by T. Williams in *The Harmonist*.

Knyvett, Mrs William the second, Deborah, née Travis *d. 1876, singer.*

The Miss Travis who was listed in Doane's *Musical Directory* in 1794 as a singer from Lancashire who participated in the Handel performances at Westminster Abbey in London was most probably Deborah Travis of Shaw, near Oldham, Lancashire. The Mrs Travis who also sang at the Abbey was very likely her aunt, who was, as Grove notes, one of the Lancashire chorus singers engaged in London in the Concerts of the Academy of Ancient Music. Miss Travis sang in the Concerts of Ancient Music in 1813, and the directors were so impressed that they articled her to Thomas Greatorex. By 1815 she appeared at the concerts as a principal singer and was considered one of the best singers of her day. She was especially acclaimed for her singing of works by Handel.

She sang at the Derby Festival in 1816, at Worcester in 1818, and at Birmingham in 1820. In 1826 she became the second wife of the musician William Knyvett, who was acclaimed as a conductor of Handel's oratorios. In 1834 Mrs Knyvett sang in the Handel Festival at Westminster Abbey. She retired in 1843, as did her husband. He died on the Isle of Wight in 1856; Mrs Knyvett died on 10 February 1876.

Deborah Travis Knyvett was pictured by an anonymous engraver on a music sheet of the *Song of the Fisher's Wife*, published in New York by William Hall and Son.

Koczwara, Franz *c. 1750–1791, instrumentalist, composer.*

Franz Koczwara (or František, Francis, Kotzwara, Kothwara) was probably born in Prague about 1750, according to the *New Grove*. Beginning about 1775 some of his musical compositions were published in London; the composer was living at Bath then, but about 1776 he was in London. He went to Dublin as a violist in 1783, playing in the band at the Smock Alley Theatre. While in Ireland the Bohemian musician composed a number of works, including *The Battle of Prague*, which became extremely popular. Koczwara played at the Chester Musical Festival from 16 to 19

By permission of the British Library Board

Susannah Hill and FRANZ KOCZWARA
artist unknown

September 1783, and in 1789 he performed for the Irish Musical Fund, though the records of that organization show that he was not a subscriber. Fétis claimed that Koczwara was accomplished not only on the viola but also the double bass, piano, violin, violoncello, oboe, flute, bassoon, and cittern.

In 1790 Gallini engaged Koczwara to play at the opera in London (at the Haymarket Theatre until the new King's Theatre was completed); the musician was serving as a double-bass player in 1791. On 2 September of that year, the *St James's Chronicle* reported, Franz Koczwara visited a house of ill repute in Vine Street, St Martin's, and paid a whore a guinea to hang him. Harold Schonberg in the New

York *Times* on 30 August 1970 brought readers the full story. On 16 September Susannah Hill was tried at the Old Bailey for the composer's death, since it occurred at her lodgings. A bizarre book titled *Modern Propensities; or, an Essay on the Art of Strangling* contained Miss Hill's memoir and a picture of Susannah putting a noose around Franz's neck, while he sat holding a glass in one hand and his flask in the other. On the floor before him was depicted what appeared to be a whip. The book indicated that a lack of potency could sometimes be cured by hanging. Susannah Hill, a native of Somerset, testified at her trial that the strange man who came to her on 2 September, drank a great deal of brandy and water and, when taken to her back room, asked to be hanged for five minutes in order to get the blood going to the proper places and raise his passion. She obliged, but when she cut him down after five minutes, he was dead. Miss Hill's case was dismissed, and later, more polite generations, spoke of Franz Koczwara's death simply as a suicide.

Koerbitz, Christiano Tedeschini [*fl.* 1754–1755], *singer.*

Christiano Tedeschini Koerbitz (or Korbitz) was in a burletta troupe that played a few times at the Covent Garden Theatre in 1754–55 with little success. He was seen as Foresto in *L'Arcadia in Brenta* on 18 November 1754 at the opening performance. The troupe spent part of January and February 1755 performing at the Haymarket for their own benefit, hoping to recoup their losses.

Kolowiky, Mr [*fl.* 1761], *flutist.*

On 28 January 1761 at the Haymarket Theatre *David and Jonathan* was presented, with Mr Kolowiky playing the German flute in the band. At the same house on 5 February Kolowiky played the same instrument in *Paradise Regained*.

Kontzen. See KUNZEN.

Kopp, Henry [*fl.* 1749?–1755], *trumpeter.*

The establishment lists in the Lord Chamberlain's accounts name Henry Kopp as a trumpeter in the King's Musick, but his date of appointment is not certain. He may have entered the royal service earlier than 1749, by which year he was certainly at court. On 22 July 1755 he was given leave to go to Frankfort on private business for six months.

Korbitz. See KOERBITZ.

Kothwara or **Kotzwara.** See KOCZWARA.

Kremberg, James *c. 1650–c. 1718, instrumentalist, composer, impresario.*

Jacob (later James) Kremberg, a German, was born in Warsaw about 1650, the son, perhaps, of a Leipzig violinist. Young Kremberg was at Leipzig University in 1672; then in 1677 he became a chamber musician for the Administrator of Saxony, first at Halle and then at Weissenfels. He remained at his post until February 1680, then went to Sweden for a few years and in 1688 was back in Germany. By 1689 he had published a number of songs, some of them set to his own lyrics. Kremberg was a court musician in Dresden in 1691. He helped Kusser with the management of the Hamburg opera from 1693 to 1695, and about November 1697, perhaps with Kusser, Kremberg went to London and took a post in the Queen's Musick.

The *Post Boy* of 18–20 November 1697 advertised that "James" Kremberg, recently arrived from Italy, would "keep" a new concert of vocal and instrumental music at Hickford's Dancing School in Panton Street on 24 November, and his concerts would continue weekly "always with New Compositions." He may well have continued serving as a musical impresario in later years. Kremberg spent much of his time in England composing, most of his works being secular in nature and some of them theatrical. He composed a masque, *England's Glory*, for the Queen's birthday in 1706 and provided some of the music for a short masque called "Bacchussess Revells" in *The Entertainment*, a lost work dating probably from the early years of the eighteenth century.

The Lord Chamberlain issued a warrant dated 12 April 1706 swearing Kremberg a musician in ordinary in the Queen's Musick in place of George Hill, deceased. That may have been a second appointment for Kremberg, for he seems to have been at court from his arrival in England in 1697, or he may have been serving without fee until 1706. The *Calendar of Treasury Books* show that Kremberg was paid £35 19s. 5¼d. for his service as a court musician for 237 days at £40 annually, from 1 August 1714 to 25 March 1715. Grove states that Kremberg died sometime after 1718; a warrant in the Lord Chamberlain's accounts states that James Moore replaced Kremberg in the King's Musick on 23 September 1715.

Krumpholz, Mme Johann Baptist, Anne-Marie, née Steckler   *b. c. 1755, harpist.*

Madame Johann Baptist Krumpholz was born Anne-Marie Steckler in Metz about 1755 and married the Bohemian harpist Krumpholz (1742–1790) some time before 1786. About that year she played a new harp, built to her husband's specifications, before the Académie in Paris, with her husband accompanying her on the violin and a special "pianoforte contrebasse" which had also been built to his specifications. Mme Krumpholz ran off with a young man to London in 1788, and two years later her husband, in a fit of grief over her behavior, drowned himself in the Seine.

Mme Krumpholz made her first appearance in England on 2 June 1788 at the Hanover Square Rooms. At the Enthoven Collection is a clipping stating that she played the pedal harp at Drury Lane Theatre on 27 February 1789. Then, on 6 March, she played a solo harp serenata there. The following 2 April she was at the King's Theatre, accompanying the singer Marchesi. In 1793 Mme Krumpholz appeared at the Oxford Meeting. Doane's *Musical Directory* of 1794 noted that she had also performed in the Covent Garden oratorios. He gave her address as No 59, New Bond Street. She may have retired after 1802. The *New Grove* states that she died sometime after 1824. Anne-Marie and Johann Baptist Krumpholz had three children, one of whom was also a harpist.

Mme Krumpholz is pictured with a large group of musicians in an engraving from the studio of Bettelini, after a design by L. Scotti, published about 1805.

Kühnel, August   *1645–c. 1700, viola da gamba and baritone player, composer.*

August Kühnel was born in Delmenhorst on 3 August 1645, according to the *New Grove*, the son of the musician Samuel Kühnel. August was a viol player in the court chapel at Zeitz beginning in 1661, a post which he held until 1686, though he made trips elsewhere during his tenure. In 1665 he studied in Paris; later he was in Dresden; in 1669 he was in Frankfort on the Main; and in 1680–81 he was in Munich, where he had to turn down an appointment at the Bavarian court because it would have required his conversion to Catholicism.

Kühnel came to London as early as 1682. The London *Gazette* of 19–23 November 1685 advertised a concert at York Buildings at which "Keenall" would perform on the "baryton," a kind of bass viol furnished with sympathetic strings. The music was of his own composition. He also played the viola da gamba.

From 1686 to 1688 Kühnel was director of the musicians at Darmstadt, after which he went to Weimar. From 1695 to 1699 he was Kapellmeister at Kassel. He died about 1700, leaving a son, Johann Michael Kühnel, who was also an instrumentalist.

Kuntze, Christian   [*fl. 1739*], *musician.*

Christian Kuntze was one of the original subscribers to the Royal Society of Musicians when that organization was founded on 28 August 1739.

Kuntzen. *See* KUNZEN.

Kunzen, Adolph Carl   *1720–1781, harpsichordist, organist, singer, composer.*

Adolph Carl Kunzen was the son of Johann Paul Kunzen. He was born in Wittenberg on 22 September 1720, according to the *New Grove*, and studied under his father and W. Lustig, becoming at a very early age a virtuoso. On 28 January 1729 he and his father performed at the Haymarket Theatre in London, the advertisement claiming, evidently incorrectly, that the lad was seven years old. The puff said that Adolph Carl "plays on the Harpsichord in a surprising manner." He accompanied his father, who played the violin, in some sonatas and concertos, and then the boy sang a cantata. On 7 February 1729 at the Lincoln's Inn Fields playhouse young Master "Kontzen" again performed on the harpsichord.

Adolph Carl Kunzen was made konzertmeister to the Duke of Mecklenburg-Schwerin in 1749 and kapellmeister in 1752. While he was again in London from 1754 to 1757 he published 12 sonatas for the harpsichord, dedicated to the Prince of Wales. At his father's death in 1757 Adolph Carl succeeded to the post of organist at the Marienkirche in Lübeck, where he remained until his death, composing a number of oratorios, cantatas, and other works. He had a son, Friedrich Ludwig Aemilius Kunzen (1761–1817), who was also an accomplished keyboard player and accompanied his father to London in 1768. Adolph Carl Kunzen was buried at Lübeck on 11 July 1781.

Kunzen, Friedrich Ludwig Aemilius *1761–1817, clavier player, composer.*

The son of Adolph Carl Kunzen, Friedrich Ludwig Aemilius Kunzen, was born, according to the *New Grove*, on 4 September 1761 (the fifth edition of *Grove* had given the date as 24 September) in Lübeck. Friedrich studied under his father and was brought by him to London to perform in 1768, though discovered London bills do not corroborate that assertion by Grove.

Kunzen studied law at the University of Kiel in 1781, but Professor K. F. Cramer persuaded him to devote his life to music, and with Cramer's help Kunzen gained a position in Copenhagen, which he held from 1784 to 1789. There he was a keyboard performer, composer, and organizer of concerts. His first opera, *Holger Danske* failed in 1789, and he moved to Berlin and set up a music shop. In 1792 he was made kapellmeister at the theatre in Frankfort on the Main, and two years later he was director of the theatre in Prague. In 1795 he returned to Copenhagen as kapellmeister and composed music for a number of Danish plays. He died there on 28 January 1817.

Kunzen, Johann Paul *1696–1757, organist, harpsichordist, singer, violinist, composer.*

Johann Paul Kunzen (or Kuntzen) was, according to the *New Grove*, born in Leisnig, Saxony, on 31 August 1696 (the fifth edition of *Grove* gave 30 August). He was the son of a cloth manufacturer and attended the University of Leipzig after learning violin and harpsichord at school in Torgau. At Leipzig he came under the influence of Kuhnau and Telemann and performed as a singer and instrumentalist at the opera. In 1718 Kunzen was appointed kapellmeister at Zerbst, and in 1719 he founded a concert society at Wittenberg; he served as the opera composer at Hamburg beginning in 1723.

With his son Adolph Carl he came to London where, on 28 January 1729 at the Haymarket Theatre, for his benefit, he played "Some Sonatas & Concertos" on the violin—apparently of his own composition. His son accompanied him on the harpsichord. In September 1732 Kunzen accepted the post of organist at the Marienkirche in Lübeck, where he served also as a composer and conductor until his death on 20 March 1757.

Kurz, Mr [*fl. 1758–1759*], *singer.*

Mr Kurz sang in the *Messiah* at the Foundling Hospital chapel on 27 April 1758 and in May 1759 for 10s. 6d.

Kydwell. *See* **KIDWELL.**

Kynaston, Edward *1643–1712, actor.*

A letter signed "Philalethes" and dated 1 August 1736 from Will's Coffee House was published in *The History of the English Stage* in 1741:

THAT excellent Actor, Mr. *Edward Kynaston*, was well descended.

The *Kynastons* were anciently possessed of a genteel Estate at *Oteley* in *Shropshire*.

Mr. *Kynaston*, to whom we have more immediate Relation, acquired a handsome Fortune by the Stage. He left an only Son, whom he bred a Mercer. He liv'd in *Covent-Garden*, greatly improved his Patrimony, and in that Parish both Father and Son lie interr'd.

A grandson of Edward Kynaston the actor was bred a clergyman and thought "it beneath him to give any Account" of the Kynaston family—which is most unfortunate, for some details about the family might help determine more certainly which of the many parish register entries citing Kynastons refer to the actor. Kynaston, and the many variant spellings of it that one finds in the seventeenth century, was a very common name.

The Dictionary of National Biography guessed that Edward Kynaston was born about 1640. A note in the Burney Collection at the British Library states that he was born on 20 April 1643. Both the prompter John Downes and

KYNASTON

Harvard Theatre Collection

EDWARD KYNASTON

engraving by Parkes, after Cooper (after Lely?)

Charles Gildon tell us that Kynaston was Thomas Betterton's under-apprentice at John Rhodes's bookshop in Charing Cross at the Sign of the Bible; Betterton told Pope years later that he was not apprenticed to Rhodes but rather to John Holden, a friend of Sir William Davenant and father of the actress Miss Holden. Kynaston, therefore, apparently worked for Holden, not for Rhodes. But if Betterton's apprenticeship came at the normal time, he served from about 1649 to 1656, and if Edward Kynaston was born in 1643, or even in 1640, his service as an under-apprentice to Betterton must have come close to the end of Betterton's apprenticeship.

It was under John Rhodes, ex-bookseller and before that a theatrical wardrobe keeper for the pre-Commonwealth King's Company, that Kynaston may have first performed. Rhodes had a troupe at the Cockpit in Drury Lane, probably by 24 March 1660, when official theatrical activity was just being revived. Young Edward was one of the boys selected to play female parts, in the old tradition. Also in the company was Thomas Betterton. With Rhodes's company Kynaston acted Aglaura, the Princess in *The Mad Lover*, Ismena in *The Maid of the Mill*, Arthiope in *The Unfortunate Lovers*, "and several other Womens Parts," Downes said. Kynaston "being then very Young made a Compleat Female Stage Beauty," noted Downes, "performing his Parts so well, especially Arthiope and Aglaura, being Parts greatly moving Compassion and Pity; that it has since been Disputable among the Judicious, whether any Woman that succeeded him so Sensibly touch'd the Audience as he." Cibber later wrote that Kynaston had spoken of his early success as Evadne in *The Maid's Tragedy*.

From Cibber, too, we get an anecdote about Kynaston as a boy actor: Charles II came to the theatre to see a tragedy and found the performance delayed because, the manager explained,

the Queen was not *shav'd* yet; The King, whose good Humour lov'd to laugh at a Jest as well as to make one, accepted the Excuse, which serv'd to divert him till the male Queen cou'd be effeminated. In a word, *Kynaston* at that time was so beautiful a Youth that the Ladies of Quality prided themselves in taking him with them in their Coaches to Hyde-Park in his Theatrical Habit, after the Play. . . . Of this Truth I had the Curiosity to enquire, and had it confirm'd from his own Mouth in his advanc'd Age.

At the Cockpit on 18 August 1660 Kynaston acted the Duke's Sister in *The Loyal Subject*; Pepys saw the performance and assured his diary that Kynaston "made the loveliest lady that ever I saw in my life, only her voice not very good."

By 6 October a troupe made up of a mixture of future King's Company and Duke's Company performers acted at the Cockpit, and John Payne Collier (perhaps not to be trusted) in his manuscript "History of the British Stage" at Harvard conjectured that during the month Kynaston may have acted Desdemona in *Othello*. By 5 November 1660 the two Restoration companies had finally crystallized: the Duke's players under Davenant and the King's under Thomas Killigrew. Kynaston acted for the latter, first at the old Red Bull playhouse but by 8 November at the Vere Street Theatre, a converted tennis court apparently set up after the pattern of a sceneryless pre-war public theatre.

Davenant had chosen to convert *his* tennis court into a playhouse with scenes and machines, and with actresses in the female roles.

Kynaston's career as a male playing women's parts was not to last long, for the novelty of actresses, once Davenant brought them forth at the rival house, became the fashion. For a while Kynaston evidently took either a male or female part; on 19 November, for example, he was seen as Arthiope, and on 6 December he played Otto in *The Bloody Brother*. Pepys saw him in an ideal character on 7 January: Epicoene in *The Silent Woman*. "Kinaston, the boy," Pepys wrote, "had the good turn to appear in three shapes: first, as a poor woman in ordinary clothes, to please Morose; then in fine clothes, as a gallant, and in them was clearly the prettiest woman in the whole house, and lastly as a man; and then likewise did appear the handsomest in the house." The 1661–62 season may have been the last in which Kynaston played female parts. That season, from the sparse records, he is thought to have acted Corporal Cocke in *The Royal King*, and as of 28 December 1661 he was still playing Aglaura.

The Burney notes that gave Kynaston's birth as 20 April 1643 also stated that he was married in 1661. Was he the Edward "Kinaston" from the parish of St Giles in the Fields who received a license to marry Mary Carter, the daughter of Henry Carter of the same parish, on 27 February 1662 (that is, 1661/62)? There is no way to be certain, but the Burney notes say Kynaston's wife was named Maria, and the Edward Kynaston (believed to have been the actor) who was buried in 1712 at St Paul, Covent Garden, was described as from St Giles in the Fields, from which parish he was, indeed, "Carryed away" the previous day. And, as will be seen, Kynaston's fellow actor Charles Hart carefully specified in his will that Kynaston was from St Giles in the Fields.

If the Edward Kynaston who was married in February 1662 was the young actor, then a number of entries in the registers at St Giles may refer to him. The wedding of Edward "Kinnaston" and Mary Carter took place on 6 March 1662. John, the son of Edward "Kinnaston," gentleman, and his wife Mary, was born on 1 January 1664 and christened on the fourteenth. A daughter Elizabeth was christened on 17 December 1665 (possibly she was the Mrs Elizabeth "Keyniston" buried on 26 November 1688). A daughter Arabella was christened on 7 August 1668; a daughter Mary was christened on 15 September 1669 and buried ten days later; a daughter Sarah was christened on 9 December 1670; and a daughter Frances was christened on 23 January 1672 and buried on 18 October 1676. Anne "Kineston" was baptized on 15 October 1674; Edward "Kennaston," was baptized on 4 April 1680 (and may have been the Edward "Kayniston," son of Edward, who was buried on 27 December 1689); "Henery" Kynaston was baptized on 25 March 1682 and buried on the following 30 August (but there was also a Henry, son of Edward "Kennestone," buried on 22 November 1678; though that could have been an earlier son of Edward and Mary whose baptismal record has not been found). James Kynaston was born on 1 March 1684, baptized on the following day, and buried on 22 March. That last entry in the registers at St Giles in the Fields described Edward "Keynaston" as of "g^t Queen"—that is, Great Queen Street. So, too, on 16 September 1685, Susanna, a daughter of Edward "Kenyston" of "g^t Qu:str," was buried.

Those would seem to have been the children of the Edward and Mary Kynaston of St Giles in the Fields we have been following, but the burial registers at that church list also Kynaston burials of Isabella on 8 February 1676, Nossr (?) on 6 May 1676, Francis on 17 November 1677, Sharlot on 11 February 1688, and Edward on 27 December 1689. On 17 April 1682, not long after the baptism of Henery Kynaston, Mrs Mary "Kennaston" was "carry'd away" to be buried in some other parish. If that was Edward Kynaston's wife, then he remarried soon, and to another woman named Mary, for an Edward and Mary Kynaston, as noted above, christened a son James at St Giles in March 1684.

Kynaston the actor quickly rose to a position of importance in the King's Company in the 1660s. As early as 1664 he had a whole acting share in the troupe, inherited, perhaps, from Walter Clun—or purchased by Kynaston after Clun's death. At that point, however, Kynaston, though a sharer in the acting company, seems not to have been one of the building sharers, to whom the troupe regularly paid a fee. But he was an important actor in the company and was given significant roles. The troupe moved from the Vere Street playhouse to their new theatre in Bridges Street, Covent Garden, in 1663. There or at the old Vere Street Theatre he acted Roseilli in *Love's Sacrifice*, and at Bridges Street until it burned in 1672 he played Caraffa in *Love's Sacrifice*, possibly Acacis in *The Indian Queen*, Peregrine in *Volpone*, Guymor in *The Indian Emperor*, probably La Fleur in *Desmoiselles à la Mode*, Dauphin in *The Silent Woman*, Young Loveless in *The Scornful Lady*, the title role in *The Black Prince*, the King in *The Island Princess*, roles in *Catiline* and *The Heiress*, Placidius in *Tyrannick Love*, Florus in *The Roman Empress*, Antony in *Julius Caesar*, Mahomet Boabdelin in both parts of *The Conquest of Granada*, Valentine in *Love in a Wood*, Signor Flaminio in *Generous Enemies*, and probably Volscius in *The Rehearsal*.

During that period Kynaston's ability as a mimic got him into trouble with Sir Charles Sedley. Pepys went to the Bridges Street playhouse on 1 February 1669, expecting to see Cavendish's *The Heiress*, but the theatre was closed: ". . . Kinaston, that did act a part therein, in abuse to Sir Charles Sedley, being last night exceedingly beaten with sticks, by two or three that assaulted him, so as he is mightily bruised, and forced to keep his bed." The following day Beeston read Kynaston's role (not named, but apparently a part that provided Kynaston an opportunity to ape Sedley), and Pepys was there again. All he could report, though, was that the show went on, and that the King was "very angry with Sir Charles Sedley for Kynaston's being beaten, but he do deny it." The whole town must have understood, however, that Sedley was responsible, for on 9 February, when Kynaston was well enough to act in *The Island Princess*, Pepys noted that he did "very well, after his beating by Sir Charles Sedley's appointment." Exactly what Kynaston did that offended Sedley is not certain.

After the burning of the Bridges Street playhouse the King's Company worked temporarily at Lincoln's Inn Fields, the playhouse recently deserted by the Duke's players when their new theatre in Dorset Garden was finished. At Lincoln's Inn Fields Kynaston played Leonidas in *Marriage à la Mode*, Prince Frederick in *The Assignation*, Harman Junior in *Amboyna*, Antonio in *The Maides Revenge*, and doubtless a number of other roles that were not recorded. In 1673–74 he, along with his fellow actors, agreed to act at the new Drury Lane playhouse that was then under construction. The Mr "Kinnaston" who owned a piece of property in St Martin's Lane measuring about 400' by 40', as shown on Lacy's 1673 map of the parish of St Paul, Covent Garden, may have been Edward the actor.

At the new Drury Lane Kynaston acted Doran in *Brennoralt*, Harcourt in *The Country Wife*, Cassio in *Othello*, Tigranes in *A King and No King*, Scipio in *Sophonisba*, Count Sforza in *Love in the Dark*, Morat in *Aureng-Zebe*, Marcellus in *Gloriana*, Freeman in *The Plain Dealer*, Titus Vespasian in both parts (probably) of *The Destruction of Jerusalem*, and Cassander in *The Rival Queens*, after which, about 1677, he gave notice that he intended to retire. Between then and the union of the King's troupe with the Duke's Company, no new roles are recorded for Kynaston, though he did, in the event, continue acting after the union.

Kynaston became more heavily involved in the operation of the King's Company in the last half of the 1670s. The Lord Chamberlain's accounts contain references to him as one of the members of the troupe responsible for company debts. In May 1676 a new sharing agreement was reached (detailed in a 1696 suit involving Kynaston and William Clayton); by that time Kynaston held one and a quarter shares in the troupe and agreed to accept 6s. 3d. every acting day for life plus £100 to his executors upon his death. This new agreement was engineered by Charles Killigrew for his father Thomas, the notion being that Charles would receive the patent and governorship of the troupe, but when old Tom Killigrew refused to hand the power over to his son, the Lord Chamberlain put Kynaston, Hart, and Mohun—the three leading players in the company at that time—in charge of the troupe. That happened on 9 September 1676, but the triumvirate did not long continue, and shortly Charles Hart was given sole control. Still, the Lord Chamberlain's accounts contain warrants that name Kynaston, usually with Hart, Mohun, and Cartwright, in connection with affairs concerning the running of the King's Company.

What is one to make of the scurrilous "Satyr

upon the D. of Bucks" about 1678, a manuscript lampoon at Harvard, supposedly by Dryden, that includes the line, "And Kenastons arse knows its own Buggerer"—the inference being that the Duke of Buckingham and Kynaston had had a homosexual relationship? That, at any rate, seems to have been the assumption of Montague Summers, who was quick to spot deviant behavior in his readings of seventeenth-century sources. In *The Playhouse of Pepys* he commented in a footnote that "Kynaston was of a bisexual temperament, for on 8th February, 1691, when he was aged nearly fifty, he married Hannah Bunhead at S. Mary le Bone." The registers of that parish show that Summers was a year off—the year was 1691/92—and Summers provided no proof that the scurrilous poem had any validity (though it may have had) or that the Edward Kynaston in the St Marylebone registers was the actor and not one of a number of other men of that name.

In the early 1680s the King's Company finances were most unstable, and Kynaston, along with the leading actor of the troupe, Charles Hart, played an underhanded game with the rival Duke's Company. On 14 October 1681 they entered into a contract:

> IT is hereby agreed upon, between Dr. *Charles D'Avenant*, *Thomas Betterton*, Gent. and *William Smith*, Gent. of the *one* Part: and *Charles Hart*, Gent. and *Edward Kynaston*, Gent. on the *other* Part. That, the said *Charles D'Avenant*, *Thomas Betterton* and *William Smith*, do pay, or cause to be paid out of the Profits of Acting, unto *Charles Hart* and *Edward Kynaston*, five Shillings a-piece for every Day there shall be any Tragedies, or Comedies, or other Representations acted at the DUKE'S Theatre in Salisbury-Court; or wherever the Company shall act during the respective Lives of the said *Charles Hart* and *Edward Kynaston*, excepting the Days the young Men or young Women play for their own Profit only; but this Agreement to cease, if the said *Charles Hart* or *Edward Kynaston* shall at any time play among or effectually assist the KING'S *Company* of Actors; and for as long as this is payed, they *Both* covenant and promise not to play at the KING'S Theatre.
>
> If Mr. *Kynaston* shall hereafter be free to act at the DUKE'S *Theatre*, this Agreement with him, as to his Pension, shall also cease.
>
> In Consideration of this Pension, Mr. *Hart* and Mr. *Kynaston* do promise to make over, within a Month after the Sealing of this, unto *Charles D'Avenant*, *Thomas Betterton* and *William Smith*, all the Right, Title and Claim which they or either of them may have to any Plays, Books, Cloaths, and Scenes in the KING'S *Playhouse*.
>
> Mr. *Hart* and Mr. *Kynaston* do *Both* also promise, within a Month after the Sealing hereof, to make over to the said *Charles D'Avenant*, *Thomas Betterton* and *William Smith*, all the Title which they, or each of them, have to six Shillings and three Pence a-piece for every Day there shall be any Playing at the King's Theatre.
>
> Mr. *Hart* and Mr. *Kynaston* do *Both* also promise to promote with all their Power and Interest an Agreement between both Playhouses; and Mr. *Kynaston* for himself, promises to endeavour, as much as he can, to get free, that he may act at the DUKE'S Playhouse, but he is not obliged to play unless he have ten Shillings *per* Day allowed for his Acting, and his Pension then to cease.
>
> Mr. *Hart* and Mr. *Kynaston* promise to go to Law with Mr. *Killigrew* to have these Articles performed, and are to be at the Expence of the Suit.

The merger of the two troupes doubtless would have taken place whether Kynaston and Hart had entered into that traitorous agreement or not, for the King's troupe was in a very shaky condition and probably only a union with the stronger Duke's players could have saved it. The union took place in 1682, and after not having performed for a few years (so far as the records show), Kynaston began to act regularly.

On 10 July 1683 the actor Charles Hart wrote his will, leaving to "Edward Kynaston of St Giles in the Fields" his one share in the Drury Lane Theatre for the rest of the 41 years "which I have therein yet to round out. . . ." Kynaston was to use the revenue to pay the Earl of Bedford, who owned the land on which the theatre was built, £50 ground rent annually. Hart also left Kynaston £5 for mourning. The will was proved on 6 September 1683.

His first appearance with the United Company may have been as Freeman in *The Plain Dealer* or Tigranes in *A King and No King* (manuscript casts showing him in those parts cannot be very precisely dated) or as Henry IV (which he may have performed in the 1680s). The King in *The Duke of Guise* on 28 November 1682 is the earliest performance that can be pinpointed. After that Kynaston played the Colonel in *Dame Dobson*, Antony in *Julius Cae-*

sar, Maximus in *Valentinian*, Sir Phillip Luckless in *The Northern Lass*, Rollo in *The Bloody Brother*, Lord Beaugard in *Sir Courtly Nice*, Don Antonio in *The Banditti*, Belmour in *The Lucky Chance*, the King of Tedore in *The Island Princess*, Clermont in *The Fool's Preferment*, Tom Wealthy in *The Fortune Hunters*, the Cardinal of Lorrain in *The Massacre of Paris*, Muley Moloch in *Don Sebastian*, Lord Wiseman in *The English Friar*, the Duke of Venice in *Othello*, Clarence in *Richard III*, Fable in *The Merry Devil of Edmonton*, Otrantes in *Distressed Innocence*, Sir Thomas Delamore in *Edward III*, Rant in *The Scowrers*, the Duke of Guise in *Bussy D'Ambois*, Merlin in *King Arthur*, Wellvile in *The Wives' Excuse*, Lorenzo in *The Traytor*, Pantheus in *Cleomenes*, Metellus in *Regulus*, Verulam in *Henry II*, probably the Earl of Pembroke in *The Innocent Usurper* (that was the intended casting), Lord Touchwood in *The Double Dealer*, Veramond in *Love Triumphant*, and Count Baldwin in *The Fatal Marriage*.

Colley Cibber in his *Apology* in 1740 remembered some of Kynaston's performances:

He had something of a formal Gravity in his Mien, which was attributed to the stately Step he had been so early confin'd to, in a female Decency. But even that in Characters of Superiority had its proper Graces; it misbecame him not in the Part of Leon, in *Fletcher's Rule a Wife, &c.* which he executed with a determind'd Manliness and honest Authority well worth the best Actor's Imitation. He had a piercing Eye, and in Characters of Heroick Life a quick imperious Vivacity in his Tone of Voice that painted the Tyrant truly terrible. There were two Plays of *Dryden* in which he shone with uncommon Lustre; in Aureng-Zebe he play'd Morat, and in Don Sebastian, Muley-Moloch; in both these Parts he had a fierce Lion-like Majesty in his Port and Utterance that gave the Spectator a kind of trembling Admiration!

In that role, Cibber wrote, when Kynaston pronounced the line "*I'll* do't, to shew my Arbitrary Power," it was "impossible not to laugh and reasonably too, when this Line came out of the Mouth of *Kynaston*, with the stern and haughty Look that attended it."

"But," Cibber wrote, "above this tyrannical, tumid Superiority of Character there is a grave and rational Majesty in *Shakespeare's Harry the Fourth*, which, tho' not so glaring to the vulgar Eye, requires thrice the Skill and Grace to become and support." Cibber was much impressed with what Kynaston was able to do with that kind of role:

Of this real Majesty *Kynaston* was entirely Master; here every Sentiment came from him as if it had been his own, as if he had himself that instant conceiv'd it, as if he had lost the Player and were the real King he personated! a Perfection so rarely found, that very often, in Actors of good Repute, a certain Vacancy of Look, Inanity of Voice, or superfluous Gesture, shall unmask the Man to the judicious Spectator. . . . This true Majesty Kynaston has so entire a Command of, that when he whisper'd the following plain Line to *Hotspur, Send us your Prisoners, or you'll hear of it*! He convey'd a more terrible Menace in it than the loudest Intemperance of Voice could swell to. . . . But the Dignity of this Character appear'd in *Kynaston* still more shining in the private Scene between the King and Prince his Son; There you saw Majesty in that sort of Grief which only Majesty could feel! there the paternal Concern for the Errors of the Son made the Monarch more rever'd and dreaded: His Reproaches so just, yet so unmix'd with Anger (and therefore more piercing) opening as it were the Arms of Nature with a secret Wish, that filial Duty and penitence awak'd, might fall into them with Grace and Honour. In this affecting Scene I thought *Kynaston* shew'd his most masterly Strokes of Nature; expressing all the various Motions of the Heart with the same Force, Dignity and Feeling, they are written; adding to the whole that peculiar and becoming Grace which the best Writer cannot inspire into any Actor that is not born with it.

The United Company, chiefly because of the tyrannical managership of Christopher Rich, split in 1695, with Thomas Betterton and the older players, including Kynaston, seceding to form their own troupe and to play at the reconverted Lincoln's Inn Fields tennis-court theatre. The legal depositions filed by both sides in the theatrical dispute brought out that Kynaston acted but seldom in the 1690s prior to the division of the company. Rich and his partner Sir Thomas Skipwith complained that Kynaston and other seceders had been paid a weekly salary of £3 but acted infrequently. Yet at the Lincoln's Inn Fields Theatre under Betterton Kynaston seems to have worked full time. His first known part there was Hystaspes in *Cyrus* in mid-December 1695, after which he is known to have played Friendly in *The Country Wake*, the Prince of Libardian in *The Royal Mischief*, Michael Perez in *Rule a Wife and Have a Wife* (Cibber spoke of his playing Leon, but we are not sure when), Paulinus in *Boadicea*, Chryses in *Heroick Love*, Sir Bellamour Blunt in *The Pretenders*, Duke Ferdinand in *Beauty in Distress*, Count Roquelaure in *Fatal Friendship*, and the Earl of Warwick in *Queen Catharine*.

We are not certain when Kynaston ceased acting; a manuscript cast in a copy of *The Fatal Marriage*, dated by hand 24 April 1701, significantly gives Kynaston as playing Count Baldwin, and Colley Cibber said that "even at past Sixty his Teeth were all sound, white, and even, as one would wish to see in a reigning Toast of Twenty." But, "*Kynaston* staid too long upon the Stage," Cibber wrote, "till his Memory and Spirit began to fail him. I shall not therefore say any thing of his Imperfections, which, at that time, were visibly not his own, but the Effects of decaying Nature."

It seems clear that Kynaston did not continue acting much after the beginning of the new century, though he maintained a certain interest by holding one of the 36 shares of ground rent in Drury Lane Theatre. *The Dictionary of National Biography* has it that Kynaston died in January 1706. But that report would appear to have been of a child, for the registers of St Paul, Covent Garden, show the baptism of Edward Kynaston, son of Edward and Maria on 11 January 1706 and the child's burial on 18 January. That child may have been a son of the actor. Indeed, the registers of St Paul, Covent Garden, contain a great many entries concerning various Kynastons during the first 30 years or so of the eighteenth century, but they seem to concern a later generation of Kynastons, though possibly related to the actor. The one entry in those registers which would seem to relate to our subject is the burial on 30 July 1712 of Edward Kynaston from the parish of St Giles in the Fields. Was the Mary Kynaston, widow, who was buried at St Paul, Covent Garden, on 1 August 1718 the actor's widow? The administration of the estate of that Mary Kynaston was granted on 21 October 1718 to her son Thomas.

When Edward Kynaston was young he sat for a portrait for Peter Lely, but the work is evidently lost. An engraving by R. B. Parkes, of R. Cooper's copy after Lely, was published as a plate to Cibber's *Apology* in 1889. That portrait was reproduced in *Country Life*, 20 May 1960, as from an engraving in the collection of Mander and Mitchenson.

Kynaston, Nathaniel? [*fl.* 1711?–1718], *singer, composer?*

At York Buildings on 5 December 1718 a Mr Kynaston sang, with Hughes, at his benefit concert. That singer may have been the composer Nathaniel Kynaston, who published *Twenty Four New Country Dances for the Year 1711* and brought out new collections in 1716 and 1718.

Kytch, Jean Christian *d. c.* 1737, *oboist, bassoonist, flutist.*

A Mr Kytch (or Keitsh, Kitch, Kites, Creitch, etc.) was recorded in the Coke papers about 1708 as asking £1 5*s.* nightly for playing in the band at the Queen's Theatre, which was what many of the musicians were asking the opera house to pay them. Kytch was probably the Kytes who was listed as an instrumentalist at the Queen's on 24 December 1709; a similar document shows "Kaite" at 10*s.* each evening.

On the previous 18 June, Kytch had had a benefit concert at the Hand and Pen. Kytch was a bassoonist, and by about 1713 at the theatre he was being paid 11*s.* 6*d.* daily. At the Lincoln's Inn Fields Theatre on 10 May 1716 Kytch played a concerto on the oboe, and eight days later he offered at the same playhouse two new concertos on the oboe and "double cortell." He was cited for other concerts from time to time during the years that followed at that theatre and at Stationers' Hall, Hickford's Music Room, Coignand's Great Room, and Merchant Taylors' Hall. From about 1717 to 1720 Kytch played oboe at Cannons for £12 10*s.* per quarter, and his nephew, evidently a child, was provided with a special small harpsichord to play there.

Kytch's full name was Jean Christian Kytch. He was a native of Holland, according to Deutsch's *Handel*. He appeared regularly in the 1720s at the theatres, especially the Haymarket and Lincoln's Inn Fields but also at Drury

Lane, at the various London concert rooms, and at Marriott's Great Room on Richmond Green, while continuing as first oboist at the King's Theatre (a post he may have held continuously for many years; the records are too sporadic to tell). At a benefit concert for him at Hickford's on 16 April 1729, for example, Kytch was cited as the opera's first oboist, and there were performed that evening songs from the operas, "All the Vocal Parts performed by Kytch on Hautboy, also Little Flute and Bassoon." He continued performing in the 1730s, but he did not prosper. About 1737 Kytch was found dead one morning in St James's Street. Michael Christian Festing and some other fellow musicians, observing the destitute situation of the oboist's two boys, raised a subscription for their benefit. Out of that act of compassion grew the idea for the Royal Society of Musicians; the organizers first met on 23 April 1738, the purpose of the group being to provide for "Decay'd" musicians and their families.

The introduction to the laws governing the Royal Society of Musicians states that Kytch's

performance was held in such high estimation that he was engaged at two or three private parties in an evening to play songs from favorite Operas and other pieces, which he executed with exquisite taste and feeling; but with all the patronage that Kytch enjoyed he was very improvident; he neglected his family then himself, consequently he became totally incapable of appearing before any respectable assembly; and at last, one, morning, he was found dead in St. James's Market.

The Society eventually held yearly benefits and the Minute Books show the great extent to which the benevolent association helped musicians in financial difficulty, especially after their retirement. The group was especially concerned, from the first and over the years, with the care of the widows and children of indigent musicians, even to the point of locating appropriate people to whom young boys and girls could be apprenticed.

= L =

La Bach, Mons [*fl. 1736*], *dancer.*
Monsieur La Bach (or La Back) danced *Two Pierrots* with Smith for Pritchard's benefit at the Lincoln's Inn Fields playhouse on 31 March 1736.

La Bane. *See* L'ABBÉ.

"La Barbarini." *See* CAMPANINI, BARBARINA.

L'Abbé, Mons [*fl. 1705–1712*], *dancer.*
On 20 February 1705 Anthony L'Abbé's brother danced at Lincoln's Inn Fields Theatre. He was probably the "Young" L'Abbé who appeared the following season at the new Queen's Theatre in the Haymarket. Among the papers of Vice Chamberlain Coke at Harvard is a company list for the Queen's that probably dates about 1708; among the dancers is "Labbe's brother." The "l'Abbe Jr" who danced in a turn called *Four Scaramouches* at Drury Lane on 30 May 1712 was probably the same man.

L'Abbé, Anthony *d. c. 1741?, dancer, choreographer.*
The *Post Boy* of 14–17 May 1698 reported that "On Friday night last [13 May] there was fine Dancing at Kensington, where his Majesty was present, as also His Excellency the French Ambassador: The Frenchman, who is lately come over and Dances now at the Play-House, was sent for to dance there, and performed his part very dexterously." The French dancer referred to was Anthony L'Abbé, one of the earliest of the flood of foreign dancers and singers who enriched themselves and the English theatre in the eighteenth century. He was brought over by Thomas Betterton to perform at the Lincoln's Inn Fields Theatre, and despite occasional difficulties with Betterton on the one hand and the resistance to foreigners on the other, L'Abbé made England his home and became one of the most important dancers and choreographers of the first quarter of the eighteenth century.

The English struggled with his name, spelling it Abbé, La Bane, La Bee, Labree, etc. L'Abbé, filed a complaint with the Lord Chamberlain in 1703 concerning his three-year contract, which expired on 22 June. "Je Vous prie," he wrote, "de croire que J'ai toutes les raisons du monde di n'être pas content de la mainère d'agir du Sieur Batardon, à mon égard." He said it was not just caprice that made him wish to leave Betterton's employ but a matter of honor; "le dit Sieur Batardon m'ayant toujours manqué de parole . . ." Just what the misunderstanding was is not clear, but there was evidently a language barrier, despite Betterton's presumed knowledge of French. *A Satyr Against Dancing* in 1702 contained the lines:

The fair thus wave what Betterton will say,
And only talk how finely danc'd L'Abee;
Those cuts in th'air, how sudden nice and clean;
These Entertainments ruin ev'ry Scene.

Whatever backstage bickering there may have been, L'Abbé, like most of the continental performers who came to England about that time, was a crowd-pleaser. He was regularly cited in the bills at Lincoln's Inn Fields as well as at Drury Lane in 1702–3 through 1704–5, and though the bills are very scarce and uninformative, we can assume that if L'Abbé had a three-year contract ending in 1703, he was busy dancing right from the turn of the century. His brother, called Young L'Abbé, danced in England too, from at least 1704–5 to 1712. When the new Queen's Theatre opened in 1705, L'Abbé appeared there that year, after which he returned temporarily to the Continent; he was not mentioned in the discovered bills again until 16 August 1710, when he appeared at the Queen's, hailed as lately arrived from the Paris Opéra.

After that the records of his public performances are sporadic: he offered a *Dutch Skipper* at Drury Lane on 12 June 1713 and danced at the new Lincoln's Inn Fields playhouse on 22 December 1714—and he probably made many other appearances for which no records have been found. How much he was able to demand in salary during the first two decades of the eighteenth century is not certain. A document in the Lord Chamberlain's accounts dating about 1703 (previously thought to belong to the summer of 1707) lists a prospective company with L'Abbé at the head of the list of dancers at £60; he was to have been the dancing master for the troupe as well as choreographer. Upon the death of Queen Anne in 1714 L'Abbé became the court dancing master, succeeding Isaac.

Anthony was highly regarded as a choreographer. Pemberton's *Essay for the Further Improvement of Dancing* in 1711 included only three examples of dances, one of them a "Passacaille" by L'Abbé. *A Collection of Minuets, Rigadoons, & French Dances* in 1721 contained "Mr. L'abee's new Dance for his Majesty's Birth Day 1721." He was similarly cited about 1725 when *A New Collection of Dances* included some of his works. By that time L'Abbé was dancing master to the three princesses, a post that brought him, according to Deutsch's *Handel*, £250 annually (£50 more than Handel received as their music master). L'Abbé held the position until 1741, when Leach Glover succeeded him.

It is unlikely that "Le Sieur Labisle from France" who danced at a booth at Tottenham Court in the summer of 1730 was L'Abbé, considering L'Abbé's high position in court circles. Anthony composed a dance called the *Prince's Saraband* for the Queen's birthday; it was danced at Drury Lane by Essex and Mrs Booth on 22 March 1731. His *Prince of Wales's Saraband* was presented at Covent Garden on 25 April 1737. Dance compositions by L'Abbé were published regularly from 1711 to 1733, as the *Catalogue of Printed Music in the British Museum* indicates.

Ifan Kyrle Fletcher in *Famed for Dance* states that L'Abbé died about 1737, though we are more inclined to accept Deutsch's statement that implies a death date for L'Abbé no earlier than 1741, when Glover succeeded him at court.

L'Abbree. *See* L'ABBÉ.

La Bee. *See* L'ABBÉ.

"La Belle Espagnole." *See* REDIGÉ, MME PAULO.

Labisle, Sieur [*fl.* 1730], *dancer*.
Le Sieur Labisle, advertised as from France, danced a *Mad Dance* and a *Pierrot* at Tottenham Court on 1 August 1730 with a troupe made up chiefly of performers from the Goodman's Fields playhouse.

La Borde, Mons [*fl.* 1707], *musician*.
In the papers of Vice Chamberlain Coke at Harvard is a document dating about late December 1707 listing performers at the Queen's Theatre. Mons La Borde, evidently an instrumentalist, was cited as receiving an annual salary of £40.

Labordi, Mr [*fl.* 1782], *acrobat*.
A Mr Labordi was a member of Andrews's troupe from London and appeared in an acrobatic turn called "Egyptian Pyramids" at Bristol in March 1782. It is very likely he was related in some way to the dancer L'Aborie.

Laborie, Master [*fl.* 1798], *dancer*.
Master Laborie (or L'Aborie) danced in the pastoral ballet *Elisa* at the King's Theatre on 10 May 1798. Both Monsieur and Madame Laborie were also in that work, so it is almost certain that Master Laborie was their son.

Laborie, Lombard *b. c. 1771, dancer*.
According to Julien's *L'Opéra Secret* (1880), the dancer Lombard Laborie (or L'Aborie) was 17 in 1788 and thus was born about 1771. He was surely the Master Laborie who made his first appearance in England dancing a pas de deux with Miss Simonet at the King's Theatre from 10 through 23 December 1782. It is likely that the acrobat "Labordi" (if that spelling is correct) who performed in Bristol in March 1782 and was in a troupe from London was related in some way to our subject. We believe, too, that the Mr Laborie who was in a *Dance of Coopers* at the Royal Circus on 9 October 1784 was Lombard Laborie.

Laborie was in the company at the King's Theatre during the full 1786–87 season, appearing first in a *Divertissement* on 23 December

1786 and then dancing in *Le Berger inconstant*, *L'Heureux événement*, *Zemira and Azor* (he was the Genius of the Arts), a Russian pas de deux with Mlle Mozon, *Sylvie*, *Le Cossac jaloux*, and *Le Divertisement Asiatique*. In 1789 Laborie made his debut at the Paris Opéra in *Aspasie*; then he returned to London for the 1789–90 season, to dance with the King's Theatre company at the Haymarket and Covent Garden theatres. He appeared in such dances as *La Bergère des Alpes*, *Les Mariages Flamands*, *Les Caprices*, *La Jalousie sans raison*, a pas Russe with Mlle Hilligsberg (for his solo benefit on 22 April 1790), *The Generous Slave*, and a potpourri that had been performed at Ranelagh Gardens.

He returned to London again for the 1791–92 season, appearing on 17 December 1791 at the Pantheon as Alcindor in *L'Amant déguisé* and at the Haymarket on 14 February 1792 in *La Fête villageoise* and on 14 April as Laboriski in *La Foire de Smirne*. Later in 1792 he was again at the Opéra. Indeed, on 4 May 1793 the London opera manager Gallini tried to get a judgment against Laborie for £50 for not dancing according to his contract, but the case was set aside on the grounds that the opera house had not been properly licensed. Laborie had probably broken a contract for the 1792–93 season. The opera house accounts make no mention of him between 1791–92 and 1795–96, when he was engaged at the King's Theatre at a season salary of £800 (according to *The Italian Opera* by William C. Smith; *The London Stage* does not list Laborie there that season). Madame Laborie was also named at the same salary in 1795–96, according to Smith. Smith does not show the couple as having been in London in 1796–97, but both were at the King's Theatre in 1797–98.

On 28 November 1797 Laborie danced in *L'Offrande à Terpsichore* and was Bacchus in the new *Bacchus et Ariadne*. The bill that night incorrectly stated that Laborie was making his first appearance since 1790. *The London Stage* corrects that date to 1792. If Smith is correct about the Labories being in London for the 1795–96 season, the bill was even further off. During the rest of the season Laborie danced in such pieces as *Le Triomphe de Thémis*, *Constante et Alcidonis*, *La Vengeance de l'Amour*, *Enée et Didon*, *Peggy's Love*, *Elisa*, and *Le Déserteur* (in which he danced the character of Skirmish). The dancers from the opera company appeared once in May at Drury Lane and once in June at Covent Garden.

Laborie and his wife danced at the King's Theatre through 4 April 1805, his last appearance there. He was in such new dances as *Tarare et Irza*, *Les Jeux d'Églé*, *Témire*, *Le Mariage Mexicain*, *Hyppomène et Atalante*, *Telasco and Amgahi* (at Drury Lane), a *Divertisement Bayadaire*, *Rinaldo e Leonora*, and *Laura et Lenza*. Goede in *The Stranger in England* wrote of seeing Laborie perform on 2 May 1799: "D'Egville, Laborie and St. Pierre are excellent dancers and fine manly figures. Laborie possesses more elegance than St Pierre; but the latter greater animation."

The Master Laborie who danced with Lombard Laborie and his wife in May 1798 was surely their son. The dancer Anne Laborie who was born about 1769 and performed in France from 1783 to 1789 may have been Lombard's sister.

Laborie, Mme Lombard [*fl.* 1795?–1805], *dancer.*

Madame Lombard Laborie (or L'Aborie) was first mentioned in London playbills on 28 November 1797, when she danced in *L'Offrande à Terpsichore* and was Ariadne in the new ballet *Bacchus et Ariadne*. Dancing with her was her husband, who had appeared before in London. The bill did not state that Mme Laborie was making her initial London appearance, so we should suppose that she, too, may have danced there before. She danced in *Constante et Alcidonis* on 6 February 1798, *Enée et Didon* on 19 April, *Peggy's Love* on 26 April, *Bacchus et Ariadne* at Drury Lane on 9 May, *Elisa* at the King's on 10 May, *Peggy's Love* at Covent Garden on 11 June, and *Le Déserteur* (she was Louisa) at the King's on 14 June.

Mme Laborie was similarly engaged in the 1798–99 and 1799–1800 seasons, adding to her dancing repertoire such works as *Les Deux Jumelles* ("Mesdames Laborie and Hilligsberg, who appeared as the Twin Sisters, were most happily successful," said the *Morning Chronicle* on 30 January 1799), *Télémaque* (she danced as Vénus), *Tarare et Irza*, *Les Jeux d'Églé*, *Témire*, *Le Mariage Mexicain*, *Hyppomène et Atalante* (she was Zelie), *Telasco and Amgahi* (at Drury Lane), *Rinaldo e Leonora*, and *Laura et Lenza*. According to William C. Smith's *The Italian Opera*, she and her husband danced at the King's Theatre through the 1804–5 season. (Smith also lists Mme Laborie as at the King's in 1795–96 at a season salary of £800, but *The London Stage* does not cite the Labories there that season, and Smith may have erred in the year.)

Labusierre, Timothy [*fl. 1739*], *musician*.

Timothy Labusierre was one of the original subscribers to the Royal Society of Musicians when it was organized on 28 August 1739.

Lacey. *See also* LACY.

Lacey, Charles *d. 1757, actor, dancer.*

Perhaps Charles Lacey had acted elsewhere in the provinces before he appeared at the New Concert Hall, Edinburgh, as Hamlet on 16 November 1747. Other roles he played that 1747–48 season at Edinburgh included Cassio in *Othello*, Coupee in *The Virgin Unmask'd*, Fribble in *Miss in Her Teens*, Hotspur in *1 Henry IV*, King Lear (on 9 March 1748), Lothario in *The Fair Penitent*, Lusignan in *Zara*, Macbeth (on 2 February 1748), Marc Antony in *Julius Caesar*, and Tancred in *Tancred and Sigismunda*.

Lacey's first appearance at Covent Garden was on 25 October 1748, when he acted Marcus to Quin's Cato before the Prince and Princess of Wales and other members of the royal family. It was Lacey's only London performance that season, however, and on 14 December 1748 he was back in Edinburgh playing Hotspur. During 1748–49 there he acted a number of capital roles, including Jaffeir in *Venice Preserv'd*, Hamlet, Lear, Richard III, George Barnwell in *The London Merchant*, and Myrtle in *The Conscious Lovers*.

In the summer of 1749 Lacey played at the Jacob's Wells Theatre, Bristol, taking a benefit on 5 August, and then he went to act at Richmond, Surrey, where he was advertised somewhat pretentiously as from Covent Garden. When the 1749–50 season had begun, Lacey had indeed been a member of the Covent Garden company; on 29 September 1749 he was paid £1 for the first two nights the theatre was open, 25 and 27 September, though his name did not appear in those bills. Still no mention of him in the bills had occurred by 14 October 1749, when the *General Advertiser* announced that "On Thursday evening 12 October as Mr Lacey belonging to Covent Garden Theatre was coming from Marybone, he was stopt by three fellows armed who robb'd him of 18s. some half pence, his Buckles and a Key." Finally, on 11 November 1749 he was advertised for Marcus, again to Quin's Cato. Then he was seen as Barnwell on 26 December, as Charles in *The Non-Juror* on 4 January 1750, and subsequently as Burgundy in *Henry V*, Chamont in *The Orphan*, Tybalt in *Romeo and Juliet*, Hastings in *Jane Shore*, and Pembroke in *Lady Jane Gray*. He returned to Richmond in the summer of 1750.

Lacey spent the next season, 1750–51, at Covent Garden and the following summer he was again at Richmond. Among his characters at the patent house that season were Paris in *Romeo and Juliet*, Tressel in *Richard III*, the Dauphin in *King John*, Buckingham in *Henry VIII*, and Chatillon in *Zara*. On 23 April 1751 he acted Hastings for Miss Falkner's benefit when Barry refused to appear. Lacey's name was not to be found in a London bill in 1751–52, for he spent that season at Bath, but he was again acting in the metropolis in 1752–53, this time engaged at Drury Lane, where he first appeared on 26 September 1752 as Surrey in *Henry VIII*, followed by Paris, Axalla in *Tamerlane*, Adam in *As You Like It*, Macduff in *Macbeth*, and a character in *The Rehearsal*. On 1 May 1753, sharing a benefit with Wilder (gross receipts where £170), Lacey acted Hamlet and danced a minuet with Mme Auretti. Lacey's last season at Drury Lane was 1753–54, when he added to his repertoire Varole in *The Relapse* and the Gentleman Usher in *King Lear*. On 6 May 1754, he shared £130 in gross benefit receipts with Miss Thomas and three other performers and acted Macduff and the Frenchman in *Lethe*; additionally, by desire, he and Mrs Addison offered a minuet.

In October 1754 Lacey was engaged at Smock Alley Theatre in Dublin. Reed's "Theatrical Obituary" in the Boston Public Library states that Charles Lacey died in December 1757, but five months earlier the *Public Advertiser* of 18 July 1757 had reported that the life insurance was to be paid following his recent death and identified him by full name as formerly of Drury Lane.

La Chapelle. *See* DE LA CHAPELLE.

"La Charmante, Mlle," [stage name of Mlle Beaumaunt?] [*fl. 1736*], *actress.*

On 29 April 1736 at the Haymarket Theatre Colombine in *Tumble Down Dick* was performed by "Mlle La Charmante," "piping hot from Paris." The 1736 edition of the work listed Mlle Beaumaunt in the part; that was probably the actress's real name.

Lackit, Mr [*fl. 1746*], *actor.*

Mr Lackit played Squire Numps in *The Imprisonment of Harlequin* at Warner's booth at Southwark Fair on 8 September 1746.

"La Coghetta." *See* GABRIELLI, CATERINA.

La Cointe. *See also* DE LA COINTRIE.

La Cointe, Mr [*fl. 1756–1757*], *dancer.*

Mr La Cointe (or Le Cointe) danced a hornpipe at Covent Garden Theatre on 22 April 1756 and subsequent dates and was in a new dance called *Les Savoyards* on 18 May. The dancer Miss Vallois was cited in the Haymarket bill of 14 September 1757 as having been a scholar of La Cointe.

Lacon, Mr *d. c. 1757, puppeteer.*

In the summer of 1739 the eccentric Charlotte Charke journeyed to Tunbridge Wells to exhibit her puppets only to find that a Mr Lacon had been established there for some years with a successful puppet theatre. On 28 November 1741, according to David Jenkins in *Theatre Notebook* 23, Lacon put on his puppet show at the James Street Theatre in London. Jenkins describes Lacon as a waxwork exhibitor from Bath and Tunbridge Wells. The puppeteer Jobson bought Lacon's figures at some point. According to Bryan's *Dictionary* Lacon was a painter of watercolor portraits as well as a puppeteer at Bath and died about 1757.

La Count, David [*fl. 1691*], *musician.*

David la Count was sworn a Gentleman of the Chapel Royal extraordinary (without fee, waiting for a vacancy) on 31 August 1691. He evidently never received a salaried position.

Lacourt. *See* DE LA COUR.

Lacrig, Mr [*fl. 1688*], *musician.*

Mr Lacrig, a Gentleman of the Chapel Royal, was paid riding charges of 6s. on 20 December 1688 for his journey to Windsor on the previous 25 July and back to London on 19 September, presumably in musical attendance on the King.

La Croix. *See also* DE LA CROIX.

La Croix, Mons [*fl. 1741–1750s?*], *dancer.*

On 21 October 1741 at Drury Lane Theatre Monsieur La Croix, recently arrived from Paris, danced in *Le Généreux corsaire*. He was also seen during the 1741–42 season in a number of specialty dances: *Les Jardiniers Suédois*, *Les Satires puny* (he was a Shepherd), *Les Masons et les sabotiers*, *The Peasants* (again he was a Shepherd), and unnamed ballets. He was perhaps the La Croix mentioned in Michael Kelly's *Reminiscences* as performing at Penzance, perhaps in the 1750s:

Before [Jefferson] became proprietor of the Plymouth theatre, he was manager of a strolling company of comedians, who acted on shares. When they were at Penzance, in Cornwall, performing in a barn, and miserably off for audiences, a French dancer, of the name of La Croix, who had come from St. Malo's, to seek his fortune in Plymouth, finding the theatre there shut, and hearing of Monsieur Jefferson's company at Penzance, formed a resolution to pack up his very "little all," and *chassé* on foot to join them.

When he arrived at Penzance, he waited upon Mr. Jefferson, offered his services, and said, that he had no doubt he should draw crowded houses by the excellence of his performance; for Monsieur La Croix, in his own opinion, was "Le Dieu de la danse." He was accordingly enrolled in the company on the usual terms, that is to say, that all should share and share alike. He made his appearance in a fine pas seul; but, unluckily, in one of his most graceful pirouettes, a very important part of his drapery, either from its age or slightness, or from the wonderful exertion of its wearer, became suddenly rent in a most unmendable manner. Shouts of laughter and applause followed, which Monsieur La Croix imagined were given for his jumping; nor was the supposition at all unjustifiable, for the higher he jumped, the more he was applauded. At last some one behind the scenes called him off the stage; and he was so shocked at the mishap which had befallen him, that he could never be induced to appear again. But, in the sequel, when he came to receive the recompence of his exertions and exposure, the salvo for his shame amounted only to a few bits of candle ends, which he would not accept; he said, he was a French artiste, and not a Russian, and therefore could not be expected to live on candles, and that Monsieur *Jeff* (as he called the manager) had imposed upon him with false pretences. The poor fellow made his way to Totness, where, as I heard, he got some scholars; but nothing would induce him to hear Mr. Jeff, or his tallow provender, ever spoken of again.

"La Cuochetina." *See* GABRIELLI, CATERINA.

La Curtz. *See* CURTZ.

Lacy. *See also* LACEY.

Lacy, Mrs [*fl. 1696*], *actress.*
A Mrs Lacy, apparently not Margaret Lacy, the widow of the actor John, played Mrs Ventre in *The City Bride* in March 1696 at the Lincoln's Inn Fields Theatre.

Lacy, James *1696–1774, manager, patentee, actor.*
James Lacy was born in 1696 to an Irish family "at once *splendid, loyal,* and *unfortunate*," according to a contemporary memoir. His family had remained faithful to Charles I and consequently were ruined. Its members then followed the military, and James's grandfather married the daughter of John Russel and Grace Cromwell. James's father settled in the eastern part of England, so by 1722 young James was living in Norwich. Having failed at business, James turned to acting with the Norwich company, then came to London, where by 18 March 1724 his name was in the account books of John Rich's Lincoln's Inn Fields Theatre. The first notice of his name on a surviving bill, however, was on 2 May 1727, when he acted Herodorus in *Philip of Macedon*, which he followed on 19 May with Cunedag in *The Ancient History of Caradoc the Great,* for a benefit shared with Morgan at which gross receipts of £103 18s. were taken.

At Lincoln's Inn Fields during the next season, 1727–28, Lacy acted Robin of Bagshot in *The Beggar's Opera,* the First Outlaw in *The*

Harvard Theatre Collection

JAMES LACY
artist unknown

Pilgrim, Rigadoon in *Love in a Bottle,* Laelius in *Sophonisba,* and Bob Cash in *The Wife's Relief.* In 1728–29 he was at the Haymarket Theatre playing Acasto in *The Orphan,* Truck in *The Lottery,* John in *Don Carlos,* Renault in *Venice Preserv'd,* and Worthy in *The Recruiting Officer.* On 13 June 1729 he acted Gage in *Phebe* at Drury Lane Theatre. In 1729–30 he joined the new venture at Goodman's Fields Theatre and also played on several occasions at the Haymarket. During the 1730s Lacy made the rounds of every London theatre (save Drury Lane where he would eventually co-manage), providing useful but uninspired service. He was not "an *absolute fixture,* as an actor," as one memoirist wrote, and "his performances were of the middling cast." In 1729–30 he was with the Haymarket company, 1731–32 with Rich at Lincoln's Inn Fields and then in 1732–33 and

1733–34 at Covent Garden. In the summer of 1735 he was again at Lincoln's Inn Fields. His brother Theophilus Lacy acted occasionally in London in 1730.

With Mrs Lacy (fl. 1727–1737), whom we take to have been his first wife, Lacy performed at the Bartholomew and Southwark fairs in the summer of 1730 and in Fielding's booth at Bartholomew Fair in 1734. He was with Fielding's company at the Haymarket in 1735–36 and acted Fustian in that author's *Pasquin*, a satirical farce which opened on 5 March 1736 for a long run. That summer at the Tottenham Court Fair Lacy, who advertised himself as "the Poet Fustian," and Jones, who styled himself "the Mayor of Pasquin," led a troupe that played Aaron Hill's version of *King Henry the Fifth* (within which was given a ballad opera called *The Amorous Old Widow*). Again with the "Great Mogul's Company of Comedians" at the Haymarket in 1736–37, Lacy acted Sourwit at the premiere of Fielding's *The Historical Register* on 21 March 1737 and the same character in Fielding's "very short, but very merry Tragedy" *Eurydice Hiss'd* on 13 April. On 4 May 1737 Lacy had a benefit at the Haymarket at which was performed his "a new Satyrical, Allegorical, Political Farce" called *Fame; or Queen Elizabeth's Trumpets; or, Never plead's Hopes of being a Lord Chancellor*. A letter had appeared in the *Daily Advertiser* of 30 April signed "James Lacy, Alias Fustian, Alias Sour-Wit." The writer asserted that inasmuch as he knew neither "Mr Lacy the Author" nor the manager, he could not "be accus'd of Partiality, in affirming, that I think this the best Farce this Age had produc'd. It seems to be writ in Imitation of Shakespear, and entirely calculated for the present Taste."

With the passing of the Licensing Act, Fielding's Haymarket season was cut a bit short, and Lacy, who had taken no small part in that drama over theatrical liberties, now turned his mind to other ventures. Soon, however, Lacy brought the authorities down upon himself. On 12 December 1737 Lacy tried to evade the Licensing Act by presenting his *Oratory* at the Long Room, in York Buildings, Villiers Street. The "lecture" was announced to be on "The Trial of John Philpot (Alderman of London in the reign of Richard II) for destroying the Pirates without a Commission, who had for many years plundered the Merchants of England. . . ."

Mr Professor Lacy (having been qualified himself at the Sessions of Justices, according the memorable Act of Toleration) begs leave to inform the Publick, that to avoid the tediousness of one sole speaker, the Lecture is artificially divided among his Assistants, and cannot fail of being greatly to the Edification of his Auditory.

The subterfuge fooled nobody and Lacy was arrested. On 15 February 1738 the *London Daily Post and General Advertiser* reported:

On Monday last 13 February Mr Lacy, who set up the Oratory in York Buildings, and was committed to Bridewell some time since, by two of his Majesty's Justices of the Peace on the late Act of Parliament, was brought up by Habeas Corpus to the King's Bench, in order to be bail'd, but after several Learned Arguments by his Council, which were answer'd by the Attorney and Solicitor-General, the Court remanded him back again.

But on 2 March the paper reported that Lacy "is got out of Custody." He wasted little time in asserting his small triumph, for on 26 March he returned to York Buildings with "An Oration: On a passage from St. Matthew by Lacy. . . . In Regard to the Expences of the late Prosecution, the Seats will be 2s." Lacy repeated the program on 29 and 30 March, seven times in April, and three times in May, including some Sunday evenings.

Though Lacy was not again seen on the London stage until 22 August 1741, when he played Captain Strut in *The Modern Pimp* in Hallam's Bartholomew Fair booth, he remained, as Davies described him in his *Life of David Garrick*, "active and enterprising." Lacy developed his scheme for an outdoor place of entertainment, first attempting to buy the site of Beaufort House in Chelsea and then settling, in partnership with one Solomon Rietti, a lease of the house and gardens of the late Earl of Ranelagh, near the river adjoining the Royal Hospital. Evidently it was Lacy who planned the Rotunda, and about 1741–42 the pleasure garden proved to be a great success. Horace Walpole claimed that "Every night . . . I go to Ranelagh, which has totally beat Vauxhall. Nobody goes anywhere else—everybody goes there." Despite Walpole's enthusiasm and Davies's description of the Rotunda as "a standing monument" of Lacy's taste and ingenuity, again he was unfortunate for he had been "yoked with a wicked partner." But Lacy managed to escape from the Ranelagh adventure with £4000 profit, and by 1742 William Crispe and James Myonnet had taken over the lease.

On 12 May 1742, announced as the "Inventor of the Theatre in Ranelagh Gardens," Lacy acted the title role in *Oroonoko* to a very small house (40) at Drury Lane. For a while, according to a memoir in *European Magazine* for April 1809, Lacy became assistant manager to Rich at Covent Garden, but there was no contemporary commentary as evidence of that.

Late in 1744 Lacy became entangled for the first time in the financial and managerial complication created by Charles Fleetwood's tenure at Drury Lane Theatre. Sometime in mid-December, before the eighteenth, Fleetwood sold out to the bankers Norton Amber and Richard Green, who entered into partnership with Lacy. Amber and Green advanced the money to Lacy for purchasing the patent and effects of the house. As security for £2250, plus interest, they held two third-parts of the patent, scenes, wardrobes, and house lease, along with a covenant for sharing any new patent that should be obtained. Additionally, Fleetwood was to receive a £600 annuity. David Garrick had come near buying the patent and theatre but had decided against doing so at that time, writing to John Hoadley on 29 December 1744 that Fleetwood had sold to "Orator Lacy," though it was yet a secret who had furnished funds.

Though Garrick remained in the Drury Lane company for the balance of the season, he soon had contract disagreements with Lacy which must have made him regret his decision to remain a mere employee. The main dispute revolved around two contentions: Lacy refused to pay Garrick £250 in arrears, a debt due him from Fleetwood's days, and Lacy also insisted on his prerogative to order Garrick to play any night the manager desired, an arrangement which Garrick insisted would injure his health. In the summer of 1745 the quarrel had its most violent eruption and Garrick forsook Drury Lane for a triumphant 1745–46 season in Dublin. (For details see K. A. Burnim, "Garrick's Quarrel with Lacy," *Yale Library Gazette*, July 1958.)

The year 1745, of course, also brought the Jacobite Rebellion. The *General Advertiser* of 28 September 1745 announced that "Mr. Lacy, Master of his Majesty's Company of Comedians, at the Theatre Royal in Drury Lane, has apply'd for leave to raise 200 men in Defense of his Majesty's Person and Government, in which the whole Company of Players are willing to engage," but nothing came of that patriotic intention.

Business went poorly for Lacy at Drury Lane in Garrick's absence. Houses declined from bad to worse, and Mrs Cibber wrote to Garrick several times in 1746 of the abuse being heaped upon her and Garrick by Lacy in the press. She repeatedly urged Garrick to take advantage of the opportunity to scoop up the patent provided by Lacy's insolvency. She had heard a rumor that Garrick was intending to take Quin as a managing partner, but Garrick was stalling, keeping information close to his vest, all the time dealing for a partnership with Lacy himself.

Moreover, Lacy had acquired some influence by having ingratiated himself—at hunting it seems—with the Duke of Grafton, who as Lord Chamberlain controlled the patent, which was scheduled to expire in several years. The Duke made clear his intention to renew the patent if Lacy could find a substantial partner. Lacy's other important patrons were Lady Burlington, Lord Hartington, and John Roberts, Secretary to Henry Pelham, Minister of the Treasury. Lacy realized he needed Garrick, so despite their former differences he again offered him a half-interest in the operation. The negotiations were tortuous, but on 9 April 1747 an agreement was concluded, by the terms of which James Lacy and David Garrick became "jointly and equally possessed" of an interest in the patent, the property lease, the furniture, scenes, costumes, and other accoutrements of the theatre. Though they had an oral understanding concerning the division of their responsibilities, at Lacy's insistence another written agreement in 1750 stipulated that "the settling or altering of the business of the Stage be left entirely to Mr. Garrick" and that Lacy would assume the general maintenance of the theatre, its properties, and "the economy of the household." They were to concur on the hiring, discharging, and fixing of salaries of their employees, but Garrick seems eventually to have done most of the negotiating. Procedures were established for arbitrating disputes. Either party, if ever dissatisfied, could sell, first offering the other the option to buy. On 14 May 1747 a King's Warrant was issued "to prepare a 21 years' patent from 2nd Sept. 1753 for James Lacy and David Garrick, Esqr, to form a Company of Comedians to perform Tragedies, Plays, Operas, & other Performances of the Stage at Drury Lane Theatre or elsewhere," and on 4 June 1747 the patent was issued.

Lacy had sold Garrick half interest in the patent for £12,000, of which Garrick raised £8000 immediately and signed for the balance. A financial statement drawn up on 11 April 1747 details the incumbrances which Garrick and Lacy assumed at the beginning of their partnership. Total liabilities were £8808 14s.; of that amount £2447 14s. constituted salary arrears, a mortgage made up another £4700, tradesmen were due £1100, another £400 was due Lacy for money he had borrowed to keep the theatre going, and the balance consisted of miscellaneous debts. In addition to this total it was agreed to pay Fleetwood £4000 to relinquish his interest in the patent.

The operation of a major London theatre in the eighteenth century was an enterprise of high finance. In addition to a company of some 70 to 100 performers and 40 to 70 house servants, the inventory was unstable in value and the consumers exceedingly fickle. No one had succeeded at Drury Lane since the triumvirate of Cibber, Wilks, and Booth had dissolved in 1732. Recently Charles Fleetwood had proved woefully inadequate. Lacy and Garrick took on the theatre in the ebb of its prestige and credit was the lowest it had been in 15 years.

In view of those liabilities, the financial prosperity of the partnership, which became evident almost from the outset, is remarkable. The Drury Lane account books reveal that at the end of their first year Garrick and Lacy realized a net profit of £6334 for the season. By the close of their fourth season, 1749–50, they had their investments back. For the eight years in the period of the partnership for which the account books are available, the profits averaged some £4850 per season; it seems to have been the partners' policy to divide the profits of each season and to begin each campaign afresh. Each manager drew £500 per year in salary, and Garrick an additional £500 and a clear benefit for acting. By 1764–65 each drew a salary of £16 13s. per week.

While the great success of Drury Lane Theatre for 27 years must, of course, be credited in very large measure to Garrick's talents and genius, the behind-the-scenes contributions of Lacy, ably assisted by Pritchard and Wood in the treasury, should not be underestimated. The partners had little in common; they often were suspicious of each other's motives; and they constantly reaffirmed their own prerogatives. But as Charles Wyndham informed Garrick's brother Peter at Lichfield two months after the first season commenced: "Lacy and he [Garrick] agree very well; and every thing is done just as David pleases. . . . there is a satisfaction and joy in all the folks at Drury Lane Theatre, that show they are under good government, & in a thriving way. And I think every year must make it better."

Even if the co-managers had not had antipodal natures, some minor differences and a major quarrel or two were inevitable in such a long relationship. Davies characterized Lacy as uncultivated but a man of good understanding, with clear notions of business and judicious observations on men and manners. He was liberal in his sentiments, though rough and sometimes boisterous in his language. Lacy was a determined person, not diverted from his purpose by reversals of fortune or disappointments. While the town thought Garrick the political director—the author of the *Theatrical Examiner* (1757) followed the *Inspector* in calling Lacy a cipher who only mechanically followed Garrick's lead—Lacy maintained the self-delusion that he was "the main politician." He sometimes assumed a lordly attitude, as when he would remind Garrick in letters that "you were received by me as a Partner," or "I say NOW what I said when I admitted you FIRST, that no partner shall have a greater share of POWER."

In 1751 Lacy began negotiations to engage the rope dancer Anthony Maddox. Garrick complained of bringing "this defilement and abomination into the house of William Shakespeare" in a letter to friend Somerset Draper and called Lacy a "mean mistaken creature," adding "Oh, I am *sick, sick, sick of him*!" On the same subject Garrick later wrote to his brother George that Lacy "ought to have a thorough Scouring before his inside will be tolerably clear from Y^e filth & Nastiness that he has been gathering from his Youth upward until now." In another letter to George he labeled Lacy "Timbertop." Lacy, however, proved to be correct and Garrick wrong in at least one decision: he had been vigorously but unsuccessfully opposed to engaging Noverre's company to perform the ill-fated *Chinese Festival* which in 1755–56 provoked riots that led to the destruction of the interior of Drury Lane Theatre.

A really serious conflict between the partners occurred when Garrick returned in 1765 from his two-year grand tour. That fall Joseph Reed heard that Garrick was determined to "have nothing to do with the theatre at the end of this season, Mr. Lacy will then have sole management." On 9 November 1765 David wrote George, "my resolution is to draw my Neck as well as I can out of ye Collar, & sit quietly with my wife & books by my fireside." A contract of dissolution was drawn up in which Garrick's share of the patent was computed to be worth £27,500; but James Clutterbuck, Garrick's financial counsel, advised a reconciliation, since the paradox was that Lacy's share was worth more than Garrick's, simply because Garrick came with it, whereas a purchaser of Garrick's share would get only Lacy. The partnership survived, but rumblings of dissatisfaction continued to be heard. In a letter to George on 8 March 1766 David expressed his repugnance for his partner's "maggot-breeding pericranium." According to the *Universal Museum and Complete Magazine* for November 1767 both Lacy and Garrick were to sell and the purchasers would be George Garrick one half, Charles Holland one fourth, and Thomas King one fourth—"Everything was so near a conclusion, that the writings were drawn, and the money ready, when Mrs. Lacy protested against her husband's parting with his share; and the bargain for that time dropt." The *Theatrical Monitor* of 16 December 1767 reported that it was well known the Drury Lane patent had been up for sale for some two years and that "*Caesar* and *Pompey* had been in their hearts at continual variance for a long time." All seemed peaceful again, however, by January 1769, when the *Town and Country Magazine* observed: "This association has generally subsisted with the utmost harmony, as both are equally satisfied with their authority and power, and are too sagacious to enter into any altercation by which their mutual interest would be greatly injured."

After Lacy had acted Oroonoko at Drury Lane on 12 May 1742, we find no evidence that he ever performed again. James Lacy was not, as many theatre historians have suggested, the person of that name acting at Dublin in 1745–46; that player was Thomas Lacy (fl. 1745–1747), who also acted at Drury Lane under James Lacy's management in the spring of 1746 and occasionally in 1746–47. It was Charles Lacey (d. 1757), and not James Lacy, who was a member of the Smock Alley Company at Dublin in 1754–55.

In 1762 the managers made major alterations to the theatre because of Garrick's resolution to drive the spectators from their accustomed seats on the stage during benefit performances, a move with which Lacy concurred. The capacity of the house was increased to compensate for the loss of seating on the stage. The alterations were under the direction of Lacy, who, according to Davies, had "a taste for architecture." Garrick was sufficiently enthusiastic to write brother Peter on 6 November 1762, "our theatre is most amazingly improved, &c. I really think it is the first Playhouse in Europe." In January 1769 the *Town and Country Magazine*, recalling Lacy's work years before on the Rotunda at Ranelagh, affirmed that he was "very properly qualified for the regulation and inspection of alterations, repairs, and occasional embellishments of the theatre," tasks he had always executed "to the constant satisfaction of his colleague." Lacy had taken a hand in the remodeling of his own estate, called Turk's House, which was situated on the Thames at Isleworth, Middlesex, a few miles from Garrick's Hampton villa. The actor West Digges had been there several days prior to his writing on 27 June 1753 to Mrs Ward that Lacy "is a very worthy gentleman, and has improved his house, (which commands the river up to Richmond Hill,) to very great advantage."

James Lacy died at Turk's House on 21 January 1774, at the age of 78, according to the *Gentleman's Magazine* of that month. He was buried on 30 January in the churchyard of St James, Paddington, where a monument was erected to his memory.

In his will dated 20 May 1768 Lacy left £400 a year to his second wife Ann Lacy, the former Mrs Willoughby, who had acted at Drury Lane between 1748 and 1752. (The Mrs Lacy who acted in London with him between 1727 and 1737 was probably his first wife.) Perhaps he had never actually married Ann Willoughby, though he called her his wife in the will; she still used the name Willoughby in 1751–52. To their son, called Willoughby Lacy, otherwise Morris, born in 1749, Lacy left the bulk of the substantial estate, which included his "moiety of Drury Lane Theatre Patents Leases Cloathes Scenes and Whatever else appertains to my partnership with David Garrick Esq!.," the "Manors of Eynsham Newland and Tylgersleigh in Oxfordshire," his house, barn, three fields and gardens consisting of about ten acres called the Turk's House, at Isleworth, a freehold estate purchased from Mr Deval at Eynsham, bringing about £500 per year, his diamond ring "weight about fourteen grains," and his books. To Mrs Lacy he left the furniture, plate, and other effects in his house in Berners Street, Marylebone. He left a shilling each to his "unhappy brother" Theophilus Lacy and his sister Grace James and recommended them to the care of his son and wife.

Mrs Lacy died on 11 November 1768, a few months after Lacy had made out his will and some five years before he died. The will was proved and administration granted on 17 February 1774 to "Willoughby Lacy otherwise Morris, Esqr.," a widower, after "May Sainsbury spinster Sarah Hayward spinster William Sainsbury and Thomas Sainsbury the Cousins German once removed and only next of kin of the said deceased having first respectively renounced the Letters of Administration."

By the terms of their agreement Garrick was to have the option of buying Lacy's half at his decease. According to the *Gentleman's Magazine* of January 1774 Lacy's share of the patent was valued at £32,000. Garrick refused to exercise the option and, over the next several years, was to suffer more grief from the machinations and idiosyncracies of young Willoughby, who fancied himself an actor as well as a manager, than he had ever had from the father.

James Lacy, it seems, also had owned some interest in the Theatre Royal, Bristol, which he had sold to the actor Samuel Reddish in the early 1770s and which thus was not mentioned in his will. But young Lacy profited from that sale also. On 20 September 1775 Reddish wrote to Garrick that he felt himself "bound by Mr Lacey's very kind indulgence to clear all the arrears due him upon the shares of the Bristol Theatre, which I purchased of his Father." The elder Lacy had been a great loser, however, in a speculation which prospected for coal in Oxfordshire. According to the *European Magazine* of April 1809, Garrick held a mortgage for £20,000, representing money by which Lacy had pursued his abortive scheme. The sum was probably eventually paid to Garrick and later Mrs Garrick out of the ultimate sale by Willoughby Lacy of his half of the patent to Sheridan and his colleagues.

A portrait of James Lacy by an unknown engraver was published by J. Sewell as a plate to the *European Magazine*, 1802. The same picture, with a decorated oval and with a verse below, also was published in the *European Magazine* in April 1809. According to a memoir of Lacy in the latter publication, he was also pictured in a hunt scene with the Duke of Grafton by Wooton. Lacy appeared in a satirical print entitled "A New Muster of Bays's Troops," by an unknown artist, published in 1745. The print satirizes Lacy's announcement of his intention to raise a volunteer company of "200 men in Defense of his Majesty's Person and Government" in 1745.

Lacy, Mrs James, the first [*fl.* 1727–1737], *actress.*

The Mrs Lacy (sometimes Lacey or Leacy) who performed in London between 1727 and 1737 was the first wife of James Lacy (1696–1774), then a journeyman London actor but subsequently Garrick's co-patentee at Drury Lane Theatre. She was first noticed in the surviving bills on 11 December 1727 at Lincoln's Inn Fields Theatre, when she acted Beatrice in *The Cheats*. At the same theatre on 29 January 1728 she played Dolly Trull in a performance of *The Beggar's Opera* in which Lacy played Robin of Bagshot. During the remainder of the season she was seen as Valeria in *The Rover*, Mrs Dainty in *The Country Wife*, and Belinda in *Tunbridge Walks*.

On 23 June 1730 she acted Mrs Staff in Henry Fielding's new play *Rape Upon Rape* at the Haymarket. That summer she performed with Lacy at the Bartholomew and Southwark fairs and then returned in 1730–31 to the Haymarket, where her characters included Honoria in *Love Makes a Man*, Lucilla in *The Fair Penitent*, Harriet in *The Author's Farce*, Huncamunca in *Tom Thumb*, Dorinda in *The Stratagem*, Mrs Stitch in *The Jealous Taylor*, Lady Wronghead in *The Provok'd Husband*, and Mrs Foresight in *Love for Love*, among others.

After playing again at Bartholomew Fair in the summer of 1731, Mrs Lacy seems not to have returned to a patent house stage until 26 March 1733 when she acted Jenny in *The Beggar's Opera*, at Covent Garden Theatre, where James Lacy was also engaged. There on 15 January 1734 she played Lady Wronghead and then appeared in an unknown character in several performances of *The Distress'd Wife*, a comedy by Gay first presented on 5 March 1734. After the summer fairs in 1734 she played Mrs Frail in *Love for Love* on 7 October at the Haymarket. Again at Bartholomew Fair, in Fielding and Hippisley's booth, she appeared during the last weeks of August 1736.

Mrs Lacy's last known role was one of the Ladies in *The Historical Register*, Fielding's dramatic satire, which premiered on 21 March 1737 and helped close down Fielding's Haymarket venture when the Licensing Act was passed that year. Mrs Lacy appeared in the final performance of *The Historical Register* for the season on 23 May 1737. Her subsequent activities and the record of her death are unknown to us. By 1749 James Lacy was living with the Drury Lane actress Mrs Willoughby, who was eventually called his wife and bore his son Willoughby Lacy (1749–1831).

Lacy, Mrs James [the second?], **Ann, earlier Mrs Willoughby** *d. 1768, actress.*

Announced as making her first appearance on any stage, Mrs Ann Willoughby acted Jacintha in *The Suspicious Husband* on 27 September 1748 at Drury Lane Theatre. She appeared next on 18 October as Belinda in *The Provok'd Wife*, and during the season she was seen as Alithea in *The Country Wife*, Cynthia in *The Double Dealer*, and Harriet in *The Miser*. She remained at Drury Lane for another three seasons, adding to her repertoire Mrs Foresight in *Love for Love*, Hippolito in *The Tempest*, Camilla in *Friendship in Fashion*, and Victoria in *The Fatal Marriage* in 1749–50; Alinda in *The Pilgrim*, Hero in *Much Ado about Nothing*, Mrs Fainall in *The Way of the World*, Clarinda in *The Double Gallant*, and Sylvia in *The Recruiting Officer* in 1750–51; and Violante in *Sir Courtly Nice*, Charlotte Weldon in *Oroonoko*, Doralice in *The Comical Lovers*, and Lady Grace in *The Provok'd Husband* in 1751–52.

After 1751–52 Mrs Willoughby retired from the stage, for by 1749 she had become the second wife of, or at least had begun to live with, James Lacy, the co-manager of Drury Lane Theatre. In his will dated 20 May 1768, Lacy left to his wife Ann Lacy £400 a year for life and appointed her executrix. But he did not die until 1774, outliving his wife, who died on 11 November 1768, a few months after Lacy had made his will. Their son, Willoughby Lacy, was born in 1749 and eventually inherited his father's interests in Drury Lane, where he also acted.

The Mrs Willoughby who earned 1s. 6d. per day or 9s. per week as a dresser at Drury Lane in 1764–65 was not, it would seem, the manager's wife but probably was related.

Lacy, James [*fl. 1794–1815*], *musician.*

The name of James Lacy of Salisbury was on the list of subscribers to the New Musical Fund in 1794, 1805, and 1815.

Lacy, John *c. 1615–1681, actor, dancer, choreographer.*

John Lacy was born, according to Aubrey's *Brief Lives*, near Doncaster in Yorkshire and came to London in 1631 to join an unnamed playhouse, possibly the Cockpit. He became an apprentice to the dancer John Ogilby, perhaps at his dancing school in Gray's Inn Lane near the Cockpit or, as Aubrey seems to imply, at the theatre. If Lacy was the usual age to begin an apprenticeship, perhaps he was born about 1615. Aubrey said that Ben Jonson "took a Catalogue from M. Lacy (the Player) of the Yorkshire Dialect. 'Twas his Hint for Clownery to his Comedy called The Tale of a Tub. This I had from Mr. Lacy." A list of players, dated 10 August 1639, shows "John Lacie" as the third man on the list of "ye young Company" at the Cockpit. During the civil war Lacy was "lieutenant and quartermaster to the Lord Gerrard," later Earl of Macclesfield.

In the spring of 1660 Lacy was a member of Beeston's troupe at Salisbury Court, and as of 6 October he was a member of the King's

By gracious permission of Her Majesty Queen Elizabeth II

JOHN LACY, in three roles
by Wright

Company under Thomas Killigrew. By December the troupe was at the converted tennis-court playhouse in Vere Street, where Lacy acted Ananias in *The Alchemist*—the earliest role we know for him. Sometime during that season he may have played Cleobulo in Flecknoe's *Erminia*—that at any rate was the author's intended casting. Other references to Lacy at this early period concern a debt he owed Edward Man, for which on 1 March 1661 Man was granted permission by the Lord Chamberlain to go to court. And, as a member of a royal patent company, Lacy received a livery grant on 29 July 1661 to cover the period 1660 through 1662.

John was one of the leading members of Killigrew's troupe from the beginning. On 20 December 1661 he was a signer of a three-part indenture to lease the land on which the company's new theatre in Bridges Street was to be built. A month later he became one of the building sharers, holding four of the 36 shares; only Sir Robert Howard and Thomas Killigrew held more (nine each), and all the other sharers had two each. Separate from the building shares were the acting shares, which totaled 12¾; Killigrew held two, Mohun, Hart, and Lacy owned one and a quarter each, and five other actors held one each. Two shares were apparently held for others outside the company, perhaps Dryden and Robert Lewright. Lacy's income from his acting shares may have been as high as £280 annually during the company's prosperous years.

Before the troupe moved to their new playhouse in 1663 Lacy acted (or probably acted—some of the information comes from manuscript casts not easily dated) a Welshman in *The Royall King*, the Dancing Master in *The French Dancing Master* (*The Variety?*), Brancadoro in *The Surprisal*, Johnny Thump in *The Changes*, Maurico in *Love's Sacrifice*, Teague in *The Committee*, and Scruple in *The Cheats*. Once during the period, on 28 November 1661, he found himself in trouble: the Lord Chamberlain's accounts indicate that he was arrested at the request of a Mr Serle—perhaps for debt. Most of the time, however, Lacy basked in the admiration of audiences. Of his work in *The Surprisal*, a weak play, an anonymous poet wrote

> Be it never so good the Actors say
> But they may thanke God with all their hart
> That Lacy plaid Brankadoros part.

The manuscript poem at the British Library was quoted by Hotson in *The Commonwealth and Restoration Stage*.

Pepys was captivated by Lacy. After seeing "The French Dancing Master" (which may be Cavendish's *The Variety*) Pepys wrote on 21 May 1662, "The play pleased us very well; but Lacy's part, the Dancing Master, the best in the world." The following day the diarist saw *The Changes*, which he thought "hath little in it but Lacy's part of a country fellow, which he did to admiration." When Pepys saw the play again a year later, he told his diary "the life of the play is Lacy's part, the clown, which is most admirable; but for the rest, which are counted such old and excellent actors, in my life I never heard both men and women so ill pronounce their parts, even to making myself sick therewith."

Teague in *The Committee* brought Lacy more praise than perhaps any other role he undertook. On 27 November 1662 John Evelyn saw it at court: "a ridiculous play of Sir R: Howards where that Mimic Lacy acted the Irish-footeman to admiration: a very Satyrus or Roscius." Pepys, who saw it later at Bridges Street, called it "a merry but indifferent play, only Lacey's part, an Irish footman, is beyond imagination." The prompter John Downes years later wrote a bad triplet in praising Lacy's "Teg" and other parts:

> For his Just Acting, all gave him due Praise,
> His part in the Cheats, *Jony Thump, Teg* and *Bayes,*
> In these four Excelling: The Court gave him the *Bays.*

The new theatre in Bridges Street, the first of the playhouses built on the present site of Drury Lane, opened with *The Humorous Lieutenant* on 7 May 1663, and, oddly, Lacy did not participate. But the following day he took over Clun's title role and continued playing it thereafter. Before the plague closed the theatre in 1665 Lacy is known to have delivered the epilogue to *The Vestal Virgins* and played Sir Politick in *Volpone*, and he surely played far more than the scanty records reveal.

By 1663–64 Thomas Killigrew had delegated the actual direction of the King's Company to Lacy, Mohun, and Hart, the three leading players. As Hotson revealed, they appropriated an acting share from someone (or they may have taken portions from several to make up one for themselves) and divided three-fourths of it among themselves as payment for their services. That meant, evidently, that one or more of the actors had been deprived of their shares and turned into hirelings at £100 annual wages. When the Lord Chamberlain discovered these facts, the share and the delegated powers were withdrawn.

Of Lacy's private life very little is known. We find from the *Diary and Will of Elias Ashmore* that on 17 March 1664 (1664/65?) Ashmore "christened Secundus, [that is, John, Jr] son to Mr. Lacy the Player." John's wife, unless he married a second time later in his life, was named Margaret. Davenport Adams in *A Book About London* says that Lacy from 1665 to his death in 1681 lived in a house that was "the third from the mansion of the Earl of Anglesey (Lord Privy Seal)" near Cradle Alley, off Bow Street.

After the resumption of theatrical activity in 1666 and until the Bridges Street Theatre burned in January 1672 Lacy revived his favorite old parts—Ananias, Teague, Thump, and doubtless others—and played for the first time Sganarelle in *Damoiselles à la Mode*, Sauny in his own *Sauny the Scot* (on 9 April 1667; published in 1698), Asinello in *The Change of Crownes*, a Plebeian in *Julius Caesar*, Gripe in *Love in a Wood*, and Bayes in *The Rehearsal.* Lacy is said to have been Nell Gwyn's instructor in dancing (and perhaps one of her early lovers) and probably served the troupe as a dancing coach.

His first play, obviously an adaptation of *The Taming of the Shrew*, prompted Pepys to write on 9 April 1667 that "the best Part, 'Sawny,' done by Lacy, hath not half its life, by reason of the words, I suppose, not being understood, at least by me." Perhaps the players laid on the Scottish accent too heavily. But at *The Committee* on 13 August 1667 Pepys found ". . . Lacy's part . . . so well performed that it would set off anything," and at *The Changes* on 28 April 1668 he laughed at the "very good mirth of Lacy, the clown." Satirists had more praise for the players than for the playwrights; in the *Session of the Poets* (1665) Apollo found most of the dramatists wanting and could give the laurel to none,

> But when Apollo was quite withdrawn,
> The wits, for fear of the critics' scoff,
> The laurel on Lacy and Harris put on,
> Because they alone made the plays go off.

And Dryden in the prologue to *1 Conquest of Granada* in 1670–71 spoke of Lacy and his compatriot Joe Haines:

> Thus two, the best Comedians of the Age
> Must be warn out, with being blocks o'th Stage.
> Like a young Gurl, who better things had known,
> Beneath their Poets Impotence they groan.

But Lacy came in for criticism, even from his admirer Pepys. On 11 January 1669, for example, *The Jovial Crew* was "ill acted to what it was heretofore, in Clun's time [the early 1660s], and when Lacy could dance." Lacy's age, perhaps, was to blame, though he continued active as a dancer and choreographer. On the following 19 January Pepys saw the tragedy *Horace* and reported that ". . . Lacy hath made a farce of several dances—between each act, one: but his words are but silly, and invention not extraordinary, as to the dances; only some Dutchmen come out of the mouth and tail of a Hamburgh sow."

The most notable events during that period from 1666 to 1672, however, concerned Lacy's participation in *The Change of Crownes* and *The Rehearsal*. The former was banned after one performance, but Pepys was lucky enough to find standing room at the premiere on 15 April 1667: ". . . Lacy did act the country-gentleman come up to Court who do abuse the Court with all the imaginable wit and plainness about selling of places, and doing every thing for money." The following day his actress friend Mrs Knepp told Pepys that "the King was so angry at the liberty taken by Lacy's part to abuse him to his face, that he commanded they should act no more." On the twentieth the King's Company did not act. Pepys learned from his friend Rolt that the reason was that

> Lacy had been committed to the porter's lodge for his acting his part in the late new play, and that being thence released he come to the King's house, there met with Ned Howard, the poet of the play, who congratulated his release; upon which Lacy cursed him as that it was the fault of his nonsensical play that was the cause of his ill usage. Mr Howard did give him some reply, to which Lacy [answered] him, that he was more a fool than a poet; upon which Howard did give him a blow on the face; on which Lacy, having a cane in his hand, did give him a blow over the pate. Here Rolt and others that discoursed of it in the pit this afternoon did wonder that Howard did not run him through, he being too mean a fellow to fight with. But Howard did not do any thing but complain to the King of it; so the whole house is silenced, and the gentry seem to rejoice much at it, the house being become too insolent.

A newsletter among the Fleming manuscripts noted that the reason for Lacy's arrest was that "on his own head" he added some indecent expressions to his role in Howard's play. The Lord Chamberlain's accounts show that on 20 April Lacy was to have been re-arrested for abusing Howard; he was discharged from the Marshalsea on 25 April and was back on stage at the latest by 1 May 1667. Indeed, on that date Pepys saw him in *The Changes*: "a sorry play: only Lacy's clowne's part, which he did most admirably indeed; and I am glad to find the rogue at liberty again."

On 13 July 1667 Pepys reported that "yesterday Sir Thomas Crew told me that Lacy lies a-dying of the pox, and yet hath his whore by him, whom he will have to look on, he says, though he can do no more; nor would receive any ghostly advice from a Bishop, an old acquaintance of his, that went to see him." (Nahm in his edition of *The Cheats* transferred that anecdote to Lacy's death in 1681.) Lacy recovered; in fact he was acting within a month if not sooner, and his illness may have been feigned in order to regain the favor of the King, who did, apparently, forgive him for the *Change of Crownes* affair and continued to count Lacy as one of his favorite actors.

The original Bayes in *The Rehearsal* received direction in the playing of the role from the author himself. In Spence's *Anecdotes* we find a note: "It is incredible what paines Buckingham took with one of the actors, to teach him to speak some passages in Bayes' part, in *The Rehearsal* right." Lacy was evidently a splendid mimic and aped Dryden in the role to the delight of most members of the audience, if not of Dryden himself.

Though Lacy probably performed at the Lincoln's Inn Fields Theatre, the temporary home of the King's Company after the Bridges Street fire and before the opening of their new theatre, Drury Lane, we have no record of the roles he may have played. He had a skirmish in 1672 and 1673 with a Mary Bennet, who sued him for some reason, a debt, perhaps. A manuscript cast in a Bodleian copy of *Brennoralt* indicates that sometime between 1673 and 1675 Lacy acted Grainevert in that work, but we cannot be certain when or where. Shortly before the new Drury Lane playhouse opened on 26 March 1674, Lacy, as one of the shareholders, contributed £200 toward the building of a new scene house in Vinegar Yard.

In May 1674 Lacy became embroiled in a dispute with some French dancers from the court of Charles II, who, through the Master of the King's Musick, Louis Grabu, had agreed to act at Drury Lane for 10s. per day. Killigrew, Hart, and Lacy made what was apparently a separate agreement with them whereby they were to receive 5s. daily even if they did not perform. They refused their money, claiming that their previous arrangement through Grabu was binding. What was very likely a communications problem was settled on 6 May 1674 by the Lord Chamberlain, who ordered the dancers to attend Killigrew and obey his commands. That was perhaps some indication of the internal disorders of the troupe. A year

LACY

later Thomas Killigrew's son Charles entered into a new agreement with some of the old and disgruntled King's Company players, including Lacy, but the new group did not materialize, and the shaky King's troupe continued to deteriorate until a union with the rival Duke's Company became inevitable in the early 1680s.

At Drury Lane, before his death in 1681, Lacy played Bessus in *A King and No King*, Intrigo in *Love in the Dark*, and doubtless other roles of which we have no record. He seems to have retained an interest in company affairs, since he was a sharer, but after 1674 he may not have been very active on stage. On 23 February 1681, a few months before his death, Lacy sued the King's Company for his share of the profits, which action suggests that in their unstable financial state they may have been trying to cope with their problems by squeezing out the inactive sharers. Though it was too late for him to enjoy it, on 19 October 1681 the crown ordered that Lacy be paid for the plays that had been performed—his right as a sharer in the acting company, whether he performed or not.

A *Satire* (1677) was for a while thought to have been the work of Rochester, but according to the editors of *Poems on Affairs of State* Lacy may have written it. It is an invective against Charles II and his mistresses Nell Gwynn and the Duchess of Portsmouth, but at that date Lacy, so far as we know, had little reason to show open bitterness against the King. Yet Rochester seems not to have been the author, either.

By 1681 the situation in the King's Company was desperate. In February a number of the shareholders complained that they were being denied their profits, though there were at that point few profits to share. It did not matter in Lacy's case, for he was close to death; his widow, on the other hand, had to spend many years trying to secure the profits due her as the inheritor of his four shares.

John Lacy, according to Aubrey, "made his exit on Saturday September 17 1681, and was buried in the farther churchyard of St. Martyn's in the fields on the Monday following, age [blank]." Would that Aubrey had recorded Lacy's age, but he did not. His widow Margaret inherited his four shares in the troupe, and when the United Company was formed out of the old King's and Duke's companies, she retained the shares, supposedly enjoying an income of £7 daily for the Dorset Garden playhouse and £3 daily for Drury Lane for every acting day at either house (both of them were operated by the United Company). That was a profitable arrangement, even though Dorset Garden was little used, but the Lord Chamberlain's accounts show that Margaret was regularly complaining that her widow's pension was not being paid and that her income from the shares was in arrears. She was still alive in the first decade of the eighteenth century.

In addition to *Sauny the Scot*, John Lacy wrote *The Old Troop* (probably produced at Bridges Street about December 1664; published in 1672), *The Dumb Lady* (possibly performed at Bridges Street in 1669–70; published in 1672), and *Sir Hercules Buffoon* (posthumously performed about 1 June 1684; published 1684).

Langbaine in 1691 said of Lacy that he was

> A Comedian whose Abilities in Action were sufficiently known to all that frequented the King's Theatre, where he was for many years an Actor, and perform'd all Parts that he undertook to a miracle: insomuch that I am apt to believe, that as this Age never had, so the next never will have his Equal, at least not his Superiour. He was so well approv'd of by King Charles the Second, an undeniable Judge in Dramatick Arts, that he caus'd his Picture to be drawn, in three several Figures in the same Table. viz. That of Teague in the Committee, Mr Scruple in The Cheats, and M Galliard, in the Variety:

We learn also from Langbaine that Lacy played Falstaff, "and never fail'd of universal applause." The Falstaff referred to was probably in *The Merry Wives of Windsor*, which was the property of the King's Company.

Gould in the version of *The Play-House, a Satyr*, reprinted by Summers in *The Restoration Theatre*, wrote:

> *Another You may see, a* Comick *Spark,*
> *That wou'd be Lacy, but ne'r hits the Mark,*
> *Not but his Making Sport must be confess'd,*
> *For where the Author fails, he is Himself the Jest.*
> *To be well laught at is his whole Delight,*
> *And there, indeed, we do the Coxcomb Right.*
> *Tho' the Comedian makes the Audience roar,*
> *When off the Stage, the Booby tickles more:*
> *When such are born some easy Planet rules,*
> *And Nature, dozing, makes a Run of Fools.*

The portrait of Lacy in three characters was painted for Charles II by M. Wright between

The CASE of Margaret Lacy Widow and Relict of John Lacy Deceas'd.

Humbly Sheweth,

THat *Thomas Killegrew*, Esq; did Beg of King *Charles* the 2d. of blessed memory (by the assistance of her Husband *John Lacy*, *Michael Mohun*, *Charles Hart*, and others, old Servants and Sufferers for King *Charles* the 1st, of Blessed memory, in his Wars) a Pattent for Erecting a Company for His Majesty, by vertue of which Pattent and Covenants, Mr. *Killegrew* had two Shares, two Voyces, and two Parts of the Cloaths, Scenes and Books, of which her Husband *John Lacy* had One share and a Quarter, and by the Order and Direction of His Majesty King *Charles* the Second, *Thomas Killegrew*, Esq; *John Lacy* her Husband, and Five more of the Principall Actors, Did build a House betwixt *Drury Lain* and *Bridges-street*, call'd the *Theatre Royal*, which was twice built and cost above 7000 *l.* the Rent whereof was Six pound a Day, and her Husbands part was Thirteen Shillings and four pence a Day. Her Husband did also purchase of *Thomas Killegrew*, Esq; and the rest of His Majestys Company of Actors Three Shillings and four pence a Day to be payd for the Life of *Margaret Lacy* his Wife for every day His Majestys Company of Actors should Act at the *Theatre Royal*, or any other Place where His Majestys Company should be Erected, or any under them, for which her Husband payd Two hundred Pounds.

Sr. *William Davenant* did also Beg of His Majesty a Pattent for raising a Company, call'd the *Duke of Yorks*.

Soon after the Death of her Husband, Mr. *Charles Killegrew* and Doctor *Davenant*, the two Pattentees, did joyn the two Companys, upon which Mr. Ch. *Killegrew*, Dr. *Davenant* and others did possess themselves of her Rent of Thirteen Shillings and four pence a Day, and also of the Three Shillings and four pence a day Annuity, And the share of the Cloaths, Scenes and Books, which cost her Husband for his part near 1000 *l.* In consideration of which she has Articles to Produce for the payment of 200 *l.* which was to be payd at the Death of her Husband, upon demand of which they told her that *Westminster-Hall* was open and she might go to Law, she not being able, haveing at that time four Children and deprived of all her Subsistance, The shares of the Rent also under a Considerable Mortgage, which brought her into such a miserable condition, that she and her Children had perished without the assistants of her Friends.

And whereas the Rent was Thirteen Shillings and four pence a Day for her part, they brought it without her consent to Six Shillings and eight pence a Day, and detain'd it from her near two years, as also her Three Shillings four pence a day Annuity.

Upon her petitioning King *James* the Second for her Three Shillings and Four pence a day, His Majesty was pleased, by an Order of Counsel, to Referr to the Right Honourable the Lord *Mulgrave*, now Marquess of *Normanby*, then Lord Chamberlain, to Examin her Allegations and Redress her; And upon the hearing of Counsell on both sides, the Earl of *Mulgrave* made an Order for the payment of it, which was confirm'd by another Order afterwards made by the Right Honourable the Earle of *Dorset*, and since there is no Lord *Chamberlain* (notwithstanding they cannot Act without His Majesties permission) Sir *Thomas Skipwith* and Mr. *Rich*, (Assignees of Mr. Ch. *Killegrew* & Dr. *Davenant*) they do unjustly detain from her the Three Shillings and Four pence a day Annuity, being all she has left her for her Subsistance.

And She does in all humility Humbly beseech this Honourable Board they would be so Charitable as to grant an Order for her Releif, She not being able to go to Law.

Courtesy of the Public Record Office

The Case of Margaret Lacy

1662 and 1675, and according to Millar's catalogue of Tudor and Stuart portraits in the Royal Collection, it is "entirely autograph." Some confusion has surrounded the identification of the three characters, but they seem to be Parson Scruple in *The Cheats*, Galliard in *The French Dancing Master*, and Monsieur De Vice in *The Country Captain*. Some identifications give Teague in *The Committee* instead of Monsieur De Vice in *The Country Captain*. The portrait now hangs at Hampton Court. Two versions were offered for sale at Edinburgh in 1698. Perhaps these were the smaller copies which have found their way to present collections: one is in the Garrick Club (No 122); another was sold at Sotheby's to an unknown buyer on 18 May 1949, when it was reported to be from the collection of Lt Col G. Bryant and formerly at Ettington Park. A copy by Wright was recorded by Vertue to have been in the possession of the Duke of Norfolk. Another copy was made by Ranelagh Barret for Lord Foley. An engraving of the portrait, made by W. Hopkins, was published by W. Smith in 1825; another engraving, by an unknown artist, was published as a plate to the *Dramatic Magazine* on 1 December 1830.

Lacy, John *d. 1871, singer.*

It is hardly possible that the singer John Lacy was born, as *The Dictionary of National Biography* states, in 1788. For if he had gone to Italy about 1798, as the same source indicates (quoting the *Dictionary of Music*, 1824), to master entirely "both the language and style of singing of the natives," he would have been barely ten years of age at the time. *The Dictionary of National Biography*, moreover, mistakenly gives Lacy's Christian name as William. His early training with Rauzzini at Bath must have occurred prior to 1794, in which year he was listed in Doane's *Musical Directory* as a bass singer, a member of the Choral Fund and the Portland Chapel Society, and a performer in the Covent Garden oratorios and the Handel Memorial Concerts at Westminster Abbey. Lacy's address was given by Doane as No 2, Nevill's Court, Fetter Lane.

After returning from Italy, presumably about 1800, Lacy sang regularly in the Lenten oratorios and in other concerts. Though he possessed great talent and range in both voice and style, the poor health he chronically suffered prevented him from attaining special fame.

In 1812 Lacy married Jane Bianchi (1776–1856), the widow of the composer and musician Francesco Bianchi (c. 1751–1810) and the daughter of an apothecary in Sloane Street, Chelsea, named John Jackson. As Miss Jackson she had sung as a soprano in the Concerts of the Academy of Ancient Music on 25 April 1798, and as Mrs Bianchi she performed at the King's Theatre from 1809 to 1812. After her marriage to Lacy she appeared professionally as Mrs Bianchi Lacy at the King's Theatre between 1812 and 1815. She is noticed in this dictionary as Mrs Francesco Bianchi.

With his wife, Lacy participated in the concerts at Willis's Rooms and the Hanover Square Rooms. In 1818 they took an engagement at Calcutta where they frequently performed at the court of the King of Ouda. After eight years there they returned to England to retire into private life. Subsequently they lived for several years in Florence and elsewhere on the Continent, and Lacy, it is said, declined offers from the opera companies of Florence and Milan.

Lacy's wife died at Ealing on 19 March 1858. He died on a visit to Devonshire in 1871. According to the *Dictionary of Music* (1824), Lacy was then considered by competent judges

without question, the most legitimate English bass singer, the most accomplished in various styles, and altogether the most perfect and finished that has appeared in this country. He is endowed by nature with organs of great strength and delicacy; his voice is rich and full-toned, particularly in the lower notes; his intonation perfect, and his finish and variety in graces remarkable.

Lacy, Mrs John, Jane. *See* BIANCHI, MRS FRANCESCO.

Lacy, Theophilus [*fl. 1727–1768*], *actor.*

Little is known of Theophilus Lacy, an obscure brother of James Lacy, the co-patentee of Drury Lane Theatre with David Garrick. Information on the family background will be found in James Lacy's notice. At the time that his brother James was acting in various London theatres in the early 1730s, Theophilus appeared for his own benefit at Goodman's Fields Theatre on 26 May 1730 as the Bastard in *King*

Lear. On 23 June 1730, according to the bills, a Mr F. Lacy acted Sotmore in *Rape Upon Rape* at the Haymarket Theatre, but we suspect that the "F" was a scribal or printer's error for "T." James Lacy did not perform that evening, but Mrs Lacy, whom we take to have been James's first wife, acted Mrs Staff in that new piece by Fielding which was repeated on 24 June and 1, 2, 10, and 21 July.

In his *Wandering Patentee*, Tate Wilkinson placed Theophilus Lacy at York in 1727. He was probably the Lacy who played at Norwich in 1738. Thereafter, we lose track of him until he was mentioned in his brother's will dated 20 May 1768, when James left him one shilling and asked his son Willoughby Lacy to take care of "my unhappy Brother," who was evidently incapacitated. It is not known to us whether or not Theophilus was alive when James's will was proved on 17 February 1774.

Lacy, Thomas [*fl.* 1745–1747], *actor.*

The actor whom George Anne Bellamy called a "young adventurer named Lacy" made his debut under Thomas Sheridan's management at the Aungier Street Theatre, Dublin, on 4 November 1745 as Moneses in *Tamerlane.* He was advertised as "A Gentleman, being the first Time of his appearing on the Stage." At his second appearance on 7 November, when he acted Laertes in *Hamlet*, his name was given as Mr Lacy, but he was not James Lacy, the Drury Lane manager, as some historians have believed; the latter was busy in London that autumn. The novice was Thomas Lacy, who next acted Polydore in *The Orphan* on 11 November, Bertram in *The Spanish Fryar* on 2 December, and, after the company moved to the Smock Alley Theatre on 5 December 1745, Altamont in *The Fair Penitent* on 2 January 1746.

Several months later Thomas Lacy was in London, making his debut at Drury Lane Theatre on 12 April 1746 as Chamont in *The Orphan.* Next he acted Richard III on 29 April for the benefit of Ray, "the oldest actor now belonging to the House." The following season at Drury Lane he was seen as Moneses on 4 November 1746, Malcolm in *Macbeth* on 7 November, Chamont on 15 November, and the Elder Brother in *Comus* on 24 January 1747, after which this actor, who seems to have attracted no critical notice, was not heard from again.

Lacy, Willoughby 1749–1831, *actor, patentee, manager.*

Willoughby Lacy was born in 1749, probably in London, the son of the Drury Lane Theatre co-patentee James Lacy (1696–1774) and the actress Ann Willoughby (d. 1768). It is not clear that his parents ever married. But his mother acted at Drury Lane as Mrs Willoughby through 1751–52 and she was referred to by James Lacy in his will of 1768 as his wife. On his father's side, Willoughby was descended from an Irish family that had been ruined by their loyalty to Charles I. Willoughby's great-grandfather had married the daughter of John Russel and Grace Cromwell and the family had eventually settled in Norwich, where James Lacy failed in business and consequently turned to the stage, eventually becoming manager and then co-patentee with David Garrick of Drury Lane Theatre.

When James Lacy died in January 1774 (Ann Lacy having died in 1768), Willoughby became the principal legatee of his father's estate. The questionable status of his legitimacy, however, is reflected in the will, in which he is referred to as Willoughby Lacy, otherwise Morris. He inherited the "Manors of Eynsham Newland and Tylgersleigh in Oxfordshire," another estate at Eynsham bought by his father from Mr Deval, which brought £500 a year, a house in Berners Street, Marylebone, a ten-acre estate at Isleworth called Turk's House, a diamond ring "of fourteen grains," his father's books and other effects, and most significantly his father's "Moiety of Drury Lane Theatre Patents Leases Cloaths Scenes and Whatever else appertains to my partnership with David Garrick Esq."

The will was proved by Willoughby on 17 February 1774, and he immediately came to loggerheads with his late father's partner David Garrick concerning the division of responsibilities; for clearly, though but 25 years old and very inexperienced, he felt himself as qualified as Garrick for the direction of theatrical affairs. On 1 February 1774, just over a week after James Lacy died, Garrick wrote to Richard Cox that he had been dealing with "three Lawyers & my Partner's Son." On 25 February 1774 Lacy wrote from Berners Street to Garrick that his counsel Mr Mansfield, having studied the original articles of agreement, "was clearly of opinion that I have an equal right with you in the management of every branch of the business relative to the theatre." The next day Garrick replied tactfully but firmly from the Adelphi that he was surprised Lacy had "consulted counsel in a less amicable way than I proposed" and that he had no desire to deprive Lacy of his rights, but he would "follow your example" and seek legal advice. On 28 February Lacy wrote in a more conciliatory manner, advising Garrick that he had some proposals for the theatre's operation which he thought would "prove *very* acceptable."

Evidently the differences were resolved; at least the correspondence between the partners simmered down and they proceeded for a while on amicable if tentative terms. On 18 May 1774 Lacy, along with David and George Garrick and Tom King, was named a trustee of the new Drury Lane Fund. Lacy meanwhile married Maria Ann Orpen at St Marylebone Church on 22 March 1774 in a ceremony "attended by a prodigious concourse of people." She was the seventeen-year-old daughter of Daniel Orpen, "an eminent hatter," who gave his consent, according to the marriage register. The Lacys then, it seems, began to live extravagantly on his father's old estate at Isleworth and in a new town house in Great Queen Street.

In the summer of 1774 Lacy prepared to launch his acting career. On 31 August 1774 Garrick wrote to brother Peter asking if he would take a look at Lacy, who was scheduled to make his debut at the Theatre Royal, Birmingham, on Wednesday 7 September—"I think you will be pleas'd . . . let me know your opinion." The debut, according to Reed's manuscript notes in the British Library, was delayed until 9 September, on which night Lacy acted the title role in *Alexander the Great*. The *London Chronicle* of 13–15 September reported a very large audience. Lacy, like all other young actors on a first night, had seemed confused, but after he recovered himself a little he was received with general applause, having shown promise of making a "good player." Soon afterward he acted at Norwich, probably the same role.

A month later, on 8 October 1774, announced as "a Young Gentleman, first appearance on this stage," Lacy acted Alexander at Drury Lane. To introduce him, King spoke a "New Occasional Prologue" written by Garrick. That night the prompter Hopkins wrote in his diary: "He is very Tall, & Thin, a good Voice but His Fright took away from it's power—he was rec'ed with Applause." The *Westminster Magazine* of October 1774 offered more details:

His performance was far from answering the expectations we had been taught to form from a friend and pupil of our English Roscius. Indeed Mr Lacy is a very young man. . . . His figure is at present lank, awkward, and unengaging; his voice distinctly powerful but inharmonious; his action *outre*, vulgar and forced; his attitudes unnatural, affected and disgustful; and his delivery a continued rant, without proper change, a pleasing variety, or a just discrimination of the necessary difference of tone demanded by the different passions. These . . . capital defects . . . are not unsurmountable. . . . The play was prefaced by a new *Prologue*, evidently the production of Mr Garrick. . . . The purport of it was to beg favor for the hero of the evening, whom it compared to a young swimmer, who had tried to float in two shallow streams, and was now about to venture himself in the great deep. This image is certainly an apt one, though, it is no great compliment to the audiences of Norwich and Birmingham.

After repeating Alexander on 11 October—"Mr Lacy much the Same as first time," wrote Hopkins—he took on Oroonoko on 27 October 1774, announced as the "Young Gentleman who performed Alexander." Hopkins noted that he was "very tolerable" and "met with applause." On 2 November he played Alexander again, before the King and Queen. In his *Miscellanies in Prose and Verse* (1775), William Hawkins wrote that Lacy, not having met with "so much indulgence as was literally expected," had "cordially relinquished all thoughts of any future trial on the stage." But Lacy had not given up. On 14 March 1776, still billed as a Young Gentleman, he acted the title role in *Cyrus*. According to Hopkins's report, though he "Spoke too Low and wanted Spirit," he was "receiv'd with Applause." In an act of extreme presumption, it would seem, Lacy then insisted on performing Richmond in what was announced as the last performance of *Richard III* to be given by Garrick, on 3 June 1776, during the rounds of his farewell appearances. Next morning Garrick wrote to Hannah More,

"My Partner Lacy would play Rich^d with me last Night & was hiss'd." Garrick, however, acted Richard once more on 5 June, by command of the King and Queen, that time with Palmer as Richmond.

In January 1776 Garrick had sold his interest in the theatre and patent to Richard Brinsley Sheridan, Thomas Linley, and Dr James Ford for £35,000. Lacy now had new partners, and immediately he began thinking of selling out part of his share, but to some friend who would help him maintain a balance of power in the management. Garrick, though his last rounds were completed and he was legally separated from the management, maintained a special interest in the problem of ownership, for he held mortgages from the new partners, including Lacy. On 27 June 1776 he wrote to wish Lacy well but to warn him against precipitous action, pointing out that he was "very Young & inexperienc'd in the ways of Men, you have done some things & I am afraid are doing more, which I very warmly caution'd you against." Furthermore Garrick assured Lacy that the new partners were men of their word, and that such suspicions on his part would be "a very bad foundation for good fellowship."

Ignoring Garrick's advice, Lacy arranged to sell one half of his share to Edward Thompson, a naval officer and author of verses and theatrical pieces, and Robert Langford, an auctioneer. His determination was prompted by the pressure Garrick put on him to pay the interest on a £22,000 mortgage note which Garrick had taken from James Lacy, an obligation Willoughby had inherited. Actually, Garrick seems to have been cooperating at this point with Sheridan, who wanted complete control over the theatre but could not obtain it as long as Lacy refused to transfer his share of the mortgage debt, as Garrick had suggested. When Lacy failed to pay the interest on time Garrick sent him a notice of foreclosure. On 27 September 1776 Lacy wrote to request more time, which Garrick granted. Then Lacy decided to go through with his plan to sell to Thompson and Langford, without telling Sheridan.

The maneuvers that ensued were complex and devious. On 9 October 1776 Hopkins entered in his diary: "Mattocks came and told me that Lacy had sold Half his Share of the Patent to Mr Langford (The Auctioneer) and Captain Thomson (*Author of the Syrens &c.*). I acquainted Sheridan of it—he had not heard it before." The following day Sheridan requested that Lacy put off his sale and was denied, whereupon he informed Lacy that he would withdraw from active management, throwing the affairs of the theatre into confusion by leaving all the responsibility to the inexperienced Lacy. Mrs Abington refused to act as advertised, for she would play, she said, for no other manager than Sheridan. Hopkins, the Drury Lane prompter, entered in his diary on 15 October 1776:

The Managers met again to-day, but nothing settled. Hamlet was given out. I saw Mr Sheridan, he told me that Mr Lacy and he had agreed that no Play should be given out, nor any Bills put up, till they had settled this Affair, which was to be done to-morrow at Mr Wallis's (the Attorney's) where they were all to dine. I waited on Mr Lacy, who agreed to the same, and no Bills or Paragraph were sent to the Papers. All the Business of the Theatre is at a Stand, and no Rehearsal called. *Wed. 16th*—Mr Sheridan, Dr Ford and Mr Linley dined today by Appointment with Mr Wallis where Mr Lacy was to have met them; about four o'clock he sent a verbal Message that he could not come to Dinner, but would wait upon them in the Evening, and about nine o'clock he came, and everything was settled to the Satisfaction (of them all) and a Paragraph sent to the Papers, and the Hypocrite and Christmas Tale was advertised for Friday, but no Play was to be done on Thursday—Covent Garden did not play on Friday.

A long letter from Sheridan to Garrick, dated 15–16 October 1776, provides a further account of the circumstances.

Central to the dispute was the insistence by Sheridan and his colleagues that an original agreement between Garrick and James Lacy still prevailed; to wit, that in case of any one party's intention to sell any or all shares of his patent, he must offer first refusal to the other party. By selling to Thompson and Langford, the Sheridan party contended, Lacy was acting illegally. The pressure on Lacy evidently became too great, for on 17 October 1776 in a letter to the *Public Advertiser* he denied that he was bound by the original agreement but announced that in the theatre's best interests he had persuaded Thompson and Langford to withdraw from the contract of sale. Langford, however, continued to figure in Lacy's deteriorating personal finances. By 1778 Lacy was in debt to the extent that he had to secure Langford a £500 annuity, and by 1785 he had signed over to him Eynsham Hall, inherited from his father. (In the Forster Collection at the Victoria and Albert Museum is a series of letters by Lacy's auditors concerning attempts to get the Oxfordshire estate surveyed and evaluated for the purpose of disposing of it.)

The crisis with Sheridan having been settled, Lacy had turned once more to acting. On 3 February 1777, with his name now in Drury Lane bills, he acted Hamlet, a role he repeated on 8 February. He played Alexander on 17 February, Lord Hardy in *The Funeral* on 13 March, Lord Townly in *The Provok'd Husband* on 20 March and 5 April, Othello on 11 April, Lord Hardy again on 15 April, Don Alonzo in *The Revenge* on 24 April, Hamlet on 5 May, and Lord Townly on 28 May. The account books indicate no salary for him for acting that season, but at the end of June 1777 he was paid £40 6s. 3d. as "proprietor." In the next season, on 21 April 1778 he was paid £200. Two nights later he acted Marc Antony in *All for Love* (for Palmer's benefit), his last performance at Drury Lane while still a co-patentee.

In 1778 Lacy's affairs reached a crisis state. On 26 May the *Public Advertiser* reported that "Lacy has parted with his entire Moiety" in the theatre to Sheridan. The sale brought £31,500 and life annuities in the amount of £500 each to Lacy's wife and to Robert Langford. The transaction is documented in a long letter from Sheridan to Albany Wallis and in other papers now in the Harvard Theatre Collection. Soon after, Lacy sold his share in the Bristol Theatre, also inherited from his father, to John Moody. Then in July 1778 Lacy went off to act for Heaphy at Cork, playing Lord Townly and Hamlet.

After the summer of 1778, nothing survives about Lacy's activities until his reappearance in London on 13 September 1784, playing Hamlet at the Haymarket Theatre and delivering an address written for the occasion by the elder George Colman:

> As some poor mariner by tempest tost,
> Shipwreck'd at last, and in the sea near lost,
> Cleaves to one plank, and braving shoal and sand,
> Buoy'd up by Hope, attempts to gain the land;
> Thus I, my treasures on the waters cast,
> Guided by Hope, seek here a port at last.
> Oh! might I cast secure my Anchor here!
> Should Kindness sooth my Grief and ease my Fear!
> Warm Gratitude, all anxious to repay
> The soft restorers of my happier day,
> Within my swelling breast new Pow'rs may raise,
> And guide my feeble Aims to gain your Praise!

The reviewer in the *European Magazine* that month reported that the personal nature of the address overwhelmed Lacy as he spoke it, and that, as Hamlet, "he did many things much better, and some things much worse than any representation of that character now on the stage." Moreover, the critic wrote: "his voice is better calculated for the recitation of tragedy than that of any male performer at any of our theatres. All he wants . . . is the proper *modulation* of that voice: for his lower tones . . . are deficient, and sometimes scarcely audible. . . . Like Barry, he is *too* tall, and somewhat awkward in deportment, though his figure, on the whole, is handsome and engaging." In the summer of 1785 he returned to Colman's Haymarket to play Hamlet on 24 June and 13 July and Othello on 9 September.

In 1785–86 he acted at the Smock Alley Theatre in Dublin. He was probably the Lacy who read poetry at the Free Masons' Hall in Great Queen Street, London, on 13 June 1786. A month later, on 14 July, at the Haymarket he again acted Othello. In *The Children of Thespis* published that year, John Williams (under the pseudonym "Anthony Pasquin") wrote of Lacy:

> See he fondly returns to indulge the last view
> Of his father's domains, ere he bids them adieu.
> . . . .
> With an excellent heart, and a credulous head,
> The man is affectionate, kind, and well bred;
> . . . .
> If question'd the cause of his woes and decay,
> 'Tis answer'd, Such ills mark the course of each day.
> UNPRINCIPLED VARLETS, unblessed with a guinea,
> Have seiz'd on his rent-roll, and laugh at the ninny;
> But Destiny's womb strange events disembogues,
> And FIDLERS and WITS may be—eminent rogues.

Lacy spent some of the remainder of the century as an itinerant actor. On 14 May 1791 he made his first appearance on the Nottingham stage as Oroonoko, for the benefit of Mrs Pero. An anonymous manuscript in the Folger Shakespeare Library, dating about July 1795, indicates that "Poor Lacy is reduc'd to great Distress, & laments too late the credulous Confidence he placed in those he *thought his Friends*." In the summer of 1795 he was in the company at Richmond, Surrey. The *How Do You Do* of 13 August 1796 reported that Lacy was "in captivity," for debt—"He is about to publish an essay on *Poetry, Painting, and Acting*, which we sincerely hope will meet a good sale, and benefit an unfortunate, but honest man." The number for 27 August 1796 stated that Lacy had intended to give the essay as a lecture, "had circumstances proved propitious to his wishes."

A Public Record Office document reveals that a license had been issued to a Mrs Lacy for plays and entertainments at the Haymarket on 27 April 1796. That evening at the Haymarket were given performances of *The Earl of Essex* and *The Citizen*, but Lacy's name was not in the bills. The performance was permitted by the Lord Chamberlain for the benefit of "a widow," perhaps a subterfuge, and Rutland in the former and Maria in the latter piece were played by "A Young Lady" announced as making her first appearance on any stage. There is no hard evidence to assume that this young lady or the licensee was actually Mrs Willoughby Lacy, though it is quite possible she was. If she was, then she was Willoughby's second wife Elizabeth Lacy (née Jackson), whom he had married at Hanwell on 16 August 1789. (His first wife, Maria Ann, née Orpen, whom he had married in 1774, had died at Brompton on 11 January 1788, at the age of 31.) According to the *Gentleman's Magazine* of August 1789, at the time of her marriage to Lacy, Elizabeth Jackson was a member of the Hanwell company.

A license was issued to Lacy for a play and entertainment at the Haymarket on 16 November 1798, but the event was postponed until 17 December, when for his own benefit he acted Oakly in *The Jealous Wife* and gave an address. Several important London performers rallied to the cause that night by acting for him, including Mrs Abington, Robert Palmer, the younger Bannister, and Richard Suett. Lacy received another benefit, this time at Drury Lane, on 18 June 1800, when he acted Othello. The total receipts were a very modest £97 3s., but the manager gave the house free of charge. Again on 18 June 1801 he was given a free house, playing Reginald in *The Castle Spectre*, and his son, the younger Willoughby Lacy, acted Osmond. The bills announced that the performance was "Under the Patronage of His Excellency The Algerine Ambassador By Grant from the Proprietors of the Theatre Royal Drury Lane, For the Benefit of Mr Lacy, formerly of the Theatre." On 15 June Lacy had written from No 12, Martlet Court, to Mrs Garrick hoping she would honor the occasion by being present "in her Box."

From 1804–5 through 1808–9 Lacy's name appeared in the Drury Lane account books for payments of £6 6s. per week. These payments were not for acting but in fulfillment of an agreement that he was to receive one guinea from every performance. He also was paid periodically on his annuity but, as was usual with Sheridan, those payments frequently were in arrears. The Drury Lane Fund Book at the Garrick Club reveals some of Lacy's subsequent misfortunes. On 2 December 1809 he asked for relief, a request he repeated on 20 January 1810, when he was granted one guinea per week. A committee meeting was called for 25 March 1810 "for Poor Mr Lacys affairs." Dated 29 June is a notation that "Poor Lacy intends to lay his Benefit at the discretion of Com^{ee}." and on 30 June he sent word that his allowance had been stopped "without calling a Committee." On 16 July 1810 Maddocks, the Fund treasurer, was instructed "to continue Lacy until the opening of Theatrical Season." The next entry was made at a later, unspecified date: "Maddocks discontinued Mr Lacy."

Lacy was granted licenses for plays, recitations, and music at the King's Theatre on 22 June 1809, 28 June 1810, and 25 March 1813. He had been granted similar licenses for performances in Richmond (with Sidley, Harper, and Hill) in 1805, and for the Assembly Rooms in Brewer Street, Golden Square, on 8 July 1811. The last such license we note was for the Haymarket on 13 April 1814. In 1813 Lacy published *A Memorial, humbly addressed to the Public, by Willoughby Lacy, formerly one of the patentees of the Theatre Royal, Drury Lane, to be had at Mr. Eber's circulating library; Mr Earle's circulating library; and Mr Asperne, Bookseller*, an account of his financial difficulties, with an appeal for help.

The *Gentleman's Magazine* for September 1831 reported Willoughby Lacy's death in Mornington Place on the seventeenth of that month, at the age of 82. The date of his second wife's death is unknown to us. His son Willoughby Lacy (1775–1817), by his first wife, had acted occasionally in London and had managed a company at St Neots in the first decade of the nineteenth century; he had acted at Edinburgh from 1813 to 1815 and had died at Skibbereen, Ireland, in 1817. The younger Lacy had married a Covent Garden actress named Miss Hopkins in 1796; their daughter Maria Ann Lacy acted in London beginning in 1822 and married the dramatist George William Lovell.

The elder Willoughby had a daughter by his second wife Elizabeth Lacy about August 1802; she died at the age of 15 months in November 1803 and on the sixteenth of that latter month R. B. Sheridan wrote to Downs, an undertaker in Lower James Street, Golden Square, that he would be responsible for the funeral expenses, since Lacy was not receiving his annuity from the theatre as usual.

Lacy, Mrs Willoughby the second, Elizabeth, née Jackson [fl. 1789–1804], actress?

The *Gentleman's Magazine* of August 1789 reported that the elder Willoughby Lacy (1749–1831), late joint patentee of Drury Lane Theatre, had married Miss Elizabeth Jackson of the Hanwell company on the sixteenth of that month. (Lacy's first wife, Maria Ann, née Orpen, had died on 11 January 1788 at the age of 31.)

A Public Record Office document indicates that a Mrs Lacy was issued a license for plays and entertainments at the Haymarket Theatre for 27 April 1796, similar to licenses periodically granted to Willoughby Lacy. The performance was permitted by the Lord Chamberlain for the benefit of "a widow," but that may have been the use of a not-unfamiliar subterfuge. The characters of Rutland in *The Earl of Essex* and Maria in *The Citizen* were acted by "A Young Lady," announced as making her first appearance on any stage, who quite possibly was Elizabeth Lacy.

The second Mrs Lacy is an obscure figure in the remaining years of her husband's career, which was punctuated by financial distress. She had a daughter by him about August 1802 who died at the age of 15 months in November 1803. On 25 November 1804, R. B. Sheridan sent Mrs Lacy a brief note and 18 guineas due on her husband's annuity, addressed to No 9, Duke Street, Lincoln's Inn Fields. Willoughby Lacy died in Mornington Place in 1831. It is not known to us whether Mrs Lacy was then still alive.

Lacy, Willoughby 1775–1817, actor, manager, scene painter.

Born in 1775, Willoughby Lacy the younger was the son of the actor and sometime patentee Willoughby Lacy (1749–1839) by his first wife Maria Ann Lacy (1757–1788), née Orpen. He was the grandson of James Lacy (1696–1774), who had been Garrick's co-patentee for 27 years. Announced as Lacy Junior and making his first appearance in London, young Lacy acted Palamon in the premiere of F. G. Waldron's farce *Love and Madness* at the Haymarket Theatre on 21 September 1795. Thereafter he retreated to the provinces, whence no doubt he had come. At Plymouth in late June 1796 he married a Miss Hopkins, of Bath, a Covent Garden actress and singer. The marriage was reported in the *Monthly Mirror* of July 1796.

The Lacys passed the remainder of their careers in the provinces, with several exceptions. In 1799 they were members of a company circuiting Barnstaple, Taunton, Poole, and Guernsey. Lacy also served the troupe as a scene painter. He did, however, return to London on 4 June 1801 to act Hamlet at Covent Garden Theatre, where he was announced as "Mr Lacy Jun," making his first appearance in London, his earlier single performance in 1795 having been forgotten or conveniently ignored. Two weeks later he acted Osmond in *The Castle Spectre* at Drury Lane on 18 June 1801, for the benefit of his father who had returned to the theatre to act Reginald that evening. The younger Lacy was that time advertised as making his first appearance on that stage and his "Second in London."

In 1801–2 Lacy was engaged at Covent Garden for £2 10s. per week. One of his roles that season was Sir Philip Blandford in *Speed the Plough* on 13 January 1802. Genest related a practical joke at a rehearsal, which poked fun at his great height:

. . . he was remarkably tall, and if any passage in a play had reference to height, he was desirous of cutting it out—one morning when he was rehearsing Sir Philip Blandford, H. Johnston procured the longest cloak he could find in the wardrobe, and came upon the stage with Simmons on his shoulders covered by the cloak, so as to give the appearance of there being but one person—Simmons, who had a loud voice, began some ridiculous speech—this set the performers into such a violent laughter, that they could not go on with the Rehearsal . . .

In the summer of 1802 Lacy assumed management of the theatre at St Neots, where he, according to the *Monthly Mirror*, "managerlike, played everything." By 1803 he was also co-manager with Miss Dorell of the theatre at nearby Wellingborough. He was still operating in that part of England when Thomas Gilliland published his *Dramatic Mirror* in 1808. Probably he was the Lacy who was a busy member of the company at the Theatre Royal, Shakespeare Square, Edinburgh, from 1813 to 1815, where his roles included Bassanio in *The Merchant of Venice*, Captain Absolute in *The Rivals*, Claudio in *Much Ado about Nothing*, Jeremy Diddler in *Raising the Wind*, Kalig in *The Blind Boy*, Mercutio in *Romeo and Juliet*, Valcour in *The Point of Honour*, and Young Rapid in *A Cure for the Heart-Ache*.

Lacy died at Skibbereen, Ireland, of typhus fever on 12 November 1817 at the age of 42. In his obituary notice, the *Gentleman's Magazine* of December 1817 observed: "He filled his situation in the theatrical department for many years in the several towns in this kingdom with much credit, and he left a wife and four young daughters totally destitute." One of the daughters, Maria Ann Lacy (1803–1877), made her debut as Belvidera in *Venice Preserv'd* at Covent Garden on 10 October 1822 and enjoyed a successful career; she married the dramatist George William Lovell. Lacy's father, the elder Willoughby, did not die until 1831.

Lacy, Mrs Willoughby. See HOPKINS, MISS [*fl.* 1790–1817].

Ladd, Mr [*fl.* 1739–1741], *dancer.*
Mr Ladd danced a few small roles at Covent Garden in 1739–40 and 1740–41, and it is likely that he danced more regularly than the bills show. His earliest notice was on 10 December 1739, when he was one of the Bacchanals in *Cupid and Psyche*. Then he was seen as a Swain and a Villager in *Orpheus and Eurydice* and Coxen in *The Parting Lovers*.

Ladd, Mr [*fl.* 1733], *actor.*
Mr Ladd played one of the Arval Brothers in *Ambarvallia* at Marylebone Gardens on 3, 6, and 9 September 1773.

Lade, Nicholas *d.* 1783, *singer.*
The song *Love alone shall here alarm you* was published about 1735 as sung by a Mr Lad at Sadler's Wells. He was very likely Nicholas Lade (or Ladd), who was sworn a Gentleman of the Chapel Royal on 15 August 1743. A Mr Ladd, also a singer and also probably Nicholas Lade, sang in the *Messiah* at the Foundling Hospital in May 1754 and again in the springs of 1758 and 1759, each time for a fee of 10*s.* 6*d.* Nicholas Lade died at Windsor on 9 July 1783 and, stated the notes to the Westminster Abbey registers, was described by the journals of the time as a "senior gentleman of H. M.'s Chapel Royal at St. James, a member of St. Peter's, Westminster, father of the choir of H. M.'s free Chapel of St. George in Windsor Castle, and a member of the Collegiate Chapel of Eton."

Lade left a will, dated at Windsor Castle 2 June 1783 and proved on the following 18 September. He requested a simple burial at either St George's Chapel in Windsor or at Westminster Abbey, where his daughter and her grandmother (Nicholas's mother-in-law, Mary Smith, who died September 1773) were buried. Evidently Lade was buried in Windsor, for there is no record of his burial in the Abbey in London. His daughter Maria had been buried in the West Cloister of Westminster Abbey on 8 May 1770 at the age of 11 years and 5 months. Lade left his entire estate to his wife Frances, except for a bequest of £100 to Hannah Lade, widow of Nicholas's brother Charles. After Frances Lade died, the children of Charles and Hannah Lade (Frances, Ann, and Hannah) were to receive £100 each.

"La Droghierina." See CHIMENTI, MARGHERITA.

La Duke. See LE DUKE.

"Lady Flame." See HAYWOOD, MRS VALENTINE.

"Lady Isabella" [*fl. c.* 1712?], *rope dancer.*
George Speaight in his *History of the English Puppet Theatre* observes that the puppeteer Martin Powell about 1712 fleshed out his presentations of puppet plays with such other en-

tertainments as a puppet imitating a rope dancer called "Lady Isabella."

"Lady Isabella" *1724–1745, posture maker, dancer.*

W. R. Chetwood in his *General History of the Stage* in 1749 told of

the Lady *Isabella* [who] was born in Italy, sprung from a noble Family in the City of *Florence*: She was put into a Nunnery at twelve Years of Age, in order to take the Veil; but a Posture-master unluckily came to that City, gained her Affections, and found Means to carry her off, and marry'd her; instructed her in his unseemly, dangerous Employment (if we may call it so), and brought her to *England*; where Lady Isabella was greatly admir'd, for her Postures, and Feats of Activity. The last, fatal, Time of her Performance, she was eight Months gone with Child; but the covetous Husband loved Money so well (as it is reported), that he would not allow her the necessary Repose required in her Condition; so that, in one of her Dances on a slack Rope, she fell on the Stage, where the Mother and Infant, newly born with the Force of the Fall, expired in a Moment, fatal Catastrophe! in the Twenty-first Year of her Age. This was the running Account of the poor Lady Isabella, after her Death, whose End was much lamented: For, notwithstanding her disreputable Employment, she was esteemed as a Woman of strict Virtue.

She is said to have died in 1745. Where she performed in England, Chetwood did not say, but he made it clear that she appeared in theatres. Some features of the story are open to doubt.

"Lady Mary." *See* FINDLEY, MR.

Lady Morgan. *See* MORGAN, LADY.

La Faver. *See* LE FEVRE.

La Fay. *See* LE FEVRE.

"La Ferrarese." *See* FERRARESE, SIGNORA.

Laferry. *See* LA FOREST.

La Fevre *See* LE FEVRE.

La Folle, Mrs W. *See* PLACIDE, MRS ALEXANDER THE SECOND.

La Fond, Mlle [*fl.* 1764–1773], *dancer.*

According to the *Lexique* of Fuchs, a Mademoiselle "Lafont," a dancer, made her debut at the Comédie Italienne in Paris on 25 April 1764. Perhaps she was the Mlle La Fond who danced at the King's Theatre in 1772–73. That dancer's first appearance was on 1 December 1772, when she participated in an unnamed serious ballet. She appeared regularly throughout the season in such pieces as a *Pastoral Dance*, an allemande, a pas de cinq, and *La Fête du Village*. Her final appearance was on 19 June 1773, the last day of the season.

La Font, Mons. *See* LA FONT, MME.

La Font, Mme [*fl.* 1742–1750], *dancer.*

Madame La Font (or Le Font, L'Font) was first noticed in London playbills on 26 November 1741 as an Amazon in *Perseus and Andromeda* at Covent Garden Theatre. On 8 January 1742 "Mlle La Fond" was a Sylvan in *The Rape of Proserpine*. On 22 February "Mrs" La Font was in a ballet entitled *Mars and Venus*. Mme La Font danced at Sadler's Wells on 19 June and 3 July (and doubtless other dates). She returned to Covent Garden in October and during the season was in an unnamed ballet, played her Sylvan part again, and participated in a specialty dance called *The Peasants*. Her 1743–44 season was similar: her Sylvan role, participation in *A New Scotch Dance*, the chorus roles of a Villager and a Country Lass in *Orpheus and Eurydice*, and participation in the dances in *Comus*. On 4 May 1744 she shared a benefit with four others. *The London Stage* again lists her in one bill as Mlle La Font—which may have been an error in the original bill, of course—but there appears to have been only one female dancer named La Font in London in the 1740s.

Mme La Font seems not to have performed in London again until December 1746, when she was once more at Covent Garden, though perhaps not a regular member of the troupe. She was not named in any bills then, but the account books cited her as having danced in three performances of *The Rape of Proserpine* for 5s. per performance. *The London Stage* lists performances on 24 and 26 November and 2 December; Mme La Font (or La Fons) was paid on the sixth, with the notation that she was not to be put on the regular paylist. On 20 December 1746 she was paid 5*s*. for the previous night (when *The Royal Chace* was given), and on 27 December she received 15*s*. for three performances, probably also of *The Royal Chace*.

On 3 March 1748 and subsequent dates Mme La Font was a Follower of Daphne in *Apollo and Daphne* at Covent Garden, and that spring she also danced in *The Muses' Looking Glass*. *The London Stage* incorrectly lists Mme La Font as Mlle in the 1747–48 season roster. *The London Stage* is also in error listing a male dancer named La Font in the Drury Lane troupe in 1748–49; the bill for 27 October 1748 has Mme La Font dancing in the ballet *Vertumnus and Pomona*, which was repeated several times through November. She also danced Justice in *The Triumph of Peace* in February 1749 and shared a benefit with three others on 11 May. She returned to Drury Lane in 1749–50 to dance in *Comus*, a *Rural Dance* in *The Chaplet*, *Acis and Galatea*, and a *Dance of Aerial Spirits* in *The Tempest*.

La Font, Mlle. *See* LA FONT, MME.

La Forest, Mons [*fl.* 1702–1707], *dancer.*
The dancer "Laferry" who was first noticed in the bills on 23 October 1702 when he danced with Miss Campion at Drury Lane was very likely the Monsieur La Forest (or Laforrest, Lafory) who danced there from 1703–4 through 1705–6. So far as can be determined from the scarce and often uninformative bills, La Forest danced only at Drury Lane. He was usually in dances that were not titled, though from time to time the bills specified that he danced a *Scaramouch Man and Scaramouch Woman* with Mrs Lucas, or a *Harlequin Man and Woman* with Mrs Bicknell, or that he was in a *Fury's Dance* or in dances in *Psyche*. The Lord Chamberlain issued an order on 31 December 1707 restricting operas to the Queen's Theatre; a petition by the players against a union of the companies was signed by, among many others, "La Forest."

La Forest, Mons [*fl.* 1727], *dancer.*
"Monsieur La Forest and his Wife, just arriv'd in England," danced at Drury Lane Theatre on 31 May 1727 when *Julius Caesar* and *Harlequin Doctor Faustus* were performed.

La Forest, Mme [*fl.* 1727], *dancer. See* LA FOREST, MONS [*fl.* 1727].

La Foy, Mons [*fl.* 1729], *dancer.*
On 15 October 1729 at the Lincoln's Inn Fields Theatre Monsieur La Foy danced a French(man) in *The Triumphs of Love*, which was added to *Apollo and Daphne*. St Luce replaced him on 15 November.

La Foy, Mrs [*fl.* 1732], *dancer.*
Mrs La Foy danced a Sylvan in *The Rape of Proserpine* at Lincoln's Inn Fields Theatre on 8 November 1732, but she was replaced by Mrs Baston the following day.

"La Francesina." *See* "FRANCESINA, LA."

La Fronde. *See* LEFRONDE.

La Garde. *See also* DELAGARDE *and* LA-GUERRE.

Lagarde, Signor [*fl.* 1720–1724], *singer.*
Signor Lagarde sang the bass part of Farasmane in Handel's *Radamisto* at the King's Theatre on 27 April 1720 and subsequent dates in April and May and in December and January in the 1720–21 season. On 20 February 1724 he sang Curio in *Giulio Cesare*. The singer Legar who performed in 1731 seems not to have been Signor Legarde but rather John Laguerre. The *New Grove* gives those Handel roles to Laguerre, but we have found no evidence to support his singing in Italian operas.

Lagaronne, François [*fl.* 1719–1725?], *actor. See* LAGARONNE, MME.

Lagaronne, Mme [François, Marthe, née Farraguet?] [*fl.* 1719–1725], *actress.*
The French troupe calling themselves "Italian" comedians who held forth at the Haymarket Theatre from 17 December 1724 to 13 May 1725 included a Mme Lagaronne, who was the company's Isabella in their *commedia dell' arte* pieces. She shared a benefit with Laniere on 7 April 1725. She may have been the wife of the Scaramouch François Lagaronne; if so, she was born Marthe Farraguet. The François Lagaronnes had performed—she as a Col-

LAGARONNE

umbine—at the Hague in 1719. In the troupe which came to London in 1724–25 Philippe was the Scaramouch, but a new young Scaramouch, lately arrived, danced on 29 March 1725. Could he have been François Lagaronne?

Laggat, Mr [*fl.* 1799], *actor.*
Mr Laggat played Hastings in *She Stoops to Conquer* and Eugene in *The Agreeable Surprise* at Wheatley's Riding School, Greenwich, on 17 May 1799.

"L'Agile, Mons" [*fl.* 1740–1750], *dancer.*
Harlequin in *The Chymical Counterfeits* at the Goodman's Fields playhouse from 6 to 29 November 1740 was performed by a dancer named "L'Agile"—which one supposes was a pseudonym. He was Harlequin again on 15 December in *The Imprisonment, Release, Adventures, and Marriage of Harlequin.* Hailed as from Paris, Monsieur L'Agile played Harlequin at the New Wells, Clerkenwell, on 16 April 1750 in *Harlequin Mountebank.*

La Grange, Claude [*fl.* 1660–1688], *singer.*
Claude La Grange (or Degranges, Des Granges) was sworn a musician in ordinary in the King's Musick on 19 October 1663; Eleanor Boswell in *The Restoration Court Stage* noted that the French singer had been in England at least since June 1660. In the Lord Chamberlain's accounts he was often listed as a bass; indeed, one warrant, dated 18 September 1671, reappointed him as a French musician in ordinary, "being established among the violins for singing the basse" at £100 annually, a very handsome salary for a court musician. He sang in the court masque *Calisto* on 15 February 1675, had his certificate renewed in March 1681, and on 5 July 1687 in the retrenched King's Musick was listed as a Gregorian at £50 annually. The last mention of him in the accounts was on 20 October 1688, when he was listed as having attended the King at Windsor the previous summer.

Laguerre, John *c.* 1702–1748, *actor, singer, dancer, composer, scene painter.*
John Laguerre, according to Roger Fiske's *English Theatre Music*, was born in London about

By permission of the Trustees of the British Museum
JOHN LAGUERRE
artist unknown

1702 (the *New Grove* says about 1700), the son of the painter Louis Laguerre (1663–1721). The elder Laguerre came to England in 1683 and married the daughter of Jean Tijou, a worker in iron. After the death of his first wife Laguerre married again; it is not known whether John (originally Jean) was the son of the elder Laguerre's first or second wife. John was given instruction in painting by his father and for a time worked under Hogarth, and though he dabbled in art during his life, turning out some engravings and painting some scenery, he was best known to eighteenth-century Londoners as a tenor (though Grove says baritone) singer and actor.

John was probably the Mr "Legar" (a common variant spelling of his name) who, with

Leveridge, sang *See the yielding fair*, a song published about 1720. On 20 April 1721 at Lincoln's Inn Fields Theatre, a benefit was held for "Le Garde" (another common variant) at which he and Pack offered "The *Enthusiastick Song* and Dialogues" at a performance of *The Island Princess*. To that performance John's father went; the elder Laguerre had grown dropsical in his late years and died of apoplexy before the performance began. We do not know whether or not John Laguerre went on anyway. (The *New Grove* credits Laguerre with roles in Handel's *Radamisto* in 1720 and *Giulio Cesare* in 1724, but there is no other evidence to support his having sung in Italian operas, and we take the Handel singer to have been Signor Lagarde.)

"Le Gar" played the Valet in *The Magician* at Lincoln's Inn Fields on 10 May 1721; the work was written by the manager of the theatre and chief pantomime dancer, John Rich, for whom Laguerre worked throughout most of his career. A roster of performers at Rich's theatre in April 1722 included John "Lequerie"—yet another spelling of Laguerre's name. Not until the 1730s did the printers manage to get his name right with any regularity.

Laguerre was customarily cited in the Lincoln's Inn Fields bills as an entr'acte singer, though too often the bills said little more than "several new collected Songs by Mr Legare, never performed by him before"—which is not very helpful. Occasionally the song titles were mentioned, as on 2 November 1723 when Laguerre and Leveridge sang "In Praise of Love and Wine." He probably offered as entr'acte specialties songs he sang from plays and pantomimes that proved popular enough to warrant publication, such as *This great World is a Trouple* (sic) and *What Scenes of approaching delight* (1723) from *Jupiter and Europa*, *While on ten thousand Charms I gaze* (1724) from *The Necromancer*, *Fortune often wooes us* (1725?) from *The Rape of Proserpine*, and *How pleasant a Sailors life passes* (1730?) from *Perseus and Andromeda*.

Over the years at Lincoln's Inn Fields Jack Laguerre built up a list of roles in pantomimes and other entertainments: Mercury in *Jupiter and Europa*, the Beau in *The Beau Demolished*, Apelles in *The Union of the Three Sister Arts*, the Petit Maitre in *Harlequin Sorcerer*, a Spirit in *The Necromancer*, Damon in *The Capricious Lovers*, Pan and Mystery in *Apollo and Daphne*, the title role in *The Sultan*, a Sylvan in *Pan and Syrinx*, Metius in *Camilla*, Mercury in *The Rape of Proserpine*, the Burgomaster in *Apollo and Daphne*, Harry Pyfleet in *The Cobler's Opera* ("his first attempt in the dramatic way" on 17 March 1729), a Noble Venetian in *Italian Jealousy*, Hob in *Hob's Opera*, Hob in *Flora*, a Scots Servant in *The Dutch and Scotch Contention*, Coridon in *Acis and Galatea*, Timothy Stitch in *Sylvia*, a Fury in *Orestes*, Geta in *The Judgment of Paris*, and other parts left unnamed in the bills.

Laguerre rarely performed elsewhere, though on 11 May 1722 he sang at a concert at the Haymarket Theatre. And though his specialty was singing, he was noted in the playbills in May 1728 as dancing. Laguerre also tried his hand at composition. He wrote a song for *Perseus and Andromeda* for a performance, oddly, at a rival house—Goodman's Fields—on 1 April 1731.

Over the years at Lincoln's Inn Fields Laguerre did fairly well at benefit time. In April 1723, for example, with the Prince and Princess present, his gross receipts came to £122 14*s*.; his shared benefit with Hall in May 1724 brought in £114 16*s*. 6*d*.; with his wife in 1725 Laguerre shared £98 15*s*. 6*d*.; with her in 1726 he shared £120; and in 1731 they took in £87 12*s*. 9*d*. In 1731 the Laguerres were living at No 22, Old Boswell Court. Jack's salary, in the mid-1720s at any rate, was about £2 2*s*. weekly (the account books are somewhat ambiguous). Mrs Laguerre was Mary, the widow of the dancer Rogeir; she and Laguerre were married sometime between 3 June and 25 September 1724.

The Covent Garden Theatre opened in December 1732, and John Rich moved his troupe from Lincoln's Inn Fields. Laguerre performed there through the 1733–34 season, then joined the Drury Lane troupe in 1734–35 and began the following season, only to return to Covent Garden in mid-season. There he remained, except for rare activity elsewhere, to the end of his life. At Covent Garden he played such new parts as Diomedes in *Achilles*, Squire Somebody in *The Stage Coach*, a Priest of Hymen in *The Nuptial Masque*, Bacchus in *Apollo and Daphne*, Mercury in *The Rape of Helen*, Gubbins in *The Dragon of Wantley*, Mercury in *The Royal Chace*, Gaffer Gubbins in *Margery* (for which

Harvard Theatre Collection

"The Stage Mutiny"
JOHN LAGUERRE

he wrote some or all of the music), Ascalax in *Orpheus and Eurydice*, Dreadnaught in *The Parting Lovers*, and Wall in *Pyramus and Thisbe*. Laguerre continued as an entr'acte singer, one of his most popular songs being, with Leveridge, "The Black and White Joke." On 24 August 1734 Laguerre tried his hand at co-managing a booth at Bartholomew Fair with Ryan, Chapman, and Hall. There he acted Gunner in *The Barren Island*.

His brief stint at Drury Lane began on 28 September 1734, when he played Hob in *Flora*, one of his most popular parts, about which he engraved a number of plates. Two days before his debut at Drury Lane he had played the role at Richmond. While at Drury Lane in 1734–35 Laguerre was seen as the Burgomaster's Servant in *The Burgomaster Trick'd*, Coupee in *An Old Man Taught Wisdom*, the title role in *Merlin*, and the Petit Maitre in *Harlequin Orpheus*. A benefit bill, attributed to Hogarth but possibly not by him, for *An Old Man Taught Wisdom* names Laguerre, though he is not known to have had a benefit during his stay at Drury Lane. The bills did not list him as singing any entr'acte songs. He began the 1735–36 season at Drury Lane on 6 September 1735 with Coupee in *The Virgin Unmask'd*, but after three performances he left the troupe. By 6 March 1736 he was back at Covent Garden. His benefit bill in April indicated that he had lodgings beside the King's Arms in George Street, York Buildings.

Laguerre's wife died in the spring of 1739 in Chelsea. Jack finished the season at Covent Garden, joined Hippisley and Chapman in the operation of a booth at Bartholomew Fair in August (and played the Petit Maitre in *The Top of the Three*), and performed his usual heavy schedule at Covent Garden in 1739–40. Then his career became erratic. On 10 July 1740 he placed a plea in the papers:

This is to give notice that on Wednesday next I shall prepare an Entertainment for the reception of my friends at the Dog & Duck in St. George's Fields. All Gentlemen who please to honour me with their Company, the favour will be gratefully acknowledged by their most obedt. humble servant.

J Laguerre

The nature of the entertainment is not known. But he was obviously trying to raise money. He did not return to Covent Garden in the fall of 1740, but on 6 February 1741 at Goodman's Fields he played Hob in *Flora* and the Father in *Nancy*. On 16 April with Mrs Jones he sang a "Dialogue of the Widow and the Rake." He repeated Hob again on 23 April at a special benefit for himself. He was, his benefit bill said, a prisoner in the King's Bench and had been for "some time past." "It being in Term time I shall by the common license of a Day Rule, have the liberty to personally perform the part cast for me. . . ." Tickets, he said, would be available at John's Coffee House, conveniently located next door to the King's Bench, Southwark. On 12 May 1742 he had another benefit at Covent Garden.

Laguerre's name disappeared from London bills for two years. In February 1743 at Southwark he played Trapland in *Love for Love* at a benefit he shared with Boman on the eighteenth, and on 25 February he appeared as Hob in *Flora*. On 6 April he shared a benefit with four others at Lincoln's Inn Fields. Then he again dropped out of sight until January 1745, when he renewed his association with Covent Garden, playing regularly to the end of the season. He returned on 27 September 1745 to play in *Pyramus and Thisbe*, then his name again disappeared from the bills. In this instance, perhaps we have found a reason: at St Paul, Covent Garden, on 25 October 1745 Frances, the daughter of John "Legauree" was buried. The following spring at benefit time Laguerre shared a benefit at Covent Garden with three others.

Though Jack was not mentioned in the Covent Garden bills in 1746–47, he was on the payroll at £1 weekly as a scene painter, and he continued receiving pay as a painter through December 1747. The accounts also indicate that he was renting lodgings from the theatre management at £20 annually. In December 1747, just after receiving his last pay as a painter, his name reappeared in the bills as a performer, and he acted and sang through February 1748.

Laguerre, along with Leveridge, Hogarth, Charles Fleetwood, Theophilus Cibber, and James Quin, belonged to the distinguished Freemasons' lodge that met at the Bear and Harrow in Butcher Row, east of the Tower.

The *General Advertiser* on 29 March 1748 reported that "Yesterday morning died Mr. John Laguerre, an eminent Painter, belonging to the Theatre Royal in Covent Garden; a facetious companion universally esteem'd in every scene of life." Laguerre was buried at St Paul, Covent Garden, on 1 April. Most sources claim that he died in poverty. Widow Laguerre (he had evidently married again) was granted a benefit at Southwark on 5 March 1750.

John Laguerre's claim to fame today is an etching called "The Stage Mutiny" (June 1733), which wittily depicts Theophilus Cibber's revolt from Drury Lane. It was copied in small

By permission of the British Library Board

JOHN LAGUERRE, singing "Poor Children Three"
artist unknown

by Hogarth and used as a show cloth in the engraving "Southwark Fair."

Laguerre, Mrs John, Mary, formerly Mrs Rogeir *d. 1739, dancer, actress.*

Mary Rogeir Laguerre's maiden name is not known. By the time she was first mentioned in playbills, on 1 August 1721 when she danced at Drury Lane, she was already married to a Mr Rogeir (sometimes Rogier). On 4 August she played Dorcas in *The Fair Quaker*, and she continued that month appearing as an entr'acte dancer. Mary performed at Lincoln's Inn Fields Theatre from 1721–22 through 1723–24 as Mrs Rogeir, offering specialty dances (such as a *Dutch Skipper* with Pelling, *Tollet's Ground* and a *Stripping Dance* with Newhouse, a *French Peasant* and the *Running Footman's Dance* with Nivelon), appearing in pantomimes that called for dancing, and playing a number of important roles in plays.

In addition to Dorcas in *The Fair Quaker*, she acted Cherry in *The Stratagem*, Peggy in *The London Cuckolds*, Cynthia in *The Double Dealer*, Frolick in *Injured Love*, Araminta in *The Old Bachelor*, Colombine in *The Magician*, Ann Page in *The Merry Wives of Windsor*, Rose in *The Recruiting Officer*, Prince Edward in *Richard III* (she must have been petite), Jessica in *The Merchant of Venice*, Lucia in *The Squire of Alsatia*, Lucy in *Oroonoko*, Jaqueline in *The Beggar's Bush*, Europa in *Jupiter and Europa*, Venus in *Mars and Venus*, Colombine in *Amadis*, and Colombine in *The Robbers*. Her benefits brought her fair returns: £87 17s. in 1722, £123 15s. 6d. with Newhouse in 1723 and £102 2s. 6d. with Hippisley in 1724—all presumably before house charges.

The London *Journal* on 8 February 1724 reported that her husband Rogeir had hanged himself. Details are lacking, but it may be significant that between 3 June and 25 September of that year she married John Laguerre, who had been a performer with Mary at Lincoln's Inn Fields from her first notices there. Her salary as Mrs Laguerre in the fall of 1724 was 16s. 8d. daily.

Mrs Laguerre continued under John Rich's management at Lincoln's Inn Fields until the troupe moved to Covent Garden Theatre in December 1732. Some of the new parts that came to her over the years were a Harlequin Woman, a Mezzetin Woman, a Scaramouch

Harvard Theatre Collection

MARY LAGUERRE and FRANCIS NIVELON in *Perseus and Andromeda*

Frontispiece to *Harlequin Horace*, artist unknown

Woman, and the Miller's Wife in *The Necromancer*, a Mad Lady in *The Humours of Bedlam*, Atropos, Clotho, and Colombine in *Harlequin Sorcerer*, Miss Whiffle in *Bath Unmask'd*, Florinda in *The Rover*, Miranda in *The Busy Body*, Mademoiselle in *The Provok'd Wife*, a French Woman, the fourth Nymph, Daphne, and Flora in *Apollo and Daphne*, Jenny Staple in *The Dissembled Wanton*, a Sylvan and a Female in *The Rape of Proserpine*, Damaris in *The Amorous Widow*, Corinna in *The Confederacy*, Sylvia in *The Old Bachelor*, a Noble Venetian Lady in *Italian Jealousy*, a Highlander's Wife in *The Dutch and Scotch Contention*, Parly in *The Constant Couple*, and an Amazon in *Perseus and Andromeda*. She also continued offering entr'acte dances and sharing reasonably profitable benefits each spring, her best being on 28 April 1731 when she and her husband shared gross receipts of £162 8s. 6d.

At Covent Garden she continued to the end of her career, save for a few performances in the fall of 1734 at Drury Lane. She retained her old parts but apparently added only two new ones: Phaedra in *The Necromancer* and Psyche in *The Royal Chace*. She played the Italian Lady's Servant in *Merlin* at Drury Lane in the fall of 1734 (her husband had changed over to Drury Lane that season and played the title role in *Merlin*). After that Mrs Laguerre left the stage temporarily. On 27 April 1736 at Covent Garden for her husband's benefit she returned to the stage to play in *The Provok'd Wife*. The bill offered an explanation: "N. B. Mrs. Laguerre being lame & incapable of Dancing hopes that her endeavouring to appear in the character of Mademoiselle will be accepted by her friends in lieu of any other performance." The bill noted that Mary had not appeared at Covent Garden for two years. Tickets were available at Laguerre's house next to the King's Arms in George Street, York Buildings. Mrs Laguerre returned to play the entire 1736–37 season at Covent Garden, after which she left the stage for good.

The *Daily Post* on 27 March 1739 reported that Mrs Laguerre had died the week before in Chelsea "after a most tedious and expensive Illness." She was identified as "formerly a celebrated Dancer on the Stage." She was buried on 19 April at St Martin-in-the-Fields.

The frontispiece to *Harlequin Horace* (1731), according to the *Grub Street Journal*, shows Mrs "Legar" dancing with Nivelon.

Lahante, Mons [*fl.* 1794–1796], *dancer.*

Monsieur Lahante danced at the King's Theatre from the spring of 1794 through the end of the 1795–96 season. He was in *Don Giovanni* (by Gazzaniga, not Mozart) and the ballets *Les Ruses de l'amour*, *L'Espiègle soubrette*, *L'Amant retrouvé*, *Paul et Virginie*, *L'odio vinto dall' eroismo*, *La Villageoise*, and *L'Heureux naufrage*.

La Haussage. *See* LAHOUSSAYE.

Lahoussaye, Pierre-Nicholas 1735–1818, *violinist, conductor, composer.*

Pierre-Nicholas Lahoussaye (sometimes Housset; cited in *The London Stage* as La Haussage) was born in Paris on 11 April 1735 (according to the *New Grove*; the fifth edition of *Grove* gave 12 April). He taught himself to play the violin when he was very young, but by the age of eight he was a pupil of J.-A. Piffet, a violinist at the Opéra. At nine Lahoussaye made his debut at the Concert Spirituel, and later, at a musical party at the house of Count Senneterre, he amazed some of the best violinists in Paris with his ability to perform portions of a Tartini sonata he had just heard played by André Pagin. Pagin took Pierre as a student and recommended him to Count Clermont, at whose concerts young Lahoussaye played.

About 1753, attached to the household of the Prince of Monaco, Pierre went to Padua, met Tartini, and was accepted as a pupil. With the Prince he stayed for some years at the court of Don Philip in Parma, where he studied composition under Traetta. Later he returned to Padua to study further under Tartini; then he conducted orchestras in a number of Italian towns. Grove states that Lahoussaye came to England in 1768 or later; Sainsbury gives 1769 and van der Straeten 1772. Pierre's position in London may have been leader of the orchestra at the King's Theatre. He was cited in bills on 8, 22, and 29 March 1770 as playing concertos on the violin at the King's, so van der Straeten's dating of his arrival in England is clearly incorrect.

Lahoussaye was appointed *chef d'orchèstre* of the Concert Spirituel in Paris under the directorship of Joseph Legros in 1777 (says Grove; van der Straeten dates it 1779). He gave up his post to conduct the band at the Comédie Italienne in 1781. In 1790 he began conducting at the Théâtre de Monsieur (later the Théâtre Feydeau). When the Feydeau merged with the Favart in 1801 Lahoussaye lost his position, as he did his professorship in violin at the Conservatoire when it was reconstituted. He ended up in his old age playing second violin at the Opéra, from which he was dismissed in 1813, chiefly because of age and growing deafness. He died in Paris toward the end of 1818.

Fétis, who knew Lahoussaye personally, described him toward the end of his life as a handsome man with flowing locks of white hair, still capable of playing Tartini's "Devil's Trill Sonata" with astonishing aplomb. Lahoussaye composed six violin sonatas, which were published about 1765, and a comic opera, *Les Amours de Courcy*, which was given at the Théâtre de Monsieur on 22 August 1790.

"L'Aigle." See "L'Agile."

Lair, Mr [*fl.* 1744], *dancer.*
Mr Lair danced the Swiss Servant in *The Amours Goddess* on 1 February 1744 and subsequent dates at Drury Lane, but he was replaced on 6 February.

Laithfield, Mr [*fl.* 1704], *dancer.*
Mr Laithfield danced at the Lincoln's Inn Fields playhouse on 27 July 1704.

Lalauze, Mr [*fl.* 1787–1788], *dancer.*
Among the newspaper clippings in Lysons's *Collectanea* at the Folger Shakespeare Library are a number concerning the Royalty Theatre in 1787 and 1788. A dancer named Lalauze appeared at the Royalty, but we do not know precisely when. He was very likely a son of Charles Lalauze.

Lalauze, Miss. See Masters, Mrs, née Lalauze.

Lalauze, Charles *d. 1775, dancer, actor.*
It seems probable that Charles Lalauze was the son of the Lalauze who appeared in London as a harlequin in 1726 and was, perhaps, Philippe or Marc-Antoine Lalauze. In the troupe with the elder performer was a Lalauze Junior who danced with the visiting players several times during their engagement at the Haymarket Theatre. He was first mentioned on 18 April 1726, and on 27 April at the elder Lalauze's benefit, the younger man was a Fury in a *Gardiner's Dance* and participated in a dance titled *La Triomphante*. On 9 May young Lalauze was in the "Rival Pierros" with Boudet and Mlle Violante and danced a *Moor's Dance* with the latter.

Young Lalauze returned to the Haymarket two years later, on 21 February 1728, to play Pierrot in *The Rivals* with Mme Violante's troupe. At his shared benefit with Leger on 27 March the bill stated that *The Rivals* was composed by the two beneficiaries. The work was last performed on 10 April, after which the company seems to have disbanded, though other entertainments continued to be put on by various members of the group. It is our guess that the "Pagod" listed in *The London Stage* as dancing at the Lincoln's Inn Fields playhouse on 22 April 1728 and the "La Loge" who offered a *Peasant Dance* there on 30 April was Lalauze and that the printers were simply having difficulties with his name. In Bristol on 20 July 1728 was advertised *The Rivals* at the Theatre at St Augustine's Back, with "Lallauz" as Harlequin and Mme Violante as Colombine; it was to be performed on 22 July. Monsieur Lalauze was also advertised in Bristol as dancing on 5 August.

Lalauze then went to Dublin, where he performed at the Smock Alley Theatre in 1729–30 and was in Mme Violante's Children's Company in Dame Street in 1730–31. Just how young a performer had to be to qualify for that troupe is not known, and the group's name suggests that Lalauze may still have been a minor; his accomplishments in London in previous years, on the other hand, would suggest a more mature person.

In 1732–33 Lalauze was in London at the Haymarket again, still with Violante's company, which on 4 September 1732 was advertised as just arrived (from Ireland?). With Tobin on that date Lalauze danced *Two Pierrots*, and on the eleventh he danced Pierrot in *The White Joke*. His attachment to the pierrot character is what suggests that he was the junior, not the senior Lalauze in the visiting foreign troupe in 1726; the elder Lalauze was clearly a harlequin, and the younger, as has been seen, seems to have played that character only once.

On 23 October 1734 Lalauze made his first appearance at Drury Lane Theatre, dancing *Pierrots* with Nivelon. During the 1734–35 season he busied himself offering entr'acte turns and appearing as a Pierrot in *Cephalus and Procris*, *Columbine Courtezan*, and *Harlequin Orpheus*, and playing an Italian in *Merlin*. He was, it is most likely, the Charles "Latouze" who was one of the original 24 members of the Sublime Society of Beefsteaks when it was formed in 1735 by the harlequin John Rich.

Indeed, beginning in the fall of 1735 Lalauze began an engagement at Covent Garden Theatre, which was managed by Rich. His first appearance there was on 3 October; with Nivelon, who had also joined the troupe, he danced *Two Pierrots*. Rich paid Lalauze 16s. 8d. nightly for performing 150 nights in 1735–36; the contract did not include a benefit, according to the account books, though he had a rather special one in the spring. During the season he offered as usual his entr'acte specialty dances and played a Clown in *The Rape of Proserpine*, a Boor Servant in *Apollo and Daphne*, the Doctor's Servant in *The Royal Chace*, and Petit Maître in *Perseus and Andromeda*—all probably pierrot characters. On 8 April 1736 *Le Mariage forcé* was performed as an afterpiece at Lalauze's benefit. The performers were French comedians, most of whom had just arrived. Lalauze played Pierrot and between the acts danced *French Peasants* with Mlle D'Hervigni. His gross receipts for the evening came to £131 18s. 6d.

He continued at Covent Garden through the 1738–39 season, adding to his repertoire such new parts as a Fury in *The Necromancer*, Shift in *The Cheats of Scapin*, and Pierrot in *The Jealous Farmer Deceiv'd*. He played Shift on 2 April 1737, and the bill observed that it was his first attempt at acting in English. He may not have been successful, for he did not try the part again, nor do the records suggest that he attempted many other roles in English. On 14 November 1739 Lalauze rejoined the Drury Lane Company, performing specialty dances, often with Leviez, and appearing as a Pierrot in *Columbine Courtezan*, *The Fortune Tellers*, and *Harlequin Skeleton*.

He returned to Covent Garden in 1740–41 at £1 10s. daily and a benefit with £50 house charges. When he danced Pierrot in *The Royal Chace* on 21 January 1741, the bill noted that he had not appeared on that stage for three years, a rather gross exaggeration. That spring he also danced Pierrot in *Harlequin a Statue* and was the Petit Maître in *Perseus and Andromeda*. *Faulkner's Dublin Journal* on 27 June reported that "This week arrived here from London, *Mr Lalauze*, the famous Comick Dancer, who intends to perform with Madam Chateauneuf, in Aungier Street." One of his appearances there was as Pierrot in *L'Arlequin mariner*. During the 1741–42 season at Covent Garden Lalauze pulled a tendon in his leg and could not dance; Rich gave him an early benefit on 1 March 1742, tickets for which were available from Lalauze at his lodgings at Widow Gwinn's in Drury Lane near the Castle Tavern. His dancing was curtailed until the following winter.

During the 1740s and 1750s Lalauze continued appearing in pantomimes and entr'acte turns. He occasionally added to his repertoire—Earth in *The Rape of Proserpine*, Drudge in *Orpheus and Eurydice*, a pierrot in *Merlin* and *The Perplex'd Husband*—but for the most part he kept to his earlier roles. He introduced a number of his pupils to Covent Garden audiences; many of them were young boys and girls not named in the bills ("A Ball Minuet by La Lauze and two of his scholars, of three months learning only, who never appear'd before," or dancing "By the English boy and Girl"), but sometimes names were mentioned, as in the case of Lalauze's apprentices Dennison, Master Settree, and little Miss Toogood. Oddly, the bills did not provide a Christian name for Lalauze's own daughter, who was born in 1753 and made her debut at her father's benefit on 25 April 1759. (She performed occasionally as Lalauze's daughter and later married a Mr Masters; under that name she sang and acted to the end of the century.) A letter in the *Daily Advertiser* of 30 April 1747 said that the pupils of Lalauze did very well in their performances at Covent Garden; the writer praised Lalauze for being "a modest Man, though a Frenchman. . . ."

In the Burney papers at the British Library is a clipping belonging to 1757 regarding Lalauze's teaching:

Mr. Lalauze, Dancing-Master, of the Theatre Royal in Covent-Garden, is removed from Great Suffolk-street to Leicester-square, where he has a large convenient Room separate from the House, and proposes to teach young Gentlemen and Ladies, from six or seven years of Age to twelve, twice a Week, at Two Guineas a Quarter, and private Scholars as usual.

His work as a teacher caused him to reduce his schedule at the playhouse, as the bills indicate. By the early 1750s he appeared only occasionally. He was, however, earning £100 annually or 12s. daily in 1760 at Covent Garden, and that was evidently only part of his salary, for a paylist in 1761 shows him receiving a total of £210 annually.

Lalauze rarely performed elsewhere during the 1740s and 1750s. He is recorded as playing a Frenchman in *Harlequin Hussar* at Tottenham Court in August 1743, and he may have made a few other appearances that were not recorded. And though his specialty was dancing, he tried again an acting role: on 23

LALAUZE

April 1745 for his benefit at Covent Garden he attempted Shylock in *The Merchant of Venice* and spoke a new prologue.

His benefit bill on 29 April 1763 stated that he had been extremely ill and would not be able to perform that night. Tickets were available from him "at his house the Two Green Lamps, in Leicester Fields." He did not perform again for some time. On 26 December 1768 the Covent Garden playbill noted that he would dance the Boor Servant in *Apollo and Daphne* for his first appearance in six years. Fanny Burney went to an elegant masquerade at Lalauze's house on 10 January 1770—probably an affair not unlike those run by Mrs Cornelys and something he did for profit. By that time he was no longer a member of the Covent Garden company.

On 14 February 1770 Foote allowed Lalauze a benefit at the Haymarket Theatre. The *Gazetteer* on 8 February had contained a lengthy explanation of the dancer's situation. Lalauze told his public that he had been a resident of the country for 42 years and had been retained by the late John Rich of Covent Garden Theatre for 27 years. Rich had promised Lalauze that whenever age or infirmity forced him to retire from the stage he would give Lalauze an annuity of £50. Unfortunately, Rich's will did not confirm the agreement. His successors at Covent Garden gave Lalauze the annuity for three years, however, on the odd condition that he should not perform at Covent Garden or at any other theatre. Lalauze had hoped the annuity would continue, but the patent had been sold and his income stopped. The managers of Covent Garden had employed Lalauze in 1768–69, he said, but he was not hired for 1769–70. Samuel Foote then generously offered him the Haymarket for the February 1770 benefit, free of house charges.

The *Town and Country Magazine* reviewed the benefit performance:

On the 14th instant was performed for the benefit of Mr. Lalauze, at the theatre royal in the Haymarket, *The Lovers of their Country; or, Themistocles and Aristides*.

Whether the patriotic title of this play, or the particular interest of Mr. Laulauze effected it, we cannot decide, but the house was as full as if Mr. Garrick was to have appeared in one of his first characters. The person who spoke, or rather attempted to speak the prologue, was so intenacious in his memory, that before he had repeated four lines he hitched; and, notwithstanding the utmost assiduity of the prompter, joined to every effort of the speaker's recollection, he could not get a single line farther: the audience seeing his distress, very good naturedly remitted this part of the entertainment, not to delay the succeeding piece, which was represented with *equal accuracy* and *propriety*.

The performance, given by "A Set of Gentlemen and Ladies who never appeared on any stage," must have been a disaster. And Lalauze in his old age dancing a louvre and minuet with his daughter and appearing as Pierrot in *The Country Farmer Deceiv'd* may not have saved the day. But at least the house was full and the dancer must have made a handsome sum.

Lalauze's last benefit, and perhaps his last public appearance, was at the Haymarket on 24 April 1771. The afterpiece was *Cupid's Friendship*, in which Lalauze presumably danced Pierrot. With his daughter he offered a louvre, minuet, and allemande. Reed in his "Notitia Dramatica" copied a newspaper article of April 1775 which reported that sometime the previous month Charles Lalauze, "the celebrated Pierrot," had died near Paris.

Lalauze, [Philippe?] *d. c. 1751?, dancer, actor.*

At the Haymarket Theatre from 24 March to 11 May 1726 a troupe of comedians from the Continent performed a variety of entertainments, mostly *commedia dell' arte* pieces. The harlequin of the troupe, and possibly the master of it, was a Monsieur Lalauze. He offered entr'acte dances and appeared as Harlequin in *Les Deux Pierrots* (on 27 April 1726: "In which Monsieur Lalause the Arlequin will perform without a Mask") and presumably many other pieces. In the troupe was a Lalauze Junior, who danced and was, it appears, a pierrot. The younger Lalauze we take to have been Charles, who returned to England in 1728 and spent the ensuing 42 years entertaining English audiences.

The elder Lalauze may have been Philippe Lalauze, who was a harlequin. Fuchs in his *Lexique* notes that Philippe was performing as early as 1701 on the Continent with Maurice and Allard. He worked as a supernumerary, then danced with Allard in 1706 and 1711. He was with Octave's company from 1713 to 1716 and toured the provinces after that. He has been traced to Prague in 1718, the Hague in 1727, Hamburg in 1741, and Strasbourg in 1742. He died about 1751. Fuchs thought that the Lalauze who was the father of Charles may have been Marc-Antoine Lalauze rather than Philippe, but the known facts about Philippe's specialty and his whereabouts, especially in 1727, point to his having been the performer who came to London with his son.

"L'Allemand, Mme" [fl. 1779–1780], *dancer.*

In the Burney Collection at the British Library is a list of dancers at the opera house (the King's Theatre) in 1779–80. On it is a Madame "L'Allemand"—very likely a pseudonym—who was called one of the first dancers, *demi-caractere*. She is not listed in *The London Stage*.

Lalli. *See also* LOLLI.

Lalli, Mr [fl. 1778–1806], *dancing master.*

The accounts for Drury Lane Theatre name a Mr Lalli (or Lolli) as a dancing master from as early as 4 October 1778, when he was paid £1 17s. 6d., to 1805–6, when he was on the paylist at 6s. 6d. (probably daily).

L'Allouette, Mons [fl. 1793–1797], *dancer, equestrian.*

Monsieur L'Allouette was a member of Astley's troupe at the Amphitheatre Royal in Peter Street, Dublin, on 31 January 1793, and took a role in the pantomime *La Forêt noir*. At Astley's Amphitheatre at the south end of Westminster Bridge in London he served as an equestrian in May and August 1793, and on 22 August 1795 he danced the Spanish Lover in *Harlequin Invincible*. L'Allouette was with Handy's company from London in March 1796 at the Amphitheatre in Limekiln Lane, Bristol; he was given a benefit on 29 March. He returned to Bristol on 6 February 1797 in a new circus troupe of combined Handy and Astley performers. The last reference to him that we have found is in a Manchester bill dated 19 August 1799; he was the Clown in *Harlequin Phoenix*.

Lally, Mr [fl. 1720–1722], *dancer.*

On 21 and 23 May 1720 "Lally's brother" danced at Drury Lane. Lally would have been Edward (or Edmund?) Lally, we would guess, who had been performing at Drury Lane since the previous November. The brother's Christian name, unfortunately, was not given. Lally's brother danced again at Drury Lane on 23 May 1721 (Edward was still with the troupe) and on 2 May 1722 at Lincoln's Inn Fields (where Edward was then performing). The bills contain no further references to Lally's brother.

Lally, Edward [or Edmund?] c. 1677–1760, *dancer.*

Though John Weaver in his *Lectures* in 1721 listed among the important dancers in England Edward *and* Edmund Lally, Charles Beecher Hogan in *Shakespeare in the Theatre* takes that to be an error and treats Edward and Edmund as variant names for the same man. Though the evidence is not conclusive, we take Hogan to be correct. Edward Lally was born about 1677. On 10 November 1719 at Drury Lane Theatre was presented a "Pastoral Dance from Myrtillo, in which Mr Lallie performs a Part, it being the first Time of his Appearance on any Stage." He was then about 42, rather old to be making a stage debut, but perhaps he had pursued a career as a dancing master, shunning public appearances.

He danced regularly at Drury Lane throughout the 1719–20 season, offering such entr'acte turns as *Forlanta* with Miss Smith, a *Shepherd and Shepherdess* with Miss Tenoe, and many dances not given titles in the bills. One of his pupils also danced at Drury Lane that season. At Lally's benefit on 21 May 1720 his brother (name not known) danced, as he did again in May 1721 and May 1722.

Edward Lally again danced at Drury Lane in 1720–21, but he and his brother moved to Lincoln's Inn Fields in the fall of 1721 and performed there through 1722–23 and part of 1723–24. As at Drury Lane, he was used as an entr'acte entertainer in dances usually not titled in the bills. On 10 April 1722 at his benefit his gross receipts were a very handsome £129 0s. 6d. The Lincoln's Inn Fields manager and harlequin John Rich gave Lally his first pantomime role, Leander (Mars) in *Jupiter and Europa*, probably on 23 and certainly on 25 March 1723. At his benefit on 29 April, which brought

LALLY

in £155 14s., the bill provided his full name: Edward Lally. On 27 January 1724 he was paid £20 for performances given by his two sons the previous season. The sons would presumably have been Michael and Samuel. Lally, along with his son Michael, evidently began the 1723–24 season, but they were never named in any bills. A letter at Harvard, written by John Rich, officially discharged the two Lallys on 3 December 1723. The Lally who danced a Follower of Mars in *The Loves of Mars and Venus* at Drury Lane on 27 January 1724 and subsequent dates may have been Edward.

On 16 October 1724 at Lincoln's Inn Fields "Ed. Lalley" was back, dancing a *Passacaille* with Mrs Wall. In the Lincoln's Inn Fields accounts are entries concerning "H." Lally—which may be an error for E. Lally. On 9 October 1724 he was paid £1 (perhaps his weekly wage, for he received the same amount on 16 September 1726).

During the 1724–25 season Edward Lally offered entr'acte dances and played a Fury in *Harlequin Sorcerer* and a Follower of Mars in *Mars and Venus*. At his benefit on 20 April 1725 he danced a new *Polonese* with Mrs Wall and took in a total of £167 11s. 6d. He remained at Lincoln's Inn Fields through 1726–27, adding such parts to his repertoire as Mezzetin (Apollo) in *Jupiter and Europa*, a Mezzetin Man in *The Necromancer*, a Frenchman in *Apollo and Daphne*, and the Mad Dancing Master in *The Humours of Bedlam*. After the spring of 1727, Edward left the stage.

The *Public Advertiser* on 18 January 1760 reported that "Edmund" Lally, formerly a dancer at Drury Lane and the father of Michael Lally, had died the previous day in his eighty-third year at his house in Chapel Street, Bedford Row.

Lally, Michael *d. 1757?, dancer, choreographer.*

On 17 October 1721 at the Lincoln's Inn Fields Theatre Lally Junior danced between the acts. He was, we take it, Michael Lally, whose father Edward (or Edmund?) was a dancing master and member of the Lincoln's Inn Fields troupe. The senior Lally also danced on that date. The following 26 April 1722, according to Latreille, Lally Jr composed a new dance of two harlequins, two punches, and a Scottish highlander for Mrs Rogeir's benefit. *The London Stage*, however, transcribes that bill as simply being a *Scotch Highlander* dance performed by the senior Lally. The younger Lally's work at that early stage in his career seems not to have been important enough to have been cited in the bills more than a few times during the season. He was at Lincoln's Inn Fields again in 1722–23, dancing entr'acte turns regularly, and probably on 23 and certainly on 25 March 1723 he played Mezzetin (Apollo) in *Jupiter and Europa*; his father was Leander (Mars). He and his father must have remained on the roster into the 1723–24 season, though they were not named in any bills; a letter now at Harvard from John Rich notes that Edward and Michael Lally were discharged from Lincoln's Inn Fields on 3 December 1723.

The elder Lally appeared briefly at Drury Lane Theatre the January following that discharge, and then he returned to Lincoln's Inn Fields in the fall of 1724. Michael was not active—or at least not mentioned in any London playbills—until 20 February 1725, when he danced a Shepherd in *Apollo and Daphne* at Drury Lane. Perhaps he was one of the minor dancers at that house throughout the 1724–25 season; not until 1725–26 was he very frequently mentioned in the bills. He participated in entr'acte dances and repeated the part of the Shepherd in *Apollo and Daphne*, and on 13 May 1726 the benefit bill provided his full name, Michael Lally, and indicated that he danced that night in a *Spanish Dance* and performed a *Pastoral* with Mrs Walter. That he was given a solo benefit signifies his importance in the troupe; in addition to performing he probably served as a dancing master and choreographer. In 1726–27 he was seen as Mercury in *Harlequin Doctor Faustus*, the Statue in *The Miser* (later called *Harlequin's Triumph*), and a number of specialty dances between the acts. At his solo benefit on 20 April 1727 he performed the *Coquet Shepherdess* with Mrs Booth and danced in *The Fawns*.

Michael Lally continued dancing at Drury Lane through the spring of 1734, several of his roles in pantomimes being those he had essayed earlier. Among the new ones he tried were Mephistophilus and Mars in *Harlequin Doctor Faustus*, a Brideman in *Harlequin Happy and Poor Pierrot Married*, Perseus in *Perseus and Andromeda*, a Sea God, a Gormogon, and a Gardener in *Cephalus and Procris*, Vertumnus in *Cupid and Psyche*, a Wind in *The Tempest*, a Yeoman and Colin in *The Country Revels*, and a Shepherd, a Fingalian, and Le Coutillion in *The Harlot's Progress*. At his benefit in May 1728 he danced in a new *Spanish Entry* and performed a muzette with Mrs Booth; "Young Master Lally" also danced. He was, we believe, Samuel Lally, Michael's younger brother, who had been appearing as a dancer in London since 1727. When he and Michael were at Drury Lane together, the bills distinguished the two by using Master or Junior for Samuel and sometimes Lally Senior would be mentioned—not a reference, we think, to their father, but to Michael, the elder brother.

The *Daily Journal* reported on 3 April 1732 that "Mr Michael Lally, an eminent Dancing Master & a man of an universal good Character, was lately married to a Berkshire lady of a handsome fortune." His good luck did not cause him to leave the stage, however. Indeed, he continued as busy as ever, dancing his pantomime roles and appearing in such entr'acte turns as *La Badine*, *Two Pierrots*, *Le Badinage champêtre*, *Grand Dance in Momus*, *Revellers*, and *English Maggot*.

Beginning in 1734–35 Lally performed at Covent Garden under John Rich, his first appearance being on 2 October 1734 as a Fury in *The Necromancer*. His association with Covent Garden continued through the 1742–43 season, though after 1735–36 he seems to have done very little performing. For two seasons, however, at £100 annually, he was seen as a Demon and Water in *The Rape of Proserpine*, an Infernal in *Perseus and Andromeda*, a Rural Swain in *The Royal Chace*, and his role in *The Necromancer*. He was chiefly employed as an entr'acte dancer, appearing in such dances as *La Coquette François*, *Les Bergeries*, *La Tambourine*, *Pigmalion*, a *Scot's Dance*, *Shepherd and Shepherdess*, a *Pastoral Dance*, and dances "appropriate" to *Macbeth*. Many times his partner was Mlle Salle. At benefit time his address was given as in Southampton Row, Bloomsbury, where he lived until 1740. In 1741 he was living in Great Russell Street, beside Montague House.

Though Lally seems not to have danced regularly during the winter seasons in the late 1730s (he may have been serving as dancing master, for he still exhibited pupils) he appeared at benefit time and usually offered a dance or two. In 1738 he danced a minuet, and the bill noted that it was his first appearance "since his lameness." His last benefit was on 14 April 1743, when he danced a louvre and minuet with Anne Auretti.

A Michael Lally, Esq, Common Hunt, became a freeman in the Worshipfull Company of Musicians on 25 October 1752 and was admitted to livery on 7 August 1754. The Common Hunt had originally been the title of a position as keeper of the city's hounds but its holder had become an attendant on the Lord Mayor's Lady; the Common Hunt served as a master of ceremonies at public balls and other entertainments. It seems probable that Michael Lally the dancer after his retirement from the theatre was granted the post and, in consequence, was made a freeman in the Worshipfull Company of Musicians. Lally was specified as the Common Hunt in the *Gentleman's Magazine* when it reported his death on 2 September 1757.

A Michael Lally, Esq, drew up his will on 26 August 1757, and though there is no proof positive that he was the dancer, it seems almost certain. The date is about right; the mention in the will of a son Edmund fits with the fact that Michael's father was named Edward or Edmund; and Michael cited a daughter Elizabeth, a name we know to have been his wife's. Lally left to his "poor Dear ffather" an annuity of £30. To his wife (not cited by name) he left his house, stables, and land at Mill Hill, Hendon. To his daughter Elizabeth and his son Edmund (when he should reach the age of 23) Lally gave £2000 each. He provided for an annuity of £10 for his sister Catherine Lally and gave £10 each to his sisters Mary Lally and Ann Lowes and to his brother Thomas. To his friend James Hutton he left a ring and £10. Lally specified that his son William Michael Lally and his daughter Elizabeth Lally should inherit the remainder of the estate. The marriage Michael Lally the dancer made in 1732 was to a Berkshire lady of good fortune, and the will certainly suggests a man of means. Further, since the dancer was married in 1732, his children by 1757 would not have been much beyond their majority; the will indicates that his daughter Elizabeth had not yet married, that his son Edmund was not yet 23, and that his son William Michael was apparently unmarried. The will was proved on 15 September 1757.

LALLY

The will of Hester Booth, made on 2 February 1769 and proved on 3 March 1773, provides us with the Christian name of Lally's wife. Hester Booth left a diamond ring to Elizabeth Lally, widow of Michael Lally.

Lally, Samuel *1714–1735, dancer.*

Lally Junior, described in the Drury Lane playbill of 9 November 1727 as "a young Son of Mr Lally's" made his stage debut dancing with an unnamed little girl. The young man was Samuel Lally, who was born in 1714 and could be correctly described in 1727 as Master Lally; he was the son of the Mr Lally who lived in Chapel Street in 1735—that is Edward (or Edmund?) Lally, who had just retired from the stage. At Drury Lane was Michael Lally, another son of Edward Lally; he had begun his dancing career in 1721 and was, one guesses, older than Samuel by some years. Though Samuel supposedly made his debut in 1727, an entry in the Lincoln's Inn Fields accounts dated 27 January 1724 suggests that he may have appeared earlier. That note directs that "H." Lally (an error for E. Lally?) should be paid £20 for performances given by his two sons the previous season. The sons in question may have been Samuel and Michael Lally.

Master Lally or Young Master Lally or Lally Jr, as some bills called Samuel, continued offering entr'acte turns, and on 19 March 1728 in *Harlequin Happy and Poor Pierrot Married* he and Miss Brett were "Children of Love, representing two Harlequins." He repeated that role the following season and again offered specialty dances. He played the Gardener in *Cephalus and Procris* in 1730–31, and in 1731–32 he was a Gorgon, Brideman, and a Mezzetin Man in *Perseus and Andromeda*, and a Triton in *Cephalus and Procris*, in addition to his entr'acte chores. In 1732–33 he added to his list of parts a Peasant in *The Country Revels*, a Scaramouch Man in *Harlequin Restored*, a Shepherd in *The Judgment of Paris*, and Scaramouch and a Companion of Paris in *The Harlot's Progress*.

The bills in 1733–34 sometimes cited Lally as Junior and sometimes as S. Lally. He had to be distinguished from Lally Senior (Michael, we take it), who danced some of the same kinds of pantomime roles and entr'acte specialties. Samuel continued in his old parts and also was seen as Scaramouch and Mercury in *Harlequin Doctor Faustus*, a Hungarian in *The Harlot's Progress*, Wind and Water in *The Tempest*, and a Sylvan in *Cupid and Psyche*. Some of the specialty dances he appeared in were *La Badine*, a *Polish Dance*, *English Maggot* (a great favorite, which he danced with Mrs Walter), *La Badinage champetre*, the *Dutchman and His Wife*, and *Revellers*—many of those having been dances in which Michael had appeared.

Samuel and Michael Lally both moved to Covent Garden in 1734–35 where Samuel was seen in *Pigmalion*, *The Medley*, a *Scot's Dance*, *Grecian Sailors*, and *English Maggot*, and was an Infernal in *Perseus and Andromeda* and a Demon and Earth in *The Rape of Proserpine*. On 14 December 1734 a dance called *La Coquette François* was performed; the bill said that Lally and S. Lally danced in it. On the same bill in *The Medley* "Lally Jr" danced. The manner in which the names were specified would seem to suggest that three Lallys performed that evening, but it is the only such instance we have found, and since on other nights S. Lally appeared in *The Medley*, we take Lally Jr to have been Samuel.

The London *Daily Post and General Advertiser* on 30 June 1735 reported that "On Tuesday last [24 June] died at Islington, in the 21st year of his age, Mr. Samuel Lally, a very pretty dancer at the Theatre in Covent Garden." He was buried in Lamb's Conduit Fields "in a brick vault not yet finish'd; he was youngest son to Mr Lally of Chapel Street."

Laloge. *See* LALAUZE.

Lalouette. *See* L'ALLOUETTE.

"La Lucchesina." *See* MARCHESINI, MARIA ANTONIA.

L'Amand, Mlle. *See* ST AMAND, MLLE.

"La Margerita." *See* DE L'ÉPINE.

Lamarre, John Billon [*fl.* 1671–1676], *singer.*

The Lord Chamberlain's accounts show that John Billon Lamarre was admitted to the King's Musick as one of the Gentlemen of the Chapel Royal on 23 July 1671. *The Old Cheque Book of the Chapel Royal*, however, cites Lamarre as being sworn a Gentleman of the Chapel Royal in ordinary on 19 February 1676. He may have served in an "extraordinary" (without salary) position between those two dates, waiting for a salaried post to become vacant.

Lamash, Philip d. 1800, actor.

According to the unreliable *Secret History of the Green Room* (1790), Philip Lamash was the son of a French tutor to the Duke of Gloucester's children. Taught fencing and "some polite languages" by his father, young Philip was also trained as a teacher, but he determined to go on the stage instead. Lamash's first appearance of record occurred at the Haymarket Theatre on 21 July 1773 as James in the premiere of Foote's comedy *The Bankrupt*. That night he also acted James in the afterpiece *The Mock Doctor*. On 28 July he played Lord Brilliant in *The Register Office*, and during the remainder of that summer in Foote's company he was also seen as Young Inkle in *A Trip to Portsmouth*, a comic sketch by G. A. Stevens that premiered on 11 August, and as an unspecified character in *The Orators* on 1 September.

During the next year Lamash probably gained some experience in the provinces, perhaps at Brighton, and then was engaged by Garrick at £1 10s. per week for the 1774–75 season at Drury Lane. Garrick gave him some instruction, according to *The Secret History of the Green Room*, and brought him on as Rovewell in *The Fair Quaker* on 29 September 1774. He played an unspecified role in *A Christmas Tale* on 5 October, Lord Lurewell in *The Miller of Mansfield* on 8 October, and Dapper in *The Alchemist* on 24 October. After repeating Rovewell on 31 October, Lamash appeared on 5 November 1774 as one of the Shepherds in the premiere of *The Maid of the Oaks*, a highly successful piece by General Burgoyne which received a number of performances that winter, mainly because of the superb scenery provided by De Loutherbourg and his painters. Lamash also appeared that season as Biondello in *Catharine and Petruchio*, an unspecified role in many performances of *Harlequin's Jacket*, Conrade in *Much Ado about Nothing*, Harry in *The Male Coquette*, an unspecified character in *A Peep behind the Curtain*, Jessamy in *Bon Ton*, Bowman in *Lethe*, a Brother in *Comus*, Spruce in *The School for Wives*, and Flimsy in Waldon's unsuccessful farce, *The Contrast; or, The Jew and Married Courtezan*, which had its single performance on 12 May 1775.

At Drury Lane over the next eight seasons, Lamash failed to achieve the distinction that his handsome face and figure promised, but he did serve as a useful player of many tertiary roles, such as Paris in *Romeo and Juliet*, Radel in *A Christmas Tale*, Harwood in *The Register Office*, Guildenstern in *Hamlet*, Solerino in *The Merchant of Venice*, Fabian in *Twelfth Night*, Borachio in *Much Ado about Nothing*, Sellaway in *The Gamesters*, Jack Meggot in *The Suspicious Husband*, Roderigo in *Othello*, and Sebastian in *The Tempest*. On 23 January 1776 he acted the title role in *Epicoene* and on 8 May 1777 he created the role of Trip in the first performance

By permission of the Trustees of the British Museum

PHILIP LAMASH, as Colombine's Lover
artist unknown

of *The School for Scandal*, a part he subsequently held in the repertory. On 5 May 1779 he shared £104 12s. 6d. in benefit receipts with Giuseppe Grimaldi. At that time Lamash lodged at No 3, Air Street, Piccadilly.

From 1779 through 1781 Lamash also acted with Colman's summer company at the Haymarket. His roles there included, among others, the Squire in *Piety in Pattens*, Eustace in *Love in a Village*, Robin in *The Suicide*, Junius in *Bonduca*, Lord Trinket in *The Jealous Wife*, Idle in *The Son-in-Law*, Vane in *The Chapter of Accidents*, Spruce in *Summer Amusement*, and Colonel Frankly in *Man and Wife*.

In reviewing his performances at the Haymarket in the summer of 1781, the *Public Advertiser* on 7 August was of the opinion that Lamash did "well enough in *every* thing—if he would learn to stand *upright*, and dispose properly of his *Hands*." But Lamash, it seems, was not inclined to work at improving his craft, preferring to occupy himself in pleasurable pursuits. His handsome head, according to *The Secret History of the Green Rooms*, was turned by the adoration of women. At one time he was the "uncommon favourite" of the beautiful and controversial actress, Sophia Baddeley. Then he was "doated on" by the mistress of a foreign ambassador. For a while he enjoyed the lavish attentions of the celebrated courtesan, Catherine Frederick, who, though she was being kept by the Duke of Queensberry, lavished presents upon the actor and "often desired his Grace to wait in the next room until Lamash was gone." When she and Lamash were attempting to leave together for a continental sojourn, the Duke had her arrested on Westminster Bridge. His nontheatrical enterprises kept Lamash in debt, for the Drury Lane account books in 1776–77 and 1777–78 reveal his attempts to pay back large amounts in loans, such as £19 1s. 9d. on 1 December 1777, a difficult feat when he was earning but £1 10s. per week.

Lamash began the 1782–83 engagement at Drury Lane as usual, playing some of his regular characters, such as Fabian, Trip, and Biondello. On 17 October 1782 he appeared as Jessamy in *Bon Ton*, but on 24 October his name was omitted from the bill of *Robinson Crusoe*. He had gone to Dublin, where he made his debut at the Crow Street Theatre on 5 November. By February 1783 he joined the company at the Theatre Royal, Edinburgh, playing there until May as Belcour in *The West Indian*, Courtwell in *Woman's a Riddle*, Flutter in *The Belle's Stratagem*, Jessamy in *Bon Ton*, La Nippe in *The Belle of the Manor*, Lissardo in *The Wonder! A Woman Keeps a Secret*, Lord Foppington in *A Trip to Scarborough*, Sir Brilliant Fashion in *The Way to Keep Him*, Sir Harry Muff in *The Rival Candidates*, Squire Groom in *Love à-la-Mode*, Squire Turniptop in *Piety in Pattens*, Vermilion in *The Wives Revenged*, and Macheath in *The Beggar's Opera*.

After playing briefly at Leeds and York in 1783, Lamash returned to Edinburgh for three seasons, through 1786–87. Among his more important roles during that period were Captain Bobadil in *Every Man in His Humour*, Doricourt in *The Belle's Stratagem*, Lothario in *The Fair Penitent*, Mercutio in *Romeo and Juliet*, Sir Andrew Aguecheek in *Twelfth Night*, and Young Meadows in *Love in a Village*. Though he was well received as an actor at Edinburgh, his conceit, self-importance, and pretentions as sportsman, beau, and man of fortune made him obnoxious socially.

Acting with him in the Edinburgh company in 1787 was "Mrs Lamash." According to *The Secret History of the Green Room*, written in 1790, after Catherine Frederick died Lamash took in a Miss Smith, a linen draper's daughter, "who has lived with him ever since." Presumably she was the Mrs Lamash acting at Edinburgh. Often in debt and social disfavor, Lamash, it is said, had her pose as the disowned daughter of an Irish peer in order to persuade the compassionate Lady Elphinstone to support his benefit and introduce them to the best Edinburgh society.

In 1787–88 Lamash returned to Drury Lane, reappearing on 2 October 1787 as Sir Brilliant Fashion in *The Way to Keep Him*. He acted Sparkish in *The Country Girl* the next night, and the Marquis in *The Englishman in Paris* on 6 October, on which night his name was added to the paylist for 10s. per day, or £3 per week. For his benefit on 14 May 1788, at which he shared net receipts of £163 4s. with Staunton, Lamash acted Petulant in *The Way of the World*; tickets could be had of him in Queen Court, Great Queen Street, Lincoln's Inn Fields.

Over the next several seasons at Drury Lane, Lamash offered his customary repertoire. According to notations in the Winston papers at the Folger Library, he could not play lords well, but his "menial countenance" made him excel at valets and coxcombs. The author of *The Secret History of the Green Room* (1792) thought that his chief merit was in representing Frenchmen, but in both fops and gentlemen "he bawls too much to please a London audience." (But he may have learned in time to subdue his voice, for in 1800 G. F. Cooke remarked in his manuscript diary [now in the Harvard Theatre Collection] that not only were his portrayals of Jessamy and Trip "sufficient to stamp him an actor" but that in fine gentlemen "he stood unequalled by any actor I ever saw.") Lamash was no special favorite in 1788–89; his benefit on 2 June 1789, shared with Burton, brought net receipts of only about £59.

In the middle of the 1789–90 season, while employed at £4 per week, Lamash suddenly deserted Drury Lane. An entry in the account books dated 30 January 1790 reads, "Mr. Lamash Run away List low:^{d} 13:4 p^r. diem." Evidently Lamash owed someone a debt of £17 and decided to flee rather than pay, though on the day before his departure, according to *The Secret History of the Green Room*, he had paid 16 guineas for two miniatures. He had gone to Edinburgh, where on 6 February 1790 he appeared as Sparkish in *The Country Girl* and Bagatelle in *The Poor Soldier*. On 10 February he acted Tom in *The Conscious Lovers*, on 15 February Lord Miniken in *Bon Ton*, and on 27 February Cloten in *Cymbeline*.

On 6 December 1793, Isabella Abercromby, age 26, who had "Died of a Cramp in the Stomach" and was identified as "Late Spouse of Mr Lamash Comedien from Lieth Walk," was buried in the Calton Burying Ground, Edinburgh. She was perhaps his second "wife," for the Mrs Lamash who had acted at Edinburgh in 1787 presumably had been Miss Smith.

Still at Edinburgh in 1794, Lamash solicited an engagement from Tate Wilkinson at York, writing "that his life was a torment in the Edinburgh theatre . . . and that he was much improved in his acting, as in his private conduct, which was quite reformed with every attention to oeconomy." Wilkinson engaged Lamash and asked him to join the York company at Doncaster in September. Lamash played for a while at Lancaster in the summer but did not show up in Doncaster as agreed. He went so far as to borrow £10 from Wilkinson and promised in letter after letter to join the company at Hull, where he was advertised by Wilkinson to make his debut on 26 September as Ranger in *The Suspicious Husband*. Again he failed to arrive, causing Wilkinson to write sarcastically in his *Wandering Patentee*:

I have not made any comments on such behaviour, but must observe that it was the most wanton and unprovoked I ever experienced. I did, as in duty bound, print a few severe lines, to explain to the public how ill I judged he had behaved. . . . No,— I leave Mr. Lamash to be his own judge and juror, and think he must feel contrition; for surely he has pride and spirit superior to imagine a 10l. bill an object sufficient as to certainly taint his integrity and honour, if any remains of such qualities are in his possession. There is no one propensity which I despise more than envy, detraction, and malevolence. . . . He urges, in a letter to me, dated Monday January 5, 1795, that I have much endeavoured to *injure* him, but *such* efforts *have*, and always must, prove BARREN against a MAN who fame in his profession, and his independence in his present circumstances, make him the envy of *some*, and the *delight* of others. I wish I could say the same myself, as he must be a happy man indeed.

Lamash, in any event, though he did not keep his commitment to Wilkinson, repaid the £10 in February 1795.

Lamash remained with the Edinburgh company through at least 1796. In the summer of 1797 he went to play at Crow Street, Dublin, where he remained for three years. He died at Dublin on 28 January 1800. In his diary G. F. Cooke recorded on 29 January having been informed by Hamerton of Lamash's death the previous evening: "He had been in a declining state for some weeks past, partly as supposed, from living too fast." On 30 January 1800 Lamash was buried in St Mark's churchyard, Dublin, near the grave of the actor Thomas Blanchard. The expenses of his funeral were paid by Mr Jones, the Crow Street patentee, who had continued to provide Lamash's salary during his illness.

On 16 February 1800, Cooke recorded in his diary that "Cornely's called upon me, respecting Mrs Lamash." She was, it seems, at least the third woman of that name. In his *Memoirs*, Edward Cape Everard described her as a Miss Loftis of Newcastle, whose parents kept in that city a hotel and tavern called The

Turf. Probably she did not benefit from the Drury Lane Theatrical Fund, for though Lamash had subscribed 10s. 6d. to it beginning in 1775, he had, according to Winston's Fund Book (at the Folger Library), neglected payment in 1797. Everard reported that the widowed Mrs Lamash returned home to her parents; soon after, this "accomplished and most amiable young lady" was suddenly taken ill while swimming one morning and was "brought home a corpse."

Lamash was pictured as Colombine's Lover in *Harlequin's Frolick* by an unknown engraver in 1790.

Lamb, Mr [fl. 1774], *actor.*

At the Haymarket Theatre on 24 January 1774 a Mr Lamb played Whisper in *The Busy Body* and Dapper in *The Citizen* in a performance specially licensed by the Lord Chamberlain.

Lamb, [Matthew?] [fl. 1757], *organist? violinist?*

David Garrick on 2 February 1757 addressed a letter to his friend John Butcher, Esq, a functionary at Bedford House, pressing him to request the favor of the Duke of Bedford in preferring a Mr Lamb to some musical post. "I have long known him," wrote Garrick; "he is a Lichfield man, & of great Reputation in his profession. You will see by y^e [enclosed] Papers that he has often supply'd M^r [Matthew] Du[bourg's] place, & I flatter myself would most worthily supply it now, if his Grace would be pleas'd to favour him." What the post was for which Lamb was being considered and whether he was awarded it are unknown. The violinist Dubourg was at this time leader of the King's Band and an organizer of concerts in London but was also trying to hold down several positions in Dublin, where he lived most of the year. Perhaps Lamb acted as his London deputy in one or more of his enterprises. Little and Kahrl in *The Letters of David Garrick* identify him as Matthew Lamb, "eventually canon-residentiary of Lichfield."

Lamb, William [fl. 1727–1739], *singer.*

A warrant in the Lord Chamberlain's accounts dated 30 June 1727 named William Lamb as one of the former children of the Chapel Royal. His voice had changed, apparently shortly before that date, and he had left the Chapel. Alexander Pope recommended Lamb to Dean Swift in a letter dated 12 October 1738, and Swift sent word back on 19 April 1739 that he had given Lamb "a full vicar-choralship in my choir." On 10 May, however, Swift wrote Pope that Lamb had only a half position, at almost £50 annually, but was a most deserving young man.

Lamball, Mrs [fl. 1739–1743], *actress, singer.*

Mrs Lamball (or Lambell) made her first stage appearance on 3 May 1739 as Lady Townly in *The Provok'd Husband* at Drury Lane Theatre. She joined the Goodman's Fields troupe for the 1740–41 season, acting Lady Wronghead in *The Provok'd Husband*, Lady Sadlife in *The Double Gallant*, Lucinda in *Love and a Bottle*, Nottingham in *The Unhappy Favorite*, Lady Macduff in *Macbeth*, Dorinda in *The Stratagem*, Mrs Coaxer in *The Beggar's Opera*, Emilia in *Othello*, Melpomene in *Harlequin Student*, and Elvira in *Love Makes a Man*.

On 7 May 1742, after a year's absence from the London stage, Mrs Lamball played Madam Bernard in *The Country House* at Covent Garden, but she seems not to have made any other appearances there. On 12 October she turned up at the James Street Theatre as Lappet in *The Miser*, a role she repeated at Lincoln's Inn Fields on 4 April 1743. Four days later she was seen there as Lady Easy in *The Careless Husband*. At Bartholomew Fair on 23 August 1743 she played Miss Humility in *The French Doctor Outwitted*, her last known appearance in London.

Lambe, John [fl. 1769–1788], *musician.*

The records of the Royal Society of Musicians show that John Lamb of the "Lord Mayor's Office," musician, was admitted on 14 November 1769. On 22 April 1788 was entered the following notation: "John Whalley Lambe Son of John Lambe Citizen & Musician was this day bound apprentice to his said father for seven years." The address of the Lambes was given as No 153, New Broad Street.

Lambell. *See* LAMBALL.

Lambert, Mr [fl. 1773], *singer.*

A Mr Lambert performed one of the Arval Brothers in *Ambarvalia*, a musical piece presented at Marylebone Gardens on 3, 6, and 9 September 1773.

Lambert, Edward [*fl.* 1711?], *prologue speaker.*

At some performance of Settle's *Pastor Fido*, Edward Lambert spoke the prologue. The work was presented at the Dorset Garden playhouse in December 1676, but as Robert Hume has pointed out to us, a reference in the prologue to "*Ladies* of the *May*" suggests a different time of year. A production of the work at Greenwich on 21 May 1711 may have been the one. Lambert's name was included in the undated separately published prologue printed by Wiley in *Rare Prologues and Epilogues*.

Lambert, George 1699?–1765, *scene painter, landscape painter.*

Most biographical sources place George Lambert's birth in Kent in 1710, but Ronald Paulson in *Hogarth: His Life, Art, and Times* states that he was two years younger than Hogarth (b. 1697) and that Lambert was first mentioned by Vertue in September 1722 as a pupil of Warner Hassells and "a young hopefull Painter in Landskape, aged 22, much in Imitation of Wotton, manner of Gaspar Poussin." The armorial bookplate designed by Hogarth for Lambert in the 1720s suggests a connection with the Lamberts of Banstead and Woodmansterne, an old Surrey family, or possibly with the Earls of Cavan. As a young man Lambert worked with Samuel Scott on panels for the India Office and, probably with Hogarth, on landscapes for Westcombe House, Blackheath. A landscapist in the style of Claude and Salvator Rosa, he also followed the manner of Poussin but, as Horace Walpole said in his *Anecdotes of Painters*, "with more richness in his compositions."

At the age of 16 or 17, Lambert was employed by John Rich as a scene painter at Lincoln's Inn Fields Theatre; he was paid £50 on account on 28 December 1726, another £50 on 9 March 1727, and £48 for the balance on 14 March 1727. Young Lambert's main efforts that season were expended on *The Rape of Proserpine*, a spectacular pantomime which premiered on 13 February 1727 and included the destruction of the palace of Ceres by an earth-

By permission of the Trustees of the British Museum
GEORGE LAMBERT
engraving by Faber, after Vanderbank

quake, the eruption of Mount Etna, and the rising of Pluto and Proserpine from hell. In its enthusiasm, *Mist's* of 18 February 1727 reported that the production "far exceeds all ever yet shewn, in the Magnificence and Beauty of the Scenes, the Number and Richness of the Habits, as well as the Fable, which is purely poetical, as the Italian Operas ought to be."

Possibly Lambert helped Amiconi with the house and ceiling decorations of the new Covent Garden Theatre which Rich had built and opened on 3 December 1732. Certainly he was responsible, with Harvey, for the scenery which graced the new stage. The *Daily Journal* of 18 September 1732 announced that "We hear that Mr. Harvey and Mr. Lambert have been employed some time in painting the scenes for the new Theatre in Covent Garden." These scenes, according to Tom Davies, were "extremely well painted."

Though Lambert was employed as a Covent Garden scene painter for at least 29 years (the last known payment to him was on 26 November 1761), very little of his work is documented. It is said that when the theatre opened

Rich had given Lambert a dispensation "to render the stage as imposing as the collateral aid of painting, machinery, and costume could raise it," and to that end he "wrought day and night in his vocation." He was paid £100 per year, in quarterly installments of £25. Among his scenes were those for a revival of *Harlequin Sorcerer* on 11 February 1752 and a "New Scene of a Fountain" in the same on 13 January 1753. Lambert also painted new scenes for Ross's company at the Manchester Theatre in the spring of 1762, according to advertisements in the Manchester *Mercury*. In 1763 *Mortimer's London Directory* listed him as a landscape painter with an address in the Great Piazza, Covent Garden, where he had lived since at least 1757.

According to a story told by Edward Edwards and adopted by *The Dictionary of National Biography*, Lambert, a man of convivial disposition, often held court at suppers he gave in the scene-painting room of Covent Garden Theatre, where his business kept him evenings. His friends from aristocratic society or the theatre would join him in beefsteak broiled over a fire, and from these social gatherings evolved the famous Beefsteak Club, founded with John Rich and 23 others in 1735. (Allen, in *Clubs of Augustan London*, gives Rich the chief role in the foundation of the Beefsteaks.) The place of assembly was later changed to the Shakespeare Tavern, where the Beefsteaks met for many years. Lambert was also a member of the club that met at Old Slaughter's Tavern in St Martin's Lane.

Many of Lambert's large landscapes, in the manner of Poussin (for whose works Lambert's were sometimes sold), were engraved by Vivares and Mason, including views of Plymouth, Saltwood Castle in Kent, another of Dover, and a landscape which he presented to the Foundling Hospital. In 1735 he had been associated with Vertue, Pine, and Hogarth in

Private Collection, England

"Hilly River Landscape with a Ferry and Wayfarers"
by GEORGE LAMBERT

obtaining from Parliament the Engravers' Act, granting artists a copyright in their works. He exhibited with the Society of Artists in Great Britain, of which he was a founding member and chairman of the committee from 1761 to 1764. When the Society of Artists was chartered on 26 January 1765, Lambert served as its first president, but for less than a week before his death.

Lambert died in his house in the Great Piazza, Covent Garden, on 30 January 1765 (not on 30 November as stated in *The Dictionary of National Biography*). He was buried on 5 February at St Paul, Covent Garden, "in the Church Close at the End of the Church Wardens Pew Door," according to the burial register.

The manuscript papers of the actor William Havard, now at the Folger Shakespeare Library, contain "A Character of my Ingenious, & much esteem'd Friend Mr George Lambert Landscape Painter":

On Wednesday last, died at his apartments in the Great Piazza, Covent-Garden, M^r: George Lambert an eminent Landscape Painter & A Gentleman of many Virtues:—The Goodness of his Heart was conspicuous in his Countenance, & his known Beneficence was a Confirmation of that Goodness. His Judgment & his Candor were equal; and so happily did he temper the one with the other, that he never sacrific'd his Sincerity to his Complaisance, nor suffer'd ill Nature to prevail over Humanity. As his Acquaintance was not large, he number'd not many Friends—But every one who knew him, lov'd him. Numbers admired ye Character who were Strangers to the Man. He was modest to a Fault—for it hurt him in his Profession; yet he chose rather to wear that Fault, than ye Effrontory of successful Importunity. He lov'd Society, & honor'd Temperance:—His Disposition was easy, for his Conscience was clear;— —In a Word, he had all ye Requisites to excite Reverence in this World, and all ye Virtues to insure him Happiness in the next.—As to his Profession—I shall content myself to say of his Works, that what the present Age has only prais'd—Posterity will Admire.

In a short will made on 29 December 1764 and proved on 6 February 1765 Lambert left all his property to his "servant Ann Terry as a Reward of her care of me in several dangerous fitts of Illness and for her other good and faithful Services to me." He named his "dear good Friend John Moody Esq. of the parish of Twickenham" executor. On 18 December 1765 over 100 of his paintings and other effects, including some elegant furniture, were sold at Langford's. His pupil John Inigo Richards reported that Lambert's library consisted of "seven or eight hundred volumes."

It is not known whether or not Lambert ever married. No family is mentioned in his will. At St Martin-in-the-Fields a George Lambert and Ann Holt were married on 20 February 1718; their son Marmaduke, born on 20 November 1720, and their daughter Margaret, born on 28 December 1721, both died within a year of their births.

After his death, Lambert's scene of the eruption of Mount Etna was used again at Covent Garden in a revival of *The Rape of Proserpine* on 4 November 1769. Other scenes of his were repaired and brought out in productions of *Harlequin's Chaplet* on 21 December 1789 and *Harlequin's Treasure* on 24 October 1796. These perished in the Covent Garden fire of 1808. His scene for the farmhouse in *Harlequin Sorcerer* is reproduced by Sybil Rosenfeld in *A Short History of Scene Design in Great Britain*.

A portrait of Lambert by Thomas Hudson used to hang in the rooms of the Beefsteak Club when they met at Covent Garden Theatre, but apparently it was destroyed in the fire of 1808. In 1782 his portrait by Hogarth was in the possession of Samuel Ireland. A portrait of Lambert by J. Vanderbank, present location also unknown, was engraved by J. Faber in 1727; subsequent engravings were by A. Bannerman as a plate to Walpole's *Anecdotes* in 1762 and by H. Robinson as a plate to the same work published by Major in 1827 and reissued in 1862. Edward Croft-Murray cites, in *Decorative Painting in England*, the sale of John Inigo Richards's collection of paintings by Squibb on 14 March 1811, in which sale was "a Portrait of Mr [George] Lambert by Wilson." An exhibition of Lambert's paintings was held at Kenwood in 1960; Elizabeth Einberg's introduction to the exhibition catalogue offers information and an appreciation of his works.

"Lame Tumbler, The" [*fl.* 1720], acrobat.

At the King's Theatre on 29 April 1720, between the acts of a performance of *Le Bourgeois Gentilhomme* by De Grimbergue's French players, a group of tumblers, newly arrived in

London, exhibited their abilities, "particularly . . . a lame tumbler who never performed before in England."

La Mercier or **La Merieux.** *See* LEMERCIER.

Lamert, John $_[fl.\ 1710_],$ *musician?*
According to an article by E. H. Coleman in *Notes and Queries* (15 July 1905), John Lamert was one of the founders, along with Dr Pepusch, Galliard, and Gates, of the Academy of Ancient Music, instituted at the Crown and Anchor in the Strand in 1710.

Lamkin, John $_[fl.\ 1739_],$ *musician.*
John Lamkin was one of the original subscribers to the Royal Society of Musicians when it was founded on 28 August 1739.

Lammerton, Hugh $_[fl.\ 1699_],$ *wrestler.*
The *Post Boy* of 30 March–1 April 1699 advertised that at the New Red Theatre in Winchester Street, Southwark, next door to the Pair of Tongues and Keys, would be performed, among other athletic and theatrical entertainments, "a Wrestling Match, between the famous Welch Will, of Kidwelly (who had the Honour last Year to divert the Elector of Bavaria) and Hugh Lammerton, Tinman, near Lestiethill [Leith Hill?], for Twenty Pounds."

Lamoire. *See* HAMOIR.

La Montagn. *See* FELIX, SIEUR.

La Montagne, Mme $_[fl.\ 1786_],$ *dramatic lecturer.*
Mme La Montagne lectured and read scenes from Racine's *Phèdre* at the Free Masons' Hall on 16 November 1786.

Lamotte, Franz 1753?–1780, *violinist, composer.*
In his *History of the Violin* van der Straeten dates the birth of the violinist Franz Lamotte (or Lamotta) about 1751, but Grove gives 1753. Lamotte may have been born in Vienna, or perhaps in the Netherlands; he was sold by his mother to an English merchant and educated in London. Dr Burney said that Lamotte was a pupil of Giardini. He made his debut in Vienna on 31 December 1766, says van der Straeten; Grove dates the concert 29 December and places it at the Burg Theater. In any case, the *Wienerisches Diarium* called him a young Englishman and said he was then 13 years old. About 1767 Gerber heard him at Hiller's in Leipzig, and at some point Lamotte performed in Paris.

By 1772 he had appeared in Naples, and from that year until his death Lamotte was a member of the court chapel at Vienna. But he toured on occasion and was in London from 1776 to 1779. His first appearance was at the King's Theatre on 15 February 1776, when he played a concerto on the violin at the annual benefit for indigent musicians and their families. On 23 February he appeared at Covent Garden Theatre, and he played there regularly to the end of the oratorio season on 27 March. Lamotte was engaged to play at the Oxford Music Room in May 1776, but he became ill and was replaced by Cramer. He was at Oxford in January 1777, however, and *Jackson's Oxford Journal* on the eighteenth spoke of "that great execution in octaves that he first introduced into England." He returned to Covent Garden for the oratorios in February and March 1777. On 30 August for Rauzzini's benefit he performed in Brighton. Michael Kelly heard him play in the Rotunda concerts in Dublin in the 1770s.

In March 1778, according to the *Early Diary of Frances Burney*, Lamotte and others "played several Quartettos divinely" at a morning concert at Mr Harris's house. In 1778–79, Grove says, Lamotte and Rauzzini gave a number of subscription concerts in London, and Lamotte conducted some concerts at Bath in cooperation with Rauzzini. At the Assembly Room in Princes Street, Bristol, on 19 October 1779 Lamotte joined the oboist Fischer in a concert. Fétis in his *Biographie* claimed that Lamotte contracted heavy debts in London, chiefly because of dissipation, and was imprisoned for several years. The Gordon rioters brought about his release, and he fled to Holland. According to van der Straeten, Lamotte died in Vienna in 1781, but the *Gentleman's Magazine* reported that he died at the Hague on 7 September 1780.

Dr Burney heard Lamotte in 1772 and called him the "best solo player and sightsman upon the violin in Vienna." The violinist was famous for his staccato playing and was apparently capable of performing entire pages of music without changing his string. Charles Dibdin, on the other hand, was not impressed. In his *Musical Tour* he wrote:

I will venture to say *solos* and *solo concertos* have done but little good to the cause of music. La Motte's great merit was to figure away in *alt*, till at last, approaching to the bridge, he played himself, as it were, *out of sight*. The *dexterity* was *wonderful*, but for heaven's sake where was the *pleasure*?

Lamotte composed a number of works for the violin, including three concertos and several sonatas.

Lamotte is pictured in a large group of musicians in an engraving by the studio of Bettelini, after a design by L. Scotti, published about 1805.

Lamound, Mons [*fl.* 1743–1748], *dancer*.

A dancer named Lamound, evidently a Frenchman, was Pluto in *The Royal Chace* at Covent Garden from 20 December 1743 to 7 February 1744. It is our guess that the same performer, cited as "Le Mont," was the dancer who participated in a *Grand Dance of Furies* at Phillips's booth at Southwark Fair on 7 September 1748.

Lamour. *See* LATOUR.

Lamp, Mr [*fl.* 1789–1792], *house servant*.

Mr Lamp, a house servant at Covent Garden Theatre, had benefit tickets out on 13 June 1789, 9 June 1791, and 1 June 1792.

Lampe, Charles John Frederick *c.* 1740–1767?, *organist, composer*.

Charles John Frederick Lampe was born about 1740, the son of the musician and composer John Frederick Lampe and his wife Isabella, a singer who was one of the performing daughters of the organist Charles Young. In 1758 Charles succeeded his maternal grandfather as organist of All Hallows, Barking by the Tower, an appointment he held until his death. Lampe's name was on the Covent Garden Theatre list of musicians for 3*s*. 4*d*. per night in 1760–61.

On 14 May 1763 the press announced that Mr Charles Lampe, of Covent Garden Theatre and All Hallows, had married a Miss Smith, a singer at Marylebone Gardens on Saturday, 7 May 1763. Thereafter she was sometimes advertised as "Mrs Lampe Junr" to distinguish her from her mother-in-law.

The younger Lampe's published songs included *Britannia's Invitation to her Sons, to partake of the Glory of the intended Expedition* (1760?), *Six English Songs as sung by Mr Lowe and Mrs Lampe Junr at Mary-bone Gardens* (1764), and songs included in published collections of the Catch Club.

In the Burney papers at the British Library is a notation of the death of "Christopher" Lampe on 10 September 1767, probably a transcription error for Charles, for on 10 March 1768 a commission was granted by the Consistory Court to "Ann Beaumont, wife of Henry Beaumont the Relict of Charles James Frederick Lampe late of the Parish of St Giles in the ffields . . . to administer the goods chattels and credits of the deceased. . . ." Lampe's widow evidently married Beaumont, also a Covent Garden musician, soon after her first husband's death. She continued to perform on the stage as Mrs Beaumont until about 1773. She was dead by 1782, when Henry Beaumont had another wife, much younger than Ann Lampe would have been.

Charles and Ann Lampe had a child, Esther Isabella Lampe, named as a minor in the will of her grandmother Isabella Lampe on 19 May 1780.

Lampe, Mrs Charles John Frederick, Ann, née Smith, later Mrs Henry Beaumont [*fl.* 1763–1773?], *singer*.

Ann Smith, a singer at Marylebone Gardens, married the musician and composer Charles John Frederick Lampe on 7 May 1763. When Marylebone Gardens opened that month under Thomas Lowe's directions she was still advertised as Miss Smith. One of the songs, *Now the Summer advances*, sung at the opening by her, Lowe, Miss Catley, and Miss Miles, was published that year. Her name appeared with those of Lowe, Legg, Miss Plenius, and Miss Catley in announcements of Handel's *Alexander Feast* on 28 June. Also published the following year were *Six English Songs as sung by Mr Lowe and Mrs Lampe Junr at Mary-bone Gardens*. She was so billed to distinguish her from her mother-in-law, Isabella Lampe, wife of John Frederick Lampe, who was also a singer. Ann Lampe was at Sadler's Wells in September 1765 and 1766.

Soon after Charles Lampe died on 10 September 1767, she married his fellow Covent Garden musician Henry Beaumont. In March 1768 the Consistory Court granted a commission to "Ann Beaumont, wife of Henry Beaumont the Relict of Charles James Frederick Lampe late of the Parish of St Giles in the ffields . . . to administer the goods chattels and credits of the deceased. . . ."

The widow Lampe's career as Mrs Beaumont was given in the first volume of this dictionary before we discovered she had previously been married to Charles Lampe and had been born Ann Smith, but for the sake of convenience we repeat that information and make additions here. In Mrs Beaumont's notice we suggested that the Henry Beaumont who was a musician at Sadler's Wells and Covent Garden was probably not her husband, but our discovery of the Consistory Court commission for administration of Charles Lampe's estate clearly establishes her as the wife of one Henry Beaumont, who we are now persuaded was the musician also noticed in volume I.

Still known as Mrs Lampe, she was singing at Sadler's Wells in September 1767. That year the song *The Matrons Advice* was published as sung by her there. In 1769, now Mrs Beaumont, she sang at the Wells, where she returned in 1771. At the Haymarket on 8 December 1770 she sang the part of Mary in *Love and Resolution*, a musical dialogue by Dr Arne, who was the uncle, by marriage, of her first husband. In 1769 her address was No 7, Bull-Head Court, Newgate Street, though in that same year Henry Beaumont's address was No 10, Turnagain Lane, Fleet Market. Perhaps she was the Mrs Beaumont who performed at Bristol in 1773.

Ann Beaumont died sometime before 1781, the year in which Henry Beaumont died, for on 1 January 1792, his widow and second wife Sally Beaumont petitioned the Royal Society of Musicians for relief; this second Beaumont wife at that time had three children, the oldest of which had been born in January 1782. Sally Beaumont, the second wife, died in 1826, about 64 years of age, and thus had been born about 1762.

By her first husband Charles Lampe, Ann had at least one child, Esther Isabella Lampe, mentioned as a minor in the will of Isabella Lampe on 19 May 1780.

Lampe, John Frederick *c. 1703–1751, bassoonist, harpsichordist, composer.*

Born about 1703, John Frederick (Johann Friedrich) Lampe was a native of Saxony, and the fact that Hawkins wrote that "he affected to style himself sometime a student of music of Helmstadt" has suggested that city as his birthplace. Lampe also seems to have attended St Catherine's School at Brunswick. Nothing more is known of his education or early career until he arrived in London about 1725. He was soon well known, it appears. Roger Fiske in *The New Grove's Dictionary* points out that by 1726 Henry Carey had cited him in one of his poems about London composers, calling him "my learned friend."

Lampe was engaged in the opera band at the King's Theatre and became recognized as one of the premier bassoonists of his time. (He is

By permission of the Trustees of the British Museum
JOHN FREDERICK LAMPE
engraving by McArdell, after Andrea

not to be confused with another Johann Friedrich Lampe, b. 1744, who never came to England.) Thomas Busby in *Concert Room and Orchestra Anecdotes* (1825) remembered that

The great bassoon, sixteen feet long, which at the grand commemoration of Handel at Westminster Abbey [in 1784], was erected in the centre of the orchestra, and attempted to be performed on that occasion by John Ashley, had been made by order of Handel himself, for the use of John Frederick Lampe, an excellent bassoonist. . . . The stupendous bassoon manufactured expressly for his use, had, in his hands, a powerful and astounding effect; but, in the band at the Abbey performances, the current jest was, that *no doubt Ashley would do every justice to the powers of the instrument, if he could but once make it speak.*

Few records survive of Lampe's London performances. On 7 March 1729 an instrumental and vocal concert was offered for his benefit at the Haymarket Theatre.

By 1730 Lampe turned his talents to composing for the theatres. His first known contribution was the music for *Diana and Acteon*, a pantomime entertainment concocted by Rogers which played at Drury Lane on 23 April 1730. Probably he provided music for other pantomimes about that time. Soon Lampe became involved with Henry Carey in a scheme to present "English Operas" at the Haymarket Theatre. On 25 February 1732 the *Daily Post* reported that "there is a subscription for a new English opera called *Amelia*, which will be shortly performed at the new theatre in the Haymarket, by a set of performers who never yet appeared in public." *Amelia*, written by Henry Carey, with music by Lampe ("after the Italian Method"), opened on 13 March 1732. Making her stage debut in the title role was Susanna Arne, later to become the renowned tragedienne Mrs Cibber. On 17 and 19 May 1732 Lampe and Carey produced Handel's *Acis and Galatea*, "With all the Grand Chorus's, Scenes, Machines, and other Decorations; being the first time it was ever produced in a Theatrical Way." Lampe's next effort was for *Britannia*, Lediard's opera which opened with elaborate settings and decorations at the Haymarket on 16 November 1732, after a public rehearsal on 14 November. In the title role that time was Cecilia Young, who would marry the composer Thomas A. Arne and who was the sister of Lampe's future wife, Isabella Young. On 23 February 1733 the new opera *Dione* was performed to music by Lampe.

On 7 November 1733 an operatic adaptation of Fielding's *Tragedy of Tragedies* was brought out at Drury Lane under the title *The Opera of Operas*, announced as "Set to Musick After the Italian Manner by Mr John Frederick Lampe." *New Grove* credits the altered text to Eliza Haywood. (Interestingly enough, a musical burlesque similarly titled *The Opera of Operas* had been first played at the Haymarket the previous season on 31 May 1733, during Lampe and Carey's "English Operas" stint. Music for the earlier version, in which Master Arne played Tom Thumb, has usually been credited to Thomas A. Arne, but Lampe may well have had a hand in it.) During that 1733–34 season at Drury Lane select pieces by Lampe were played as entr'acte music on 7 December 1733. He also provided new songs for a revival of Vanbrugh's *The Cornish Squire* on 3 January 1734 and music for the new pantomime *Cupid and Psyche; or, Columbine Courtezan* on 4 February 1734. *Grove's Dictionary* (5th edition) credits him with music for Hewitt's new tragedy *Fatal Falsehood* on 11 February 1734, but *New Grove* does not mention the work. On 22 February, Lampe's new overture and some songs were introduced in the premiere of Carey's farce *Chrononhotonthologos*. At a benefit for Clarke and Messing at Hickford's Rooms on 5 April 1734, "Adonis Chace, consisting of two Aubaden for four French Horns," composed by Seedo and Lampe, was performed. Some of Lampe's music was heard at Lincoln's Inn Fields on 9 May 1734. It was a busy season for the composer. On 16 May his works were produced at two theatres on the same night: at Drury Lane his "new Comic-Medley-Overture" was played, and at Lincoln's Inn Fields "A Masque of Pastoral Musick," composed by him, was introduced into a revival of Tate's *The Island Princess*. That season the theatres were preparing special entertainments to celebrate the marriage of the Prince of Orange and Princess Anne. Several postponements of the marriage, which finally occurred on 14 March 1734, caused confusion in the theatres' schedules. A masque entitled *Aurora's Nuptials*, which was set to music by Lampe, was published in 1734; it was intended as Drury Lane's contribution to the festivities but we find no record in *The London Stage* of its performance.

A "Comic Medley Overture" by Lampe was played at Drury Lane on 29 April 1737. In the middle of the following month, after a public rehearsal on 10 May, Lampe and Carey enjoyed their greatest success at the Haymarket on 16 May with the two-act musical burlesque *The Dragon of Wantley*. Enormously popular, and a favorite of Handel, the opera was written in the tradition of *The Beggar's Opera* insofar as it mocked the current passion of the town for Italian opera. As described in *Biographia Dramatica*, it involved "all the incidents of love, heroism, rivalry, and fury, which most of the Italian operas indiscriminately were stuffed with. To help it forward, the characters were dressed in the utmost extravagance of theatric parade: the machinery, truly burlesque, and the songs, though ludicrous to the highest degree, were set perfectly in the Italian taste." In October 1737 Rich took *The Dragon* into Covent Garden, where this all-sung English opera ran 67 performances, exceeding by seven the first run of *The Beggar's Opera*. The full score of Lampe's songs and duets was published in 1738; a title page of that edition published by J. Wilcox and signed on the reverse by Lampe is in the Enthoven Collection. The full manuscript score survives at the Royal College of Music. Lampe and Carey were less successful with a sequel entitled *Margery: or A Worse Plague than the Dragon*, produced at Covent Garden on 9 December 1738. That full score was published by Wilcox that year.

On 31 January 1738 Lampe married the singer Isabella Young at St Benet, Paul's Wharf. She was the daughter of Charles Young, organist of All Hallows, Barking by the Tower, and the sister of Cecilia Young, who in the previous year had married Thomas A. Arne. Thus the two eminent composers of English theatrical music became brothers-in-law. Isabella and Cecilia also shared sisters named Esther and Mary, who also appeared on the concert stage as well.

Lampe wrote music in the 1740s for *Orpheus and Eurydice* at Covent Garden on 12 February 1740 (with Mrs Lampe as Rhodope); *The Sham Conjuror* at Covent Garden on 18 April 1741 (with Mrs Lampe as Bell Banter); *The Queen of Spain* at the Haymarket on 19 January 1744 (with Mrs Lampe as the Queen); *The Kiss Accepted and Returned* at the Haymarket on 16 April 1744 (with Mrs Lampe as Phoebe); and *Pyramus and Thisbe* at Covent Garden on 25 January 1745 (with Mrs Lampe as Thisbe). In 1741 Lampe and his wife, along with her sister, Sullivan, the two Messings, and Worsdale, went to Preston and to Chester, where they performed several of Lampe's operas, heard by Dr Burney, then a lad of 15. Lampe's grand martial music composed in honor of Admiral Vernon's victory at Carthage was performed at Marylebone Gardens on 23 May 1741. By 1740 the Lampes lived at the Golden Bull in Brownlow Street. In March 1743 their address was the Golden Unicorn in Hanover Street, Longacre, and in April 1748 at "the Sign of the Holy Lamb in Drury Lane near Long Acre." In 1746 Lampe's anthem celebrating the failure of the Jacobite rebellion was performed at the Lutheran church in the Savoy.

In 1748 the Lampes, together with Mr and Mrs Macklin, Pasquali, Sullivan, and several others of a group that Victor called "the Musical Tribe," were engaged for two years by Thomas Sheridan for the Smock Alley Theatre in Dublin. On 29 November 1748 Lampe conducted his *Dragon of Wantley* there, and on 29 April 1749 *Theodosius* was presented with "all the original Songs set to Musick by Mr Lampe and now first performed." In his second season, 1749–50, he newly set the original songs for *Oroonoko* on 27 October 1749 (sung by Mrs Lampe and Mrs Storer "in the Habits of American Slaves"), and his *Pyramus and Thisbe* was revived on 19 January 1750. On 12 March a new serenata by Lampe graced *Damon and Amanthe*, and on 4 April at the end of each act of *King John*, new choruses sounded out "in the manner of the Ancients, set to Musick by Mr Lampe." Before the 1750–51 season began the Lampes left the company, evidently having been victimized by some of Sheridan's managerial shenanigans, of which Charles Macklin had so vociferously and publicly complained. Sheridan, according to Kirkman's *Memoirs of Macklin*, refused to pay the Lampes the full amount agreed upon and Lampe was forced to accept Sheridan's terms "rather than abide the distant event of a Chancery suit in a strange country."

On 24 September 1750 the *Caledonian Mercury* announced that a concert and a performance of *The Beggar's Opera* would be presented at the New Concert Hall in Edinburgh on 29 October, featuring Mrs Storer and Mrs Lampe, and that the "Orchestra will be enlarged, and the voice accompanied with a Harpsichord, on which Mr Lampe is to perform." The Lampes' departure from Dublin, however, was delayed by a serious fever which kept Isabella in bed for 16 days, so the event announced for 29 October at Edinburgh had to be postponed until some time after their arrival on 5 November. Burney tells us that Lampe settled at Edinburgh "very much to the satisfaction of the patrons of Music in that city, and of himself." He served as *maestro di capella* for the concerts of the Edinburgh Musical Society and conducted concerts in Heriot's Gardens when the weather was not unfavorable. On 14 January 1751 he organized and conducted a performance of *Comus* at the New Concert Hall in which his wife sang Euphrosyne and spoke the epilogue.

Lampe died in Edinburgh of a fever on 25 July 1751 and was buried on 28 July in the Canongate churchyard, where a monument to him was raised with a lengthy and effusive inscription (reported in *Notes and Queries*, 30 January 1864):

> Here lie the mortal Remains of John Frederick Lampe, whose harmonious Compositions shall outlast monumental Registers, and with melodious Notes through future Ages perpetuate his Fame, 'till Time shall sink into Eternity. His Taste for moral Harmony appeared through all his Conduct. He was a most loving Husband, an affectionate Father, Friend, and Companion. On the 25th Day of July 1751, in the 48th Year of his Age, he was summoned to join that heavenly Concert with the blessed Choir above, where his virtuous Soul now enjoys the Harmony which was his chief Delight upon Earth.

Evidently a good musician and a good man, Lampe enjoyed the affection and esteem of his colleagues. Upon Lampe's death, Charles Wesley wrote a hymn beginning "'Tis done! the sov'reign will's obeyed!" which was later set to music by Samuel Arnold. Lampe and his wife had been converted to Methodism by Mrs John Rich soon after the production of *Orpheus and Eurydice* in 1740.

In addition to his compositions for the theatre Lampe wrote numerous songs, some of which were collected and published in *Wit Musically Embellished* (1731), *British Melody; or, the Musical Magazine* (1739), and *Ladies' Amusement* (c. 1748, Dublin). He also wrote and published *The Art of Musick* (1740) and *A Plain and Compendious Method of Teaching Thorough Bass* (1737). According to Hawkins, Lampe wrote the anonymous cantata "In Harmony would you excel" to words by Swift. Twenty-four of his tunes in two parts, composed to words by his close friend Charles Wesley, were published in *Hymns on the Great Festivals and other Occasions* (1746). A long list of Lampe's compositions may be found in the *Catalogue of Printed Music in the British Museum*.

Lampe's wife continued to perform on the London stage until 1773 and did not die until 1795. Their son Charles John Frederick Lampe, a sometime musician at Covent Garden and a composer of songs for the pleasure gardens, in 1758 succeeded his maternal grandfather Charles Young as organist at All Hallows. He married in 1763 the singer Miss Ann Smith, who then performed as Mrs Lampe and thus is often confused with her mother-in-law Isabella Lampe. In the Burney papers at the British Library is the notation of the death on 10 September 1767 of a Christopher Lampe, whose relationship, if any, to the musical family is not known by us; perhaps Burney may have intended to write "Charles."

A portrait of John Frederick Lampe was bequeathed by his wife (in her will drawn on 19 May 1780 and proved on 12 March 1795) to the singer John Beard but was not to be delivered to him until after the death of her two sisters Cecilia Arne and Esther Jones. Mrs Lampe, however, outlived Beard and her sisters, and the present whereabouts of the portrait is unknown to us. Probably it was the painting by S. Andrea which was engraved by J. McArdell.

Lampe, Mrs John Frederick, Isabella, née Young *d. 1795, singer, actress.*

Isabella Young was one of the daughters, probably the second eldest, of Charles Young, organist of All Hallows, Barking by the Tower. She and her sisters, Cecilia, Esther, and perhaps a Mary Esther, all began their stage careers in the 1730s as "Miss Young," so it is often difficult to discriminate among their respective professional activities. The eldest and most talented daughter, Cecilia Young, married Thomas A. Arne, the eminent composer, in 1737. Esther Young (d. 1795), no doubt younger than Isabella, in 1762 married Charles Jones (d. c. 1784), a musician and music seller in Russell Street. Further complicating the matter of sorting out these women is the fact that a brother, Charles Young, a clerk in the treasury, also had three daughters, each of whom at some time sang as "Miss Young" before they married: Isabella to the Hon John Scott in 1757, Elizabeth to Ridley Dorman in 1762, and Polly (or Mary) to François Hippolyte Barthélemon in 1766.

Our Isabella Young was probably the Miss Young who, having "never appeared on any stage before," sang the role of Amphitrite in a production of *The Tempest* at Drury Lane Theatre on 26 November 1733. At Mercers' Hall on 13 December 1734 and 11 February 1736 Isabella and her sister Cecilia performed for their father's benefit. Again for his benefit, on 26 November 1736, they sang ("songs and duets") at the Swan Tavern.

On 16 May 1737 Isabella "created" the role of Margery in Henry Carey's *The Dragon of Wantley* at the Haymarket Theatre. This all-sung English opera, with music by John Frederick Lampe, was enormously popular, and after it transferred to Covent Garden Theatre on 26 October 1737 it enjoyed a run of 67 performances, which outstripped by seven the original run of *The Beggar's Opera*. Also in the cast, as Mauxalinda, was Esther Young. In the middle of the run Isabella married the composer Lampe on 31 January 1738 at St Benet, Paul's Wharf, and thereafter appeared in all his subsequent productions.

Singing as Mrs Lampe, she was regularly engaged at Covent Garden Theatre for a decade, through 1747–48. In 1738–39 she played Helen and her sister Esther played the Shade of Hero in *The Necromancer*, and on 9 December 1738 they were Margery and Mauxalinda again in the premiere of the Carey-Lampe sequel to *The Dragon of Wantley* called *Margery; or, a Worse Plague than the Dragon*. For their benefit on 28 April 1739, Mrs Lampe performed Polly and Esther Young Lucy in *The Beggar's Opera*, when the bills announced the occasion of "the first time of their attempting to speak on the Stage." In 1739–40 Isabella added to her repertoire a vocal part in *The Rehearsal*, Cupid in *Cupid and Bacchus*, and Nancy in *The Parting Lovers*. The last piece, by Carey, opened on 18 March 1740, but embryonic portions of it had been sung as a vocal interlude on 1 December 1739 by Mrs Lampe, Laguerre, and Salway. Also that season, on 12 February 1740, Mrs Lampe sang Rhodope in *Orpheus and Eurydice*, when new music by her husband was added. After that production the Lampes were converted to Methodism by Mrs Rich and became friends of Charles Wesley. For her benefit on 30 April 1740, shared with Miss Young, she sang Tom Thumb in a revival of her husband's *The Opera of Operas*, and tickets could be had of her in their house in Brownlow Street.

On 1 August 1740 Mrs Lampe joined a host of singers, dancers, and musicians who performed in the *festa teatrale* organized by the Prince of Wales for the birthday of the Princess Augusta of Brunswick in the gardens of Cliveden. Thereafter in the 1740s at Covent Garden her new roles included Bell Banter in Lampe's *The Sham Conjuror* on 18 April 1741, Andromeda in *Perseus and Andromeda* on 26 November 1741, Proserpine in *The Rape of Proserpine* on 8 January 1742, and Thisbe in Lampe's *Pyramus and Thisbe* on 25 January 1745. In 1742–43 she made appearances at Drury Lane in *Comus* and *The Dragon of Wantley* and at the Haymarket sang the Queen in Lampe's *The Queen of Spain* on 19 January 1744 and Phoebe in his *The Kiss Accepted and Returned* on 16 April 1744. In 1741 she had accompanied her husband and her sister, with Sullivan and Worsdale, to Preston and Chester for performances of Lampe's operas. By March 1743 the Lampes had moved from Brownlow Street to the Golden Unicorn in Hanover Street, Longacre, and by April 1748 to "the Sign of the Holy Lamb" in Drury Lane. Mrs Lampe's salary at Covent Garden in 1746–47 was £2 10s. per week.

After the 1747–48 season the Lampes left London to take up a two-year engagement with Thomas Sheridan at the Smock Alley Theatre, Dublin, arriving in the Irish capital in mid-September. They were joined by Pasquali, Sullivan, and other members of a group which had been imported at great cost by Sheridan to boost attendance and which was dubbed by Victor "the Musical Tribe." During her time in Dublin Mrs Lampe performed some of her London roles, especially Margery and Thisbe, and also was heard in such parts as Peg in *A Cure for a Scold*, Jack in *Jack the Giant Queller*, the title role in *Lady Moore*, and vocal parts in *The Chaplet*, *Macbeth*, *The Triumphs of Hibernia*, and *The What D'Ye Call It*.

A salary dispute with Sheridan drove the

Lampes from Dublin to Edinburgh. Their departure from Ireland was delayed by a serious fever which Mrs Lampe suffered for 16 days, so they did not arrive at Edinburgh until 5 November 1750. The northern capital in 1750–51 witnessed her performances of Lucy, Margery, Tom Thumb, and Jessica in *The Merchant of Venice* (on 28 January 1751), among other roles.

The "satisfaction" which Burney tells us the Lampes found in Edinburgh was shattered when Lampe caught a fever and died on 25 July 1751. Three days later he was buried in the Canongate churchyard. His widow returned to London that autumn to resume her engagement at Covent Garden, where, deprived of the support of her husband's prestige, she was relegated to a variety of chorus roles for almost 25 years. In 1762 *The Rosciad of C–v–nt G–rd–n* called her "useful . . . / To join in chorus, or to scream an air." She had occasional benefits as the Widow Lampe. In 1760–61 her salary was 13s. 4d. a day and by 1767–68 it had been reduced to 5s. per day.

During the 1760s Mrs Lampe's daughter-in-law, the wife of her son Charles John Frederick Lampe, sang in London, thereby creating some confusion. But that younger Mrs Lampe, who before her marriage in 1763 had sung as Miss Ann Smith, was in the bills as Mrs Lampe only until 1767, when Charles Lampe died, and she soon married the musician Henry Beaumont; moreover her singing seems to have been limited to the pleasure gardens and Sadler's Wells.

Though her name did not appear in the regular bill after 1774–75, Isabella Lampe must have continued to serve Covent Garden in some modest capacity, for she shared in benefit tickets with minor personnel each year from 19 May 1781 through 8 June 1790. Her career in the theatre seems to have spanned 57 years.

The *European Magazine* for January 1795 reported the death of Isabella Lampe on the fifth of that month. (Reed's notation in a British Library manuscript that it was the widow of "Charles" Frederick Lampe who had died on that date is incorrect.) Clearly it was Isabella, widow of John Frederick Lampe, whose will was proved at London on 12 March 1795. In that will, originally drawn on 19 May 1780, Isabella had left £100 in three per cent bank annuities in trust to her "Granddaughter Esther Isabella Lampe the daughter of my late Son Charles ffrederick Lampe," a minor in 1780. To John Beard, the singer, she bequeathed the portrait of her late husband, to be delivered to Beard after the death of her sisters Cecilia Arne and Esther Jones. (But Isabella outlived Beard and the sisters.) Administration of the estate was granted to the executor Richard Hewetson, a laceman of St Paul, Covent Garden.

Lampman, Newel [*fl.* 1724], *house servant?*

On 5 October 1724 in the Lincoln's Inn Fields accounts was entered 15s. for Newel Lamp(m)an for a bill and salary. He was apparently one of the house servants, but his position is not known. Related to him in some way, no doubt, was Thomas Lampman, possibly one of the employees in the theatre business office. He was cited on the free list (as "Tom" Lampman) in 1726–27 and occasionally was noted for a business transaction, probably involving complimentary tickets: "Ch. Rich by Tom Lampman" was the usual rubric.

Lampman, Thomas [*fl.* 1726–27], *house servant. See* LAMPMAN, NEWEL.

Lampugnani, Giovanni Battista 1708–c. 1786?, *composer, harpsichordist.*

Giovanni Battista Lampugnani was born at Milan in 1706, and possibly he was the son of the composer of the same name who was active in Italy from 1690 to 1698. His first opera, *Candace*, was produced in 1732 at Milan, where he had studied music. By 1741 some ten of his operas had been heard in Italy, including *Ezio* in 1736 and *Antigono* in 1737 at Milan, *Demofoonte* at Piacenza in 1738, *Angelica* at Venice in 1738, and *Didone abbandonata* at Padua in 1739. Lampugnani came to London to succeed Galuppi as composer to the King's Theatre in the autumn of 1743. Some of his airs had already been performed at the King's Theatre in *pasticci* productions of *Alessandro in Persia* on 31 October 1741, *Meraspe o L'Olimpiade* on 20 April 1742 and *Gianguir* on 2 November 1742.

During 1743–44 and 1744–45 Lampugnani shared the duties of conductor at the King's Theatre with other composers, including Gluck. Some musicologists have suggested that the opera *Rossane*, produced at the King's on 15 November 1743, was by Lampugnani, but

Deutsch (*Handel*) is persuaded that it was a revival of Handel's *Alessandro nell' Indie* (and not until 15 April 1746, after he had left London, was Lampugnani's version of *Rossane* played at the King's). Lampugnani's first work in London was *Alfonso* on 3 January 1744, an opera that was performed a total of eight times through 28 January. Recalling that opera, Burney wrote of Lampugnani:

> Upon a cool and fair examination of the works of this composer, I now find more genius and merit of various kinds, than I used to allow. He was thought slight and flimsy when he was here. . . . Lampugnani's is not a grand style; but there is a graceful gaiety in the melody of his quick songs, and an elegant tenderness in the slow, that resemble no other composer's works of that time. If any defect is more prominent than another in all his productions, it is want of dignity and richness of harmony. This composer, who was very young at this time [actually 37] . . . rioted too much with comedy, for a serious drama. There is more bravura for Monticelli in the songs of Alfonso, than I ever remember that singer to attempt in any other.

Lampugnani's next composition at the King's was *Alceste* on 24 April 1744, repeated 11 times in May and June. This opera, according to Burney, deserved praise and was in great favor "with the votaries of the new lyrical style of Italy." On 10 May 1745 his air "Scherza quest' Alma Mia" was sung at Covent Garden Theatre by Sga Frasi. By July 1745, Lampugnani probably had left England, for his *Semiramide o Nino* was produced at Padua that month. He was probably in Milan for the preparation of his new opera *Il Gran Tamerlano* on 20 January 1746.

During the remainder of his career on the Continent, Lampugnani's operas, about 29 in all, were produced at Venice, Copenhagen, Lisbon, Barcelona, and elsewhere, and especially at Milan, where in 1760 he settled first as conductor of the Teatro Regio Ducal and then at La Scala. The *Enciclopedia dello spettacolo* states that he returned to London in 1754–55, when *Ipermestra*, with music by him and Hasse, was produced on 9 November 1754 and his *Siroe, re di Persia* was produced on 14 January 1755. Burney, who did not note Lampugnani's presence in London that second time, found the music of *Siroe* to be "light, airy, and pleasant. . . . It wants dignity, as is usual with the compositions of this master, but it is never vulgar or tedious; it is the Music of a gay man of the world; no study or labour appear, though fashion or elegance are never wanting."

Lampugnani died, probably at Milan, in 1784, according to the *Enciclopedia dello spettacolo*, but according to *New Grove* he was still playing harpsichord in the Milan opera in 1786. Details of his continental career may be found in the former work and an appreciation of his music in the latter. In addition to his operas, he wrote some instrumental works; his Opus 1 was published during his first visit to London. Selections and airs by Lampugnani were also performed in various London productions over the years, including in Cumberland's *The Summer's Tale* at Covent Garden on 6 December 1765. A list of his operas may be found in Grove.

Lancashire, Richard [*fl. c.* 1670s?], *rope dancer, acrobat?*

In *Notes and Queries* in January 1859 John Payne Collier quoted a bill for one of Jacob Hall's performances, probably in the 1670s:

> These are to give Notice to all Gentlemen and Others, That there is Joyned together Two of the Best Companies in England, viz. Mr. Jacob Hall (Sworn Servant to his Majestie), and Mr. Richard Lancashire, with several Others of the Companies; by Whom will be performed Excellent Dancing and Vaulting on the Ropes; with Variety of Rare Feats of Activity and Agility of Body upon the Stage; as doing of Somersets, and Flip-flaps, Flying over Thirty Rapiers, and over several Men's heads; and also flying through severall Hoops: Together with severall other Rare Feats of Activity, that will be there presented: With the Witty Conceits of Merry Will: In the performing of all which They Challenge all Others whatsoever, whether English-men or Strangers, to do the like with them for Twenty Pounds, or what more They please.

The Hall-Lancashire booth was presumably at Bartholomew Fair. But the authenticity of the bill must be questioned in view of Collier's penchant for forgery.

Lance, Mr [*fl.* 1783–1785], *dresser.*

Mr Lance was a men's dresser at the King's Theatre from at least 1783, when his name appeared on a company list, through the 1784–85 season.

Lancetti. *See* LANZETTI.

Lander, Mr ₁*fl.* 1760s₁, *singer.*

The Rendel manuscript notes concerning Southwark at the Folger Library list Mr Lander as one of the vocal performers at Finch's Grotto Gardens, George Street, St George's Fields, Southwark, sometime between 1760 and 1769.

Lane, Mr ₁*fl.* 1778–1787₁, *conjuror.*

Morley's *Memoirs of Bartholomew Fair* contains a picture of Mr Lane, "his Majesty's Conjuror," who appeared at the Fair in 1778. His advertisement carried the following poem:

It will make you to laugh, it will drive away gloom,
To see how the egg it will dance round the room;
And from another egg a bird there will fly,
Which makes the company all for to cry,
O rare Lane, Cockalorum for Lane, well done Lane,
You are the Man.

Lane's entertainment concluded with the two Misses Lane, presumably his daughters. One exhibited "Surprising Posturing," and the other, Ann, danced a hornpipe.

In August 1787 Lane performed feats of magic at Flockton's booth at Peckham Fair.

Lane, Mr *d.* 1782, *actor.*

Mr Lane spent the summer of 1775 playing in Foote's company at the Haymarket Theatre. Between 24 May and 20 September he was seen as George Bevil in *Cross Purposes*, Leander in *The Mock Doctor*, unnamed characters in *Eldred* and *The Rehearsal*, Hortensio in *Catherine and Petruchio*, Elliot in *The Lyar*, Young Loveit in *The Commissary*, Woodford in *The Lame Lover*, Sharper in *The Old Bachelor*, and Charles in *The Busy Body*. He must also have appeared at Covent Garden Theatre, for he was described as from there when he appeared in Dublin in 1781, but we have found no mention of his name in the Covent Garden bills at any time.

Lane appeared as Sir Charles Seymour in *The Runaway* on 7 June 1776 in Birmingham, and from October to December of that year he was earning £1 1*s*. weekly at the Theatre Royal, Liverpool. He was the second lead at Edinburgh in 1779–80 and was seen in such parts as Aimwell in *The Beaux' Stratagem*, Bellamy in *The Suspicious Husband*, Carlos in *The Revenge*, Cleremont in *The Double Gallant*, Courtall in *The Belle's Stratagem*, George Bevil in *Cross Purposes*, Laertes in *Hamlet*, Sir George Airy in *The Busy Body*, Spritely in *The Author*, Stanley in *All the World's a Stage*, Valerius in *The Roman Father*, and Young Wilding in *The Citizen*.

Tate Wilkinson engaged Lane for Hull, Edinburgh, and York in 1780. In *The Wandering Patentee* Wilkinson said of Lane:

In Sir John Melville, Lord Morelove, and many gentlemanlike characters in that cast, he was truly unexceptionable. His temper, deportment, nice honour, without affection, and ever strictly sober and attentive, with many good qualities, added to a handsome and expressive face, with a good person, rendered him not only a credit to my theatre, but to every one he was ever to know. He did not continue with me above a year; he went to Ireland, being seduced by the alluring Mr. Hitchcock, who at that time drained my forces.

Lane played with Wilkinson's troupe at Sheffield in June 1781 before leaving for Ireland.

Lane made his debut at the Smock Alley Theatre, Dublin, and was also at Cork, in 1781. But in Dublin, Wilkinson heard, "the young, the spirited, the good Mr. Lane, formed a fatal attachment, fell into a decline, and died." His death came on 23 January 1782 at his lodgings in Bachelor's Walk, according to the *General Evening Post*.

Lane, Miss ₁*fl.* 1778₁, *posture maker. See* **LANE, MR** ₁*fl.* 1778₁.

Lane, Ann ₁*fl.* 1778₁, *dancer. See* **LANE, MR** ₁*fl.* 1778₁.

Lane, George ₁*fl.* 1675?–1696₁, *dancing master, dancer.*

Perhaps the Mr Lane who danced in the court masque *Calisto* on 15 February 1675 was the dancing master George Lane. When Dryden's *Albion and Albanius* was produced at the Dorset Garden Theatre in June 1685, with music by Louis Grabu, one critic-wit penned a poem ridiculing the effort, blaming most of the spectacle's failure on Grabu. The poem appeared in *Wit and Mirth* in 1719. One stanza concerned the dancing by one Lane, again probably George:

Lane thou has no Applause for thy Capers,
Tho' all without thee would make a Man spew;

*And a Month hence will not pay for the Tapers,
Spite of Jack Laureat and Monsieur Grabeu.*

The *Post Boy* of 4–6 February 1696 advertised that George Lane the dancing master was the teacher of William Cox, who had recently studied under St André in Paris and was about to set up dancing classes himself in London.

It may be that the following entry in the registers of St. Paul, Covent Garden, concerned our subject, though his name was too common to be certain: on 2 April 1685 Elizabeth, the wife of George Lane, was buried.

Lane, Mary. *See* WHITFIELD, MRS JOHN.

Lane, William *d. 1795, actor.*

At the Haymarket Theatre William Lane played Captain Sommerville in *The Double Amour* on 26 September 1791 and Dapper in *The Citizen* on 16 April 1792. The *Gentleman's Magazine* in April 1795 reported that Lane had died and identified him as a Canterbury actor.

Laneare. *See* LANIER.

La Neeves, Edmond [*fl. 1739*], *musician.*

Edmond La Neeves was one of the original subscribers to the Royal Society of Musicians when it was established on 28 August 1739. He may have been related to Corbet and William Neeves.

Lang, John Christopher [*fl. 1794*], *violist, harpsichordist.*

Doane's *Musical Directory* of 1794 listed John Christopher Lang, of Berwick Street, Soho, as a violist and harpsichordist who performed for the New Musical Fund.

Langdon, Mr [*fl. 1784*], *singer.*

A Mr Langdon from Peterborough sang bass in the Handel Memorial Concerts at Westminster Abbey and the Pantheon in May and June 1784.

Langfield. *See* LAYFIELD.

Langley, Mr [*fl. 1774*], *performer.*

Mr Langley was a supernumerary at Drury Lane Theatre in 1774 and possibly later.

Langley, Jacob [*fl. 1675–1692*], *drummer.*

The Lord Chamberlain's accounts show that on 20 December 1675 Jacob Langley was admitted to the King's Musick as a drummer in ordinary but without fee (that was usually styled an extraordinary post). Eventually, he must have been given a salaried position, for he was active in the King's Musick into the following decades. At the coronation of James II, Langley and three of his colleagues were described by Francis Sandford as "Four drums, in the same livery as the fife, with His Majesty's arms depicted on the drums, with scarves of crimson taffeta fringed with silver, all in one rank." Jacob got into debt, it seems, in the winter of 1691–92; on 22 January 1692 Henry Robinson petitioned against Langley for a rental payment, and both were ordered to appear before the Lord Chamberlain. The accounts contain no further references to the drummer.

Langley, John [*fl. 1685*], *proprietor.*

The London *Gazette* of 24 September 1685 reported that John Langley, a London merchant, had purchased "the rhinoceros and Islington Wells." It is not known how long he remained proprietor of the Wells.

Langlois, Francis [*fl. 1770–1777*], *dancer.*

Monsieur Francis Langlois was cited in Langford's *Century of Birmingham Life* as a performer in Birmingham in 1770. In 1770–71 he was a dancer at Drury Lane, but he apparently did not have assignments large enough to warrant his being named in the bills. His benefit tickets were admitted on 21 May 1771. He may have labored obscurely at Drury Lane in the years that followed, but we find no other notice of him until 24 May 1776, when the benefit tickets of "L'Englois" were accepted. He evidently worked at Drury Lane in 1776–77, but on 19 July 1777, the account books show, he was one of three performers who were not engaged for the ensuing season.

Langrish, Master [*fl. 1767–1782*], *dancer, actor.*

Master Langrish was one of 11 children who received £2 2s. each from Covent Garden Theatre on 10 March 1767 for dancing ten nights in *The Fairy Favour*, a masque by Thomas Hull that was first performed on 31 January 1767.

Though he may have performed again over the following several seasons, his name was next found in the Covent Garden bills on 26 April 1773, when he was advertised as a scholar of Aldridge making his first appearance in "A New Dance." He danced again on 30 April, several times in May, and then in the summer of 1773 he performed at Bristol.

Over the following several seasons he made occasional appearances at Covent Garden. In 1776–77, when Timothy Langrish (his brother or father) also danced in the company, Master Langrish performed in *Mirth and Jollity* and *The Villagers*. In 1780–81 he appeared as Eumenes in *The Siege of Sinope*, a tragedy by Frances Brooke which had its premiere on 31 January 1781 and ran ten nights. On 2 April 1781 he played the young Duke of Gloster in *King Charles the First*, according to a notation in the Enthoven Collection, though his name was not in the bills. On 7 January 1782 he played the Duke of York in *Richard III*, and on 6 May 1782 in *The What D'Ye Call It* he represented the Ghost of a Child Unborn.

Master Langrish also made occasional appearances at Drury Lane Theatre, though his name was in the bills there only once, for the Duke of York in *Richard III* on 18 September 1781. That theatre paid him and Miss Langrish (presumably his sister) 5*s*. each on 18 November 1780 for appearing on the "13th inst," apparently in *The Camp*. The same payment was repeated to each on 23 December 1780.

Langrish, Mary *b. 1769, actress.*

Mary Langrish, probably the daughter or sister of the dancer Timothy Langrish, was first noticed in the bills on 11 October 1779, when she played the Page in *The Orphan* at Covent Garden Theatre. At that time she was about ten years old. Her next role was the Duke of York in *Richard III* on 1 November 1779, and subsequently that season she appeared as a Page in *The Merry Wives of Windsor*, Lord William in *The Countess of Salisbury*, and an Attendant Genius in *A Fête*. In 1780–81 she reappeared in these roles and played a principal character in *The Touchstone*. On 12 May 1780 she acted the Duke of York in *Richard III* at Drury Lane, a role she repeated there on 8 March 1781. Occasional payments to her are noted in the Drury Lane account books: 5*s*. on 28 October 1780, for one night; 5*s*. each to her and Master Langrish on 18 November 1780, for the "13th inst"; another 5*s*. to each on 23 December 1780, for one night; and 5*s*. to her on 19 May 1781, again for one night.

Other roles for Miss Langrish in 1781–82 at Covent Garden were Prince Edward in *Richard III*, Joyce in *The What D'Ye Call It* (on 6 May 1782, when Master Langrish acted the Ghost of a Child Unborn), and a principal Fairy in *The Merry Wives of Windsor*. On 19 August 1783 she played Honoria in *The Lawyer* at the Haymarket Theatre. That autumn, on 18 October 1783, she appeared at the Royal Circus and then went to Ireland to play at the Capel Street Theatre, Dublin, where she made her debut on 18 December 1783. The *Public Register* of 10 January 1784 described her as scarcely 15 years old.

In the summer of 1785 Miss Langrish was back in London performing at the Haymarket Theatre, where her characters were Miss Winterbottom in *Hunt the Slipper*, Lucinda in *Love in a Village*, Miss Di in *Seeing is Believing*, Theodosia in *The Maid of the Mill*, Charlotte in *The Apprentice*, Arabella in *The Honest Yorkshireman*, Harriet in *The Devil upon Two Sticks*, the title role in *The Genius of Nonsense*, and Lucy in *The Beggar's Opera*, a busy season for a sixteen-year-old professional.

Again crossing the Irish Sea, she made her debut at the Smock Alley Theatre, Dublin, on 15 November 1785. She signed her name as Mary Langrish on a letter from Smock Alley performers in the *Hibernian Journal* on 30 January 1786, after which date we lose track of her.

Langrish, Timothy [*fl. 1776–1790?*], *dancer, dancing master.*

Timothy Langrish was probably the Langrish who was a member of the summer company at Birmingham in 1776. He was a chorus dancer at Covent Garden Theatre by 1776–77, earning £1 10*s*. per week. On 25 April 1777 he danced a comic dance, *The Coopers*, with Master Jackson and Miss Nicolo. There seem to have been both a Mr Langrish and a Master Langrish in the Covent Garden dancing corps that season—either father and son or brothers. While it is possible that there was only one male dancer of that name, we are assuming an elder dancer named Timothy and a younger one, "Master" Langrish (scholar to Aldridge), who had been dancing at Covent Garden since 1767. It was Timothy who appeared, we believe, in various specialty numbers at that theatre through 1781–82, during which period his salary remained a constant £1 10s. per week. On 29 December 1777 one Langrish had replaced Aldridge in a dancing part in *Norwood Gypsies*, a pantomime which first had been performed on the previous 25 November. This substitution for a mature dancer—indeed Master Langrish's teacher—and the fact that Master Langrish continued to dance at Covent Garden until 1782 would seem to confirm the presence of two dancers of that name.

Langrish also danced at Sadler's Wells in May 1777, April 1779, and May 1781. An undated advertisement (but probably from 1780) surviving in a press clipping in the Finsbury Public Library announced his benefit at Sadler's Wells and gave his address as No 14, Bow Street, Covent Garden.

In 1790 the *Universal British Directory of Trade and Commerce* listed Timothy Langrish (probably our subject) as a dancing master in Liverpool.

The Miss Mary Langrish (b. 1769) who acted in Dublin and London during the 1780s was probably his sister or daughter.

Langsdale. *See* LONSDALE.

Languishe. *See* LANGRISH.

Lanier, Andrea *d. 1660, wind instrumentalist.*

Andrea Lanier was the son of the Nicholas Lanier who died in 1612 and who was responsible for founding the English branch of the extensive Lanier clan. Andrea had a brother Alfonso and a brother John, both of whom were musicians at the English court. Pulver cites as the earliest reference to Andrea Lanier the Cotton manuscript at the British Library, in which Lanier was listed as receiving an annual salary of £17 9s. 2d. in 1603. It is possible, however, that that citation concerns an earlier Andrea Lanier, for the earliest reference to our subject in the Lord Chamberlain's accounts is many years later, on 20 September 1618, when "Andrew" Lanier was appointed to his deceased father's position as flutist in the King's Musick. Yet *Grove* (fifth edition) dates his appointment 1612 and notes that Lanier had been receiving payments as a cornetist from about 1603.

On 6 June 1626 Lanier received £59 13s. 4d. for summer and winter liveries for two boys in his keeping and under his instruction in wind instruments. Lanier also received the usual £16 2s. 6d. livery allowance. From time to time he was given money for the purchase of materials for teaching, as in January 1629, when the accounts show him to have been paid £23 for four sets of music books and two Italian music cards to compose on. By 1630 Lanier was receiving quarterly £29 16s. 8d. for maintaining and teaching his two students. A payment to him on 19 December 1630 would suggest that he may have been in charge of the wind instruments at court: he was paid £16 10s. for three tenor and three treble cornets. In 1633 Andrea took under his tutelage his nephew and namesake, Andrea, the son of Henry Lanier. As one warrant in 1637–38 put it, Lanier taught his students "the science of lez flutes and cornetts." By 1640 Andrea had two other Lanier boys as his pupils, William and Thomas.

At the Restoration, Lanier, on 13 July 1660, was reappointed a "musician upon the flute in ordinary" and a tutor for two boys, but he did not live to enjoy the reestablishment of the King's Musick. Lanier was buried at Greenwich on 2 November 1660. By 15 November Thomas Lanier, Andrea's son and executor, succeeded to his father's position in the wind instruments and received the money due his father for the maintenance and teaching of his two pupils.

Andrea Lanier had made his will on 2 (22?) September 1660 at East Greenwich, Kent. Andrea's late sister, Katherine Farrant, had left him a legacy of about £30, to be paid after the death of his sister Mary Lanier. Of that amount he left £10 to his wife Joyce, £10 to his son Thomas, and £10 to his daughter Margaret (a Margaret Road was a witness to his will, but she signed with her mark, so she may not have been his daughter). Andrea left £100 and all his land and buildings in East Greenwich to his son Thomas; the rest of his estate he bequeathed to his wife Joyce. Thomas and his mother proved the will on 14 February 1661.

Lanier, Clement *d. 1661, recorder, cornet, and sackbut player.*

Clement Lanier was the son of the Nicholas Lanier who died in 1612 and was a sackbut player in the King's Musick. According to Grove and *The Dictionary of National Biography*, Nicholas Lanier left five daughters and six sons; the sons were all court musicians: John (d. 1616), Alphonso (d. 1613), Innocent (d. 1625), Jerome (d. 1657), Clement (d. 1661), and Andrea (d. 1660). Possibly our subject was the Clement Lanier who, according to Pulver, played the recorder at court about 1600 and was in 1604 receiving an annual salary of £20 as a sackbut player. Though double positions were not uncommon, the dates seem very early, for the Lord Chamberlain's accounts make no further mention of Clement Lanier until 1625, when he was listed among those court musicians who played "windy Instruments" for James I. On 19 December of that year he was granted a livery allowance of £16 2s. 6d. as a musician to Charles I. On 15 July 1628 he was listed as one of the musicians for the recorders. A warrant dated 4 March 1633 indicates that Lanier also played the cornet. In 1636 he succeeded to his deceased brother Alphonso's hay-weighing monopoly.

With the outbreak of the civil war the court musical establishment was disbanded. Clement Lanier's arrears in salary the Commonwealth government in 1651 promised to pay, and in 1652 his wife Hannah received £10 on account. His annual salary, as of 1640, had been £46.

At the Restoration Clement Lanier was granted livery as a wind instrumentalist at the coronation of Charles II, and on 4 October 1661 he was officially readmitted to the King's Musick. But Lanier died between then and 13 November, on which date Stephen Strong replaced him as a musician on the double sackbut. Lanier had made his will on 2 February 1659, describing himself as then of East Greenwich, Kent, and sick and weak of body. He left everything, including his house in East Greenwich, to his daughter Susannah, who had been caring for him and for his small children, her brothers. He asked that she sell the property in order to obtain money enough for the following legacies: £40 to herself, £5 to Clement's son Nicholas if he demanded it in person, £10 to his daughter Elizabeth Lanier, £10 for Susannah to divide among the younger children when they should reach 21, £5 each to his sons Nicholas, John, and Robert if each made demand in person £5 to his son Lionel if he should complete his apprenticeship under Thomas Mabb (if he should fail to do so and become a freeman, he was to get only 12d.), £5 to his son William, and £5 to his daughter Frances Lanier. If any of the younger children should die before reaching 21, their portion was to be divided among the surviving daughters only. Susannah Lanier proved the will on 3 December 1661. Lanier made no mention of a wife, so we can assume she died before he wrote his will. The only mention of any wife was in 1652 when Hannah Lanier received money for Clement from the government. The wording of the will suggests that Hannah had been a second wife, the mother of Clement's younger children, and that he had had Susannah and the others, who sound like adults, much earlier.

Lanier, Nicholas *1588–1666, singer, lutenist, composer, scene painter.*

Nicholas Lanier was the son of the second John Lanier, a sackbut player who died in 1616, and his wife Frances, née Galliardello. Nicholas was born in Greenwich (?) and christened on 10 September 1588 at Holy Trinity, Minories, in London. Until 1607 he was indentured to the Earl of Salisbury, and from 1605 to 1613

Faculty of Music, Oxford

NICHOLAS LANIER
self-portrait

he received payments from the Cecil family. He may have journeyed to Italy in 1610 with William Cecil.

Lanier, Coperario, and Campion collaborated on a masque celebrating the marriage of Robert Carr, Earl of Somerset, and Lady Frances Howard; it was presented at Whitehall on 26 December 1614 (*Grove's Dictionary*, 5th edition; the *New Grove* says only 1613) with Lanier participating as a singer. Lanier composed the music for Ben Jonson's masque *Lovers Made Men*, which was performed on 22 February 1617 at the house of Lord Haye; in it he used the *stilo recitativo*, already popular in Italy and eventually to become the fashion in England. Lanier sang in the performance, for which he had also painted the scenery. He composed music for Jonson's masque *The Vision of Delight*, which was given at court at Christmas 1617, *Gypsies Metamorphosed* (1621), and the *Masque of Augurs* (1622). In 1618 Nicholas was made Master of the Musick to Prince Charles at an annual salary of £200. By 1615 Lanier was a singer in the King's Musick, and among the wind instrumentalists were his uncles Andrea and Clement. All of them were part of a large family of French (and possibly Italian) origin who were an important part of the English musical scene for a hundred years.

In June 1625 Charles I sent Nicholas Lanier to Italy with the Duke of Buckingham to purchase paintings and statues for the royal collection. Though Lanier is said to have remained on the Continent for three years (or made three continental trips between 1625 and 1628) helping to gather art works, he was still on the books as a musician in London. The Lord Chamberlain's accounts show a livery payment of £16 2s. 6d. on 6 June 1626 to Lanier as one of the court lutenists. The following 22 June he was named Master of the King's Musick, and on 11 July he was granted an annual salary of £200 for that post. He returned to England in October 1627, then made another trip to the Continent later that year. The impressive collection Lanier brought back to England cost the King about £35,000, though he was delinquent in some of his payments, and at the outbreak of civil war some years later, the collection was auctioned off—with Lanier and other members of his clan buying as much as they could afford.

Back in London on 6 February 1629 Nicholas, his brother John, and his uncles Andrea, Clement, and Jerome were apprehended for disorderly conduct on the street; the case created considerable hubbub in town. In 1630 Nicholas set to music the Herrick poem celebrating the birth of Prince Charles (later Charles II). Lanier was made keeper of the King's miniatures, and in 1636 he and some of his musical colleagues were granted permission by the King to form what came to be called the Corporation of Music, of which he was the first Marshall.

The civil war brought an end to Lanier's musical activities in London. He crossed the channel several times during the period before 1660, but much of his time was spent in Holland. He was in Antwerp, the Hague, and Utrecht in 1646. That year he described himself to Huygens as "old, unhappye in a manner in exile, plundered not only of his fortune, but of all his musicall papers, nay, almost of his witts and vertue." He kept up with his painting, developing a technique for making his works appear aged. In 1658, in *Graphice*, William Sanderson wrote of Lanier working in Paris: "by a cunning way of tempering his colours with Chimney Soote, the Painting becomes duskish, and seems ancient; which done, he roules up and thereby it crackls, and so mistaken for an old Principall, it being well copied from a good hand."

On 28 August 1660 Nicholas Lanier was reappointed Master of the King's Musick and Marshall of the Corporation of Music (or, more correctly, of The Marshall, Wardens, and Cominality of the Arte and Science of Musicke in Westminster, or sometimes the Corporation of Westminster Musicians). As Master of the King's Musick Lanier had the

power to order and convocate the [musicians] at fitt time of practize and service as is expressed in [the King's] privy seal given him by his late Majesty when he was Prince of Wales, and that if any of them refuse to wayte at such convenient tymes of practize and service as he shall appoint, and for such instruments, voyces and musick, as he in reason shall think them fitted to serve in, upon his just complaint, [the Lord Chamberlain] shall punish them either in their persons or their wages as [he] shall think the offence deserves.

Lanier's position also concerned expenditures for instruments, the purchase and repair of which he had to approve. He continued receiving his annual salary, plus two separate livery payments, one as Master and one as a lutenist. With four other prominent members of the King's Musick—Henry Cooke, Matthew Locke, the elder Charles Coleman, and George Hudson—Lanier paid annually £50 for the rental of two rooms for practice and storage of instruments—perhaps in premises outside the court. Possibly it was one of those rooms from which Lanier barred six of his court musicians, for they complained to the Lord Chamberlain, and on 2 December 1661 Lanier was told to allow the musicians to use the practice room assigned for violin rehearsals.

From time to time the court musicians were ordered to accompany the King on trips outside London, as in the summer of 1663, when Lanier and a number of other musicians went to Windsor. Like many other musicians in the royal employ, Lanier probably lived a much richer musical-social life than surviving records reveal. We get a glimpse of Lanier in the diary of Samuel Pepys. Pepys first mentioned the musician on 30 October 1665. On the following 6 December he wrote of visiting his friend Mrs Pierce, "where Captain Rolt and Mrs Knipp [the actress], Mr Coleman and his wife [musicians], and Laneare, Mrs Worshipp and her singing daughter met. . . . Here the best company for musique I ever was in in my life, and I wish I could live and die in it. . . ." A month later he had Lanier and some of the same group at his own home. "Laneare sings in a melancholy method very well, and a sober man he seems to be."

Nicholas Lanier died in February 1666. The registers at his home parish in Greenwich show that on 24 February he was "buried away"—but there was no indication where. Wheatley's notes to Pepy's *Diary*, citing the *Somerset House Gazette*, state that Nicholas Lanier died at the age of 78 on 4 November 1646 (*sic*) and was buried at St Martin-in-the-Fields. Pelham Humphrey replaced Lanier as a lutenist, and Louis Grabu succeeded him as Master of the King's Musick. Lanier had made his will on 5 March 1661, with Charles Coleman and John Hingeston, both court musicians, serving as witnesses. To his wife Elizabeth he left all of his household goods, including his "drawings Paintings [and] moveables." Oddly, he made no mention of music or instruments, though he was careful to describe himself as master of his majesty's music. Nicholas Lanier's widow was to distribute £2 to charity; a 20*s*. piece of gold to his brother John Lanier's son and 10*s*. to his daughter; and 20*s*. to Nicholas's sister and 10*s*. each to her son and three daughters. From a debt of £450 owed to Lanier by Thomas, Earl of Arundell, Lanier had by an earlier memorandum made a bequest to his niece Elizabeth Atkins; to Elizabeth's brother and sister he left 10*s*. each; and to "our goodfriend Mr William Towers" he gave £2 for a pair of gloves. Elizabeth Lanier proved the will on 21 March 1666.

Some of Lanier's songs and other short pieces were included in popular collections that appeared from 1653 to 1685, and much of his music in manuscript is at the British Library, Oxford, and Cambridge.

Portraits of Nicholas Lanier include:

1. By W. Dobson, of Lanier with Sir Charles Cotterell. At Alnwick Castle, Northumberland.

2. By Inigo Jones. Some sketches of Lanier with a damsel and a dwarf.

3. By Nicholas Lanier. Self-portrait inscribed "Made & paynted by Nich. Lanier." At the Music School, Oxford. Engraving by J. Caldwall.

4. By J. Livens. Location unknown. An engraving was done by L. Vorsterman (n.d.); copies were engraved by T. Chambars for a plate to Walpole's *Anecdotes*, 1762, and by R. Cooper for a plate to a later edition of the same work, 1862.

5. By Isaac Oliver. Miniature once in the collection of James II.

6. By Van Dyck. Half-length. In the Vienna Kunsthistorisches Museum. A preparatory chalk study is in the National Gallery of Scotland.

7. By Van Dyck. As "David playing the harp before Saul." Location unknown.

Lanier, Thomas *1633–c. 1686, lutenist, violinist, wind instrumentalist.*

Thomas Lanier was baptized on 23 June 1633, according to *Grove* (fifth edition), the son of Andrea Lanier (d. 1660) and his wife Joyce (at least Joyce Lanier was named as Thomas's mother in 1677). Thomas studied music under his father as a member of the court music of Charles I, beginning on 12 January 1640; also under Andrea Lanier's tuition was

LANIER

William Lanier, perhaps Thomas's brother. At the Restoration Lanier petitioned for "the three places of music in which in 1643 the late king joined him with his father." Also in 1660 Lanier applied, unsuccessfully it seems, for the receivership of Suffolk, Cambridgeshire, Leicestershire, and Warwickshire, or some other county.

Andrea Lanier died in 1660, leaving Thomas as his executor. On 15 November 1660 Thomas Lanier was admitted to the King's Musick as a musician for the flutes and cornets—that is, the wind instruments—replacing his father. In some documents in the Lord Chamberlain's accounts Lanier was listed also among the violins. He was granted 1s. 8d. daily or £7 11s. 8d. yearly for board wages, plus 1s. 8d. daily and £16 2s. 6d. annually for livery, plus £29 9s. 2d. annually for "apparrell." On 30 November Thomas received £59 13s. 4d. as his father's executor for teaching and maintaining two students.

The accounts show that Thomas Lanier did not manage his finances well and was frequently in debt. The earliest such occurrence was on 12 January 1661, when Thomas Arthur petitioned against Lanier for a debt. A year later Mr and Mrs Bartholomew Audley went against Lanier for a debt for £20, and in September 1662 Thomas Johnson petitioned against the musician. In May 1663 Lanier was to be apprehended "at the suit of a blind man," and a month later Lanier, the tables turned, petitioned against Joseph Alexander. Thomas Johnson still had some cause outstanding against Lanier in January 1664. Lanier's financial troubles were shared by other court musicians; Charles II was behind in his payments of livery allowances to his employees, though the records indicate that the King's delinquency did not get serious until the middle of the 1660s. In 1666, for instance, Lanier was still owed livery payments for 1663, 1664, and 1665. As of 9 January 1669 he was owed £67 9s. 2d. It is worth noting that he had encountered financial difficulties even before the King fell behind in his payments.

Grove states that after 1668 Lanier held only a position among the lutes. On 7 December 1677 Thomas wrote to a Mr Townsend requesting that his debenture for his 1677 livery allowance be sent to his mother, Mrs Joyce Lanier. His finances seem to have stabilized somewhat after his difficulties in the early 1660s, however, despite the lateness with which the crown paid his allowances. His yearly salary (as of 13 December 1679) of £46 10s. 10d. as a member of the wind group at court seems to have been paid on time; the livery allowance regularly ran about three or four years behind. Perhaps there was an error in the report of arrears on 25 February 1686, for it shows Lanier was still owed for the periods 1660 to 1667 and 1678 to 1684, whereas earlier livery warrants had not indicated any arrears dating back into the 1660s. On 21 September 1686 King James, in an attempt to clear up his late brother's debts to court musicians, ordered the payment of £170 10s. to Lanier.

But it is likely that the money came after Lanier had died. The previous 13 May he had appointed Mrs Francis Emps his lawful attorney, and after 1686 citations of Lanier in the Lord Chamberlain's accounts cease.

Grove states that Thomas Lanier was the father of General Sir John Lanier, Governor of Jersey.

Lanier, William   *1618–1660?, sackbut player.*

William Lanier was baptized on 21 September 1618. He was the son of Jerome Lanier, and on 28 January 1626, when William was yet a boy, a place among the sackbut players was granted to William and his father. The post was evidently held for him over the years. On 22 December 1637 a warrant in the Lord Chamberlain's accounts indicates that by then William was a member of the court wind instrumentalists and was required to wait on the King at chapel and at table. He may at that time have held a position without salary, for on 6 and 7 July 1640 he was sworn a musician for the wind instruments in ordinary (salaried) in place of John Adson, deceased. Lanier's salary was set at 1s. 8d. daily, and he was to receive the customary livery allowance of £16 2s. 6d. annually.

Lanier was briefly in the court musical establishment at the Restoration, or so it would seem. On 3 August 1661 a warrant was issued for William Lanier and others to remain in their places in the wind music. Yet Grove states that John Singleton had replaced Lanier on 3 June 1661; that warrant is not listed in

Cart de la Fontaine's *The King's Musick*. And the *New Grove* dates William Lanier's death abut 1660. (It was not uncommon for warrants to cite replacements a year or more after the deaths of previous incumbents.)

Lanière, Mons [*fl.* 1724–1725], *actor.*
In the French troupe of "Italian" comedians that performed from 17 December 1724 to 13 May 1725 at the Haymarket Theatre Monsieur Lanière was the lover in the *commedia dell' arte* tradition. No roles were named for him, but he shared a benefit with Mme Lagaronne on 7 April 1725 when *Le Festin de Pierre* and *Arlequin embassadeur d'amour* were performed.

Lankman. *See* LARKMAN.

Lanthoife, John [*fl.* 1794], *singer?*
Doane's *Musical Directory* of 1794 listed John Lanthoife, of No 24, Bacon Street, as a tenor (singer, presumably, though he may have been a violist) who participated in the Handel performances at Westminster Abbey.

Lany, Jean-Barthélémy 1718–1786, *dancer, ballet master, choreographer.*
The dancer Jean-Barthélémy Lany was born at Paris on 24 March 1718, the son of the dancing master Jean Lany and his wife Françoise Hallé. He was a dancer at the Académie royale de musique (the Paris Opéra) by 1741, that year performing in *Issé* and *Nitétis*. In 1743 he was engaged by Frederick the Great in Berlin as *maître de ballet* and *premier danseur* for a salary of 2000 crowns. With his two sisters, Lany first danced at Berlin in November 1743 and met with Frederick's approval. But the Prussian ruler mistreated his players and paid them poorly, so at the end of 1747 Lany and others broke their contracts and fled Berlin.

On 3 December 1747, the Marquis d'Argenson in Paris wrote to Frederick: "Nothing can be so dreadful as the action of Lany, he deserves that your Majesty should make him feel the full weight of his indignation. I have said throughout Paris what I had to say about this low fellow and his companions in desertion and knavery. . . ." The Marquis's efforts to the contrary, in 1748 Lany became ballet master at the Opéra, where he staged and danced

Bibliothèque de l'Opéra

JEAN-BARTHÉLÉMY LANY
by Bouquet

in many ballets and operas until 1770, when he left with a pension of 2500 livres. According to Compardon, who in his *Académie royale de musique* provides a long list of the productions in which Lany appeared in Paris, he was one of the best ballet masters of his time.

In 1774–75 Lany was engaged as ballet master at the King's Theatre, London, where he first appeared on 8 November 1774 as Zephir in the ballet *Le Baillet de Fleur*. On 19 November he danced with Mlle Baccelli in a new pastoral ballet. His most important assignment that season was as ballet master and principal dancer in *Motezuma*, which opened on 7 February 1775. His other choreography included *Le Bal masquer* with Mme Vallois, *La Mascherata*, and *Champêtre comique*. On 27 April 1775 he enjoyed a benefit at the King's.

Upon returning to Paris, Lany was a member of the *Académie de danse*. He died at his house in the Rue de Richelieu on 29 March

1786 and was buried at St Eustache. Of Jean-Barthélémy Lany, Noverre wrote that his "superiority excites our admiration and raises him above anything I could say of him."

One of the Lany sisters, Louise-Madeleine Lany, born in 1733, danced for the first time at the Opéra in 1743 and enjoyed a successful career there until 1763, when she retired with a pension of 1500 livres. In 1764 she married Nicolas Gélin, a singer at the Opéra. Louise-Madeleine, whom in his *Lettres* Noverre called "the first dancer in the world," died in 1777. Another sister, Charlotte Lany, also danced at the Opéra during the middle years of the century.

A sketch of Jean-Barthélémy in a dancing pose drawn by costume designer René-Louis Bouquet abut 1760 is in the Bibliothèque de l'Opéra.

Lanyer. *See* LANIER.

Lanyon, Mr [*fl.* 1723–1741], *dancer.*

A dancer named "Lanyam" played the Doctor (Neptune) in *Jupiter and Europa* at Lincoln's Inn Fields Theatre probably on 23 and certainly on 25 March 1723. That would appear to be a citation for Mr Lanyon, who danced in London until 1741. On 22 May 1723 he shared a benefit with Mrs Edzard which brought in only £54 4s. He did much better a year later, when he shared with Huddy gross receipts of £124 5s. Lanyon's daily salary at Lincoln's Inn Fields was 5s., at least in the fall of 1724. He continued at that theatre through the 1729–30 season, dancing in entr'acte turns and appearing as Scaramouch (Pan), a Doctor (Neptune), and Punch (Pluto) in *Jupiter and Europa*, a Scaramouch Man and Mezzetin Man in *The Necromancer*, a Fury in *Amadis*, the Mad Astrologer in *The Humours of Bedlam*, Ixion in *Harlequin Sorcerer*, a Follower of Mars in *Mars and Venus*, a Peasant and a Bacchanal in *Apollo and Daphne*, a Sicilian, Demon, and Countryman Gardener in *The Rape of Proserpine*, and an Infernal in *Perseus and Andromeda*.

After that Lanyon turned to teaching, one of his scholars, Master Davey, making his first appearance on 9 April 1741 at Goodman's Fields Theatre for Lanyon's benefit. That was the first mention of Lanyon in any playbill since 1730 and the last mention of him that has been found.

Lanze. *See* LALAUZE..

Lanzetti, Salvatore *c. 1710–c. 1780, violoncellist, composer.*

Salvatore Lanzetti was born in Naples about 1710, according to Grove, and after studying music at the Conservatoire of Santa Maria di Loreto in his native city he came to London. Grove dates his London journey about 1739, but surely the following news clippings as transcribed by Latreille refers to him: at Lincoln's Inn Fields Theatre on 7 May 1733 was held a "Benefit of Signor Lancetti, Vertuoso of the Violoncello & servant to His Majesty, King of Sardinia. A Concert of vocal and instrumental musick by Signori Arigoni, St. Martini, Fratelli, Castrucci, Carbonelli . . . The said Signor Lancetti will play several solos on the Violoncello." Burney credited Lanzetti with popularizing the 'cello in England.

Grove states that Lanzetti performed in Germany at Frankfurt on the Main in May 1751. He returned to England in 1754 and at the Haymarket Theatre on 13 February played a violoncello solo at a performance of *Acis and Galatea*. After his stay in London he went to Turin and became a member of the royal chapel. Lanzetti composed some sonatas for his instrument and wrote a tutor for it. He died in Turin about 1780. Lanzetti was pictured in an anonymous engraving showing a quintet of musicians in an outdoor concert, published as the frontispiece to Michel Corrette's *Les Amusements du Parnasse* (Paris, c. 1740). He is shown playing the 'cello, with Scarlatti at the harpsichord, Tartini on the violin, San Martini playing the oboe, and Locatelli on the violin.

Lanzoni, Vincenzo *b. 1757, violinist, violist.*

Vincenzo Lanzoni was recommended for membership in the Royal Society of Musicians on 1 February 1784 and was described then as 27 years old, single, a violinist and tenor (viola) player, and a participant in "Lord Abrilbons concerts." He was admitted in June, and though the minutes indicate that he withdrew, he must have been readmitted later, for in May 1790 he played violin in the Society's annual concert at St Paul's. In May and June 1784 at Westminster Abbey and the Pantheon, Lanzoni had played in the Handel Memorial Concerts. Smith

Courtesy of the Reasearch Center for Musical Iconography, City University of New York

"The Musical Ensemble," about 1740
ALESSANDRO SCARLATTI, harpsichord; Giuseppe Tartini, violin; GIUSEPPE SAN MARTINI, oboe; Locatelli, violin; and SALVATORE LANZETTI, violincello.

artist unknown

in *The Italian Opera in London* lists Lanzoni among the musicians playing at the Haymarket and Covent Garden theatres in 1790.

La Pierre, Mons [*fl.* 1740–1744], *dancer.*
Monsieur La Pierre danced the character of Pan in *The Rural Sports* at Drury Lane Theatre on 27 October 1740 and was seen during the rest of the 1740–41 season in *Comus* and a solo dance called *Le Paisan*. He began the 1742–43 season with an appearance at Drury Lane on 21 September 1742 in a *Tyrolean Dance*, but by December he had moved to Lincoln's Inn Fields Theatre. There he appeared in a comic ballet beginning on 3 December and was seen during the season in a solo entr'acte number, *Le Sabotier*. In *The Imprisonment of Harlequin* he danced a Shepherd and a Peasant. La Pierre concluded his appearances in England performing a *Wooden Shoe Dance* at the Pinchbeck and Fawkes booth at Bartholomew Fair on 23 August 1743. The bill claimed that the dance had never been performed by anyone but him. He also danced *Le Paissans léger* with Mlle Mariette.

Campardon lists La Pierre as a "danseur anglaise" and notes that he danced *Le Sabotier* on 2 September 1744 at the Saint Laurent Fair and was engaged by the Opéra Comique.

Laravier. *See* LA RIVIERE.

Larbor, Mr [*fl.* 1767], *dresser?*
The account books for Drury Lane Theatre show a payment of £2 2s. to a Mr Larbor for attending Guidetti the dancer. Perhaps Larbor was a dresser.

Laremouth, Robert [*fl.* 1794], *violist, violinist.*
Doane's *Musical Directory* of 1794 listed Robert Laremouth, of Church Street, Ostend

(*sic*), as a tenor player (violist) and violinist who performed in London for the Choral Fund, Cecilian Society, and Surrey Chapel Society.

La Revier. *See* **LA RIVIERE.**

Larfay, Mr [*fl.* 1725], *house servant?*
Mr Larfay shared a benefit with three others at Lincoln's Inn Fields Theatre on 22 May 1725 that brought in £101 before house charges.

Largeau, Master [*fl.* 1756–1757], *actor.*
At Drury Lane Theatre from 3 December 1756 to perhaps 8 March 1757 Master Largeau played Fripperel in *Lilliput.*

La Rich, Francis [*fl.* 1685–1700], *bass player.*
On a warrant dated 10 September–22 October 1685 in the Lord Chamberlain's accounts Mons La Rich was listed as having been appointed to the private music of James II as a bass player. From time to time the accounts referred to La Rich (or Le Rich, La Rush, Li Rich): in the autumn of 1685 he attended the King and Queen on a trip to Hampton Court and Windsor; he was with the King at Windsor again in the summer of 1688; and he apparently went to Holland with William III in January 1691. For such service court musicians were paid extra daily fees. La Rich served as a Steward for the St Cecilia Day Festival in 1689 while still retaining his post in the King's Musick. His annual salary at court was £30 under William III, but court records of La Rich stop after 1691.

A benefit concert was given for La Rich and Jeremiah Clarke at Hickford's Dancing School on 9 December 1697. He had that year again been a Steward at the St Cecilia Day Festival, and the popular music Clarke had written was played at that concert and again, for La Rich's benefit alone, on 16 December. On 23 March 1698 James Brydges reported going to a concert at Frank Roberts's at which La Rich was one of the performers. La Rich went to the Continent after that, for on 25 September 1700, when he played at the Lincoln's Inn Fields playhouse, he was described as "lately arrived from the Court of Poland: being the only and last Time of performing the said Entertainment [of Musick], or any other, by reason of his sudden return to the said Kingdom."

La Riche, Mrs. *See* **LA ROCHE, MRS.**

Larini. *See* **VIOLANTE..**

La Riviere, Mons [*fl.* 1764–1784], *dancer, choreographer, dancing master.*
One La Riviere (sometimes denominated Laravier, La Revier, La Rivere, Revier, Ravier, Revilly, or Restier) was from time to time a dancer or choreographer at London's patent theatres and opera house from 1764 to 1784.

He was said to be making his first appearance on an English stage when, on 9 May 1765, he danced a *New Turkish Dance* at Covent Garden Theatre. He was also on the list of the corps de ballet of the opera at the King's Theatre that spring. He was doubtless the "Restier" who danced with three others following performances of the opera *Berenice* on 5 January and following. But because of the paucity of records concerning the opera in London at that time it is impossible to determine how constantly he was employed at the King's Theatre over the years. He danced at Covent Garden Theatre in 1766–67 and 1767–68 for 16s. a week, according to Arthur Murphy's list of that theatre's salaries for those seasons.

When La Riviere next appeared in the records he was at Drury Lane Theatre. He created the short ballets introduced in the *fête champêtre* in *The Maid of the Oaks* on 5 November 1774 and repeated on many successful nights following. "The ballets are very Grand," the prompter Hopkins wrote in his diary; and the *Westminster Magazine* thought them "elegant." But La Riviere did not himself dance at Drury Lane until 3 April 1775, in his own new ballet *The Force of Love*, with Signor and Signora Como and two children. He appeared with Mrs Sutton dancing a pastoral and a comic dance on her benefit night, 28 April. In the next season, 1775–76, he seems to have been a choreographer at Drury Lane, but he danced on only two nights, so far as the bills show. On 15 April 1776, at the end of the play, there was "A *Comic Dance* by the two Miss Stageldoirs, scholars to M. La Riviere." On 10 June, when he received a payment, his name was spelled "Larivere."

The listing in *The London Stage* of "Mad LaRiviere" dancing with Miss Wilford and others in *The Female Archer* on 16 March 1767 at Covent Garden Theatre is a mistake for Mons La Riviere.

Larken, Mr [fl. 1756], *actor.*

On 12 August 1756 a Mr Larken, otherwise unknown, played a principal role in a performance of *Love and Duty* at Drury Lane Theatre. The work was not repeated.

Larken, Mr [fl. 1771–1772], *actor.*

At Drury Lane Theatre on 17 April 1771 a Mr Larken made his first stage appearance, playing Abel in *The Committee*. His second attempt seems to have been on 12 May 1772 at Covent Garden Theatre, when he played Richard III. The *Theatrical Review* that year made short work of him: ". . . Mr Larken . . . is an Engraver by profession. We hope he cuts a better Figure on Copper than he does upon the Stage."

Larken, Edmund [fl. 1744], *musician?*

At Stationers' Hall on 9 February 1744 a benefit concert was presented for Edmund Larken. He was probably a musician, though the bill made no mention of his participation in the concert.

Larkin, Mr. See LARKEN, MR [fl. 1771–1772].

Larkman, Mr [fl. 1793–1813], *doorkeeper, boxkeeper.*

The Covent Garden Theatre accounts cited a Mr "Lankman" as a house servant earning 12s. weekly in 1793–94. That was surely a reference to the doorkeeper Larkman, named in the accounts the following season at that salary and mentioned regularly to 16 October 1813. By 1805 he was working as a boxkeeper, though his salary remained a constant 12s. weekly to the end of his career. He may have been related to the Mr Larkman who was active at the Theatre Royal, Edinburgh, in 1807–8.

L'Armand. See ST AMAND.

La Roche, Mrs [fl. 1767], *actress.*

Mrs La Roche made her first appearance on any stage at Covent Garden Theatre on 4 November 1767 as Arpasia in *Tamerlane*. She repeated the role the following day; then on 12 December she announced her "Last time of appearing this season" and acted Monimia in *The Orphan*. Those three performances seem to be the extent of her London career. *The London Stage* mistakenly listed her as Mrs La Riche in the 1767–68 Covent Garden season roster.

Laroche, James c. 1688–1710?, *singer.*

When James Laroche was first noticed in playbills in late December 1695 he was described as a boy of seven, so we can place his birth about 1688. He sang "So well Corinna likes the joy" in *The She-Gallants* at the Lincoln's Inn Fields Theatre. He was probably "the Boy" who was sometimes cited in printed songs in 1696. In March of that year he sang in *The City Bride*, and on 14 November and subsequent dates "Jemmy Laroche" played Cupid in *The Loves of Mars and Venus*. He was the Child of Hercules in "Hercules," a section of *The Novelty* presented in June 1697. Young James was a Savoyard in *Europe's Revels* on 4 November of that year. In the latter work he sang "The Raree-Show," which became exceedingly popular.

Caulfield in his *Remarkable Persons* stated that

Harvard Theatre Collection

JAMES LAROCHE
artist unknown

Laroche exhibited a raree show in London and the provinces about 1710, in competition with a showman called "Old Harry." Laroche was described as "a fellow of great ingenuity." Perhaps the James "La Roach" who was buried at St Paul, Covent Garden on 4 July 1710 was our subject.

The Dictionary of National Biography cites a print of Laroche entitled "The Raree Show, sung by Jemmy Laroch in the Musical Interlude for the Peace [of Utrecht] with the Tune set to Music for the Violin [by John Eccles]. Ingraved, Printed, Culred, and Sold by Sutton Nicholls . . ." (brackets theirs; the peace the original song referred to was that of Ryswick in 1697). The *DNB* says the interlude was played at Lincoln's Inn Fields in April 1713, but that is well after any other record of Laroche's activity and, in any case, the old Lincoln's Inn Fields playhouse was not then in use and the new one had not yet opened. Marcellus Laroon printed in his *Cryes of the City of London* the same or a similar picture of Laroche presenting his raree show to a group of children, according to Grove. But Laroon's work first appeared in 1688 and was reprinted in 1711.

La Romaine, Mme [*fl.* 1786–1789], *rope dancer.*

Mme Romaine was a rope dancer at Sadler's Wells from at least 1786 to 1789. Surviving advertisements indicate that she danced on the rope with the Little Devil, La Belle Espagnole, and others on 9 October 1786, 23 April 1787, 14 September 1787, 7 June 1788, and 13 April 1789.

Laroon, John *b. c.* 1676?, *bass player.*

John Laroon was the elder brother of the artist Marcellus Laroon (in whose entry more details are provided of the Laroon family) and was probably born about 1676—or between his father's marriage about 1674 and Marcellus's birth in April 1679. In his autobiographical sketch Marcellus Laroon said that as boys he and John were taught painting by their father and also schooled in French, writing, arithmetic, fencing, and dancing. His father entertained in his house a very good master of music, whose name was Moret, who performed on several instruments,—with design, as my father had a very good ear, to learn of him to play on the six-stringed viol; but my eldest brother [John], ten years old, took up the instruments, and executing Moret's instructions better than my father, he ordered him to teach my brother. We had frequent concerts of music at our house. I was then about seven or eight years of age, and was judged to have an inclination to music, by being often found scraping on a fiddle in some private place. I was then put under Moret's discipline, to learn to play on the violin. We both made such progress, that in about two years we could perform *à livre ouverte.*

Robert Raines in his *Marcellus Laroon* cites evidence that John Laroon was a ne'er-do-well who at some point studied under Michael Dahl.

Jacob Campo Weyerman said Laroon could have earned four or five guineas a day as a painter, but he loved music more and enjoyed "scraping on the four-stringed Bass." The Duke of Beaufort hired John at Badminton, but, said Weyerman, Laroon's "Spanish idleness, British drunkenness and Flemish carelessness" lost him his job, and he returned to London to play bass, Raines says, in the Drury Lane band. John wrote to Weyerman,

there is no delight in love or in art to compare to music. Music masters the soul and the soul rules all the passions. But just as beauty is no beauty without virtue and music is no music unless accompanied by art, so will I who am a superlative musician, practise the art as long as there is breath in my body.

Inasmuch as Weyerman was in England about 1718–20, that letter presumably dates from a period much later than that for which we have documentary evidence of John playing bass in a theatre band.

In Vice Chamberlain Coke's papers at Harvard are several documents citing a Mr Laroon, certainly John, as a bass player for the operas, which were usually at the Queen's Theatre but for part of the 1707–8 season at Drury Lane. The earliest references to Laroon date from January 1707 (probably 1707/08) and the latest from 1711–12. He was paid 8*s.* daily for a season salary of £30. He may have continued playing at London theatres after the 1711–12 season; the records for the early eighteenth century are far from complete.

In 1702, when John's father died, John served as executor of his estate. Among the bequests to John was the elder Laroon's bass viol. John and his two brothers (Marcellus and James) shared the art works of the elder Marcellus "Laroun."

Laroon, Marcellus *1679–1772, singer, painter.*

Marcellus Laroon was the son of Marcellus "Laroun" (for so his father usually spelled his name), and the work of the two was often confused until Robert Raines's fine book on the younger man established the facts. The elder artist was probably born about 1648 or 1649 and died in 1702. He was from a French family that had settled at the Hague, and he came to England and settled for some years in Yorkshire before coming to London. By 1674 he was a member of the Painter-Stainer's Company and about that year he married Elizabeth Keene. Elizabeth and the elder Marcellus had a son John, whose birthdate is not known, and a son Marcellus, our subject, who was born on 2 April 1679. In time, the family settled in Bow Street, Covent Garden, where four more children were born, two of whom, James and Elizabeth, survived.

The elder Marcellus had learned painting from his father and had a modest career as a painter, one of his works being a large oil of Charles II. He also drew the series of pictures for *The Cryes of London*. He gave Marcellus the younger a good musical and artistic training, and in 1697, when young Marcellus was 18, his father arranged for him to serve Sir Joseph Williamson as a page on Williamson's trip to Ryswick. Later Laroon wrote a brief autobiography (which was printed in J. T. Smith's *Nollekins and his Times* in 1829), but in it he said almost nothing of art works or artists he might have seen at the Hague. Then, in the service of the Earl of Manchester, young Laroon received a grand tour of Europe: Cologne, Frankfort, Innsbruck, and over the Alps to Venice.

Laroon had an opportunity to go to operas in Venice, which suited his lifelong interest in music. Then, on the return journey to London the boy was able to see Padua, Vicenza, Verona, Milan, Turin, Lyons, and Paris.

Laroon in his autobiographical sketch was vague about the years that followed:

As my father's circumstances were not such as would enable him to give us fortunes, we were obliged to learn to earn a living; we then went on in painting; but a quarrel I had with my younger brother, (for we were three), which I thought unjustly supported on his side by my father, made me resolve to leave him. Having some knowledge in music, I threw myself on the theatre in Drury-Lane, about the year 1698, where I continued, not as an actor, but a singer, for about two years.

Laroon may not have remembered the date of his theatrical activity correctly, for the first reference the late Emmett L. Avery found, which he communicated to Raines and is not in *The London Stage*, is about February 1700 in *The Grove* at Drury Lane. Avery did, however, list a Mr Laroon as a singer in the Drury Lane troupe during the 1699–1700 season. Daniel Purcell's *Plenty Mirth & gay Delight* was indeed later published as sung by Mr Laroon and Mrs Lindsey, and it was that song, Avery told Raines, that was sung in *The Grove*. Avery was, perhaps, supposing that "The Boy" who was listed in *Songs in the New Opera Called The Grove* (1700) was young Laroon, though the boy referred to may have been Jemmy Laroche.

In any case, records of the early eighteenth century show a Mr Laroon as a singer, certainly in 1702, if not earlier, and as late as 1706. Just when he sang *As a Tyrant when degraded* we cannot tell, but the song was probably published about 1702. At Drury Lane on 8 December 1702 "Sing, Sing All ye Muses" was sung by "Laroone" and Hughes. Laroon was noticed in playbills as singing in a revival of at least one act of *The Fairy Queen* at Drury Lane in February 1703; with Hughes he sang a duet at that house that month and also appeared as a singer at Barker's Great Dancing Room in Mincing Lane, Fenchurch Street; and in March 1704 he was in a concert at York Buildings. Laroon sang Sylvander in *The Temple of Love* at the Queen's Theatre on 7 March 1706; *The London Stage* cites the 1706 edition of the work as listing him as F. Laroon, and Raines states that he was variously advertised as F. and J. Laroon. A misprint could, of course, explain matters, but since as a painter in later years Marcellus often signed himself "Laroon F" (sometimes spelled out, "Fecit") it seems quite possible that for some reason he asked to be identified in a cast list as not just a singer but an artist. After the spring of 1706 Laroon's name disappeared from cast lists and bills; interestingly, about a year or so later his brother John began to be cited as a bass player at the theatres.

In early 1702, when Marcellus was having (or about to have) his first fling at theatre work, the elder Marcellus Laroun died at Richmond. He left his property to be shared by his children and Mrs Burgess, a kinswoman. Marcellus inherited, as did his brother John, some of his father's jewelry, and the three sons (James was the third) were left all their father's art work, most or all of which was sold in 1725.

Marcellus said in his autobiography that he tired of the stage. He spent some time in the army in 1704, as a letter from "N. Laroon" to his brother "Jan" dated July of that year indicates. The letter was written on the night before the battle of Schellenberg. We know that he was back in London performing by 1706, but apparently only briefly. By September 1707 he was again active in the army, attached to a battalion of the first regiment of Foot Guards in Holland. Then he was given a commission as Lieutenant in the Royal Scots regiment, in which he served until 1709, twice suffering wounds but occasionally taking time to sketch scenes from the campaigns he was in. He served at Malplaquet, though in his autobiography he neglected to mention it.

Back in London in 1709 he gave up his commission in the Royal Scots and joined James Craggs, Resident at the court of Barcelona, where he arrived in May 1710. There he served as Deputy Quartermaster General of the English troops. He described in some detail in his autobiography the battles at Balaquer and Almenara and the march on the retreat from Madrid. When his regiment was disbanded in August 1712 Laroon returned to London and became a member of the Academy of Painting, recently established. Oddly, he seems to have done little painting during the three years he was in London, and he may not have taken full advantage of the contacts and instruction the Academy would have offered him.

In July 1715 he was commissioned a Captain-Lieutenant under Col William Stanhope to help cope with the threat of a Jacobite invasion from Scotland. In January 1718 he was promoted to Captain, but by the end of the year the regiment was disbanded and he was on half-pay for a number of years. In 1724 he served as Captain in Brigadier Kerr's Dragoons, and at some point, perhaps in the early 1720s, he visited Venice again. He concluded his military service in 1732, when he retired at the age of 53 at a full Captain's pay of £4 weekly.

Laroon gave more of his time now to painting, but he only dabbled. Vertue said Laroon

lately has amused himself more particularly to painting & drawing. conversations. in small with much variety & pleasant entertainment of musick. some portraits in large from the life. whereby he woud not be uneasy if he coud, (stoop to it) not to make some benefit of it. which seems a little aukard to begin with, after 50 four or five.

Yet Laroon was apparently able to command higher fees than more serious artists of the time. He also on occasion bought and sold paintings.

He did not lose touch with theatrical activities, though, as Raines argues, it is improbable that he did any more performing after his few years early in the century. Among his paintings are several theatre pieces: *Dancers and Musicians*, showing two dancers, a harlequin with a violin, and a bass player (c. 1750–1755); a *Commedia dell' Arte Scene* (c. 1735); a scene from *1 Henry IV* (1746); and a *Stage Figure* (c. 1740). *A Music Party*, with the impresario Heidegger at the harpsichord (1736) and a number of other music party drawings are semitheatrical in nature. (All of his music party drawings date from 1731 to 1736).

Probably the Falstaff shown in Laroon's scene from *1 Henry IV* is James Quin. His *Lovers in a Park* (c. 1745) and *The Rencontre* (c. 1750) may have theatrical origins. Some of the figures in *The Musical Assembly*, Laroon's earliest known painting, dating about 1720, may represent real people; Raines sees possible representations of the Earl of Peterborough, who married the singer Anastasia Robinson in 1722, and possibly of Anastasia herself, of William Croft the organist, and of Pope, hunchbacked, playing a violin. In *A Musical Tea Party* (1740) it has been suggested that Handel is shown at the harpsichord with "Orator" Henley close by. Vertue said that Laroon painted Owen Swiney, the theatrical manager, but the portrait has not been found.

Hawkins in his *General History of Music* listed Laroon as one of those skilled musical amateurs, noting that he "played on the violoncello and composed solos for that instrument." Vertue mixed comments on music and art when speaking of Laroon's talent: "a genius to Art. well educated in Learning—in Musick & other branches of Gentil Education. a man of strength spirrit & vigour. . . ." Vertue's last mention of Laroon was dated 1742, after which Laroon continued painting, though evidence of his movements is harder to come by. He may have spent some time in the provinces at some point. When he wrote his will on 8 August 1768 he was residing in Oxford but still considered himself of the parish of St Paul, Covent Garden, in London. On 11 June 1770 he added a codicil, describing himself then as of the parish of St Mary Magdalen. Marcellus Laroon died at the age of 94 on 1 June 1772 and was buried at St Mary's.

In his will he stated that all his pictures, prints, and drawings should go to Gherard Bochman, but Bochman died in 1773 and the collection was sold in 1775 and 1778. Laroon's collection included some of his own works plus those of such artists as Kneller and Watteau. His two violins and violoncello and all his music books and papers he left to his friend Richard Combes. All his fishing gear he gave to Thomas Langford. His servant Christopher Yeates received £200 and many household goods; Mrs Elizabeth Long received £300 for the purchase of an annuity; and £50 went to the poor of Laroon's parish.

Laroon painted his own portrait (c. 1730), now in the collection of Mr and Mrs Paul Mellon. Laroon may have been pictured, but not clearly, in the Ashmolean Group of Artists, artist unknown, but the identification is not certain. Robert Raines's *Marcellus Laroon* reproduces a great many of Laroon's paintings and drawings and provides a very complete biography, upon which much of this entry is based.

La Rosa, Signor and family [*fl.* 1782], *acrobats*.

In *Revels in Jamaica* Wright reports that on 3 July 1782 Signor La Rosa and his family, fresh from Sadler's Wells in London, performed balancing acts, tumbling, and feats of strength at their first island appearance. They were in the surviving bills through 17 August. We have found no evidence to corroborate their boast that they had performed at Sadler's Wells, but bills for that theatre are very scarce.

La Rovere. *See* DE LA ROVERE.

La Rush. *See* LA RICH.

La Sal. *See* LE SAC.

"La Santina," stage name of Signora Santa Tasco [*fl.* 1735–1736], *singer*.
On 25 November 1735 at the King's Theatre, Idalma in *Adriano* was sung by Signora Santa Tasco (or Tasca), called "La Santina" (or "Santini"). On 24 January 1736 she sang Ismene in *Mitridate*, and she probably sang in other works the casts for which were not advertised. She was in excellent company: in the troupe that season were "Senesino," "Farinelli," and Signora Cuzzoni.

Lascelles, Miss [*fl.* 1800], *actress*.
The celebrated singer Ann Catley met Col Francis Lascelles in Dublin in 1768, had two children by him by November 1770, married him in 1771, and subsequently had at least seven other children. Her will, proved in October 1789, named three sons and four daughters, Charlotte, Elizabeth, Frances, and Jane.

Very likely it was one of those girls who came out as Lady Eleanor Irwin in *Every One Has His Fault* at Covent Garden Theatre on 3 June 1800, billed only as "A Young Lady (1st appearance)." The next morning's *Morning Post* identified her as a Miss Lascelles. The identification was confirmed by the *Monthly Mirror* for June, which reported that "She has an elegant figure, and possesses capabilities, that may, hereafter, be turned to account." Thomas Dutton in his *Dramatic Censor* (1800) added that she was "related, if we are rightly informed, to a well-known family" and thought "her features expressive, and her voice distinct, audible, and capable of great inflexion. On the whole, her performance, for a first appearance, was entitled to commendation." She was entered on the salary list for £2 per week.

The *Morning Post* had understood that "This lady is engaged . . . for the ensuing season," and she was on the list for £2 again at the beginning of 1800–1801. But according to *The Thespian Dictionary* (1805) she appeared only once more, on 24 October 1800 as Clarinda in *The Suspicious Husband*, and then quit the stage. She did not appear on the Covent Garden salary list for 1801–2.

Lascelles, Mrs Francis. *See* CATLEY, ANN.

Lascelles, Thomas [*fl.* 1735–1742], actor.

Thomas Lascelles must have had some theatrical connections well before he attempted a stage career, for on 14 May 1735 at Lincoln's Inn Fields he and Daniel Boyes, "who have been for many Years under Confinement for Debt," were given a benefit. Perhaps he was released by 29 March 1736, or it may be that he was given a day's liberty; on that day at Lincoln's Inn Fields, then little-used, Lascelles (the same man, we assume) made his first stage appearance, as Cato, for his benefit. He repeated the role at Goodman's Fields on 5 May. Then he made his first appearance on the Covent Garden stage on 1 April 1741 as Aboan in *Oroonoko*. During the 1741–42 season he was seen at that house as the Governor in *The Pilgrim*, Saygrace in *The Double Dealer*, Aegon in *Damon and Phillida*, and Gratiano in *Othello*.

Laschi, Filippo [*fl.* 1748–1750], singer, actor.

John Francis Croza managed a burletta troupe that opened at the King's Theatre on 8 November 1748 with *La comedia in comedia*. Singing Dorinna was Anna Laschi and singing Florillind was her husband Filippo. Dr Burney thought Filippo was one of the best *buffo* actors he had ever seen; Horace Walpole agreed, but he wrote to Mann on 2 December that "the women are execrable, not a pleasing note among them." But the company continued with some success to 10 June 1749. Filippo on 28 February 1749 had offered "A new Interlude between the Acts" of *La Maestra* and on 21 March sang two songs at the benefit for "decay'd" musicians and their families. Anna had a benefit on 22 April.

The troupe returned to the King's Theatre in 1749–50, and though no roles are known for Anna, Filippo was listed for Latino in *Il trionfo di Camilla*, sang again at the annual benefit, and, according to Burney, was given a benefit on 27 April 1750 (which is not listed in *The London Stage*). The Laschis doubtless appeared in many productions, the casts for which were not announced in the bills. Fuchs in his *Lexique* lists a Laschi at Lyon about 1760, but there is no way of knowing if he was Filippo.

Laschi, Signora Filippo, Anna [*fl.* 1748–1750], actress, singer. *See* LASCHI, FILIPPO.

Lasci, Mr [*fl.* 1757–1761], dancer.

Mr Lasci participated in *A Medley Concert* organized by "Mrs Midnight" (Christopher Smart) at the Haymarket Theatre beginning 15 June 1757 and continuing into September. The bill for 17 June indicated that Lasci danced in a comic ballet called *The Marine Boys Marching to Portsmouth*. He was no doubt the Mr "Lassy" who according to a paylist drawn up on 22 September 1770 earned £35 (at 3s. 8d. per day) for dancing at Covent Garden Theatre in 1760–61.

La Sere, Mons [*fl.* 1707], musician.

Among Vice Chamberlain Coke's papers at Harvard is a document dating about late December 1707 listing Mons La Sere as one of the instrumentalists at the Queen's Theatre at an annual salary of £20—the lowest on the list.

La Serre, James [*fl.* 1733?–1759?], musician.

The Lord Chamberlain's accounts show James La Serre as a musician at court as early as 20 January 1733, when he replaced George Powell, though he may have been active at court before that year. His annual salary was £40. The establishment list for 1759 shows that John Gordon replaced La Serre, but the exact date was not given; the replacement may have taken place after 1759.

"La Spiletta." *See* GIORDANI, NICOLINA.

Lassa, Signor [*fl.* 1784–1785], performer.

Among the Lord Chamberlain's papers is a note to the effect that Signor Lassa, a performer at the King's Theatre in 1784–85, received a season salary of £350. He must have been either a singer or a dancer.

Lassells, Master [fl. 1792–1803?], dancer. See LASSELLS, D.

Lassells, D. [fl. 1788–1803], dancer.
D. Lassells and his wife, dancers, joined Tate Wilkinson's company on the York circuit at Pontefract in the summer of 1788. Wilkinson in *The Wandering Patentee* remembered that "Mr. Lassells was excellent as a clown in Pantomime, I may say equal I think to any I ever saw; was clever also as a Harlequin; and was a well-behaved industrious man."

Lassells expended his talent and industry for Wilkinson also in 1789 and 1790, as did his wife. The pair (and eventually their children) popped up in provincial playhouses and the patent and minor theatres of London from time to time over the next 15 years. Though the provincial records are woefully incomplete, if we judge from those we have seen the Lassells were favorites.

At Derby on 9 August, 1792, Mr, Mrs, and Master Lascells (*sic*) danced the "Italian Cow-Keepers," and the bill promised that "Mr. and Master Lascells will appear on STILTS FOUR FEET HIGH." They were said to be from "the Opera House, London." In the season of 1792–93 Mr and Master Lassels, dancers, were on the roster of the Crow Street Theatre, Dublin. The scattered bills of Astley's Amphitheatre in London show the name in 1794 and 1795. On 8 September 1794 *The Indian Triumph; or, The Rival Slaves*, a pantomime farce, was "composed and arranged" by Mr Lassells, and the same evening he presented his *Harlequin in His Element*. On 27 July 1795 was advertised "a new dance composed by Lassells called "Rustic Sports; *or Win Her and Wear Her*," which he performed with Mrs Mercerot. In an Astley's bill of 16 May 1796 Lassells is listed as Harlequin in *The Magician of the Rocks*. (There were also in the early 1790s a dancer-choreographer Lascelles Williamson and his son Lascelles at Sadler's Wells. They were perhaps related to the family Lassells.)

A Royal Circus bill of 17 April 1795 listed both a Mr and a Master Lassells, and Mr Lassells was listed again on 11 May. The name was not seen again until the season of 1801–2 when a Mr Lascells was given small parts in pantomime and musical drama at Drury Lane. Perhaps that was the younger man, for on 5 October 1801 "Lassells Sen." was Justin (Harlequin) in *Puss in Boots* at the Royalty Theatre. In 1802 and 1803 Mr and Mrs Lassells, two sons, and Miss Lassells were all dancing at the Norwich Theatre Royal.

Lassells, Mrs D. [fl. 1788–1803], dancer. See LASSELLS, D.

Lassels, Mrs [fl. c. 1690?–1697], actress, singer.
A manuscript cast in a Harvard copy of *The Man of Mode*, dating about 1690–1692, has Mrs Lassels down for the role of Emilia. The play was probably done at Drury Lane by the United Company. She played the Duchess of Guise in *Bussy D'Ambois* in March 1691, and from then to the dissolution of the United Company in 1694 Mrs Lassels (or Lascelles, Lassells) was seen as Violante in *Greenwich Park*, Berenice in *The Marriage-Hater Match'd* (a role which required her to sing), Oriana in *The Traytor*, the prologue speaker for *The Wary Widow*, and Carroll in *A Very Good Wife*.

Mrs Lassels joined Betterton and his group of seceders at Lincoln's Inn Fields Theatre for the remainder of her career. In June 1697 she played Dorinda in "Thyrsis," part of *The Novelty*, and in late June was Mrs Flywife in *The Innocent Mistress*.

Lassy. See LASCI.

La Strada. See STRADA DEL PÒ.

Lates, Charles 1771– c. 1810, pianist, organist, singer, composer.
Charles Lates, the son of the Oxford violinist and composer John James Lates (or, on his will, just James Lates), was born in 1771, according to *The Dictionary of National Biography*. The elder Lates made his will on 8 November 1777, leaving most of his estate in trust for his wife Mary; after her death the Lates house and musical instruments were to be sold and the money divided equally between the two sons, Charles and John James Lates, when they should reach the age of 21. From some four per cent annuities the elder Lates held, Charles was to receive, in addition, £200, John James £150, and their (step-?) sister Charlotte £100. Since the will specified that Mrs Lates was to be appointed guardian to Lates's daughter Char-

lotte, Charlotte would seem to have been the issue of a previous marriage. The elder Lates died on 21 November 1777; his will was proved the following 2 January 1778.

Charles Lates matriculated at Magdalen College, Oxford, on 4 November 1793 at the age of 22, according to the *DNB*, and graduated bachelor of music on 28 May 1794, at which time he described himself as an organist of Gainsborough. His music teacher at Oxford was Philip Hayes, who had been a friend and a debtor of the elder Lates. Doane's *Musical Directory* of 1794 cited a Lates—Charles, we would assume—who sang bass at the Oxford Meeting in 1793 and in the Handel performances at Westminster Abbey in London. Grove says he died about 1810.

But on 3 January 1824 Charles Lates gave biographical sketches of his father and himself to Sainsbury for his *Dictionary*. The manuscript letter, now at the Glasgow University Library, was written from Walsall, where Charles Lates was then organist. He wrote Sainsbury that he was known to be "an able extempore fuguist, on the organ, & a capital player on the Piano Forte." He published some sonatas and songs in his early years.

Lathbury, Mr [*fl.* 1743–1747], *house servant?*

Mr Lathbury, probably a house servant, was cited in the Drury Lane benefit bills in May 1743, 1745, 1746, and 1747.

Latherbourg. *See* DE LOUTHERBOURG.

La Tour, Miss *d. 1735, dancer, actress, harpsichordist.*

On 26 October 1725 at Lincoln's Inn Fields Theatre "Young Le Sac and Miss La Tour, being the first Time of their Appearance on the Stage," entertained with a dance between the acts. The *Daily Courant* the day before had noted that the young dancers were "Scholars of Mr Dupre." Miss La Tour, in addition to her dancing abilities, which were displayed in entr'acte turns throughout the 1725–26 season, was also a "scholar of Mr Troas" and on 11 May 1726 at her shared benefit with Le Sac played some Handel lessons on the harpsichord. That night the pair also offered a dance called *Shepherd and Shepherdess representing Acis and Galatea*, which they had performed with success during the season, and Miss La Tour danced a solo chaconne.

Beginning in December 1732, Miss La Tour danced at Covent Garden through the 1732–33 season, appearing as an Old Woman and a Sylvan in *The Rape of Proserpine*, Lachesis, Clotho, and Atropos in *Harlequin Sorcerer*, a Harlequin and a Mezzetin Woman in *The Necromancer*, a Nymph and Colombine in *Apollo and Daphne* (and a Spaniard in "The Triumphs of Love," which concluded that pantomime), a Masquerader in *Italian Jealousy*, an Amazon in *Perseus and Andromeda*, the Burgomaster's Wife in *The Dutch and Scotch Contention*, and other pantomime parts. And she was regularly seen in entr'acte turns and dances within plays. Occasionally she danced with her teacher Dupré, and at her benefits (always shared) she sometimes offered a solo, such as *Tamo Tanto*, but she seemed to have preferred dancing a pas de deux with Glover, Dupré, or Poitier—sarabandes, minuets, and occasional character dances such as *Harlequin* or *French Peasant*. The titles of some dances she was in do not reveal much: *Numidian*, *Grand Dance*, *The Furlong*, and *La Mariee*.

Miss La Tour began the 1733–34 season at Covent Garden, dancing her Nymph role in *Apollo and Daphne* (but she did not appear in her other parts in that piece). On 27 October 1733 she danced *La Bagatelle* with Essex and was in a *Mock Minuet* with a larger group at the Haymarket Theatre, it being her first appearance on that stage. The *Daily Advertiser* had her still dancing in *Apollo and Daphne* at Covent Garden that day, but the *Daily Journal* noted that Miss Rogers substituted for her—a notation which was evidently correct.

The troupe at the Haymarket Theatre in the fall and winter of 1733–34 was made up of malcontent Drury Lane personnel under the leadership of Theophilus Cibber. With them she danced in no pantomimes but confined her activity to entr'acte specialities: the popular *Bagatelle* with Essex, a Nymph in *Grand Dance in Momus*, *Les Ombres des amants fidèles*, *Revellers*, and some untitled pieces. A peace was made with the Drury Lane management and the company returned there in March. Miss La Tour's first appearance was on 12 March 1734 in the group dance *Revellers*. After that she was in several of the entr'acte dances she had appeared in at the Haymarket and was seen as a

Reveller in the masque *Britannia* but in no other new pieces. On 29 May 1734 after the Drury Lane season had concluded, Miss La Tour danced at Lincoln's Inn Fields in *Revellers* with other Drury Lane performers, after which she seems to have left the stage. The *London Daily Post* on 11 January 1735 reported that Miss La Tour, formerly a celebrated dancer, had died the day before.

La Tour, Peter [*fl.* 1699–1726], *oboist.*
As of 23 October 1699 Peter La Tour was a musician serving Princess Ann of Denmark; he and other court musicians on that date were paid for playing at two balls and a play. On 19 April 1703 at the Drury Lane playhouse was offered "A new Entertainment by the whole Band, in which Paisible, Banister, and Latour play some extraordinary Parts upon the Flute, Violin, and Hautboy." La Tour apparently continued as a member of the Drury Lane band at a salary of £1 10*s.* weekly at least until the end of 1707, when he and other musicians at that house were accused of negotiating with the Queen's Theatre for posts in the opera band. Occasionally he appeared at concerts elsewhere, as in February 1706 and April 1707, when he played the German flute at York Buildings.

On 1 December 1707 La Tour and a number of other musicians were permitted by the Lord Chamberlain to perform at the Queen's Theatre. He had asked for £1 10*s.* nightly but like most of his fellows had to settle for less—in his case 11*s.* 3*d.* By about 1713 he had inched up to 11*s.* 6*d.* nightly. It would appear that he may have continued all along as a court musician, or at least received pay, for the Calendar of Treasury Books show pension payments to La Tour and others who were "late Prince of Denmark's Musick" covering the period from 1 October 1714 to 24 June 1716. On 2 June 1716 La Tour and two other Drury Lane musicians had been dropped from the paylist. He had obviously been playing at both Drury and the Queen's and perhaps at court as well. Possibly Peter was the La Tour who composed some of the dance music published in 1721 in *A Collection of Minuets, Rigadoons, & French Dances.*

One of La Tour's close associates in the London musical world during the first 15 years of the eighteenth century was the musician James Paisible. On 17 January 1721 Paisible wrote his will, naming Peter La Tour as one of his two executors. The will was proved on 5 June 1722 by Peter Bressan, the other executor, Peter La Tour renouncing. La Tour was last cited in the Lord Chamberlain's accounts on 18 July 1726, when he and others were paid for attending the installation at Windsor of the Duke of Richmond and Sir Robert Walpole.

Latourdy, Mons [*fl.* 1705], *dancer.*
Monsieur Latourdy danced at Drury Lane Theatre on 7 November 1705.

La Touze. *See* LA LAUZE.

Latter, Edward [*fl.* 1784–1815], *singer.*
Edward Latter was one of the tenors who sang in the Handel Memorial Concerts at Westminster Abbey and the Pantheon in May and June 1784. Doane's *Musical Directory* in 1794 gave Latter's address as Angel Alley, Little Moorfields, and noted that the singer was a subscriber to the New Musical Fund. He was still a member of that organization in 1815.

Latter, James [*fl.* 1784–1794], *singer.*
When James Latter sang in the Handel Memorial Concerts at Westminster Abbey and the Pantheon in May and June of 1784, Dr Burney listed him as Master Latter. He was a "Treeble." By the time Doane's *Musical Directory* came out in 1794 James was evidently out of his minority. He was cited as James Latter Junior and a tenor who had participated in the Handel performances at the Abbey. He lived in Swallow Street.

Lauchery, Mons [*fl.* 1755–1778], *dancer.*
Mons Lauchery was among the several French dancers led by Noverre whom Garrick engaged in 1755. Lauchery was first named in a Drury Lane playbill on 3 November 1755, when he danced with Boletti, Miss Noverre, Mrs Vernon, and others in a ballet called *Lilliputian Sailors*, which Cross in his prompter's diary said was "pretty well receiv'd." But Noverre's ballet *Les Fêtes Chinoises* provoked chauvinistic catcalls at its introduction on 8 November and full-blown anti-Gallic riots on 15 and 18 November. The interior of the theatre was heavily damaged. Garrick was "oblig'd to give up the

LAUCHERY

Dancers," and several of them, including Lauchery, returned to the Continent.

Lauchery came back to Drury Lane in 1761. It was surely he who, at the end of Act III of the mainpiece of 19 November 1761, presented "A New Comic Dance call'd *The Blacksmiths*," though his name was now spelled "Lockery" and this was said to be his "first appearance in England." For the next couple of seasons Lauchery was merely one of the corps of dancers at Drury Lane, seldom being featured. Perhaps he was also dancing at the King's Theatre in the ballets of the opera, for which the records are almost nonexistent. He was also named (as "Lochery") in the fragmentary bills of Sadler's Wells of 1762, 1763, and 1765. He was making £2 per week at Drury Lane, according to a Drury Lane paylist of 9 February 1765. (The account placed him in the fourth level of dancers, below Grimaldi and Georgi at £6, Miss Baker and Aldridge at £4, Slingsby at £3, and, with Berardi, above 16 other dancers paid amounts down to 12s. per week.)

One Lauchery, probably the same, acquired substantial recognition in France as a choreographer in the 1760s and 1770s. He devised nearly 40 scenarios for the ballet music of Christian Cannabich. Charles Burney, in *The Present State of Music in Germany* . . . (1773), furnished a brief description of one of them—*La Foire de village hessoise*—which he saw at Schwetzingen in July 1772 and thought "the most entertaining I ever saw."

In 1774 a Lauchery was once again at Drury Lane. He was cited—"Dancing by Giorgi, Lauchery, Mrs Sutton, &c."—on 27 September 1774. His name did not appear again that season, but the ampersand—et cetera—on that bill probably demonstrates why. He was still (or again) there on 30 September 1775, when the list of dancers was again truncated: "Giorgi, Lauchery, Mrs Sutton, &c." The only other occurrence of his name in a London playbill was on 1 November 1775, when the same notation concerning dancers was repeated.

A manuscript in the Forster Collection at the Victoria and Albert Museum (among the Garrick papers) lists him on 25 February 1775 as earning £1 per week.

An extract taken by James Winston from the register book of the retirement fund of Drury Lane Theatre (now in the Folger Library) shows that Lauchery contributed 10s. 6d. to the fund in 1775 and "left theatre 1776." Yet Additional Manuscript 29,709 in the British Library shows a payment (for choreography? for disbursement to other dancers) in June 1777: "Lauch^y—41.13.4," and on 2 February 1778, "Lauch^y—1 wk. 41.13.4."

Lauchrie, Mr $_[fl.\ 1789]$, *actor, singer?*

A Mr Lauchrie played a Waiter in the pantomime *I Don't Know What* at the Royal Circus, St George's Fields, "for the fifth time" on 12 May 1789. He is otherwise unrecorded.

Laud, Squire $_[fl.\ 1778]$, *musician.*

In the Lord Chamberlain's papers is a power of attorney dated 19 May 1778 by Squire Laud, "musician in Ordinary to HM."

Lauder, James *d. 1769, actor, singer, licensee.*

James Lauder, a Scottish performer, received his first known London benefit at the Haymarket Theatre on 7 March 1752. The piece was *The Gentle Shepherd; or, Patie and Roger*, a traditional pastoral by Allan Ramsay, in which Lauder probably played Sir William Worthy. Perhaps he had been in the cast that had played *The Gentle Shepherd* at the Haymarket three months earlier on 10 January 1752.

Probably he was the Lauder who had a benefit at the Jacob's Wells Theatre, Bristol, on 8 August 1752, when *Macbeth* was performed. He returned to the Haymarket on 14 April 1753 to sing a Mason's song and several Scottish songs for his benefit. Over the next 15 years Lauder sang such songs at the Haymarket several times almost every season. On 22 April 1757 he sang in *Patie and Roger* and in September of that year offered selections on several nights. That year the song *The Gear and the Bragie o't* was published as sung by him at the Haymarket.

Several times in almost every year from 1758 to 1769 Lauder also played Sir William Worthy and often sang Mason's songs for his own benefit at the Haymarket. In January 1758 he lodged at the Rising Sun opposite Hungersford Market in the Strand. His first name, James, is on documents in the Public Record Office, granting him licenses to perform *Patie and Roger* in 1759 and 1760. Lauder also sang at Finch's Grotto Gardens in 1765.

His last performance as Sir William Worthy,

was on 27 February 1769. He was dead by 18 December of that year when *Patie and Roger* was given at the Haymarket for the benefit of "the Widow and child of the deceased Lauder." His widow received subsequent benefits there on 21 September and 21 December 1773.

Laudermey, Miss [*fl.* 1792], *actress.*

On 26 November 1792 at the Haymarket Theatre Miss Laudermey played Leonora in *The Mourning Bride* and Charlotte in *The Apprentice.*

Laurence. *See also* LAWRENCE.

Laurence, [Herbert?] [*fl.* 1719–1757], *boxkeeper.*

The Mr Laurence (or Lawrence) who served John Rich as a boxkeeper at Lincoln's Inn Fields Theatre and then Covent Garden Theatre from 1719 to 1757 was very likely Herbert Laurence, who in 1743 was elected to membership in the Sublime Society of Beefsteaks and who witnessed the will of the actor Dennis Delane about 1750. Laurence was first cited in the bills on 13 May 1719, when he and three others shared a benefit at Lincoln's Inn Fields. He was similarly cited over the years at benefit time, and from time to time the bills specified that he was one of the boxkeepers. In the 1720s the gross receipts at his benefits rarely dropped below £70 and often went over £100, and he normally shared the profits with only one other person. Presumably he made more after the opening of the larger Covent Garden playhouse in 1732. His daily salary in the 1735–36 season appears to have been 2s., and in 1746–47 his season salary was £10. But boxkeepers were in a position to do very well financially through their benefits and gratuities from the nobility and gentry, which often raised them on the economic and social scale.

It is not surprising, then, to find that on 1 October 1743 Laurence was elected to the Sublime Society of Beefsteaks, which had been founded by the harlequin and theatre manager John Rich. Indeed, one of the other witnesses to the will of Dennis Delane in 1750 was Alexander Crudge, a Covent Garden doorkeeper and housekeeper and also a member of the Beefsteaks (as was the third witness, the oboist and dancing master John George Cox). Laurence was last mentioned in the bills on 10 May 1757, when he shared a benefit with Crudge and the actress Jane Ferguson.

A Mrs Laurence, probably his wife, was mentioned in the theatre's free list in 1726–27, and seems to have had a business of her own; on 15 April 1727 she was paid £7 7s. by Lincoln's Inn Fields for a gown, petticoat, and embroidery.

Laurent, Charles [*fl.* 1787], *house servant?*

On 3 January 1787 Charles Laurent, Thomas Webb, J. White, and Edward Silvester signed a letter to Edward Jerningham concerning a complaint Jerningham had evidently made about the lack of sufficient light in either his box or the whole auditorium of the King's Theatre. They assured him that the same number of candles were being used as in previous seasons, when there had been no complaints. The four men spoke for the manager, Gallini. Since Silvester was the theatre's property man, Webb a box and lobby keeper, and White a journeyman carpenter or box and lobby keeper, it is probable that Charles Laurent was also a house servant.

Laurent, Jean-Baptiste 1763–1822, *dancer, equestrian, manager, acrobat?, designer?*

In Winter's *Pre-Romantic Ballet*, Jean-Baptiste Laurent's birth and death dates are given as 1763 and 1822. The earliest theatrical citation we have found for him is in a bill for Astley's Amphitheatre dated 6 May 1791: Laurent danced in a turn called *The Irish Fair.* On 3 June and in July he was the clown in a rope-dancing exhibition. In 1792 he was not mentioned in London bills, so we take him to have been the Monsieur Laurent listed in *Le Petit Almanach* as a dancer at the Opéra in Paris that year. Laurent was at Astley's Amphitheatre Royal in Peter Street, Dublin, on 31 January 1793, performing in the pantomime *La Forêt noire.* That piece was probably the work called *Maternal Affection* (subtitled *Dark Forest*) in which Laurent appeared at Astley's in London in April. He was advertised as one of Astley's equestrians in the summer of 1793. Laurent's last notice in an Astley bill was on 16 May 1796, when he played Count Umpressa in *The Magician of the Rocks.*

A bill for the Royal Circus, dated only 1798, listed Laurent as Paraquetto ("the Grand Pur-

Harvard Theatre Collection

JEAN-BAPTISTE LAURENT, as the Clown
artist unknown

and in 1805 he took over both buildings of the Lyceum, turned them into one theatre, and dubbed the place the Theatre of Mirth. The enterprise proved to be a financial disaster, and by 1807–8 Laurent had joined the Drury Lane company as a clown at £8 weekly. His articles provided for graduated raises to £10 weekly by the end of the 1809–10 season. Also performing at Drury Lane was his son, who was cited as Laurent Junior. He was probably Philippe (1801–1872), who became an eminent harlequin in Paris. For Drury Lane Jean-Baptiste Laurent seems also to have helped design some of the costumes and decorations. In Edmund Simpson's notebook in the Folger Shakespeare Library is a reference of 1818 to "Mr. Laurent's son," a harlequin—again, probably Philippe.

In February 1820 Jean-Baptiste Laurent and his family appeared in Calais, according to a bill reproduced in Winter's *Pre-Romantic Ballet*. Jean-Baptiste's son John was called "le jeune Roscius," the Harlequin Philippe was cited as the "fils ainé," and in Le Troupe Sédentaire de Calais were also two Misses Laurent. The Laurent who was manager of Covent Garden Theatre in 1845 (according to the entry on Thomas Archer in *The Dictionary of National Biography*) may have been one of our subject's sons, but Winter claims that both remained in France for the rest of their lives.

An anonymous engraving of Laurent as the Clown in *Furibond* in 1807–8 was published by J. Scales. An engraving by C. Tomkins, after I. F. Roberts, shows Laurent as Rolla in *Cora* at the Royal Circus. It was published by Beauclerk in 1799.

veyor") in a spectacle called "The Knights of Malta. He also played Pierrot in *Mirth's Medley*; the bill did not make clear whether he or Simpson (whose benefit it was) performed a leap through a hogshead of water, a flight across the stage from balcony to balcony, and an escape through a cask of fire. On 28 May 1799, ("for that night only"), Laurent made his first appearance at Covent Garden Theatre, playing Pierrot in *The Norwood Gipsies* for Farley's benefit. He was at the Royal Circus in June and drew praise from the *Monthly Mirror*, whose critic liked Laurent's "admirable tricks and grimace."

Laurent was at the Royalty Theatre in Wellclose Square in 1801 and at Astley's in 1802,

Laurenti, Marianna [*fl.* 1790], *singer.*

Signora Marianna Laurenti sang the title role in *Ninetta* at the Haymarket Theatre on 7 January 1790. The following day the *World* said, "The Laurenti, the new Buffa, is a scholar of Giardini, she comes from Rome, and not very heavy laden with voice or figure." As the opera troupe's first *buffa assoluta* Signora Laurenti also sang that season Zeffirina in *Li due castellani burlati*, which opened on 2 February.

Lava, John [*fl.* 1775], *musician.*

In the Forster Collection at the Victoria and Albert Museum is a note endorsed by David Garrick showing that John Lava was a member of the Drury Lane band as of 20 August 1775.

La Val. *See* DE LA VALLE.

Lavenu, Lewis August *1768–1818, violinist, violist, flutist, publisher.*

According to information supplied to the Royal Society of Musicians when Lewis August Lavenu was proposed for membership, he was born in Carnaby Street in the parish of St James, Westminster, on 2 March 1768, the son of John Lavenu. By 1791 Lewis was playing second violin in the band at the opera house, and on 30 March 1791 at Covent Garden Theatre he was in the oratorio band. He had been recommended for membership in the Royal Society of Musicians on 1 January of that year, at which time it was reported that he was single and had engagements not only at the opera house and Covent Garden but at Ranelagh Gardens. He was listed as a violinist and violist; Grove does not name those instruments for him but calls him a flutist. On 1 April 1792 Lavenu was elected to the Society by a vote of eight to five. On 10 and 12 May he played violin in the Society's St Paul's Concert, and he continued performing in those annual programs and in the Covent Garden oratorios to the end of the century.

Doane's *Musical Directory* of 1794 noted that Lavenu had played at the Oxford Meeting in 1793 and had participated in the Handel concerts at Westminster Abbey. His address was in Titchfield Street, Cavendish Square. Lavenu played viola at the Oxford Music Room on 18 November 1794, and we assume he was the Lewis "Lavenue" of No 11, Great Pultney Street, Golden Square, who became a freeman of the Worshipfull Company of Musicians on 21 November. From about 1796 Lavenu was a music seller and publisher at No 23, Duke Street, St James's. About November 1798 he moved his shop to No 26, New Bond Street, and about 1805 he moved to No 28, on the same street. From about 1802 to 1808 he was in partnership with Charles Mitchell, first at No 29, New Bond Street and then at No 26. They ran a "Musical Circulating Library" as well as a music selling and printing shop.

Lewis Lavenu was a member of the Court of Assistants of the Royal Society of Musicians in 1815, 1816, and 1817. He died on 17 August 1818, and his widow Elizabeth carried on his publishing business. She operated the shop at No 28, New Bond Street until about 1821, then she set up at No 24, Edwards Street, Manchester Square, until 1827. About 1827 or 1828 she was again at No 28, New Bond Street. In 1819 she had married the violinist Nicholas Mori, and the shop name was changed to Mori and Lavenu about 1828.

Lewis and Elizabeth Lavenu had a son, Louis Henry (1818–1859) who became a violoncellist, composer, and, from about 1839, owner of the shop at No 28, New Bond Street.

Laver, Mrs [*fl.* 1797], *singer.*

Mrs Laver sang in the chorus at the Haymarket Theatre on 23 and 26 January 1797 when performances of *The Battle of Eddington* were presented.

Lavigny, Mons [*fl.* 1734–1735], *scene mover.*

Monsieur Lavigny was a scene mover in the troupe of French players who performed at the Haymarket Theatre from 26 October 1734 to 3 June 1735 and at Goodman's Fields Theatre on 23 May and 4 June 1735. Rosenfeld in *Foreign Theatrical Companies in Great Britain* states that Lavigny and the other scene movers in the troupe received a benefit, but *The London Stage* does not list one. The company was under the leadership of Francisque Moylin.

Laving, Mr [*fl.* 1705], *dancer.*

A Mr Laving danced at Drury Lane Theatre on 17 December 1705. There is not sufficient evidence to identify him accurately, though it is worth noting that Julien de Lavigne, a rope dancer, was active in France from 1706 to 1732.

Lavoy, Denis de [*fl.* 1655–1688], *actor, manager.*

A French troupe was granted a pass on 25 August 1663 to bring their scenes and decorations into England. The company may have been that headed by Alcidor and Denis de Lavoy, who in 1662 in France styled themselves the Comédiens du Roy d'Angleterre. Mongrédien notes that Lavoy had been a comedian for the Queen of Sweden in Brussels on 14 April 1655, had been in Rosidor's company in 1660, and then had joined the company of the Elector of Cologne at the Hague in 1660–61. He was in Brussels in 1662 and in Rochefort's troupe in 1663 playing comic parts. He played at the Marais Theatre in Paris from 1667 to 1669 and in 1668 was again acting under Rosidor's management. About 1673 Lavoy was in the company of the Duke of Brunswick and Lunebourg; in 1683 he performed in the troupe of the Prince of Orange at Haarlem and Amsterdam. He played in Brussels in 1685 and in 1687–88.

Law. *See also* **LAWS**.

Law, Edmund [*fl.* 1794], *violinist.*
Doane's *Musical Directory* of 1794 listed Edmund Law, of Peter Street, Saffron Hill, as a violinist who played for the Handelian Society.

Lawder. *See* **LAUDER** and **LOWDER**.

Lawes, Henry *1596–1662, singer, actor, lutenist, composer.*
The *New Grove* states that Henry Lawes was born in Dinton, Wiltshire, on 5 January 1596 (*The Dictionary of National Biography* has it that he was baptized on 1 January). Henry was the son of Thomas Lawes and his wife Lucris, née Shephard. He may have studied music in London under Giovanni Coperario, but he was influenced by the works of Ferrabosco. On 1 January 1626 Henry was sworn epistler of the Chapel Royal, and on the following 3 November he became a Gentleman of the Chapel. The Lord Chamberlain's accounts cited him on 6 January 1631 as a musician for voices in the King's Musick, replacing Robert Marsh, who had recently died. The following 28 February he was granted a stipend of £20 annually plus a livery allowance of £16 2s. 6d. Lawes was a countertenor, as a list of musicians appointed to wait on the King on his journey to Scotland in 1633 shows. A payment of £20 for two lutes was made to Henry and his brother William, also a court musician, on 4 March 1636. Under Charles I, Lawes also served as Clerk of the Cheque of the Chapel Royal and a member of the royal band.

By 1633 he had probably become connected with the household of the Earl of Bridgewater, serving as music teacher. Henry's (?) music for the masque *Coelum Britannicum* was heard at Whitehall on 18 February 1634 when the work was produced with Bridgewater's two sons as participants. Lawes certainly composed the music for Milton's *Comus*, which Peck in his *New Memoirs* said was written at Henry's request. *Comus* was produced at Ludlow Castle on 29 September 1634 with Lawes taking the role of the Attendant Spirit. The Earl of Bridgewater's sons and Lady Alice Egerton also performed. When *Comus* was published Lawes's name, not Milton's, was attached to it.

Lawes was much attracted to setting English words to music. In addition to the works already cited, he wrote music for Strode's *The Floating Island*, a tragicomedy which was acted at Oxford on 29 August 1636 before the King and was published in 1655. In 1637 was published his setting of Sandys's *Paraphrase upon the Psalms of David*. Henry and his brother William (who died in 1645) set a number of psalms to music; in 1648 Lawes published those, along with a setting of an elegy on William's death, and some canons. He set the Christmas songs in Herrick's *Hesperides*, and in 1651 the plays of William Cartwright were published, the "Ayres and Songs set by Mr. Henry Lawes." Playford's *Select Musical Ayres* in 1653 contained songs by Lawes, and Henry published three volumes of his own *Ayres and Dialogues* in 1653, 1655, and 1658.

Faculty of Music, Oxford
HENRY LAWES
artist unknown

Milton was so enamoured of Henry's way with setting English words that he wrote a sonnet to him, dating, it is believed, 1646:

> Harry *whose tuneful and well measur'd Song*
> *First taught our English Musick how to span*
> *Words with just note and accent, not to scan*
> *With* Midas *Ears, committing short and long;*
> *Thy worth and skill exempts thee from the throng,*
> *With praise enough for Envy to look wan;*
> *To after age thou shalt be writ the man,*
> *That with smooth aire couldst humor best our tongue.*
> *Thou honour'st Verse, and Verse must send her wing*
> *To honour thee, the Priest of* Phoebus *Quire*
> *That tun'st their happiest lines in Hymn, or Story.*
> Dante *shall give Fame leave to set thee higher*
> *Then his* Casella, *whom he woo'd to sing*
> *Met in the milder shades of Purgatory.*

Grove notes that to achieve his desired blend of words and music Lawes "employed a kind of *aria parlante*, a style of composition which, if expressively sung would cause as much gratification to the cultivated hearer as the most ear-catching melody would to the untrained listener." Dr Burney held a very different opinion.

Burney disliked his work sufficiently to devote several pages to Lawes in his *General History of Music*. He found Henry's predecessors Tallis, Bird, and Gibbons "infinitely superior to Lawes" even though contemporary poets praised Lawes more, much to Burney's consternation. His view was that poets like Milton and Waller were perhaps "pleased with Lawes for not pretending to embellish or enforce the sentiments of their songs but setting them to sounds less captivating than the sense."

But bad as the Music of Lawes appears to us, it seems to have been *sincerely* admired by his contemporaries, in general. It is not meant to insinuate that it was pleasing to poets *only*, but that it was *more* praised by them than any other Music of the same time. Though that of Laniere, Hilton, Simon Ives, Dr. Child, and others seems preferable; and the poets, whose praise is fame, perhaps taught others to admire.

Burney's feelings toward Lawes were so strong that he launched into an essay on music and poetry. What bothered Burney, evidently, was that Lawes did not write melodies as good as the poems he set.

The civil wars brought an end to the court appointments that Lawes held. In his second book of *Ayres and Dialogues* in 1655 Henry said, "although I have lost my Fortunes with my Master (of ever blessed memory) [Charles I], I am not so low to bow for a subsistence to the follies of this Age." He taught during the interregnum, and contributed to Sir William Davenant's historical *First Day's Entertainment* at Rutland House, which was performed on 23 May 1656. He and Coleman composed the music for the songs. A spy from the government attended and reported that nothing untoward happened. "The Musick was aboue in a loouer hole," he wrote, "railed about and couered wth Sarcenetts to conceal them, before each speech was consort Musick. At the end were songs relating to the Victor [Cromwell] . . . The first song was made by Hen: Lawes, ye other by Dr Coleman who were the Composers." When *The Siege of Rhodes* followed at Rutland House, Lawes composed the first and fifth entries. (Grove seems to lump the two Rutland House productions into one.)

At the Restoration Lawes was restored to his posts in the King's Musick and appointed a composer for the lutes and voices. For the coronation of Charles II Lawes composed an anthem, *Zadok the Priest*, one of his last works. He was getting on in years, and Samuel Pepys reported on 30 December 1660 that his friend William Child had gone to see Henry Lawes, "who lies very sick." Henry Lawes died in London on 21 October 1662. Dr Charles Coleman replaced him in the King's Musick as a singer; Thomas Purcell was appointed to Henry's second post in the private music for lutes, viols, and voices. Henry's position as composer at court was worth £40 annually at his death. Lawes was buried in the cloisters of Westminster Abbey on 25 October.

Lawes had drawn up his will at his lodgings in the Almonry, Westminster, on 14 October 1662. To Nicholas Johnson and Francis Sambrooke of the Close of Sarum he left in trust £340, which he asked them to dispose of as follows: £100 to Margaret Crispe, the widowed daughter of Henry's brother John Lawes (Joseph and Charles Crispe, her sons, were residuary legatees); £40 toward the binding of Thomas Lawes Crispe (another of Margaret's sons) to an apprenticeship, and the remaining £200 to him when he reached 24, or sooner if the trustees thought fit. The trustees were granted 40s. each for rings. To the poor of Dinton, Wiltshire, Lawes left £10. He gave his viols, a bass viol, a book of pavanes and allamandes and six books of lessons—all the works of his late brother William, who was killed in the civil war—to Francis Sambrooke. Everything else Henry left to his wife Elianor.

Two paintings of Lawes, one showing him when young and the other when older, were exhibited at Kensington in 1867. One is at the Music School at Oxford. It was engraved by Faithorne for Lawes's *Ayres and Dialogues* (1653). Another portrait, painted in 1622, is in the bishop's palace at Salisbury. *The Dictionary of National Biography* lists another portrait at Salisbury in the possession of A. R. Malden; it was apparently painted by Charles Hambro.

Willa Evans's biography, *Henry Lawes*, was published in 1941.

Lawley, Mr [*fl.* 1743], *house servant?*

Mr Lawley's benefit tickets were accepted at Drury Lane Theatre on 24 May 1743. He was probably one of the house servants.

Lawr, Mrs [*fl.* 1775–1776], *actress.*

Mrs Lawr's benefit tickets were admitted at Covent Garden Theatre on 11 May 1775, though she had not to that point been mentioned in any bills. On the following 13 October she played the Maid in *Orpheus and Eurydice*, which ran through 19 December, and on 11 May 1776 she was again on the list of beneficiaries.

Lawrence. *See also* LAURENCE.

Lawrence, Mr [*fl.* 1706–1718], *singer.*

Mr Lawrence was first mentioned in the bills at the Queen's Theatre on 7 March 1706, when he played Thyrsis in *The Temple of Love*. He also offered entr'acte songs that spring; then, in 1706–7, he performed at Drury Lane. There on 24 February 1707 he, Leveridge, and others sang between the acts; the following 4 March he was the Messenger in Clayton's new opera *Rosamond*; and on 1 April he sang Tigranes in *Thomyris*. Until the management of the two theatres settled down in 1710 Lawrence performed now at one house and now at the other, entertaining audiences with songs between the acts and singing, in addition to his earlier English opera parts, Roderigo in *Clotilda*.

Lawrence also appeared at concerts at Hampstead Wells, Stationers' Hall, and York Buildings. The accounts of the Queen's Theatre show that he was earning £50 as of March 1708, but he was, "if he learns a thro Base by y^e End of y^e year to have 10$^£$ more." Other documents among Vice Chamberlain Coke's papers at Harvard show Lawrence to have been earning 15s. daily, a wage which placed him almost at the bottom of the pay scale for singers (Mrs Tofts, for example, was paid £7 10s. per diem).

By 1710, if not earlier, Lawrence was singing in Italian, according to Dr Burney; he was Arbaces in *L'Idaspe fedele* on 23 March of that year at the Queen's in a cast that featured mostly Italian singers. His other opera roles in the second decade of the eighteenth century at the Queen's (later King's) Theatre were Delbo in *Etearco*, the Herald in *Rinaldo*, Ormonte in *Antioco*, probably Oronte in *Creso*, Germanicus Caesar in *Arminio*, Amiceto in *Lucio Vero*, Fileno in *Cleartes*, and, at the Lincoln's Inn Fields Theatre, Wall in *Pyramus and Thisbe*. At Stationers' Hall on 4 April 1712 Lawrence and Leveridge sang in a concert. Lawrence was at the King's Theatre in 1716–17, according to the accounts, but no specific roles are known for him that season. He sang in *The Prophetess* at Lincoln's Inn Fields on 31 October 1717 and sang entr'acte songs there during the 1717–18 season.

Lawrence, Mr [*fl.* 1743], *actor.*

A Mr Lawrence acted the Prince in *The Glorious Queen of Hungary* at Tottenham Court on 4 August and at Bartholomew Fair on 23 August 1743.

Lawrence, Mr [*fl.* 1761], *fire eater.*

The fire eater Lawrence was paid 7s. 6d. (nightly, apparently) for doing his stunt for 23 nights in *The Fair* at Covent Garden Theatre through 9 November 1761.

Lawrence, Mr [*fl.* 1766–1770], *wire dancer.*

Mr Lawrence (or Laurence) was with a troupe from Sadler's Wells in London performing Mondays, Tuesdays, Thursdays, and Saturdays in July and August 1766 at the Old Assembly Room at St Augustine's Back in Bristol. He and Baker shared a benefit on 5 August, at which he performed, as usual, on the slack wire. In 1770 he was back at Sadler's Wells,

Lawrence, Mr $_{[fl.\ 1796–1808]}$, *bell ringer.*

On 2 June 1796 at Covent Garden Theatre in a dance within *The Shipwreck*, "Lawrence, that inimitable Performer, will introduce accompaniments on his Bells." He played his bells again in *The Village Fête* beginning 18 May 1797. The nature of the bells Lawrence used is not certain; Charles Beecher Hogan in *The London Stage* suggests he may have been playing a glockenspiel, though one would suppose that if that was his instrument it would have been so named in the bills. The reference to Lawrence's performances over the years suggest the possibility of chimes or chime-bells or hand bells.

When *The Magic Flute; Or, Harlequin Champion* was performed on 23 June 1800 at the Royal Circus, accompaniments were provided by Lawrence on "the Musical Bells"; and on 6 October, when Mr Masters sang "The Merry Merry Bells," he was accompanied on "the Harmonic Bells" by Lawrence. The Drury Lane accounts show that on 27 April 1802 "Lawrence, Musical Bells" was paid £8 8s. He was at the Royal Circus in October and November 1803 and again in October 1804. Royal Circus bills for 31 August 1807 and 19 September 1808 noted that tickets for performances were available from Lawrence (presumably the bell player) in High Timber Street. In those two instances he was not named as performing.

Lawrence, Miss $_{[fl.\ 1770–1772]}$, *dancer.*

Miss Lawrence was paid 5s. on 22 March 1770 "for walking" two nights in *Harlequin's Jubilee* at Covent Garden Theatre. She danced a Country Girl in a "pantomimical dance" called *The Recruits* on 1 May 1772.

Lawrence, Miss $_{[fl.\ 1791–1795]}$, *dancer.*

Miss Lawrence (or Laurence) appeared in a comic dance called *The Irish Fair* at Astley's Amphitheatre on 6 May 1791; at that performance Joseph Lawrence was in a tumbling act, and it is probable that he was her father. Miss Lawrence danced again on 22 August 1795 as a Haymaker in *Harlequin Invincible*, in which Joseph Lawrence played a Mountebank Doctor.

Lawrence, Joseph $_{[fl.\ 1785–1800]}$, *acrobat, dancer, actor, manager.*

Joseph Lawrence (or Laurence) was sometimes called "The Great Devil" or "Le Grand Saut du Trampolin." He was presumably the father of the Miss Lawrence who danced in the early 1790s at Astley's Amphitheatre and of the Master Lawrence, who was, we believe, Moses Lawrence, a performer there in the late 1780s. The youngsters were usually cited in bills only when the elder Lawrence also performed. According to Findlater, there was another son named Richard; but there is no record of his having performed.

Joseph Lawrence's earliest discovered notice is dated 7 April 1785, when he was in a tumbling act at Astley's with Master Lawrence. Lawrence was at Astley's the rest of the summer and returned in 1786 to play an Old Man in *At the Village Sports*. Philip Astley boasted in a bill on 13 June that "One day last week Mr. Lawrence threw 14 somersets," and a critic in an unidentified news clipping of 1786 wrote that "If tumbling and rope dancing can please, Mr. Astley has to boast of the most noted families in all the world, namely Mess. Lawrence and Lonsdale."

In 1786–87 Lawrence performed at Sadler's Wells, and in 1787–88 is known to have appeared there as an Officer in *The Four Valiant Brothers*, a spectacle that involved dancers, tumblers, swordsmen, singers, and rope-dancing clowns. The 1788–89 season found him dancing at the Crow Street Theatre in Dublin.

Lawrence was back at Astley's Amphitheatre in May 1791 in a tumbling act, and Miss Lawrence appeared there as a dancer. "The Great Devil," as he was called in a bill in June, performed somersaults "over Twelve mens heads," and another time he somersaulted over 12 horses. His French nickname was also attached to him that summer as he entertained the crowds with acrobatics and rope dancing. With the Astley troupe at the Amphitheatre Royal in Dublin in January 1793, Lawrence performed in a pantomime entitled *La Forêt noir*, and in August 1795 at Astley's in London he is known to have played a Mountebank Doctor in *Harlequin Invincible*.

In view of the fact that Lawrence is known to have built a theatre in Grantham in 1800, it is possible he was the Lawrence who produced a pantomime at Bartholomew Fair in London in 1791. The Grantham theatre was described by Winston in *The Theatric Tourist* as a handsome building with two tiers of circular boxes and a capacity of £50, "at the prices of 3s. 2s. and 1s." The season there began in December and ran for five weeks, but we do not know whether or not Lawrence performed.

Lawrence, Moses [*fl. c.* 1784–1824], *acrobat, composer.*

De Castro said in his *Memoirs* that Moses Lawrence, who in 1824 was a composer and leader of the band at the Royal Amphitheatre, had been an attendant at Astley's Amphitheatre when he was a lad. Moses was probably the Master Lawrence who was cited in Astley's bills beginning 7 April 1785 as in a tumbling act with Lawrence Senior, presumably his father. The younger Lawrence tumbled at Sadler's Wells in 1787 and 1788. The elder Lawrence was Joseph, "The Great Devil," and he also had a daughter who danced at Astley's. Nicoll lists as composer for three early nineteenth century productions M. Lawrence, and we take him to be Moses. He composed the music for the spectacle *Zittau*, which was performed at the Royal Adelphi in 1804, *Pyramus and Thisbe*, done at the Royal Amphitheatre the same year, and *Harlequin Plagiarist*, a pantomime performed at the Olympic Pavilion in 1807.

Lawrence, [**Thomas?**] *c.* 1766–1826?, *actor.*

The *Public Advertiser* on 1 December 1785 noted that at Drury Lane Theatre that night would appear a young gentleman who had had a commission in the army but was now on half-pay and would play the title role in *Philaster*. The *European Magazine* identified the actor as a Mr Lawrence, who had on 20 August 1784 as an amateur played Algernon Sidney in Thomas Stratford's *Lord Russel*. (Another Lawrence had acted the Earl of Bedford in that fiasco; he was the father of Thomas Lawrence the painter.) It would seem that after appearing in Stratford's play young Lawrence had signed on with Drury Lane, for on 7 October 1784 an entry in the account books stated that Lawrence, "on acct. of an Eng^t" received £10. After his appearance as Philaster in December 1785 he was added to the paylist at 10s. daily. It seems probable that he acted small parts not mentioned in bills throughout the 1784–85 and 1785–86 seasons. And he was advertised as playing Allworth in *A New Way to Pay Old Debts* on 13 January 1787, which fact suggests that he was at Drury Lane for the 1786–87 season as well.

During the summer of 1787 Lawrence acted at the Haymarket Theatre playing Harry in *The Two Connoisseurs*, Easy in *The Manager in Distress*, Spinosa in *Venice Preserv'd*, a Brother in *Comus*, Horace in *A Beggar on Horseback*, Salanio in *The Merchant of Venice*, Captain Wilmot in *English Readings*, Charles in *The Village Lawyer*, and Harry Bevil in *Cross Purposes*. The *Gentleman's Magazine* in February 1826 reported the death on 8 February at the age of 60, at Brighton, of Thomas Lawrence of Drury Lane; there seems to be no other Lawrence to whom that could refer than the Lawrence whose career we have followed here.

Laws, Mr [*fl.* 1741–1747], *actor.*

A Mr Laws was the Porter in *The Imprisonment, Release, Stratagems, and Marriage of Harlequin* at Goodman's Fields Theatre on 9 October 1741 and subsequent dates. His benefit tickets were accepted on 22 March 1746, and one supposes that he had been playing walk-ons and bit parts over the years without being named in the bills. On 26 March 1747, the last citation for him, "Law" shared a benefit at Goodman's Fields with four others.

Lawson, Mr [*fl.* 1693], *actor.*

Mr Lawson played Crack in *A Very Good Wife* in late April 1693 with the United Company at Drury Lane Theatre. The play was given five performances. Lawson was very likely related to the actress Abigail Lawson, whose theatrical career had begun at Drury Lane the previous year.

Lawson, Mrs [*fl.* 1755], *dancer.*

Mrs Lawson danced in the performances of *The Chinese Festival* when it was presented— or, rather, when against a rioting audience it was attempted—at Drury Lane Theatre on 8 November 1755.

Lawson, Mrs [fl. 1794], actress.

The *Morning Herald* listed a Mrs Lawson as playing Laura in *Tancred and Sigismunda* and Nancy in *Three Weeks After Marriage* at the Haymarket Theatre on 22 May 1794, but the *Oracle* had it that Miss Herbert played Laura and Mrs Jones played Nancy. In any case, the plays were not repeated.

Lawson, Miss [fl. 1753], singer? dancer?

At Sadler's Wells on 13 August 1753 for the benefit of Mr Maddox, an entertainment of music and dancing called *An English Night's Entertainment* was presented (along with acrobatic performances by Maddox). One of the characters in the entertainment was played by a Miss Lawson; the bill did not specify whether she sang or danced or did both.

Lawson, Abigail [fl. 1692–1705], actress.

Abigail Lawson played Margery in *The Marriage-Hater Match'd* in January 1692 with the United Company at Drury Lane Theatre. In late September 1694 she was listed for Mrs Dazie in *The Canterbury Guests* at the same house. Though she did not join with some of the disgruntled actors who signed a complaint against the managers Skipwith and Rich, she joined the rebel group headed by Thomas Betterton and left Drury Lane in 1695 for Lincoln's Inn Fields Theatre. There on 30 April she was the original Jenny in the first performance of *Love for Love*. Before the end of the century with Betterton's troupe she appeared as Doll in *She Ventures and He Wins*, Sprightly in *Lover's Luck*, the Nurse in *The City Bride*, Altea in *Rule a Wife and Have a Wife*, Beatrice in *The Anatomist*, Fidget in *The City Lady*, La Busque in *The Intrigues at Versailles*, Dorothy in "All Without Money" and Lysette in "The Unfortunate Couple"—sections of *The Novelty*—Eugenia in *The Innocent Mistress*, an English Country Woman in *Europe's Revels*, Nibs in *The Pretenders*, and Zelide in *The False Friend*.

In December 1700 Abigail Lawson was one of the players cited by the authorities as having uttered blasphemies on the stage; just what she said was probably no more or less shocking than "'E God," which was one of the examples cited. The case provided us with Mrs Lawson's Christian name and the fact that she was of the parish of St Clement Danes. She continued acting during the first years of the new century, though cast lists are so rare that we know of only a few parts for her: Mrs Junket and Lady Weepwell in *The Ladies Visiting Day*, Laura in *The Stolen Heiress*, Larea in *Love Betray'd*, Claius in *The Fickle Shepherdess*, Lady Gaylove in *The Different Widows*, and Mrs Scribblescrabble in *The Biter*. She seems not to have continued acting after the 1704–5 season.

Lawson, Henry [fl. 1744–1751], flutist, trumpeter.

Mr Lawson's first notice was on 26 April 1744 at Covent Garden Theatre, where he played a concerto on the German flute. At the Haymarket Theatre on 5 November of that year Lawson and Burke Thumoth played a concerto for two flutes. That Lawson was, we believe, the court trumpeter Henry Lawson, who was listed in the Lord Chamberlain's accounts beginning in 1744, when he replaced Daniel Hopkins. Lawson was cited as offering a flute performance in April 1748 at Covent Garden, and Latreille copied out a notice, dated only 1750, of Lawson performing at a benefit for young Jonathan Snow, held at Snow's father's house in St Margaret Street, Westminster. The musicians who performed there appeared again on 23 April 1751 at the Haymarket, according to Latreille, though *The London Stage* does not list that event. Henry Lawson was replaced in the King's Musick by John Turner, but when that was done, or when Lawson died, is not clear.

Lax, Mr [fl. 1715–1719], dancer.

Mr Lax danced at Lincoln's Inn Fields Theatre on 1 March 1715. "Lux" danced there again on 9 January 1719. He rejoined the troupe in October and November, performing with several others some untitled entr'acte dances. He was last mentioned in the bills on 12 November 1719.

Lax, Mrs [fl. 1714], actress.

Mrs Lax played Calista in *Injured Virtue* at Richmond in the summer of 1714 and at the King's Arms in Southwark on 1 November the same year.

Lax, Mrs [fl. 1738–1740], dancer.

Mrs Lax was in a *Peasant Dance* on 5 September 1738 at Hallam's Southwark Fair booth;

and on 23 August 1740 at the Lee-Phillips booth at Bartholomew Fair she was one of three performers representing Tragedy in *Harlequin Restored*.

Laye, George *d. 1765, singer.*

On 23 July 1712, according to *The Old Cheque Book of the Chapel Royal*, George Laye, a countertenor from Windsor, was sworn a Gentleman of the Chapel, replacing the deceased Thomas Richardson (though Laye was cited in the Lord Chamberlain's accounts as early as 17 February 1710 as attending the Queen at Windsor in 1709). Laye was still active at court in April 1725, when he was paid for attending at Windsor in 1724. On 2 February 1726 he sang in a concert at the Inner Temple in London, and it is possible that he engaged in other concert activity as well. He became on 28 August 1739 one of the original subscribers to the newly formed Royal Society of Musicians. According to a manuscript at the Chapel Royal, says Rimbault, the editor of the *Cheque Book*, George Laye died at Windsor in September 1765.

Layfield, Lewis *d. 1751, actor, dancer, musician, manager.*

Lewis Layfield was first mentioned in London bills on 10 January 1704, when he danced a new *Italian Scaramouch* at Lincoln's Inn Fields Theatre. Chetwood in his *General History* in 1749 recalled that Layfield had been born in England. He may have served in the army. He had, Chetwood said, "been in many Employments both by Sea and Land, and was formerly very active and strong, able to go through Fatigues.... I remember him in Drury-lane, when I was in my Youth, a nimbel active Scaramouch...." Layfield's period of military duty probably came between his London activity in the first decade of the century and his work in Dublin from 1719 onward.

In London from January to August 1706 he danced between the acts at the new Queen's Theatre, regularly offering his Scaramouch specialty. In 1709–10 he was at Drury Lane, where Chetwood evidently saw him. His first appearance, in his *Scaramouch* dance, was on 15 December 1709, and that season, in addition to entr'acte turns, he danced Scaramouch in *The Emperor of the Moon* and played Pyracmon in *Oedipus*, Pedro in *The Successful Strangers*, and Toledo in *The Mistake*. At his 1710 shared benefit with Mrs Cox he danced *Harlequin Man and Woman* with Hester Santlow (later Mrs Booth) and his *Italian Scaramouch* and spoke the epilogue. On 23 May he danced an *Italian Night Scene* and *Scaramouch*, and three days later, in imitation of the imitator Clinch of Barnet, Layfield gave impressions of a horn, huntsman, and pack of hounds. On 12 August 1710 he appeared in Greenwich at Pinkethman's playhouse.

Clark's *The Irish Stage in the County Towns* places Layfield at Smock Alley in Dublin from 1717 onward, though the first certain record that has been found is a Smock Alley cast for *Wexford Wells*, dated 7 November 1720, with Layfield as the Innkeeper. He performed there through the 1727–28 season, but the only roles that have been discovered for him are Captain Strut in *The Double Gallant*, Sir Peter Pride in *The Amorous Widow*, Townsman in *The Island Princess*, and Sir Paul Squelch in *The Northern Lass*. In the W. J. Lawrence papers that W. S. Clark investigated is a notice that on 9 April 1723 Layfield was appointed overseer of the City Music and called the "major haut-boy."

The Layfield who at the Haymarket Theatre in London played Dominic in *The Spanish Fryar* on 26 October 1728 and Plowshare in *The Lottery* on the following 19 November was probably Lewis. His wife played Mrs Subtle in the latter piece. But Lewis was back in Dublin for most of the 1728–29 season, during which he is known to have performed, at Smock Alley, Leon in *Rule a Wife and Have a Wife*, Sullen in *The Beaux' Stratagem*, Ned Sneak in *Chuck*, and Hunter in *The Beggar's Wedding*. At Dublin that season, on 7 December 1728, Thomas Benson published a picture of Macheath and Polly in *The Beggar's Opera*, and W. J. Lawrence guessed that the performers represented may have been Lewis Layfield and Mrs Sterling—but no copies of the print have survived, Lawrence said.

On 10 December 1729, according to Reed's "Notitia Dramatica," Layfield was appointed State Kettledrummer to the Lord Lieutenant of Ireland. He was living at the time in Finglas, Dublin, from which address in November he had advertised the loss of a horse. The season at Smock Alley in 1729–30 was curtailed in the winter due to an epidemic (flu?)

which in November afflicted several members of the Smock Alley Company, including Layfield; but on 30 March 1730 he acted the Gravedigger in *Hamlet* and a month later was seen as Hob in *Flora*. He remained at Smock Alley through 1733–34 playing T. Peascod in *The What D'Ye Call It*, Squire Somebody in *The Stage Coach Opera*, Hilliard in *The Jovial Crew*, Cosmez in *Love and Ambition*, Damon in *Damon and Phillida*, Jobson in *The Devil to Pay*, Rovewell in *The Contrivances*, and Bumbardo in *All Vows Kept*. The Dublin Assembly Roll in 1733 tells us that "Certain of the Commons, [set] forth that Lewis Layfield, one of the city music, has greatly neglected the duty of his office in attending on public days, and therefore prayed to have the said Layfield displaced for his said neglect; whereupon it was granted."

There may have been more to that request than the petition stated, for as one of the managers of the Smock Alley Theatre, Layfield was high-handed and violent. Gilliland wrote that Layfield, whom he called the original Macheath in Dublin, shared the Smock Alley management with two others. At some point (perhaps November 1729)

he became sick, and his colleagues, refusing to supply him with money, he sallied forth on one of the evenings of performance, with his broad-sword under his cloak (for he had been a trooper), and going to the different door-keepers, demanded all the money, which he took from the box, pit, and gallery offices, and then walked demurely home, and waited patiently the return of his health.

During a representation at Smock-alley theatre, the brother of an Irish nobleman, who was among the crowd of spectators upon the stage, . . . took some indecent liberties with the wife of one of the managers, which coming to the ears of Layfield, he publicly declared that had the intruder abused his wife in a similar way, he would have wrung his neck off.

The gentleman, hearing that, engaged 12 Dublin chairmen to horsewhip Layfield; they enticed him to the Rose and Crown in Dame Street, where the gentleman was waiting, but Layfield had been warned of the plot by a cook and had helped himself to one of the cook's carving knives. Thus armed, Layfield entered the room where the gentleman was, repeated his threat, and when the chairmen began to make their move, Layfield seized the young gentleman and told the chairmen he would "cut off the scoundrel's head" if they attacked. The chairmen remained passive spectators as Layfield "dragged his opponent into the street, where he kicked and rolled him in the kennel, until his life was endangered by the severe castigation."

The Aungier Street playhouse in Dublin opened on 9 March 1734 with *The Recruiting Officer*, in which Layfield played Balance. He performed there through 1741–42, though the records are scanty; he may not have been there every season, and he is known to have performed in Carlow in July 1735. His parts included Henry VIII, Hob in *Flora*, Jobson in *The Devil to Pay*, and the King of Spain in *The Queen of Spain*. In 1743–44 Layfield was at the Smock Alley Theatre, though a Layfield was also listed at Aungier Street; since both Lewis and his son Robert were active in Dublin that season, it is not always easy to distinguish the two, but Robert would appear to have been at Aungier Street and Lewis at Smock Alley. At any rate, a Layfield received a benefit at Smock Alley on 2 February 1744.

The bills for the Dublin theatres up to 1746 usually provided an initial to help distinguish between Lewis and Robert Layfield, but after that the distinction was not clearly made. One would suppose that the Layfield Senior who was at Smock Alley in 1746–47 was Lewis; he received a benefit on 23 March 1747. A Layfield was at that playhouse in 1748–49, and the 23 May 1749 benefit for a Mr Layfield was advertised with an apology which makes him sound very like the aging Lewis: "As the Indisposition which Mr. Layfield has sometime languished under, deprives him of the Pleasure of waiting on his Friends, to solicit their Favour, on this Occasion; he most humbly hopes, from their known Humanity and Benevolence, that they will give him the Honour of their Company at his Approaching Benefit Play." He was not listed as performing at his benefit, and it is probable that he did not act at his last recorded one, on 19 April 1750 at Smock Alley.

Chetwood said that as of 1749 Layfield "was loaden with that Burden of Flesh" that he did not have in his younger years. Yet he was "a main Pillar, Time past, in supporting Dublin Theatre," Chetwood wrote, and though now in his decline ought to be respected. Chetwood said that Layfield "is happily engaged for Life, and of Consequence (if Articles are binding) will receive his Salary to the Day of his Death." Even in 1749, Chetwood stated, Layfield was still filling some parts satisfactorily, such as Hob and Jobson.

Robert Layfield was Lewis's son, and there was a Layfield Junior who acted in Dublin (but not in London) in 1728–29 and again in 1746–47 and who was surely related. British Library Manuscript Add. 18586 states that Lewis Layfield died insane in Dublin in 1751.

W. J. Lawrence declared that a print, showing Lewis Layfield and Mrs Sterling as Macheath and Polly in the *Beggar's Opera*, had been published by Thomas Benson in Dublin on 7 December 1728. We have seen no copy.

Layfield, Mrs [Lewis?] [*fl. 1728*], actress.

A Mrs Layfield played Mrs Subtle in *The Lottery* at the Haymarket Theatre on 10 December 1728. Three days earlier it had been reported that she was indisposed. Perhaps she was Mrs Lewis Layfield, but we cannot be certain that the Mr Layfield who performed in London in October and November 1728 was Lewis and not another person.

Layfield, Robert *d. 1761, actor, dancer, singer, trumpeter.*

Lewis Layfield's son Robert was probably just a lad when he played Tom Chuck in *Chuck* on 27 January 1729 at the Smock Alley Theatre in Dublin, for he was called Master Layfield as late as the 1732–33 season. Few other roles are known for him in the early part of his stage career, though in December 1731 he acted Mopsus in *Damon and Phillida*, and in February 1733 he played a boy in *The Contrivances*. The Dublin bills did not cite him again for over two years (though only a handful of bills have survived). In 1735–36 Robert was playing at the Ransford Street Theatre, where two of his roles were a Boor in *The Royal Merchant* and Macheath in *The Beggar's Opera* (a role his father had played). Robert was at Aungier Street in 1737–38, during which season he acted Fountain in *Wit Without Money*. He remained there through 1743–44.

At Aungier Street some of his parts were Scaramouch in *The Emperor of the Moon* (again he took after his father, who had been a Scaramouch in the early years of the century), Knockmedown in *The Female Officer*, Hob in *Flora* (another of his father's parts), Sir Trusty in *Rosamond*, Grizzle in *The Tragedy of Tragedies*, the Dragon in *The Dragon of Wantley*, and the Conjurer in *Hussar*. With the United Company in 1744–45 Layfield played Charos in *The Necromancer*. From 1745–46 to 1758–59 he performed at Smock Alley with occasional appearances at Capel Street and Crow Street. Layfield was a state trumpeter, from which position he was at least once, in September 1757, given a six-month leave of absence, presumably to perform. Like his father he also had a hand in theatre management, at least in 1749–50 at Capel Street.

On 3 November 1750 Robert Layfield began an engagement at Drury Lane Theatre in London playing Kite in *The Recruiting Officer*. During the season of 1750–51 he was also seen as Hecate in *Macbeth*, Waitwell in *The Way of the World*, Charon in *Lethe*, Charles in *As You Like It*, Harlequin in *Queen Mab*, Lovewit in *The Alchemist*, and Blister in *The Virgin Unmask'd*. Sybil Rosenfeld has placed Layfield in Simpson's troupe at Bath in 1751, and it is possible that the Mr "Langfield" who was cited in W. J. Lawrence's notes as playing in Belfast and Lisburn in the winter of 1754–55 was Robert Layfield. In 1757–58 Layfield acted at the New Concert Hall in Edinburgh, taking such roles as Capulet in *Romeo and Juliet*, Sullen in *The Beaux' Stratagem*, Wingate in *The Apprentice*, Antonio in *Twelfth Night*, Colonel Bully in *The Provok'd Wife*, the Drunken Cook in *The Lying Valet*, the Ghost in *Hamlet*, Mat in *The Beggar's Opera*, the Old Shepherd in *Douglas*, a Physician in *The Rehearsal*, Ventidius in *All for Love*, and Duncan in *Macbeth*. Gentleman and Boswell in their *View of the Edinburgh Stage* pronounced Layfield "the best Duncan that ever trod the Edinburgh, if not any, Stage."

Faulkner's Dublin Journal on 3 February 1761 reported that Robert Layfield, "one of the State Trumpets," had died the previous week. Mrs R. Layfield, presumably Robert's wife, acted at the Aungier Street playhouse in 1743–44 but never appeared in London. The "Langfield" who acted at the Vaults in Belfast in July 1761 may have been Lewis Layfield Junior, Robert's brother. Chetwood in his *General History* in 1749 spoke of Robert Layfield as "a very good Player in several Cast of Parts, particularly Serjeant Kite, &c."

Layley, Mr [fl. 1775], *house servant?*
Mr Layley was one of many whose benefit tickets were admitted on 30 May 1775 at Covent Garden Theatre. He may have been one of the house servants.

Lazzari, Antonio [fl. 1756], *singer.*
Antonio Lazzari sang in Giordani's burletta troupe at Covent Garden beginning 12 January 1756. *La comediante fatta cantatrice* and *Gli amante gelosi* were performed, but no roles for Lazzari were given in the bills.

Lazzarini, Gustavo c. 1765–c. 1801, *singer.*
Gustavo Lazzarini was born in either Padua or Verona about 1765 and made his debut in 1789 in *Ifigenia in Aulide* (by Zingarelli) in Lucca. During 1790–91 and 1791–92 Lazzarini sang with the opera company at the Pantheon and Haymarket theatres in London. His initial appearance was as Ubaldo in *Armida* at the Pantheon on 17 February 1791. The *Morning Post* on 10 January had reported after a rehearsal that "Lazzarini, the new Tenor, does not disgrace his Tutor; and this is not slight praise, when it is known that the Tutor was Paisiello." The critics found Lazzarini good in both serious and comic roles, and Lord Mount-Edgcumbe noted that he had a "sweet tenor voice."

At the Pantheon during the rest of the season Lazzarini sang Cavaliere Cedidoro in *La bella pescatrice*, Palmoro in *Idalide*, Don Calloandro in *La molinarella*, Lucio Papirio in *Quinto Fabio*, and Riccardo in *La locanda*. On 17 December 1791 he appeared as Il Marchese in *La pastorella nobile* at the Pantheon; then, after the Pantheon fire in January 1792, the troupe had to move to the Haymarket, where Lazzarini sang Don Nardo in *Le trame deluse*, Don Ridolfo in *La discorida conjugale*, and some of his earlier parts. In 1792 he also participated in the Professional Concerts.

He was in Milan in 1794 during the Carnival singing in *Artaserse* and *Demofoonte*, and he returned there in 1795 and 1798, singing in the latter year in *Orazi* and *Meleagro*. He was in Paris in 1801. Charles Beecher Hogan has informed us that Lazzarini died about 1801. An engraved portrait of him by the singer Nitôt Dugrêne was published in Paris, where two volumes of Italian airs and a pastoral had been published by Lazzarini.

L'Cler, Mr [fl. 1751], *flutist.*
Mr L'Cler played a concerto on the German flute on 11 and 16 April 1751 at Drury Lane.

L'Clert, Mons [fl. 1755], *dancer.*
Monsieur L'Clert was one of the French dancers in the ill-fated production of *The Chinese Festival* which opened at Drury Lane on 8 November and played to—or was interrupted by—rioting audiences through 18 November 1755.

L'Contri. *See* DE LA COINTRIE *and* LA COINTE.

Leach, Mr [fl. 1746], *house servant?*
The Drury Lane bills for 23 April 1746 announced that "Tickets deliver'd by Mr Leach will be taken." His function in the theatre, if any, is unknown to us; perhaps he was a house servant.

Leach, Mr [fl. 1780], *actor.*
A Mr Leach was a member of a company that performed at the Crown Inn, Islington, for at least seven nights between 29 February and 19 April 1780. Leach's roles were Captain Dudley in *The West Indian* on 29 February, King Henry in *Richard III*, the Clown in *Death and Restoration of Harlequin*, and Puff in *Miss in Her Teens* on 6 March, Friar Lawrence in *Romeo and Juliet* and Puff on 13 March, Sir Jealous Traffick in *The Busy Body* on 17 March, the Uncle in *The London Merchant* and O'Daub in *The Camp* on 27 March, Whittle in *The Irish Widow* on 5 April, and Tester in *The Suspicious Husband* on 19 April.

Leach, James 1762–1798, *composer, singer.*
James Leach, who was born at Wardle, near Rochdale, Lancashire, in 1762, became a handloom weaver, but then turned to the profession of music, which he had studied in leisure time. Soon he became attached to the King's band and earned some reputation as a choir leader. On 18 October 1779 he and Miss Mitchell sang the two-part song "Damon and Clora" at the Haymarket Theatre. He was listed by Dr Burney as one of the countertenors (Grove calls him a tenor) who sang in the Handel

Memorial Concerts at Westminster Abbey and the Pantheon in May and June 1784. Leach took part in subsequent Abbey concerts and in various other music festivals.

After teaching at Rochdale from 1789, Leach moved to Salford about 1795. On 8 February 1798 he was killed in a coach accident at Blackney, near Manchester, and was buried in the cemetary of the Union Street Wesleyan Chapel, Rochdale, where his grave was marked by a stone on which was cut his short-metre tune "Egypt."

Leach published *A New Sett of Hymn and Psalm Tunes* in 1789 and *A Second Sett of Hymn and Psalm Tunes* about 1794. The latter was reissued posthumously in 1798 with a solicitation for subscriptions by which his sundry manuscripts would be published for the benefit of his family. A reprint also was issued in 1886 with a sketch of his life by Thomas Newbigging. Many of his tunes were published in America in such collections as *Easy Instructor* (Albany, 1798), *Bridgewater Collection* (Boston, 1802), and *The David Companion, or Methodist Standard* (Baltimore, 1810). Leach also published some anthems and trios for a bass viol and two violins.

Leach's music was especially popular at various Methodist meetings. He was, in the words of the *New Grove*, "one of the best practitioners of the Methodist style of church music."

Leach, Mrs M.   *1780–1807, actress.*

Announced as "A Young Lady" making her first appearance on any stage, Mrs Leach acted Miss Harriet in *The Guardian* at the Haymarket Theatre on 15 August 1800. She is identified as Mrs Leach in a manuscript notation on the night's playbill in the Harvard Theatre Collection. No other performances by her in London are known.

In the summer of 1802 Mrs Leach acted at Brighton and in September of that year joined Collins's company in which she played principal parts at Portsmouth, Southampton, Chichester, and Winchester. Early in 1806 she left Collins to play in Ireland, acting at Waterford, Younghall, and Tralee. Having received an offer from Dublin, she made a hard winter journey of 160 miles "in a common Irish car" but did not please the audiences there, so after several performances she returned to London without money or prospects. "The vexation produced by these and other unfortunate circumstances brought on a disorder which soon terminated her existence," reported the *Gentleman's Magazine* of June 1807, where her obituary described her as Mrs M. Leach, "a beautiful but unfortunate young woman," who died in her twenty-seventh year in Westmoreland Street, Marylebone.

Leach, Thomas   [*fl. 1794–1815*], *harpsichordist, violist.*

Thomas Leach of Cheshunt was listed in Doane's *Musical Directory* in 1794 as a harpsichordist and violist who was a member of the New Musical Fund. His name was on the list of subscribers to that fund in 1794, 1805, and 1815; in the last year he served on the Committee.

Leacy. *See* LACY.

Leadbetter, Mr   [*fl. 1726*], *house servant.*

The performance of *The Spanish Fryar* at Lincoln's Inn Fields Theatre on 16 May 1726 was for the benefit of Mr Leadbetter. He was, noted Latreille, a house servant, and the benefit brought him a modest £71 1s. 6d. before house charges.

Leader, Mr   [*fl. 1755*], *actor.*

A Mr Leader played Simon Pure in *A Bold Stroke for a Wife* at Widow Yeates's "large Theatrical BARN Facing the Boarding-School in CROYDON" on 2 October 1755.

Leak. *See also* LEEKE.

Leak, Elizabeth   *b. c. 1778, singer, actress.*

Elizabeth Leak was born about 1778 in Beckham, Norfolk, the daughter of a farmer. Contemporary biographical notices were contradictory in respect to her early upbringing. The *Monthly Mirror* of January 1799 and Thomas Gilliland in the *Dramatic Mirror* (1808) stated that because her parents died young, Miss Leak was raised by an aunt and uncle; the *Authentic Memoirs of the Green Room* (1799) claimed, on the other hand, that once she became a professional, she supported her parents. According to Reed's manuscript notes in a copy of *Roach's Authentic Memoirs of the Green Room* (1796) in the British Library, Miss Leak's father "was hanged at Newgate 1797 for an unnatural crime." There is some certainty, however, to

Harvard Theatre Collection
ELIZABETH LEAK
engraving by Ridley, after Beechey

the report that she learned the rudiments of music from the Norwich oboist Michael Sharp (d. 1800) and that in December 1792, at about the age of 13 or 14, she came to London and was articled to Dr Samuel Arnold for five years.

Her early memoirs also stated that Miss Leak's first essay in public was in a concert at Freemasons' Hall at the age of 14. When, however, she sang in the oratorios conducted by Arnold at the King's Theatre on 15 February 1793, the advertisements announced she was then making her first public appearance. That night she sang the solos "Full fathom five" and "Come unto these yellow sands" by Purcell (from *The Tempest*) and with Master Hummel the duet "My faith and truth" by Handel (from *Samson*). In the *Messiah* on 20 February her airs were "Behold! a Virgin," "O thou that tellest," and "How beautiful," and, with Harrison, "O! Death." In the King's oratorio on 22 February she rendered "There beneath a lowly shade" from *Alexander Balus*. That same season she also performed in the oratorios at the Haymarket Theatre, again conducted by Arnold, singing "O magnify the Lord" on 27 February 1793 and songs by Handel and Arne on 6, 13, and 20 March.

Miss Leak's debut in a stage character occurred at the Haymarket Theatre on 21 January 1794 when she played Rosetta in *Love in a Village*. At the time she was "not yet fifteen," acording to a biographer in the *Monthly Mirror* of January 1799, who claimed to have been present in the audience that night, "but she proved a capacity equal to the trial, and gained . . . unbounded applause." Her extreme youth and talent, it was reported, made her "the darling of the audience" and brought her "instant fame." After repeating Rosetta on 28 January, she performed the title role in *Rosina* on 11 February and several other nights and then was seen as Sally in *Thomas and Sally* on 24 February.

Several months after her Haymarket debut, Miss Leak was one of the singers in the impressive concert of Handelian music with which the new Drury Lane Theatre was inaugurated on 12 March 1794, and she was awarded an encore in "O magnify the Lord." She sang in several other oratorio programs at the new house that spring and then on 28 April performed Sally there. Her subsequent characters at Drury Lane before the end of that season, during which she earned £6 per week, included Louisa in *No Song No Supper*, Gillian in *The Quaker*, and Susan in *The Glorious First of June*.

In the summer of 1794 Miss Leak joined Colman's company at the Haymarket, repeating Rosina and Sally and adding Eliza in *The Flitch of Bacon*, a Villager in *The Battle of Hexham*, Caroline Sanford in *The Dead Alive*, Jenny in *Auld Robin Gray*, Laura in *The Agreeable Surprise*, Louisa in *The Farmer*, a Peasant in *The Mountaineers*, Florella in *My Grandmother*, Amelia in *Summer Amusement*, the First Bacchant and a Pastoral Nymph in *Comus*, and Ismene in *The Sultan*. That year Doane's *Musical Directory* listed her as a soprano living at No 28, Southampton Street, the Strand, who sang at the Haymarket and for the Academy of Ancient Music.

In the autumn of 1794 Miss Leak commenced a long engagement at Drury Lane at a salary of £6 per week, which was raised in 1795–96 to £7 and in 1797–98 to £8. She supported "with great credit" several characters of the absent Sga Storace. Typical of her repertoire were such sprightly heroines as Fanny in *The Cherokee*, Josephine in *The Children in the Wood*, Flora in *Hob in the Well*, and Phillis in *The Smugglers*. In his *Candid and Impartial Strictures on the Performers* (1795), F. G. Waldron described her as "A bewitching little syren, and a very pretty actress, as well as a sprightly, agreeable woman. Her person low, but pleasing; her manners engaging and unembarrassed." Waldron thought her "a most excellent second" to Sga Storace, while Bellamy in his poem *The London Theatres* (1795) likened her to the celebrated Anna Maria Crouch:

Of pleasing form of tender years
In LEAKE *another Crouch appears*
And sooth to say the comic muse
In Leake another Darling views

Miss Leak's popularity may be suggested by her good net benefit receipts: £153 12s. 4d. on 23 May 1798 (when she made her first appearance as Hero in *Much Ado about Nothing*), £339 14s. 6d. on 9 May 1799, and £235 12s. 1d. on 3 June 1800. Between 1795 and 1800 she lived in Upper Mews Gate, Castle Street, Leicester Fields.

By January 1799, however, according to her champion in the *Monthly Mirror*, she was not being employed by the Drury Lane management to best advantage—"a charge of neglect lays somewhere, and if so, a deserving performer is materially wronged and the public greatly insulted." Her roles so far that season had been Florella in *My Grandmother*, Laura in *The Agreeable Surprise*, Theodosia in *The Maid of the Mill*, Margaretta in *No Song No Supper*, Beda in *Blue-Beard*, and Angelica Goto in *The Shipwreck*, among some others. In October 1799 the *Monthly Mirror* hinted that a cabal was keeping Miss Leak from being engaged at Drury Lane that season, but at the bottom of the page an italicized note was added to the effect that "While revising the press, we had the satisfaction to hear that Miss Leak has been restored to her situation in Drury Lane theatre." She made her first appearance of that season on 6 November 1799 as Theodosia in *The Maid of the Mill*.

At the Haymarket Theatre Miss Leak played a total of three summers between 1794 and 1796, appearing in her usual line. Some of her roles there included Rachel in *Zorinske*, Lady Lauretta in *The Apparition*, Emma in *Peeping Tom*, and Phebe in *The Three and the Deuce* in 1795, and Mrs Goodwill in *Banian Day* and Barbara in *Love and Money* in 1796, in addition to several of the characters she regularly played at the winter house. She also sang at Norwich in 1795. When Colman would not grant her a benefit at the end of the 1796 summer season at the Haymarket, Miss Leak quit that employment. Subsequently she passed her summers engaged at Birmingham, where in 1797 she played a line of first characters, giving—as the *Monthly Mirror* of July reported—"great satisfaction." That summer she also acted at Liverpool for a month. She returned to Birmingham in 1798 for two weeks, during which she acted Ophelia to Kemble's Hamlet, then proceeded to Manchester for a few days and subsequently to Newcastle and to Liverpool again. In the summer of 1799 she was once more at Liverpool, where her benefit brought £183.

Harvard Theatre Collection

ELIZABETH LEAK, as Peggy
engraving by Wilson, after Roberts

Songs published as sung by her at Drury Lane included *To welcome Mirth and harmless Glee* in *The Stranger* (1798), Linley's *Last Whitsunday they brought me* in *Vortigern* (1796), and Hook's *Orphan Bess the Beggar Girl* (1800?). At her Drury Lane benefit on 3 June 1800, when she performed Rosara in *She Wou'd and She Wou'd Not* and Clarinda in *Robin Hood*, she "gratified her numerous friends" by singing new songs by De Lanza and Dr Arnold; in the latter she accompanied herself on the tambourine.

In June 1800 the *Monthly Mirror* announced that "Miss Leak quits Drury Lane, and, we believe the stage altogether." According to Gilliland, she had retired because her voice had failed. In 1808 she was still alive, teaching music.

In his anatomization of her in *A Pin Basket to the Children of Thespis* (1797), John Williams indicated that she had never lived up to her unqualified puffs at the beginning of her career:

When she acts, I'm impell'd to take much upon trust;
When she sings, her sweet voice shuts the eyes of Disgust,
Her dulcet contralto *exacts Fame's confession*
To her feminine graces and manly expression.
In her onset her name met the Public too proudly,
She was injur'd by zeal—she was lauded too loudly!

She was, according to Williams' testimony, very pretty, with "ebon-hued locks." A charming portrait of her holding a mask was painted by Sir William Beechey and exhibited at the Royal Academy in 1797. It was owned by Knoedler & Co sometime in the twentieth century, but its present location is unknown to us. Perhaps this was "Miss Leake's picture" given by the Covent Garden prompter James Wild to his daughter Elizabeth in his will dated 4 July 1801. W. Ridley's engraving of the Beechey portrait was published in the *Monthly Mirror* in January 1799. An engraving by Wilson, after J. Roberts, of Miss Leak as Peggy in *The Gentle Shepherd* was published as a plate to *Bell's British Theatre*, 1796.

Leander, Lewis Henry *1769–1830, horn player, violinist, violist.*

Lewis Henry Leander, the elder son of the musician Thomas Leander and his wife Mary, was born on 28 February 1769 and was baptized on 26 March next at St Anne, Westminster. Probably he was trained in music by his father. On 27 April 1784 at the Haymarket Theatre, Lewis Henry and his younger brother Vincent Thomas played a new concerto for two French horns composed by Barthélemon. The two brothers and their father were paid £12 12*s.* for playing in the concerts of the Academy of Ancient Music in 1787–88.

During the last decade of the eighteenth century the Leander brothers were ranked with the most celebrated horn players in Europe. They appeared frequently as soloists in the Oxford Music Room and performed in the Covent Garden oratorios between 1790 and 1794 and in 1798. In June and July 1795 they were musicians at the King's Theatre.

On 6 May 1792 the brothers were recommended for membership in the Royal Society of Musicians and were unanimously elected on 5 August 1792. At the time, Lewis Henry Leander was described as age 23, a single man, and a performer on the horn, violin, viola, and violoncello, with engagements at Salomon's concerts, those of the Academy of Ancient Music, and "a variety of other Engagements." In 1794, noticed as "H. Leander Junr," he was listed in Doane's *Musical Directory* as having appointments with the above-mentioned institutions as well as participating in the Handelian performances at Westminster Abbey; his address in Wells Street, Oxford, was the same as that of his father and brother.

Though his brother eventually resigned from the Royal Society of Musicians, Lewis Henry served that organization for many years. He played viola or violin in the Society's annual May concerts at St Paul's in 1794 and 1795, from 1798 to 1800, and from 1802 to 1804. In 1806 he was elected a Governor.

From 1794 Lewis Henry and his brother were principal players in the concerts of the Academy of Ancient Music. His brother did not perform there after 1811, but Lewis Henry continued in those concerts until 1820.

Probably Lewis Henry was the horn player employed in the Haymarket band at £2 per week in 1815. By 4 May 1823 he was too ill to work and applied to the Royal Society for relief, for he "was deprived of all business." In view of his age he was granted £5 relief on 2 April 1826. He was subsequently given occasional grants of £5 each for medical aid until 1 June 1828, when he was awarded a permanent allowance of £30 per year because of continuing poor health. On 6 December 1829 he was refused assistance to move from his residence at Tiverton and to satisfy his creditors there. The Society's Minute Books for 5 December 1830 record Lewis Henry Leander's death.

Leander, Thomas [fl. 1752–1798], *horn player, violinist, violist.*

The horn player Thomas Leander was performing in concerts in England as early as 1752, when, no doubt as a young man, he played in the Assembly Room, St Augustine's Back, Bristol, on 18 October. At Marylebone Gardens on 21 August 1770, Master Rogers of Bath, age 12, announced as Leander's scholar, played a concerto on the French horn. In 1775–76 Leander was a member of the band at Drury Lane Theatre. By 1783 Leander was employed in the opera band at the King's Theatre. He was listed by Dr Burney as one of the horn players in the Handel Memorial Concerts at Westminster Abbey and the Pantheon in May and June 1784.

In 1787–88 Leander received £12 12s. on behalf of himself and his two sons for playing in the Concerts of the Academy of Ancient Music. In 1794 Doane's *Musical Directory* listed "Thomas Leander, Senr," living at Wells Street, Oxford, as a member of the Royal Society of Musicians. He played the violin or viola in the Society's annual May concerts at St Paul's from 1793 to 1796. On 5 August 1798 the Governors of the Royal Society of Musicians appointed a committee to inquire about any property that Thomas Leander might have inherited by the death of his wife Mary, an action that suggests Leander may have been receiving benefits from the Society at the time.

His two sons, Lewis Henry Leander (1769–1830) and Vincent Thomas Leander (b. 1770), who became celebrated horn players, are noticed separately.

Leander, Vincent Thomas *b. 1770, horn player, violist, violoncellist, violinist.*

Vincent Thomas Leander, the younger son of the musician Thomas Leander and his wife Mary, was born on 25 February 1770 and baptized on 25 March at St Anne, Westminster. Like his elder brother Lewis Henry, he was probably educated in music by his father. On 27 April 1784 at the Haymarket Theatre he played with his brother a new concerto for two French horns composed by Barthélemon. The three Leanders were paid a total of £12 12s. for playing in the concerts of the Academy of Ancient Music in 1787–88. They also performed in the Covent Garden oratorios between 1790 and 1794 and in 1798. In June and July 1795 they were engaged at the King's Theatre.

The Leander brothers became two of the most celebrated horn players in Europe, according to Mee, who places them as frequent soloists in the Oxford Music Room. When they were both recommended on 6 May 1792 for membership in the Royal Society of Musicians (to which they were unanimously elected on 5 August 1792), Vincent Thomas Leander was described as a single man, 22 years old, a performer on the French horn, viola, and violoncello, with engagements at the oratorios and the concerts of Ancient Music. In 1794 he was listed in Doane's *Musical Directory*, where in addition to the engagements abovementioned it was stated that he also played in the Handelian concerts at Westminster Abbey and lived in Wells Street, Oxford, the same address as that of his father and brother.

The younger Leander played the violoncello in the Royal Society of Musicians' annual May concert at St Paul's in 1793. In 1795 he failed to attend at St Paul's but was put on the list for the violin in 1796 and 1797. On 4 June 1797, he asked to be allowed to withdraw from the Society, a request which the Governors granted.

Between 1794 and 1811 he and his brother were principal horn players in the Concerts of the Academy of Ancient Music.

Lear, Mr [fl. 1778], *actor.*

At China Hall, Rotherhithe, from 22 to 26 June 1778 a Mr Lear played Tyrrel in *The Fashionable Lover*, the Nephew in *The Irish Widow*, the Lawyer in *The Miser*, and Stanley in *Richard III*.

"Learned Dog, The" *d. 1800, trained animal.*

The *Monthly Mirror* for March 1800 reported on the fire in Panton Street which destroyed Chapman's (previously De Loutherbourg's) *Ei-*

dophusikon, including, "we are sorry to add, that . . . *learned dog*, whose sagacious tricks were so much admired."

"Learned French Dog, The" [*fl.* 1751–1752], *trained animal*.

At the Great Room adjoining the Guildhall in Bristol from 13 to 24 July 1751 was exhibited "Le Chien Savant, or, The Matchless Learned French Dog from London. . . ." An engraving by Morellon la Cave, after Nicholls, of "The new CHIEN SAVANT, Or LEARN'D DOG, that reads, writes, & casts Accomps &c." was published in 1752 and sold "at all the Print Shops, and at the Place [in London?] where the Dog is exhibited."

"Learned Horse, The Little Military" [*fl.* 1768–*c.* 1775], *trained animal*.

The Little Military Learned Horse, originally called Billy, was one of two horses purchased by Philip Astley at the Smithfield beast market in 1768. He was to become the center of the most popular of all the circus acts of the day. From various bills and accounts we learn that the horse could compute, feign death, fire a pistol, read minds, dance, and spell out "ASTLEY" with a forehoof in the tanbark. His feats are apt to be confused with those of the white charger Gibraltar, also called the Spanish Horse, which was General Elliot's present to Astley and which lived for 42 years.

"Learned Little Horse" [*fl.* 1766–1769], *trained animal*.

An "amazing" Learned Little Horse "from Courland" was exhibited by Mr Zucker, "a high German" at Taylor's Hall, Broad Street, Bristol, on 19 January 1765, at the Belvidere Gardens, Pentonville, London, in 1766–67, and again at Bristol in March 1766.

On 8 August 1769, according to a newspaper puff quoted in Pinks's *History of Clerkenwell*, Mr Zucker was still exhibiting his horse, but just where in Clerkenwell was not said. The Little Horse would "be looking out of the windows up two pairs of stairs every evening before the performances" began. What the sagacious equine did when he began performing was not revealed.

"Learned Pig, The" [*fl.* 1784–1786], *trained animal*.

Under the date of November 1784 Boswell recorded a discussion of "The Learned Pig" at Dr Johnson's at Lichfield:

> I told him (says Miss Seward) in one of my latest visits to him, of a wonderful learned pig, which I had seen at Nottingham; and which did all that we have observed exhibited by dogs and horses. The subject amused him. "Then," (said he,) "the pigs are a race unjustly calumniated. *Pig* has, it seems, not been wanting to *man*, but *man* to *pig*. We do not allow *time* for his education, we kill him at a year old." Mr. Henry White, who was present, observed that if this instance had happened in or before Pope's time, he would not have been justified in instancing the swine as the lowest degree of grovelling instinct. Dr. Johnson seemed pleased with

By permission of the British Library Board
THE LEARNED FRENCH DOG
engraving by La Cave, after Nicholls

By permission of the British Library Board
THE LEARNED PIG
engraving by Rowlandson

the observation, while the person who made it proceeded to remark, that great torture must have been employed, ere the indocility of the animal could have been subdued.—"Certainly," (said the Doctor;) "but," (turning to me,) "how old is your pig?" I told him, three years old. "Then," (said he,) "the pig has no cause to complain; he would have been killed the first year if he had not been *educated*, and protracted existence is a good recompence for very considerable degrees of torture."

There may, of course, have been more than one trained pig exhibited in England from 1784 to 1786, but it is quite possible that all of the several references we have found are to the same animal. According to the *Cornhill Magazine* in 1868, as quoted by Powell in a note to his edition of Boswell's *Life*, Captain Edward Thompson of the Royal Navy spoke of a "wonderful learned pig," in his journal on 17 March 1785, which "now draws the attention of the beau monde—women of the first Fashion waited four hours for their turn to see him. I am much flattered in this classick pig—he was bred at Beverley."

On 6 April 1785, not quite four months after Dr Johnson died, the *Public Advertiser* published some tasteless verses:

On the Learned Pig

Though Johnson, learned Bear, is gone,
    Let us no longer mourn our loss,
For lo, a learned Hog is come,
    And wisdom grunts at Charing Cross.

Happy for Johnson—that he died
    Before this wonder came to town,
Else had it blasted all his pride
    Another brute should gain renown.

The pig's learning was described by Sylas Neville in his diary on 3 May 1785, but Neville, alas, did not care for trained animals:

Another part of the morning's entertainment was the learned pig—any thing will do in London. This animal, one of the least docile in nature, has been taught to spell any word from an alphabet laid on the floor in a semi-circle, to tell the hour of the day, the day of the month &c. The keeper rewarded the docility of his pig with bread from his jacket. I was never much entertained with exhibitions of this kind of learning in dogs horses &c—very superior animals to this.

Neville did not say where he saw the Learned Pig, but the animal was exhibited doing those tricks, says Arundell, at Sadler's Wells in 1785. Altick in *The Shows of London* says the animal made his London debut at No 55, Charing Cross, after being exhibited in York and Scarborough in 1784. He was advertised as "well versed in all Languages [and a] perfect Arethmatician & composer of Musick. . . ." Robert Southey claimed that the pig was "in his day far greater object of admiration to the English nation than ever was Sir Isaac Newton."

In Bristol an advertisement on 13 August 1785 said that "The AMAZING PIG of KNOWLEDGE" was being exhibited by J. Fawkes in a room at the Plume-of-Feathers in Wine Street that month, and perhaps that animal was the one shown in London. A Bristol notice on 4 March 1786 said a "Learned Pig" was being shown at a room in Temple Street every day during the fair. Perhaps the pig shown by Philip Astley in Paris in December of that year was again our subject. Astley, the popular London showman, wrote on 4 December from Paris, "I hope our Pig will take as he performs very well."

An engraving by Rowlandson of "The Wonderful Pig" was published by L. W. Jones in London on 12 April 1785.

Learoyd, Mr [*fl.* 1794], *violoncellist.*

Doane's *Musical Directory* of 1794 listed Mr Learoyd, of No 1, Chapel Street, "in the back Road," Islington, as a violoncellist who played for the Choral fund and Cecilian Society.

Leary, Miss [*fl.* 1786–1793?], *singer, organist.*

A news-bill hand-dated 11 June 1787 by James Winston advertised a "concert of Vocal and Instrumental Music" at Vauxhall Gardens in which Parke played the oboe and there were songs by Incledon, Miss Poole, Miss Bertles, and Miss Leary. Miss Leary also played an "organ concerto."

Miss Leary sang with Darley and Miss Newman in a concert at the Crown and Anchor Tavern in the Strand on 6 April 1789. In an edition of James Hook's Vauxhall songs published in 1790, she was listed as one of the singers. Hook's *Then cease ye fine fellows* was published about 1793 as sung at Vauxhall by Miss Leary.

An engraved portrait of Miss Leary by T. Trotter, depicting her with music in her right

Harvard Theatre Collection
MISS LEARY
engraving by Trotter

hand and her left hand resting on a balcony rail, was published in 1786. Another portrait by an unknown engraver showing her standing in the orchestra at Vauxhall was published by W. Locke in 1792.

Leasy. *See* LACY.

Leathes, Mr [fl. 1744], *scene painter.*

In a letter from David Garrick to the fourth Earl of Bedford on 11 September 1744 an accounting was given of the expenses of some private theatricals Garrick had been presenting for Bedford. One note said that Mr Leathes, a painter, had been paid £31 5s. 6d. The scene painter John Devoto was also noted as painting a flat scene and wings.

Leaver, Mrs [fl. 1790–c. 1796], *singer.*

Among the clippings at the Garrick Club is one dated 18 May 1790 advertising Mrs Leaver's first appearance at Vauxhall Gardens as a singer. The Vauxhall lists at the Minet Library, probably written by the music copyist John Foulis, contain a quaint note dated 15 June 1790: "Song, Mrs Leaver, *My heart from my bosom wou'd fly.* Mem.: The above song is in D—about the middle of the Ist Stanza, Mrs L. got too sharp & continued rising—the Orchestra finish'd the song in E." Yet Mrs Leaver continued at Vauxhall Gardens through August and was at the Apollo Gardens in 1792.

Some songs to which Mrs Leaver's name was attached were *The Tear*, published about 1790, "Twas the Morning of May," in manuscript at the Minet Library, and Joseph Willson's *Oh yes, Sir, if you please*, published about 1796. Mrs Leaver was probably the mother of Miss A. Leaver and Miss E. Leaver, who played Amazons in *The White Witch* at Sadler's Wells in 1808.

"Le Barbarini." *See* CAMPANINI, BARBARINA.

Le Benico. *See* SEBENICO.

Le Beuf. *See* LE BOEUF.

Le Blanc, Mrs [fl. 1777], *actress.*

The "Lady" who played Emma in *St Helena* at Drury Lane on 28 and 29 May 1777 was identified by the *London Magazine* in July as Mrs Le Blanc. She seems not to have performed in London again.

Leblanche, Mons [fl. 1733–1734], *dancer.*

Monsieur Leblanche (or Le Blanc) danced Harlequin in *Riddoto al'Fresco* on 4 September 1733 at the Cibber-Griffin-Bullock-Hallam booth at Bartholomew Fair. He evidently left England for the winter season, for when he and Mlle Violante danced *Harlequin and Harlequinette* at Goodman's Fields Theatre on 27 April 1734 they were advertised as making their first appearance "since their arrival in this Kingdom." The wording would suggest that they had been not on the Continent but in Ireland or Scotland.

Le Blond, Mons [*fl. 1735*], *dancer.*
Monsieur Le Blond was hailed as making his first appearance in England when he danced *Two Pierrots* with Monsieur Chatillion at the Haymarket Theatre on 17 September 1735.

Le Boeuf, Mons [*fl. 1783–1784*], *dancer.*
At Covent Garden Theatre on 9 October 1783 the ballet *The Rival Knights* was performed as the evening's second piece by ". . . Performers who never before appeared in the Kingdom." Later in the season playbills identified some of the performers—from Audinot's troupe in Paris—among whom was the dancer Le Boeuf. *The Rival Knights* was evidently composed by the members of the company. On 17 April 1784 Le Boeuf and Mlle Constance entertained with a dance between the acts, and on 8 May Le Boeuf shared a benefit with Mons and Mme Bithmere. Tickets were available from all three from Stacy the colourman at the "corner of Longacre," the bill said.

Lebon, Mr [*fl. 1795–1796*], *violoncellist.*
William C. Smith, in *The Italian Opera in London*, lists the violoncellist Lebon as a performer at the King's Theatre in 1795–96.

Le Brun, Mr [*fl. 1717*], *scene painter.*
For the performance of the opera *Cleartes* at the King's Theatre on 30 March 1717 the scenery was painted by a Mr Le Brun. He provided a palace scene that involved, according to the accounts, 1000 yards of painting, and a "Room adorn'd with Tapestry, representing the famous Battle of Alexander."

Le Brun, Mons [*fl. 1726–1738*], *dancer.*
The "Company of Italian Comedians just arriv'd" opened at the new Haymarket Theatre on 24 March 1726 with *La Fille allamode* [*sic*] and *L'Ombre d'Arlequin*. The troupe gave 18 performances through 11 May, in many of which Mons and Mlle Le Brun probably participated as dancers. But there are few casts surviving. She was not mentioned in the bills until she danced in *Arlequin a bonne fortune* and *Roy de Tripoli* on 20 April; and he was not cited until 9 May, when he was the Fourth Harlequin in *Les Quatre Arlequin*[*s*] *par magie*. She also danced that night in "A new *Chacoon* [*sic*] *of All Characters*" with seven others.

On 17 November 1732 Le Brun danced Harlequin in *The Country Revels* at Drury Lane Theatre and a hornpipe on 18 December, and on 22 December he performed Harlequin in *Cephalus and Procris*. On 31 March 1733 he was Harlequin in *The Harlot's Progress* and on 24 May, Harlequin in *The Country Revels*. He performed entr'acte dances several other times that season and took a benefit with Mullart on 24 May.

At Bartholomew Fair in August 1733, Le Brun furnished dancing to the Fielding-Hippisley booth in George Inn Yard and did his *Drunken Peasant* dance for the same entrepreneurs on 4 September.

Le Brun remained with the "loyal" company at Drury Lane after the secession of part of the troupe in 1733–34. He repeated his former roles and added Harlequin in *Harlequin Grand Volgi* and was a Waterman and Chief Spirit in a *Grand Dance of the Spirits* in *The Tempest*. He was employed almost incessantly that season, as he was in 1734–35, when he added Harlequin Faustulus in *Merlin* and harlequins in the pantomimes *The Plot*, *Cupid and Psyche*, *Columbine Courtezan*, *The Harlot's Progress*, *Harlequin Orpheus*, and *The Burgomaster Trick'd* and danced countless times between acts and after the play, especially in his *Drunken Peasant* and (with Miss Brett) *The Burgomaster and His Frow*. He was also steadily employed in many of the same pantomimes and specialty dances in 1735–36 and added harlequins in *Harlequin Restored* and *The Fall of Phaeton* and several comic dances, notably "The new comic Dance called *Fye! nay prithee John*; *or, Handel's Jig*," with Mrs Anderson.

The identification of Le Brun as Phillips by *The London Stage* (in commenting on Le Brun's benefit of 24 May 1733) is incorrect, though it is tempting because of the facts that Le Brun's name left the Drury Lane bills shortly after William ("Harlequin") Phillips began to appear in them, and that they appeared in a number of the same roles and dances. But on both 12 January and 3 May 1736 both Le Brun and Phillips are named in the same playbills at Drury Lane.

On 7 August 1738 a "Le Brune" and a "Mlle Le Brune" were in Fielding and Hallam's company in their "Great Booth, Near the Turnpike in Tottenham-Court" for the fair; he was a Bride Man in *The Mad Lovers*, and both danced a *Peasant Dance* with others. On 23 August, during Bartholomew Fair they turned up with the same group of dancers at Penkethman's booth. On 5 September many of the same, including the Le Brunes, were at Southwark Fair in Hallam's booth "at the bottom of Mermaid-Court." Mlle Le Brun went on dancing until 1746–47 (after 1735–36 as "Mrs" Le Brun, which was perhaps her proper designation but was more likely a recognition of her having reached her majority). Perhaps the dancer Le Brun who performed a few times at Drury Lane in 1756 or 1757 was the same as the earlier one, but that is unlikely.

Le Brun, Mr [*fl. 1755–1757*], *dancer.*

A Mr Le Brun was a chorus dancer at Drury Lane Theatre in 1755–56 and 1756–57. He shared benefit tickets on 20 May 1756 and 18 May 1757.

Le Brun, Mlle or Mrs [*fl. 1726–1747*], *dancer.*

Mlle (after 1735–36 Mrs) Le Brun appeared in the company of the "Italian Comedians" in some or all of the 18 performances that troupe gave at the New Haymarket Theatre on and after 24 March 1726. Few casts survive. *Arléquin Homme a bonne fortune* and *Roy de Tripole* and *Colombine docteur endroit* were given on 19 April ("Joue par Mademoiselle Le Brun"). A Le Brun, probably her brother, possibly her husband, was also in the company.

"Mrs" Le Brun (so-called, probably because she had now reached her majority) was identified as Nivelon's "Scholar" when she performed a *Serious Dance* with him at Covent Garden Theatre on 9 November 1736. But she had already appeared there, as one of five Sylvans in *The Rape of Proserpine* on 8 October. Such chorus parts in pantomimes were to be for the most part her function for the following 11 seasons, 1736–37 through 1746–47: country lasses, followers of Daphne, villagers, nymphs, aerial spirits, Amazons. She was doubtless also the "Mlle Le Brune" who, with (her brother?) "Le Brune," danced at the Fielding-Hallam booth at the Tottenham Court Fair on 7 August 1738, at Penkethman's booth at Bartholomew Fair on 23 August, and at Hallam's booth at Southwark Fair on 5 September.

Lebrun, Ludwig August 1752–1790, *oboist, composer.*

Born in Mannheim and baptized there on 2 May 1752, Ludwig August Lebrun was the son of Jacob Alexander Lebrun, from Brussels, who was an oboist in the Mannheim orchestra from 1747 until his death in 1771. Having been taught by his father, the young Lebrun was admitted as a "scholar" to the same orchestra in 1764 and became a full member in 1767, a position he held at a substantial salary throughout his life.

By the beginning of 1778 Lebrun had left his post at Mannheim and had come to London. He was first noticed in the bills at the King's Theatre on 7 February, when he accompanied the soprano Franziska Danzi on the oboe for an air in Act II of *Erifile*. On 6 March 1778 he played an oboe concerto in the oratorio program at Covent Garden Theatre and on 19 March at the King's he again accompanied a song by Sga Danzi. On 4 April he was joined by the violinist Cramer, the violoncellist Cervetto, and the flutist Florio, when all four accompanied Sga Danzi's air in Act II of *La clemenza di Scipione*. By 30 May 1778 Lebrun had married the soprano, for on that date when she sang in *Il re pastore* the bills listed her as Mme Lebrun, late Sga Danzi.

The Lebruns returned to the Continent in 1778–79, where she appeared in Paris and Milan, and then they were back in London for two seasons, 1779–80 and 1780–81. On 15 March 1781 a song of his composition was sung by Mme Lebrun for her benefit, when their address was No 36, Great Suffolk Street. He appeared occasionally as an accompanist or soloist, the last time being on 16 June 1781. He also composed some ballet music for *Armida* and *Agus*, according to Grove, but we find no record of performances of those ballets in London during his years there. The ballet *Adela of Ponthieu* was staged by Noverre at the King's on 11 April 1782 with music by Lebrun, but the composer seems already to have departed London.

During the 1780s Lebrun traveled to his wife's engagements throughout Europe, which in the autumn of 1789 brought them to Berlin, where he died on 16 December 1790. Lebrun published seven concertos, six trio sonatas, and other pieces.

His wife survived him by six months, dying

also at Berlin, on 14 May 1791. Their daughter Sophie Lebrun, who had been born in London on 20 June 1781, became a celebrated pianist on the Continent billed as Mme Dülken, having married a famous Munich piano maker on 18 April 1799. Another daughter, Rosine Lebrun, born at Munich 13 April 1785, also sang; but after marrying the Munich actor Stenzsch on 30 November 1801, she gave up the opera stage for comedy; she retired in 1830 and died at Munich on 5 June 1855. Both of Ludwig August Lebrun's daughters are noticed in the *New Grove*.

Lebrun, Mme Ludwig August, Franziska, née Danzi 1756–1791, *singer, composer*.

Franziska Danzi was born at Mannheim and baptized there on 24 March 1756. She was the daughter of the celebrated violoncellist Innocenz Danzi and the elder sister of the composer Franz Danzi. At the age of 16, in 1772 she made her debut as Sandrina in *La contadina in corte* at Swetzingen, the summer residence of the Elector Palatine. The performance of 9 August 1772 was attended by Dr Burney on his grand tour, and he was very impressed, describing her as:

a German girl whose voice and execution are brilliant; she has likewise a pretty figure, a good shake, and an expression as truly Italian, as if she had lived her whole life in Italy; in short she is now a very engaging and agreeable performer, and promises still greater things in future, being young, and never having appeared on any stage till this summer.

Over the next five years she rose to prominence in the Mannheim court opera. In 1777 Reichard's *Theaterkalender* acclaimed her the "most admirable songstress who had ever been heard" and announced that by permission of the court she was able to accept an engagement in London. Sga Danzi made her debut at the King's Theatre on 8 November 1777 in Sacchini's *Creso*, singing Ariene, a role she performed five times more that season. On 7 February 1778 she sang the title role in Sacchini's *Erifile* and was accompanied in an air in Act II by Ludwig August Lebrun on the oboe. After eight performances of *Erifile*, she sang Arsinda in *La clemenza di Scipione* on 4 April 1778, repeated seven times. While still pleased with her, Burney now had some criticism of the soprano, which he expressed in his *General History of Music*:

As Signora Danzi . . . had a voice well in tune, a good shake, great execution, a prodigious compass, and great knowledge of Music, with youth, and a face and figure far from disagreeable; it seems difficult to account for the little pleasure her performance afforded to persons accustomed to good Italian singing. However, the problem certainly admits of a solution, if it is to be considered, that the natural tone of her voice is not interesting; that she had never been in Italy, and had been constantly imitating the tone and difficulties of instruments; that her chief labour and ambition had been to surprise, concluding perhaps that wonder however excited includes pleasure; . . . in short, forgetting that she is not a bird in a bush or a cage, and that from a human figure, representing a princess or great personage, it is natural for an audience to expect human passions to be expressed in such tones, and with such art and energy, as will not degrade an individual of our own species, into a being of an inferior order.

When Sga Danzi performed Elisa in *Il re pastore* on 30 May 1778, the King's Theatre bill advertised her as Mme Lebrun, late Sga Danzi, she having recently married the oboist who had accompanied her that season.

After leaving London, the Lebruns went that summer to Paris, where she sang in the Concert Spirituel, and then to Milan, where she sang with Pacchierotti, Rubinelli, and Balducci in Salieri's *Europa riconosciuta*, the inaugural opera at the Teatro alla Scala on 3 August 1778. At Milan in 1778–79 she also sang in *Troja distrutta*, *Calliroe*, and *Cleopatra*.

In the autumn of 1779 Mme Lebrun and her husband returned to London. At the King's Theatre in 1779–80 she performed Cleofide in *Alessandro nelle Indie* (for her reappearance on 27 November 1779), a principal role in *Il Soldano generoso*, Emilia in *Quinto Fabio*, a role in *L'Olimpiade*, Armida in *Rinaldo*, and Euridice in *Orfeo* (Bertoni's new opera, in the manner of an oratorio, on 31 May 1780). In 1780–81 she again sang in *Rinaldo* and appeared as Almira in the premiere of *Mitridate* on 23 January 1781, as Zémire in the premiere of Grétry's *Zémire et Azor* on 8 March, and as Tisbe in the premiere of Rauzzini's *Piramo e Tisbe* on 29 March. While in London the Lebruns lived at No 36, Great Suffolk Street. (In her first visit to London in 1777–78 she had lived, when Sga Danzi, at No 8, the same street, near Charing Cross.)

In Burney's judgment, Mme Lebrun had not been improved by her experience in Italy, "but travelling with her husband, an excellent performer on the hautbois, she seems to have listened to nothing else; and at her return to London she copied the tone of his instrument so exactly, that when he accompanied her in divisions of thirds and sixths, it was impossible to discover who was uppermost."

Mme Lebrun's last London performance was as Tisbe on 29 March 1781. When the opera was repeated on 3 April, Sga Prudom sang in place of Mme Lebrun, who was announced as "extremely indisposed." She was, in fact, pregnant, and on 20 June 1781 she gave birth to her first daughter, Sophie. She was not engaged at the King's Theatre in 1781–82, but according to Mee she sang at the Oxford Music Room in April 1782. She performed at Munich from 1782 to 1786. Then, at the San Carlo opera in Naples, she was heard during 1786–87 in *Olimpia*, *Giulio Sabino*, *Mesenzio re d'Etruria*, *La distruzione di Gerusalemme*, and, on 12 January 1787, in the premiere of Paisiello's *Pirro*.

In the autumn of 1789 she accepted an invitation to join the Royal Opera in Berlin, where her husband died on 16 December 1790. Mme Lebrun died there six months later on 14 May 1791. Information on their children is in her husband's notice.

While in London, Mme Lebrun had composed and published two sets of six sonatas for harpsichord and violin. More information on her continental career may be found in the *Enciclopedia dello spettacolo*.

Le Cler. *See* L'CLER.

Le Cointe. *See* LA COINTE.

Le Coudrière, Mons [*fl.* 1727], *dancer.*
Monsieur Le Coudrière was advertised as "lately arriv'd from Paris" when he danced Harlequin in *The Wheel of Life* on 21 August 1727 at the Bartholomew Fair booth operated by Miller, Hall, and Milward.

Le Couteux, Mons [*fl.* 1773], *bassoonist.*

At Marylebone Gardens on 15 June 1773 Monsieur Le Couteux, making his first appearance in England, played a solo concerto on the bassoon.

Le Croix. *See* DE LA CROIX and LA CROIX.

Le Det, Mons [*fl.* 1778–1779], *dancer.*
During the 1778–79 season at the King's Theatre Monsieur Le Det danced in a number of ballets, beginning on 24 November 1778 with the character of Bailly in *Annette et Lubin*. After that he was seen in *Pas de deux Anacréontique*, *La Noche Hollandoise*, *Les Oiseleurs*, a ballet of the Fairies of the Count of Azore at the end of Act II of *Zemire e Azore*, the character of a Cyclopes in *Les Forges de Vulcain*, *La Sérénade interrompuée*, and *Les Paisans volés*. The bills were so consistent in spelling the dancer's name that one supposes he was not the dancer Ledai, who was at Lyon on 21 August 1784 in *La Mort d'Hercule*, according to Fuchs's *Lexique*. That dancer was probably the Ledai who was the first dancer and ballet master at Brussels in the Bultos and Adam troupe in 1789–91.

Ledger. *See also* ST LEDGER.

Ledger, John 1749–1808, *actor.*
Born in 1749, John Ledger was perhaps the son of John Ledger and Mrs Frances Calvert, of St George, Bloomsbury, who were married at St George's Chapel, Hyde Park Corner, on 15 April 1743. He was first noticed in a London bill on 5 January 1776, when at Covent Garden Theatre he replaced Jones in an unspecified role in the pantomime *Prometheus*. By the next performance, on 12 January, however, Jones had reclaimed his part and Ledger was not seen until 30 April 1776, when he acted Mendlegs in *The Man of Quality*, a role he repeated on 4 May, the night he shared benefit tickets with eight other performers.

Absent from London for almost two years, during which period he was engaged at Liverpool for £1 10s. per week in the summers of 1776 and 1777 (and perhaps also during the winter months), Ledger returned to Covent Garden by 23 February 1778, when he appeared as an unnamed character in *Mother Shipton*, a pantomime in which he performed 19 times before the season ended. Those performances marked the beginning of an uninterrupted period of 30 seasons in which, at that theatre, he would play a host of modest gentlemen, servants, coachmen, and anonymous characters. His salary in 1777–78 was £1 12*s*. per week; in 1782–83 it was raised to £2, and then in 1796–97 to £2 10*s*., where it remained through his last season, 1807–8. Ledger also provided similar humble service at the Haymarket Theatre every summer from 1781 through 1807.

A list of his many roles at Covent Garden includes, among others, a Gentleman in *The Deaf Lover* and one of the Mob in *The Siege of Gibralter* in 1779–80, Lopez in *The Castle of Andalusia* in 1782–83, Gadshill in *1 Henry IV* and Sam in *The Man of the World* in 1783–84, a Footman in *The Choleric Fathers* in 1785–86, a Sailor in *Inkle and Yarico* in 1789–90, and a Coachman in *The Honest Thieves* in 1796–97. His roles at the Haymarket were even more numerous but of the same undistinguished kind; for example, in 1800 he acted a Waiter in *The Heir at Law*, Sailor in *Inkle and Yarico*, Kilderkin in *The Flitch of Bacon*, Crier in *The Surrender of Calais*, a Passenger in *Ways and Means*, Father Frank in *The Prisoner at Large*, and a Goatherd in *The Mountaineers*.

By 1799, according to the *Authentic Memoirs of the Green Room*, Ledger was "more employed behind the scenes than on the stage," serving as the prompter's messenger. When onstage he filled his coachmen and servants roles "very respectably." The 1806 edition of the same memoirs described his "urbanity of manners" and his "unimpeachable integrity," qualities that earned him the "respect and good will of the whole theatre." The *Thespian Dictionary* in 1805 stated that he was commonly called "Honest Ledger" by the other actors. The Covent Garden prompter James Wild left his "best Silver Snuff box" to Ledger in 1801 and named him a co-executor of his estate.

Ledger received his last weekly salary of £2 10*s*. from Covent Garden on Saturday, 2 April 1808. That night he attended to his job but became ill. According to a manuscript notebook by James Winston now at the Huntington Library, Ledger soon felt better and went a few doors to "Bankers." Soon after his return, about "9 at night" he suddenly died. His obituary in the *Gentleman's Magazine* for April stated that he had been "upwards of 50 years a diligent and faithful servant" of Covent Garden Theatre—an exaggeration, certainly, since he was 59 years old when he died—and "had, by his integrity and good conduct, obtained not only the regard and confidence of his employers, but the esteem of every one who knew him." He was buried on 8 April 1808 at St Paul, Covent Garden, where the registrar described him as "Aged 59 Years" and from St Anne, Westminster.

In his will, drawn on 27 February 1806, John Ledger described himself as a "Gentleman" of the Theatre Royal, Covent Garden. To his "natural son John James Darenett now residing with Mr. Walker of Tabernacle Row Moorfields . . . Pawnbroker," he left £100 and all his wearing apparel. The remainder of his unspecified estate he bequeathed to Anna Maria Leserve of Covent Garden Theatre, whom he also appointed his sole executrix. She was probably his mistress or common-law wife. Administration was granted to her on 12 April 1808, when she was described as a "Spinster."

In 1799 a Mr Ledger, who had not appeared on the London stage, was acting at Liverpool, according to the *Monthly Mirror* of June 1799; perhaps he was related to our subject, as may have been Richard Ledger, a Covent Garden house servant between 1778 and 1787.

Ledger, Richard [*fl.* 1778–1787], *house servant?*

Richard Ledger was named with other Covent Garden personnel, most of whom were house servants, for sharing in benefit tickets on 22 May 1778. He next shared tickets on 15 May 1779, when he was advertised as "Ledger Jun," a description which suggests that he was the son of, or otherwise related to, John Ledger, who served as a utility actor at Covent Garden for some 32 years. Specified as R. Ledger, he had benefit tickets again on 24 May 1780, 25 May 1781, 28 May 1782, 29 May 1783, 30 May 1786, and, evidently for the last time, 5 June 1787. A British Library manuscript which states that on 7 June 1783 he received one-half value of his tickets for 29 May 1783, also provides his first name. Richard Ledger was not named in John Ledger's will in 1808.

Lediard, Thomas 1684–1743, *scene designer, manager, architect, author.*

Thomas Lediard, the son of Thomas and Dorothy Lediard, was baptized at St Dionis Backchurch, off Fenchurch Street, on 20 October 1684. The family name is also in the parish registers variously as Ledyard, Lidiard, Lydyard, and Lydiard. An elder son named Thomas had been buried on 9 March 1676. Four daughters were christened: Elizabeth on 9 February 1679 (buried on 17 October 1684), Dorothy on 6 August 1680 (buried on 21 February 1681); Mary on 2 May 1683; and another Elizabeth on 6 July 1688.

Nothing is known of Lediard's education, though his professional life certainly points to his having received training in architecture, drawing, and letters. By 1707 Lediard was a member of the staff of the Duke of Marlborough, whom he accompanied that year when the duke visited Saxony to negotiate with Charles XII of Sweden. In the preface to his *Life of John, Duke of Marlborough*, Lediard claimed personal knowledge of the transactions and the important papers, and also described himself as a gentleman of sufficient means "who travelled for his pleasure at his own expense, without having or desiring any reward or gratification for it in any shape or under any denomination whatsoever."

Subsequently Lediard served for many years as "secretary to his majesty's envoy extraordinary" in Hamburg. From 1724 to 1727 he was also involved in the management of the Hamburg Opera House, in the Goosemarket, of which his chief, Sir Cyril Wych, was a proprietor. Since there appears to have been no scenic artist attached to the theatre at that time, Lediard took over the visual aspects of the productions. Though he had made some study of architecture and painting in his youth, he wrote in his preface to *The German Spy* (1738) that such endeavors were "out of my Way, and what I should never have attempted but by the express command of Sir Cyril Wich and some other Persons of Distinction." For the celebration at Hamburg of the birthday of George I in June 1724 he presented an illuminated theatre for a specially composed Serenade, the first of his known designs. Wych wrote home that the music, dance, and decorations rendered the production the most brilliant ever seen in that city's theatre. The ambassador's dispatch was accompanied by an engraving of Lediard's design, described by Sybil Rosenfeld in "The Career of Thomas Lediard" (*Theatre Notebook*, II, 1948)—to whom this notice is much indebted—as in a "much cruder and sketchier form" than the plate which appears in the later collection of his designs.

In 1725 and 1726 he produced scenes, transparencies, and illuminations for several royal marriages and birthdays, in the latter year taking over the Opera House's direction. For the birthday of George I in June 1727 he created scenes for the prologue and epilogue of Handel's *Julius Caesar in Aegypten*, an opera which Lediard had translated from the Italian of Haym in 1725. In that production he employed extensive transparencies and displayed views of Oxford, London, and the Thames in moonlight. The *German Spy* described the beginning:

the Curtain drew up leisurely under a softer Symphony of Flutes and Violins, and discover'd the most noble and beautiful Prospect I ever saw on any stage. The whole Theatre was illuminated with several Thousands of Lamps, dispos'd, however, in such Manner, behind transparent Scenes, that none of them were to be seen, and yet the Light they gave

By permission of the Trustees of the British Museum

THOMAS LEDIARD

engraving by Fritesch, after Wahl

was extremely penetrating by Reason of their Great Number.

He provided four scene changes and four illuminations for *Great Britain Rejoycing*, a specially composed three-act drama which was presented on two nights in October 1727 to observe the coronation of George II.

His final design at Hamburg was in August 1730. That year, claiming he had spared neither cost nor pains to assure their accuracy, he published at Hamburg a collection of plates and descriptions, *Eine Collection Curieuser Vorstellungen in Illuminationen und Feuer-Wercken*. His designs also had been published in *Eine Collection Verschiedener Vorstellungen in Illuminationen und Feuer-Wercken* (Hamburg, 1729, with seven plates); and *A particular Description of four curious Illuminations; An Exact and particular Description of the beautiful Illumination, Prospect of the City of London, and Fire-Works . . . in a Prologue and Epilogue . . . to Julius Caesar in Aegypt*.

During his tenure at Hamburg, Lediard also published his *Grammatica Anglicana Critica, oder Versuch zu einer volkommen Grammatic der englischen Sprache* (1726), with a portrait dated 1725 and bearing the arms of Lediard of Cirencester. On the title page of N. Bailey's *Dictionarium Britannicum* (1736), to which he had contributed in "the etymological part," Lediard was described as a "professor of modern languages in Lower Germany."

Sometime between 1730 and 1732 Lediard returned to London, settling in Smith Square, Westminster. On 16 November 1732 his new English opera, *Britannia*, set to music by J. F. Lampe, was premiered at the Haymarket The-

Harvard Theatre Collection

Stage design by THOMAS LEDIARD
engraving by Fritesch

atre: "The Scenes and Cloaths are entirely New. With the Representation of a Transparent Theatre. Curiously illuminated, and adorn'd with a great Number of Emblems, Mottos, Devices, and Inscriptions; and embellish'd with Machines, in a Manner entirely new." The opera was repeated on 20, 23, and 27 November, and published that year with an engraving of a setting.

Britannia proved to be Lediard's last effort for the stage. He then turned to his historical and architectural interests, publishing *The Life of Sethos* (translated from J. Terrasson) in 1732; *The Naval History of England. In all its Branches; from the Norman Conquest, 1066, to the Conclusion of 1734* (2 vols) in 1735; his *Life of John, Duke of Marlborough* (three volumes, 1736); *The History of the Reigns of William III and Mary and Anne* (in continuation of the *History of England* by Rapin de Thoyras) in 1737; a translation of J. J. Mascon's *History of the Ancient Germans* (2 vols) in 1737; and a translation of J. B. Fischer's *Plan of Civil and Historical Architecture* in 1738. He also edited in 1738 *The German Spy, in familiar letters . . . written by a Gentleman on his Travels to his Friend in England*, containing lengthy accounts, perhaps written by himself, of Lediard's scenery for Hamburg. Therein it was reported of Lediard that "his Architecture, tho' very beautiful, has a little too much of the *Gothick* in it, I mean of the Extravagances of an irregular Fancy."

During the 1730s Lediard was also working with Thomas Cotton and Nicholas Hawksmoor on a plan for building a bridge at Westminster. After Hawksmoor's death, Lediard and Cotton published their scheme in 1738, the consequence of which was Lediard's appointment as "Agent and Surveyor of Westminster Bridge" and on 13 July of that year "the crown lands from Westminster Bridge to Charing Cross" were granted to him and Sir John Ayloffe, "in trust to the Commissioners appointed" to build the bridge. Lediard was made a Fellow of the Royal Society on 9 December 1742.

Lediard never saw Westminster Bridge completed, for failing health forced his resignation as "Surveyor of the Bridge" early in 1743 and he died that June. He was succeeded in his surveying office by his son Thomas, who died at Hamburg on 15 December 1759.

"The Discovery of Thomas Lediard" by I. K. Fletcher and "Lediard and Early 18th Century Scene Design" by Richard Southern, with reproductions of Lediard's engraved designs accompany Sybil Rosenfeld's article in *Theatre Notebook*.

A portrait of Lediard by J. S. Wahl was engraved by C. Fritesch in 1725 and published with his *Grammatica Anglicana Critica*. The Fritesch engraving was again published in 1730, surrounded by emblematical subjects designed by Lediard, and later was issued in a variant by an anonymous engraver as frontispiece to Lediard's *Naval History of England* (1735).

Lediger, Henry [*fl.* 1673–1675], *violinist.*

Henry Lediger (or Ledger, Ledgier, Leiger) was one of the musicians from the "Nursery" for young performers who were ordered apprehended on 15 April 1673. He was discharged four days later. Lediger was one of the violinists who participated in the court masque *Calisto* on 15 February 1675.

Le Duke, Mons [*fl.* 1675], *dancer.*

Monsieur Le Duke danced in the court masque *Calisto* on 15 February 1675. Could he have been the Lewis Laduke whose daughter Jane was buried at St Paul, Covent Garden, on 27 October 1680?

Ledwith, Mr [*fl.* 1770], *actor.*

Mr Ledwith played a Servant in *The Busy Body* at the Haymarket Theatre on 5 October 1770.

Lee. *See also* LEIGH.

Lee, Mr [*fl.* 1722], *singer.*

A Mr Lee sang at Westminster Abbey on 14 August 1722 at the funeral of the Duke of Marlborough.

Lee, Mr [*fl.* 1726–1727], *trumpeter.*

The Lincoln's Inn Fields Theatre's accounts for 23 September 1726 show a payment of 10s. for three nights to a musician in the band named Lee. The free list on 4 January 1727 cited Lee as a trumpeter.

Lee, Mr [*fl.* 1729–1748?], *boxkeeper.*

Mr Lee was given a solo benefit at the Haymarket Theatre on 14 May 1729 and designated a boxkeeper. He was recorded at that house for benefits in 1730, 1731, 1732, and 1733, and in the last year, on 23 April, he shared his benefit with his brother Mason Fulwood, also a boxkeeper. The Lee who shared a benefit at Drury Lane on 21 May 1734 was probably our subject, in view of the fact that his benefits there in 1736, 1737, and 1744 were again shared with Fullwood. He was probably the "Leigh" named in the benefit bill there on 4 May 1748, when he shared the income with Ray and with the house servant Dickenson. Lee's position at Drury Lane was never stated in the bills.

Lee, Mr [*fl.* 1747], *actor.*

A Mr Lee acted Gadshill in *1 Henry IV* to Spranger Barry's Hotspur at Drury Lane Theatre on 15 and 16 January 1747. Possibly that actor was John Lee, longtime London performer and provincial manager who died in 1781, but according to the bills that same night the latter was acting Robin of Bagshot in *The Beggar's Opera* and Gonzalo in *The Tempest* at Goodman's Fields. *1 Henry IV* was repeated at Drury Lane on 17 and 19 January, on which night *The Tempest* was again at Goodman's Fields. The two theatres were located too far apart for the same Mr Lee to have played at both the same night.

Lee, Mr [*fl.* 1769–1777], *musician, composer, proprietor.*

In 1769 and 1770, and probably before and after, a Mr Lee was a musician at Finch's Grotto Gardens. For Neeve's benefit concert there in August 1769, which was supported by brother Masons, Lee wrote a new song set to music by Mr Smart, Junior. The advertisements called the brethren to meet at Brother Lee's, Sun Tavern, Ludgate Street, at five o'clock, before the concert, to go in procession with the music. At Hickford's Room on 22 May 1771, in a concert given under the direction of Bach and Abel, Lee had a benefit; his address was in Theobald's Row, Red Lion Square. In 1778 a Mr Lee, perhaps the musician, leased Prospect House (built by the late Sir Thomas Robinson opposite Ranelagh House), with a pleasant and extensive view of the river and the Surrey and Kentish hills. Calling it the Ranelagh Subscription House, Lee laid in an assortment of good wines and advertised *petits soupers*. The operators of Ranelagh Gardens published notices repudiating any connection, and a correspondent to the *Town and Country Magazine* suggested that Lee's establishment was a place from which "old husbands" would be well-advised to keep their young wives.

Lee, Mr [*fl.* 1799], *actor.*

Advertised as "A Young Gentleman" making his first appearance, a Mr Lee acted Richard III at Covent Garden Theatre on 6 May 1799. The *Monthly Mirror* identified him as Mr Lee, the "hero" of a group that was playing in a barn at Camberwell under Osborne's management. In June the same periodical, stating that Mrs Crespigny, a grande dame of Camberwell, had been his patron, reviewed Lee's performance as Richard:

Though the character demands infinitely more than Mr. Lee will ever be able to give, we are not altogether displeased with the performance. Some of the bye-play was very good, and the part appeared to have been studied by him, though not always to the purpose, with great care. His countenance is expressive; but it expressed but one character. Whether he flattered, scowled, rejoiced, raged, or despaired, the same disposition of the features presented itself. So also of his voice:—it never yielded to the passion of the character; where it should have been rapid it drawled; in perturbation, in anger, in haste, in the heat of battle, the same dull uniformity prevailed. Upon the whole, however, we do not think the attempt so discreditable to his conception, or his powers, as has been generally stated.

We do not know whether or not the Lee of that review continued as an actor, but if he did, he could have been any one of the several of the name acting in the provinces in the early decades of the nineteenth century.

Lee, Miss [*fl.* 1742–1743], *actress.*

Announced as making her first attempt on any stage, Miss Lee acted Corinna in *The Confederacy* at Drury Lane Theatre on 3 April 1742. On 25 May she played Miss Prue in *Love for Love* and shared in benefit tickets with some house servants and minor performers. Perhaps she was the Miss Lee who was paid 4*s.* per performance for acting at the Jacob's Wells Theatre, Bristol, between 16 June and 27 August 1742. In the following season at Drury Lane she probably performed in minor unnoticed roles; her name did appear on the bills for Melissa in *The Lying Valet* on 2 May 1743, when she shared benefit tickets with Owen.

Lee, Miss b. 1759, actress.

On 23 March 1776 at Covent Garden Theatre a "Young Gentlewoman" made her first appearance on any stage as Cordelia in *King Lear*. Reed's notations at the British Library and the *Morning Chronicle* of 22 March identified her as the daughter of John Lee, who acted Lear that night for his benefit. The *Morning Chronicle* gave her age as 17.

Lee had four daughters, or five, depending on which source is believed. We know the names of three: Sophia, the eldest, born in 1750 and thus 27 in 1776; Harriet, born in 1757 and thus 19 in 1776 (and possibly the Miss Lee who acted Cordelia); and Ann, birth date unknown, who committed suicide in 1805. One daughter, neither Sophia nor Ann, had acted Lucy in *The Recruiting Officer* at Covent Garden on 8 May 1761.

If the Covent Garden Cordelia of 1776 was Harriet Lee (1757–1851), then the *Morning Chronicle* misstated her age by two years; however, it may have been reporting on a daughter who placed in age between Sophia and Harriet. Harriet Lee became an important novelist and dramatist, and with her sisters ran the Belvidere School at Bath for some years. She is noticed in *The Dictionary of National Biography*, and a list of her theatrical pieces is in Nicoll's *History of the English Drama*.

Lee, Miss [fl. 1761], actress.

A Miss Lee made her first and evidently only appearance on the stage at Covent Garden Theatre on 8 May 1761 as the maid Lucy in *The Recruiting Officer*. Though she may have been one of the daughters of the actors Mr and Mrs John Lee (Mrs Lee was then engaged at Covent Garden), she would not have been, it would seem, one of the future authors Sophia or Harriet, who at that time were only 11 and seven years of age, respectively.

Lee, George [fl. 1719–1749], booth operator, printer.

King Egbert was produced at Bartholomew Fair on 20 August 1719 by Spiller and Lee and *The Siege of Bethulia*, a droll, was put on at the "Lee-Walker Great Booth" at Southwark Fair on 5 September 1720. The Lee in question was active at the late summer fairs for many years after that and was, it seems, George Lee. He operated booths in August and September 1721, offering the public a revival of *The Siege of Bethulia* at Bartholomew Fair and *The Noble Englishman* at Southwark Fair; in the first instance his booth was beside the Hospital Gate, and in the second it was in the Queen's Arms Tavern yard. Lee joined with Spiller and Harper at Bartholomew Fair in 1722. In the summer of 1723, in partnership with Bullock at Luffingham's Great Room in Hampstead Wells, Lee presented *The Stage Coach*, *Love for Love*, and *Tunbridge Walks*. At Bartholomew Fair in August, Lee alone ran a booth at which he produced *The Wisdom of Solomon*. *The Prodigal Son* was his offering there in August 1724. On 7 September of that year at Southwark Fair, Lee presented *Robin Hood* at one booth and, with Harper, produced *The Siege of Troy* at another. His relation to Hannah Lee, who prepared *The Siege of Troy*, is not clear; they were not husband and wife, though they may have been related by marriage. They seem to have worked in friendly competition.

Lee was not mentioned in the fair bills in 1725, but with Harper and Spiller in August 1726 at Bartholomew Fair and with Harper only in September at Southwark Fair, Lee put on *The Siege of Troy* again. In 1727 he worked with Harper at Bartholomew Fair, performing *The Unnatural Parents*. In 1728 he and Harper put on *Hero and Leander* and *The Quaker's Opera* in August and then in September managed two booths at Southwark Fair, offering *The Quaker's Opera* at one and *The Royal Champion* at the other. Morley in his *Memoirs of Bartholomew Fair* identified Lee as George Lee; "an adventurous printer, who did business in Blue-Maid Alley, Southwark. His name, except as manager, appears only as printer of the Drolls." In 1729 Lee and Harper revived *The Siege of Bethulia* at both fairs, and Lee also ran a second booth at Southwark Fair, where he produced *The Beggar's Wedding* and *The Stratagems of Harlequin*.

Lee continued during the 1730s in much the same fashion, usually operating at one or both late summer fairs and sometimes exhibiting at Tottenham Court as well. Harper was often his partner, but at Tottenham Court in September 1733 they were joined by Pettit.

LEE

For a few years in the middle of the decade Lee operated alone; in 1737 he joined Hallam; and in 1739 and 1740 he was in partnership with Phillips. Lee produced during the decade such works as *The Stratagem, The Unhappy Libertine, Guy, Earl of Warwick, The Devil to Pay, Whittington, Female Innocence, Jeptha's Rash Vow* (the book of that droll was advertised as printed by G. Lee in Bluemaid Alley, Southwark), *Bateman, The Harlot's Progress, The Fall of Phaeton, The Drummer,* and *Columbine Courtesan,* plus a variety of song and dance entertainments between the acts. As before, he sometimes operated two booths, as in September 1735 when the bills cited "Lee's Old Theatrical Playhouse on the Bowling Green, running down Axe and Bottle Yard" and "Lee's Old Theatre on the Bowling Green, behind Marshalsea Prison, down Mermaid Court, next Queen's Arms Tavern." The Lee-Harper booth is pictured among the end-illustrations of our volume III.

Lee and Woodward ran a booth at Tottenham Court Fair in 1741 and remained in partnership for Bartholomew and Southwark fairs, producing, among other things, *Darius, King of Persia; or the Noble Englishman, with the Comical Humours of Sir Andrew Aguecheek, at the Siege of Babylon.* Lee joined with Phillips again in 1742, with Yeates the younger in 1746, with Yeates and Warner in 1747, with both Yeateses in 1748, and with Yeates and Warner again in August and September 1749. After that Lee seems to have given up management.

Lee, Hannah, née Leigh?, [later Mrs Thomas Yeates?] [*fl. c. 1705–1739*], *booth operator.*

According to her own testimony in later years, Hannah Lee and her mother were operating booths at the late-summer fairs in London from about 1705. It is probable that her mother, who had evidently remarried, was then Mrs Mynns and, if so, Hannah was a (younger?) sister of the Elizabeth "Leigh" who worked with Mrs Mynns from as early as 1681 to as late as 1718. Hannah, then, continued the family tradition into the 1720s and 1730s. That her name was spelled differently is not unusual; "Leigh" was the most common spelling in the seventeenth century, but a noticeable change to "Lee" began after the first decade or two of the eighteenth century. The fact that Hannah called herself *Mrs* Lee in many advertisements raises a pretty question; if her maiden name was Leigh, perhaps she married a man named Lee. In 1735 she described herself as a widow.

The *Original London Post* on 28 August 1724 carried the following advertisement for *The Siege of Troy*:

Mrs Lee, daughter of Mrs Minns, at the Great Booth on Bowling Green. With all the Scenes and Machines, with Additions. Mrs Lee has spared no Cost, but used her utmost Care, and most elaborate Industry in this droll, to surpass even her Mother, the Booth coming as near the Perfection of the Theatre as possible, being adorned by the most ingenious Workmen: Her Head Characters are all Dress'd in real Gold and Silver, beyond what was ever worn at the Fair before, but by her own People.

Mrs Lee had intended the production for Bartholomew Fair a week earlier but had not been able to get the production ready. There seems to be no proof to the suggestion that Hogarth may have painted some of her scenery. *The Siege of Troy* was advertised for the following 7 September for "Lee's and Harper's Great Theatrical Booth, on the Bowling Green, the Lower End of Blue Maid Alley." That Lee was George, who had been operating booths at the fairs for several years. He was not the husband of the Mrs Lee who placed the advertisement in the paper on 28 August, but the two were perhaps related in some way and may have been friendly competitors at the fairs. (Could they have been in-laws?) Mrs Lee was not mentioned in Lee and Harper's advertisement; they may have purchased her show from her.

Mrs Lee operated a booth at Southwark Fair on 8 September 1725. *Parker's Penny Post* on the thirteenth reported an accident at her establishment:

At about 11 a Clock at Mrs Lee's great Booth on the Green in Southwark, happen'd a very sad Accident: The Gallery over the Stage not being thoroughly secured, gave way, when between Twenty and Thirty People fell with it . . . It is high Time for Authority to interpose, to suppress those Nurseries of Lewdness, if so little Care is taken that those who resort to their Entertainments, must be in Jeopardy.

That accident seems not to have discouraged Mrs Lee from working the fairs, for she was at Southwark Fair in 1726 and 1727. On 8 October 1730 Mrs Lee produced *The Recruiting*

Officer at Southwark for the benefit of Charles "the Merry Trumpeter." In December at her booth, Nicoll tells us, she put on the pantomime *The Nuns Turn'd Libertines*, and she ran a booth again in October 1733.

Hogarth's "Southwark Fair" shows "Lee & Harpers Great Booth"; in *Hogarth's Graphic Works* Paulson suggests that the booth was run by the actor John Harper and Hannah "Leigh." That seems to be an error, for the bills carefully distinguish the advertisements of Lee from those of Mrs Lee.

In connection with the hearings on Barnard's bill to tighten control over theatres, "Hannah Lee, Widow," submitted a petition in April 1735 in which she said that she and her mother (deceased) had lived in the parish of St George, Southwark, for upwards of 30 years and had every year during Southwark Fair performed drolls. She pleaded that she had at great expense erected two booths and spent £2000 on costumes, scenes, and decorations. She stated that she was old and infirm and that if the Barnard bill should pass she would be ruined. Mrs Lee claimed that her companies and those of her mother in earlier years had served as nurseries for some of England's great actors—and she cited in particular Barton Booth. She begged to be allowed to be heard by counsel, but her petition was rejected. She ran a booth in September anyway, in defiance of the law, and at Southwark Fair in 1738 she presented *Merlin*.

Sybil Rosenfeld in *The Theatre of the London Fairs* quotes a possibly (we would say probably) satirical report in the *Daily Post* of 19 April 1739 that Mrs Lee, "well Known for her agreeably entertaining the Town with Drolls at Bartholomew and Southwark Fairs etc." had married the showman Yeates on 10 April, "on which occasion considerable fortune in South Sea Stock was made over to the Bridegroom." Then Miss Rosenfeld traces Mrs Lee's fair booth activity (cited usually as Lee, not Mrs Lee in the advertisements) through 1749. But we take references to Lee in the 1740s to be to George Lee, and both *The London Stage* and Morley's *Bartholomew Fair* treat Lee the booth operator (with various partners) as a male. It seems very unlikely, if Hannah Lee was old and infirm in 1735, that she would marry in 1739 and then continue her activity at the fairs for another ten years under her old name, not even identifying herself as the Mrs Lee who had entertained fairgoers over the years. We are inclined to believe that she ceased her work at the fairs about 1738 or 1739.

She was not forgotten, however, for in August 1748, when *The Unnatural Parents* was performed at the Bartholomew Fair booth of Lee and the two Yeateses, it was advertised that the droll was the same one that Mrs Lee had produced 15 years earlier with great success.

Lee, Henry *1765–1836, actor, manager, playwright.*

Henry Lee was born on 27 October 1765 at Nottingham, where he received his schooling. While Henry and his brother were quite young, their father died and two years later their mother married John Timm. But soon she also died. Her daughter by Timm, who married Captain Eminson of the 15th Light Dragoons, also died young. John Timm, Henry Lee's stepfather, had a handsome fortune, but none of it was inherited by Lee—"he made us (myself and brother) work pretty handsomely," wrote Henry in his *Memoirs*. For a while Lee was superintendent of Timm's farm at Normanton, about seven miles from Bingham. Then he had a brief literary career, contributing poetical articles to Moore's *Almanacks*.

At about the age of 21 Lee became an actor. His first engagement was with James Shatford's company, which he joined at Newport Pagnall on 1 August 1787 and traveled with in the west. At Christmas-time that year a one-act piece by Lee founded on the personification of cards was played at Bedford. In his *Memoirs* Lee claimed he could not remember what had become of the manuscript. Perhaps he was the Lee who took £47 7s. 6d. at his benefit at Liverpool on 1 December 1786. In January 1789 Lee was acting at Abingdon and by the summer of 1789 he was at Brighton, where he was also engaged the following year.

In 1791 Lee left Brighton to become Shatford's partner in the theatre at Salisbury and the circuit that encompassed Lymington, Wells, and Devizes. By 1793 he also managed at Dorchester, and by 1799 he was manager on the Taunton circuit, which included Barnstaple, Poole, and Guernsey.

According to the *Thespian Dictionary* and several other contemporary accounts, Lee "belonged to Covent Garden in 1795," but we have not found his name in the bills there until 26 September 1796, when he appeared as one of the Witches in *Macbeth*. Also playing that night as one of the Murderers and a singer in the chorus was James Nathaniel Lee (fl. 1788–1815), a busy but obscure singer who may have been related. Henry Lee's other roles at Covent Garden that season seem to have been Zorayda in *The Mountaineers*, Ammon in *Mahomet*, Mahogany in *Abroad and at Home*, Rob in *The Deaf Lover*, Biondello in *Catherine and Petruchio*, Simon Snuffle in *The Mayor of Garratt*, and Henry Bevil in *Cross Purposes*. Though *The London Stage* suggests he was again at Covent Garden in 1797–98, we believe that he had only one season there and that the performer there in 1797–98 was James Nathaniel Lee.

Henry Lee's musical farce called *Throw Physick to the Dogs!* (which he had written and played in, in the provinces about 1789 under the title of *Jack of All Trades*) was produced by the younger Colman at the Haymarket Theatre on 6 July 1798. The author seems not to have acted in that version, which was not published but survives in Larpent MS 1221. After being repeated on 7 July, the piece was withdrawn for a revision, which Colman refused. Later Lee accused Colman of stealing the character of Caleb Quotem for his own musical farce *The Review; or The Wags of Windsor*, produced at the Haymarket on 1 September 1800. When Colman published his piece Lee claimed the edition was "quite different from what it is always represented." Consequently, Lee published his *Caleb Quotem and his Wife! or Paint, Poetry, and Putty! . . . To which is added a Postscript, including the Scene always play'd in the Review, or Wags of Windsor, but omitted in the Edition lately published by G. Colman, Esq.* (London and Barnstaple, 1809).

Lee had acted at Birmingham in the summers of 1796, 1797, and 1798. He was at Liverpool in 1801 and December 1802, when his benefit brought him £126. He continued to manage at Taunton for many years and there in 1830 published his two-volume *Memoirs of a Manager, or Life's Stage with new Scenery*, full of anecdotes and miscellaneous verse but with few facts or dates. Lee wrote of himself as eccentric and irregular, but in her *Memoirs* the actress Anne Catherine Holbrook praised him as a pleasant gentleman who conducted the business of the stage "in the most regular manner, and entirely free from the disgusting haughtiness which I have often experienced from others. In short, his behavior made . . . him universally respected." James Shatford, partner in the theatres of Taunton, Bridgewater, and Wells, left Lee £100 at his death in 1810 "as a mark of respect for his long and faithful friendship."

Henry Lee died in Longacre, London, on 30 March 1836, at the age of 71. His first wife, whom he had married at Salisbury in July 1793, was Sarah Keys, daughter of the actor Simon Keys. As Mrs Lee she acted in London in the mid-1790s and died on 6 March 1797, without known issue. In 1814 Henry Lee married a Miss Lloyd, by whom he had a son and several daughters.

Lee, Mrs Henry, Sarah Jane, née Keys *d. 1797, actress, singer.*

Sarah Jane Lee was one of the daughters of the provincial actor and manager and sometime London performer Simon Keys, by an actress who may have been his first wife. Sarah Jane's sister, also an actress, married the actor Henry Mills, and her brother was an obscure musician.

Evidently Sarah Jane Keys made her first appearance about 1792 on the Salisbury stage. Her marriage to Henry Lee, her Salisbury manager, was announced in the *Salisbury and Winchester Journal* on 22 July 1793. Her success in the provinces won her a trial in the metropolis in the spring of 1795. On 7 February 1795 the London press announced that Mr and Mrs Lee "of provincial fame" had been engaged at Covent Garden. Though her husband seems not to have played there until 26 September 1796, Mrs Lee made her debut on 19 March 1795 as Fanny in the premiere of O'Keeffe's *Life's Vagaries*. (That year the song *I can dance and sing* from that comedy was published as sung by her.) Her next role was Moggy in *The Highland Reel* on 21 March. She appeared as Julia Melcombe in the premiere of O'Keeffe's *The Irish Mimick* on 23 April, and before that season was over she acted Miss Jenny in *The Provok'd Husband*, Sally Flounce in *The Bank Note*, Edward in *Every One Has His Fault*, Rosa in *How to Grow Rich*, and Marianne in *The Dramatist*. She earned £4 10s. per week.

In 1795–96 Mrs Lee was not at Covent

Garden but acted on the Salisbury and Taunton circuits. At Weymouth she became a favorite of the royal family. She suffered a severe illness at Sudbury, made worse by quack medicines. She recovered, however, to enjoy success at Bristol and on the isles of Portland and Guernsey.

Mrs Lee returned to Covent Garden in 1796–97, again at a salary of £4 10s. per week, making her reappearance on 14 October 1796, when she acted Sophia in *The Road to Ruin*. Next she was seen as Catalina in *The Castle of Andalusia* on 21 October and Julia in *The Irish Mimick* on 29 October. On 10 November she took over the role of Paris in *Olympus in an Uproar*. Her last performance seems to have been as Julia on 20 February 1797, soon after which she died of consumption, on 6 March. Her death was announced in the March *Monthly Mirror*.

Mrs Lee had been a high-spirited and promising actress whose premature death, according to the *Thespian Dictionary* (1805), "deprived the public of her abilities before they had scarcely witnessed them." In his *Pin Basket to The Children of Thespis* published in 1797, John Williams wrote of Mrs Lee:

> Meritorious LEE, who's suppress'd in her song,
> Sure the finger of Malady's smote her fine form—
> She looks bruis'd, like a reed roughly us'd by the storm
> . . . .
> She's exceedingly graceful, though weak 'mid that grace,
> And her smile has its charms, though the bloom's left her face.

No children are known by her marriage to Henry Lee, who survived her by 39 years. He was remarried in 1814, to a Miss Lloyd, by whom he had a son and several daughters.

An engraved portrait by Mackenzie of a "Mrs M. Lee," published by Vernor, Hood, & Sharp, 1 January 1810, may actually be a picture of Sarah Jane Lee.

Lee, James Nathaniel [*fl.* 1788–1815], singer, actor.

The singing actor James Nathaniel Lee probably was the Mr Lee described by James Winston in his *Theatric Tourist* as the son of a Liverpool blacksmith. A somewhat effeminate young man, according to Winston, Lee played in the Liverpool company, where one night he was to make his debut in his first speaking role, Mat o' the Mint in *The Beggar's Opera*, but Barrymore, the Macheath that night, being imperfect in his own role, cut him out entirely. When the manager inquired why the scene had been omitted, Barrymore "coolly replied that Lee had not studied it, and therefore he passed it by."

By 1788–89 Lee was acting small roles and singing in the choruses at Covent Garden Theatre for a salary of £1 per week. No doubt he was the Lee who had played the Servant in *The Jealous Wife* the previous season on 23 April 1788. In 1788–89 he appeared as Satin in *The Miser*, Rupert in *Love in a Camp*, a Recruit in *The Funeral*, Apollo in *Poor Vulcan!*, and a Spanish Grandee in *Don Juan*.

During the rest of the eighteenth century Lee continued in similar service at Covent Garden. In 1790–91 his salary was raised to £1 5s. per week. By 1796–97 he was earning £1 10s., an amount that remained his constant salary in the account books through 1814–15. A pay sheet now in the Harvard Theatre Collection indicates that he received £47 15s. for 191 nights in 1797–98; it is endorsed "settled James Nat Lee."

A selection of Lee's numerous assignments at Covent Garden includes the Carpenter in *Harlequin's Chaplet* and a Shepherd in *A Peep behind the Curtain* in 1789–90; a principal character in *The Provocation* and a Bailiff in *The School for Arrogance* in 1790–91; a Spanish Officer in *The Governor* in 1792–93; a Waiter in *Harlequin's Treasure* in 1795–96; an Irish Peasant in *Bantry Bay* in 1796–97; an Irish Chief in *The Round Tower* and a role in *Harlequin and Quixotte* in 1797–98; a Man Milliner in *The Magic Oak* and a Friar in *Raymond and Agnes* in 1798–99; and a Sailor in *The Death of Captain Cook* in 1799–1800.

Winston provided several anecdotes about Lee, whose colleagues at Covent Garden were fond of playing tricks upon him. When he complained of the cold in the dressing room he shared with Fearon and Thompson, they would open the window; if he was hot, they would close the window and place more coals on the fire. He was nearly seriously injured one night during a pantomime when "they let the trap go & down he went by the run." In a notebook now at the Folger Shakespeare Library, Winston called him "Natty Lee."

Described as a bachelor, James Nathaniel Lee married Mary Butler of St Luke, Chelsea, widow, by license at St Paul, Covent Garden, on 3 April 1791. She seems not to have been a performer.

Lee, John [fl. 1673–1680], actor.

Summers, in his edition of Aphra Behn's *Works*, said that John Lee never rose above minor parts in the Duke's Company, was the husband of Mary Lee, later Lady Slingsby, and died in 1678. Typically, Summers did not indicate what evidence he had for that death date; *The London Stage* lists John Lee as a member of the Duke's Company in 1679–80, but neither does it offer proof. Lee was first cited for a role about August 1673 at Dorset Garden, Alexas in *Herod and Mariamne* (Robert Hume has shown that *The London Stage* date of September 1671 is too early).

He was mentioned sporadically over the following years: Dumain in *Love and Revenge*, Marcellus in *Hamlet*, Sebastian in *Abdelazer*, the title role in *Tom Essence* (unless that was an error for Anthony Leigh; but it was a late summer production and the troupe may have let him try a title part), Titiro in *Pastor Fido*, Sancho in *The Rover*, Pedro in *The French Conjurer*, and Noddy in *The Counterfeit Bridegroom*. The last-mentioned role was in September 1677 and is the last notice of Lee that has been found in cast lists. Since Mary Lee probably married Sir Charles Slingsby between February and September 1680, John Lee's death very likely came sometime before that.

Lee, Mrs John, Mary, née Aldridge, later Lady Slingsby d. 1694, actress.

Mary Aldridge joined the Duke's Company at the Lincoln's Inn Fields Theatre about 1670 and soon married the actor John Lee. She seems not to have been named in any casts as Mary Aldridge, though she may well have played small parts under that name before she married. Her first named role may have been Olinda in *The Forc'd Marriage*, performed on 20 September 1670, though Robert Hume has argued that *The Women's Conquest*, in which she acted Doranthe, may have been performed in September or earlier. In any case, Mary Lee quickly achieved popularity in romantic and tragic roles and breeches parts, as J. H. Wilson in *All the King's Ladies* points out. Before the Duke's players moved to their new Dorset Garden Theatre in November 1671, Mary was seen as Eugenia in *The Six Days Adventure*, Leticia in *The Town Shifts*, and Salome in *Herod and Mariamne*.

At Dorset Garden her first recorded role was Aemilia in *The Reformation*, perhaps in May 1673, though Hume suggests it may have been acted a year earlier. Before her remarriage in 1680 and her subsequent appearances as Lady Slingsby (John Lee having died), Mary appeared in such new parts as Mariamne in *The Empress of Morocco*, Nigrello in *Love and Revenge*, Amavanga in *The Conquest of China*, Deidamia in *Alcibiades*, Christina in *The Country Wit*, Roxalana in Settle's *Ibrahim*, Mrs Loveit (probably) in *The Man of Mode*, the Queen of Spain in *Don Carlos*, Isabella in *Abdelazer*, the title part in *Madam Fickle*, Berenice in *Titus and Berenice*, Corisca in *Pastor Fido*, Cleopatra in Sedley's *Antony and Cleopatra*, the title part in *Circe*, Astatius in *The Constant Nymph*, Roxana in *The Siege of Babylon*, Elvira in *The Counterfeits*, Eurydice in *Oedipus*, Cassandra in *The Destruction of Troy*, Laura Lucretia in *The Feign'd Curtizans*, Cressida in *Troilus and Cressida*, Bellamira in *Caesar Borgia*, possibly Cleomena in *The Young King*, Arviola in *The Loyal General*, Julia in *Loving Enemies*, and Queen Margaret in *The Misery of Civil War*. In addition, she was a popular speaker of prologues and epilogues.

Sometime between February and December 1680 she married (most authorities say) Sir Charles Slingsby, Bart, of Bifrons in Patrixbourne, near Canterbury, Kent—but, as will be seen later, her new husband may have been another Slingsby. As Lady Slingsby she played Marguerite in *The Princess of Cleve*, Sempronia in *Lucius Junius Brutus*, Regan in *King Lear*, Queen Margaret in *1 Henry VI*, Lady Elizabeth Blunt in *Vertue Betray'd*, Lucia in *Mr Turbulent*, Tarpeia in *Romulus and Hersilia*, the Queen Mother in *The Duke of Guise*, Lady Noble in *Dame Dobson*, Calphurnia in *Julius Caesar*, Clarinda in *A Commonwealth of Women*, and, according to Genest, Gertrude in *Hamlet*.

Again she was a popular speaker of prologues and epilogues, and one, the epilogue to *Romulus and Hersilia*, which contained reflections on the Duke of Monmouth, caused her to be taken into custody in August 1682, but that seems to have been her only recorded brush with the law. Satirical poems of the day referred to her, however. *A Satyr on both Whigs and Tories* of 1683 (quoted by Summers in his edition of Otway) speaks of Sir Gilbert Gerrard and Lady Slingsby having an intrigue; Gerrard is called

> *Thou Thing made up of Buttons, Coach, and Show,*
> *The Beasts that draw thee have more sense than*
>   *thou.*
> *Yet still thou mightst have fool'd behind the Scenes,*
> *Have Comb'd thy Wig, and set thy Cravat Strings,*
> *Made love to Slingsby when she played the Queen,*
> *The Coxcomb in the Crowd had passed unseen.*

The Satyr on Players of 1684 (as transcribed by J. H. Wilson) was typically obscene:

> *Imprimis Slingsby has ye fatall Curse*
> *To have a Lady's Honour, with a Players purse:*
> *Tho' now she is so plaguy haughty grown*
> *Yet Gad my Lady, I a time have known*
> *When a dull Whiggish Poet wou'd go down.*
> *That Scene's now chang'd, but prythee dowdy Beast*
> *Think not thy Self an Actress in the least*
> *For sure thy figure ne'r was seen before—*
> *Such Arse-like Breasts, Stiff neck, & menstruous*
>   *Gore,*
> *Are certain Antedotes against a Whore.*

Or did she, as Wilson suggests in *All the King's Ladies*, have something like the beauty that her character of Bellamira in *Caesar Borgia* was described as having?

> *. . . such a skin full of alluring flesh!*
> *Ah, such a ruddy, moist, and pouting lip;*
> *Such dimples, and such Eyes, such melting Eyes,*
> *Blacker than Sloes, and yet they sparkl'd fire.*

The Dictionary of National Biography noted that a Dame Mary Slingsby, widow, from St James's parish, was buried at St Pancras on 1 March 1694, and that has been taken by most authorities as a reference to the actress. But, according to the *Post Boy* of 13–15 September 1698, Sir Charles Slingsby died on 13 September, so our subject would not have been a widow in 1694. Dame Mary Slingsby of St Pancras could have been another woman. The Patrixbourne registers, for instance, show the baptism on 26 April 1666 of Mary, daughter of Lady Slingsby, widow of Sir Arthur Slingsby.

Lee, John [*fl.* 1794]. See JEE, JOHN.

Lee, John 1725–1781, *actor, manager, playwright.*

Nothing is known of the early years of John Lee, from his birth in 1725 until he appeared at Goodman's Fields Theatre, at the age of about 20, as Conde in *The Massacre at Paris* on 28 October 1745. That season at Goodman's Fields, which was then under the management of the struggling Hallam tribe, Lee also acted Richmore in *The Twin Rivals*, Gayless in *The Lying Valet*, Sir Charles in *The Stratagem* (on 13 November, a performance which *The Dictionary of National Biography* calls his first in London), Jacomio in *The Humours of Purgatory*, Sharper in *The Old Bachelor*, Fantome in *The Drummer*, Pedro in *The Spanish Fryar*, the Ghost in *Hamlet*, Alonzo in *The Tempest*, Catesby in *Jane Shore*, Southampton in *The Earl of Essex*, and Juan in *Rule a Wife and Have a Wife*. His performance as Richard III on 3 March 1746 was announced as his last on that stage, and on 9 May 1746, for a benefit he shared with several house servants, he appeared for the first time at Drury Lane Theatre, as Hotspur in *1 Henry IV*. Announced as from Goodman's Fields,

Harvard Theatre Collection

JOHN LEE as Aboan and WILLIAM POWELL as Oroonoko

artist unknown

Lee again played Hotspur at Southwark Fair on 20 October 1746.

In 1746–47 Lee was back with the Hallams at Goodman's Fields, playing Richard III again on 11 November 1746 and adding to his repertoire several important roles, such as Cassio in *Othello* on 9 December 1746, the Bastard in *King Lear* on 2 March 1747, and Hamlet, for his benefit, on 12 March. Other parts included Carlos in *The Revenge*, Axalla in *Tamerlane*, Young Gerrard in *The Anatomist*, Woolsort in *The Royal Merchant*, Bertran in *The Spanish Fryar*, the Governor in *Love Makes a Man*, Guildenstern in *Hamlet*, Jack and Hotman in *Oroonoko*, Bully in *The Provok'd Wife*, Freeman in *A Bold Stroke for a Wife*, Robin of Bagshot in *The Beggar's Opera*, Lothario in *The Fair Penitent*, Malcolm in *Macbeth*, Fenton in *The Merry Wives of Windsor*, Gonzalo in *The Tempest*, Marcus in *Cato*, Bedamar in *Venice Preserv'd*, Trueman in *The London Merchant*, the Conjurer in *The Devil to Pay*, Morelove in *The Careless Husband*, Dick in *The King and the Miller of Mansfield*, Rodolpho in *Tancred and Sigismunda*, Cabinet in *The Funeral*, and Flash in *Miss in Her Teens*. On 5 March 1747 he played an original but unspecified role in the premiere of Mrs Hoper's *The Battle of Poictiers*.

According to the bills, a Mr Lee acted Gadshill in *1 Henry IV* to Spranger Barry's Hotspur at Drury Lane on 15 and 16 January 1747; possibly that actor was John Lee, but the bills also reveal that on those nights he was at Goodman's Fields acting Robin of Bagshot and Gonzalo, respectively. *1 Henry IV* was given again at Drury Lane on 17 and 19 January, and on the latter night presumably John Lee played Gonzalo at Goodman's Fields. The two theatres were located much too far apart, it would seem, for Lee to have played at both on the same night. On 22 April 1747, however, John Lee joined the Hallams and Foote, in the latter's *The Diversions of the Morning*, and as Bellmour in *The Credulous Husband* at the Haymarket Theatre. Foote's *Diversions* was repeated frequently until mid-June. Then Lee joined the company at Richmond, where the surviving bills show his debut on 3 October 1747 as Ranger in *The Suspicious Husband*. On 13 October at Richmond he acted Hamlet and Flash.

Garrick was already two months into his first season of Drury Lane management when Lee joined his company, making his first appearance on 14 November 1747 as the Bastard to Garrick's Lear. Then followed Myrtle in *The Conscious Lovers*, the King of France in *Henry V*, Ferdinand in *The Tempest*, Belmour in *Jane Shore*. For his benefit on 14 April 1748, when tickets could be had of Lee at Mr. Oliphant's in Exeter Street, he acted Standard in *The Constant Couple* and Young Rakish in *The School Boy*.

In the summer of 1748 Lee returned to Richmond, but the engagement there was marred by a squabble, probably not the first and certainly not the last that he was to have with his professional colleagues. Lee refused to appear for Miss Ferguson's benefit on 2 September in a part he thought unsuitable, so a paper war followed, when he seems to have had the better of Miss Ferguson. In a pamphlet entitled *An Apology for Mr Lee's Behaviour* (laid into British Library Burney MS 938. C.9, but not listed in Arnott and Robinson), he claimed that in late August 1748 he had "withdrawn myself from the Company" and "consequently shall sustain the Loss of my Benefits, and a whole Summer's Performance, without having receiv'd One Shilling." Lee's name, however, was in the Richmond bills as Lothario and Flash for his benefit on 7 September 1748.

In his second season at Drury Lane, 1748–49, Lee seemed to have established himself as a solid member of the company, acting among other roles Young Fashion in *The Relapse*, Claudio in *Much Ado about Nothing*, Paris in *Romeo and Juliet*, Ross in *Macbeth*, and the Bastard in *King Lear*. The next summer Lee was once more, despite his problem of the previous year, ensconced at Richmond in an even stronger position, for his roles were now Romeo, Lear, and Captain Squib in *Tunbridge Walks*, as well as Ranger in *The Suspicious Husband*. On 19 September 1749 he began a third season at Drury Lane as Young Fashion. He then played Claudio in *Much Ado about Nothing*, but on 5 October that role was taken by King, for Lee had deserted to Covent Garden, a move which very much disturbed Garrick. A person of some vanity, Lee perhaps felt that Garrick had suppressed his talents by denying him roles in which Garrick himself excelled. Whether or not that was true, Lee had probably defected for a higher salary and certainly for greater professional opportunity. On 6 October 1749 his name was placed on the Covent Garden list for £10 per week, but not until 23 October 1749 did he make his debut as Ranger (a role in which Garrick was very accomplished) and was, according to one press report, "greatly received." During the remainder of the season at Covent Garden he acted Axalla, Essex in *The Unhappy Favourite*, Heartly in *The Non Juror*, the Dauphin in *Henry V*, Campley in *The Funeral*, Alexas in *All for Love*, Flash, Archer in *The Stratagem*, and Carlos in *The Revenge*. On 1 March 1750, he played Romeo and on 2 April Richard III, roles he probably never could have hoped for at the other house. *Richard III* was performed for his benefit, when tickets could be had of him at Mr Christmas's in Maiden Lane. His net proceeds were £90 3s.

Lee performed at least once at Richmond in the summer of 1750, as Ranger on 8 September. He began the winter season at Covent Garden as Standard in *The Constant Couple* on 13 October 1750 and acted Granger in a revival of Cibber's *The Refusal* on 31 October. He repeated Granger on 3 November, then played Axalla on 5, 6, and 7 November, and appeared once more as Granger on 9 November. Garrick and the law finally caught up with him for breach of articles, thus compelling him to return to Drury Lane on 13 November 1750 when he was seen in the modest role of Ross in *Macbeth*. There he remained for two seasons, for the most part relegated to the likes of Valerius in *The Roman Father*, Lycon in *Phaedra and Hippolitus*, Surrey in *Henry VIII*, and Carlos in *The Fatal Marriage*. He did, however, get the chance to act George Barnwell, Castalio in *The Orphan*, Hamlet and the Poet in *Lethe* for his benefit on 23 April 1751, Buckingham in *Richard III*, Aboan in *Oroonoko*, and, for his benefit on 6 April 1752, when tickets could be had at Mr Reynolds's Crane Co in Crown Court, Little Russell Street, Lear and the title role in *Don Quixote in England*. On 23 February 1751 he was the original Earl of Devon in the premiere of Mallet's *Alfred*.

He had returned to Richmond (and Twickenham) once more, in the summer of 1751. There he was joined by his wife Anna Sophia Lee (she had been a member of the Goodman's Fields Company with him in 1745–46). Together at Richmond they acted Archer and Mrs Sullen in *The Beaux' Stratagem*, Osmyn and Zara in *The Mourning Bride*, Romeo and Juliet (for their benefit on 3 September 1751), Lothario and Calista in *The Fair Penitent*, and Benedick and Beatrice in *Much Ado about Nothing*.

His "peculiar oddity of temper"—as Genest put it—and his resentment of Garrick prompted Lee to finish out his stormy contract at Drury Lane in mid-April 1752. Quickly he went to Dublin to join his wife at the Smock Alley Theatre, where she had been acting under Thomas Sheridan's management since the previous September. On 20 May 1752 he made his debut as Romeo to her Juliet. That proved to be his only performance there that season, for soon he was off to Scotland, intent on becoming a manager.

He arrived at Edinburgh in midsummer 1752, evidently at the invitation of a group of aristocrats and influential business persons who desired to see the condition of management and the level of production at the Canongate Concert Hall raised from the decay into which it had fallen. Assisted by Lord Elibank, Andrew Pringle, and other patrons, Lee secured excellent terms for the lease and began to operate the house under his management probably by 16 July 1752, on which night he acted Hamlet. Surviving bills and advertisements for his first season are scarce. The company played *The Beggar's Opera* in November and *Romeo and Juliet* in December. The latter piece probably had Lee gracing the juvenile leading role and was evidently the version of the play which the *Biographia Dramatica* claimed was arranged by Lee for the Edinburgh stage. If so, it was the first of Lee's so-called "Literary Murders," and the only one not published. (According to *The London Stage* and Nicoll it was this version of *Romeo and Juliet* which was acted at Covent Garden on 29 September 1777.)

Other Canongate productions that season included Pasquali's *The Enraged Musician*, *Much Ado about Nothing* (perhaps in an alteration by Lee), *Herminius and Espasia* (a new play by a Scottish gentleman), *The Suspicious Husband* and *Miss in Her Teens* for Mrs Lee's benefit on 4 March, *The Conscious Lovers* with Lee as Young Bevil, and *The Rehearsal*. On 15 April 1753 Lee acted Shylock and his wife acted Portia in *The Merchant of Venice*, "newly alter'd from

Shakespear and Lord Landsdown, and adapted for the stage." The bills cautioned that gentlemen passing over the stage to the boxes "are not to make continuance behind the scenes, as the new painted scenes are scarce dry."

In his four years at Edinburgh Lee proved a capable theatrical manager and administrator, displaying energy, economy, imagination, and even tact. His reforms included improvements in scenery and decorations and the elimination of seats on the stage and visits behind the scenes. In his *Annals of the Edinburgh Stage* Dibdin credits Lee with "having been the first to raise the status and *morale* of the theatre in Edinburgh."

Lee's adaptation of *Macbeth* as produced at Edinburgh was published in 1753. Among other leading roles played by him in the northern capital were Archer, Benedick, Macheath, Othello, Captain Plume in *The Recruiting Officer*, Castalio in *The Orphan*, Richard III, Pierre in *Venice Preserv'd*, Ranger, Sir John Brute in *The Provok'd Wife*, and Touchstone in *As You Like It*. Because the actors had signed articles for periods longer than the Edinburgh season, Lee took them each spring and summer to Glasgow, Newcastle, Scarborough, and other places, and he claimed that consequently in the first summer he was £500 out of pocket.

Despite Lee's apparent artistic and administrative success, he suffered financial reversals which brought about his professional demise at Edinburgh, aided and abetted by a cabal against him. The details are laid out in Dibdin's *Annals* and in Lee's own eloquent and blistering attack on the conspirators in his *Narrative of a Remarkable Breach of Trust committed by a Nobleman, Five Judges, and Several Advocates of the Court of Session in Scotland* (London, 1772). In this thirty-six-page pamphlet, Lee convincingly describes the long process of law by which some of the principal men of Edinburgh conspired to wrest from him profitable control of the patent and considerable real property.

As a result of the arbitration over Lee's original purchase of the theatre property, on 7 March 1753 it had been determined that for the lease and scenes and other equipment Lee should pay a total of £645, plus interest, as follows: £200 down, £100 payable at Whitsuntide 1753, £200 at the same time in 1754, and a final £145 a year later. Lee purchased the property from Thomas Robertson, a factor for the previous proprietors. Lee was very encouraged by the easy terms which Lord Elibank, Andrew Pringle, and others had arranged for him. The terms also included a £100 annuity for Lee for five years provided he would remain at Edinburgh to act and manage.

When the third installment of the purchase was due in May 1754, Lee found himself short, and tradesmen seized his goods. His application to Lord Elibank for relief met with cordial assurances that Elibank and some friends would furnish security by taking an assignment of the theatre. Lee's request for a trust rather than an assignment was rejected, but, instead of becoming very suspicious at that juncture, Lee agreed to the assignment on 27 December 1754. Lee still believed in the "friendliness" of the transaction, which he assumed was intended to protect his property against tradesmen, who—as Lord Elibank had explained to him—"would badger you if the theatre was your property, but they will be frightened to do so when it belongs to us."

Either Lee did not see that he was becoming the victim of a confidence scheme or, if he did, he could do nothing about it. In February 1754, after a very detailed inventory had been provided by Lee, Lord Elibank sent him a document allowing him "to continue as manager" but declaring that the gentlemen who had the assignment would not be responsible for any of his debts. The "gentlemen" had advanced Lee £500, of which they paid £316 by a bond granted to Moubray and Clapperton, tradesmen. So Lee now owed that £500 in addition to the balance of the original purchase money. He had, indeed, been entrapped, for they had already engaged West Digges as manager and only awaited an opportunity to evict Lee. On 23 February 1756 his creditors seized the theatre while Lee was on stage, even taking in hand the money at the door. When Lee exposed the whole perfectly legal but very shady scheme, they promptly had him arrested, and on 26 February they sold off his furniture and turned his wife and children into the street. Lee was two months in jail, where he had leisure to reflect

that within the space of a few hours, I was, by an unparalleled act of fraud and barbarity, thrown from the possession of a considerable property, with an income of £600 a year, into a loathsome gaol; with about £8 in my pocket; two children destitute in Edinburgh; and my wife (unable to form a true idea of this oppression) with two more, waiting in London for supplies from me;—nay, with an absolute certainty, all the time, of *my effects exceeding, by many hundreds of pounds, every debt I owed*.

After languishing for two months, Lee was released and in July entered a suit for restitution, whereupon he was immediately re-arrested for debts owed to a stonemason, but next morning was again set free. The courts upheld the legal plunder, though the litigation dragged on for some 10 years.

Realizing that Edinburgh held no future for him, Lee accepted an engagement at Smock Alley, Dublin, where he made his appearance as King Lear on 3 November 1756. He had been negotiating by post with Thomas Sheridan, the Irish manager, over the summer of 1756. Soon he was embroiled in another controversy as the result of his Irish venture, the details of which he offered in his pamphlet *Letter from Mr. Lee to Mr. Sheridan* (Dublin, 1757), reputedly a verbatim transcript of the letters that had passed between them. According to Lee's side of the story, Sheridan had originally proposed a salary of £300 and expressed hopes that Lee would soon replace him as Smock Alley manager: "From the Accounts I have had of Mr. *Lee's* Assiduity, Regularity of Discipline, Punctuality of Dealings, and his other Merits, I know no Theatrical Person whom I would so readily chuse for a Successor." Lee countered with a demand for £400, since Digges (who had replaced Lee as Edinburgh manager) had that much from Sheridan. The manager argued in reply that in his initial Irish season Digges had been paid £300 and in subsequent years about £180. Lee and Sheridan finally agreed on £400 for Lee and his wife—whom Sheridan was persuaded reluctantly to accept, for she had not really pleased in her previous engagement—and the first benefit, with assurances that Lee's terms were "*far superior* to any *Person's* in the *Company*."

Sheridan had urged Lee's arrival well before the start of the season, but "opposite Winds" detained him for some three weeks, so that the season opened on 18 October 1756 without him. Lee accused Sheridan of having lured him to Ireland on false pretenses in a desperate attempt to bolster his tottering enterprise. He had made life impossible for Lee and by all manner of underhanded devices had reneged on every article of their agreement. After trying to break the contract with Lee, Sheridan's "next Endeavor was to *smooth* me into a *Subordination*: if that fail'd, then let *Disuse* be productive of *Obscurity*, and by such Means temper me into an Acquiescence with whatever Evasion of Promises [Sheridan] might hereafter think necessary to suggest."

There was, however, another side to the story, told in the anonymous pamphlet *Remarks on Mr. Lee's Letter to Mr. Sheridan* (1757). When Lee made his second appearance, as Archer in *The Beaux' Stratagem*, on 11 November, hissing nearly drove him from the stage. A delegate from the audience met with Sheridan to request that Lee not reappear in principal characters; since "he was but indifferently qualified to be set at the Tail" of a theatre, it was not sensible he should be at the head. Because of Sheridan's "Delicacy and Tenderness," he could not bear to have Lee "degraded." Sheridan, however, knowing that Lee was not suited to succeed him as manager, had already begun his campaign to interest Spranger Barry as Lee's successor. Lee appeared about 30 times during the season, playing Myrtle in *The Conscious Lovers*, Old Norval in *Douglas* (on 12 and 18 May, unsuccessfully), Hastings in *Jane Shore*, Cassius in *Julius Caesar*, Hotspur in *1 Henry IV*, the Frenchman in *Lethe*, Sir Paul Pliant in *The Double Dealer*, Don Cholerick in *Love Makes a Man*, Flash in *Miss in Her Teens*, Polydore in *The Orphan*, and Benedick in *Much Ado about Nothing*.

By 1757 almost every engagement of Lee's career of some 22 years had ended acrimoniously. The next would be no exception. Announced as making his first appearance on the Covent Garden stage in five years (actually seven), Lee began the 1757–58 season on 11 November as Richard III. Though he was articled to act four times per week, Lee appeared only four times during the entire season: his opening Richard, Ranger on 18 November and 21 December, and Bayes in *The Rehearsal* (with a new prologue) on 24 January 1758, when benefit tickets could be had from him at the Golden Ball in Bow Street. In his folio, *Mr. Lee's Case against J. Rich*, published on 13 November 1758, Lee charged Rich, the Covent Garden manager, with breach of agreement and refusal to meet with him or respond to his letters. Lee's articles, by his account, had stipulated that he and Spranger Barry should appear in certain plays together and that Lee "should receive a *third* Share of each Night's Account after the deducting of an hundred Pounds, or (when Mr. *Barry* played with me) an hundred and twenty." But with Barry already a main attraction, Rich had avoided scheduling the plays—*Venice Preserv'd, The Fair Penitent, King John*, and *The Siege of Damascus*—in which it had been stipulated that Lee would act, thus preventing Lee from earning, as he claimed, even a shilling, save his benefit money (which was £208 18*s*., less house charges of about £65). Lee's prospects, he asserted, were sacrificed by Rich when he engaged Barry.

By the time that Lee published his case with John Rich, however, he was already acting with the company at the Orchard Street Theatre in Bath, where according to Winston's *Theatric Tourist* the management had also "devolved" to him. Lee remained at Bath for three seasons, still unable to suppress his penchant for trouble. In 1759 the late Bath prompter John Brownsmith published *The Danger of a Lee Shore*, in which he detailed his difficulties with John Lee. The manager, Brownsmith complained bitterly, paid slave wages, treated Mrs Brownsmith like a neophyte despite her 12 years of acting experience and subsequently discharged her. In 1761 Lee carried a company, probably from Bath, to Winchester to play every Saturday in August. He also acted again at Edinburgh in 1760 and 1761. On the morning of 2 May 1761, by way of farewell, he read Milton's *Paradise Lost* in Mr La Motte's large room in James's Court, for 2*s*. 6*d*. a ticket.

Lee's peregrinations brought him back to Drury Lane Theatre on 22 February 1762, when he made his first appearance there in ten years, playing Pierre in *Venice Preserv'd*. Perhaps he acted there several other times that season, but his name was in only one more bill, on 11 May 1762, as Norval in *Douglas*, for his own benefit, which surprisingly, in view of their enmity, Garrick granted. In the autumn, with his differences with Garrick evidently patched up, he became a regular member of the Drury Lane Company, for four years. His roles for that engagement included among others Paris in *Romeo and Juliet*, Garcia in *The Mourning Bride*, Prince John in *2 Henry IV*, Laertes in *Hamlet*, Bertran in *The Spanish Fryar*, Buckingham in *Richard III*, the Bastard in *King Lear*, Perdiccas in *The Rival Queens*, and Traverse in *The Clandestine Marriage* (in the premiere on 20 February 1766). On 26 April 1765 he acted Pinchwife in his own two-act adaptation of Wycherley's *The Country Wife*, for his benefit shared with Miss Slack, when tickets could be had of him at La Grange's Medicinal Warehouse in New Street, Covent Garden. The version was published in 1786, after Lee's death.

Lee's salary at Drury Lane in 1764–65 was 10*s*. per night, or £3 per week, in about the middle range of the pay list. He subscribed £1 1*s*. to the Drury Lane Fund in 1766. In his *Thespis* of 1766, Kelly deplored the defects many found in Lee's acting, but nevertheless approved his "stage struck heat, so vehemently strong" and welcomed his return:

> *For five long years in dark oblivion thrown,*
> *Has* LEE *remain'd, neglected and unknown,*
> *Unless, when chance, on some capricious start,*
> *Has kindly blest him with a decent part*
> ....
> *'Tis true that* LEE *has fatally imbib'd*
> *A mode of speech not easily describ'd;*
> *A nice affected drawlingness of phrase,*
> *A wire-drawn tone in everything he plays;*
> *With which, too oft, most execrably fine,*
> *He racks a word, and tortures out a line;*
> *Yet still has* LEE *a consequence of form,*
> *A voice and look so capable to warm*
> ....
> *Hence, mean so'er, as managers may prize,*
> *I look on Lee with very different eyes,*
> *And freely place, however they disdain,*
> *His chair next* GARRICK'S *high in Drury-Lane.*

Kelly's final generous compliment, however extravagant, must have warmed the heart of Lee who always thought himself in Garrick's class as an actor, but it did little for his future at Drury Lane. For whatever reason, Lee was not in the company in 1766–67. During his last years at Drury Lane, Lee had acted at Manchester in the summers of 1762 and 1764, and had managed there in 1765. In the summer of 1766 he worked with Barry's company at the King's Theatre, London, where he was seen as Iago, Pierre, Edmund, Myrtle, Lothario, Chamont, and Jaques in *As You Like It*. In the early months of 1767 Lee made an ill-advised attempt to regain the Edinburgh management, but circumstances there were still much muddled, and he failed. He did act, however, at Edinburgh at that time.

In April 1768 the press announced that Lee had been appointed by Palmer, the patentee, as manager of the Theatre Royal at Bath. On 30 April of that year Lee had a benefit at Bath, and that summer played as a member of Foote's company at the Haymarket, acting Archer in *The Stratagem*, Copper Captain in *Rule a Wife and Have a Wife*, Lorenzo in *The Spanish Fryar*, and Bayes in *The Rehearsal*.

In the autumn of 1768 he began his tenure as Bath manager, a situation he held through 1770–71. At Bath, Lee once again became entangled with the law, though the circumstances remain obscure to us. They seem to have related to an attempt made by Lee back in 1766 to buy some land upon which to build a theatre. In the Boston Public Library are several published items about the matter, including *An Address to the Judges and the Public, on a decision lately made in our courts of judicature*, dated by Lee 18 July 1772 from debtor's prison of the King's Bench. With the *Address* was printed "AN AGREEMENT made this 29th of *March*, 1766, between *John Cottell* and *Cecilia Walker* of *Bath*, Widow, and one of the beneficial Devisees, &c. of the one Part; and *John Lee, John Pritchard*, and *Charles Davis*, of the same City, of the other Part." A Bath scene-and-house painter named Charles Davis had offered to secure a parcel of land for Lee, but evidently never carried out the commission.

In January 1770 some "frequenters of Drury Lane playhouse" used the pages of the *Freeholder's Magazine* to implore Garrick "to engage Mr Lee, if at liberty," suggesting somewhat tactlessly that, "As Mr Garrick's reputation as a player, and a fortune, are now established upon a basis sufficiently firm and solid, he need not entertain those jealous apprehensions of Mr Lee he formerly did." Despite the appeal, which carried with it a reminder that since the public had provided Garrick with an immense fortune, he should, in gratitude, give them this satisfaction and pleasure, the manager did not oblige.

Subsequently Lee became involved with Jonathan Battishill and Joseph Baildon in a scheme which produced at least five concerts of music and readings at the Crown and Anchor Tavern in the Strand in April 1772. For a benefit taken by Lee, at which he offered select pieces from Milton, Dryden, Pope, and Shakespeare, tickets could be had of him at Mr Mitchell's, hosier, in Chandos Street, Covent Garden. "The whole entertainment was highly rational and refined," remembered Busby in his *Anecdotes* (1825), "and the encouragement it received, till interrupted by Mr. Lee's indisposition, proved that the metropolis of England possessed a pure and elevated taste." On 27 April 1773 Lee's adaptation in two acts of Vanbrugh's *The Relapse* was produced at Covent Garden under the title of *The Man of Quality*. Lee did not act in it, though he may well have been present. It was published that year with Lee's title.

Lee seems to have acted in Ireland for a year or so. The autumn of 1774 found him back at a London patent house, this time at Covent Garden, where he began a three-year engagement on 11 October as Bayes, followed by Richard III on 22 October. The reviewer in that month's *Westminster Magazine* was greatly disappointed in both characters:

Never did we see the part of *Bayes* attempted by a performer so entirely destitute of spirit, taste, and pleasantry. The sallies of wit (pretended to be extempore) usually thrown out by the Actors in this play, were . . . very sparingly sprinkled this evening. . . .

We never remember to have heard before so tame a recital of the character of Richard, or to have seen so inactive a representative of this bustling Monarch. Whether ignorance or inattention was the cause, we will not determine; but never were scenes of such ample latitude for the abilities of the Performer, so faintly marked, or so shamefully trifled with. That admirable soliloquy—*Now are our brows bound with victorious wreaths, etc.*—gave but a poor example of Mr. Lee's oratory, for which he has been so repeatedly cried up to the Public by the puffs of dunces.——When Richard, impatient to encounter Richmond, hastily commands his tent to be pitched in Bosworth field, Mr. Lee issues out these royal orders with all the composure of a Common Council-man, who bids his servant lay the cloth in his gazebo, that he may regale himself with Yorkshire ham and capons; Nay, the last scene where he falls, with—*Perdition catch thy arm*—*the chance is thine*—resembled but the situation of a greasy Freeholder of Middlesex laid sprawling by the club of a Brentford rioter.

By December Lee also had acted Benedick, Osman in *Zara*, and Adam in *As You Like It* and William Hawkins, more impressed than the earlier critic, wrote in his *Miscellanies in Prose and Verse* (1775):

> This established veteran from Ireland . . . has great abilities: he has numberless beauties which are entirely his own, as he appears to be free from imitation. . . . I think him too corpulent and masculine, notwithstanding his features are expressive, his voice articulate and powerful, his action just [and] . . . free from that stiffness (considering his part) many actors are subject to . . .

In Downman's poem "Drama" (1775), however, Lee was not treated so sympathetically:

> . . . tho' their Lee boasts some faint strokes of art,
> Does he e'er touch with sympathy the heart?
> . . . .
> His person's vulgar, his deportment's bad,
> And tame correctness all he ever had.

Supposedly Lee's portrayal of Sir Lucius O'Trigger was one of those bad performances, along with Shuter's Sir Anthony Absolute, which caused disapproval of *The Rivals* at its premiere on 17 January 1775. Lee's other Covent Garden roles during that period included Lycon in *Phaedra and Hippolitus*, Wolsey in *Henry VIII*, and the Duke in *Measure for Measure*.

Following 1776–77, his last season at Covent Garden, Lee returned to Bath and Bristol to finish out his career. He managed at Bath in 1778–79 and also acted Richard III, Macbeth, Jaques, and Comus. His last role was Macbeth at Bristol on 14 July 1780. (A Mr Lee acted Nym in *Falstaff's Wedding* at the Haymarket Theatre, London, on 27 December 1779, but we doubt that he was our subject. He perhaps was the northern actor, John Lee, who died in 1784.)

In 1780 Lee's failing health prevented his performing. He died at Bath of a "mortification of the bowels" in his fifty-sixth year on 20 February 1781, according to an extract of a letter of that date in the Enthoven Collection—("This morning died here Mr. Lee, the once celebrated tragedian . . ."). Manuscripts in the Burney and Reed papers at the British Library give his death date as 19 February. In reporting his demise, the *Bath Chronicle* of 21 February 1781 eulogized: "He was long contemporary with Mr. Garrick and extremely admired for the propriety, force and justness of his delivery. In a variety of parts he was excellent, in a few, perhaps, unequalled; and in the course of his theatrical progress has distinguished himself on many occasions as a capital performer and worthy man."

His wife, Anna Sophia Lee, an actress with whom he had shared much of his career, had died at Craven Hall on 3 September 1770. Their son George Augustus Lee (1761–1826) became a partner in the Manchester cotton-spinning firm, Philips and Lee; he was responsible for many working reforms in his plant and adopted new inventions for manufacturing, including fine specimens of the steam engines of Boulton and Watt, his friends. According to *The Dictionary of National Biography* John and Anna Lee had five daughters. The best known of these were Sophia Lee (1750–1824), a novelist and dramatist, author of *The Chapter of Accidents*, and Harriet Lee (1757–1851), also a novelist and dramatist. Both are noticed in *The Dictionary of National Biography*. A third daughter, Anna Lee, assisted her sisters with the Belvidere School at Bath. Despondent, she hanged herself from the top railing of her bed on 23 October 1805; her death is described in a letter from William Siddons to Mrs Piozzi on 29 October 1805 (published as No 22 by K. A. Burnim, *Bulletin of the John Rylands Library*, 52, Autumn). The fourth daughter—and fifth, if there was one—remain unknown to us. The Miss Lee who made her first and evidently only appearance at Covent Garden as Lucy in *The Recruiting Officer* on 8 May 1761, at a time when Mrs Lee was acting at that theatre while John Lee was at Bath may have been one of the sisters. She could not, however, have been Sophia or Harriet, who were then 11 and four, respectively, though she could have been the unfortunate Anna. A daughter, who may have been Harriet or one of the unknown girls acted Cordelia for her father's benefit at Covent Garden on 23 March 1776.

It is difficult to form an assessment of John Lee's acting, for there are few direct accounts of it and the general testimony is contradictory. No doubt he was a worthy performer with great professional knowledge. But all those who praised him were at pains to point out that he had been kept in the shadow, as did the author of *The Rational Rosciad* (1767):

All the great requisites with Lee were born,
An universal actor to adorn;
But much oppressed by managers and fate,
He now maintains a mere unnoticed state;
But if his hands by favour were unbound,
By Truth he'd be our modern Roscius crowned.

Other commentators, like Reed in his *Biographia Dramatica* (1812), found his talents "hardly above mediocrity." It is true that Lee scarcely ever associated himself with any theatre where he did not have a falling out with the manager or the proprietor. His quarrelsome nature and his sometimes paltry disputes made him unwelcome in many theatres and on several circuits. As an actor he possessed peculiarities of speech, and according to the author of *The State of the Stage* (1753), he was "emphatically wrong in almost everything he repeated." In his *Memoirs of Charles Macklin* (1804), William Cooke offered an assessment of Lee which perhaps is the most balanced:

Lee's Iago was very respectable, and showed a good judgment and thorough representation of the character—this actor was not without considerable pretentions, were they not more than allayed by his vanity—he had a good person, a good voice, and a more than ordinary knowledge in his profession, which he sometimes showed without exaggeration; but he wanted to be placed in the chair of Garrick, and in attempting to reach this he often deranged his natural abilities—he was for ever, as Foote said, "doing the honours of his face"—he affected uncommon long pauses, and frequently took such out-of-the-way pains with emphasis and articulation that the natural actor seldom appeared.

In addition to the "literary murders" and his various argumentative tracts cited above, Lee probably put his hand to other creative efforts or adaptations. It is said that when he was manager at Bath he so mangled the promptbooks of some plays that J. P. Kemble, when he came to that city, refused to act until they were properly restored. It was also said by some at Bath that Lee, and not his daughter Sophia, had really written *The Chapter of Accidents*, but, as Genest judged, "the play is so good, that it is not likely he should have written any considerable part of it," though he may have helped. *The Bath Comedians. A Poem: in Two Cantos: Written in Imitation of Hudibras*, which was printed for the author at London in 1753, is sometimes tentatively attributed to John Lee because it is initialed "J. M. L."; but at that period in his career Lee was in Edinburgh and seems to have had no connections whatever with the Bath theatre.

John Lee was pictured as Aboan, with William Powell as Oroonoko, in an anonymous engraving published in the *Universal Museum*. Lee and Powell appeared together in those roles at Covent Garden on 9 May 1764.

Lee, Mrs John, Anna Sophia *d. 1770, actress.*

By 1745–46 Anna Sophia Lee was acting with her husband John Lee in the Hallam Company at Goodman's Fields Theatre, but in a very obscure function. Probably her early career was closely connected with that of her husband, but we do not find her name in the advertisements until the summer of 1751, at Richmond, where she acted Mrs Sullen in *The Beaux' Stratagem* to her husband's Archer on 6 July. There she was also seen as Arabella in *The Wife's Relief*, Zara in *The Mourning Bride*, Juliet to Lee's Romeo, Calista in *The Fair Penitent*, Millamant in *The Way of the World*, Alicia in *Jane Shore*, Beatrice in *Much Ado about Nothing*, Lady Percy in *1 Henry IV*, Bisarre in *The Inconstant*, and Lady Townly in *The Provok'd Husband*.

Such an array of capital roles in her Richmond summer would seem to have shown that she had great promise, but we have no reviews of these performances. Evidently she had done well enough for Thomas Sheridan to engage her as a leading lady for the Smock Alley Theatre in Dublin, where she made her debut as Juliet to Digges's Romeo on 30 September 1751. But she failed to please, being in the shadow of Peg Woffington's success, and soon was assigned more secondary roles. Among her parts there were Lady Graveairs in *The Careless Husband*, Lady Dainty in *The Double Disappointment*, Nottingham in *The Earl of Essex*, Bisarre in *The Inconstant*, Lady Townly in *The Man of Mode*, Mrs Page in *The Merry Wives of Windsor*, Araminta in *The Old Bachelor*, Lady Wronghead in *The Provok'd Husband*, Mrs Strictland in *The Suspicious Husband*, and Mrs Fainall in *The Way of the World*. Her benefit scheduled for 22 April 1752 was delayed for the arrival of her husband from his Drury Lane engagement until 20 May when they appeared as Romeo and Juliet. The prompter Hitchcock later wrote satirically that Mrs Lee "chose to treat the town with an exhibition of her own Juliet."

In 1752–53 Mrs Lee was with a company at the Canongate Concert Hall in Edinburgh, where her husband had become manager. Among her roles that season were Clarinda in *The Suspicious Husband* and Juliet. Over the next three seasons at Edinburgh she was seen in many roles, including Almeria in *The Mourning Bride*, Beatrice, Cordelia, Indiana in *The Conscious Lovers*, Desdemona, Portia in *The Merchant of Venice*, and Mrs Sullen in *The Beaux' Stratagem*. When Lee retreated from the management at Edinburgh, he engaged at Smock Alley. In the negotiations Thomas Sheridan's determination not to hire Mrs Lee was dissuaded. After a delay of three weeks caused by unfavorable winds, the Lees arrived at Dublin by early November 1756. Mrs Lee, however, again failed to please and played only Beatrice, Lady Graveairs, and Lady Froth in *The Double Dealer*.

In 1758–59 she became a member of the Orchard Street Theatre Company at Bath, now under her husband's management. Though she continued to act at Bath regularly until her death, on 20 December 1759 she began her first real London engagement as Dorinda in *The Stratagem* at Covent Garden Theatre. On 29 December she was paid £5 5s. for that service, which she repeated on 15 January 1760. She acted Bertha in *The Royal Merchant* on 20 March and 12 April, then Rutland in *The Earl of Essex* for her benefit shared with Saunders on 19 April when her share came to £49 19s. Her other role that season was Britannia in *The Siege of Quebec* on 14 May. The following season at Covent Garden offered her Dorinda, Bertha, Clara in *Rule a Wife and Have a Wife*, Aurelia in *The Wife's Relief*, Princess Sachema in *The English Tars in America*, and Imoinda in *Oroonoko*.

In 1762–63 Mrs Lee transferred to Drury Lane for a six-season engagement. Her husband also was there from the middle of 1762–63 through 1765–66. Between 1764–65 and 1766–67 Mrs Lee was earning 6s. 8d. per day, or £2 per week. Her first role at Drury Lane was Melissa in *The Lying Valet* on 21 September 1762. That was followed by Camilla in *The Mistake*, Jacintha in *The Suspicious Husband*, Doll Tearsheet in *2 Henry IV*, Sophia in *The Male Coquette*, Lettice in *The School Boy*, and Tag in *Miss in Her Teens*. Some of her roles during subsequent years there were Maria in *Twelfth Night*, Mrs Bruin in *The Mayor of Garratt*, Goneril and Regan in *King Lear*, Millwood in *The London Merchant*, Alithea in *The Country Wife*, Lady Loverule in *The Devil to Pay*, and the Chambermaid in *The Clandestine Marriage*.

In the summer of 1765 Mrs Lee had acted at the new theatre in Richmond, Surrey, managed by James Love. The *Universal Museum* for August praised her Queen in *Richard III* and regretted that upon her return to Drury Lane she would be "frequently thrust on to carry a message to a person of infinitely less talents than herself." In 1763 the anonymous author of *The Smithfield Rosciad* had been less cordial:

Beg Mrs Lee would not be quite so proud,
Or, 'midst her acting, talk aside—so loud:
Nor to forget amidst her regal train,
She's but a Chamber-maid in Drury-lane.

In her will, drawn on 24 May 1767, the popular dancer Nancy Dawson left a mourning ring and a suit to her friend, Mrs Lee of Martlett Court.

After leaving Drury Lane in 1767–68, Mrs Lee continued to act in the Bath company through 1769–70. She died at Craven Hall on 3 September 1770.

Information on her children by John Lee, who died in 1781, can be found in his notice. Mrs Lee's full name was entered in the baptismal register of St Paul, Covent Garden, on 13 May 1750, when her daughter Sophia was christened.

Lee, [**John?**] [*fl.* 1779], *actor.*

An actor named Lee played Nym in a performance of *Falstaff's Wedding* given at the Haymarket Theatre on 27 December 1779. It is unlikely that he was John Lee (d. 1781), the Bath manager and sometime London performer. Perhaps he was the John Lee who acted at Dublin between 1767 and 1774 and at Edinburgh in 1777 and 1778, but we have no evidence. The latter John Lee was executed at Newgate on 4 April 1784 for forgery. His wife, who acted as Mrs Lee in the provinces, had previously been Mrs Jefferies, under which name she is noticed in this dictionary.

Lee, Mrs John [*fl. 1771–1778*]. *See* JEFFERIES, MRS.

Lee, Mary. *See* LEE, MRS JOHN, MARY.

Lee, Michael *d. 1721, musician.*

The burial of Michael Lee, "musishener aged," was recorded in the registers of St Giles, Cripplegate, on 6 May 1721.

Lee, Nathaniel *c. 1646?–1692, actor, playwright.*

There has been much disagreement about the date of Nathaniel Lee's birth: *The Dictionary of National Biography* tentatively suggests 1653. A. L. McLeod in *Modern Language Notes* in 1954 made a case for 1651, and Stroup and Cooke in their edition of Lee's plays argue for early 1646, which seems to fit best with what we know of Lee's schooling. A reference to Capricorn in the prologue to Lee's *Constantine* could be taken as an indication of the time of his birth—between 22 December and 19 January. Lee was the son of the Reverend Richard Lee (1612–1684), who inclined toward Catholicism during his years at Cambridge but became a deacon in the Church of England and who during the Commonwealth was an ardent Puritan but became a Royalist at the Restoration. The same turncoat pattern was followed by his son Nathaniel. Richard Lee's family consisted of at least 11 children, Nathaniel being one of the elder. Richard Lee's parish was Walthamstow, Essex, and perhaps Nathaniel was born there before his father moved to a post at Bishop's Hatfield, Hertfordshire.

Nathaniel was nominated by the Earl of Salisbury for a vacancy at Charterhouse on 20 May 1658, and he probably began his studies there soon afterward. He entered Trinity College, Cambridge, graduating A.B. in January 1668, according to the *DNB* (1668–69 according to McLeod and Stroupe and Cooke). Buckingham was Chancellor of Cambridge when Lee was there and is said to have taken an interest in young Nathaniel and to have brought the lad to London, but then to have lost interest in him. Just when Lee came to London is not certain, for he seems to have stayed at Cambridge for a while after graduating and to have contributed a poem to a collection eulogizing General Monck, who died on 3 January 1670. After being dropped by Buckingham, Lee turned to the stage for employment.

His first recorded role was the Captain of the Watch in *The Fatal Jealousy* at Dorset Garden on 3 August 1672. The following 18 February 1673 he attempted Duncan in *Macbeth*. The prompter Downes wrote later that Lee had the same fate as Otway and failed as an actor (Dennis called them both "wretched Actors"). Yet Cibber wrote in his *Apology* (1740) that Lee was

so pathetick a Reader of his own Scenes, that I have been inform'd by an Actor who was present, that while *Lee* was reading to Major *Mohun* at a Rehearsal, *Mohun*, in the Warmth of his Admiration, threw down his Part and said, Unless I were able to *play* it as well as you *read* it, to what purpose should I undertake it? And yet this very Author, whose Elocution rais'd such Admiration in so capital an Actor, when he attempted to be an Actor himself, soon quitted the Stage in an honest Despair of ever making any profitable Figure there.

The Lord Chamberlain's accounts show Lee to have served with the King's Company in 1674–75, after his failure with the Duke's players.

His association with the players of both companies no doubt helped him get his early plays produced. His *Nero* was presented at Drury Lane, the King's Company house, in May 1674, but was not well received by the critics, as Lee indicated in his dedication to the play when it was printed: "From the Criticks, whose Fury I dread, those Kill-men, and more than Jews, I appeal to your Lordship [the Earl of Rochester], as the Saint did to Caesar." Lee's second work, *Sophonisba*, was a success at Drury Lane in late April 1675. His third, *Gloriana*, appeared in late January 1676, but, as Lee put it in his dedication to the Duchess of Portsmouth, he was "blasted in my hopes, and press'd in my growth by a most severe, if not unjust Fortune." In the "Session of the Poets" (1676) in *Poems on Affairs of State*,

> Nat Lee stepp'd in next in hopes of a prize;
> Apollo remember'd he had hit once in thrice,
> By the rubies in's face he could not deny
> He had as much wit as wine could supply,
> Confess'd that indeed he'd a musical note,
> But sometimes strain'd so hard that he rattl'd i'the throat.
> Yet owning he had sense, to encourage him for't,
> He made him his Ovid in Augustus's court.

Harvard Theatre Collection
NATHANIEL LEE
engraving by Warren, after Thurston

By 1677 Lee had become friends with Dryden and with the Earl of Mulgrave, to whom his next play, *The Rival Queens*, was dedicated. That work, often called, *Alexander the Great* (its subtitle) was first performed on 17 March 1677 at Drury Lane, with the King and Queen in the audience. It was a stunning success and held the stage into the nineteenth century. *Mithridates* was produced in February 1678 and was thought by Lee's newest patron, the Earl of Dorset, to be the playwright's best work. Lee's position was so strong that Dryden asked him to collaborate on *Oedipus*, which was well received at the rival Dorset Garden playhouse in September 1678. Dryden and Lee had both given the King's Company first refusal of their earlier plays, and Dryden had agreed to supply his future works to that troupe. The desertion of Dryden and Lee to the Duke's players was an indication of the growing instability of the King's Company that was in 1682 to lead to a union of the two groups. After *Oedipus*, Lee gave his works to the Duke's players, despite the fact that he was a pensioner of the King's Company. Dryden in his preface to *Oedipus* said "I writ the First and Third Acts . . . and drew the Scenery [i.e. scenario] of the whole Play," and Lee did the rest.

Lee's next work was *The Massacre of Paris*, written in 1679 but banned and not produced until November 1689. His *Caesar Borgia* was given at Dorset Garden in May 1679. His next play, *The Princess of Cleve* is listed in *The London Stage* under September 1680, but Robert Hume has argued that it probably did not get produced until December 1682 or later, under the aegis of the United Company. In any case, it was not successful. Lee's *Theodosius*, Hume argues, probably belongs to the early summer of 1680 rather than September of that year; it was well received, especially, said Downes, by the court ladies. *Lucius Junius Brutus* was acted on 8 December 1680, but its antimonarchical sentiments caused it to be banned after six performances. After that Lee turned his coat and supported the King.

The Duke of Guise was written in collaboration with Dryden and presented by the United Company at Drury Lane on 28 November 1682. Dryden said in his vindication of the play that Lee had approached him about the project and that two-thirds of the play was Lee's work; Dryden claimed responsibility for the first scene,

Harvard Theatre Collection
NATHANIEL LEE ?
engraving by Watts, after Dobson?

the fourth act, and a little more than half of the fifth act. That did not quiet those who thought Dryden had seduced Lee into Toryism. Lee's new political stance was stated even more clearly in his last play, *Constantine*, which appeared at Drury Lane in November 1683.

Not long after *Constantine* was performed Lee went insane. Anthony Wood on 30 September 1684 said "Nathaniel Lee the playmaker endeavouring to reach high in expression in his plays broke his head and fell distracted." Lee was committed to Bedlam the following 11 November. His breakdown was perhaps facetiously stated by Wood, though at the time some thought that was why he went mad. Stroup and Cooke believe that a combination of excessive drinking and some inherited instability may have been the cause. Oldys said Lee's drinking went "beyond all Reason which flying up into his Face broke out into those Carbuncles which have been observed the rein and also touch'd his Brain Occasioning that Madness so much to be lamented in so rare a Genius." Lee remained in Bedlam until 11 April 1688. Poets made up descriptions of his state there, but they were probably fanciful, and one cannot know whether or not to believe Tom Brown, who claimed that Lee wrote a 25-act play while in the asylum. It has never been found, in any case.

After his release Lee had only his weekly pension of 10*s*. from the theatre to sustain him. He wrote no more, but in 1689 he published *The Princess of Cleve*, and on 7 November of that year *The Massacre of Paris*, which had been banned earlier, was given a performance at Drury Lane at which the new King and Queen were present. The anti-Catholicism of the work no longer offended. After that Lee languished. He had lodgings in Duke Street and took the short walk to Drury Lane each week to get his pension. In May 1692 he died. He was found on the street, literally dead drunk. Nathaniel Lee was buried at St Clement Danes on 6 May 1692.

R. G. Ham provided Lee with a modern biography in *Otway and Lee* in 1931, and Stroup and Cooke's edition of his *Works* is the only modern one. Yet in the Restoration and eighteenth century there were dozens of editions of some of Lee's plays—*Alexander the Great* and *Theodosius* being perhaps his most popular works—and during the 1700s his collected works were published. Today he is largely forgotten in the theatre, though scholars have still found him interesting, as the bibliography of Lee in 1962 in *Restoration and 18th Century Theatre Research* testifies.

The portrait in the Garrick Club (No 468), attributed to William Dobson, has been called the only authentic portrait of Nathaniel Lee. If the painting is by Dobson, however, it cannot be of Lee, for the artist died in 1646, before Lee was born. Gyles Isham in *Notes and Queries* in September 1953 claimed that the portrait is indeed by Dobson, but probably is of some courtier in the time of Charles I. Engraved versions of the Garrick Club picture were made by J. Watts, 1728; by B. Reading, published by T. & H. Rodd, 1820; and by an unknown engraver (n.d.). A crayon copy of the Dobson portrait was drawn by W. Faithorne; a photograph of it is in the British Museum. In the Dulwich Art Gallery is a canvas by an unknown artist (No 569), also said to be of Lee, about 1680. There is some similarity between the sitter of the Dulwich picture and the Garrick Club one, so, again, the former may not be of Lee. The Dulwich picture was the gift of Fairfax Murray in 1911. An eighteenth-century portrait, said to be a more romantic treatment, but similar to the Dulwich picture, was sold at Christie's in 1954. An engraved portrait by W. Ridley, said to have been made from an original drawing of Lee, was published as a plate to the *Monthly Mirror* in February 1802; but it is manifestly a late eighteenth-century concoction, and probably does not represent the playwright. A copy of the Ridley engraving, made by A. W. Warren, was published as a plate to *Effigies Poetical*, 1824; that engraving was described as made after a drawing of an original picture in the possession of Thomas Ashworth.

Lee, "Natty." *See* LEE, JAMES NATHANIEL.

Lee, Samuel [*fl.* 1794], *singer.*

Doane's *Musical Directory* of 1794 listed Samuel Lee, of No 218, Borough (High Street?), as a tenor who sang for the Cecilian Society.

Lee, William [*fl.* 1772–1807], *box bookkeeper, concessionaire.*

In a letter to the *Public Advertiser* on 7 November 1775, William Lee stated that since 1772 he had served refreshments in a room at the King's Theatre which provided a passage to the boxes. In 1773 alterations had been made to enclose the passage, and subsequently Lee was charged £60 per year for the room (with fire and light at his own expense). After Elizabeth Smith, who had charge of the concessions, died he was charged £160 plus £80 for coal and light. Lee lost £130 and was rescued only by a benefit sponsored by members of "the nobility."

No doubt the concessionaire was also the King's Theatre box bookkeeper of that name in the 1790s, but whether or not he was serving in the latter function in the 1770s is unknown. When the opera was playing at the Pantheon in 1790–91, after the King's Theatre burned in 1789, he published *The Plan and section of the boxes at the King's Theatre, Pantheon with An alphabetical list of the subscribers are most respectfully submitted to the nobility & gentry by their most humble, dutiful & obed.! serv.! William Lee. N° 51, G! Marybone Street, Portland Place*. In 1794 from the same address he published *A Plan of the boxes at the King's Theatre,*

Haymarket, which was opened for the 1792–93 season. The plan of the boxes of the King's Theatre, Haymarket, was reissued by Lee in 1804, 1805, and 1807. Lee's address was No 8, Walnut Tree Walk, Lambeth, in 1804 and No 18, in 1805 and 1807.

Lee-Lewes. *See* LEWES, CHARLES LEE.

Leeke. *See also* LEAK *and* LEAKE.

Leeke, Henry [*fl.* 1671–1672], *scenekeeper.*

The London Stage cites the scenekeeper Henry Leeke as a member of the King's Company at the Bridges Street Theatre and, after it burned, at Lincoln's Inn Fields Theatre in 1671–72. The Lord Chamberlain's accounts noted Leeke's membership in the troupe on 20 March 1672.

Leeming, Robert [*fl.* 1744–1768], *proprietor.*

Robert Leeming was the proprietor of the Lord Cobham's Head public house in Cold Bath Fields, where, in 1744, he erected in the main room an organ and offered concerts of selections from *Saul* and *Samson* with Blogg as one of the singers and a concert on the organ by Master Strologer. After the concert a ball was held. On 20 July Leeming advertised a concert ending with a "set of fireworks by several gentlemen lovers of that curious art—Rockets, line ditto, Katherine wheels, and many other things; likewise will be shewn the manner of Prince Charles's distressing the French after he passed the Rhine."

In an extra-illustrated copy of Daniel's *Merrie England* at the Huntington is a bill, pendated by Daniel 19 August 1762:

Lord Cobham's Head, Cold-Bath-Fields
THE Season of the Year being far advanc'd, I take this Opportunity of acquainting the Town, that the Musical Entertainment in the Gardens will be continued till Tomorrow Night, and no longer; during which short time I humbly hope my kind Benefactors will continue their Indulgence, by favouring me with their Company as they have hitherto done; and they may be sure of the best Liquor and Attendance, from
Their much-oblig'd humble Servant,
Robert Leeming
Note, As I have hitherto carry'd this Affair on, and spar'd no Expence that might render the Place Agreeable to the Company, I have made an extraordinary Addition for these two Nights to the Band of Musick, with several celebrated Performers, both Vocal and Instrumental, in particular Mr. Hockbroker [i.e. Hochbrucker], the famous Italian [*recte*: Bavarian] Harper, will perform several grand Pieces on the Harp, and Mr. Crosman on the Violdemore [*sic*], he being the only Performer on that Instrument in England.

Perhaps Robert Leeming was the Mr Leeming who played Wat Dreary in *The Beggar's Opera* at the New Concert Hall in Edinburgh on 23 March 1768.

Lees, T. [*fl.* 1794], *singer?*

Doane's *Musical Directory* of 1794 listed T. Lees, of Prestwich, Lancashire, as a bass (singer, presumably) who participated in the Handel performances at Westminster Abbey.

Leeson, Henrietta Amelia. *See* LEWIS, MRS WILLIAM THOMAS.

Leete, Mr [*fl.* 1793–1808], *singer.*

Mr Leete made his first appearance in public on 27 February 1793 singing at the Haymarket Theatre in Sedgwick's place in the Handel Memorial Concert. He was listed on 1 March as singing "He layeth the beams," "Jehovah Crowned," and "He was brought as a lamb" in *Redemption*, and on 8 March he sang for Sedgwick in *L'allegro ed il Penseroso*. He sang in the oratorio selections performed on the thirteenth and in the first part of the *Messiah* and other oratorio selections on the fifteenth.

Doane's *Musical Directory* of 1794 listed Leete as a principal bass who sang not only at the Haymarket (which Doane described as Colman's theatre) but also in the oratorios at Westminster Abbey and in concerts presented by the Academy of Ancient Music and the Concert of Ancient Music. On 15 January 1798 Leete sang in the *Messiah* at the Haymarket, and he sang in the oratorios again in January and March 1799. At Cambridge in the summer of 1808, according to a letter from Samuel Wesley to Dr Burney, Leete was a principal singer when Carnaby took his doctor's degree in music.

Leete, Mr [*fl.* 1794], *singer.*

Doane's *Musical Directory* of 1794 listed Mr Leete, of No 27, Surrey Street, Blackfriars, as a tenor (singer, presumably) who performed for the Cecilian Society.

LeFèvre, Mr [fl. 1728], *performer.*

At the Haymarket Theatre on 20 March 1728 Mr LeFevre (or LaFevre) shared a benefit with Mme Violante's daughter, it "being the only Reward allow'd them for Performing the whole Season." Perhaps LeFevre was the father of the Master LeFevre who danced with Mme Violante's troupe a few years later.

LeFèvre, Mr [fl. 1730–1750], *dancer.*

The Master LeFevre (or Lefavre, LaFevere) who was in Mme Violante's children's company at the Dame Street Theatre, Dublin, in 1730–31 was probably the Mr LeFevre of the later 1730s. Master LeFevre played the Butler in *The Cobler of Preston's Opera* in Dublin in February 1732 and came with Violante's troupe to London in the autumn of that year. At the Haymarket Theatre on 4 September he danced *Harlequin* with Miss Violante, and on 12 September the pair performed the same dance at the Great Assembly Room at Richmond Wells. Our subject was probably the Mr Lafayer who was in *Harlequin a Statue* in Edinburgh about February 1736. With his sister, Mlle LeFevre, he danced (or tried to) at the Haymarket in London on 9 October 1738. But a xenophobic audience, objecting to foreign performers, threw dried peas onto the stage, making dancing impossible.

In 1742 Mr Sturrock wrote to Lord Hertford from Lyon, speaking of the two LeFevres, "who came unluckily to London only a few days before the French Strollers were demolished in the Haymarket" in October 1738. Sturrock called LeFevre and his sister good dancers. Fuchs in his *Lexique* lists a Lefèvre dancing at Lyon in Mangot's troupe in 1749–50. He may have been our subject.

Lefèvre, Mrs [fl. 1778–1792], *actress, singer.*

Announced as making her first appearance in the town, Mrs Lefevre acted Alicia in *Jane Shore* at the Haymarket Theatre on 9 February 1778. Her second appearance there was on 24 March 1778 as Lady Anne in *Richard III* and Emily in *The Deuce Is in Him*. At the same theatre five weeks later, on 29 April, she acted Flora in *The Country Lasses*. Mrs Lefevre then

Harvard Theatre Collection

Mrs LEFÈVRE, as Richard III

artist unknown

joined a company that played 14 nights, from 25 May to 26 June 1778, at China Hall, Rotherhithe, where her known roles were Isabella in *The Wonder* and Mrs Gadabout in *The Lying Valet* on 25 May and 10 June, Miss Neville in *She Stoops to Conquer* on 29 May, and Lucy in *The Devil to Pay* on 3 June.

Mrs Lefevre's occasional appearances in specially-licensed performances at the Haymarket in 1778–79 included Goneril in *King Lear* on 17 September 1778, an unspecified character in *The Macaroni Adventurer* and Stormandra in *The Covent Garden Tragedy* on 28 December (when she had benefit tickets out), Lucetta Sharp in *Wit's Last Stake* on 8 March 1779, and Lady Science in *The Humours of Oxford* and Jacinta in *The Wrangling Lovers* on 15 March.

From 1779 to 1784 and again from 1787 through 1789 Mrs Lefevre was a regular member of Colman's summer company at the Haymarket. There in her first summer she acted Ina in Mrs Cowley's tragedy *Albina, Countess of Raimond* on 31 July 1779 and Dolce in O'Keeffe's musical farce *The Son-in-Law* on 14 August, both premieres. On 31 August 1779 she was the original Mrs Fustian in the elder Colman's comedy *The Separate Maintenance*. Among her other roles at the Haymarket during that period were a Lady in an Upper Box in Colman's *The Manager in Distress* (first performed on 30 May 1780); the male role of Peachum in *The Beggar's Opera* and Plumante in *Tom Thumb* in 1781; Signora Crotchetta in *Polly*, the Queen of Common Sense in *The Life and Death of Common Sense*, a character in *Tunbridge Walks*, a character in *Harlequin Teague*, and Lady Loverule in *The Devil to Pay* in 1782; Fadladinida in *Chrononhotonthologos* in 1783; a character in *Here There and Every Where* in 1785; Mrs Cheshire in *The Agreeable Surprise* and Mrs Honeycomb in *Polly Honeycomb* in 1787; Mrs Bruin in *The Mayor of Garratt*, Mrs Goodman in *The English Merchant*, and a character in *The Gnome* in 1788; Duenna in *The Spanish Fryar* and the Player Queen in *Hamlet* in 1789.

Upon occasion during the winter months in the 1780s Mrs Lefevre appeared in specially-licensed performances at the Haymarket: as Lady Science in *The Humours of Oxford* and Kitty in *High Life below Stairs* for her benefit on 28 March 1780 (when she lived at No 25, Frith Street, Soho); Widow Heedless in *The Artifice* and Dorothy in *The Ghost* on 16 October 1781; the Queen in *Richard III* and Widow Brady (with an epilogue song) in *The Irish Widow* on 15 December 1783; Mrs Willoughby in *A Word to the Wise* and a character in *The Talisman* on 21 January 1784; Lucetta in *Wit's Last Stake* on 9 February 1784; Molly in *The English Merchant* and Melissa in *The Lying Valet* on 22 March 1784; and Lady Randolph in *Douglas* on 18 December 1786. She played at King's Lynn in the summer of 1786. In a somewhat extraordinary instance, for her own benefit at the Haymarket on 4 March 1782 (when she still lived on Frith Street) Mrs Lefevre had acted the title character in *Richard III*, perhaps the only time in the eighteenth century that the role was played in London by a woman. Lady Ann was acted by Miss Shelburne and the Queen by Mrs Jackson. That night between the acts of the afterpiece, *Don Quixote in England*, Mrs Lefevre introduced a demonstration called *The Manual Exercise*.

When the younger Colman took over his father's interests in the Haymarket at the end of the summer of 1789, Mrs Lefevre was one of the performers discharged. Immediately, however, she was taken on at Covent Garden Theatre as a singer at £1 10s. per week. There, from 1789–90 through 1791–92, she assisted in the choruses of such pieces as *Harlequin's Chaplet* and *Macbeth*. On 16 November 1789 she acted the Player Queen in *Hamlet*, a role she performed several other times. On 5 March 1791 she played the Duchess in *Barataria*. On 12 May 1792 she shared in benefit tickets with other minor performers.

It is possible that the actress was the Mrs Lefevre, described as a prostitute, who became involved with Mrs Curtis, another lady "of the Cyprian Corps," in a fracas at Vauxhall in July 1791. Mrs Lefevre and a colleague, Mrs Fane, were brought by Mrs Curtis before the Bow Street Magistrate. According to *The Oracle* of 15 July 1791, Mrs Curtis had several months before threatened to throw Mrs Fane out of the green boxes at Covent Garden Theatre into the pit. The matter was resolved when the Magistrate persuaded Mrs Curtis to withdraw her action.

An anonymous engraving of Mrs Lefevre as Richard III was published by Torre & Thane, 1782.

LeFèvre, Master [fl. 1753], *dancer.*

On 1 November 1753 (not 1 October, as Fuchs reports in his *Lexique*) Master LeFevre and Mlle Prud'homme, two French children, danced at Drury Lane Theatre. They offered two turns, *The Neapolitans* and a "Dance in Demi-Charactère." The prompter Cross noted that they danced well and were much applauded. On 17 November young LeFevre was added to the dances in *The Genii*, and on 19 December he was a Savoyard in a dance called *The Savoyard Travellers*.

LeFèvre, Mlle [fl. 1711], *dancer.*

Mlle LeFevre (or LaFevre), announced as recently arrived from Brussels, danced at the Queen's Theatre on 20 March 1711. On 21 April she made her last appearance in England.

LeFèvre, Mlle [fl. 1736–1742], *dancer.*

Compardon in *Les Spectacles de la Foire* lists a Mlle LeFèvre as a dancer at the Opéra Comique at the time of the St Laurent Fair in 1736. She was probably the Mlle LeFevre who, with her brother, danced at the Haymarket Theatre on

9 October 1738 (*The London Stage* cites her, in error, we believe, as Mme LeFevre). The audience rioted against the French players. In 1742 Mlle LeFevre and her brother were evidently at Lyon, for Mr Sturrock wrote from there to Lord Hertford, commenting on the sad plight the brother and sister had been in when they appeared in London in 1738. They were called good dancers by Sturrock.

LeFèvre, Daniel [*fl.* 1685–1714?], trumpeter.

Daniel LeFevre (or Leffebre, LeFever, LaFaver) was sworn a trumpeter in the King's Musick on 18 May 1685. Sworn with him was the younger William Shore, who became a close friend of LeFevre and was in 1700 appointed Sergeant Trumpeter. The Lord Chamberlain's accounts cited LeFevre from time to time and showed that in 1697 his annual salary was £91 5s. When William Shore died in 1707 he left two broad pieces of gold and his silver snuff box to his "walking mate" LeFevre. Perhaps our subject was the Daniel LeFevre from the parish of St Giles in the Fields who married Jane Lenain of the Liberty of the Tower on 23 April 1714 at St Martin-in-the-Fields.

LeFèvre, Elias [*fl.* 1686], trumpeter.

Elias LeFèvre (or LeFeure) was one of four trumpeters in the King's Musick who, on 12 October 1686, were issued silver trumpets. That was the only citation of LeFèvre in the Lord Chamberlain's accounts.

LeFèvre, Elizabeth. See BRIDE, ELIZABETH.

LeFèvre, Joseph [*fl.* 1788–1790?], cittern player.

At the King's Theatre on 22 May 1788 in Act II of the ballet *Richard Coeur de Lion*, Joseph Lefèvre played on "a new French instrument, Le Cistre" (the cittern or cither). His full name is on the title page of his treatise, *A concise method to attain the art of playing on the cistre*, published in London about 1790, according to the British Library catalogue.

LeFèvre, Stephen d. 1717, musician.

Stephen LeFèvre (or LaFever) was cited on 23 October 1699 as one of several musicians serving Princess Ann of Denmark who were to be paid for performing at two balls and a play. The *Calendar of Treasury Books* shows that by 1 October 1714 LeFèvre was on a pension. In the *Historical Register Chronicle* is the report that on 19 October 1717 "Monsieur Le Fevre, a French Musician, being extreamly afflicted with the Gout, shot himself thro' the Head and dy'd immediately."

Leffebre. See LEFEVRE.

Leffler, J. Adam [*fl.* 1784?–1805], instrumentalist.

At the Handel Memorial Concerts at Westminster Abbey and the Pantheon in May and June 1784, the Leffler who played bassoon may have been J. Adam; a Leffler Junior played oboe, but it seems that he was probably James Henry, presumably Adam's brother. But distinguishing the two musicians is difficult, for they played many of the same instruments. J. Adam Leffler did not list the oboe, however, as one of his specialties when he was being considered for membership in the Royal Society of Musicians.

Leffler was proposed for membership in the Society on 6 February 1785 but was roundly rejected a month later by a vote of 19 to 6. Doane's *Musical Directory* of 1794 listed him as a violinist, violist, clarinetist, and bassoonist who played for the New Musical fund, in the oratorios at Drury Lane, and at the Handelian Concerts at Westminster Abbey. He was probably the "Leffler sen." who, with "Leffler Jun.," played in *The Thespian Panorama* at the Haymarket Theatre on 4 March 1795. His address was Green Street, Leicester Square, where James Henry Leffler also lived. Adam was still a subscriber to the New Musical Fund in 1805.

Leffler, James Henry c. 1764–1819, instrumentalist, composer.

James Henry Leffler was born about 1764 and was probably the Leffler Junior who played second oboe at the Handel Memorial Concerts in May and June of 1784 at Westminster Abbey and the Pantheon. He was proposed for membership in the Royal Society of Musicians on 2 January 1785 and elected unanimously a month later. His specialties at that time were listed as violin, viola, clarinet, and oboe, but he was also a bassoonist of reputation in later years. In 1785 he declared to the Society that he was single, 21 years of age, and playing at Covent Garden Theatre. He was, we think, the younger brother of J. Adam Leffler, who was ignominiously rejected by the Society (by a vote of 19 to 6) about the same time James Henry was accepted.

For the Society's St Paul's concerts in May of 1785 Leffler played violin, but from May 1789 to May 1794 he was the Leffler, we believe, who played oboe. Doane's *Musical Directory* of 1794, strangely, cited James Henry Leffler only as a bassoonist. His address was given as Green Street, Leicester Square, where Adam Leffler also lived. James Henry was cited as a performer at Drury Lane and in the Handelian Concerts at Westminster Abbey. He was probably the "Leffler Jun." whose music was used in *Mago and Dago* at Covent Garden Theatre on 26 December 1794 and who played in *The Thespian Panorama* at the Haymarket Theatre on 4 March 1795. He would seem to have been the Leffler who played violin at the St Paul's Concerts in 1795, 1796, and 1797, for Adam and Thomas Leffler, both of whom also played the violin, were not members of the Royal Society of Musicians. The playbills at Covent Garden Theatre cited Leffler playing in *Alexander's Feast* in February 1796, the *Messiah* in March 1797, *L'allegro ed il Penseroso* in February 1798, and the oratorio programs of February 1799 and February 1800. The theatre accounts show that Leffler was paid 6s. 8d. some nights and 5s. 10d. others, and in 1799–1800, at least, he appears to have been a regular member of the band, not just an oratorio performer.

In the summers of 1804, 1805, and 1807 through 1810 (and perhaps the missing years as well) a Leffler, probably James Henry in view of his other known theatrical playing, was in the band at the Haymarket Theatre, and in 1817 he played viola in the opera orchestra at the King's Theatre. According to Grove, Leffler also held the post of organist at St Katherine's Hospital by the Tower, the German Lutheran Church in the Savoy, and Streatham Chapel.

The minutes of the Royal Society of Musicians reveal a good deal of information about Leffler's family, for when Leffler died suddenly about March 1819 the Society needed to gather vital statistics in order to judge in what way they should support Leffler's widow and children. At Leffler's death his wife Elizabeth, née Shiel, was left with 11 children, three of whom were under 14. She and James Henry Leffler had been married at St Mary, Lambeth, on 21 July 1791. The three children whose births and baptisms were reported to the Royal Society of Musicians were Adam, born on 19 October 1806 (Grove dates his birth 1808); Edmond, born on 21 January 1809 and baptized on 5 March at St Mary, Lambeth; Francis Mark, born on 15 November 1810 and baptized at St Mary's on 16 December. Adam Leffler was not baptized until 16 November 1816 at St Mary's. He grew up to be a fine bass singer and died in 1857; Adam is the only Leffler given an entry by Grove (5th edition; Leffler is not in the *New Grove*).

Leffler, Mrs James Henry, Elizabeth, née Shiel *d. 1837, singer?*

Mrs Leffler sang at Sadler's Wells on 7 June 1788 and participated in *The What Is It?* at the Royal Circus on 12 May 1789. She was listed by Doane in his *Musical Directory* of 1794 as a singer who had participated in the Handelian Concerts at Westminster Abbey. Her address was given as Green Street, Leicester Square, where both J. Adam Leffler and James Henry Leffler lived.

Elizabeth Shiel and James Henry Leffler had married at St Mary, Lambeth, on 21 July 1791. When Leffler died in 1819 she applied to the Royal Society of Musicians for aid, and that organization investigated her case. The information they gathered concerning the three of her 11 children who were under the age of fourteen is set forth in James Henry Leffler's entry. She was left with eight other children over 14 and they, presumably, had been apprenticed or were otherwise cared for. Her application for aid from the Society was written on 6 April 1819, probably very soon after her husband's death. A note in the Society minutes in January 1821 shows that by then Mrs Leffler was receiving £41 annually from some other source, hence the Society reduced whatever it had been giving her as an allowance to £20 10s. annually.

By November 1822 her son Edmond (or Edmund) was soon to become 14 and wished to be apprenticed to a musician; Mrs Leffler sought from the Society the apprentice fee. In

September 1824 she applied for a fee for her son Francis, who was bound in January 1825 to Mr Simcock—probably the M. Simcock who in 1819 had certified that James Henry Leffler's dues were paid up and his widow was eligible for a pension. Francis must not have liked apprenticeship under Simcock, however, for in November 1828 Mrs Leffler assured the Society that Mr Barber, a perfumer of Bishopsgate Street, would accept Francis as an apprentice.

In March 1832 Edmund Leffler (spelled Edmund regularly now) was granted £10 for being a good apprentice. But Francis seems to have been a problem. On 4 November 1832 Henry Leffler (evidently one of the elder Leffler offspring) told the Society that his brother Francis's master, Mr Barber the perfumer, had gone out of business. The Society was not unwilling to grant permission for Francis to be bound to yet another master. On 6 January 1833 the Society learned that Francis was apprenticed to Mr Boucher, a hairdresser. On 7 February 1836, when Francis would have been 26 years old, he requested a £10 apprentice gratuity. The minutes show that on 6 March 1836 Francis Mark Leffler was granted £10 by the Society when they learned that his master Mr Boucher was dead. The minutes say nothing more about that peculiar sequence of events.

On 3 September 1837 the society was advised that Elizabeth Leffler had died, but no application had been made for funeral expenses. Perhaps her son Adam, who was by then a successful singer, paid for her burial.

Leffler, Thomas *1773–1819?, violoncellist, violinist.*

Thomas Leffler was born in London on 2 December 1773 and baptized at St Martin-in-the-Fields on the nineteenth. He was the son of Adam and Jude Leffler, according to the files of the Royal Society of Musicians, which needed such information when they considered Thomas's proposed membership on January 1798. Thomas was put up for membership by James Henry Leffler, who was perhaps his elder brother, though the relationship cannot be certainly established. Thomas was elected unanimously on 1 April 1798, at which time he was described as a violoncellist and violinist, 24 years old, who was then employed at the Covent Garden Theatre. Thomas played 'cello at the Society's St Paul's Concert in May 1799 and again in May 1800.

At St George, Hanover Square, on 15 December 1800 Thomas Leffler married Elizabeth Thompson. Leffler played in the St Paul's Concerts each May from 1802 to 1806, but after that something unfortunate must have happened to the Thomas Lefflers. On 6 December 1812 his wife applied to the Royal Society of Musicians for support for herself and her two children. She was granted two guineas, but in March 1813, when she applied again for help, she was refused.

Thomas Leffler must have died in 1819, the same year James Henry Leffler died. His wife Elizabeth was granted the usual widow's allowance (whatever that was) by the Royal Society of Musicians on 3 May 1819. At that time she had two children over the age of 14—and they, according to the Society rules, would not have been a burden on the Society. The Society minutes indicate donations to her over the years through 1838. She died, senile, on 15 April 1851 at No 4, Robert Street, Bedford Row, St Andrew Holborn, at the age of 80.

Le Fillier, Mons *[fl. 1675], musician.*

On 27 May 1675 Nicholas Staggins was paid £221 for his participation and that of his band members in the court masque *Calisto* the previous February. Among those to be paid by Staggins was Monsieur Le Fillier, one of five musicians simply listed as Frenchmen.

Le Fond. *See* LA FOND.

Le Font. *See* LA FONT.

Lefronde, Mons *[fl. 1733], dancer.*

Monsieur Lefronde made his "first appearance on any stage" in England on 16 March 1733 at the Haymarket Theatre dancing Harlequin in *Love Runs All Dangers*. The work was repeated through 26 March.

Le Gagneur. *See* GAGNEUR.

Legar or **Legard.** *See* DELAGARDE, LA GARDE, LAGUERRE.

Leger. *See also* ST LEGER.

Leger, Mons [fl. 1728], *dancer, choreographer.*

Mme Violante's troupe presented an entertainment called *The Rivals* at the Haymarket Theatre on 21 February 1728, with Monsieur Leger, who with Lalauze composed the work, playing Harlequin. The two dancers shared a benefit on 27 March when *The Rivals* was repeated.

Léger [Jean Marie?] [fl. 1762?–1782], *dancer.*

A dancer named Léger was employed at the King's Theatre from 23 February to 22 June 1782. He danced in 14 performances of Noverre's ballet *Rinaldo and Armida*, which premiered on 23 February. On 9 March he replaced Slingsby in *Les Amans réunis*. He also danced in *La Rosière de Salency* on 19 March and seven other times.

While in London Léger occupied the large room of the piazza of the King's Theatre, which he used for a dancing school. By 1783 he vacated the premises, which were then occupied by a Mr Ridaut, and subsequently, beginning in 1785, by Harry Angelo.

Possibly this Léger was the dancer of that name who had been engaged as a *figurant* in 1762 at Stuttgart and later was among the ballet personnel at the Paris Opéra in 1776 or the Jean Marie Léger who in 1780 was dancing at the Théâtre des Grands Danseurs du Roi. At the latter place the title dance in *Le Sabotier*, a comedy, was performed by Léger on 15 September 1781. In 1780, according to Campardon's *Les Spectacles de la foire*, Léger had been arrested twice, once over the loss of money belonging to his employer and again, with Nicolet, when both were charged with having neglected their service. There is no evident connection between our subject and the Mons Legé who, accompanied by his wife, was a member of a French ballet company that performed at the Haymarket Theatre in Boston, Massachusetts, in 1796–97.

Legg, Miss. *See* DUNCAN, MRS TIMOTHY.

Legg, Jonathan *d. 1778, singer, actor.*

Announced in the bills as making his first appearance on any stage, Jonathan Legg played an Infernal Spirit in a revival of *The Necromancer* at Covent Garden on 11 November 1751. After several other appearances in that role, Legg performed Silenus in *Apollo and Daphne* on 4 December 1751, a Witch in *Harlequin Sorcerer* on 11 February 1752, and in the choral sections of *Macbeth* on 17 March 1752. On 25 April 1752, when he shared a benefit with Desse and Mrs Chambers, Legg offered "Honour and Arms" as a solo and "Old Chiron" as a duet with Lowe. In 1752–53, when his name was sometimes printed in the bills as Legge, he sang in the solemn dirge in *Romeo and Juliet* and also appeared again in the above-named pieces. On 2 May 1753 he sang in *Theodosius*.

At Covent Garden a total of 21 seasons, through 1772–73, Legg's bass voice was heard in many pantomime choruses and dozens of roles, among which were a Recruit in *The Fair* and Pluto in *The Rape of Proserpine* in 1759–60, Merlin in *Harlequin Skeleton* in 1760–61, Morpheus in *Apollo and Daphne* in 1761–62, and Cepheus in *Perseus and Andromeda* and Jupiter in *Midas* in 1763–64. His salary between 1760–61 and 1767–68 was 5s. per night, or £1 10s. per week. On 7 May 1760, for his shared benefit with Bennet, Legg's net receipts were about £62. On 6 May 1762, when he again shared a benefit with Bennet, the receipts for which are unknown, tickets could be had from him at the Crown and Anchor Tavern in the Strand.

Legg also sang in performances of the *Messiah* at the Foundling Hospital in May 1754, for which he was paid 10s. 6d., and at Marylebone Gardens in 1763 and 1765. At the latter place on 28 June 1763, he was identified as a Free Mason in a bill for *Alexander's Feast*, and on 6 August 1765, he had a benefit while singing in *Solomon*. In the summer of 1768 he performed again there and also at Ranelagh Gardens.

In 1774–75 Legg transferred to Drury Lane Theatre for a salary of £2 per week. He made his first appearance there on 5 October 1774 as Nigromant in *A Christmas Tale*, a role he often played thereafter. That season he also performed vocal parts in *The Genii*, *The Maid of the Oaks*, *Harlequin's Jacket*, *A Peep behind the Curtain*, *Timanthes*, and *Comus*, in addition to Grumble in *The Cobler*, Hecate in *Macbeth*, Cant in *Phebe*, and a Soldier in *The Deserter*. Over the next several seasons he sang in *Old City Manners*, *May Day*, *Harlequin's Invasion*, *The Tempest*, and other pieces. On 6 May 1777, when tickets were available from him in Market Street, St James's Market, Legg shared net benefit receipts of about £164 with Fawcett and Kear. In the summer of 1778 he played Jupiter in eight performances of *Midas* at the Haymarket Theatre, making his first appearance there on 12 June.

Legg began the 1778–79 season at Drury Lane in his usual modest capacity, singing several times in *The Tempest*, in which on 27 November 1778 he seems to have made his last stage contribution. The *Gentleman's Magazine* for December reported his death on 19 December 1778.

Administration of Jonathan Legg's estate, value unspecified, was granted on 4 January 1779 to his widow, Mary Legg, of the parish of St James, Westminster. At Drury Lane on 19 May 1779 Widow Legg (who was not a performer) shared net benefit receipts of £125 15s. with Mrs Colles and Miss Kirby. The Miss Legg who married the provincial actor Timothy Duncan at Chester Cathedral on 3 October 1778 may have been the daughter of Jonathan and Mary Legg; as Mrs Duncan she passed most of her career in the provinces but acted in London in 1788. Joseph Legg, an actor at Boston and Providence in 1814 and 1815 and at Baltimore in 1816 may also have been related; he married a Miss Banister of Boston, a wealthy young lady who turned actress and who, after Joseph Legg's death in Louisiana, became Mrs Stone.

Le Grand, Mrs [*fl.* 1677–1678], *actress.*
Mrs Le Grand played Eugenia in *The Counterfeit Bridegroom* and Hesione in *The Siege of Babylon* in September 1677 at the Dorset Garden playhouse. In January 1678 she appeared as Phrinias in *Timon of Athens*.

Le Grange. *See also* LA GRANGE.

Le Grange, Mons [*fl.* 1736], *dancer.*
Monsieur Le Grange danced Punch in a new comic turn called *The Pastoral* when it was performed at the Haymarket Theatre on 20 February 1736.

Le Guerre. *See* LAGUERRE.

Leicester, Mr [*fl.* 1735], *actor?*
Venice Preserv'd was performed at the Haymarket Theatre on 10 July 1735 for the benefit of a Mr Leicester and the entertainment of the "Grand, and the rest of the Brethren of the Antient and Honourable Society of Gregorians." Pierre was played by "a Gentleman," who may have been Leicester, and Jaffeir was acted by the Bard of the order, evidently Henry Giffard.

Leicester, Eliza, [Mrs Thomas?] [*fl.* 1769–1794], *actress.*
Eliza Leicester performed in Miller's troupe in Derby on 17 February 1769, was probably active in the provinces in the years that followed, and acted the Duchess of York in a single performance of *Richard III* at the Haymarket Theatre in London on 24 March 1778. She was perhaps the Mrs "Leister" at Manchester in February 1783 and at Newcastle in 1789.

On 7 October 1793 Mrs Leicester began an engagement at Covent Garden Theatre as the Nurse in *Romeo and Juliet*. The *European Magazine* noted that she seemed to be a veteran of the stage and had passed the heyday of life. Her salary, according to the account books, was £2 weekly or £69 6s. 8d. for the season. In addition to the Nurse, she played Mrs Drugget in *Three Weeks after Marriage*, Margaret in *The Deserter*, Marcelina in *The Follies of Day*, Mrs Fardingale in *Grief à-la-Mode*, Dorcas in *Rosina*, Fidget in *Rose and Colin*, Lady Pride in *Barnaby Brittle*, Deborah in *Love in a Village*, a Spanish Lady in *Barataria*, and a Landlady in *The Chances*. Her last appearance was as Marcelina on 5 June 1794.

The *Index to The London Stage* calls her Mrs Thomas Leicester, but we have no evidence of her marriage.

Leicester, Thomas [*fl.* 1673], *musician.*
On 17 July 1673 the Lord Chamberlain ordered the apprehension of Thomas Leicester and six other musicians for playing music without permits.

Leidler, Johan Christopher *d.* 1793, *musician.*
On 3 February 1793 the widow of "Johan Christr Leidler" reported to the Royal Society of Musicians, of which her husband had been a member, that he had died. She requested the

usual allowance, and on 7 April she was granted £8 for funeral expenses. Her case, however, was apparently severe, for the Board of Governors referred it to the full membership, which on 7 July voted her an allowance of 15 guineas per year.

Leiger. *See* LEDIGER.

Leigh. *See also* LEE.

Leigh, Anthony *d. 1692, actor.*
The History of the English Stage (1741) said that Anthony Leigh (or Lee) was born of a good Northamptonshire family. He came to London and on 27 December 1671, along with Philip Griffin, George Bristow, William Scott, and John Perin, was ordered arrested by the Lord Chamberlain for having performed plays in and about London without a license. It is not certain whether or not Leigh was at that time a member of the Duke's Company. *The London Stage* cites him as Polites in *Herod and Mariamne* in September 1671, but Robert Hume has made a convincing case for dating that performance August 1673. Leigh was named in a cast list as Pacheco, the Fop, in *The Reformation* at the Dorset Garden playhouse. Again, Hume has argued that *The London Stage* dating of May 1673 may be as much as a year too late. Anthony's bride, Elinor Dixon Leigh, was first cited as Mrs Leigh in *The Citizen Turn'd Gentleman* in July 1672 at the latest (Hume argues for December 1671 or January 1672). All we can say is that perhaps Anthony was a member of the Duke's Company in the 1671–72 season or a part of it.

In any case, the scanty records reveal no mention of Leigh in casts again until 10 January 1676, when he played Rash in *The Coun-*

National Portrait Gallery

ANTHONY LEIGH, as Father Dominic
by Kneller

Harvard Theatre Collection

Called JOHN DUNSTALL, as Dominic
engraving after Dodd

try *Wit* at Dorset Garden. After that he was regularly named in cast lists and became a popular speaker of prologues and epilogues. His parts before 1682, when the Duke's and King's Company were united, included the title role in *Tom Essence*, Old Bellair in *The Man of Mode*, Sir Formal Trifle in *The Virtuoso*, Count de Benevent in *The Wrangling Lovers*, Zechiel in *Madam Fickle*, the title role in *The Cheats of Scapin*, Old Fumble in *The Fond Husband*, Monsieur in *The French Conjurer*, Sir Oliver Santloe in *The Counterfeit Bridegroom*, Aelius in *Timon of Athens*, the title part in *Sir Patient Fancy*, Malageen in *Friendship in Fashion*, Don Gomez in *The Counterfeits*, Sir Frederick Banter in *Squire Oldsapp*, Petro in *The Feign'd Curtizans*, Pandarus in *Troilus and Cressida*, possibly Gripe in *The Woman Captain*, Ascanio Sforza in *Caesar Borgia*, Sir Lubberly Widgeon in *The Virtuous Wife*, Paulo in *The Loving Enemies*, Sir Jolly Jumble in *The Soldier's Fortune*, Mr Dashit in *The Revenge*, St André in *The Princess of Cleve*, Dominic in *The Spanish Fryar*, probably Teague in *The Lancashire Witches*, Guilion in *The False Count*, Dashwell in *The London Cuckolds*, Abednego Suck Thumb in *Mr Turbulent*, Sir Oliver Oldcut in *The Royalist*, Antonio in *Venice Preserv'd*, and Sir Anthony Meriwell in *The City Heiress*. Montague Summers conjectured that Leigh may also have acted Wariston in *The Roundheads* and Ballio in *The Jealous Lovers*.

Not only was Leigh given important roles, mostly comic, beginning in 1676–77, but he quickly established himself with the public and was alluded to frequently in prologues, epilogues, and other writings. For example, the epilogue to *1 Rover* in 1677 poked fun at the fops in the audience:

Oh that our Nokes, or Tony Lee could show
A Fop but half so much to th' Life as you.

In 1679 Mulgrave and Dryden's *Essay Upon Satire* made another reference:

Yet he will laugh at his best friends and be
Just as good company as Nokes or Lee.

The epilogue to *The Feign'd Curtizans* the same year spoke of Nokes and Leigh as specialists in "Fops of all sorts."

With the United Company at Drury Lane (and sometimes Dorset Garden) from 1682 until his death ten years later Leigh acted Major Oldfox in *The Plain Dealer*, Bessus in *A King and No King*, Bartoline in *City Politics*, Jenkin in *Dame Dobson*, Beaugard's Father in *The Atheist*, a Plebeian in *Julius Caesar*, Hearty in *The Jovial Crew*, Sir Paul Squelch in *The Northern Lass*, Rogero in *The Disappointment*, Trappolin in *A Duke and No Duke*, Sir Nicholas Callico (*The Dictionary of National Biography* says Crack) in *Sir Courtly Nice*, Security in *Cuckold's Haven*, Frugal in *The Commonwealth of Women*, Teague in *The Committee*, Harlequin in Mountfort's *Doctor Faustus*, Don Ariell in *The Banditti*, Sir Feeble Fainwou'd in *The Lucky Chance*, Fribble in *Epsom Wells*, Scaramouch in *The Emperor of the Moon*, a Soldier in *The Injured Lovers*, Justice Grub in *The Fool's Preferment*, Sir William Belfond in *The Squire of Alsatia*, Chylas in *Valentinian*, Sir William Wealthy in *The Fortune Hunters*, La Roch in *Bury Fair*, Mustapha in *Don Sebastian*, Don Francisco in *The Successful Strangers*, Lord Stately in *The English Frier*, Teague in *The Amorous Bigotte*, Geta in *The Prophetess*, the Host in *The Merry Devil of Edmonton*, an Abbe in *Sir Anthony Love*, Mercury in *Amphitryon*, Tarleton, Bishop of Hereford in *Edward III*, Tope in *The Scowrers*, Lady Addleplot in *Love for Money*, Falstaff in *The Merry Wives of Windsor*, Sir Thomas Reveller in *Greenwich Park*, Truman Senior in *Cutter of Coleman Street*, Waspish in *Win Her and Take Her*, Myn Heer Van Grin in *The Marriage-Hater Match'd*, Cleonidas in *Cleomenes*, Gisgon in *Regulus*, Sir Thomas Vaughan in *Henry II*, Major General Blunt in *The Volunteers*, Coligny in *The Villain*, Ralph in *Sir Solomon*, and possibly Aldo in *Mr Limberham*.

The version of the *Satyr on the Players* (c. 1684) at Ohio State has a verse devoted to Leigh that runs:

But now ye Character of one you'l read,
Who strove so long a fool to be believ'd,
That at ye last he is a fool indeed,
Witness his bant'ring Nonsence, & his Noise,
Stealing from Stalls, and Fooling with ye Boys.
If still thou play'st such Tricks, the world shall see
The diff'rence 'twixt Jack Sparks & Tony Lee,
Which is the Sillyest Cur, ye Dog or thee.

Leigh, like any good comedian, introduced touches of his own in parts he played. Aphra Behn, when criticized for the bawdiness of *The Lucky Chance*, replied, "they cry, *That Mr. Leigh opens his Night Gown, when he comes into the Bride-Chamber*; if he do, which is a Jest of his own making, and which I never saw, I hope he has his Cloaths on underneath? And if so, where is the indecency?" Leigh's ad-libbing once displeased James II. The United Company performed *The Committee* at Oxford at some point. The head of University College was Obadiah Walker, who had turned Catholic during James's reign. In the performance Leigh, as Teague, dragged in another character, Obadiah, with a halter about his neck, threatening to hang him for refusing to drink the King's health. Leigh ad-libbed a line, saying he was going to hang Obadiah because, "Upon my Shoule, he has shanged his Religion." The Oxford audience was delighted, but Leigh was made to understand that James II was highly displeased.

Anthony Leigh and his wife Elinor were close friends of Thomas Shadwell and spent some time in the autumn of 1690 in Chelsea, where Shadwell lived. When Shadwell drew up his will that year the Leighs were witnesses, and after the playwright's death, they testified on 13 December 1692 to the authenticity of the will. Ironically, Anthony Leigh at that time had only about a week to live. Narcissus Luttrell reported on 24 December 1692 that "Anthony Lee, the famous comedian died on Wednesday last," 21 December (Wood dated his death 22 December). Cibber reported later that Leigh had died of a fever brought on by shock over the death of his fellow actor William Mountfort on 9 December. Leigh was buried at his parish church, St Bride, Fleet Street, on 25 December 1692.

The church registers contain a number of references to Leigh and his wife Elinor, but there was another Anthony Leigh in the parish; he was buried at St Bride's on 27 July 1684. Perhaps he was the actor's father. Marmaduke, the son of "Anthony Lee and Elianor" was christened on 15 March 1676. Their daughter, "Eleanor" was christened on 26 April 1678 but must have died in infancy. Their son Francis, who became an actor in the early eighteenth century, was christened on 28 July 1680. A second "Elenor" was christened on 10 September 1681; a son Anthony was christened on 3 July 1684 and was doubtless the Anthony Leigh who was buried on 23 May 1710. A daughter Charlot was christened on 23 September 1686, a son John on 22 July 1688, and a daughter Anne on 22 July 1691. The registers contain no mention of their son Michael, so he may have been born before the Leighs moved into the parish.

Fortunately some comments on Leigh's acting have survived. The Earl of Ailesbury commented on Leigh's performance as Lady Addleplot in *Love for Money* in January 1791:

My Lady Fenwick was a great intriguer, and had always castles in the air in her imagination to that degree, that I was present at a play where she was brought in. If I mistake not it was The Boarding School [the play's subtitle], and the famous comic Mr Lee, in woman's clothes represented her to the life, and so exactly had her features and complexion that one could hardly have distinguished one from the other.

Colley Cibber joined the United Company before Leigh died and remembered in his *Apology* (1740) Tony's talent; he did not agree with Ailesbury:

Leigh was of the mercurial kind, and though not so strict an Observer of Nature, yet never so wanton in his Performance as to be wholly out of her Sight. In Humour he lov'd to take a full Career, but was careful enough to stop short when just upon the Precipice: He had great Variety in his manner, and was famous in very different Characters: In the canting, grave Hypocrisy of the *Spanish* Friar he stretcht the Veil of Piety so thinly over him, that in every Look, Word, and Motion you saw a palpable, wicked Slyness shine through it—Here he kept his Vivacity demurely confin'd till the pretended Duty of his Function demanded it, and then he exerted it with a cholerick sacerdotal Insolence. . . . *Leigh* rais'd the Character as much above the Poet's Imagination as the Character has sometimes rais'd other actors above themselves! and I do not doubt but the Poet's Knowledge of *Leigh*'s Genius help'd him to many a pleasant Stroke of Nature, which without that Knowledge never might have enter'd into his Conception.

The Earl of Dorset had Kneller paint Leigh in the character of the Spanish Fryar.

Cibber also liked Leigh in *The Soldier's Fortune*: "In Sir Jolly he was all Life and laughing Humour, and when *Nokes* acted with him in the same Play, they returned the Ball so dexterously upon one another, that every Scene between them seem'd but one continued Rest [i.e. rally] of Excellence." As Sir William Belfond in *The Squire of Alsatia*, said Cibber,

Leigh shew'd a more spirited Variety than ever I saw any actor, in any one Character, come up to:

. . . the high Colouring, the strong Lights and Shades of Humour that enliven'd the whole and struck our Admiration with Surprize and Delight, were wholly owing to the Actor. . . . Leigh had many masterly Variations which [Pinkethman] cou'd not, nor ever pretended to reach, particularly in the Dotage and Follies of extreme old Age, in the Characters of *Fumble* in the *Fond Husband*, and the Toothless Lawyer [Bartoline] in the *City Politicks*, both which Plays liv'd only by the extraordinary Performance of Nokes and Leigh.

John Crown, the author of *City Politics*, would have disagreed with Colley's last statement. He said that the way Leigh spoke in the play, "which all the comedians can witness was my own invention, and Mr. Lee was taught it by me; to prove this farther I have printed Bartoline's part in the manner of spelling by which I taught it Mr. Lee."

Cibber appreciated the confidence Leigh exuded:

Now, the Judgment of *Leigh* always guarded the happier Sallies of his Fancy from the least Hazard of Disapprobation: he seem'd not to court, but to attack your Applause, and always came off victorious; nor did his highest Assurance amount to any more than that just Confidence without which the commendable Spirit of every good Actor must be abated; and of this Spirit *Leigh* was a most perfect Master. He was much admir'd by King *Charles*, who us'd to distinguish him when spoke of by the Title of *his Actor*. . . .

Godfrey Kneller's full-length portrait of Anthony Leigh as Dominic in *The Spanish Fryar*, painted and signed by the artist in 1689, is in the National Portrait Gallery (No 1280). Sold from the John Green collection at Christie's on 22 July 1871 (lot 195), it was bought by John Wylie, in whose memory it was presented to the National Portrait Gallery in November 1900. This version is said to have hung at one time at Kensington Palace. It was engraved, in reverse, by J. Smith probably soon after it was painted. A copy in the Garrick Club, three-quarter length, attributed to Kneller, is perhaps actually that by Ranelagh Barret noted by Vertue in his notebooks in 1746. It shows the box in the right hand, while the National Portrait Gallery version shows it in the left.

A picture of John Dunstall in the same role is a replica in many respects of the Kneller portrait of Leigh; the engraving of Dunstall by Walker, after Dodd, was published in 1776, clearly stipulating the subject as Dunstall. We mistakenly reproduced the Smith engraving of Leigh in the notice of Dunstall in this dictionary (IV, 506), when the Walker engraving of Dunstall was intended.

The Garrick Club version of Leigh as Dominic is stated by Joseph Knight in *The Dictionary of National Biography* to be the one commissioned by the Earl of Dorset. But the Kneller in the National Portrait Gallery seems the more likely candidate. A version or copy, which perhaps is the one that made its way to the Garrick Club, was sold in the Earl of Godolphin's collection in 1803.

Leigh, Mrs Anthony, Elinor, née Dixon? [*fl.* 1670–1709?], *actress*.

Though there seems to be no proof positive that the actress Mrs Dixon became the wife of Anthony Leigh, most sources think the marriage highly probable. There was another Mrs Leigh—Elizabeth, the daughter of Mrs Mynns—who was active in theatricals at the fairs in the 1680s, and some early sources, such as *The Dictionary of National Biography*, confused the two women and thought Anthony Leigh's wife was named Elizabeth. Elinor Dixon was probably the daughter of the actor James Dixon, who was one of the original members of Sir William Davenant's Duke's Company at the Lincoln's Inn Fields Theatre, but there is no certainty about their relationship.

Mrs Dixon (the "Mrs" did not necessarily mean she was married) played Melvissa in *The Woman's Conquest* in September 1670 or earlier, argue Robert Hume and Judith Milhous in the 1974 *Harvard Library Bulletin* (*The London Stage* dates the play November 1670). She was then seen as Orinda in *Cambyses*, Petilla in *The Six Days Adventure*, and Betty in *The Town Shifts* before the Duke's Company moved from Lincoln's Inn Fields to their new theatre in Dorset Garden in November 1671. She acted Julia in *Charles VIII* in late November as Mrs Dixon and shortly after that married Anthony Leigh. Her first billing as Mrs Leigh was for the role of Betty Trickmore in *The Citizen Turn'd Gentleman*, which *The London Stage* dates 4 July 1672 but the premiere of which, Hume and Milhous argue, may have been as early as December 1671 or January 1672. Mrs Leigh played Beatrice in *The Careless Lovers* on 12 March 1673, but after the 1672–73 season she left the stage for a while. J. H. Wilson in *All the King's Ladies* suggests that she did so probably because of the birth of her son Michael, who began his stage career in 1690. No birth record for Michael has been found, though the baptisms of several other children of Anthony and Elinor Leigh are noted in the registers of St Bride, Fleet Street.

Mrs Leigh was cited again in a cast on 10 January 1676 when she played Isabella in *The Country Wit*, according to the printed edition of the play. The 1676 edition of *The Man of Mode* listed Mrs Leigh as Lady Woodvill, and the Lord Chamberlain's accounts show that work to have been performed on 11 March 1676. But the St Bride's registers show the baptism of Marmaduke (after the actor Marmaduke Watson?), son of Anthony and Elinor Leigh, on 15 March. Either Elinor did not act at that performance, or the baptism may have been late, or the registers refer to a different woman; our guess is that the registers do concern our subject.

Elinor played Moretta in *The Rover* and Seintilla in *The French Conjurer* in the spring of 1677, then again left the stage until January 1680. Wilson suggests that the reason may have been the birth of Rachel Leigh, who is known to have acted a tiny part in 1693, but the St Bride's registers mention no Rachel. They do, however, show the christening of a daughter Elinor, who died in infancy, in April 1678. *The London Stage* dates Mrs Leigh's appearance as Mrs Dashit in *The Revenge* in late June 1680, but Hume argues for as early as January of that year, and in view of the fact that the Leighs christened their son Francis in July 1680, his arguments (on quite different grounds) suit the register information. In September 1680 Mrs Leigh, according to *The London Stage*, played Touron in *The Princess of Cleve*; Hume argues that that play was probably not performed until December 1682.

The London Stage's next listing for Elinor is as Engine in *The London Cuckolds* on 22 November 1681; Hume and Milhous suggest that the premiere took place about a month earlier. Either way, performances would not have conflicted with a pregnancy; the Leighs baptized a second Elinor in September 1681. Mrs Leigh's last known role with the Duke's Company before it united with the King's players was Mrs Closet in *The City Heiress* in late April 1682.

Montague Summers in his edition of Behn's *Works* conjectured that Elinor may have acted either Lady Cromwell or Gilliflower in *The Roundheads*, which had been given in late November or early December 1681.

Elinor's first recorded role with the United Company was Mrs Prudence in *Dame Dobson* on 31 May 1683. The 1684 edition of *The Disappointment* has her down for Clara; the play was performed in April of that year, though there is no certainty that she performed in it then; her son Anthony was christened on 3 July 1684. A University of Pennsylvania copy of *Epsom Wells* has a manuscript cast naming Mrs Leigh as Mrs Bisket; it dates 1686–87 or perhaps earlier. The Leigh's daughter Charlot was baptized in September 1686. Again Mrs Leigh absented herself from the theatre for about two years, during which time, in July 1688, her son John was baptized.

Sometime between 1688 and 1690, according to a manuscript cast at Claremont College, Mrs Leigh acted Marcellina in *Valentinian*, and in March 1689 she played Lady Sly in *The Fortune Hunters*. A manuscript cast for *Othello*, dating about 1688–89, has her listed as Emilia, and one for *Pastor Fido*, dating about spring 1689 has her as Gerana. In 1689–90 she acted Johayma in *Don Sebastian* and Lady Pinch-gut in *The English Frier*. Manuscript casts show her as Lady Clare in *The Merry Devil of Edmonton* in 1690–91 and Lady Woodvill in *The Man of Mode* (again) about 1690–92. In December 1690 she was Lady Maggot in *The Scowrers* (which the Leighs had read in manuscript, liked, and helped Shadwell get produced), and in January 1691 she played Oyley in *Love for Money*. No other roles are known for her for a year, and, as it happened, a daughter Anne was christened in July 1691. Mrs Leigh played Mrs Ford in *The Merry Wives of Windsor* on 31 December 1691. In February 1692 she played Rhadegonda in *The Rape*, and in mid-November 1692 she was Mrs Hackwell in *The Volunteers*.

When Thomas Shadwell drew up his will in 1690, the Leighs served as his witnesses and on 13 December 1692 after his death they testified to its authenticity. Elinor's husband Anthony died on 21 December and was buried at St Bride's on the twenty-fifth. Mrs Leigh did not perform, so far as the records show, until late February 1693, when she acted Siam in *The Maid's Last Prayer*. From then until the break-up of the United Company in 1694 she was seen as Lucy in *The Old Bachelor*, Marmalette in *The Richmond Heiress*, Mrs Sneaksby in *A Very Good Wife*, Lady Meanwell in *The Female Vertuosos*, Lady Plyant in *The Double Dealer*, the Nurse in *The Fatal Marriage*, Rosalin in *The Ambitious Slave*, and Teresa Pancha in both parts of *Don Quixote*.

The legal documents concerning the dissolution of the United Company brought forth the fact that after Anthony Leigh's death Mrs Leigh had been raised 10s. to a weekly salary of 30s. But, complained the managers Rich and Skipwith of the United Company, "She not appears [sic] in any pts to ye satisfaction of ye audience." She joined Thomas Betterton and his rebel players, most of them experienced performers, and was seen as the Nurse in *Love for Love* on 30 April 1695 at the opening of the Lincoln's Inn Fields playhouse. Betterton obviously did not share the view that Mrs Leigh no longer satisfied audiences, for he cast her regularly through 1706–7.

Her new parts included Mrs Beldam in *She Ventures and He Wins*, Vesuvia in *Lover's Luck*, Plackett in *The She-Gallants*, Betty in *The Country Wake*, the First Lady in *Rule a Wife and Have a Wife*, the Doctor's Wife in *The Anatomist*, Secreta in *The City Lady*, Grossiere in *The Intrigues at Versailles*, Lady Beauclair in *The Innocent Mistress*, Lady Temptyouth in *The Deceiver Deceived* (later retitled *The French Beau*), Sweetny in *The Pretenders*, Phenissa in *Rinaldo and Armida*, Lady Laycock in *The Amorous Widow*, the Hostess in *Henry IV*, Lady Wishfort in *The Way of the World*, the Mother in *The Chances*, the Aunt in *Sir Courtly Nice*, Calphurnia in *Julius Caesar*, Lady Autumn in *The Ladies Visiting Day*, Sophia in *The Czar of Muscovy*, Lady Rakelove in *The Gentleman Cully*, Goneril in *King Lear*, Plotwell in *The Beau's Duel*, Dromia in *Love Betray'd*, Adrastus in *The Fickle Shepherdess*, Chloris in *As You Find It*, Widow Bellmont in *The Different Widows*, Marama in *Abra Mule*, Sysigambis in *The Rival Queens*, Lady Stale in *The Biter*, and, at the Queen's Theatre from spring 1706 on, Peeper in *The Platonick Lady*, Mrs Day in *The Committee*, Lady Wouldbe in *Volpone*, Mrs Sentry in *She Wou'd If She Cou'd*, the Aunt in *The Tender Husband*, and Lady Sly in *The Fortune Hunters*. Mignon in *Crabbed Age and Youth* says that Mrs Leigh acted Lady Fantast in *Bury Fair*, though *The London Stage* does not cite her in that role. There is a possibility that Mrs Leigh acted Mophilda in *The Coy Shepherdess* in Dublin about 1709, though that Mrs Leigh may well have been a different woman. As of 1703 (not 1707), according to a document concerning the establishment of a new company, Mrs Leigh could command about £50 or £60 annually.

In his *Apology* in 1740 Colley Cibber said Mrs Leigh

had a very droll way of dressing the pretty Foibles of superannuated Beauties. She had in her self a good deal of Humour, and knew how to infuse it into the affected Mothers, Aunts, and modest stale Maids that had miss'd their Market; of this sort were the Modish Mother in the *Chances*, affecting to be politely commode for her own Daughter; the Coquette Prude of an Aunt in Sir *Courtley Nice*, who prides herself in being chaste and cruel at Fifty; and the languishing Lady *Wishfort* in *The Way of the World*: In all these, with many others, she was extremely entertaining, and painted in a lively manner the blind Side of Nature.

Elinor Leigh seems not to have performed after June 1707. The "Eli Leigh" on a petition of 1709 reproduced by Fitzgerald could have been Elinor, if she continued her interest in the theatre.

Leigh, Elizabeth [*fl.* 1681–1718], *booth operator.*

According to the proceedings in a law suit in April 1687, discussed in some detail in Hotson's *Commonwealth and Restoration Stage*, the playwright Elkanah Settle made an agreement in 1681 with Elizabeth Leigh, spinster, daughter of Mrs Mynns, who operated booths at the late summer fairs in London. Elizabeth provided Settle with some ideas for a play, and he agreed to complete the play within eight months. The work was to be produced by the King's Company at Drury Lane, and Settle was to pay Miss Leigh £20 minimum and more if the profits from performance and printing went over £40. He posted a £40 bond to seal the agreement.

By the time the dramatist finished the play (*The Ambitious Slave*) the King's Company was in the process of dissolution, and the piece could not be performed (when it was finally done in 1694 it was a failure). Elizabeth had Settle arrested several times over the bond, for she claimed she was supposed to get her £20 whether the play was acted or not. How the matter was finally settled is not known, but it must have been amicably resolved, for as late as 1716 Settle was writing drolls and acting in them for Elizabeth and her mother at their fair booths for an annual salary.

The *Weekly Journal or British Gazetteer* of 30 August 1718 reported that "Mrs Leigh, Daughter of the late Mrs Minns [d. 1717], is preparing for Bartholomew-Fair; but not Bullock and [Francis] Leigh as some People Imagine." That reference is the latest-dated one we have found to Elizabeth Leigh. She was supposed to have inherited her mother's fortune and booths, but *Mead's Journal* on 11 January 1718, shortly after Mrs Mynns's death, noted that since Mrs Mynns's "Husband is Living, 'tis expected he wil set aside any Will." That may account for Elizabeth's not having continued the family business.

Some authorities have identified Elizabeth Leigh as the wife of the actor Francis Leigh the elder, who died in 1719, but Hotson states that Elizabeth Leigh was a spinster in 1681; if so, her maiden name was evidently Leigh, and her mother had by that time apparently remarried. The Mrs Leigh who acted with Betterton's troupe in 1699–1700 and performed in the early years of the eighteenth century was, we believe, Elinor, the widow of the comedian Anthony Leigh. And the Mrs Lee who operated fair booths in the 1720s and 1730s was Hannah Lee, possibly a younger sister of Elizabeth, but the names Leigh and Lee were so common that it is quite possible Elizabeth and Hannah were not related.

Leigh, Francis *d. 1719, actor, dancer, manager.*

Francis Leigh was the son of the performers Anthony and Elinor Leigh, and the earliest note that has been found of him may date before the death of his father in December 1692. In James Quin's trial in 1718 Francis Leigh testified that the actor William Bowen had once made three attempts on Leigh's life, "and once particularly as he [Leigh] was sitting at his Father's Door. . . ." That testimony suggests that Anthony Leigh was still alive at the time. How old Francis may have been at the time we have no way of knowing; he was not named in cast lists until 1701.

The incident at his father's door was violent:

. . . Mr. Bowen passed by him and asked how he did . . . and coming back in about half-an-hour, while he was still sitting there, without any Provocation called him ill Names, drew his Sword, cut him over the Head, and he rising and retreating backward into the House he happened to fall, whereupon he made two Passes at him with his Sword, but happened to miss him, he putting it by with his hand, and somebody coming by, and taking hold of him, he was shortening his Sword to have stabb'd him as he lay on the ground, but was prevented by Persons running to his Assistance. That thereupon he [Leigh] advised with Sir Peter King in order to prosecute him, but by the Mediation of some Great Men on *Mr. Bowen's* Account, did make it up with him.

Francis Leigh's earliest theatrical notice came when he acted Sir Thrifty Gripe in *The Ladies Visiting Day* at the Lincoln's Inn Fields Theatre about January 1701. He apparently remained with the Lincoln's Inn Fields troupe under Betterton through the 1704–5 season, but the bills seldom provided much cast information, and we know only a few of his parts: Tristram in *The Stolen Heiress*, Dandle in *The Different Widows*, the Constable in *The Stage Coach* (according to the late Emmett Avery), Hector in *Love at First Sight*, Scribblescrabble in *The Biter*, and the Boxkeeper in *The Gamester*. In the Silver Collection at the Newberry Library is evidence that about 20 July 1704 Leigh spoke a new prologue. A conjectural new company, organized on paper about 1703 (not, as has been previously thought, 1707), showed Leigh listed near the bottom of a group of actors who were apparently not thought of as potential full-time members of the troupe; his salary was no more than £40 annually—about half what better established players could command.

In the 1705 edition of *The Confederacy* Leigh was listed as Gripe; the work was given at the new Queen's Theatre on 30 October 1705. He is not known to have acted any other parts that season, nor was he cited again in London bills until 3 April 1707, when he shared a benefit at Drury Lane with Bickerstaff and spoke an occasional epilogue. The play that day was *Tunbridge Walks*, but the bill did not indicate any participation by Leigh. On 18 October 1707 at Drury Lane Leigh ("Lee" in the bill) played both Bullock and Pearmain in *The Recruiting Officer*, and during the rest of the season he appeared as Antonio in *Love Makes a Man*, Widgeon in *The Northern Lass*, and Bumkin in

The Funeral. He shared a benefit with Mrs Willis on 29 May 1708. A Mr Leigh had been granted a benefit at a concert at York Buildings on 26 March 1708; probably that Leigh was Francis.

During the 1708–9 season at Drury Lane Leigh acted a number of new parts: Crumplin in *Bartholomew Fair*, Young Hartford in *The Lancashire Witches*, a Witch in *Macbeth*, Mercury in *Amphitryon*, Jaquelin in *The Fatal Marriage*, Cacafogo in *Rule a Wife and Have a Wife*, Sheppard in *The Libertine Destroyed*, Dominic in *The Spanish Fryar*, Crack in *Sir Courtly Nice*, Hackum in *The Squire of Alsatia*, Cook in *Rollo*, Peter in *The Chances*, Petulant in *The Fond Husband*, Appletree in *The Recruiting Officer*, and the Landlord in *The Stage Coach*. He was given a solo benefit on 31 May 1709, after which, it is believed, he went to Ireland. A "Lee" acted Melibaeus in *The Coy Shepherdess* in Dublin, probably in the summer of 1709, but he may have been another person.

The 1709–10 season at Drury Lane was a rocky one. William Collier was the proprietor, following Christopher Rich, who had been forced out of the management; but the actors were not fully loyal to Collier, and disturbances arose. Collier delegated managerial authority to Aaron Hill, and, after the season ended, Francis Leigh, along with several other actors, broke open the theatre doors and attacked Hill. In a letter to Vice Chamberlain Coke about the event Hill said that Leigh, "with an impudence unheard of . . . told me in publick Defyance that he would not only be a manager when I was none, but woud go down & act with Penkethman [in Greenwich] in spite of my Lord Chamberlain, or me, either."

Despite the unstable situation that season and the attempts during and after it to wrest control from the management, the actors continued performing. Leigh appeared in 1709–10 in such new roles as Sir Jealous Traffick in *The Busy Body*, Sir Sampson in *Love for Love*, Booby in *The Country Wit*, Obadiah in *The Committee*, a Senator in *Timon of Athens*, Chylax in *Valentinian*, Sancho in *2 Don Quixote*, Flip in *The Fair Quaker*, and Tom Shacklehead in *The Lancashire Witches*. During the season Leigh was also seen in a *Miller's Dance* with Prince, and in the summer he joined Pinkethman's successful venture in Greenwich.

His roles at Greenwich, beginning on 21 June 1710, were Jaqueline in *The Fatal Marriage*, Theodore in *Venice Preserv'd*, Hothead in *Sir Courtly Nice*, the Gravedigger in *Hamlet*, Jacomo in *The Libertine Destroyed*, Trinculo in *The Tempest*, Flip in *The Fair Quaker*, Clodpate in *Epsom Wells*, Balzaro in *The Emperor of the Moon*, Bullock in *The Recruiting Officer*, the Boxkeeper in *The Gamester*, a Plebeian in *Oedipus*, Loom the Weaver in *The Island Princess*, Sir Jealous in *The Busy Body*, Sir Roger Petulant in *The Fond Husband*, Vandunck in *The Royal Merchant*, Toledo in *The Mistake*, the Master in *The Sea Voyage*, Bumkin and a Frightened Soldier in *Caius Marius*, Sir Tunbelly in *The Relapse*, and Gripe in *The Confederacy*. (Sybil Rosenfeld in her *Strolling Players* lists the Leigh at Greenwich as John, but that surely is an error; several roles were those Francis had played earlier.) It is perhaps significant, in view of the question about a concert benefit for a Mr Leigh in 1708, that at his benefit in Greenwich on 19 August 1710 Francis Leigh scheduled a concert before the play began, played in *The Mistake*, and danced the *Miller's Wife* is an entr'acte turn called the *Whimsical Miller, his Wife, and Town Miss*.

Leigh continued acting at Drury Lane during the winter seasons until John Rich lured him to the new Lincoln's Inn Fields playhouse in 1715. Among his new parts were Isander and later Isadore in *Timon of Athens*, Old Hob in *Hob*, Lalpoop in *The Squire of Alsatia*, Sir Roger Merryman in *The Perplexed Lovers*, Nincompoop in *The Petticoat Plotter*, Jollyboy in *The Successful Pyrate*, Sir Harry Atall in *The Double Gallant*, Blunder in *The Humours of the Army*, Bulfinch in *The Northern Lass*, William in *The Wife of Bath*, Bankbill in *The Apparition*, Ralph in *The Cautious Coxcomb*, a Carrier in *1 Henry IV*, Mustacho in *The Tempest*, and Sir Oliver Muckhill in *The Puritan*. He spent the summer of 1711 in Pinkethman's troupe at Greenwich, though none of his roles are known, and on 16 June 1713 he was possibly the Leigh who was in Dublin, speaking an epilogue to *Peace Triumphant*.

There were two Leighs at Lincoln's Inn Fields from January to October 1715: Francis and John. The bills seem regularly to have supplied John's Christian name whenever he was cited, and Francis was designated either F. Leigh or just Leigh—since he was an established player and John was a newcomer. The first role Francis played was an old favorite of his, Flip in *The Fair Quaker* on 7 January 1715. He followed that with Gripe in *The Confederacy*, the Constable in *The Slip*, Octavio in *The Perplexed Couple*, Sir William Belfond in *The Squire of Alsatia*, the first Whore in *The City Rumble*, and Thump in *The Doating Lovers*. At his solo benefit on 19 April, "You^r Humble Servant Francis Leigh" took in £102 before house charges.

He returned to Lincoln's Inn Fields on 10 October 1715 to play the Constable in *The Recruiting Officer*; then two days later he danced a *Miller's Dance* with the Spillers. On 28 October he played Rashly in *The Fond Husband*, but on 9 November he returned to Drury Lane, perhaps dissatisfied at not having been given more of his old parts and some good new ones. For his return to Drury Lane he chose the title role in *The Spanish Fryar*.

Francis Leigh remained at that house until his death in 1719, essaying such new parts as Kite in *The Recruiting Officer*, the Constable in *The Cobler of Preston*, the Mad Taylor in *The Pilgrim*, Sir Joslin in *She Wou'd if She Cou'd*, Nautilus in *Three Hours after Marriage*, Don Antonio in *Love Makes the Man*, and Waitwell in *The Way of the World*. For the most part he stayed with a handful of old parts. On 5 August 1717 Leigh and Norris operated a booth at Tottenham Court Fair and produced *The History of Jane Shore* and *The Pleasant Adventures of Sir Anthony Noodle and his Little Man Weazle*. On 9 September Leigh teamed with Bullock at Southwark Fair and produced *The Noble Soldier* and *The Comical Adventures*. In the summer of 1718 Francis Leigh (and John Leigh, too) acted at Richmond. Francis played in *The Spanish Fryar* on 19 July, Obadiah in *The Committee* on 2 August, and at Drury Lane the Comical Shepherd in *Don John* on 20 August. On 3 September 1718 Leigh and Bullock shared the management of a booth at Bartholomew Fair and put on *Love's Triumph*, with Leigh as the Old Shepherd.

Leigh's last benefit at Drury Lane was on 23 April 1719. A month later he was dead. The *Weekly Journal or Saturday's Post* on 30 May reported that "On Saturday last [i.e. 23 May] died Mr Francis Leigh, one of the Comedians of Drury-Lane Playhouse, and Partner with Mr Bullock in the Entertainments of Southwark Fair, &c. He was Son of the Celebrated Tony Leigh, so fam'd heretofore for his Mastership in Comick Performances." On 8 June administration of the estate of a Francis Leigh of St Dunstan in the West was granted to his creditor Richard Morgan. There is no certainty that that Leigh was our subject, but the date is about right. The actor's widow was granted a shared benefit at Drury Lane on 1 June 1720. After Leigh's death she joined Bullock in the operation of a fair booth.

Leigh, Mrs Francis [fl. 1719–1726₁], booth operator.

In August 1719 at the Great Booth in Greyhound Inn Yard at Bartholomew Fair *The Constant Lovers* was produced by Bullock and Widow Leigh. Mrs Leigh was the widow of the elder Francis Leigh, who died that year and who had himself been a booth operator at the late summer London fairs. She seems not to have continued her interest in the fair after 1719 (though a Mrs Lee [Hannah] was busy in the 1720s), but Widow Leigh was regularly named in the Drury Lane bills for shared benefits through 17 May 1726. Drury Lane had been her husband's house, and the management evidently felt an obligation to Francis's widow for several years after his death.

Charles Beecher Hogan in *Shakespeare in the Theatre* suggests that the wife of Francis Leigh was named Elizabeth and performed in the early years of the eighteenth century, but we believe the Mrs Leigh who acted then was Elinor, the widow of Anthony Leigh. An Elizabeth Leigh was involved in booth operations in the late Restoration and early eighteenth century, but she seems to have been a different person.

Leigh, Francis [fl. 1725–1747?₁], actor, dancer, singer.

The younger Francis Leigh was first noted in the bills on 20 February 1725, when he played Cupid in *Apollo and Daphne* at Drury Lane. He repeated that part several times in 1725–26, 1726–27, and 1727–28 but seems not to have been given any new roles worth mentioning in the bills. And when he finally did get a new part, he was badly hurt in an accident. The *Universal Spectator* on 16 November 1728 reported that two days before "one Leigh, a young Lad belonging to . . . Drury-Lane, was descending in a Machine, at the

Rehearsal of the New Entertainment of Perseus and Andromeda, when the same was let down with such a Force, that the poor Boy broke both his Arms." He was out of performances for the rest of the season, though his benefit tickets were admitted on 16 May 1729.

Reed in his "Notitia Dramatica" claimed that "Lee" performed at the opening of the Goodman's Fields playhouse (in October 1729), but *The London Stage* does not list him in the troupe. Possibly young Francis was the Leigh who appeared at the Smock Alley Theatre in Dublin in 1729–30.

On 28 October 1730 at Drury Lane, Leigh danced a Wind in *Cephalus and Procris*, but he was cited for no other parts in the 1730–31 season. In 1731–32 he played Bacchus in *Perseus and Andromeda* and later added the part of Pierot's Servant. He was Filch in *The Beggar's Opera* on 1 August 1732 and the First Woman in *The Devil of a Duke* on 17 August, and he concluded the season at Bartholomew Fair playing an unnamed character in *The Envious Statesman*. After the 1731–32 season he was no longer referred to as "Young" Leigh.

Perhaps he came of age about 1732; he certainly came into more parts during the 1732–33 season: Harry in *The Mock Doctor*, Beau Brindle in *The Harlot's Progress*, and Foodle in *The Tragedy of Tragedies*. Frederick in *The Miser* and a Masquerader in *Ridotto al' Fresco* occupied him at Bartholomew Fair on 23 August 1733, and Lancaster and Simon Shadow in *Sir John Falstaff* at the same fair on 4 September.

Though he made appearances elsewhere from time to time, Leigh continued playing at Drury Lane for the rest of his career, adding to his repertoire such new roles as the Doctor's Man in *Harlequin Doctor Faustus*, Mezzetin, Bess Brindle, and later Scaramouch and Pierot in *The Harlot's Progress*, Appletree in *The Recruiting Officer*, A Cobler and a Satyr in *Cupid and Psyche*, James in *The Mock Doctor*, a Chinese Guard in *Cephalus and Procris*, a Neighbor and Dapper in *The Alchemist*, Lucilius in *Julius Caesar*, Rugby in *The Merry Wives of Windsor*, Clark in *The Plot*, a Waterman in *The Tempest*, Francis and later Gadshill in *1 Henry IV*, the Bookseller and later Abel in *The Committee*, Daniel in *The Conscious Lovers*, Porter in *The Fall of Phaeton*, Richard in *The Provok'd Husband*, a Cyclops in *Mars and Venus*, Jeremy in *The Amorous Widow*, a Forester in *The King and the Miller of Mansfield*, Crook-fingered Jack and Bagshot in *The Beggar's Opera*, a Coffee Boy in *The Coffee House*, an Attendant in *Sir John Cockle at Court*, Porter and Colombine's Father in *Robin Goodfellow*, Don Jack in *Britons Strike Home*, a Gipsy and Staytape in *The Fortune Tellers*, Tomlinson in *An Historical Play*, Young Gubbins in *The Rural Sports*, a Peasant in *Harlequin Shipwrecked*, Sparkle and List in *The Miser*, La Varole and Bull in *The Relapse*, Jaques in *Love Makes a Man*, a dancing part in *Masqueraders* within *Columbine Courtezan*, Tom Errand in *The Constant Couple*, Barnaby in *The Old Bachelor*, the King of Fiddlers in *Chrononhotonthologos*, the Cooper's Man in *The Cooper Outwitted*, Trusty in *The Intriguing Chambermaid*, Martin in *The Anatomist*, a Drawer in *The Spanish Fryar*, Whisk in *The Lottery*, an Ostler in *The Stage Coach*, a Bravo in *The Lady's Last Stake*, the Second Officer in *Twelfth Night*, Hounslow in *The Stratagem*, Wormwood in *The Virgin Unmask'd*, a Valet in *Sir Courtly Nice*, Beau Trippet in *The Lying Valet*, Jasper in *Marry or Do Worse*, and Francisco in *Hamlet*. The season of 1747–48 was his last at Drury Lane.

Though the vast majority of Francis Leigh's appearances during the 1730s and 1740s were at Drury Lane, he seems to have been the Leigh who acted Sanchio in *Rule a Wife and Have a Wife* at Lincoln's Inn Fields on 12 June 1735 and Jack in *The Twin Rivals* at the Haymarket from 22 July to 21 August of the same year. Since Francis Leigh was not cited for any parts in London in the summer of 1734, perhaps he was the Leigh who shared a benefit with Walsh at the Great Booth in George's Lane, Dublin, on 12 June of that year. Both Leigh and Walsh were called dancing masters. The "Lee" who acted Jaques in *Love Makes a Man* at York Buildings with some Lilliputians on 21 March 1735 was certainly Francis; he was advertised as from Drury Lane, and the bills show that he was not active there that month. A Leigh, perhaps Francis, had benefit tickets out at Lincoln's Inn Fields Theatre on 15 June 1737.

Leigh was in the Green Room (or "Scene Room" as they called it) at Drury Lane when Macklin murdered Thomas Hallam, and he provided the following testimony at the trial:

The deceased came into the scene-room, and said, "the prisoner had used him like a pick-pocket, about a wig." Mr. Mills, and the author of the farce, and others, advised Hallam to go up, and fetch Mr. Macklin the wig. Mr. Kitchen called the deceased to the end of the room, and lent him another wig: he shewed this wig, and said he would not change with the prisoner, for he had got a better. The prisoner replied "You are a scoundrel for taking it at all." The deceased answered, "No more a scoundrel than you are." Some other words having passed, the prisoner rose up, and, I think, said, "D——n you, you dog, do you prate!"—and then gave him the [cane] blow. The deceased clapped both his hands to his eye, and cried, "Lord, I believe my eye is put out!" and would have fallen into the fire, if Mr. Cole had not caught him. When he was set down, I asked him how he did? He said, "Lord, I believe my eye-ball is shoved to the other side of my head." I believe the prisoner had him by the hand all the while the surgeon was dressing him. He liv'd till six o'clock the next night [11 May 1735].

"**Leigh, Handsome.**" *See* LEIGH, JOHN.

Leigh, John 1689–1726, *actor.*

Chetwood in his *General History* believed that John Leigh was born in Ireland, and the *Biographia Dramatica* dated his birth 1689. A George Leigh acted in Dublin about 1673, though we cannot determine whether or not he was John Leigh's father. John acted in Dublin from about 1709 to 1714, according to W. S. Clark's *The Early Irish Stage*. Chetwood remembered two of his Dublin roles as being Demetrius in *Timon of Athens* and Axalla in *Tamerlane*. On 18 December 1714 Leigh appeared at John Rich's new Lincoln's Inn Fields playhouse in London as Plume in *The Recruiting Officer*. In the troupe also for a few months was Francis Leigh (apparently no relation), but the bills were usually careful to identify John by his first name or initial. Before the end of the 1714–15 season he appeared as Polidore in *The Orphan*, Bellmour in *The Old Bachelor*, Don Carlos in *The Mistake*, Dick in *The Confederacy*, Essex in *The Unhappy Favorite*, Valentine in *Love for Love*, Cortez in *The Indian Emperor*, possibly a role in *The Careless Husband* at his benefit on 19 March 1715, young Belfond in *The Squire of Alsatia*, Carlos in *Love Makes a Man*, Gaylove in *The Doating Lovers*, and Antonio in *The False Count*.

John Leigh remained at Lincoln's Inn Fields until his death in 1726, earning the nickname "Handsome Leigh" because of what Chetwood called "a particular amiable Form, and genteel Address. . . ." He acted heavy schedules almost every season, adding to his repertoire such new parts as Lorenzo in *The Spanish Fryar*, Volatil in *The Wife's Relief*, Loveless in *Love's Last Shift*, Freeman in *The Plain Dealer*, Ramble in *The London Cuckolds*, Heartfree in *The Provok'd Wife*, Florez in *The Royal Merchant*, Beaufort in *The Perfidious Brother*, Gamont in *The Northern Heiress*, Sir Humphrey Scattergood in *The Woman Captain*, the title role in *Aureng-Zebe*, Galliard in *The Feign'd Curtizans*, Wildish in *Bury Fair*, Southampton in *The Unhappy Favorite*, Prince Hal in *1 Henry IV*, Adrastus in *Oedipus*, Trueman in *The Twin Rivals*, Villeroy in *The Fatal Marriage*, Horatio in *Hamlet*, Colonel Manly in *Woman is a Riddle*, the Emperor and the title role in *Don Sebastian*, the title role in *Theodosius*, Lysimachus and Cassander in *The Rival Queens*, Young Valere in *The Gamester*, Captain Manworth in *The Lady's Triumph*, Sir Tunbelly in *The Relapse*, Moneses in *Tamerlane*, the Duke in *The Traytor*, Sir Charles Estcourt in *The Fair Example*, Juba in *Cato*, Mellefont in *The Double Dealer*, Careless in *The Committee*, Antony and later Caesar in *Julius Caesar*, Young Raleigh and Salisbury in *Sir Walter Raleigh*, Bellair Senior in *The Younger Brother*, and Loveless in *Tis Well If It Takes*.

Also Sir George in *The Busy Body*, the Duke in Beckingham's *Henry IV*, Lord George Belmour in Leigh's own play *The Pretenders* (originally called *Kensington-Gardens*; performed on 26 November 1719), Bolingbroke in *Richard II*, the title role in *Cymbeline*, Charles Heartfree in *Whig and Tory*, the Governor in *Oroonoko*, Bassanio in *The Merchant of Venice*, Cassio in *Othello*, apparently Banquo in *Macbeth* (he and Ryan evidently traded off that role and Macduff—Leigh's usual part—in the spring of 1720), Edmund in *King Lear*, Achilles in *Troilus and Cressida*, Saturnius in *Titus Andronicus*, Ruidias in *The Island Princess*, Ozmin in *The Fair Captive*, Richmond in *Richard III*, Sir Harry in *The Artful Husband*, Wilding in *The Quaker's Wedding*, Afterwit in *The Cheats*, Young Worthy in *Love's Last Shift*, Aelius in *Domitian (The Roman Actor)*, the Duke in *Don Quixote*, Sharper in *The Old Bachelor*, Milanes in *The Spanish Curate*, Random in *The Compromise*, Trueman Junior in *Cutter of Coleman Street*, the High Priest in *Mariamne*, Kent in *King Lear*, a Gravedigger in *Hamlet* (according to Darby's

English Theatre), the King in *1 Henry IV*, Gobrius in *A King and No King*, Scipio in *Sophonisba*, Octavio in *Love's Contrivance*, Montezuma in *The Indian Emperor*, the Cardinal in *Massaniello*, and Aegeon and Phorbas in *Oedipus*.

Leigh engaged a few times in activity at the London fairs (as did every performer named Leigh or Lee in John's day, it seems). On 5 September 1720 John played a part in *The History of Friar Bacon*, a droll presented at the "John Leigh-Hall Great Theatrical Booth, which was formerly Mr Penkethman's" at Southwark Fair. The same partners ran a booth on 10 October that year and presented *1 Henry IV* for their benefit, and in September 1721 they put on the droll *King Saul*, in which Leigh had an unnamed part. (The "Lee" who was a far more active fair booth manager in the 1720s and later was George Lee.)

Leigh also acted at Pinkethman's theatre at Richmond Hill in July and August 1718, playing Careless in *The Committee*, probably Valentine in *Love for Love*, Valere in *The Gamester*, and Reynard in *Tunbridge Walks*. Leigh's play *Kensington-Gardens, or The Pretenders* was not his only effort (that work, and Leigh himself, inspired a satire of Leigh in the character of Ludovicus in *The Stage-Pretenders; or, The Actor Turn'd Poet* in 1720; but that play was apparently not produced). On 11 January 1720 Leigh's farce *Hob's Wedding*, a sequel to *The Country Wake*, came out at Lincoln's Inn Fields. He was involved in the publication of another farce in 1724: on 5 January he paid £10 10s. "To Mr. Miars bookseller in considerasion of his damage in buying & printing the Farce of Shephard written & sold by Mr. Walker & Mr. Leigh but never acted." That work is not recorded in Nicoll or the *Cambridge Bibliography of English Literature*.

Whincop claimed that Leigh was "an actor on the stage of no great credit" and that his dramatic works gained little success. Chetwood said that *Kensington-Gardens* "walk'd consumptively six Nights, and then expir'd." He also noted pointedly that Leigh "might have been in the good Graces of the Fair-Sex, *if his Taste had led him that Way.*" John Leigh died in 1726, stated the *Biographia Dramatica* in 1812, in his thirty-seventh year, having "made no considerable advances towards theatrical excellence." Despite the negative attitudes toward Leigh as an actor, he kept a very busy schedule at Lincoln's Inn Fields at least until 1725, when he was less frequently cited in the bills, and he was thought enough of by his manager to have been given a few leading roles and a number of solid secondary parts.

Leigh, Michael *d. 1701?, actor, singer.*

The son of Anthony and Elinor Leigh, Michael Leigh was first mentioned in cast lists in late March 1690, when he played Diego in *The Amorous Bigotte* at Drury Lane with the United Company. He was called Young Leigh to distinguish him from his father. A manuscript cast dating about 1690–91 in a copy of *Richard III* has Leigh down for the part of Sir Thomas Vaughan, and another such list in a Harvard copy of *The Man of Mode*, dating about 1690–1692, cited Leigh as Young Bellair. Before the United Company split in 1694 Leigh is recorded as having played Cortaut in *Sir Anthony Love*, Springame in *The Wives' Excuse*, Valdaura in *The Rape*, Frederico in *The Traytor*, Prince Henry in *Henry II*, Jeremy in *A Very Good Wife*, Fabian in *The Fatal Marriage*, the Page to the Duke, disguised as Dulcinea, in *2 Don Quixote*, and the First Innkeeper in *The Canterbury Guests*. Manuscript notes in a British Library copy of music for *Macbeth* indicate that Leigh sang in performances of that work.

During that period in the early 1690s Michael got himself into debt at least twice: Christopher Caris went against Michael "Lee" and performer John Hodgson on 10 October 1692, and James Verdon went against Leigh in February 1694.

After the United Company divided, Leigh stayed with Christopher Rich at Drury Lane and Dorset Garden, though he seems also to have appeared at the rival Lincoln's Inn Fields playhouse as a singer. Possibly he was the Leigh who was apprehended for participating in a riot at the Dog Tavern in July 1695; Cardell Goodman the actor was one of those brought up for treason in a plot to kill the King. Goodman and Leigh were examined in March 1696 and remanded to Newgate; Michael Leigh was not mentioned in any casts from December 1695 to June 1696.

With Rich's troupe at Drury Lane or Dorset Garden Leigh played Sir Arthur Stately in *The Mock Marriage*, Macer in *Bonduca*, Gines de Passamonte in *3 Don Quixote*, Daniel in *Oroonoko*, Cleremont in *Philaster*, Swash in *The Cor-*

nish Comedy, Lorenzo in *The Triumphs of Virtue*, and Macfleer in *A Plot and No Plot*. He was surely the "M. Lee"who sang with Reading "Shou'd I not lead a happy life" in *Love's a Jest* at Lincoln's Inn Fields and the Lee who sang in *The Loves of Mars and Venus* there on 14 November 1696 and subsequent dates. At court on 4 November 1697 Leigh was Irish Reparee in *Europe's Revels*; the production was a joint effort by both London patent companies.

At least two songs were published with his name cited as singer: *Haste, haste ye Britains* [*sic*], evidently from *Europe's Revels* (1697), and *Slaves to London I'll deceive you* from *The Comical Mistake* (1700?). That information comes from the British Museum's *Catalogue of Printed Music*. *The Comical Mistake* is not otherwise known.

Leigh seems not to have performed after 1697, and in a British Library copy of *The Fatal Marriage* a manuscript cast change dated 24 April 1701 has Leigh's name deleted and Baily written in. In Behn's *Works* Montague Summers stated that Leigh died about the winter of 1701 at an early age. About this time his brother Francis began his acting career.

Leigh, Rachel [fl. 1693], *actress*.
Rachel Leigh played Judy, a walk-on role, in *The Maid's Last Prayer* at the end of February 1693 with the United Company at Drury Lane. Nothing more is known of her, nor is there any evidence to show whether or not she was related to the other Leighs of the time.

Leighborne, Robert [fl. 1672], *musician*.
The Lord Chamberlain had to order the apprehension of the musician Robert Leighborne twice in 1672, on 29 February and on 2 October; in both instances Leighborne had performed music without a permit.

Leire, Mr [fl. 1744], *musician?*
The serenata *Solomon* was performed for the benefit of Mr Leire on 17 April 1744 at Temple Bar. He was probably a musician, though there is no proof.

Leister. *See* LEICESTER.

Leitherfull, Mr [fl. 1680], *actor*.
Mr. Leitherfull played the philosopher Leontine, a fairly sizeable part, in *Theodosius* at Dorset Garden, perhaps, as Robert Hume has argued, in the early summer of 1680 (rather than September 1680 as *The London Stage* has it). In *The Playhouse of Pepys* Montague Summers, for reasons unknown, listed Leitherfull as a singer; there is no indication in the text of *Theodosius* that he sang, though the play contains songs.

Lelly, Master [fl. 1767], *dancer*.
On 24 January 1767 the Drury Lane payroll included a Master Lelly, dancer, who was earning a daily salary of 3s. 4d. for a total of £1 weekly. Could "Lelly" be a mistake for "Lally"?

Lely, Mr [fl. 1784], *horn player*.
Mr Lely played horn in the Handel Memorial Concerts at Westminster Abbey and the Pantheon in May and June 1784.

Lemaistre, Mr [fl. 1741?–1760], *impresario*.
On 19 January 1760 a license (now at the Public Record Office) was granted to a Mr Lemaistre and his company to perform a concert of music at Mr Cock's Great Room in Spring Garden on 12 February. Our subject may have been the Lemaistre who on 28 January 1741 had been granted a bill of exchange for £6 6s. to be paid at Calais.

Le March. *See* LAMASH.

Lemercier, Mr [fl. 1773–1782], *dancer*.
The Monsieur "Merci" who danced at Sadler's Wells in 1773 was probably Mr Lemercier (or La Mercier, Lamerieux), who was active at Drury Lane from 1774 to 1782 and made other appearances at Sadler's Wells. During the 1774–75 season at Drury Lane Lemercier was on the payrool at £1 5s. weekly, and he subscribed 10s. 6d. to the theatre fund. Sometime in 1775 he danced at Sadler's Wells again—probably during the summer, for he was still engaged at Drury Lane during the winter seasons in the late 1770s. The Drury Lane accounts show that his salary remained unchanged to the end of the decade. A Sadler's Wells benefit bill for Lemercier, dated only 1780, is at the

LEMERCIER

Finsbury Public Library; it gives the dancer's address as No 6, Duke Street, Lincoln's Inn Fields.

From a Drury Lane bill dated 17 May 1781 we learn that the Misses Stageldoir were scholars of Lemercier, and the theatre's bills in 1781–82 show him dancing with them in entr'acte turns on occasion. Perhaps by that season his salary had increased; certainly his notices in playbills had. He danced in the mainpiece, *The Carnival of Venice*, from 11 January 1782 on and was seen during the rest of the season in a *New Dance*, *The Distress'd Lovers*, a minuet with Miss Stageldoir in *Romeo and Juliet*, and an unnamed but principal character in a new afterpiece of unknown authorship, *Don Juan*. But after that season of emergence from the obscurity of the dancing chorus, Lemercier's name disappeared from the bills and accounts.

Lemeur, Mr [fl. 1794], *dancer.*

William C. Smith in *The Italian Opera in London* lists a Mr Lemeur as a dancer at the King's Theatre in 1794.

Lemon, Mr [fl. 1786], *gallery office keeper.*

Mr Lemon was identified as the gallery office keeper at Sadler's Wells Theatre in an advertisement dated 29 September 1786.

Lemon, A. G. [fl. 1719–1720], *trumpeter.*

A. G. Lemon was a trumpeter in the concerts at Cannons in 1719–20 at a fee of 8s. 15d. per quarter.

Le Mont. *See* LAMOUND.

Lemotte. *See* LAMOTTE.

Le Namora, Signor [fl. c. 1750–1772], *dancer, acrobat.*

An Epistle to Henry Mossop, referring to theatrical activity in Dubliln about 1750, protested the sacrifice of the immortal bards at "the Shrine of Rope-dancers, Tumblers, and Fire-Workers . . ." and asked if Shakespeare and Otway should "be kicked out of a Theatre . . . that Signor *Le Namora*, Signor *Semenzati*, and Signora *Rosalina* may enter it?" The nature of Le Namora's act was at least partly described in a bill for a performance at the old assembly room at St Augustine's Back in Bristol on 8 February 1768. The troupe was called a "Company of ITALIANS" and audiences were assured that

Each Performer will dance twice, and shew the greatest Marks of their Talents; particularly Mrs. Rossi, who will perform three different Dances on the Occasion.

Mr. Nomora, the Grand Maltese, after his surprising Dance, with an astonishing Variety of Changes, will execute that with two Children ty'd to his Feet, and one on his Shoulders; and afterwards with 2 Men.

Perhaps one of the children cited in the Bristol bill was the Miss Le Namora who performed with her father at Sadler's Wells in 1768 in some feats of activity. She was not mentioned as being with him when he performed again in Dublin in 1768–69 at the Crow Street playhouse but father and daughter joined Tate Wilkinson's troupe at Hull in November 1771 and were described as from Sadler's Wells. "They were clever in their way," wrote Wilkinson in *The Wandering Patentee*, "drew money, were well behaved, and all parties were satisfied;—the season was good, the public pleased, and we retired in good order for the remainder of the winter, and opened at York, in January 1772, in good health and spirits."

Le Namora, Miss [fl. 1768–1772], *dancer.* See LE NAMORA, SIGNOR.

Lendrick, Mr [fl. 1780], *actor.*

At the Haymarket Theatre on 5 April 1780 a Mr Lendrick played a principal but unnamed character in *A School for Ladies*. The work was not repeated.

Leneker. *See* LINIKE.

Leng. *See* LONG.

L'Englois. *See* LANGLOIS.

Lennard. *See also* LEONARD.

Lennard, Mr [fl. 1720–1729], *office keeper?*

Mr Lennard (sometimes Leonard) was a house servant at the Lincoln's Inn Fields playhouse from at least 2 June 1720, when he was cited with three others on a benefit bill, through 1728–29, when he was mentioned in the accounts. He seems to have been an office keeper, or at least someone who handled the free list for members of the troupe. Typical entries in the books read "M^r. Leveridge by Lennard" or "D^r. Pepush from the office by Lennard." In these instances he was evidently arranging for complimentary tickets. Sometimes he was also listed as a playgoer, receiving complimentary tickets himself.

Lennerd, Mr [fl. 1788], actor.

A Mr Lennerd played the French Servant in *Harlequin's Frolic* at Sayer's booth at Bartholomew Fair in 1788. In the same bill a Mr Leopard played Harry in *The Mock Doctor*, and there is a possibility that the two men were one and the same. There is insufficient evidence to connect the 1788 performer Lennerd with the actor Leonard (d. 1821) who performed in Ireland in 1796 and 1799, at Liverpool and Manchester in 1801, Manchester in 1802, and Brighton in 1807.

Lennet. See LINNET.

Lenniker. See LINIKE.

Lennox, Mrs Alexander, Charlotte, née Ramsay 1720–1804, actress, author.

Charlotte Ramsay was born in America in 1720, the daughter of Colonel James Ramsay, lieutenant governor of New York. She was sent to England about 1735 to be adopted by a wealthy aunt, but upon her arrival she found her aunt insane. Colonel Ramsay died shortly thereafter, and Charlotte had to shift for herself. On 29 January 1746 (as "Mrs" Ramsey) she made her first appearance on any stage, playing Lavinia in *The Fair Penitent* at Drury Lane. She published a book of poems in 1747, and when Horace Walpole saw her act at Richmond on 3 September 1748 he declared her "a poetess and a deplorable actress." About 1748 she married Alexander Lennox. Charlotte did not give up acting: on 22 February 1750 at the Haymarket she played Almeria in *The Mourning Bride* for her benefit, and it is possible that the Mrs Lennox who performed at Smock Alley in Dublin on 13 November 1754

Harvard Theatre Collection
CHARLOTTE LENNOX
engraving by Cook, after Reynolds

was Charlotte. As of November 1751 she was living at No 22, Plow Court, Fetter Lane.

Dr. Johnson admired Charlotte and her work greatly and celebrated the publication of her novel *Harriot Stuart* in December 1750 by giving her a supper at his club, where he also gave her a crown of laurel. In his *Dictionary* he listed her under "Talent." Her best work, *The Female Quixote*, was published in 1752. In 1760 she began turning out a magazine, *The Ladies' Museum*, and on 18 February 1769 her play *The Sister* was performed at Covent Garden, but it was received so coldly that she withdrew it after one performance.

Charlotte Lennox died on 4 January 1804, a pensioner on the Royal Literary Fund. By Lennox she had had a son, who went to America. *The Dictionary of National Biography* and *The Cambridge Bibliography of English Literature* list her works, which run the gamut: poems, novels, a dramatic pastoral (*Philander*; not written for the stage, however), *Old City Manners* (altered in 1775 from *Eastward Hoe!*; acted at Drury Lane on 9 November 1775 with success), three volumes of collections of Shakespeare's sources, and a number of translations from the French.

Sir Joshua Reynolds painted her, and Bartolozzi made an engraving of the portrait; it was published as a plate to Harding's *Shakespeare Illustrated*, 1793, and a copy engraved by H. R. Cook was also issued (n.d.). She appears in a group painted by Richard Samuel called "The Nine Living Muses of Great Britain," exhibited in 1779; the painting is in the National Portrait Gallery (No 4905). Miriam Small published a biography of Charlotte Ramsay Lennox in 1935.

Lenoir, John [*fl.* 1714], *trumpeter.*
John Lenoir was listed as a trumpeter in the royal musical establishment in 1714.

Lenoir, Peter [*fl.* 1719–1736], *trumpeter.*
Peter Lenoir (or Lanoir) replaced John Sheppard as a trumpeter in the royal musical establishment on 9 May 1719, according to the Lord Chamberlain's accounts. Lenoir was replaced by Valentine Snow on 3 April 1736.

Le Nomora. *See* LE NAMORA.

Lens, Mr [*fl.* 1765], *actor.*
Mr Lens acted at the Richmond Theatre in August 1765 and was cited in casts for *She Wou'd and She Wou'd Not* and *Miss in Her Teens*.

Lenton. *See also* LINTON.

Lenton, Miss [*fl. c.* 1750], *singer.*
About 1750 three songs by Defesch were published as sung by Miss Lenton at Marylebone Gardens: *Female Friendship*, *The Willing Maid*, and *Young Patty*.

Lenton, John 1656–1719, *violinist, flutist, composer.*
John Lenton was born in 1656. On 2 August 1681 he was appointed a violinist in the King's Musick, replacing Dorney. He was mentioned in passing in a warrant in the Lord Chamberlain's accounts in January 1685 and on 10 November of that year he was sworn a Gentleman of the Chapel Royal. The accounts cited Lenton frequently during the years that followed: attending the King at Hampton Court and Windsor in the fall of 1685 and the summers of 1686 and 1687, going with William III to Newmarket in the autumn of 1689, journeying with the King to Holland in January 1691, attending at Hampton Court in 1718, and so on. Lenton's annual salary was £30 in 1689, but it had risen to £40 by 1697, and for trips out of London he received extra pay. Each year he was also granted a livery allowance.

The *Flying Post* of 17–20 April 1697 carried an advertisement of a "three part consort," a piece of published music by Lenton which was available "at most Musick shops in Town, or [from] the Author, every day from 4 till 8, at the new Theatre in Little Lincolns Inn Fields, or at the Fountain over against it." Lenton, though he remained a member of the royal band until 1718, turned in the 1690s more and more toward musical composition. In 1694 he had published *The Gentleman's Diversion, or The Violin Explained*, which included some pieces he had composed.

Lenton composed a fair amount of music for plays in the early years of the new century, including tunes for *The Ambitious Stepmother* in 1700, *Tamerlane* in 1702, *Othello*, *Venice Preserv'd*, and *The Fair Penitent* in 1703, *Liberty Asserted* and *Abra Mule* in 1704, *The Gamester* in 1705, and an unidentified work, *The Royal Captive* (1702?). Collections of songs during the late Restoration and early eighteenth century usually included pieces by Lenton.

Rimbault's notes to *The Old Cheque Book of the Chapel Royal* state that Lenton was sworn Groom of the Vestry of the Chapel Royal. The *Calendar of Treasury Books* show in 1715–16 payments to Lenton in that post. Another entry in the *Cheque Book* records Lenton's death in May 1719.

Lenton composed a number of light songs in the late Restoration and early eighteenth century, including "Ah Phillis! cast those Thoughts away" and "When Celia wept, the Heav'ns wept too," both of which appeared in Playford's *Theater of Music* in 1685. As late as 1719 when *Wit and Mirth* was published, Lenton's "No, Silly Cloris!" was included. In 1713 Playford's *Dancing Master* was "carefully corrected by J. Lenton, one of Her Majesties Servants."

Lenz, Heinrich Gerhard c. 1764–1839, pianist, composer.

Heinrich Gerhard Lenz (or Lentz) was born about 1764 of either Polish or German parents, according to *Grove's Dictionary* (5th edition). In 1785 he played piano at the Concert Spirituel in Paris, and in 1792 he performed in Salomon's concerts in London. Haydn in his *First London Notebook* that year noted of Lenz only that he was "still very young." In 1795 Lenz went to Hamburg and was engaged by Prince Louis Ferdinand of Prussia. In 1802 he moved to Warsaw, where from 1826 to 1831 he taught at the conservatory. Lenz composed a number of concertos, sonatas, trios, symphonies, and a handbook in Polish on piano tuning.

Leonard. *See also* LENNARD.

Leonard, Mrs [*fl.* 1733], actress.

Mrs Leonard played Lady Townly in *The Provok'd Husband* on 28 May 1733 at the Haymarket Theatre.

Leonardi, Signor [*fl.* 1744–1745], dancer.

Signor Leonardi and Signora Bettini appeared at Drury Lane for the first time on 14 December 1744, offering an entr'acte dance. Leonardi danced in *Harlequin Shipwrecked* on 21 December if not earlier, and on 26 December he danced in *Robin Goodfellow*. He and Signora Bettini often danced together during December and the first part of January 1745, but after 10 January Leonardi was no longer mentioned in the bills.

Leonardi, Pietro [*fl.* 1761–1762], singer.

According to the 1761 libretto of *Il mercato di Malmantile*, Pietro Leonardi sang Berto. The opera was performed at the King's Theatre on 10 November of that year. Leonardi was presumably a member of Signora Mattei's company throughout the 1761–62 season, but the bills seldom contained casts.

Leoni, Michael d. 1797, singer, actor, dancer.

Michael Leoni was born Myer Lyon in Frankfort on the Main, according to James De

Harvard Theatre Collection

MICHAEL LEONI, as Arbaces
engraving by Goodnight

Castro in his *Memoirs*. He was the brother of Esther Lyon and consequently the uncle by marriage of her nine musically gifted children by her husband John Abraham, including the great tenor singer John Braham, who became Leoni's pupil and ward.

Leoni was "brought up for a reader in the synagogue," wrote De Castro.

The moment the German Jews [in London] heard of his reading and warbling they immediately sent to his native spot and brought him to England, where, by his great powers, he astonished all the members of the synagogue in Duke's Place: a very rich Jew, Mr. Frankle, instantly patronized him. At that time, the Rev. Mr. Hankey was so delighted with his amazing vocal powers, he introduced him to the late Earl of Sandwich, when Mr. Garrick was with that nobleman. His talents at that interview were duly appreciated by both of them, and through their influence with the Elders of the synagogue, the latter gave their permission for him to appear on the stage.

It is not known by whom the young singer was persuaded to Italianize his name, nor precisely when Garrick saw his potential for secular singing. On 12 October 1760 Garrick wrote to Joseph Austin, his assistant prompter: "I should wish that you would let *Chamnys* [the singer Samuel Thomas Champness] Mrs [Isabella] *Vincent* & ye Boy *Leoni* know that I must see 'Em to Morrow Evening about Six at ye house to run over their New Musical thing— I mean ye Business *of it*." The "thing" was Garrick's new entertainment *The Enchanter; or, Love and Magic*, with J. C. Smith's music, which had been written principally to introduce Leoni to the theatrical public in the character of Kaliel. Hopkins the prompter wrote in his diary that Master Leoni "was received with great applause."

Leoni sang in the piece eight more times over the following month, and he may also have been retained as a chorus singer, for he sang "An Italian song" at his benefit on 11 April 1761. He seems to have been in the Drury Lane chorus at least briefly, the following season, 1761–62, but was almost certainly also that Leoni who danced as one of the Croats in "A Grand Comic Ballet, call'd *The Hungarian Gambols*" at Covent Garden Theatre on 21 September 1761.

For Leoni's whereabouts during the following six or seven years we have only the word of De Castro, who claims that the lad went back to singing in the synagogue. Kathleen Barker reports to us that Master "Lion," a pupil of Aldridge, danced at Bristol on 14 June 1769 and subsequent dates and performed there again in 1770. That may have been Leoni. On 27 January 1770 our subject was listed—as Master Leoni—with Mrs Baker and Dubellamy singing in *Harlequin's Jubilee*, a new afterpiece by Henry Woodward, satirizing Garrick's Stratford Jubilee of 1769. The piece had a brief run, and Leoni was paid £10 10s. "in full" at the end of the season of 1769–70.

On 10 December 1770 a Master "Lion" danced a hornpipe at Cooke's benefit at the Haymarket Theatre. That was also probably Leoni, for there seems little doubt that he had

Harvard Theatre Collection

MICHAEL LEONI as Carlos and ISABELLA MATTOCKS as Louisa

artist unknown

been singing under his real name, Lyon, at Finch's Grotto Gardens, south of the Thames in St George's Fields, Southwark. He continued that practice through 1771. On 3 September 1771 he was given a benefit at Finch's and sang "Water Parted from the Sea." (On 1 October 1770 a "Lyon," probably our subject, had sung some role in "A new musical interlude, *The Old Women Weatherwise*, at a special benefit for Davis at the Haymarket.)

In 1771–72 Master Leoni was singing at the Crow Street Theatre in Dublin. Later in 1772 he sang at the Pantheon in London songs by Vento, published that year. During 1772, 1773, and into the season of 1774–75, he may have been employed again in the Covent Garden chorus, for on 13 October 1774 a playbill more specific than the usual ones listed him with a dozen others as singing in the "Solemn Dirge" which always accompanied Juliet's funeral in *Romeo and Juliet*.

On 25 April at Covent Garden the singer Reinhold, whose benefit night it was, conceived a novelty. He invited Master Leoni to replace George Mattocks and sing Arbaces opposite Mrs Mattocks as Arbanes in T. A. Arne's opera *Artaxerxes*. The experiment was a resounding success. Leoni was hailed as a phenomenal singer and was thrust at once into rehearsal for the role of Carlos in Sheridan's new comic opera *The Duenna; or, The Double Elopement*. In the course of a letter giving explicit instructions to Thomas Linley the elder about the singing, Sheridan delivered some opinions about Leoni's talents: "I should tell you, that he sings nothing well but in a plaintive or pastoral style; and his voice is such as appears to me always to be hurt by much accompaniment. I have observed, too, that he never gets so much applause as when he makes a cadence [cadenza]."

The Duenna was performed nearly 70 times that season after its premiere on 21 November 1775, and Leoni scored another personal triumph. In addition, he sang solos several times that season. He was a chorus singer as well as featured singer in 1775–76 and 1776–77. His benefit bill of 5 April 1777 directed ticket buyers to "Leoni, at Basire's, No. 34, Great Queen-street," and informed buyers that he was singing in the chorus supporting *Caractacus* that evening. Evidently W. J. Lawrence was in error in his Dublin notebooks in stating that Leoni spent the 1776–77 season in Dublin.

From about 1780 or a little later, Leoni seems to have assumed responsibility for the care of his nephew John Abraham (later John Braham) and was his principal instructor in singing until the lad began his illustrious professional career.

Through 1781–82 Leoni remained at Covent Garden, with an occasional excursion to other theatres, as a principal singer in choruses, supplying entr'acte diversions and broadening his repertoire of named parts in comic opera: Frederick in *The Seraglio*, Adonis in *Poor Vulcan!*, Young Meadows in *Love in a Village*, Proteus in *Calypso*, Captain Greville in *A Flitch of Bacon*, Felix in *The Islanders*, and Phillipo in *The Banditti*. But Carlos in *The Duenna* and Arbaces in *Artaxerxes* continued to be the roles in which he was most seen and most applauded. He played those two parts and Young Meadows in Edinburgh in July and August 1782.

In June 1783 Leoni began sponsoring and performing in a series of concerts in Dublin's Rotunda. He was joined in late summer by the composer Tommaso Giordani, who had just returned to Ireland. They rented the Capel Street Theatre and instituted what they called the English Opera House. Its opening night was 15 December 1783. The proprietors brought first-rate talents to the house, including the singers Elizabeth Billington and Peter Duffey, but the auditorium was so small that they failed to recover expenses. After seven months they were bankrupt and, as De Castro put it, Leoni "came to England again quite *minus*. . . ."

News of Leoni's activities after his return from Ireland is even sparser than before he left. Few performances are recorded. On 1 May 1784 he was called on to sing with William Brett "When Phoebus the tops of the hills does adorn" on the occasion of Brett's Covent Garden benefit. Sylas Neville in his diary reported that on 10 September 1784 Leoni sang "The Soldier Tired of War's Alarms" at Norwich, but that "his voice[,] always feigned, is not so good as it was." John Henry Johnstone, for his own benefit at Covent Garden on 5 April 1785, prevailed upon Leoni to assume Carlos in *The Duenna* again (for the first time in six years, claimed the bill), and the idea found some favor, for Sarah Maria Wilson had him repeat the role on 20 April and insert in Act II Giordani's song "I Blush in the Dark." Leoni was advertised in concert with Miss Twist, Incledon, Miss Wright, and others in Bristol on 20 August 1785.

There follows a two-year gap in the record. Then, on 13 January 1787 at Covent Garden, he revived his Arbaces in *Artaxerxes*. On 31 March ("for that night only") he was the Spirit in *Comus* and on 21 April he played Carlos again, for his benefit, with the bill again claiming that he sang the role now for the first time in six years. That was the evening that his brilliant nephew and pupil John Braham made his professional debut, singing two songs.

The bill of 21 April gave ticket seekers his

address, No 1, Wellclose Square. The square was also the location of John Palmer's short-lived Royalty Theatre, just then, in early 1787, preparing to open and defy the Licensing Act of 1737. Leoni and Braham his nephew were in the company and they, of course, as singers remained unaffected by the Lord Chamberlain's edict preventing spoken drama there. On 31 October 1787 Leoni sang "Water Parted from the Sea" when Braham took his benefit. Leoni's last recorded performance in London was at Covent Garden in his greatest character, Carlos, on 2 June 1788, for his final benefit.

About 1790 Leoni, deep in debt, fled to Jamaica to escape his creditors. He sang in the synagogue at Kingston and died there early in 1797, according to the *Monthly Mirror* of February 1797.

Though at the height of his popularity Leoni had been entertained at the country house at Windsor of Admiral Walsingham, sometimes with Edward Nairne the scientist and sometimes with the Duke of Cumberland, John Williams in *The Pin Basket to the Children of Thespis* (1797), sent him off with the melancholy lines:

> Neglected, appall'd, sickly, poor and decay'd,
> See LEONI retiring in life's humble shade;
> 'Tis but few little years since the charms of his voice
> Made theatres echo, and thousands rejoice;
> When the Sock and the Buskin, depress'd and dismay'd,
> From the altars of Music call'd Voice to their aid.
> And by walking approv'd th{r}o the Thespian via,
> Tho' a slave to the tribes, prov'd the Drama's Messiah;
> But, like great SOBIESKI, the service forgot,
> The Pole and the Jew knew a similar lot;
> Tho' the first drove the Turk from the gates of Vienna,
> And the last banish'd Want when he woo'd the Duenna.

The American manager Edmund Simpson noted in 1818: "Notter said Windsor the music master gave it as his decided opinion that Leoni was only second to Braham—& yet, when he was engaged with [Samuel] Arnold, he was . . . such a slouch & wretch of an actor, the audience could not bear him." That fact may furnish the reason that he was so unsuccessful in finding permanent theatrical employment.

Leoni furnished some songs to the theatre. The hymn tune known as "Leoni" was composed by him to be sung as a *yigdal* in the synagogue; it was then supplied to the hymn writer Thomas Olwers and first published in a collection in 1781.

A portrait of Leoni as Arbaces was engraved by N. C. Goodnight (undated). An anonymous engraving of him as Don Carlos in *The Duenna* was published by Bew in 1778; a copy was published by Harrison as a plate to *Vocal Magazine*, 1799. An anonymous engraver pictured Leoni as Don Carlos and Isabella Mattocks as Louisa.

The artist John Downman listed in his sketch books (now at Butleigh Court) a sketch he had done in 1777 of "Mr. Lione, the celebrated Jew Singer," as part of a series of studies he was making for Mason's *Caractacus*, which premiered at Covent Garden on 6 December 1776. But Downman noted that he "had not the time to make a picture of it as I intended."

Leonore, Mlle [*fl.* 1794], *singer.*

Doane's *Musical Directory* of 1794 listed "Demois'lle Leonore," of No 4, Green Court, Soho, as a soprano who sang at the opera. The company list at the King's Theatre that year includes no such name, nor does the roster for 1793. Leonore may have been the singer's Christian name, but it does not match any of the known first names of singers in 1793 or 1794. In the former year Signora De Mira sang, and her Christian name is not known.

Leopard, Mr [*fl.* 1788], *actor.*

A Mr Leopard played Harry in *The Mock Doctor* at Sayer's booth at Bartholomew Fair in 1788. Possibly he was the "Lennerd" who was cited on the same bill as acting the French Servant in *Harlequin's Frolic*, but we have entered the two separately.

Le Picq. *See also* PICQ.

Le Picq, Charles 1744–*c.* 1809, *dancer, choreographer.*

According to G. B. L. Wilson's *Dictionary of Ballet*, Charles Le Picq was born in Strasbourg about 1749, but Marian Hannah Winter in *The Pre-Romantic Ballet*, citing Le Picq's own statement, gives his birth as 1744 in Naples. He was the son of the dancer Charles

Picq, who was active from 1727 to 1755. The Duke of Würtemberg and Teck, Karl Eugene, placed Jean Georges Noverre in charge of his ballet troupe at the Stuttgart court opera house in March 1760. Possibly Charles Le Picq was one of the members of the small *corps de ballet* at that time; he certainly was a year later. On 5 May 1761, according to the archives there, the supernumerary Le Picq was re-engaged for six years at a salary of 600 florins plus 100 florins shoe money tax free; he was to train under Noverre in serious dance. Le Picq made his debut in Stuttgart in November 1761. By 1773 he and other pupils of Noverre had gone to other countries, carrying Noverre's name, style, and ballets. Le Picq went to his native Naples and there staged *Armide* in 1773 and *Orfeo ed Euridice* and *Adèle de Ponthieu* in 1774. In 1778 Noverre's *Les Horaces et les Curiaces* was presented simultaneously by Noverre in Milan, Gallet in Vienna, Franchi in Venice, and Le Picq in Naples.

The Neapolitans were not sure what to make of the new French style of Noverre that Le Picq brought to them. On 24 July 1773 the Abbé Galliani reported to Parisians:

we have at present with us the celebrated dancer le Picq, who is giving the ballet Armide with its choruses and all that which could be given at the Opéra of your Palais Royal. One must admit that he is as good a dancer as Vestris and Dauberval. However he has found it harder to gallicize the Neapolitans than did Aufresne. He thought at first that he would be booed[,] for the Neapolitans, in a theatre as enormous and gigantic as ours, could not see that he was dancing since he did not jump. But as he is very well built, he began by taming the Neapolitans and little by little the nation was converted.

Deryck Lynham, from whose *Chevalier Noverre* the above information is gathered, points out that the Italian style called for dancers to use as much strength of movement as they could and to continue until they dropped exhausted; by comparison, the light French style must have seemed to them not dancing at all.

In September 1776 Le Picq was in Paris, dancing under Noverre at the Opéra at the Palais Royal. Baron Grimm saw him in *Caprices de Galathée* and wrote to Frederick of Prussia that Le Picq,

as the shepherd, left nothing to be desired. A charming face, the slenderest of waists, the easiest and lightest of movements, the purest and most vivacious and yet most natural style, such are the qualities which mark the talent of this new mime. . . . [H]e dances like the King of the Sylphs. If he has not all the nobility, all the expression of Vestris, all the strength and the balance of Gardel, he has perhaps in his execution something softer and yet more Brilliant. His grace and lightness triumph above all in demi-caractère dancing and that is the *genre* of the new ballet.

Le Picq became known as the "Apollo of the Dance."

Noverre came to London for the 1781–82 season at the King's Theatre, and Le Picq joined the company late. (The *Morning Herald* of 17 April 1782, announcing Le Picq's arrival from Naples, stated that he had been born in Edinburgh.) Le Picq's first appearance in England was on 2 May 1782, dancing in the premiere of Noverre's divertissement *Apollon et les muses* and in another new Noverre dance. The *Public Advertiser* said Le Picq had

more excellencies and fewer foibles than any dancer perhaps ever seen in England.

With as much expression, he has more ease than the elder Vestris; he excels the younger Vestris in everything but mere lightness of toe. In the power of exhilaration, the best power of the art, he is a formidable rival of Slingsby. And added to all this his deportment seems to be the perfection of nature. His walk is beyond all comparison the best we know of.

On 5 June Le Picq danced a minuet with Mme Simonet and Apelles to her Campaspe in Noverre's ballet. He had recently come from his sickbed, for in late May the papers reported that he and several other performers in London had been extremely ill. An epidemic had evidently struck but quickly passed.

On 30 November 1782 a pas de deux was danced at the King's Theatre by Le Picq and Mme (Geltruda or Margherita) Rossi. She was Le Picq's (second) wife, according to Lynham, making her first appearance in England, and she had come from the Opera at Naples. (*The Enciclopedia dello spettacolo* indicates that he was married to Anna Binetti [or Binety, as her name was spelled in England] and in 1764 was with her in Venice. Winter calls Signora Binetti Le Picq's first wife. The *Enciclopedia* has it that Le Picq went to Russia about 1786 with a new wife named "Gertrude.") Mme Rossi dazzled the audience just as her husband had the previous spring at his debut, and the critics again were agog: Le Picq "discovered such profusion of talents," said the *Public Advertiser*, "if we may be allowed the expression, as 'beggar all praise.'" Throughout the season Le Picq was seen dancing in *Apelles and Campaspe*, a solo *Passacaille*, a *Grande Allemande*, *La Bégueule*, and a *Sequedilla* with Mme Rossi. But he also demonstrated his skill as a composer of ballets; during the season he brought out *Le Tuteur trompé*, *Les Epouses Persans* (in which he danced the character of Tamas), *The Amours of Alexander and Roxana*, *La Dame bienfaisante*, and *The Four Nations*. At his benefit on 13 March 1783 he gave his address as No 9, facing the King's Theatre in the Haymarket (Mme Rossi had a different address); by the following spring he had moved to No 31, Pall Mall, where Mme Rossi also lived.

The 1783–84 season was as brilliant as the previous one, and Le Picq and the splendid group of dancers who appeared with him were recognized as among the finest England had ever seen. The *Public Advertiser* on 8 December 1783, for example, commenting on the dancing two days before, said

such exquisite perfection was never seen in England before, because there certainly never was before such a band of transcendant Dancers simultaneously on the same Stage. . . . They were almost equally admirable. Thus, if Vestris and Theodore were more surprising, Lepicq and Rossi were more touching, Slingsby more exhibiting.

The same periodical on 13 May 1784 again had nothing but praise:

The Dancers, incomparably the best Groupe in Europe, exerted themselves very successfully; D'Auberval's Drunkenness was well managed; Rossi's Fainting Fit, her Agitation preceding it, and her Revival from it; Lepicq's hovering over Rossi, when in the Swoon, and in his Separation from her, were all told very expressively indeed. Lepicq is the most graceful dancer in Europe, and excells every Competitor in the Narrative and Pathos of Gesticulation.

Le Picq spent most of that season just dancing, with D'Auberval serving as the chief choreographer.

In 1784–85, however, he once again brought out several new dance compositions: a new *Divertissement*, *Il convito deglie Dei*, *Il convitato di Pietra*, dances for *Orfeo*, and a ballet based on *Macbeth*. He also busied himself dancing the title part in *The Deserter*, participating in a set of *Caledonian Reels*, and dancing in the production of Gluck's *Orfeo* (augmented with other musical selections). Reactions to his work were cooler that season, however. The *Public Advertiser* on 18 March 1785 didn't quite know what to say about the *Macbeth* piece:

We cannot think last night's effort among the most successful . . . Lepicq and Rossi were the Macbeth and Lady—and considering the narrow boundaries of their art, which is tongue-tied, they discoursed "with most miraculous organs." Still, however, the whole of the material questions of the scene were agitated with all the disadvantages of contrast with comparative inefficience.

—whatever that means.

At his benefit on 14 April Le Picq offered a new ballet of his own based on the opera *Les Amours d'été*. The *Public Advertiser* two days later did not care for the special effects: "On machinery at this Theatre the less stress is laid the better. The boat, of which, had it been good, there was too much use, was very far from good. The representation of Lepicq swimming transgressed as little the commandment. And as to the ascent of Lepicq in the bucket, that was so badly managed as to put us in heart-felt trepidation. . . ." That was a rather unfortunate note on which to end his London dancing career. Le Picq left England after the 1784–85 season.

About 1786 he was engaged as the court ballet master at St Petersburg, where he worked until his retirement in 1798. He died there about 1806. His daughter Wilhelmine, by his second wife, danced in Russia and married the choreographer Auguste Poireau, according to Winter.

Le Picq, Mme Charles. *See* ROSSI, MME [GELTRUDA? or MARGHERITA?]

Le Pierre. *See* LA PIERRE.

L'Épine. *See* DE L'ÉPINE.

Lepine, Jonequet [*fl.* 1708–1714?], tailor.

A list of bills for the Queen's Theatre, dated 10 March 1708 and now among the Coke papers at Harvard, named Mr Lepine, "Taylor," for a payment of £7 2s. The Drury Lane accounts at the Folger Shakespeare Library indicate that costume materials were delivered to Jonequet Lepine in October 1714(?).

Le Post, Mimi [fl. 1727], dancer.

Mlle Mimi le Post and Mons de Camp, "first Dancers of the Opera at Brussels, just arrived," offered serious and grotesque dances between the acts at the King's Theatre on 23 March 1727. The troupe performing there was a *commedia dell' arte* company.

Leppie, Mons [fl. 1753?–1775], dancer.

Deryck Lynham in his *Chevalier Noverre* says that "Lepy" danced in 1753 at the Opéra Comique in Paris. It is difficult to be certain that the dancer Leppie, who was active in England from 1754 to 1773, was the "Lepy" or "Lépi" who performed on the Continent, but in England the dancer's name was sometimes spelled as we find it in continental records (or close to it), so if the references are not to the same person they are very likely to a relative.

Monsieur Leppie's earliest citations come from 1754, when he performed at the Jacob's Wells Theatre in Bristol in the summer; a dancer named Lepy was in the company of L'Acadèmie Royal de Musique in Paris on 1 July 1754 and could have been the same person. In 1754–55 at Covent Garden Theatre his name was spelled "Lepy" when he performed a *Chinese Dance* with Granier and a *Peasant Dance* with Frantzel and Signora Balbi on 4 January 1755 and when he and Lucas offered a *Comic Dance* on 15 April, but the bill on 18 April called him "Lepie" when he and Lucas repeated their dance. He was Lepie again on 6 May when he and Lucas danced *Les Charbonières*. The *Dictionnaire des Théâtres* said that a "Lépy" was a dancer in the Comédie Italienne and at the Opéra Comique and was at the latter theatre in 1756. It is significant that no dancer of that name (or with any variant spelling) appeared in London in 1755–56, though Leppie was back at Covent Garden in 1756–57.

From 1756–57 through 1761–62 Leppie danced at Covent Garden, appearing in a number of unnamed dances and ballets but occasionally being cited for specific roles or titled works. He was in a *New Comic Dance*; an *Old Scotch Dance*, a minuet, and a louvre with Miss Hilliard, who was often his partner; in the dances in *Macbeth*, *The Fair*, *Comus*, *The Prophetess*, and *Romeo and Juliet* (a minuet with Miss Hilliard was usually specified); in such entr'acte pieces as *Roast Beef of Old England*, *The Threshers*, *The Woodcutters*, and a *Bohemian Dance*; and such character parts as Mercury in the pantomime ballet *The Judgment of Paris*, a Satyr in *The Feast of Bacchus*, and a Hussar in *The Hungarian Gambols*. He also danced Air and a Demon in *The Rape of Proserpine*. He and his wife were paid £4 for seven days in 1761. He set himself up as a dancing master and introduced some of his scholars to Covent Garden audiences, as in April 1761, when a young gentlewoman and young gentleman did a comic dance and were identified as his pupils, or a month later when his apprentice danced a hornpipe.

Leppie renewed his association with the Jacob's Wells Theatre in Bristol at least as early as the summer of 1758 when, on 10 July, he danced *The Haymakers* there with Mrs Granier and had a benefit the following September. He may have been there other summers as well, but we are only certain of 1758, 1761, and 1762. He was probably the "Lepee" who danced at Sadler's Wells in 1759, 1760, and 1765.

In 1762–63 Leppie joined the company at Drury Lane, appearing first on 7 October 1762 in "a proper *Dance of Slaves*" in Act II of *Oroonoko*. That season he was also in a pastoral called *The Spring*, the masque in *Cymbeline*, and perhaps other works not named in the bills, but he seems not to have been used much in performance, and he remained only for that season. His name was not mentioned in London bills again until 1764–65, when he returned to Covent Garden. In the interim it seems almost certain he was on the Continent. On 11 February 1763 in Stuttgart a "Lepy" danced Fire in *Medea et Jason*, and that month he danced Orpheus to Mlle Toscanini's Eurydice to celebrate the Duke's birthday in Stuttgart. The troupe was headed by Noverre, and in it also was Charles Le Picq, who was just beginning his career.

When Leppie returned to England he danced at Covent Garden for two seasons, 1764–65 and 1765–66, appearing as a dancer in *Love in a Village*, the ballets *Rural Love* and *Les Caprices de Galatée*, and such entr'acte pieces as *The Jealous Woodcutter* and, with Miss Pitt, a *Wooden Shoe Dance*. He was not named in London bills from 1766–67 through 1768–69, and it is probable that he was the "Leppe" who danced at Norwich, advertised as from Covent Garden, in 1768–69. When he returned to London in 1769–70 he may not have affiliated himself with any company, for that season he danced in *Cymon* at Drury Lane and in the opera *Il disertore* at the King's Theatre, and in 1770–71 his only notice was for a solo *Ballad Dance* at the Haymarket.

On 2 November 1771 the King's Theatre advertised that "Lepie" and other new dancers had just been engaged, and for two seasons he danced there. Especially popular were the ballet *La Fête du village* and a pas de cinq in which he participated. The bills occasionally styled him "Lepy Senior" to distinguish him from a younger Leppie, probably his son, who began his career in 1770. The elder Leppie danced at Bristol in 1772, probably in the summer, but he is not known to have returned in 1773. After the 1772–73 season at the King's Theatre in London he seems to have left the stage. He was probably the Mr "Lepy" whose "Annual Ball" was set for 4 April 1775, according to the *Gazetteer and New Daily Advertiser* of 22 March of that year. Tickets were available from Leppie at No 5, Dover Street, Piccadilly.

Leppie, Mrs [*fl.* 1758–1763], *dancer.*

Mrs Leppie, the wife of the dancer Leppie who was active on the Continent and in England from perhaps 1753 to 1773, was first mentioned in the bills on 1 February 1758, when she and her husband danced in *The Prophetess* at Covent Garden. She remained at that house through 1761–62, appearing in *The Threshers* and as a Bacchante in *The Feast of Bacchus*, a dancer in *The Fair* and *Comus*, and as a Hussar in *The Hungarian Gambols*. She danced also in *The Rape of Proserpine* and *Apollo and Daphne*. The last work was the only one in which her husband did not also dance. On 12 April 1760 Mrs Leppie's tickets were admitted, and the accounts show that in 1761 she and her husband were receiving £4 for seven days work. With Leppie she moved to Drury Lane, where on 23 November 1762 and subsequent dates that month she danced in *The Witches*. But she was not cited in the bills thereafter and seems to have left the stage. Presumably she was the mother of the "Leppie Junior" who danced from 1770 on.

Leppie, Mr [*fl.* 1770?–1779?], *dancer, actor.*

On 19 May 1770 a "Leppy Junior" danced in *Il disertore* at the King's Theatre. It is probable that the name was misspelled and should have been Leppie, and if so the young man was very likely the son of the dancers Mr and Mrs Leppie who had been active in London for many seasons. The name "Lapper" also appears in the 1770s, and, as will be seen, other similar names turn up in the bills, all of them concerning a young dancer. On 5 October 1770 at the Haymarket Theatre a Master Lapper played the Drawer in *The Busy Body* and danced a hornpipe between the acts. At the same house on 16 September 1771 a dancer cited as "Lepper" performed a hornpipe. And years later, on 10 May 1779 a Mr Lapper danced a hornpipe at the Haymarket.

Leprey, Mr [*fl.* 1784–1785], *performer.*

In the Lord Chamberlain's accounts is a warrant noting that a Mr Leprey was an opera performer at the King's Theatre in 1784–85 and received £850—possibly for more than one season. No performer of that name is listed in *The London Stage*.

Le Prue, Mons [*fl.* 1729], *dancer.*

Harlequin in *The Humours of Harlequin* at the Haymarket Theatre on 25 February 1729 was danced by Monsieur Le Prue (or La Prue). He also danced at the Haymarket in June, offering with St Luce on the eleventh *Pierrot and French Peasant*.

Le Pulley, John [*fl.* 1780–1794], *dancer, violinist.*

John Le Pulley of the parish of St Dunstan in the West, Fleet Street, bachelor, married Henrietta Thompson, spinster, at St Marylebone on 21 October 1780. He was almost certainly the dancer "Lepulley" who performed a hornpipe at the Haymarket Theatre on 21 January 1782, for Doane's *Musical Directory* of 1794 described Le Pulley as a violinist and dancing master living in Red Lion Court, Fleet Street.

Lepy. *See* LEPPIE.

Lequerie. *See* LAGUERRE.

Le Ragois, Benigne. *See* RAGOIS, BENIGNE.

Le Revier. *See* LA RIVIERE.

Le Rich. *See* LA RICH.

Le Roch. *See* LA ROCHE.

Le Roy, Mons [*fl.* 1675], *dancer.*
Monsieur Le Roy danced in the court masque *Calisto* on 15 February 1675.

Le Roy, Mr [*fl.* 1777], *scene painter.*
Mr Le Roy helped on the scenery for *Harlequin's Invasion* at Drury Lane on 1 January 1777.

Le Roy, Mlle [*fl.* 1737], *dancer.*
At Hallam's Bartholomew Fair booth on 23 August and Hallam and Lee's Southwark Fair booth on 7 September 1737 Mlle Le Roy performed some of the dances.

Le Sac. *See also* ISAAC.

Le Sac, Mr [*fl.* 1707–1712], *violinist.*
Mr Le Sac in late 1707 was temporarily turned out of Drury Lane Theatre, where he had been a member of the band, for having negotiated for a job at the Queen's Theatre. His pay scale at Drury Lane was £1 10s. weekly, and as things turned out he was granted permission to play for the operas at the Queen's, apparently while still performing his duties in the Drury Lane band. Le Sac earned 11s. 3d. daily at the Queen's as a "treble" player (violinist) and played at least through 1711–12.

Le Sac, Mr [*fl.* 1725–1737], *dancer.*
At the Lincoln's Inn Fields Theatre on 26 October 1725 "Young Le Sac" and Miss La Tour made their first stage appearances in an unnamed dance. They were described as scholars of Dupré. Perhaps Le Sac was close to his majority, for the bills during the months that followed style him "Young Le Sac" sometimes, but "Le Sac" at other times. He and Miss La Tour offered entr'acte turns such as a *Spanish Entry* and *Shepherd and Shepherdess* during the 1725–26 season. Le Sac danced at Lincoln's Inn Fields again in 1726–27, sharing a benefit in May 1727 with Miss La Tour and offering with her a chaconne and by himself a *Spanish Dance.* Their income was £61 5s. 6d. before house charges, which would have been about £20.

Not until 24 June 1729 was Le Sac mentioned in London bills again, it seems; on that date at the Haymarket Theatre he danced Adonis in *The Humours of Harlequin.* He rejoined the Lincoln's Inn Fields troupe for the 1732–33 season, once again dancing specialty turns with Miss La Tour. He also had the roles of Water and Fire in *The Rape of Proserpine*, his first known assignments there in a pantomime. With the company he moved to the new Covent Garden Theatre in December 1732, appearing on the eighth (the day after the grand opening) in a group comic dance. He stayed at Covent Garden through the 1733–34 season, dancing between the acts and playing a Polonese, Spaniard, Frenchman, and Bridal Swain in *Apollo and Daphne*, a Fawn, Grecian, and Harlequin Man in *The Necromancer*, and a Zephyr and Bridal Swain in *The Nuptial Masque.* Some of the specialty dances he was in were a *Scottish Dance, Pygmalion*, and *The Nassau.*

He danced a busy season at Covent Garden in 1734–35, repeating some of his old pantomime parts and entr'acte turns and appearing also in *Richmond Maggot* with Miss Rogers that was given again and again during the season. He also played an Infernal in *Perseus and Andromeda* and danced in *The Faithful Shepherd, Grecian Sailors*, and a *Grand Pastoral Dance.* On 12 September 1734 at Richmond he danced with Miss Rogers, and on 21 March 1735 he performed at York Buildings, described, oddly, as from Drury Lane. He joined the Giffard company at Goodman's Fields for the 1735–36 season, appearing in some pantomimes and dancing entr'acte pieces: *Richmond Maggot* with Mrs Woodward, a Waterman in the masque *Britannia*, a Pantaloon Man in *The Necromancer*, and a Swain and a Triton in *Harlequin Shipwrecked* (on 20 February 1736, on which night he or possibly a second Le Sac, danced Harlequin in a dance called *The Pastoral* at the Haymarket; his turn there came late in the evening, so one dancer may have been able to appear at both theatres that night). On 1 July at Lincoln's Inn Fields Le Sac danced Harlequin in *The Chymical Counterfeits.*

Le Sac moved with the Giffard troupe to

LE SAC

Lincoln's Inn Fields in 1736–37, appearing with Mrs Woodward in the popular *Richmond Maggot*, dancing in *The Worm Doctor* and *Harlequin Shipwrecked*, and serving as a member of the dancing chorus in *Hymen's Triumph*. But he appears to have left the company in early February; he danced in *The Tempest* at Drury Lane on 10 February 1737. Only a few performances were given, and after mid-February Le Sac's name disappeared from the bills. The Master Le Sac who appeared at Goodman's Fields in December 1732 may have been our subject's younger brother.

Le Sac, Master [*fl.* 1732], *dancer.*

At Goodman's Fields Theatre on 18 December 1732 a dance called *Harlequin* was performed by a Master Le Sac, who was advertised as making his first appearance on that stage. The wording would suggest that Le Sac had performed elsewhere previously. There was a dancer named Le Sac performing at Covent Garden that month—he appeared there the day after Master Le Sac danced at Goodman's Fields. The Covent Garden dancer made his first appearance as "Young Le Sac" in 1725 and would probably not be called Master in 1732, so we take Master Le Sac to be a different person, possibly a younger brother. Master Le Sac danced again at Goodman's Fields on 19 December, but then his name disappeared from the playbills.

Lesage, [Charles?] [*fl.* 1721?–1738?], *actor, manager?*

Francisque Moylin brought a troupe of French players to London to perform at the Haymarket Theatre from 26 October 1734 to 3 June 1735, and the group also appeared at Goodman's Fields Theatre on 23 May and 4 June 1735. In the troupe were, according to Sybil Rosenfeld in her *Foreign Theatrical Companies*, Lesage (or Le Sage) Senior and Junior (brothers?) and their wives. The elder Lesage played Damis in *Tartuffe*, Acab in *Sampson Judge of Israel*, Le Marquis de Polinville in *Le François à Londres*, Le Marquis du Hazard in *Le Joueur*, the title role in *Amphitryon*, Thomas Diaphoirus in *Le Malade imaginaire*, Leandre in *Arlequin Balourd*, Octave in *La Fille capitaine et Arlequin son sergeant*, Don John in *Le Festin de Pierre*, Orosmane in *Zaire*, Dorante in *Le Bourgeois Gentilhomme*, Sigismond in *La Vie est un songe*, Frederick in *Gustave Vasa*, and Le Prince Poloneus in *La Fausse Coquette*. On 13 February 1735 he and Lesage Junior shared a benefit.

The identity of the elder Lesage is not certain, but he could well have been Charles Lesage, who was in Holland in 1721 and with Mlle le Grand managed a troupe at the Hague in 1738. What makes that identification plausible is the fact that on 19 March 1735 at the Portuguese Embassy Chapel in London a Charles Le Sage witnessed the marriage of Leonard Forcade and Mary Ann Joseph Desprez; one of the other members of Moylin's troupe in 1734–35 was a Monsieur Fourcade.

The elder Lesage's wife seems to have been cited in the bills only on 13 December 1734, when she played Nerine in *Le Joueur*.

Lesage, Mme [Charles?] [*fl.* 1734–1735], *actress.* See LESAGE, [CHARLES?].

Lesage, Jean-Baptiste [*fl.* 1735–1738], *actor, manager.*

The Lesage (or Le Sage) Junior who, with his wife, was a member of Francisque Moylin's French troupe at the Haymarket and Goodman's Fields theatres from 26 October 1734 to 4 June 1735 was evidently Jean-Baptiste Lesage, who returned to London later in the 1730s. During his 1734–35 visit he played Valère in *Tartuffe*, the title role in *Sampson Judge of Israel*, Le Baron de Polinville in *Le François à Londres*, Valere in *Le Joueur*, Jupiter in *Amphitryon*, Cleanthe in *Le Malade imaginaire*, Don Rodriques in *Ines de Castro*, Don Phillip in *Le Festin de Pierre*, Nerestan in *Zaire*, Cleontes in *Le Bourgeois Gentilhomme*, the Duke of Muscovy in *La Vie est un songe*, and the title role in *Gustave Vasa*. On 13 February 1735 he and the elder Lesage shared a benefit. Judging from the roles the two Lesages played, they were probably not father and son but perhaps brothers; at least they would seem to have been close to one another in age.

On 25 September 1738 Moylin, or his younger brother Simon, and Lesage Junior brought to London a French troupe to perform at the Haymarket, which had been closed to English performers by the Licensing Act of 1737. The company opened, or tried to, on 9 October to a packed house, but most of the patrons who came were there to disrupt the performance. Someone piped up with "Roast Beef of Old England," and two justices tried to keep the peace but could not. The actors were protected by two lines of grenadiers with fixed bayonets, but the crowd was not stopped from hissing, cat-calling, ringing bells, and knocking out candles. Since the actors could not be heard (*L'Embarras des riches* and *Arlequin poli par l'amour* were scheduled), they turned the stage over to dancers, but the mob threw peas all over the stage to stop their performance. Finally the players had to escape by way of windows and back doors. (Benjamin Victor's full account may be found in Francisque Moylin's entry.)

On 8 November the leaders of the French troupe placed an appeal in the *Daily Post*:

The Case of the FRENCH COMEDIANS. Whereas we, Moylin Francisque and John Baptist le Sage, were in England in the Month of February last, and having then obtained leave to bring over a French Company of Comedians, for to represent the same in the Little Theatre in the Hay-Market this Season; we, for that Purpose, returned into France, and collected together the best Company that were to be had; being wholly ignorant of any Affairs transacted in England relating to the Regulation of the Stage, and not in the least doubting but that the Company would meet with the same Encouragement as heretofore, made us engage with several Performers abroad, at very great Expences, to come into England; and the Night the said Company were to have acted, they met with such an Obstruction from the Audience, that a Stop was put to the Performance, and the said Company discontinued, and laid aside all Thoughts of making the least Attempt, since the same was not agreeable to the Publick. Notwithstanding we the said Undertakers, by the Contracts we made, have been obliged to pay to each Performer the same Monies hitherto, and liable to the same Obligations for the Remainder of this whole Season, as if the Company had performed the whole Time, and have besides expended large Sums of Money, and contracted several Debts here which we are not in Circumstances to pay: So that we are obliged to lay our Case before the Publick, in hopes that they will be so indulgent as to permit us to perform three Nights only in one of the Patent Theatres, so as to enable us to discharge those Debts we have contracted here, and we will then humbly take our Leaves, and return to France, with grateful Acknowledgement for the Favour done to us. Suffolk-street, Nov. 6, 1738.

Their plea fell on deaf ears, according to Rosenfeld, but the *Evening Post* of 18 November 1738 reported that £600 was collected for the French players, over £300 coming from the court.

Lesage, Mme Jean-Baptiste [*fl.* 1734–1735], *actress, dancer*.

Mme Jean-Baptiste Lesage was the wife of the younger of two actors named Lesage who performed at the Haymarket and Goodman's Fields under Francisque Moylin from 26 October 1734 to 4 June 1735. She was first cited in the playbill of 20 December 1734 (as Mrs Le Sage Jr; we take references to Mrs Le Sage to be to the elder Lesage's wife); she acted Cleanthis in *Amphitryon*. On 23 December she played Antoinette in *La Malade imaginaire*. On 27 December our Mme Le Sage danced a Scaramouch Woman in a chaconne; then she was seen as Nicole in *Le Bourgeois Gentilhomme* on 13 January 1735 and Sophie in *Gustave Vasa* on 5 February. There is no evidence that she returned with her husband, Jean Baptiste Lesage, in 1738, but she may have. In any case, that engagement met with a rioting audience and had to be cut short.

Le Sal. *See* LE SAC.

Lescot, Mons [*fl.* 1753?–1758], *dancer, manager*.

Monsieur and Madame Lescot danced at the King's Theatre in January 1758, after which she seems to have been dropped from the bills, though he may have continued to 20 May. Their first notice was on 10 January, when the bill, according to *The London Stage*, designated Lescot as the "Maestri d'Balli" and his wife as one of the ballerini. Beginning 31 January Lescot played the Maestra de Balli in *Solimano*. There was a Lescot who with Fetigny and Baubour managed a troupe at Gand (Gent) in 1753–54, according to Fuchs's *Lexique*.

Lescot, Mme [*fl.* 1758], *dancer*. *See* LESCOT, MONS..

Leserve, Anna Maria *d.* 1831, *actress, singer*.

Anna Maria Leserve was first noticed in the London bills on 30 April 1787, when she acted Betty in *The Hypocrite* and Lady Scrape in *The Musical Lady* at the Haymarket Theatre, pieces performed by special permission of the Lord Chamberlain. For several subsequent seasons she evidently toured the provinces and is known to have sung in the chorus of principal Natives in *The Death of Captain Cook* in the theatre in Frankfurt Gate, Plymouth, on 17 August 1789.

Though her name was not listed for any roles at Covent Garden Theatre in 1790–91, she was an obscure member of that company, sharing in benefit tickets with Follett and Warrell on 13 June 1791. In 1791–92 at Covent Garden, she was advertised for chorus singing in *The Crusade*, *The Woodman*, *Blue-Beard*, and *Orpheus and Eurydice*. She acted Miss La Blonde in *The Romp* on 10 March 1792 and Winifred in *A Cure for a Coxcomb* on 15 May.

In the summer of 1792 Miss Leserve played at Richmond, Surrey. Among her roles were Miss Ogle in *The Belle's Stratagem*, Mrs Ledger in *The Road to Ruin*, Floretta in *The Quaker*, and Lauretta in *A Day in Turkey*. Her return to Covent Garden in the autumn of 1792 brought her some higher status, for that season she was seen as Sister Ann in *Blue-Beard*, an unspecified character in *Just in Time*, the Maid in *Two Strings to Your Bow*, the Maid in *Harlequin's Museum*, Bianca in *Catherine and Petruchio*, and on 31 May 1793 Lucy in *The Rivals*.

During the remainder of the decade at Covent Garden, earning £1 5s. per week, but raised to £1 10s. in 1799–1800, she was employed in numerous choruses of musical entertainments, played her share of maids in farces, and filled several important roles in pantomimes. A selected list of her assignments includes a principal character in *Harlequin's Chaplet*, a Biscayan Girl in *The Midnight Wanderers*, the Miller's Wife and an Aerial Spirit in *Harlequin and Faustus*, Juliette in *Love's Frailties* in 1793–94; a Country Girl in *The Mysteries of the Castle*, Helen in *Cymbeline*, Martha in *Life's Vagaries*, the Parson's Wife in *The Tythe Pig* in 1794–95; Arante in *King Lear*, Mrs Slammekin in *The Beggar's Opera*, a Maid in *Lord Mayor's Day*, and Fanny in *The Way to Get Married* (Morton's very successful comedy which premiered on 23 January 1796) in 1795–96; an Irish Peasant in *Bantry Bay*, and Lucy in *The Devil to Pay* in 1796–97; Margaret in *Much Ado about Nothing*, Florella in *The Orphan*, Mignionet in *The Way to Keep Him*, and Lesbia in *The Comedy of Errors* in 1797–98; Susan in *The Spoil'd Child*, a Country Girl in *Lovers' Vows*, and a Market Woman in *The Magic Oak* in 1798–99; and Betty in *Management*, and an Attendant in *The Volcano* in 1799–1800.

During the summers at the Haymarket Theatre among other roles she performed maids in *She Stoops to Conquer* and in *Two Strings to Your Bow* in 1797; Dolly in *Throw Physick to the Dogs* and Lucy in *The Rivals* in 1798; Jane in *Family Distress*, Toilet in *The Jealous Wife*, and Mrs Gadabout in *The Lying Valet* in 1799; and a Negress in *Obi* in 1800.

All the 1799 edition of *Authentic Memoirs of the Green Room*, had to say about her was: "As this lady's employ is entirely confined to insignificant characters, the bare mention of her name will be sufficient." Her notice in the 1801 edition, however, was, appropriately, inflated:

Bottomed on the true, genuine principles of Dutch symmetry, this actress claims the epithet of *great*, more in reference to her person, which in breeches would convey no imperfect idea of Falstaff, even without the previous ceremony of stuffing, than with a view to her professional acquirements. Yet, possessing a requisite stock of industry and perseverance, she renders herself useful, not merely as a representative of filles de chambre, and maid-servants, but even of nobility, nay, of MAJESTY itself!—where there is little or nothing to be said or done! Her countenance exhibits the very picture of good nature, and is, we make no doubt, in this respect, a faithful index of her heart.

Miss Leserve continued in this modest professional status at Covent Garden through 1814–15. Her salary from 1800–1801 through 1803–4 was £2 per week, but in the following season it was lowered to £1 10s., at which level it seems to have remained. From 1801 to 1810 she was also a chorus singer at the Haymarket. She signed her initials and surname to a Covent Garden salary receipt in 1809.

Though she seems not to have married, by 1800–1801 she was billed as Mrs Leserve, no doubt in deference to her increasingly matronly girth. She seems to have been the mistress—or perhaps common-law wife—of the Covent Garden actor John Ledger, who left the bulk of his estate in 1808 to "Anna Maria Leserve of the Theatre Royal Covent Garden." According to the *Dramatic Register*, Miss Leserve died in 1831.

Leslie, Mr [*fl.* 1774–1785], *actor.*

The "Lessley" who was named on a list of "Supernumery Men" in the Drury Lane accounts in 1774–75 was surely the Mr Leslie who was named in the bills there at benefit time from as early as 28 May 1779 to as late as 21 May 1785. Perhaps he was also the Leslie who worked at the Liverpool theatre in October and November 1777 for 15s. weekly but left there after his fourth week.

L'Espine or **L'Espini**. *See* DE L'ÉPINE.

Lessingham, Jane, née Hemet, formerly Mrs John Stott 1739?–1783, *actress.*

The inscription on Jane Lessingham's gravestone in Hampstead churchyard indicates that she was aged 44 when she died in 1783; thus it would appear that she had been born in 1738 or 1739. But if so, and if some of the stories about her are true, then she had packed a variety of experiences into her youth. Her maiden name was Hemet (though in the records of her divorce proceedings it was spelled Hamett), and reputedly she was the daughter of the king's dentist. John Taylor in *Records of My Life* (1832) claimed that prior to her marriage to John Stott in 1755 Jane had passed for Samuel Derrick's wife and had lived with him in Shoe Lane, Holborn. It was Derrick, according to Taylor, who had prepared Jane for the stage. But more likely her relationship with Derrick did not begin until after her marriage to Stott and while her husband was away at sea.

On 28 December 1755 at St Paul, Covent Garden, Jane Hemet, spinster of that parish, was married to John Stott, widower of the same parish. The marriage was allowed by license of the Bishop of London, probably because of the bride's age, which, if the birthdate of 1739 is correct, would have been short of 17 years. Jacob Hemet, perhaps the brother mentioned in a deposition given in 1765, witnessed the ceremony.

Advertised as a "Young Gentlewoman" making her first appearance on any stage, Mrs Stott acted Desdemona in *Othello* at Covent Garden Theatre on 18 November 1756. She did not reappear at Covent Garden until 1762, and then was called Mrs Lessingham. Some

Harvard Theatre Collection

JANE LESSINGHAM, as Oriana
engraving by Thornthwaite, after Roberts

facts about her during those intervening years are preserved in *Trials for Adultery* (1780), where a divorce action brought against her by John Stott in 1765 is referred to. Testimony in that trial established that Stott, a naval commander, on 17 February 1758 sailed on his ship, the *Gramont*, bound for America; in August of that year he became commander of the *Scarborough*, which remained in American waters for three years. Meanwhile, Jane Stott had remained in London, living first in Great Mattock Street, Hanover Square, and then in Dean Street, Westminster. Several women deposed that they witnessed her delivered of a female child at the later address on 7 June 1759. Recording of the baptism of the child at St Anne, Westminster, was testified to by William James, who presented a copy of the original entry to the Court; but the name and date of baptism of the child were not published in the account. The court concluded that Mrs Stott, "unmindful of her conjugal vow, and not having the fear of God before her eyes, but being instigated and seduced by the devil, did commit adultery with one or more strange person, or persons, and was by such criminal conversation begot with child." Stott was granted his divorce in April 1765.

Perhaps it was during Stott's sea duty that Mrs Stott had taken up with Derrick. Taylor's father had described her as a pretty woman of "extraordinary" character, who, after separating from Derrick, used to don men's clothes and frequent the coffee houses.

Again advertised as a young gentlewoman, she reappeared at Covent Garden on 3 February 1762 in the title role of *Jane Shore*. Still called a young gentlewoman, she played Elvira in *The Spanish Fryar* on 1 March, and then when she acted Sylvia in *The Recruiting Officer* on 9 March she was identified in the bills as Mrs Lessingham. Evidently she had adopted that alias as a stage name, for at the time she was still Stott's wife. Before the 1761–62 season ended, Mrs Lessingham also played Harriet in *The Jealous Wife*, Belinda in *The Provok'd Wife*, and a character in *The Twins*. She returned to Covent Garden in 1762–63 to act occasionally such roles as Melinda in *The Recruiting Officer*, Harriet in *The Jealous Wife*, Amanda in *Love's Last Shift*, and Dame Kitely in *Every Man in His Humour*.

Early in the next season she acted Sylvia in *The Recruiting Officer* at Covent Garden on 23 September 1763 and then went to play at Smock Alley Theatre in Dublin, where she remained for the season. Announced as from Dublin, she made her debut at Drury Lane Theatre on 29 October 1764 as Juliet in *Romeo and Juliet* and played Lady Fanciful in *The Provok'd Wife* on 23 January 1765, Clarissa in *The Confederacy* on 17 May, and Melinda in *The Recruiting Officer* on 18 May. On 18 October 1765 she acted Lady Townly in *The Provok'd Husband*. She performed at Bath and Bristol during 1765–66 and then was again at Drury Lane in the spring of 1767, when she appeared in the title role of *The Country Girl* on 29 April—Garrick, on his way home from Bath, wrote to his brother George on 2 May that he heard Lessingham was "bad." Before the season ended she also acted Lady Townly, Fidelia in *The Plain Dealer*, Imogen in *Cymbeline*, the title role in *Jane Shore*, and Jacintha in *The Suspicious Husband*. That summer she played at Richmond, Surrey.

When Garrick refused to meet her demands for a salary of £4 per week, in the fall of 1767, Mrs Lessingham engaged at Covent Garden Theatre, then under the combined management of George Colman, William Powell, the wine merchant John Rutherford, and the prosperous soap manufacturer Thomas Harris. After appearing on 26 September as Clarissa in *The City Wives Confederacy* Mrs Lessingham was seen that season as Nerissa in *The Merchant of Venice*, Lavinia in *The Fair Penitent*, Mrs Sullen in *The Stratagem*, Betty in *The Clandestine Marriage*, Oriana in *The Inconstant*, and Lady Anne in *Richard III*. She became a central figure in the

Harvard Theatre Collection

JANE LESSINGHAM as Mrs Sullen and WILLIAM T. LEWIS (?) as Archer

engraving by Walker, after Barralet

managerial disputes which quickly developed between Colman and Powell on the one hand and Harris and Rutherford on the other over the authority to hire theatrical personnel. Just when Mrs Lessingham became Harris's mistress is not clear, but the season was not far along before Harris accused Colman of being unfair in his assignment of parts to her. Evidently Colman had been dissatisfied with her acting of Mrs Sullen on 17 November 1767. He took the role from her and gave it to Mrs Bulkley. There had also been a dispute between Mrs Lessingham and Mrs Yates about the occupancy of a dressing room. Then Harris and Rutherford demanded that Mrs Lessingham and George Anne Bellamy, Rutherford's mistress, be accommodated with private dressing rooms.

On 29 December 1767 the press announced that Jane Lessingham would shortly publish her *Expostulations with George Colman*, but it seems not to have appeared as promised. Thomas Harris, however, did publish in 1768 an epistle to her called *The Ring*, in which he defended her against gossip and greenroom abuse and claimed that if her colleagues would refrain from defaming her by "pois'nous arts" she could be superior to all, including Mrs Barry, Mrs Mattocks, and Mrs Yates. In *The Ring* Mrs Lessingham was described as fine-figured, with glossy brown hair, fair skin, laughing eyes, and "Breasts that had tempted *Antony* away."

Mrs Lessingham's engagement at Covent Garden extended for 15 seasons. Among her roles were Sophronia in *The Refusal*, Flora in *She Wou'd and She Wou'd Not*, Young Clackit in *The Guardian*, Madam Florival in *The Deuce Is in Him*, Jacintha in *The Suspicious Husband*, Imogen in *Cymbeline* (a role she also played at Drury Lane on 5 April 1774 when Miss Younge became ill), Miss Neville in *She Stoops to Conquer*, Lucy in the premiere of *The Rivals* on 17 January 1775, Hero in *Much Ado about Nothing*, Mrs Conquest in *The Lady's Last Stake*, and Luciana in *The Comedy of Errors*. In 1781–82, her last full season at Covent Garden, she acted Nerissa in *The Merchant of Venice*, Hero in *Much Ado about Nothing*, Dorinda in *The Stratagem*, Lady Grace in *The Provok'd Husband*, and Florimel in the premiere of O'Keeffe's *The Positive Man* on 16 March 1782. In his *Miscellanies in Prose and Verse* (1775), William Hawkins described her as "very agreeable in some parts of comedy, but wretchedly horrible in tragedy, being destitute of voice, manner, expression, and in short, almost every requisite." Francis Gentleman wrote of her in *The Theatres*:

> *She has of managers long been the care;*
> *Oh, that regard would make her all their own,*
> *And snatch a tasteless milksop from the town;*
> *One who for parts eternally will fight,*
> *Without the sense, or talents to be right.*

Her salary was a constant £7 per week from 1776–77 through 1781–82. In the Harvard Theatre Collection is a paysheet signed by her acknowledging receipt of £206 15s. in full for acting 177 days (at £1 3s. 4d. per day) in 1777–78. At her benefit on 24 April 1778 she received £160 7s., less £64 10s. in house charges.

By April 1776 Mrs Lessingham had a house at the corner of Percy Street, Rathbone Place.

Harvard Theatre Collection

JANE LESSINGHAM, as Sylvia
artist unknown

About 1775 she also acquired, evidently from Harris, a house on Hampstead Heath and became involved in a great legal dispute with the copy holders in the area who contended that the land had been "irregularly granted for the purpose of building a house and forming pleasure grounds." The suit, at Westminster Hall, was decided in her favor (Folkard against Hemet and another, Easter Term, 16 Geo III, 1776, and several sittings for Common Pleas that year). It is said that Mrs Lessingham published a pamphlet entitled *The Hampstead Contest*. According to the *Town and Country Magazine* of May 1777, she also had developed an amorous relationship with Justice Addington of Bow Street.

Mrs Lessingham began the 1782–83 season by acting Nerissa on 29 October. The late start suggests that she may have been ill, for after playing Mlle Florival on 14 November and Jacintha on 27 November 1782 she made no further appearances. She died on 13 March 1783 and was buried in Hampstead churchyard on 17 March. A stone bearing her maiden name of Hemet was originally placed on her grave, but in 1802 her son William Frederick replaced it with a flat stone inscribed:

$$\text{M}^{\text{rs}} \text{ Jane Lessingham}$$
late of the Theatre royal
Covent Garden
Ob^{t} 13 March 1783
AE^{t} 44

In a will drawn on 12 December 1782, which she signed Jane Hemet, without witnesses, she left all her estate to Thomas Harris in trust for the sole use of her three sons Thomas, Charles, and Edwin; and she provided that should another son (William) Frederick "not be better provided for he must take his share with the rest but not otherwise." Thomas, Charles, and Edwin were likely the sons by Harris, reported by Taylor. (Harris also had a daughter who died in 1802 at the age of 15 and a son, George, who became a captain in the Royal Navy.) William Frederick, who later assumed the name of Williams, perhaps was the issue of another liaison; he died on 24 October 1805, at the age of 33, and was buried beside his mother. Mrs Lessingham did not mention in her will the bastard daughter born in 1759 when she was still married to Stott. Perhaps she was the Miss Hemet who made her debut at the Haymarket Theatre on 24 June 1780. The will was proved at London on 14 May 1784 by Thomas Harris, to whom administration was granted; John Webster, gentleman of the parish of St Thomas the Apostle, and James Brandon, the Covent Garden house servant, had appeared earlier to testify to their acquaintance with the deceased and with her handwriting.

Portraits of Jane Lessingham include:

1. By unknown engraver, on a plate with a portrait of Justice Addington, published in the *Town and Country Magazine*, June 1777.
2. By unknown engraver, on a plate with a portrait of George Colman the elder, published in the *Town and Country Magazine*, 1780.
3. As Flora in *She Wou'd and She Wou'd Not*. Engraving by Terry, published by Harrison & Co, 1779.
4. As Nerissa, with Charles Macklin as Shylock, and others, in *The Merchant of Venice*. The Trial Scene, painted by Johann Zoffany. In the Tate Gallery. For a discussion of this painting, which is reproduced in this dictionary with the notice of Charles Macklin, see Raymond Mander and Joe Mitchenson, *The Artist and the Theatre* (1955).
5. As Ophelia in *Hamlet*. Colored drawing by J. Roberts. In the British Library. Engraving by C. Grignion, published as a plate to Bell's *Shakespeare*, 1775.
6. As Oriana in *The Inconstant*. Engraving by Thornthwaite, after J. Roberts, published as a plate to *Bell's British Theatre*, 1777.
7. As Oriana. India ink drawing by unknown artist. In the British Library. Engraving by unknown engraver, published by Wenman, August 1777.
8. As Mrs Sullen, with William T. Lewis as Archer, in *The Stratagem*. Engraving by Walker, after Barralet, published as a plate to *New English Theatre*, 1776.
9. As Sylvia in *The Recruiting Officer*. By unknown engraver.

Lestant. *See* LE TEMPS.

Lester, Mr [*fl.* 1798$_1$], *house servant?*
Mr Lester's benefit tickets were accepted at Covent Garden Theatre on 5 June 1798. He was probably a house servant.

Lester, Thomas [*fl.* 1794–1815], musician.

Thomas Lester was a subscriber to the New Musical Fund in 1794, 1805, and 1815 and presumably performed in concerts sponsored by that organization.

Lestourgeon, William [*fl.* 1794], violoncellist.

Doane's *Musical Directory* of 1794 listed William Lestourgeon, of Hounsditch, as a violoncellist who played for the Choral Fund and the Cecilian Society. Nathanael Thomas Lestourgeon, possibly William's father but surely related, was buried at St Paul, Covent Garden, on 26 June 1762.

Lestrade. *See* **DESTRADE.**

L'Estrange, John [*fl.* 1732–1739], musician.

A concert for the benefit of "J. L'Estrange Jr" was played in the Great Room at the Three Tuns and Bull Head, Cheapside, on 4 March 1732. John L'Estrange was listed as one of the original subscribers ("being musicians") to the Royal Society of Musicians in the "Declaration of Trust" establishing that organization on 28 August 1739.

L'Estrange, Joseph 1724?–1804, actor.

When Joseph L'Estrange joined the company at Smock Alley, Dublin, on 26 November 1770, *Faulkner's Daily Journal* reported that he was from Drury Lane Theatre. The Drury Lane bills do not, however, reveal his name prior to his Irish debut; if he had been at Drury Lane before it would have been in a very minor, supernumerary capacity. After his first season at Smock Alley, L'Estrange and other actors from Dublin, led by Ryder, played at Waterford between September and November 1771. There on 9 October 1771 L'Estrange acted Cha-Zeba in the premiere of *Love and Despair*, a tragedy written by an unnamed gentleman of Waterford. L'Estrange returned to Smock Alley for 1771–72, and then he joined a strolling company which played at Cooper's Hall, Bristol, from November 1772 to April 1773. He returned to Dublin to play at the Crow Street Theatre in the summer of 1773 and at the Capel Street Theatre in 1773–74.

Departing Ireland after the 1774 summer season at Galway, L'Estrange was engaged at Covent Garden Theatre, where he made his first appearance on 20 October 1774 as the King in *Philaster*, a role he repeated on the twenty-sixth. His next roles were the Herald in *The Grecian Daughter* on 31 October, Orasmin in *Zara* on 3 December, and Sussex in *Lady Jane Gray* on 9 December, after which he was seen that season as the Duke in *Othello*, Catesby in *Jane Shore*, Raleigh in *The Earl of Essex*, Phoenix in *The Distrest Mother*, Cratander in *Phaedra and Hippolitus*, Zopyrus in *Cleonice, Princess of Bithynia*, Oliver in *As You Like It*, and Lucius in *Theodosius*. On 18 March 1775, L'Estrange acted the Assassin in the first performance of Thomas Hull's *Edward and Eleanora*. On 20 May he played the title role in *Cymbeline*.

That summer he joined Foote's company at the Haymarket Theatre, making his first appearance there on 22 May 1775 in an unspecified role in *The Nabob*, followed by Paduasoy in *The Commissary*, Governor Cape and Vamp in *The Author*, Bertran in *The Spanish Fryar*, Foigard in *The Beaux' Stratagem*, Face in *The Tobacconist*, and an unspecified role in *The Bankrupt*.

In the autumn of 1775 L'Estrange returned to Covent Garden, where he held an engagement through 1781–82 at a constant salary of £2 per week. Among his many supporting roles in the line of mature counselors, old soldiers, priests, governors, and the like were, to name but a few, Lavinio in *A Duke and No Duke*, the Lieutenant in *Richard III*, Sir W. Belmont in *All in the Wrong*, the Duke in *The Comedy of Errors*, the Priest in *Ethelinda*, Tigranes in *Zenobia*, Alonzo in *The Tempest*, Minos in *The Mirror*, the Chaplain in *The Orphan*, Rossano in *The Fair Penitent*, Lenox in *Macbeth*, Borachio in *Much Ado about Nothing*, the Player King in *Hamlet*, Heli in *The Mourning Bride*, and the Provost in *Measure for Measure*. Occasionally he was brought on in a younger role, the parts of Tybalt in *Romeo and Juliet* and Albany in *King Lear* being assigned him in the repertory. On 14 May 1777, when he acted Rhodolpho in *Tancred and Sigismunda* for a benefit shared with Mrs Pitt, tickets could be had of him in Bolton Street. In 1782–83, though still on the paylist at £2 per week, L'Estrange acted at Covent Garden only twice, appearing

L'ESTRANGE

as Mr Wrath in *The Wishes* on 3 and 4 October 1782. Thereafter he seems not to have been engaged again, except for one more performance on 10 June 1784, when he acted Solarino in *The Merchant of Venice* for the benefit of the prompter Wild.

In the summer of 1778 L'Estrange had acted at Richmond, Surrey, where he returned in the summers of 1781 and 1785. In the latter summer he also appeared with Buckle's company at Brighton.

In 1776 L'Estrange had acted his second summer season with Foote at the Haymarket, playing Project in *Taste*, the Colonel in *The Capuchin*, Mellefort in *The Double Dealer*, King Henry in *1 Henry IV*, and the Nephew in *The Irish Widow*, among other roles. After Foote's retirement, L'Estrange did not return to the Haymarket summer company, but he did appear in occasional specially-licensed performances there during the winter seasons: a role in *The Talisman* and Mr Willoughby in *A Word to the Wise* on 21 January 1784, Clerimont in *The Miser* on 12 February, Peachum in *The Beggar's Opera* on 15 March, Sir Patrick in *The Irish Widow* and Mr Strickland in *The Suspicious Husband* on 26 April 1785, Mr Oakly in *The Jealous Wife* and Sir Patrick O'Neale in *The Irish Widow* on 9 April and Mr Oakly again on 29 April 1788, and Bajazet in *Tamerlane* on 22 December 1788. On one occasion, 9 January 1784, he acted King John in *Edward the Black Prince* at Drury Lane. When Palmer opened the Royalty Theatre on 20 June 1787, L'Estrange played Duke Senior in *As You Like It*. He also appeared in an unspecified character in *The Deserter* at the Royalty during January and February 1788.

After 1788 L'Estrange's name was not again found in the London bills until he served as prompter and actor in the suburban Richmond theatre during the summer of 1795, probably after obscure engagements in the provinces. The next year he was recruited by Thomas Wignell for the Chestnut Street Theatre company in Philadelphia, where he made his debut on 5 December 1796 as Capulet in *Romeo and Juliet*; in the bills he was announced as from Covent Garden, whose stage he had not trod since 1784. Playing the Nurse was Mrs L'Estrange (not known ever to have played in London) and acting Juliet was Ann Brunton Merry, another of Wignell's recruits. L'Estrange appeared as Duncan in *Macbeth* on 9 December, followed by Henry in *1 Henry IV* on 14 December and the Ghost when Thomas Abthorpe Cooper, another new import, acted Hamlet on 19 December. On 21 December he played his first comedy role there, Sulky in *The Road to Ruin*. After his first season in America, L'Estrange appeared on the Chestnut Street stage less frequently, serving primarily as prompter and occasionally going on in roles requiring dignity and age. He was still with the company in the 1803–4 season.

According to Charles Durang, L'Estrange died in Baltimore in 1804; if William B. Wood's report in his *Personal Recollections* that L'Estrange was 80 at the time of his death is correct, he was born about 1724 and was about 50 when he made his first appearance at Covent Garden.

L'Estrange's widow acted with the Chestnut Street company until her death at Annapolis in 1799, sometime after 5 May, the date of her last known performance. Their daughter, Harriet L'Estrange, not known as a London player, had made her American debut with her mother and father on 5 December 1796 as a vocalist in Juliet's funeral procession. In 1800 she married a Mr Snowdon, young son of a Philadelphia merchant, who soon drowned in a storm off the Delaware capes. His widow acted as Mrs Snowdon at Chestnut Street from 1800–1801 through 1803–4. On 3 December 1804, the opening performance of a new season in Philadelphia, she was advertised as Mrs Usher, having become the wife of Noble Luke Usher, an actor in the company whom she accompanied to the Federal Street Theatre, Boston, in 1805–6. Usher, who may have been a relative of the English pantomime performer Richard Usher (1785–1843), had first appeared in Boston in 1799. The Ushers remained in Boston until after 1807–8, then played in Providence that summer, and subsequently went to Kentucky, where he was a significant force in establishing theatres in Lexington, Frankfort, and Louisville. Mrs Usher died in Louisville on 28 April 1814, followed soon after in the same year by her husband.

Joseph L'Estrange also had a son, young enough to be billed as Master L'Estrange when he made his first stage appearance in the child's role of the Duke of York in *Richard III* on 2 January 1797 at Chestnut Street; in that performance his father played Stanley, his mother the Duchess of York, and his sister Prince Edward. Over the next three years Master L'Estrange frequently performed children's roles, but nothing of him subsequent to 1800 is known. Made an orphan by the death of his father in 1804, the lad probably was cared for by his sister.

Letang. *See* LE TEMPS.

Le Telier, Mons [*fl. 1675*], *singer.*
Monsieur Le Telier (or Le Tillier) sang in the court masque *Calisto* on 15 February 1675.

Le Temps, Mons [Louis Lestang?] [*fl. 1674–1675*], *dancer.*
Monsieur Le Temps (sometimes Lestant, Letang) danced in *Ariadne* at Drury Lane Theatre on 30 March 1674. He was one of a small group of Frenchmen who became involved during the two months that followed in some misunderstandings between Louis Grabu, the master of the chamber music at court, and members of the King's Company at Drury Lane. The dancers were to dance at the theatre for 10*s.* daily but at some point claimed that they had no binding agreement with the King's players because of a previous commitment to Grabu. On 6 May came a royal order telling Le Temps and his fellow dancers to attend Thomas Killigrew, the manager of the King's Company. It is most probable that Le Temps was the dancer Letang who participated in the performance of the court masque *Calisto* on 15 February 1675.

Possibly our subject was Louis Lestang, who danced at the French court as a child in 1659, according to Winter's *The Pre-Romantic Ballet*. He made his debut in *Hermione* in April 1673 and was pictured in an engraving by Trouvain about 1690.

Le Texier, Anthony A. *c. 1737–1814, monologuist, actor, violinist, manager, pyrotechnist.*
Anthony Le Texier was born in Lyons about 1737, evidently of good (though not noble) family, according to Frank Hedgepath, who, in *Garrick and His French Friends* assembled from a variety of early French sources an outline of the early life of this mysterious and eccentric figure.

Le Texier participated in amateur theatricals in Lyons, one particular triumph being in Jean-Jacques Rousseau's little comedy *Pygmalion*, which Le Texier and Mme de Fleurieu acted in June 1770 by permission of the author. This success seems to have made Le Texier defy the social convention which in France discouraged the appearance of gentlemen on the professional stage.

For some three years Le Texier engaged in a peculiar sort of quasi-professional enterprise at Lyons, reading plays and taking all the parts. His reputation increased, and so in 1774, leaving his secure position as cashier in the office of the Ferme générale at Lyons, he went to Paris. After only two recitals there he was a sensation. His services were sought by all the Parisian fashionables and intelligentsia. Mme du Deffand praised him in letters to Walpole and Voltaire.

The adulation turned Le Texier's head and he became insufferably arrogant. Mme Du Barry arranged for Louis XV to hear him. The King, exhausted after a day's hunting, fell asleep, and the exasperated Le Texier slammed his book onto the lectern, awakening him. It was the moment of the beginning of Le Texier's Parisian decline. The King let it be known that he thought Le Texier's performances "too noisy." Courtiers took the hint, and he was no longer cossetted and favored. Official questions began to be asked about his departure from his post at Lyons without permission. Before long he was accused of peculation. Le Texier fled Paris and performed some comedies before Voltaire at Ferney. He went next to Belgium, at some point recited before the Court at Weimar, and finally, in September 1775, he arrived in England.

In London, Le Texier quickly made the acquaintance of the theatrically and socially influential David Garrick, to whom he presented letters of introduction from their mutual friend M de la Place. Le Texier was soon pressing Garrick to intercede with the French ministry to proceed against his enemies at home. Though Garrick refused to be drawn into Le Texier's political complications, he did defend him stoutly against the bitter attacks of another French exile, the Comte de Lauragais, who resented Le Texier's successes. The relationship between Le Texier and Garrick was for awhile one so respectful on one side and so complacent on the other that Garrick became in their correspondence *père* to Le Texier's *fils*. But something occurred to sour the relationship—perhaps a repetition of Le Texier's conceited behavior in Paris—and Garrick withdrew his patronage.

How Le Texier managed to exist during his first years in England is mysterious—perhaps on his charm, as a sort of professional guest. He was the guest of the Thrales, of Horace Walpole at Strawberry Hill, of Walpole's Twickenham neighbor Owen Cambridge, of Garrick, of the Topham Beauclerks, and of many others. In June 1777 he began bringing out by subscription the *Journal étranger de litterature, des spectacles et de politique*. It was especially valuable for its theatrical criticism but was discontinued after a year. In February 1777 he had planned to import actors of the Opéra Comique for the following spring, but nothing came of the scheme. A year later he tried to secure the King's Theatre for the same purpose, along with Giovanni Andrea Battista Gallini. That design led to a long paper war and his suit for some breach of contract against fellow performers, the Brookes and the Yateses. On 11 May 1779 the *Morning Chronicle* reported: "Yesterday . . . at the Public Office in Bow-street, Mr. Badini was bound over to the peace, at the suit of Mr. Le Texier." Probably that adversary was the librettist at the King's Theatre, Carlo Francesco Badini, but the cause of the squabble is not known.

On 15 March 1778 the *Morning Post* announced some details of the 1778–79 season at the King's Theatre: "The entertainments are to be the operas on the usual nights, plays twice a week, and probably a concert and ridotto on the other two nights. Mr. Le Texier is to superintend the opera and all matters of spectacle." The theatre was host to 65 nights of operas and ballets, but apparently the ridottos were not held. Le Texier presided, as acting manager for Thomas Harris and R. B. Sheridan, over a small but good company of singers and dancers in a season which saw the first performances in England of the famous *castrato* Pacchierotti. Le Texier returned for the season of 1779–80 but resigned or was discharged on or after 27 December 1779.

Le Texier had tried to supplement his income by sponsoring a subscription fête at the Pantheon in the spring of 1779, but it had failed. A letter from Paris by Edward Jerningham reported that Le Texier was "diverting himself in Paris" in (probably June) 1779 with "his valet which he calls his secretary George." The pair were closely associated in producing balls, French and English plays, and other entertainments for the fashionable English hostess Mrs Hobart. After the opera season was over in 1779, Le Texier tried another subscription *fête*, according to a letter of 8 May 1779 from Elizabeth Carter to Elizabeth Montague. There were, she said, 800 disappointed people at the opera house who had paid a guinea and a half each. Eighty people had subscribed recently five guineas each "for the enacting five plays by Mr. Texier and Co." What that company was is not clear. The account of the life of Maria Theresa De Camp Kemble in *The Dictionary of National Biography* says that she "at the age of eight" (thus around 1782) played "in a theatre directed by M. Le Texier Zélie in a translation of Madame de Genlis's 'La Colombe.' . . ."

Details of Le Texier's theatricals are difficult to resurrect, but evidently from about 1780 until past the end of the eighteenth century, at his house in Lisle Street, he was offering solo readings on his old Parisian plan, assuming all the characters, and also from time to time evading the Act of 1737 by putting on plays in French or English with other actors.

Sylas Neville, in his *Diary*, gives an illuminating description of an evening at Le Texier's:

Wed. Mar. 19 [1783] This evening at an entertainment of a kind somewhat extraordinary—a reading of a French play by a *Mons. Le Texier*. It is surprising how well this man enters into the spirit & manners of the different characters, & without the assistance of any other persons keeps up the attention of his audience during the whole time of recitation. His pronunciation is extremely pure & correct, which makes it an excellent amusement for those who wish to improve themselves in the French language. If he had greater facility of changing his voice, his readings would be without a fault. He read this evening L'Angloise a Bordeaux a favorite comedy at the ratification of a peace. The company was of the genteelest kind; it is not a place for the milion [*sic*]. The room (the same where the eidophusicon was exhibited last year) is neatly fitted up & illuminated with wax—the reader has seven lights on each side. Previous to the reading Mons. Le Texier receives his company in his in his Library, fitted up in a singular rustic taste—the chimney seems a hole in a rock; over it a small whole length figure of Voltaire in alabaster, which Le T. says was presented to him by that great genius. After the reading une petite comedie was presented—*the actors, two pretty little French girls & a lad*, played with much spirit & propriety. After the reading the company were served with tea & after the comedie with lemonade.

As A. Doyle Wallace and others have shown, Le Texier also made himself useful and agreeable in the amateur theatricals at various country houses, like the plays at the theatre of Lord Villiers at Bolney Court, Henley-on-Thames, where in 1777 he not only assumed the title role in *Pygmalion* but played the violin, or in the 1770s at the great houses of the Earl and Countess of Craven at Newberry in Berkshire and at Combe Abbey in Warwickshire.

Lady Craven was the energizing force behind theatricals at various other places where she employed Le Texier's assistance, as Sybil Rosenfeld has shown in detail in *Temples of Thespis*. At a charity performance directed by Lady Craven at Newbury Town Hall on 11 and 12 May 1778 Le Texier played the Dutch Gardener in her translation of Pont de Vile's comedy *La Sonambule* called *The Sleep Walker*. Lady Craven became the Margravine of Anspach on 30 October 1791 and she and the Margrave settled at Bradenburgh House. Le Texier read a comedy there in May 1792 and so pleased the Margrave that he was made Gentleman in Ordinary to the household. His principal duty seems to have been to organize theatricals. On 17 July 1792 he wrote a comedy, a burlesque, and a tragedy, for the Margravine and other members of the family to perform at a *fête* in honor of the Duke of Clarence. On 25 April 1793 a grand new theatre was opened adjoining Brandenburgh House. That evening Le Texier acted Champagne in the comedy *Le Poulet*. For several years thereafter, Le Texier wrote, acted, directed, and had a decisive part in arranging visual and musical effects, and his wife and daughter also took part in the presentations. But his relationship with his patrons finally cooled. A clipping in the Harvard Theatre Collection dated 26 July 1798 gives notice of a suit in chancery, "Le Texier v. The Margrave of Anspach and his Lady." "The Margravine had engaged Le Texier to furnish a variety of entertainments beyond the 4400£ per annum which was agreed between them, for providing the household." The disposition of the suit is not known.

Le Texier had been recalled as acting manager of the opera at the King's Theatre in 1795–96. He planned and conducted at Ranelagh on 25 May 1797 a celebration of the wedding of the Princess Royal to the Prince of Würtemberg. The "Grand Gala and Bal Paré" were under the patronage of the Prince of Wales, the Duke of York, and the Duke of Clarence. On that occasion there were magnificent fireworks.

That last item of information on the announcement for the celebration is not the only bit of data linking Anthony Le Texier to the production of pyrotechnic display. He was very likely the "Tessier" (said to be "of Ranelagh Gardens") who with Joseph Rossi, the opera dancer and fireworker, put on an elaborate display of pyrotechnics at Bermondsey Spa Gardens on 25 September 1792—a representation of the siege of Gibraltar. Such a representation had been given there from about 1786. The Drury Lane account books show payments in March, April, and November 1791 to "Texier and Rosse" [*sic*] for "fireworks" and "showers of fire." Finally, at Ranelagh in 1798 and 1801 were advertised "fireworks by Rossi and Tessier."

Le Texier was a considerable critic, as the prompt reprints of his reviews in several journals show. His *Ideas on the Opera, Offered to the Subscribers, Creditors, and Amateurs of that Theatre*, the English translation of which was published by John Bell in 1790, is a 66-page pamphlet reflecting with pungent wit Le Texier's great experience with varieties of musical theatre. His objections to the conduct of opera in general, and particularly at London, were directed against violations of realism and verisimilitude, and especially against anachronism in scenery and costuming. He ridiculed deaths in song "overloaded with quavers, arpegiaturas, cadences, &c. &c." He smote the "new school" which "gives it for a first rule that the words of a song are to be pronounced so as not to be understood." He was set against recitative, "the bastard offspring of declamation and singing. . . ." He criticized dancing in much the same terms, condemning embellishment ("a collection of entrechats, a series of gargouillades, and an encyclopoedia of whirlings"). He laughed at the re-use of costumes and decorations and the mindless mixture of periods and moods—what he called "theatrical anarchy."

Le Texier published 40 plays by various French playwrights in eight volumes from 1785 through 1787 under the title *Recueil des pièces de théâtre, lues par Mr. le Texier, en sa maison, Lisle street, Leicester Fields*. He translated Gretry's opera *La Caravane* into English about 1790.

The *True Briton* of 10 April 1797 published Le Texier as a bankrupt, but that probably did not interrupt his social activities. The actor and playwright Thomas Holcroft noted in his journal for 12 January 1799 that he had been at the theatre: "M. le *Texier* and his wife in the same box; he pretended to regret we each had visited when the other was not at home, and to wish a more intimate acquaintance, but I doubt his sincerity. He is a man of the world, and his world has not been of the purest kind."

The wife that Holcroft spoke of had been Mary Ross, a Drury Lane dancer. Though, as we have seen, she assisted Le Texier in the private theatricals she apparently did not perform publicly after her marriage.

Le Texier, Mrs Anthony A. *See* Ross, Mary.

Le Tillier. *See* Le Telier.

Le Tour. *See* La Tour.

Letsam, Mr [*fl.* 1757–1761], *boxkeeper*.
On 18 May 1757 the boxkeepers Letsam and Evans shared a benefit at Covent Garden Theatre. Letsam was cited regularly in benefit bills through 15 May 1760, and on a paylist dated 22 September 1760 he was down for a daily salary of 2s. On 13 May 1761 Letsam shared a benefit with three other boxkeepers.

Letteney, [William?] [*fl.* 1788–1800], *actor, singer, dancer*.
Mr Letteney (or Letteny, Latteny) performed at Richmond in the summer of 1788 before joining the Covent Garden Company to play the Clown in *Aladin* (sic) beginning on 26 December and continuing to mid-April 1789. He continued at Covent Garden in small parts in pantomimes through the fall of 1792, appearing as an Artist, a Bricklayer, and a female Porter in *Harlequin's Chaplet*, a Country Boy in *The Country Girl*, Melchion in *The Female Pursuit*, a Footman in *The School for Arrogance*, an Ensign in *Tippoo Saib*, the second Brother and a Brother to Colombine in *Blue-Beard*, a Shepherd in *A Peep behind the Curtain*, and unspecified characters in *Arden of Feversham*, *The Provocation*, *Orpheus and Eurydice*, and *The Soldier's Festival*. It seems very likely that he was the William Letteney who married Ann Medley on 22 August 1793 at St George, Hanover Square.

Perhaps Letteney performed outside London. He was not cited in London bills again until 12 and 13 February 1798, when he played a Demon in *Joan of Arc* at Covent Garden. Then his name disappeared for a year, and he was next noticed at the same house on 29 January 1799, playing a principal but unspecified role in *The Magic Oak*. That assignment occupied him for the remainder of the season; then he returned in 1799–1800 to appear as a dancer in *The Volcano*. He was last noticed in the eighteenth century as a Domestic in *Raymond and Agnes* on 24 March 1800.

The Covent Garden accounts name a Mrs "Leteny" as a performer in 1800–1801 and 1801–2 (unless that was an error for Mr Letteney).

Lettice, Mrs [*fl.* 1693], *singer*.
The Portledge papers, the Newdigate letters, and the J. R. Pine Coffin manuscripts all tell us that in June 1693 a Mrs Lettice, identified as a player, stood in a pillory in the Strand for having sung a lampoon on the Queen. Copies of the lampoon had been found in her lodgings. Mrs Lettice was offered a pardon if she would reveal the authorship of the libel. Her name has not been found in any theatrical documents.

Levace, Mons [*fl.* 1742], *dancer*.
Mosieur Levace danced at the New Wells, London Spa, Clerkenwell, on 27 December 1742.

Lever, John Ashton 1729–1788, *exhibitor*.
John Ashton Lever was the eldest son of Sir James Darcy Lever and his wife Dorothy, née Ashton. He was born on 5 March 1729 at

Alkrington, near Manchester, went to the Manchester grammar school, and on All Fools Day 1748 matriculated at Corpus Christi College, Oxford. After his university years he lived in Manchester with his mother before moving to Alkrington Hall, where he pursued a succession of passions: horsemanship, field sports, and archery, and collecting live birds (he had one of the best aviaries in England), stuffed birds, foreign shells, fossils, primitive weapons, and ancient costumes. In 1771 he was made high sheriff of Lancashire.

Richard Altick in *The Shows of London* notes that, before the end of 1772, Lever's collection included 60 species of quadrupeds, 260 birds, and 1,100 fossils. He also had a variety of "imperfect conceptions," according to the *Gentleman's Magazine*, such as an eight-legged pig and a "Pupp with two mouths and one head." Lever encountered difficulties with some of those who visited his collection, and on 13 September 1733 he advertised his new policy:

By permission of the British Library Board
JOHN ASHTON LEVER
engraving by W. Angus

This is to inform the Publick that being tired out with the insolence of the common People, who I have hitherto indulged with a sight of my museum at Alkrington, I am now come to the resolution of refusing admittance to the lower class except they come provided with a ticket from some Gentleman or Lady of my acquaintance. And I hereby authorize every friend of mine to give a ticket to any orderly Man to bring in eleven Persons besides himself whose behaviour he must be answerable for, according to the directions he will receive before they are admitted. They will not be admitted during the time of Gentlemen and Ladies being in the Museum. If it happens to be inconvenient when they bring their ticket, they must submit to go back and come some other day, admittance in the morning *only* from eight o'clock to twelve.

By 1774 Lever's collection was so large and was attracting so much attention that he took Leicester House in Leicester Square, London, and used 16 of the rooms plus staircases and nooks and crannies to display his collection, on which he had by then spent £30,000. He opened his museum, which he dubbed the "Holophusikon," from ten to four daily with an admission charge of 5s. 3d. and attracted good crowds.

Lever became quite an eccentric. David Garrick, writing to Lady Spencer from Hampton on 22 August 1777, commented on a voyage she had taken; the ship had been overcrowded, and Garrick heard that "Mr. Leaver . . . from his museum in Leicester Fields was there, and smelt so of Bird's feathers, & rabbit skins, it was no wonder if your Ladyship was sicker than usual." Smelly or not, Lever was knighted on 5 June 1778. Fanny Burney, on 31 December 1782 in her diary, reported visiting the Holophusikon:

I went this morning with my dear father to Sir John Ashton Lever's, where we could not but be entertained. Sir Ashton came and talked to us a good while. He may be an admirable natural*ist*, but I think if in other matters you leave the *ist* out, you will not much wrong him. He looks full sixty years old, yet he had dressed not only two young men, but himself, in a green jacket, a round hat, with green feathers, a bundle of arrows under one arm, and a bow in the other, and thus, accoutred as a forester, he pranced about; while the younger fools, who were in the same garb, kept running to and fro in the garden, carefully contriving to shoot at some mark, just as any of the company appeared at any of the windows. After such a specimen of

Bodleian Library, John Johnson Collection

Rotunda at the Leverian Museum

engraving by Skelton, after Stone and Ryley

his actions, you will excuse me if I give you none of his conversation.

Susan Burney inventoried some of the more interesting objects in Lever's collection:

The birds of paradise, and the humming birds, were I think among the most beautiful—There are several pelicans—flamingoes—peacocks (one quite white)—a penguin. Among the beasts a hippopotamus (sea-horse) of an immense size, an elephant, a tyger from the Tower—a Greenland bear and its cub—a wolf—two or three leopards—an Otaheite dog, a very coarse ugly looking creature—a camelion—a young crocodile—a room full of monkeys—one of which presents the company with an Italian Song—another is reading a book—another, the most horrid of all, is put in the attitude of *Venus de Medicis*, and is scarce fit to be look'd at. Lizards, bats, toads, frogs, scorpions and other filthy creatures in abundance. There were a great many things from Otaheite—the compleat dress of a Chinese Mandarine, made of blue and brown sattin—of an African Prince—A suit of armour that they say belonged to Oliver Cromwel—the Dress worn in Charles lst's time—etc—etc.

Lever also had a room full of stuffed monkeys arranged like humans doing such manual tasks as sewing, carpentry, writing, and dentistry. Between 1775 and 1784 Lever took in £13,000 from curiosity seekers.

Sophie van la Roche visited the museum and found the collection too bewilderingly displayed: "All the wonders of nature, and all the incredible conceptions of form and colour, pleasant and unpleasant, are so tightly packed, that the mind and eye are quite dazzled by them, and in the end both are overwhelmed and retain nothing at all."

Sir Ashton spent so much money on his museum that it wiped out much of his fortune, and he had to sell his Holophusikon. A parliamentary committee valued the collection at £53,000, but when it was offered to the British Museum for far less the trustees voted not to buy it. In 1788 by act of parliament Sir Ashton was permitted to sell by lottery; 36,000 tickets at a guinea each were made available, but only 8000 were purchased. James Parkinson won the museum and built a building called the Rotunda at the south end of Blackfriar's Bridge to house it. He did well as an exhibitor for a few years, but by 1806 the collection was disposed of by auction.

After the museum passed out of his hands, Lever retired to Alkrington. He died suddenly at the age of 58, on 24 January 1788 at the Bull's Head Inn, Manchester. He had married Frances Bayley of Manchester in 1746, but they evidently had no children. The novelist Charles Lever was Sir Ashton's great-nephew.

An engraved portrait of Lever by W. Angus was published in the *European Magazine* in 1784. A portrait engraved by W. Nutter, after S. Shelley, was published by R. Cribb in 1787. A portrait is reported to have been published in Baines's *Lancashire* (1833). An engraved scene by W. Skelton, after Miss Stone and C. Ryley, of Lever standing in his Rotunda, is in the Bodleian Library. Lever's portrait was sculpted by John Flaxman for a Wedgwood medallion, an example of which is in the Brooklyn Museum.

Leveridge, Richard *c. 1670–1758, singer, composer.*

Richard Leveridge was born about 1670 in London (Fiske in *English Theatre Music* suggests about 1671) and seems to have begun his

Harvard Theatre Collection
RICHARD LEVERIDGE
by Vandermyn

professional singing career in 1695, but in what work is difficult to ascertain. *Grove* (fifth edition) states that he was one of the vocalists singing John Blow's *Te Deum and Jubilate* for the St Cecilia's Day celebration that year. *The London Stage* dates his singing of Ismeron in *The Indian Queen* with Rich's company at the Dorset Garden playhouse as mid-April 1695, though Zimmerman in his study of Purcell's music dates that production late 1695. In the autumn of 1695 (October, *The London Stage* has it) *The Rival Sisters* was performed at Drury Lane, with Leveridge singing in it Purcell's "Take not a Woman's anger ill." *The London Stage* dates *3 Don Quixote* November 1695; Zimmerman notes that the music, with Leveridge's name among the singers, came out in print in mid-December. In November Christopher Rich produced *Oroonoko* at Drury Lane, with Leveridge singing "Bright Cynthia's pow'r divinely great." By the end of 1695, then, Richard Leveridge, the bass singer who entertained English audiences for the following 55 years, had already established himself as a performer in London.

Though Leveridge was associated with Christopher Rich's troupe at Drury Lane and Dorset Garden, *The London Stage* notes that he sang "Unguarded lies the wishing maid" in *The Royal Mischief* with Betterton's company in April (Robert Hume suggests about May) 1696. In June of that year Leveridge sang in *The Cornish Comedy* at Dorset Garden Theatre, and in late August at the same playhouse he and Mrs Cross sang "Fairest nymph that ever bless'd our Shore" in *The Spanish Wives*. Before the end of the century Leveridge sang with Rich's troupe in *Brutus of Alba*, *The World in the Moon*, *The Island Princess*, and *1 Massaniello*. At York Buildings in May 1698 he held a benefit for himself and in June he sang at a benefit for Daniel Purcell. He also set himself up as a composer of songs in plays, one of his earliest pieces being a second prologue to *The Island Princess*, something of a novelty, for it was introduced by an explanation:

. . . since for hum'rous Prologues most you long,
Before this Play we'll have a ballad sung.

But Leveridge was improvident. On 25 December 1699 Vanbrugh wrote to the Earl of Manchester that "Liveridge is in Ireland, he Owes so much money he dare not come over, so for want of him we han't had one Opera play'd this Winter . . ."—by which at that date Vanbrugh meant the kind of semi-operas, cited above, in which Leveridge had been singing. In Dublin Leveridge performed at the Smock Alley playhouse, for whose audience he composed "Marinda's Face like Cupid's Bow is drawn to shoot at Hearts," which was published in the March–April 1700 *Mercurius Musicus* in London, noted as set by Leveridge and sung "att the Theater in Dublin." Leveridge also wrote a duet, "You, Bellamira, we admire," for *St Stephen's Green*.

Though Leveridge seems not to have been named again in any London playbills until 1702, his stay in Dublin apparently ended after one season (1699–1700), for about 1700 a number of songs were published in London with his name given as singer: *Cou'd a Man be secure* from *The Committee*, Daniel Purcell's *Accept Maria*, *of a Heart* and *Whilst wretched Fools sneak up and down* (sung with Pate) from *1*

Massaniello, Behold the Man that with Gigantick Might (sung with Mrs Lindsey) from *The Richmond Heiress*, Henry Purcell's *You twice ten hundred Deities* from *The Indian Queen*, and *As soon as the Chaos* (with Pate) from *The Marriage-Hater Match'd*. Leveridge would hardly have been cited in so many publications dating about 1700 had he not been again in London and entertaining the public in concerts or theatrical performances.

Leveridge sang at Drury Lane through the end of 1707, offering such songs as "Let the Dreadful Engines"—the mad song from *Don Quixote*—"The Genius of England," "Since Times are so bad" with Mrs Lindsey, "The Enthusiastic Song" (his own composition), "Venus has left her Grecian isles" from *The Lying Lover*, "From Rosy Bowers," "Fill the Glass, fill, fill, fill" (his composition), "Fair Celia's Charms," "'Tis Sultry Weather" with Mrs Lindsey, "Nay pish, nay pish" (which he also set), and "From Glorious Toyls of War."

Harvard Theatre Collection

RICHARD LEVERIDGE
engraving by Saunders, after Frye

He gradually began taking more roles in musical pieces, which led to his participation in some of the early English operas. On 14 November 1702, for example, the playbill noted that Leveridge would "perform his own Parts" in *The Island Princess*; on 9 June 1704 he sang the chief characters (Pan, Vulcan, Pluto, and Apollo) in *Psyche*; on the following 6 December he played Bacchus in Purcell's masque in *Timon of Athens*; and on 16 January 1705 he sang Feraspe in Clayton's opera *Arsinoe*. He was seen as Linco in *Camilla* in March 1706, Sir Trusty in *Rosamond* in March 1707, and Baldo in *Thomyris* in April. In addition, his music "all new Compos'd" for *Macbeth* was performed by "him and others" at Drury Lane on 21 November 1702. Two versions of *Britain's Happiness* were presented in February and March 1704, the one at Drury Lane containing music by Weldon and Dieupart and the one at the rival Lincoln's Inn Fields, oddly, employing music by the Drury Lane singer Leveridge.

On 20 January 1708 Leveridge sang his role in *Thomyris* at the Queen's Theatre, which had been designated as the house for opera performances. On 26 February he was heard as Neralbo in *Love's Triumph*. Vice Chamberlain Coke's papers at Harvard show that Leveridge was paid £2 daily, which put him higher on the pay scale than some of his fellow singers but considerably below the £7 10s. which singers like Mrs Tofts were paid. Another document listed him at £100 for the season (Mrs Tofts received £400), and yet a third listed him at £30 and Mrs Tofts at £500. He remained with the opera troupe until John Rich opened the new Lincoln's Inn Fields Theatre in 1714, singing (in English) Charles in *Pirro e Demetrio*, Proteus in *Calypso and Telemachus*, Tirenio in *Il pastor fido*, an unnamed part in *Dorinda*, Minerva (*sic*) in *Teseo*, and Argantes in *Rinaldo*.

But he busied himself also at concerts; between 1711 and 1714, for example, he sang at Richmond Wells, in a St Cecilia's Day concert at Stationers' Hall, at Greenwich, with Mrs Lindsey (they sang *The Loves of Baldo and Media* "after the Italian manner"), and at Caverley's Dancing Academy in Chancery Lane. English opera after the Italian manner was something he evidently could manage well enough, but with the growing number of imported singers and their ability to offer operas in Italian, Leveridge's career as a serious opera singer withered. Roger Fiske in *English Theatre Music* is hard on Leveridge and interprets his change to Lincoln's Inn Fields as a loss of ambition, but though Leveridge seems certainly to have been blessed with a fine voice, his position in the opera troupe from the start was clearly tertiary and it is doubtful that he actually had pretentions to a career in serious operas.

From 1714 on, Leveridge sang for John Rich's company—at Lincoln's Inn Fields until 1732 and then at Covent Garden until 1751. His specialty, as earlier, was entr'acte songs and songs within plays. Among the songs he helped popularize were "Sing all ye Muses," "See, Sirs, see here!"—a "Mountebank" song of his composing—in *Farewell Folly*, "Iris beware" which he composed, Clarke's "When Maids live to Thirty," "How happy's he who weds" from *The Younger the Wiser*, "Celladon, when Spring came on" from *The Country Miss*, "Farewell my Bonny," a dialogue between a Town Sharper and his Hostess in *1 Massaniello* (sung with Pate, who is said to have studied singing under Leveridge), "Foolish Swain thy sighs forbear," "See the yielding fair" (sung with Laguerre), "Wine's a Mistress gay and easy" from *Love and Wine*, "The Tippling Philosophers," some "Chansons à Boir[e]," "Ghosts of ev'ry Occupation" from *The Necromancer*, "Flights of Cupids hover round me" from *The Rape of Proserpine*, "The Wheel of Life is turning quickly round," "Whine not, pine not" (sung with Mrs Chambers), "Tho' Envious Old Age seems in part to impair me" from *Apollo and Daphne*, "A Dialogue Betwixt a Rake and a Widow" (sung with Salway), "Ballad of the Cobler's End," "The Contented Man," "The Miser's Passport," "Advice to all Britons," "The Cure for All Grief," "Mirth Gives Courage," and "The Truly Happy Man" (the last dating from 1749).

During that same period, after 1714, Leveridge developed a number of roles, which he repeated again and again. His characters included the title role in *The Mountebank*, Damon in *Presumptuous Love*, Pyramus in his own *Pyramus and Thisbe* (and he presented the prologue and epilogue), Proteus in *Calypso and Telemachus*, Simon in *The Lady's Triumph*, Pan and later Thyrsis in *Pan and Syrinx*, Mars in *Venus and Adonis*, Homer in *The Union of the Three Sister Arts*, Linco in *The Beau Demolished*, a Witch in *Harlequin Sorcerer*, a Spirit and later Genius in *The Necromancer*, Homer in *St Ceciliae*, Strephon in *The Capricious Lovers*, Morpheus, Silenus, and later Bacchus in *Apollo and Daphne*, Bostangi in *The Sultan*, Pluto in *The Rape of Proserpine* (one of his most popular parts, first sung in February 1727), Mezzetin in *The Loves of Damon and Clemene*, Pluto in *Harlequin a Sorcerer*, Cepheus and an Infernal in *Perseus and Andromeda*, Polypheme in *Acis and Galatea*, a Fury in *Orestes*, the Gravedigger in *Hamlet* (with songs in character), Agyrtes in *Achilles*, a Priest of Hymen in *The Nuptial Masque*, Merlin and later Mercury in *The Royal Chace*, Nancy's Father in *The Parting Lovers* (later retitled *Nancy*), Pluto in *Orpheus and Eurydice*, Moon in *The Rehearsal*, and a Follower in *Comus*. He also sang fairly regularly in *Macbeth* (usually Hecate was his role), *The Provok'd Wife*, *Henry VIII*, and other productions. Though he did not keep as heavy a performing schedule in his later years as he had earlier, Leveridge nevertheless performed regularly through 1750–51, his final season at Covent Garden. (The *New Grove* is incorrect in stating that he retired during the period 1720 through 1723.)

His income at the theatre is not fully documented over the years, but *The London Stage* estimates that in the mid-1720s he was being paid about £150 yearly. The accounts list him on 25 September 1724 at £1 6s. 8d. daily. By the 1740–41 season he was receiving only 13s. 4d. daily, and in 1746–47 his weekly income was £2. His benefits were usually well attended and brought him goodly sums. On 9 April 1724, for example, his gross was £140 18s. 6d., and though in some years he dropped below £100, he could usually count on at least £130 before house charges (which were up to £50 by the end of his career); in 1728 he took in £185 16d.; and in 1730 he grossed £235.

How much he augmented his income through the songs he wrote (sometimes the words, sometimes the music, sometimes both) cannot be estimated, but he remained a popular contributor to the song world throughout his career. Some of the songs he set to music have already been mentioned, since he sang them, but he wrote many that were popularized by other singers, such as "Tho' over all Mankind" from *Caligula*, sung by Mrs Lindsey; "When Lovesick Mars the God of War" from *The Fool in Fashion*, sung by Mrs. Willis; "Tell me ye softer Powers above," sung by Mrs Campion; the words to "Cupid in search of Prey" and

"Fly, and his soft enchanting" from *Teseo*; and "Ye Commons and Peers"—a ballad on the Battle of Audenard.

Other songs of his composition were "I am a cunning Constable"; "Love is a Bauble"; "Fortune is blind"; "Of all the World's Enjoyments" from *1 Massaniello*; "Jogging on from yonder Green"; "Early in the dawning of a Winter's morn"; "One Sunday after Mass," an Irish song; "Come Fair one be kind," sung by Wilks in *The Recruiting Officer*; the words for "The Play of Love is now begun," to music by Pepusch; the English words for Haym and Handel's "Non e si vago e bello" from *Giulio Cesare*; English words for Handel's songs in *Ottone*, which came out "Bacchus God of Mortal Pleasure" and "Come to my Arms my Treasure"—evidently not attempts at translation, but simply English lyrics for the tunes; "The Bath Teazer," sung by Ray; words to a minuet by Geminiani, "Know Madam I never was born"; and a number of poems for his benefits, sung to popular tunes.

One of his benefit pieces, for 27 March 1745, to be sung to the tune of "A Cobler there was," goes:

> *Now Benefit Tickets are spread thro' the Town,*
> *More num'rous than ever since playing was known,*
> *Permit your old Servant amongst the new throng*
> *To offer his Ticket as usual——a song;*
>   *With a down, down, down derry down.*
> *Such generous Friends who my play will promote*
> *By kindly consenting to credit my note,*
> *Shall surely be paid (as I here underwrite)*
> *With songs & brisk dances my Benefit night.*
>   *With a down, down, down derry down.*

One of his last songs was for his benefit on 31 March 1748; he wrote it for the tune "Silenus, with his Bottle" from *Apollo and Daphne*:

> *Silenus, th' old, yet with Freedom and Spirit,*
> *Thus makes his Address, your Goodwill to excite,*
> *To grant him this year 'mongst the Younger of merit,*
> *Your smiles of Remembrance to Honour his Night*
> *Then, then for the Bottle, that warms the young Lover,*
> *And sets drooping Fancy again on the Wing,*
> *'Twill fire me with Joy and new Vigour recover,*
> *To tune up my Thanks, which I'll gratefully sing.*

But in addition to his work at the theatre, from 1714 to 1736 Leveridge kept a coffee house, according to *The Survey of London*. (Other sources date the opening of his coffee house much later—1722 or 1726. Lillywhite's *London Coffee Houses* cites the de Castro manuscript as mentioning a Presentment of 1718 "for Raiseing Money to pay for cleanszing the Sewers in York Street, Bridges Street, Covent Garden. . . . Mr. Richard Leveridge assessed at £40.") Leveridge's establishment was at No 2–3, Tavistock Street, in a house called the Harlequin and Pierot.

While he ran the house, he advertised it on his benefit bills as the place where his tickets could be purchased. But by his benefit on 15 April 1743 Leveridge was living at the third door on the right hand in Hanover Street turning out of Longacre. Between spring 1747 and spring 1748 he moved to the Twisted Posts in Brownlow Street, Drury Lane; by 19 April 1751 he was living beside the Red Lion in the same street. After his retirement Leveridge lived with his only daughter (some sources say daughters) in High Holborn.

Of his family we know very little. That he had a daughter or daughters at his death seems fairly certain, and the free list at the Lincoln's Inn Fields Theatre in the mid-1720s mentioned Mrs Leveridge and her daughter. Fiske notes that Charles Bannister may have been Leveridge's son, but there seems to be no evidence of that. The name Richard Leveridge can be found in the parish registers of St Martin-in-the-Fields, St James, Westminster, St Marylebone, and St Paul, Covent Garden. His will stated that his sole heir and executrix was to be Mary Parrott, widow of William Parrott. If she was his daughter, perhaps some of the register entries may have concerned the singer and his family.

The St Marylebone registers noted that on 15 July 1669 Richard Leveridge married Mary Long; since the singer's birth is thought to have been about 1670, there is a possibility that those were his parents. The registers of St Martin-in-the-Fields cited baptisms and burials of children of a Richard and Mary Leveridge in the 1670s; they could not have referred to the singer, though they may have referred to his parents. The same registers cited a Richard and Elizabeth Leveridge in 1710 and 1711; they baptized a son John on 21 September of the former year and buried a daughter Ann the following 15 February 1711. At St James,

Westminster, on 2 May 1701, Elizabeth the daughter of a Richard and Mary "Leverich" was born and baptized, and on 24 February 1706 their daughter Ann was born and baptized. Inasmuch as the singer is known to have lived in the theatrical Covent Garden area the registers of St Paul, Covent Garden, could be the most pertinent, though the names do not match with the will: on 20 April 1692 Elizabeth, the daughter of Richard and Phillis "Leveredg," was christened; on 27 September 1716 John, the son of Richard Leveridge, was buried; and on 9 April 1732 Phillis, wife of Richard Leveridge, was buried.

Dick Leveridge was apparently a most convivial fellow, as would befit the owner of a popular coffee house. *The Session of Musicians* (May 1724) included a verse on him; the scene is a court of judgment, where Apollo is trying to pick the best musician in England:

> *Amidst the Crowd gay L{eve}r{i}dge did stand,*
> *Smiles in his Face, and—Claret in his Hand;*
> *The God suppos'd he did not come to ask*
> *The Bays, but rather recommend his Flask;*
> *Old friend, says he, if that your Wine is right,*
> *Let's talk—d'ye hear? I'll sup with you to-night:*
> *The Laurel, if you hope—to do you Justice,*
> *You made—a charming Fiend in* Doctor Faustus.

Indeed, Leveridge "had no notion of elegance in singing," wrote Hawkins; "it was all strength and compass." Dr. Burney in the 1780s remembered hearing Leveridge sing "Ghosts of every occupation" and other songs "in a style which forty years ago seemed antediluvian; but as he generally was the representative of Pluto, Neptune, or some ancient divinity, it corresponded perfectly with his figure and character."

Though he did not pretend to a classical career in music (as Burney said, his listeners preferred "the rites of Comus and Bacchus [to] those of Minerva and Apollo"), Leveridge was one of the original subscribers to the Royal Society of Musicians when it was organized on 28 August 1739.

When Leveridge left the stage in 1751 he was probably past 80. An unidentified clipping in the Burney papers, dated 20 May 1752, reported that he had fallen, struck his head on a stone, and "was taken up speechless last Wednesday Evening in Prince's-street, [but] after some time recovered his Senses. He would not accept of a Chair, but walked home supported by two Men." Two days later the *General Advertiser* assured the public that Leveridge was "in as good a state of Health as he has been for some time past." A subscription of one guinea annually was opened in the singer's behalf at Garraway's Coffee House on 26 October 1751, according to the *Daily Advertiser*, and the old man was supported in the years that followed by his friends. The prompter Richard Cross wrote in his diary that Richard Leveridge died at the age of 95 on 21 February 1755, which was not true on two counts, for he died on 22 March 1758 at the age of 88, as several papers reported. He was "chearful and sensible until a few hours before his death," stated one clipping.

His will, written on 5 March 1756 (*The Dictionary of National Biography* says 1746), was a no-nonsense statement that "To prevent all disputes of claim that may arise from any Relations of mine whatsoever after my Decease" he made his sole heir and executrix Mary Parrott, widow of William Parrot, late of Chelsea, apothecary. The will was proved on 29 March 1758. Oldys said that Leveridge had written a history of the stage in his own time, but if he did, it was never published, and no manuscript has been found. He did publish numerous songs, some in collections and many in single sheets. An impressive list is in the *Catalogue of Printed Music in the British Museum*, and Grove has a useful list of his theatre pieces. Leveridge's *Collection of Songs, with Musick* in two volumes, was published in 1727, with a frontispiece by Hogarth.

Leveridge was a member of one of the most distinguished Freemasons' lodges of his day, one which met at the Bear and Harrow in Butcher Row, east of the Tower. Members included Hogarth, Quin, Theophilus Cibber, Henry Giffard, and Charles Fleetwood.

In his *General History* Hawkins said that Dick Leveridge, as he called himself, loved such characters as "Pluto, Faustus, Merlin, or in short any part in which a long beard was necessary." His portrait by Frye (which was engraved by Pether) shows no natural beard but a grave face that must have suited well the parts he enjoyed.

The portrait of Leveridge by T. Frye was

engraved by W. Pether in 1727 and published as the frontispiece to Leveridge's *Collection of Songs*; other engravings were made by D. Dodd and by J. Saunders (the latter for the *European Magazine*, 1793). A. Vandermyn's portrait of Leveridge is in the Garrick Club (No 12); a mezzotint was made by the artist in 1753. An anonymous engraver pictured Leveridge with William Pinkethman, standing in a booth at Bartholomew Fair, singing "The Mountebank Song."

Levi. *See also* LEVY.

Levi, Mr [*fl.* 1778], *actor.*

A Mr Levi played an unnamed character in *The Macaroni Adventurer* at the Haymarket Theatre on 28 December 1778.

Leviez, Charles *d. c. 1778, dancer, ballet master.*

The Frenchman Charles Leviez (sometimes Livier or Liviez), who was a professional dancer in London for almost 30 years, was first noticed in the Drury Lane bills on 28 October 1734, when he danced with Mlle Roland, newly arrived from Paris, and several other French dancers. On 1 November he danced a Triton and a Mandarin Gormogon in *Cephalus and Procris*; and during the rest of the season he was seen as a Fury in *Merlin*, a Masquerader in *Colombine Courtezan*, and an Attendant on Apollo in *Harlequin Orpheus*. In the following season, 1735–36, when he was paid £43 (5*s.* per night for 172 nights), Leviez was dancing at Covent Garden Theatre, appearing in such pantomimes by John Rich as *Apollo and Daphne*, *Perseus and Andromeda*, and *The Royal Chace*. In the summer of 1736 he danced at the Hallam-Chapman booth at Bartholomew Fair.

In 1736–37 Leviez went back to Drury Lane, where he remained engaged for 25 years as dancer. By 1748–49 he was serving also as ballet-master. Though Harry Angelo stated in his *Reminiscences* that Leviez danced early in his career in the operas at the King's Theatre, the bills extant do not reveal that he ever performed there.

Among the many ballets and pantomimes in which Leviez performed at Drury Lane were *Harlequin Grand Volgi* in 1737–38, *Robin Goodfellow* in 1738–39, *The Fortune Tellers* in 1739–40, *The Amorous Goddess* in 1743–44, *Harlequin Incendiary* in 1745–46, *The Genii* in 1755–56, and *Queen Mab* in 1757–58. In the summer of 1752 he performed in Holland, and during other summers he probably appeared in other countries on the Continent.

During his many years in London, Leviez lived next door to the Boar's Head, Henrietta Street, Covent Garden, in 1738 and 1739, at the Blue Door in Great Queen Street, Lincoln's Inn Fields, in 1742, at a house in Great Queen Street in 1749, in Martlet Court, Bow Street, in 1751, and then in a house ("the lowest . . . on the right hand") in Beaufort Buildings in the Strand from 1752 to his retirement from Drury Lane in May 1762. In *Thraliana*, Mrs Thrale, who used to take dancing lessons from Leviez in Great Queen Street, provided his first name.

According to Edward Edward's *Anecdotes of Painters* (1808), Leviez "had reputation in his profession, but employed himself much in dealing in prints and drawings." When the French painter John Pillement was resident in London he was employed by Leviez, then living in Beaufort Buildings in the Strand, who

By permission of the Trustees of the British Museum
CHARLES LEVIEZ
engraving by McArdell, after Eccardt

had a number of Pillement's drawings engraved by Ravenet and others.

According to Harry Angelo, Leviez had married an Englishwoman (whose name Angelo could not remember), who lived in Charlotte Street and whose parents kept a pew in Percy Chapel. She was a very handsome lady, in Angelo's judgment, and was the model for the figure of Elegance in Roubiliac's monument to the Duke of Argyle in Westminster Abbey.

By 1765 Leviez moved to Paris, where he was a dealer in engravings. Garrick visited with him and on 16 February 1765 in a letter to George Selwyn the actor recommended Leviez as a man of "Ability and Integrity." While in Paris in 1766, George Colman received his letters in care of "Monsr Leviez, Marchan^d des Estampes, rue des Arcs, Fouxbourgs, St Germain." Subsequently Leviez set up shop in the Rue Battois in the same district, from which he often traveled to Leipzig to collect prints. As a student in Paris Angelo lived in the Leviez house, and in his memoirs described his host as a "complete *bon vivant* and a *gourmand*" and a lover of all things English.

Leviez died about 1778 according to Edward Edwards. The dancer Nancy Leviez who danced in Noverre's company at Stuttgart in 1761 was probably his niece. The Stuttgart royal chronicles state that she was born in London; in a letter to Garrick about January 1775 Noverre claimed to have "made an excellent dancer of Levier's niece," presumably the Stuttgart performer. Nancy Leviez, however, is identified as Charles Leviez's daughter by Marian H. Winter in her *Pre-Romantic Ballet*, where it is also stated that she danced at the Pantheon, London, in 1791–92 with Antoine Trancart, whom she had married by 1772.

A portrait of Charles Leviez, after J. G. Eccardt, was engraved by J. McArdell in 1763.

Leviez, Nancy. *See* TRANCART, MRS ANTOINE.

Levy, Mr [*fl.* 1741–1743], *doorkeeper.*

The doorkeeper Levy shared benefits on 6 May 1741 and 10 May 1742 at the Goodman's Fields Theatre and on 6 April 1743 at Lincoln's Inn Fields.

Lewes, Miss. *See* WILSON, MRS RICHARD THE FOURTH.

Lewes, Charles Lee *1740–1803, actor, manager, author.*

Charles Lee Lewes was born in a house in Bond Street, in the parish of St George, Hanover Square, on 19 November 1740. His father was a hosier with a "classical education," and his mother was of Welsh descent, the daughter of William Lewthwaite of Broadgate, Cumberland, and she was related to Sir John Gilford Lawson and Lady St Aubyn. According to Lewes's *Memoirs*, his father was a friend of the author Edward Young, whose wife Elizabeth was the daughter of Edward Henry Lee, first Earl of Lichfield; Elizabeth Lee Young's first husband had been a Colonel Lee, and it was he who was our subject's godfather and from whom Lewes's middle name derived. Charles's sisters became governesses. At the age of seven Lewes was sent for schooling under the Rev Mr Mills at Ambleside, Westmoreland, whence he re-

Harvard Theatre Collection

CHARLES LEE LEWES

engraving by Hopwood

turned at the age of 14, apparently not much educated. For a while he assisted his father, who had become a letter carrier.

Lewes's interest in the stage was stimulated by visits to spouting clubs. He claimed to have appeared, as an amateur, as Cash (with Wilkinson as Kitely) in a production of *Every Man in His Humour* at the Haymarket Theatre about 1760. That performance seems to have been the one on 1 September 1764, when "C. Lewis" was in the Haymarket bills for Cash and Wilkinson for Kitely; playing Brainworm that night was Philip Lewis, unrelated. In his *Memoirs* Lewes also stated that he played Matthew Mug in *The Mayor of Garratt* with Linnett's company at the Cross Keys, a public house near Chelsea Church. That performance presumably would have occurred after the premiere of Foote's comedy at the Haymarket on 20 June 1763. *The Mayor of Garratt* was also frequently acted in the summer of 1764 but no cast was listed in the advertisements, though possibly Lewes performed in it at the Haymarket before the Chelsea presentation. *The Dictionary of National Biography* states that Lewes played Bardolph in *1 Henry IV* at Covent Garden on 26 September 1763; but that was Philip Lewis.

In his *Memoirs* Lewes relates colorful stories of his early life as a stroller but provides few specifics. In 1760 he joined Whitley's company at Doncaster. He spent some time acting at Chesterfield, Sheffield, and other country towns before he returned to London for an engagement at Covent Garden Theatre in 1767–68, at a salary of 5s. per day. He first appeared there on 23 September 1767, as Prince Henry in *King John*. His name now was given as Lewes, and it is possible that he had adopted that spelling in order to distinguish himself from Philip Lewis, still a member of the Covent Garden Company.

That season Lewes was also seen as a Recruit in *The Recruiting Officer*, Burgundy in *King Lear*, Harlequin in *Harlequin Skeleton; or The Royal Chace*, and Trinket in *The Jealous Wife*. After a summer at Bristol playing servants and low comics, Lewes returned to Covent Garden, adding to his modest repertoire in 1768–69 Ratcliffe in *Richard III*, Fenton in *The Merry Wives of Windsor*, Gloucester in *Henry V*, Melidor in *Zara*, and Welbred in *Every Man in His Humour*. He also began to exhibit his pantomime skills, appearing as Harlequin in many performances of *Apollo and Daphne*, *Harlequin Skeleton*, and *Harlequin Dr Faustus*.

Lewes remained at Covent Garden for 16 seasons, through 1782–83. Until 1770–71 his roles were Harlequin in *The Rape of Proserpine*, Luke in *Man and Wife*, a principal part in *The Spanish Lady*, Hali in *Tamerlane*, Edgar in *Edgar and Emmeline*, Aranthes in *Theodosius*, Truman in *George Barnwell*, and Loveit in *Miss in Her Teens*. His status benefited by the departure of Woodward to Edinburgh in 1770 and Dyer's death in 1774. In 1770–71 he played the principal character in *Harlequin's Jubilee*, Francis in *The Brothers*, the Dauphin in *Henry V*, Bowman in *Lethe*, Young Cape in *The Author*, Rossano in *The Fair Penitent*, Lord John in *The Englishman Return'd from Paris*, Frederick in *The Miser*, Montano in *Othello*, Harlequin in *Mother Shipton*, a Groom in *Love à-la-*

Courtesy of the Garrick Club

CHARLES LEE LEWES, as Bobadil
by De Wilde

Mode, the Citizen in *The Citizen*, Cloten in *Cymbeline*, Prattle in *The Deuce Is in Him*, Young Loveit in *The Commissary*, and Marplot in *The Busy Body* (for his benefit on 3 May 1771).

When the season opened at Covent Garden on 23 September 1771 Lewes's name was in the bills for Young Loveit in *The Commissary*, but we doubt that he played that night. He had gone to Bristol that summer (where he had also acted the three previous summers) and had fallen dangerously ill and deep in debt. On 12 October 1771 *Felix Farley's Bristol Journal* reported:

Mr. LEWIS [*sic*], of Covent-Garden Theatre, hath long languished upon a Bed of Sickness (surrounded by a Family of little ones!) whose Endeavours to please, to the utmost of his Abilities, the Public are well acquainted with. A MUSICAL ENTERTAINMENT is therefore proposed for his Benefit, in order to enable him to satisfy certain Demands, which are the natural Consequence of so long and painful an Illness, before his Return to London.

The benefit concert, organized by Thomas Linley, was given at the Assembly Rooms, Prince's Street, on 2 November, with the Linley children as principal performers.

By 22 November 1771 Lewes was well enough to resume his responsibilities at Covent Garden, appearing as Paterson in *The Brothers*. Among the roles he added to his repertoire by the end of the season were Meggot in *The Suspicious Husband*, Fabian in *Twelfth Night*, and Bertram in *All's Well that Ends Well*. In 1772–73 he added Lord Bawble in *The Country Madcap*, the Lord Chamberlain in *Henry VIII*, Chapeau in the premiere of *Cross Purposes* on 5 December 1772, Jemmy Twinkle in *A Trip to Scotland*, Gratiano in *The Merchant of Venice*, Young Fashion in *The Man of Quality*, Lofty in *The Good Natur'd Man*, and Scribble in *Polly Honeycombe*. When Smith declined the role of Young Marlowe in Goldsmith's new comedy *She Stoops to Conquer*, Lewes played it in the original production at Covent Garden on 15 March 1773. So satisfied was the author that he wrote an epilogue which Lewes spoke for his benefit on 7 May 1773, at which his net receipts were £153. The epilogue presented Lewes in the character of Harlequin removing his mask and expressing his longing to act in Shakespeare. It was used by Lewes at

Harvard Theatre Collection

CHARLES LEE LEWES, as Harlequin
artist unknown

subsequent benefits; on 28 April 1774 he took in net receipts of £190, and on 27 April 1776 the epilogue concluded "with an escape thro' the Tub, as in the Pantomime of *Mother Shipton*."

His success in *She Stoops to Conquer* brought better assignments from the management, which began to establish Lewes in the public notice. A selection of his numerous varied roles during his final ten years at Covent Garden includes: Denier in *The Man of Business*, Jeremy in *Love for Love*, and Colonel Lambert in *The Hypocrite* in 1773–74; Basset in *The Provok'd Husband*, Bussora in *The Romance of an Hour*, Young Wilding in *The Lyar*, Justice Credulous in *St Patrick's Day*, and Fag in *The Rivals* (premiere on 17 January) in 1774–75; Whitling in *The Refusal*, Stephano in *The Man's the Master*, Young Clackit in *The Guardian*, Sharp in *The Lying Valet*, Mercury in *Amphitryon*, and Brisk in *The Double Dealer* in 1775–76; Rantwell in *News from Parnassus*, Witwou'd in *The*

Way of the World, Harlequin in *Harlequin's Frolicks*, Dashwould in *Know Your Own Mind*, and Captain Savage in *The School for Wives* in 1776–77; Razor in *The Upholsterer*, Trappanti in *She Wou'd and She Wou'd Not*, Tom in *The Conscious Lovers*, Marcourt in *Man and Wife*, and Lissardo in *The Wonder* in 1777–78; Colonel Feignwell in *A Bold Stroke for a Wife*, Harlequin in *The Touchstone*, and Young Wou'dbe in *The Twin Rivals* in 1778–79; Meadows in *The Deaf Lover* and Flutter in *The Belle's Stratagem* in 1779–80; Sir Harry Beagle in *The Jealous Wife* and Lucio in *Measure for Measure* in 1780–81; Grog in *The Positive Man*, Davy Dangle in *The Walloons*, and Vane in *The Chapter of Accidents* in 1781–82; and Harlequin in *The Wishes*, and Welford in *The Capricious Lady* in 1782–83. A number of the roles specified in *The Dictionary of National Biography* as belonging to Lewes at Covent Garden were actually those of the younger and more dashing William Thomas Lewis, who played a line of fashionable gallants.

On 12 May 1778, after playing Harlequin in *Mother Shipton*, Lewes was going through a passage of Covent Garden Theatre and struck his foot on a broken bottle. A manuscript note in the Burney papers at the British Library informs that he "would probably have bled to death, if Mr. Howard, the Surgeon, had not dressed his wound skilfully." Lewes did not perform again at Covent Garden that season, which was almost over anyway, but he healed well enough to play at Liverpool the summer following.

Lewes's address in April 1778 was Charlotte Street, Rathbone Place. In 1779 and 1780 he lived in Bow Street, Covent Garden. His last two benefits he waived, preferring to accept in lieu payments of £70 on 8 April 1782 and £105 on 25 April 1783. His salary in 1782–83 was £9 15s. per week.

During the years he was a Covent Garden winter regular, Lewes took to the provinces in the summer. At York for race week in August 1773 he acted Clodio in *The Fop's Fortune*, Marplot, Harlequin, and other characters. He was engaged by Whitley for the fair at Cambridge in 1777, when he played Clodio, Chapeau, Young Marlowe, and Prince Hal in *Henry IV*. Between 1774 and 1778 he appeared each summer in Liverpool; there he earned only £2 per week but seemed to have some share in the management and had benefits. A "Lewes" is on a bill in the Guildhall, hand-dated 3 July 1776, for a production of *The Rivals* at China Hall, Rotherhithe; we believe that actor to have been Philip Lewis. Hodgkinson and Pogson in their *Early Manchester Theatre* have Lewes in that city during 1777–78, playing Falstaff in *The Merry Wives of Windsor* on 19 December 1777, but the date is impossible, since Lewes was acting in London that week. The Manchester man was, again, Philip Lewis.

Lewes possessed some talent as a deliverer of prologues, epilogues, and occasional pieces. At the opening night of the Covent Garden season on 20 September 1779 the gallery gods demanded the prologue to *The Invasion* (Pilon's farce in which Lewes had been the original Cameleon on 4 November 1778); Lewes informed them that since it was not the custom to speak a prologue after the first season of the piece he was totally unprepared. But the crowd was unrelenting, so "he stepped forward," related the next *Morning Post*, "and, to the utter astonishment of the whole house, went through the prologue very correctly, with the addition of near twenty lines, about Paul Jones, Sir Charles Hardy, and Sir John Lockhart Ross!"

In the summer of 1780 Lewes arranged with Harris to use Covent Garden for the presentation of his version of George Alexander Stevens's *Lecture upon Heads*, a monologue that satirized the follies of various contemporary types. Apparently in response to Colman's objections that a summer program at Covent Garden would injure his Haymarket business, Lewes explained in the *General Advertiser* on 9 May that his reason for choosing Covent Garden was his intention to take the lecture to different parts of England and Ireland that summer. He foresaw no harm to Colman, "under whom I have had the honour of being introduced to the Public." The announced opening night of 3 June had to be postponed because the revisions were not yet ready. Finally, on 26 June 1780, with new costumes for all the "characters" and a prologue furnished by Pilon, Stevens's *Lecture upon Heads* was offered to the public:

Delivered by Lee Lewes. The whole revised and adapted to the Times. In which the following

Characters: the Head of G. A. Stevens; the Debating Societies dissected, with the Heads of a Male and female President; a fashionable Foreigner; four national Characters, with the Heads of an English Sailor, a Spaniard, a Frenchman, and a Dutch Merchant; the Head of a Libeller.

The *Lecture* was repeated on 29 June and 3 and 6 July. In a Belfast advertisement six years later Lewes boasted that he had taken in £335 for those four nights. In August Lewes took the show to Bristol. He gave the *Lecture* at the Haymarket in London on 13 and 14 March 1781.

At the end of 1782–83 Lewes quarreled with Harris, presumably over salary. That summer (according to a notation by Joseph Reed in a manuscript at the British Library), Lewes went to France to tour with his *Lecture upon Heads*. He accepted an engagement at Drury Lane for the subsequent season, making his first appearance there on 16 September 1783, as Marplot in *The Busy Body*. Next he acted Touchstone in *As You Like It* on 16 October, followed by Lucio, Marplot, Meadows, the Copper Captain in *Rule a Wife and Have a Wife*, and Tattle in *Love for Love*. On 10 January 1784 he acted Falstaff in *The Merry Wives of Windsor* for the first time (*The London Stage* states that he acted Falstaff at Manchester on 19 December 1777, but that actor must have been Philip Lewis). His other roles were the original Colonel Quorum in *The Reparation* on 14 February 1784, Witwou'd in *The Way of the World*, and Aspin in *Love in a Veil*. On 29 January 1784 he returned to Covent Garden to substitute for Wilson as Lord Lumbercourt in *The Man of the World*, and he was "far indeed better than the man he appeared for," wrote the *Public Advertiser* on 31 January. On 27 March 1784 Drury Lane paid him £50 in lieu of a benefit.

The move to Drury Lane, where many of the roles he used to act at the other house were in Palmer's hands, proved disadvantageous for Lewes. His London career definitely declined. In September of 1784 he was in Ireland, acting in Cork. He did not return to Drury Lane until 11 October, when he acted Falstaff. That night the treasurer paid Lee Lewes £21 on canceling his engagement. His name did not appear again in Drury Lane bills that season until he played Brush in *The Clandestine Marriage* and Meadows in *The Deaf Lover* for his benefit on 9 May 1785. Receipts were disappointing: £144 6s., less house charges of £105 19s. 4d. Account books at the Folger Library show that during that season the theatre had paid him small weekly sums of £1 1s. on a regular basis.

Lewes is placed by William S. Clark at Cork in March 1786, at Waterford in August, and at Cork again in September. He then went to Belfast, where, advertised as from Covent Garden, he made his first appearance at the Rosemary Lane Theatre on 23 October 1786, as the Copper Captain in *Rule a Wife and Have a Wife*. On 23 November he gave his *Original Lecture upon Heads*—"with all the whimsical apparatus, which he purchased for the sum of Two Hundred Pounds, of the late George Alexander Stevens, and which with the additional expense of £100 in modern characters, Heads, Wigs, Pictures, &c&c., he lately revived at the Theatre Royal Covent Garden with so much approbation and success, that in four nights his receipts were £335 10. 6." On 20 December his wife (his third) Catharine Maria Lewes, billed as "a Lady (being her first appearance on any stage)," acted Rosalind to his Touchstone in *As You Like It*. Leaving Belfast in March 1787, he made his way to Edinburgh, appearing there as Captain Meadows, Marplot, Falstaff, and Young Wilding in *The Lyar*, and offering his *Lecture upon Heads* between 10 and 19 May 1787. At Palmer's Royalty Theatre in Wellclose Square, London, Lewes delivered the monologue *Hippisley's Drunken Man* on 31 October 1787. In November he performed Harlequin in *Harlequin Mungo* and also recited Cowper's *John Gilpin* and the *Lecture upon Heads*.

In hopes of finding greener pastures Lewes next took his family to India, but because he had not made the necessary arrangements in advance in London he was allowed only a few performances, and he soon returned to England.

In a manuscript at the Folger Library, James Winston wrote that it was said Lewes rashly refused a liberal offer from Harris "because it was not the highest salary he gave." In August 1789 he acted in *The Reparation* at Margate. Advertised for his first London appearance since his return from India, Lewes acted Buck in *The Englishman in Paris* at Covent Garden on 7 April 1790, for Edwin's benefit. He appeared in the same role for Hull's benefit on 18 May

LEWES

1790. At an extra night at Covent Garden on 16 July 1790 Lewes himself took a benefit, playing Trappanti in *She Wou'd and She Wou'd Not*, in which his wife acted Viletta. He also presented *A Merry Sketch of Folly and Fashion*:

The Whole to be delivered by Lee Lewes. In which will be exhibited Characters and Caricatures, many of them entirely new, and others selected from Subjects of the most Approved Wit and Humour. Two very astonishing figures will be introduced, of the late King of Prussia, and his General Ziethen; also the Propagation of a Lie, in Characters as large as life, with several whimsical Paintings in Transparency. The whole prepared for the East Indies, at a prodigious expense. The above two figures cost at Berlin 275 guineas.

On 15 February 1791 Lewes announced on the bottom of a Covent Garden bill for Mrs Esten's benefit that "on account of his not being employed at either of the theatres, the Lord Chamberlain . . . has been pleased to grant him a singular indulgence; and that the Prince of Wales has permitted Mr. Lee Lewes, to announce the performance of a Play and Entertainment, under his Royal Patronage." Lewes promised to inform the public of the specific event in a few days. The heralded benefit for Lewes occurred at the Haymarket on 7 March 1791. He acted Marplot in *The Busy Body* and a principal role in the first performance of Fennell's farce *The Advertisement; or, A New Way to Get a Husband*, in which Mrs Lewes appeared as Mrs O'Trigger. Lewes also presented his recitation *The late King of Prussia and General Ziethen* and *A Whimsical Dissertation upon Law*. Tickets were available from him at Mr Brough's, No 18, Portland Street, Soho. That night was his next-to-last appearance in London and his last there in that century.

At the age of 52 he retreated to the provinces, which witnessed the decline of his powers. At Edinburgh in 1792 he was under Stephen Kemble's management and was part manager of the theatre at Dundee. He went to Crow Street, Dublin, in 1792–93 and returned there in 1793, 1794, and 1798. At Aberdeen in December 1793 a street preacher, the Reverend Alexander Kilham, denounced him and his craft, leading Lewes into print with a pamphlet, dated 4 January 1794, entitled *The Stage and the Pulpit. The Player and the Preacher. Or, a serio-comic answer to Mr. Kilham, preacher*. Kilham replied on 6 January 1794 with a long tract called *The Hypocrite detected and exposed; and the true Christian vindicated and supported*. In December 1794 Lewes was at Belfast and Londonderry, in 1796 at Belfast (on 11 July he gave his "Comic Sketches," advertised as originally presented by him at Calcutta), Drogheda, Kilkenny, and Cork, in 1797 at Cork again, and in January and February 1800 once more at Belfast. In autumn 1800 he acted at Sheffield. The *Monthly Mirror* of December 1795 had reported: "Lee Lewis having failed in his application for a London engagement, means to set sail for America," but that voyage did not occur.

The proprietors of Covent Garden (not Drury Lane as stated in *The Dictionary of National Biography*) made the house available for Lewes's farewell benefit on 24 June 1803. Acting Lissardo in *The Wonder*, he was supported by Henry Siddons as Don Felix, Mrs Jordan as Violante, and Mrs Mattocks as Flora. A decay of Lewes's powers, according to the *Thespian Dictionary*, was now obvious. He closed out his career of about 43 years speaking an address written by T. J. Dibdin entitled "Lee Lewes's Ultimatum." The benefit evidently was a financial success, but Lewes had little time to enjoy its proceeds. In his *Reminiscences* T. J. Dibdin wrote that Lewes was found dead in his bed two mornings after his benefit—on 26 June—and in his pocket were two guineas labeled for Dibdin, from whom he had borrowed them two days before his benefit. "He ate a hearty supper, with my brother Charles, at Sir Hugh Middleton's Head, on the last night of his existence," wrote Dibdin, "and said, at parting, he feared it would do him no good, although he had been any thing but intemperate." Dibdin seems to have reminisced incorrectly, however; Boaden in his *Life of Mrs Jordan*, a Winston manuscript in the Harvard Theatre Collection, and a notation in the Burney papers at the British Library all give 23 July 1803—a month after his farewell benefit—as the date of Lewes's death. He was buried at St James, Pentonville.

Lewes had married three times. His first wife, Anne Hussey, died at Bristol on 26 August 1772. Though she had performed occasionally on the Bristol stage, she seems never to have acted in London. When Lewes was ill at Bristol in 1771 he was described as "surrounded by a Family of little ones," but only one of his children by Anne Lewes is known to us: Elizabeth Anne, daughter of Charles Lee "Lewis" by Anne his wife was baptized at St Paul, Covent Garden, on 31 March 1771. Lewes's second wife, Fanny Wrigley, the daughter of a Liverpool innkeeper, was not an actress. Their son James Wrigley Lewes was baptized on 14 January 1781. She died on 27 March 1783, a few days after the death of twin boys, no doubt from the effects of childbirth. Lewes's third wife Catharine Maria, who acted in the provinces and several times in London and died at Edinburgh on 12 March 1796, is noticed separately.

One of Lewes's daughters, by his first or second wife, became the fourth (or third?) wife of the actor Richard Wilson at St Mary, Whitechapel, on 31 July 1791. As Mrs Wilson she acted in the provinces and made her first appearance in London at the Haymarket on 28 September 1796, as Julia in *The Rivals*; she is noticed under her married name.

John Lee Lewes, one of Lewes's sons by his first or second wife, acted in the provinces in the nineteenth century. In 1805 he edited and published his father's memoirs. It is said that he inherited enough money from his parents to live in a manner which earned him the nickname "Dandy Lewes." Seven years after John Lee Lewes's death in 1818, his widow, Elizabeth (née Ashweek) married John Willim, a retired captain of the 18th Native Infantry Regiment, Bengal; she died on 10 December 1871, at the age of 83. John Lee Lewes's son, George Henry Lewes (1817–1878), acted and wrote plays and novels but is better known as one of the foremost Victorian literary critics. With his wife, Agnes Lewis, whom he had married in 1841, George Henry Lewes lived in communal marriage with the Thornton Leigh Hunts and two other couples. Mrs Lewes had two children by Hunt. Lewes separated from his wife in 1854, by which time he was living with Mary Ann Evans, the novelist George Eliot. His eldest son, Charles (1842–1891), inherited George Eliot's estate upon her death in 1880. George Henry Lewes's lawful wife, Agnes, died on 22 December 1902.

Charles Lee Lewes was regarded by Genest as a good actor whose sense of self-importance caused the loss of his career. In 1775 Lewes was, according to William Hawkins in *Miscellanies in Prose and Verse*, "a thriving and pleasant comedian," who had "a smartness in his manner" that suggested considerable potential. Anthony Pasquin (John Williams) in *The Children of Thespis* (1792) called him "Co-equal to Lun [John Rich], in the pantomime graces" and added in doggerel:

> And the harlequin jerk is to him so attracting,
> That it steals thro' his mean {sic} in colloquial acting.
> In the smart replication he mostly excels
> When snip-snappish wit in the character dwells;
> All his valets possess a bold, undescrib'd pertness,
> Appropriate conceits—a well-managed alertness:
> When he gives up Chapeau 'twill be laid on the shelf,
> And no man should be stuff'd for Sir John but himself;
> ....
> His Flutter was great, but it dignified trash,
> Like the heads of wise monarchs on base metal cash . . .

One of the few surviving critiques of Lewes's acting, found in a press clipping in the Enthoven Collection, administers a severe drubbing for his portrayal of Bobadil in *Every Man in His Humor* at Covent Garden on 1 October 1779. The critic thought him "totally inadequate," suffering from "the double misfortune of entire misconception and great incapacity of execution":

He neither attempted to adopt the extravagant solemnity of bombast and parade, which is the vital principle of the character; nor did he intimate . . . that he possessed a proper understanding of the part. . . . The Extravagance is not Mr. Lewes's forte of acting.

In addition to *The Stage and the Pulpit* (the pamphlet that he published at Aberdeen in 1794), Lewes's publications included *The London Songster, Polite Musical Companion. Containing Four Hundred and Fifty-four of the newest and most favourite Songs, Catches, Duets, and Cantatas now in Vogue at the public Theatres and Gardens* (1767); *Hippisley's Drunken Man, as altered by Charles Lee Lewes*, published by the Catch Club (1787?); a *Lecture upon Heads, as delivered by Charles Lee Lewes* (1784, with editions in 1785, 1787, 1808, and 1821); and *John Gilpin as delivered by Charles Lee Lewes*, described by *The Dictionary of National Biography* as "unmentioned by authorities and inaccessible." Some of these works reputedly were written while

LEWES

Lewes was in prison for debt. Published posthumously in 1804 was *Comic Sketches, or, the Comedian his own Manager. . . . The whole forming matter sufficient for two evenings' entertainment; originally intended for the East Indies, and as delivered by him, without an apparatus, in many parts of the three kingdoms with distinguished patronage.* The *Comic Sketches* was accompanied by a biographical account of Lewes, which his son called "false." The *Memoirs of Charles Lee Lewes, containing anecdotes, historical and biographical, of the English and Scottish stages, during a period of forty years* was edited and published in four volumes by his son John Lee Lewes in 1805. It has been described as having "an unenviable precedency of worthlessness," mostly being anecdotal—probably apocryphal—stories about other actors, with some colorful accounts of his early life. Two volumes are devoted to the struggle between Mrs Esten and Jackson over control of the Scottish stage but Lewes says little of his London career. Genest called the *Memoirs* "on the whole an abominable catchpenny."

Portraits of Charles Lee Lewes include:

1. By William Beechey? Beechey's account books, 1789, record a payment of £10 10*s*. ("paid half") by "Mr Lewes" for a portrait. Possibly that sitter was Charles Lee Lewes, but no portrait of him by Beechey can now be traced.

2. By unknown artist. In a four-panel painting with Anna Maria Crouch, Dorothy Jordan, and Joseph Munden. In the possession of the Earl of Munster.

3. Engraved portrait by J. Hopwood. Published by H. D. Symonds, 1804, as frontispiece to Lewes's *Comic Sketches.*

4. By unknown engraver. Whole length, standing to left, arms folded. Published by S. Bretherton, July 1784. Not listed in Hall catalogue, but in Harvard Theatre Collection, tentatively identified as C. L. Lewes.

5. As Bobadil in *Every Man in His Humour.* Oil painting by Samuel De Wilde. In the Garrick Club (No 249). Engraving by W. Leney published as a plate to *Bell's British Theatre,* 1791. An engraving of the same picture by H. Brocas was issued as a plate to *British Theatre,* published by William Jones, 1791.

6. As Bobadil. Watercolor by Samuel De Wilde. In the Garrick Club (No 66F). Similar to De Wilde's oil painting.

7. As Harlequin, speaking a prologue (probably the one provided by Goldsmith). By unknown engraver. Published by Fielding and Walker, 1780.

8. As Mercury in *A Hospital for Fools.* By unknown engraver. Published by Harrison & Co as a plate to an edition of the play, 1781.

9. As Sir Peter Teazle in *The School for Scandal.* By unknown artist. On a Delftware tile in the City of Manchester Art Gallery.

10. As Young Wilding in *The Lyar.* By unknown engraver. Published by Harrison & Co as a plate to an edition of the play, 1780.

11. As the "Tight Lad," with Mrs Lewes as the "Brisk Widow," in *The Road to Ruin.* Caricature by J. Kay, published 1792, probably at Edinburgh.

An engraving by Walker, after Barralet, of Mrs Lessingham in a scene from *The Beaux' Stratagem* was published as a plate to the *New English Theatre,* 1776. It is captioned Mrs Lessingham as Mrs Sullen, but the male figure, obviously the character of Archer, is not named. The picture has been catalogued and reproduced with Archer identified, we believe incorrectly, as C. L. Lewes. The more likely candidate, if indeed the male figure is intended to represent any specific actor, is William T. Lewis; the character is very much in his line, and he played it for the first time at Covent Garden on 4 May 1775, with Mrs Lessingham as Mrs Sullen.

Lewes, Mrs Charles Lee the third, Catharine Maria *d.* 1796, *actress.*

Sometime after the death of his second wife in 1783, Charles Lee Lewes married a woman whose Christian names were Catharine Maria, but about whose background nothing is known. At the Rosemary Lane Theatre in Belfast on 20 December 1786, advertised as "A Lady (being her first appearance on any Stage)," the third Mrs Lewes acted Rosalind in *As You Like It.* That night Lewes played Touchstone. The Belfast *Newsletter* reported that she acquitted herself fairly well, "seeming to comprehend the spirit of the character, by her judicious application of emphasis; but her person and voice threaten to be insuperable bars to her arriving at eminence in the profession."

Eminence was not to be hers. She played at Belfast again in March 1787, Pero's company at Derby in 1788–89 and 1789–90, and

Harvard Theatre Collection

CATHARINE LEWES as the Brisk Widow and CHARLES LEE LEWES as the Tight Lad
by Kay

Harvard Theatre Collection

CATHARINE LEWES, as Lady Sadlife
engraving by Thornthwaite, after De Wilde

probably wherever else her husband's peregrinations took him. When Lewes was given Covent Garden Theatre for his benefit on 16 July 1790, she acted Viletta to his Trappanti in *She Wou'd and She Wou'd Not*. Her only other London appearance was at the Haymarket on 7 March 1791, again for a special benefit granted to her husband, for which she acted Patch to his Marplot in *The Busy Body* and played Mrs O'Trigger in the first and only performance of Fennell's farce *The Advertisement; or, A New Way to Get a Husband*.

She made her first appearance in Edinburgh on 12 March 1792, as Mrs Oakly in *The Jealous Wife*. Her other roles at the Theatre Royal in Shakespeare Square that year included Alexina in *A Day in Turkey*, Emilia in *Othello*, Estifania in *Rule a Wife and Have a Wife*, Fatima in *Cymon*, the First Lady in *Lethe*, Kathy Pry in *The Lying Valet*, Lady Alton in *The English Merchant*, Lady Bell Bloomer in *Which Is the Man?*, Lady Macbeth, Lady Randolph in *Douglas* (with John Kemble as Douglas on 10 July), Lady Restless in *All in the Wrong*, Lisette in *Animal Magnetism*, the Marchioness in *The Child of Nature*, Miss Herbert in *The Fugitive*, Princess Catherine in *Henry V*, and Widow Warren in *The Road to Ruin*. She returned to Edinburgh in 1793, 1794, and 1795; some of her characters in those engagements included Mrs Candour in *The School for Scandal*, Mrs Frail in *Love for Love*, Mrs Page in *The Merry Wives of Windsor*, Phillis in *The Conscious Lovers*, and Flora in *The Wonder*.

The *European Magazine* of April 1796 announced the death of Mrs Lewes at Edinburgh on the previous 12 March. We know of no issue by her marriage to Lewes, who died in 1803.

A pencil drawing of Mrs Lewes by J. Roberts is in the Harvard Theatre Collection. An engraving by Thornthwaite, after De Wilde, of Mrs Lewes as Lady Sadlife in *The Double Gallant* was published by Bell in 1792; Mrs

LEWES

Lewes is not known to have played the role in London or in Edinburgh, where she displayed her largest repertoire. A caricature showing Mrs Lewes and her husband as the Brisk Widow and the Tight Lad in *The Road to Ruin* was published by the Edinburgh artist J. Kay in 1792 and no doubt depicts them in a production in that city.

Lewey. *See* LOUIS.

Lewin, Richard. *See* LEWIS, RICHARD.

Lewis. *See also* LOUIS.

Lewis, Mr [*fl.* 1779], *house servant.*
A Mr Lewis shared benefit tickets with Hodges and Gardner, house servants, at Drury Lane Theatre on 1 June 1779.

Lewis, Mr [*fl.* 1781–1792], *music copier.*
From 16 November 1781 to 22 December 1792, a Mr Lewis was paid modest amounts for copying music at Drury Lane Theatre.

Lewis, Mr [*fl.* 1784], *singer.*
A Mr Lewis was listed by Dr Burney as a countertenor in the Handel Memorial Concerts at Westminster Abbey and the Pantheon in May and June 1784.

Lewis, Mr [*fl.* 1790], *supernumerary.*
A manuscript in the British Library (Add 29,946) notes a payment of £10 10s. as "A Donation to Harley & Lewis Supernumerary Men, who fell from the Scaffold" during a performance of *The Crusade*. That musical drama by Reynolds opened at Covent Garden Theatre on 6 May 1790 and was performed a total of 13 times before the end of the season.

Lewis, Mr [*fl.* 1793–1795], *doorkeeper.*
A Mr Lewis was paid 12s. per week in 1793–94 and 15s. per week in 1794–95 as a doorkeeper at Covent Garden Theatre.

Lewis, Mr [*fl.* 1794–1804?], *dresser.*
A Mr Lewis was paid 9s. 6d. per week as a men's dresser at Covent Garden Theatre in 1794–95. A manuscript in the Folger Library lists a Lewis as a men's dresser at the Haymarket Theatre in the summer of 1804.

Lewis, Mrs [*fl.* 1711], *performer?*
A Mrs Lewis received a benefit at Greenwich on 13 September 1711 when *She Wou'd If She Cou'd* was performed at Pinkethman's theatre. The name Lewis was much too common to make identification possible, but perhaps it is worth noting that a Dorothy Lewis, widow, was one of the executors of the will of an Ursula Knight on 15 May 1711. That Ursula Knight, or another, had been an actress in the King's Company at Drury Lane in 1676–77.

Lewis, Mrs [*fl.* 1781–1789], *house servant.*
A Mrs Lewis shared benefit tickets with house servants at Drury Lane Theatre each year between 1781–82 and 1788–89.

Lewis, Miss [*fl.* 1735], *actress.*
A Miss Lewis acted Lady Loverule in *The Devil to Pay* at the Haymarket Theatre on 19 June 1735.

Lewis, Alexander [*fl.* 1682], *trumpeter.*
Alexander Lewis, a trumpeter in the King's Musick assigned to the Duke of Albemarle, received an unspecified livery allowance on 29 April 1682, according to the Lord Chamberlain's accounts. Perhaps he was the Alexander Lewis who married Mary Lowesse at St Marylebone on 24 January 1675, but the name is too common to make a certain identification.

Lewis, Mrs Anne or **Louisa.** *See* STANDEN, MRS CHARLES THE FIRST.

Lewis, [**David?**] [*fl.* 1712–1734?], *dancer, dancing master.*
In 1712 John Weaver listed in his *Essay towards an History of Dance* a dancing master named Lewis who had "arrived at true Skill and Taste of Genteel Dancing." Perhaps he was the David Lewis, dancing master (husband of Rebecca Lewis), whose child was baptized at Christ Church, Spitalfields, in 1729, when his address was in Princess Street of that parish; another child was baptized in 1734, when Lewis's address was in Grey Eagle Street. Lewis performed Harlequin in *The Amorous Adventure* at the Haymarket Theatre on 17 July and 16 November 1730 and Harlequin in *The Necromancer* at Lincoln's Inn Fields Theatre on 12, 17, and 20 January 1732.

Lewis, "Gentleman." *See* LEWIS, WILLIAM THOMAS.

Lewis, Philip *d. 1791, actor, manager, dancer?*

Philip Lewis was the son of a clergyman, the rector of Traghaire in Wales for some 30 years. His grandfather is said to have been Erasmus Lewis (1670–1754), private secretary to Robert Harley, Queen Anne's minister. In his will made in 1743 Erasmus Lewis mentioned no sons, so it is presumed that by that year Philip Lewis's father was dead.

Either Philip or his elder brother William was in "Stretch's Show" at the Capel Street Theatre, Dublin, in the 1740s. By 1750 Philip and William were members of a provincial Irish company that played in Belfast. They purchased the Newry company from James Love, but when William died in 1753, and, seven months later, his widow married William Dawson, the company was disbanded.

Probably Philip was the Lewis who was a minor member of the Drury Lane company in 1750–51; on 13 May 1751 he played Filch in *The Beggar's Opera*. Though his name did not appear in the bills for any roles in 1751–52, on 2 May 1752 Lewis shared benefit tickets with other minor theatre personnel. His name appeared in the Drury Lane bills for unspecified roles in *The Rehearsal* on 8 December 1752 and *The Genii* on 1 January 1753. On 16 May 1753 he again shared benefit tickets. For several more seasons at Drury Lane he continued virtually as an anonym except for a billing as an unspecified character in *The Englishman in Paris* on 20 October 1753. In 1754–55 his name appeared for unspecified roles in *The Rehearsal* and *The Chinese Festival*. His participation in that latter ill-fated ballet, which provoked anti-French rioting on 8 November 1755, suggests that Lewis may also have done double-duty at Drury Lane as a dancer. That season he also performed Joseph in Garrick's *Catherine and Petruchio* and the Doctor in *Chrononhotonthologos*. In 1756–57 he acted again in *The Rehearsal*.

Lewis returned to Ireland in 1757, playing at Drogheda that year and the next. In 1757–58 he was a member of Thomas Sheridan's company at the Smock Alley Theatre in Dublin, where he remained for three seasons. Among his roles there were Coupier in *The Relapse*, Duke Frederick in *As You Like It*, Wat Dreary in *The Beggar's Opera*, Thrifty in *The Cheats of Scapin*, Sir John Bevil in *The Conscious Lovers*, Sicinius in *Coriolanus*, Mopsus in *Damon and Phillida*, the Player King in *Hamlet*, Muckworm in *The Honest Yorkshireman*, an Old Man in *King Lear*, Trapland in *Love for Love*, a Witch in *Macbeth*, Old Gobbo in *The Merchant of Venice*, Hotman in *Oroonoko*, the Duke in *Othello*, Stanley in *Richard III*, Gregory in *Romeo and Juliet*, Balderdash in *The Twin Rivals*, and Alguazile in *The Wonder*.

Some of these and similar tertiary roles were his when in the autumn of 1761 he began an engagement at Covent Garden which extended for nine seasons through 1769–70. His first Covent Garden appearance was as Sir Hugh Evans in *The Merry Wives of Windsor* on 23 September 1761. That season, when his salary was £1 5s. per week, he also acted Bardolph in *2 Henry IV*, Richard Wealthy in *The Minor*, Jaques in *The Pilgrim*, and Gripe in *The City Wives Confederacy*. A selection of his subsequent roles there indicates his journeyman status: Charino in *Love Makes a Man*, the Constable in *The Recruiting Officer*, Bull in *The Relapse*, Clement in *Every Man in His Humour*, Poundage in *The Provok'd Husband*, a Plebian in *Julius Caesar*, Decoy in *The Miser*, Sir William Meadows in *Love in a Village*, and Burgundy in *King Lear*.

At the Haymarket Theatre on 11 May 1763 Lewis acted the Judge in Foote's *Trial of Samuel Foote, Esq. For a Libel on Peter Paragraph*. His other roles that summer at the Haymarket seem to have been Smith in *The Rehearsal*, Crab and Mr Ruthen in *The Englishman Return'd from Paris*, Foigard in *The Beaux' Stratagem*, Don Choleric in *Love Makes a Man*, and a part in *The Lyar*. Some of those roles, however, may have been played by Charles Lee Lewes, who seems also to have been with Foote that summer. Philip was sometimes billed as Lewis, Senior, to distinguish him from Lewes (who in the earlier years of his career spelled his name Lewis) or from William T. Lewis, Philip's nephew. Probably Philip was the Lewis who acted at the Haymarket in the summers of 1764 and 1766 and also in Barry's company at the King's Theatre in the latter year. On 7 October 1768 Lewis played Sir Jealous Traffick in a specially-licensed performance of *The Busy Body* for Bannister's benefit at the Haymarket.

After his last season at Covent Garden, 1769–70, Lewis passed a number of years in the provinces. Occasionally he reappeared in London. In the summer of 1773 he was at the Haymarket. At that theatre on 2 February 1775 he played Sir William in a performance of *Love in a Village* for the benefit of the widowed Mrs Woodman, and on 23 March 1775 he appeared there as Antonio in *The Merchant of Venice* and in a role in *The Snuff Box* for Johnson's benefit. In the summer of 1775 he was again at the Haymarket and also worked in Richmond, Surrey, where he acted in *The Recruiting Officer* on 22 July and *The Rivals* on 19 August. At China Hall, Rotherhithe, between 23 September and 18 October 1776 he acted Torrington in *The School for Wives*, Cranmer in *Henry VIII*, Coupler in *Miss Hoyden*, an Officer in *Barbarossa*, Keeper in *The King and the Miller of Mansfield*, Sackbut in *A Bold Stroke for a Wife*, Stanley in *Richard III*, Clytus in *Alexander the Great*, Drugget in *Three Weeks after Marriage*, Richard Wealthy in *The Minor*, Thoroughgood in *The London Merchant*, Syphax in *Cato*, and Philip in *High Life below Stairs*. For his benefit at China Hall on 18 October, when he acted Justice Ballance in *The Recruiting Officer*, tickets were available from him at the Europa. At the Haymarket, out-of-season, he appeared as Sir William in *The Gentle Shepherd* on 22 April 1777, a character in *Love at a Venture* on 21 March 1782, and Dervise in *Tamerlane* on 22 December 1788.

At London in 1774 was published *Miscellaneous Pieces in Verse and Prose, with Cursory Theatrical Remarks, by P. Lewis, Comedian.* An edition was published in Manchester in 1778; a fifth edition appeared in 1782 in Portsmouth, where Lewis had recently been a member of the theatre, and another edition came out in 1790. The Manchester edition at the Folger Library contains "A Prologue to the Tragedy of Douglas: Spoken at the opening of the Southampton Theatre," "A Prologue spoken at opening of Brighthelmstone Theatre, 1775," and verses on Garrick, Dunstall, Foote, Love, Shuter, Holland, Powell, and Mrs Greville.

In September 1779 Lewis was a member of Fisher's company at Sudbury, where he was known as an eccentric. His propensity for gloom and melancholy earned him the nickname of "the Stage King of Grief." Bernard described him in his *Retrospections* as a man who "took pleasure in being miserable." At the age of 75, according to Bernard, Lewis still believed himself to be an actor with talents superior to many London favorites. Probably he was the Lewis who acted at Stourbridge Fair, Cambridge, in October 1780 and at Gloucester in March 1788.

On 23 August 1788 the Bristol press reported that the King at Cheltenham promised "old Lewis the actor . . . to make some provision for him during the remainder of his days." Lewis eventually was cared for by his nephew, William T. Lewis, in whose house he lived as a vexatious and crotchety old man. On 9 September 1791 *Woodfall's Register* reported that Philip Lewis had died a few days since, near Mile End.

Lewis, Richard [*fl.* 1685–1697], musician.

On 20 January 1685 Richard Lewis, an unsalaried musician in the King's private music, was assured that he would have a fee at the next vacancy. The vacancy did not occur until 17 July 1687 at the death of Jeoffrey Aleworth, and perhaps it was to reward Lewis (or Lewys, sometimes Lewin) for his patience that on 27 October he was given the additional duty (and extra pay) of keeping the instruments for the King's Musick, a post formerly held by Henry Brockwell, who had been paid £18 5*s*. annually in addition to his regular salary and livery fee. Lewis also augmented his income on occasion with attendance on the King outside London. In the summer of 1688 he was at Windsor, earning an extra 6*s*. daily; in 1690 he went with the King to Newmarket; and in January 1691 he accompanied King William to Holland. Lewis's basic salary was £30 annually.

Lewis nevertheless got himself into debt in 1693 and was sued by John Strachan and Hans Marchant in July. That, or some unknown incident of a similar nature, may have caused Lewis to be dropped from the payroll on 22 June 1694—unless a warrant of that date in the Lord Chamberlain's accounts is an error, or unless there were two Richard Lewises. On that date Lewis was appointed to the King's Musick without fee but was assured of a salary when the next vacancy occurred. John Ridgley was told on 28 September that he would replace Lewis and have all the wages that had previously gone to him. In November 1696

Lewis appointed John Langly of St Giles in the Fields his attorney, a move court musicians often made when they were going on a trip or when they were in financial difficulty. Lewis was last mentioned in the accounts on 30 November 1697, when he was to have been paid a livery allowance.

Lewis, Robert [*fl.* 1694–1702], *musician.*

On 22 June 1694 Robert Lewis replaced the deceased Charles Coleman in the King's Musick. Lewis was an instrumentalist, though the Lord Chamberlain's accounts did not mention which instruments he played. His annual salary was £40, in addition to which he received a yearly livery allowance. Lewis was still active in the King's Musick in 1702.

Lewis, Sarah. *See* THURMOND, MRS JOHN THE YOUNGER.

Lewis, Tertullian *d. 1699, drummer.*

Tertullian Lewis was appointed a drummer in the King's Musick on 20 July 1660 and served until his death in 1699. The Lord Chamberlain's accounts rarely mentioned him. On 29 April 1699 he was replaced by John Clothier, and it is very likely that Lewis had died a day or two before that date. On 20 April he had made his will, describing himself as "sick and weak in body." He was from the parish of St Clement Danes and called himself not a musician but a salter; he evidently held two jobs. Lewis left his son John £100, his granddaughter Anne Lewis £100 when she should reach 21, and his wife Mary his house in Hammersmith (then occupied by Henry Peddar). His wife was also to receive the rest of his estate, and his son John was named residuary legatee. Mary Lewis proved the will on 5 May 1699.

Lewis, Thomas [*fl.* 1715], *tailor.*

Thomas Lewis was evidently the house tailor at Drury Lane in 1715; bills presented by him to the management of the theatre are among the manuscripts at the Folger Shakespeare Library. There was a Thomas Lewis whose daughter Catherine was buried at St Paul, Covent Garden, on 18 April 1718, but the name is too common to make a certain identification.

Lewis, William Thomas *c. 1746–1811, actor, manager.*

William Thomas Lewis was born in Ormskirk, Lancashire, but the date was in dispute among early biographers. The November 1811 issue of the *Gentleman's Magazine* declared for 4 March 1749 but stated contradictorily that he had died aged 65. *The Secret History of the Green Rooms* (1790) offered March 1756, and the *Monthly Mirror* for November 1798 testified that Lewis had been five years old when his father died, about 1753.

Lewis's grandfather, rector of Traghaire in Wales for some 30 years, was the second son of Erasmus Lewis, who had been private secretary to Robert Harley, minister to Queen Anne. Our subject's father, William Lewis, once served as apprentice to a linen draper on Tower Hill but turned actor. William Lewis may have been the player of that name who was roundly criticized by the *Tickler* on 18 February 1747 for his bad acting at the Smock Alley Theatre in Dublin.

It is said that William Thomas Lewis was

Harvard Theatre Collection

WILLIAM THOMAS LEWIS
engraving by Corner, after Brown

carried on stage as an infant in the arms of Don John in *The Chances*. Master Lewis's name was in the bills as Falstaff's page Robin in *The Merry Wives of Windsor* at the Vaults in Belfast in 1751–52. The nucleus of the company consisted of James Love the manager, Mr and Mrs William Lewis, and William's younger brother Philip Lewis. (If he had been born in 1748–49, William Thomas would have been barely three at the time, a very tender age indeed, so the birth year of 1746 seems a bit more reasonable.) The Lewises bought Love's company soon after that visit to Belfast, but when the troupe returned there in the summer of 1753 William Lewis had died, for his wife was called "Widow" Lewis at her benefit. On 14 August 1753 Master Lewis played the Duke of York in *Richard III*. Making his first recorded appearance in a 40-year career in Ireland was William Dawson, who played the title role. Not long after, Dawson married Mrs Lewis and became our subject's stepfather. By this second marriage William Thomas's mother had another son, George Dawson (c. 1756–1787), who was, according to Bernard's *Retrospections*, "the twin of Lewis in appearance."

Young Lewis accompanied his mother and stepfather when they were strolling in Ireland in the spring of 1756; at Tralee he played Prince John in *Henry IV*, the Duke of York in *Richard III*, Peter in *Romeo and Juliet*, Fleance in *Macbeth*, Dicky in *The Constant Couple*, the Boy in *The Committee* and gave the farewell address on the last night, 10 May. They were in Edinburgh in 1757 and 1758, where Master Lewis pleased audiences in his juvenile roles, according to West Digges.

Lewis was sent, about 1759, to Mr Heaphy's grammar school in Armagh, where he became a proficient student. But he was back with the strollers at Belfast in the summer of 1761; now about the age of 15, he played Squire Richard in *The Provok'd Wife*, and his half brother, George Dawson, age 5, seems to have made his debut on 24 August, as Young Sifroy in *Cleone*.

Lewis made his first appearance at the Smock Alley Theatre, Dublin, on 3 June 1761 and remained there through 1764–65. As Mr Lewis he acted at the Crow Street Theatre through 1767–68. When the Dawsons took over the Capel Street Theatre in 1770–71, Lewis's appearance there as Belcour in *The West Indian* on 19 February 1771 successfully competed against

Harvard Theatre Collection

WILLIAM THOMAS LEWIS, as the Copper Captain

engraving by Alais

Mossop in the role at the rival Crow Street house. Lewis's performance in *The West Indian* was seen in Dublin by Richard Cumberland, the play's author, who wrote to Garrick on 13 July 1771 that, though Lewis overacted, he showed spirit and promise in the coxcomical and gay walks of comedy. Cumberland suggested to Garrick that Lewis "would be an accession under your government, as he is very young, handsome, and volatile." On 5 August 1771, however, Cumberland reported that there was no probability of detaching him from his stepfather's employ, under which he earned the very high salary of eight guineas a week. The author repeated his high regard for Lewis, praising his strong tone, variety of cadence, and quick eye.

In 1771–72 and 1772–73 he was again at Crow Street, which Dawson now managed.

Tate Wilkinson saw the "sprightly lad" act Romeo on 4 May 1772. Lewis played Young Belfield in *The Brothers* for Wilkinson's benefit on 28 May 1772. Robert Hitchcock wrote in his *View of the Irish Stage* that Lewis's popularity in Dublin grew rapidly as he acted "a very extensive and varied line of business in tragedy and comedy with great ability" and applied himself "with so much good sense and propriety as to defy malice to point out a blemish." Once more Lewis's engagement at Drury Lane seemed imminent when on 11 February 1773 Richard Kelly, on his behalf, sent a list of his roles to Hugh Kelly in London, who was asked to work out terms with Garrick. But once again Garrick failed to show interest. Perhaps he had been put off by a letter the actor Thomas Wilks wrote to him from Dublin on 4 March 1773 reporting that at Crow Street "one Lewis, a very indifferent actor, who squints" was the principal performer.

The next season, however, Lewis did have a London engagement. George Colman, apparently heeding the advice of Charles Macklin, who had acted with Lewis in Dublin, hired the young actor for Covent Garden Theatre. Lewis made his debut there in his favorite part of Belcour on 15 October 1773. The critic in the *Covent Garden Magazine* that month called him "the only new performer who has raised any great expectations" but offered him some suggestions for improvement:

... Mr. Lewis is an excellent stage figure, not tall, but neat and well-proportioned. He has a pair of lively eyes, and a very pleasing countenance. His performance of Belcour was, upon the whole masterly, but rather too luxuriant, and therefore somewhat incorrect. ... Mr. Lewis occasionally suffered his spirit to get the better of him, and make his character have more levity than the author designed it. ... Upon the whole, he had great merit, and his idea of Belcour seems to us a very just one, and which on our stage has never yet been filled. We would advise him to get rid of a *Kingism* in his deportment, which he seems to have adopted; we mean an unnatural jerk with his body by no means graceful. ... We would also recommend him to curb the rapidity of his delivery, and to change the placidity of his countenance more frequently. ... Mr. Lewis is almost the only young man who has, since Mr. Powell's days been introduced on either of our stages with a sufficiency of requisites, which when matured by judgment cannot fail of completing the good comedian.

After five appearances as Belcour, Lewis acted Posthumus in *Cymbeline* on 12 November 1773, a performance which the *Covent Garden Magazine* critic could neither extol nor condemn. He complained that though Lewis possessed great fire and spirit "they carry him too far, and make his dramatic picture one universal glare, rather than a proper and judicious distribution of light and shade." He had a smile, "which is a grace to the votaries of Thalia," and other attributes which promised distinction in comedy. But the critic predicated, accurately, that as a tragedian he would be not more than "above mediocrity, and indeed respectable." In his *Miscellanies in Prose and Verse* (1775), William Hawkins echoed the same observations.

Lewis's other roles in his first Covent Garden season included the original Counsellor Witmore in Kenrick's *The Duellist* on 20 November 1773, Sir George in *The Busy Body*, Aimwell in *The Stratagem*, the original Beverly in Colman's *The Man of Business* on 29 January

Harvard Theatre Collection

WILLIAM THOMAS LEWIS
engraving by Scratch

National Portrait Gallery

WILLIAM THOMAS LEWIS
by Gainsborough Dupont

1774, Mercutio in *Romeo and Juliet*, Lothario in *The Fair Penitent*, Florizel in *The Winter's Tale*, Prince Hal in *1 Henry IV*, Don Antonio in *Don Sebastian*, Valentine in *Love for Love*, a principal character (probably Aurenge Zebe) in the premiere of Addington's *The Prince of Agra* on 7 April 1774, a principal character (probably Mowbray) in the premiere of *The South Britain* on 12 April 1774, Petruchio in *Catherine and Petruchio*, the Colonel in *The Spanish Fryar*, Don Carlos in *The Revenge*, and Campley in *The Funeral*.

Lewis remained engaged at Covent Garden Theatre for 35 consecutive seasons, during which time he played at least 194 parts, more than most other English actors could boast. The list of his characters provided in the *Theatrical Inquisitor* of December 1812 included 134 in comedy, 45 in tragedy, and 15 in farce. Since Lewis remained remarkably free of squabbles and anecdotes, and thus does not occupy much space in theatricalana of his period, his career is related largely through the listing of his roles.

A selection of the roles he played in the established repertory includes: Young Bevil in *The Conscious Lovers*, Lord Trinket in *The Jealous Wife*, Claudio in *Much Ado about Nothing*, Edgar in *King Lear*, Cassio in *Othello*, Young Norval in *Douglas*, and Archer in *The Beaux' Stratagem* in 1774–75; Don Felix in *The Wonder*, Marcus in *Cato*, and Ranger in *The Suspicious Husband* in 1775–76; Captain Plume in *The Recruiting Officer*, Hamlet, Chamont in *The Orphan*, Mirabel in *The Way of the World*, and Belville in *The School for Wives* in 1776–77; Etan in *The Orphan of China*, Lord Foppington in *The Careless Husband*, Jaffeir in *Venice Preserv'd*, and Biron in *Isabella* in 1777–78; Philaster in *Philaster* in 1780–81; Colonel Lambert in *The Hypocrite*, Sir Harry Wildair in *The Constant Couple*, and the Fine Gentleman in *Lethe* in 1784–85; Tyrrel in *The Fashionable Lover* in 1785–86; Don John in *The Chances* in 1793–94; Charles Surface in *The School for Scandal* in 1797–98; Wellborn in *A New Way to Pay Old Debts* in 1800–1801; and Brass in *The Confederacy* in 1807–8. He made a single appearance at Drury Lane to play Osmyn in *The Mourning Bride* on 2 June 1783.

Over the years at Covent Garden he created at least 85 original characters. In addition to those cited above for 1773–74, these include,

Harvard Theatre Collection

WILLIAM THOMAS LEWIS, as the Marquis
engraving by Cook, after Shee

chronologically: Faulkland in *The Rivals*, Pharnaces in *Cleonice*, and Edward in *Edward and Eleanora* in 1774–75; Wyndham in *The Man of Reason* and Sir Charles Racket in *Three Weeks after Marriage* in 1775–76; Arviragus in *Caractacus*, the title role in *Sir Thomas Overbury*, and Millamour in *Know Your Own Mind* in 1776–77; the title roles in *Percy* and *Alfred* in 1777–78; Rivers in *The Fatal Falsehood* in 1778–79; Copper Captain in *The Widow of Delphi* and Doricourt in *The Belle's Stratagem* in 1779–80; Charles Danvers in *The World as it Goes* and Egerton in *The Man of the World* in 1780–81; Sir Harry Portland in *Duplicity*, Theodore in *The Count of Narbonne*, and Beauchamp in *Which is the Man?* in 1781–82; Phillupus in *Chilodamus*, Young Loveless in *The Capricious Lady*, Charles Davenant in *The Mysterious Husband*, and Don Julio in *A Bold Stroke for a Husband* in 1782–83; Bellair in *More Ways than One* in 1783–84; Lackland in *Fontainbleau*, Count Almaviva in *The Follies of a Day*, Herodian in *The Arab*, and Welford in *The Fashionable Levities* in 1784–85; Twineall in *Such Things Are* and the Marquis in *The Midnight Hour* in 1786–87; Wildlove in *All in a Summer's Day* and Captain Daffodil in *The Ton* in 1787–88; Count Valentia in *The Child of Nature*, Aircourt in *The Toy*, Young Hazelwood in *The Pharo Table*, Marmozet in *The School for Widows*, and Vapid in *The Dramatist* in 1788–89; and Sedley in *The Force of Fashion* and Don Lewis in *The Female Adventure* in 1789–90.

He also added Count Villars in *The School for Arrogance*, Rover in *Wild Oats*, and Sir Paul Flippant in *National Prejudice* in 1790–91; Nominal in *Notoriety* and Goldfinch in *The Road to Ruin* in 1791–92; Harry Herbert in *Columbus*, Sir Robert Ramble in *Every One Has His Fault*, and Pave in *How to Grow Rich* in 1792–93; Grigsby in *The World in a Village* and Muscadel in *Love's Frailties* in 1793–94; Gingham in *The Rage*, Tippy in *The Town before You*, Hilario in *The Mysteries of the Castle*, Lord Arthur D'Aumerle in *Life's Vagaries*, and Cheveril in *The Deserted Daughter* in 1794–95; Tanjore in *Speculation* and Tangent in *The Way to Get Married* in 1795–96; Ap Hazard in *Fortune's Fool*, Young Rapid in *A Cure for the Heart-Ache*, and Bronzely in *Wives As They Were* in 1796–97; Rostrum in *Secrets Worth Knowing*, Sir George Versatile in *He's Much to Blame*, and probably Sir Francis Delroy in *The Eccentric Lover* in 1797–98; Gossamer in *Laugh When You Can*, Drooply in *The Votary of Wealth*, George Fervid in *Five Thousand a Year*, and Period in *What Is She?* in 1798–99; and Captain Lavish in *Management*, Clarensforth in *The Wise Man of the East*, and Frank Liberal in *Liberal Opinions*

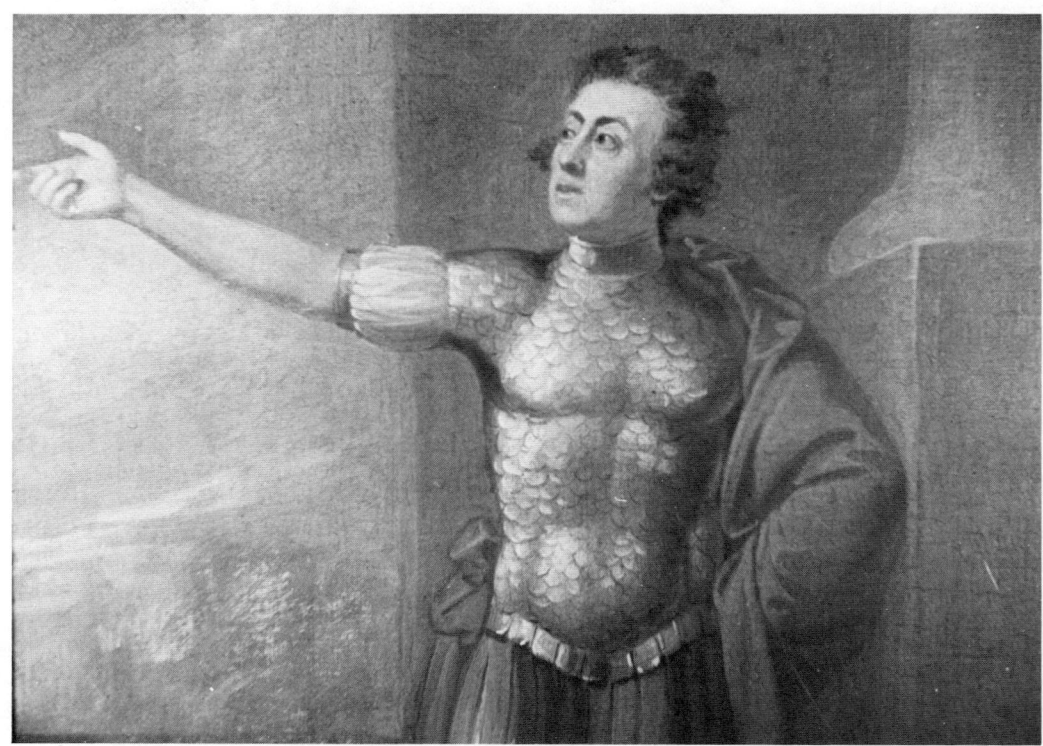

Courtesy of the Garrick Club

WILLIAM THOMAS LEWIS, as Pharnaces
by De Wilde

in 1799–1800. He continued to expand his repertoire: Sir Harry Torpid in *Life* and Frederick in *The Poor Gentleman* in 1800–1801; Tom Tick in *Folly as it Flies* in 1801–2; Henry Sapling in *Delays and Blunders* and Tom Shuffleton in *John Bull* in 1802–3; Diddler in *Raising the Wind*, an unknown character in *Love Gives the Alarm* (Holman's unpublished play for which the playbills on 23 February 1804 did not specify the characters), and Harry Hairbrain in *Will for the Deed* in 1803–4; Tourly in *The Blind Bargain*, Ferment in *The School of Reform*, and Sir Larry Mac Murragh in *Who Wants a Guinea?* in 1804–5; Young Doric in *The Delinquent* and Peerless in *The Romantick Lover* in 1805–6; Jack Familiar in *Arbitration* in 1806–7; and Modern in *Begone Dull Care* in 1807–8.

In 1782 Lewis had become the deputy or acting manager of Covent Garden, a position he held for 21 years until illness forced his resignation in the spring of 1803. Upon his assumption of those duties he began to abandon his graver stage characters to concentrate on those in mannered comedy and, toward the end of his career, extravagant ones in farce. In his managerial duties Lewis conducted himself skillfully and conscientiously in the interest of the proprietors and the performers. According to G. F. Cooke, "Billy" Lewis was a model for making everyone do his duty by kindness and good treatment.

During his career at Covent Garden he amassed a sizeable estate which allowed him to live handsomely, especially in his later years. Evidently he sensibly saved a certain part of his income for contingencies. In addition to the £200 per year he earned as acting manager between 1782 and 1803, he enjoyed a salary for acting that was usually among the highest in the company. Until 1778–79 his salary was £8 10s. per week; it rose steadily until it was £16 in 1791–92. In 1793–94 he began to receive £20 per week, a sum that remained constant throughout the remainder of his career.

Between 1777 and 1799 he lived in a house in Broad Court, Bow Street, near the theatre. In 1800 he moved to No 52, Great Queen Street, Lincoln's Inn Fields. In the summer of 1801 he rented a weekend house on Barnes Green from which in fair weather he would walk to Covent Garden and back. He performed this weekly walk, wrote T. J. Dibdin in his *Reminiscences*, "with a little switch in hand, skipping across the roads like a lad of eighteen." Subsequently he lived at No 35, King Street, Covent Garden, in a house which became a hotel run by a Mr Probett, mentioned in *The Picture of London* in 1818. It later became the original home of the Garrick Club. Lewis's last house was in Westbourne Place, King's Road, Pimlico.

Lewis's summer excursions included acting at Crow Street in 1775, 1778, 1792, 1796, and 1797, and at Smock Alley for a few nights in 1792. According to the *Monthly Mirror* of May 1796, Lewis was to receive £600 for 12 nights at Dublin in the latter end of July. He and his wife acted for Wilkinson at York and Leeds in late summer of 1775 and at York in 1779 and 1780. He went to Wakefield to perform on 6 September 1779 but refused to go

Harvard Theatre Collection
WILLIAM THOMAS LEWIS
engraving by Daniell, after G. Dance

on when he discovered there were but 30 shillings in the house. Edinburgh audiences saw him in July 1780 (as Archer, Ranger, Douglas, and Doricourt, among other roles) and in June 1793. His associations with Birmingham began in the summer of 1779, when he and his wife acted under Mattocks's management. His benefit on 2 August brought in only £9. Leaving his wife in Birmingham, he went to Liverpool, where he found larger audiences and more money, according to Genest, and then returned to Birmingham to act for his wife's benefit. Lewis visited Birmingham each summer from 1795 through 1801. In the latter summer he also acted at Richmond, Surrey, for Mrs Dibdin's benefit, when "he electrified the Richmond folks by his exquisite performance of Marplot."

During the late summer of 1802 Lewis and his Covent Garden colleague Thomas Knight obtained the lease of the Liverpool theatre for 14 years. The rental fee of £1,500 per year was considerably higher than the £360 paid by the previous lessee Francis Aickin. The *Monthly Mirror* of December 1802 reported the closing of the Liverpool season on 24 November 1802, "being the last performance, previous to the alterations that are to take place for our new managers, Messrs. Lewis and Knight."

Meanwhile, however, Lewis's health was reported as declining. At a rehearsal at Covent Garden one morning in October 1802 he "suddenly fell down in a fit." Physicians bled him and he recovered. The *Monthly Mirror* was relieved that he was restored to perfect health. "As an *actor* his loss would be irreparable, and as a *manager* his gentlemanly habits have so endeared him to the profession, and his attention to the duties of that situation have been so close and indefatigable," declared that journal, that a successor would be difficult to find. In the spring of 1803 Lewis resigned his managerial duties at Covent Garden (but not his place in the company) because of what the *Gentleman's Magazine* of January 1811 called "a severe fit of illness." More likely, Lewis wanted the time for his Liverpool venture.

Apologizing for slightly raised prices, Lewis and Knight opened the Liverpool theatre on 6 June 1803 with *Speed and Plough* and *No Song No Supper*. Knight left Covent Garden after 1803–4 to devote his full energies to the management at Liverpool. That enterprise prospered, and before his death Lewis, in conjunction with Knight, also obtained an interest in the Manchester theatre.

Lewis's farewell performance in London occurred on 29 May 1809 at the Haymarket Theatre, where the Covent Garden company was compelled to play after the loss of their theatre by a terrible fire on 20 September 1808. For his benefit he played Roger in *The Ghost* and the Copper Captain in *Rule a Wife and Have a Wife*, and before an overflowing house he made an affecting final speech expressing his gratitude that in his 36 years on the London stage he could not recollect "to have once fallen under your displeasure."

After his London retirement Lewis gave attention to the Liverpool theatre, but his precarious health was further shaken by the death of a daughter. On 16 September 1809 Dorothy Jordan wrote to her Clarence from Liverpool: "Lewis *is here* and attended the rehearsal himself. He has lately lost *a daughter*. I never saw a man so broke; he is shrunk to nothing and can hardly hobble across the stage. . . ."

Lewis died at his house in Westbourne Place, King's Road, Pimlico, on 13 January 1812. The *Morning Post* of 14 January announced that his remains were to be buried in the family vault, Christ Church, Liverpool. He left a widow and, according to the *Theatrical Inquisitor* of December 1812, two daughters and three sons.

Lewis had married the Irish actress Henrietta Amelia Leeson about 1780. According to *The Secret History of the Green Room*, "they lived together many years, and when they had produced several fine children, and had fully proved and approved each other's temper, they married." She had been a pupil of Macklin, and after acting in Ireland she made her debut on 3 November 1775 at Covent Garden, where she was engaged until 1791. She died in 1826, at the age of 75.

By his wife Lewis had at least six children. Their eldest son William became a major in the service of the East India Company. The second son, Thomas Denison, baptized at St Paul, Covent Garden, on 23 October 1787, became the Liverpool co-manager upon his father's death; more about him will be given below. Henry Lewis, the third son, began his career in the provinces in the last years of the eighteenth century and made his debut at Covent Garden on 10 October 1805, but he did not prove to be a talented actor. Henry Lewis seems to have been dead by the time his mother made her will in 1819. The death of Henry's wife on 25 July 1804, at the age of 24, was announced in the *Gentleman's Magazine* that August. They had at least one child, Mary Lewis; in 1849 her uncle Thomas Denison Lewis left £1000 to Mary Lewis of Manchester, eldest daughter of his late brother Henry.

William Thomas Lewis's three daughters included one who died in 1809; she was probably Frances, daughter of W. T. Lewis and Henrietta, baptized at St Paul, Covent Garden, on 29 March 1789. The other daughters were Rosa Frances Lewis, who was still alive in 1857, unmarried; and Henrietta Lenthal Lewis, who was alive in 1819, when her mother made her will, but was dead by 1857.

In his will drawn on 29 March 1810 and proved at London on 27 April 1811, William Thomas Lewis made substantial bequests. His son Thomas Denison Lewis received £5000 in eight per cent stock and the shares in the Circus Theatre and Tavern at Liverpool. Son William received £2000, and daughters Rosa Frances Lewis and Henrietta Lenthal Lewis each received £7500 in eight per cent stock. Son Henry Lewis was granted only 50 guineas a year. Small sums were bequeathed to a grandson Henry and to half brother William Dawson Flease. The remainder of the estate went to Lewis's wife Henrietta, "mother of all my children," and included the house in Westbourne Place and £22,000 in three per cent stock. Lewis directed that his interests in the Liverpool and Manchester theatres be sold, and after his debts were paid the excess from that sale was to revert to his wife.

Actually his son Thomas Denison Lewis eventually acquired those theatrical interests, which he continued to co-manage with Thomas Knight for some years. He, too, died a wealthy man, on 7 September 1849, and was buried in the family vault at Christ Church, Liverpool. A bachelor, he made large bequests in his will to charities and institutions, including £10,000 intended for the National Gallery after the death of his sister Rosa Frances Lewis. As his executrix she proved the will on 10 November 1849.

The executors of William Thomas Lewis's will were Francis Const, a Covent Garden proprietor, and Frederic Reynolds, the dramatist. When the latter died in 1841 he was still trustee of the investment of £2000 which had been bequeathed to Major William Lewis in 1811. By 1851 the investment had grown to £2750; on 12 August of that year that money was transferred by the probate court from Reynolds's estate to Rosa Frances Lewis and Rosamond Lewis, widow of Major William Lewis.

William Thomas Lewis was an eminently attractive actor of fashionable and flippant characters. In the anonymous poem *A Trip to Parnassus* (1788), Apollo spoke to Lewis:

> *I should ne'er find a man, if I search'd thro' the nation,*
> *Can so well represent the polite man of fashion.*
> *What others must toil at, with ease you can do.*
> *Since they but assume what is nature in you.*

Similar elegies to Lewis appeared in John Williams's *The Children of Thespis*.

Not all contemporary comment was flattering, of course. For example F. G. Waldron in his *Candid and Impartial Strictures on the Performers* (1795) described him as bad-limbed and knock-kneed. Waldron complained of a "continual exhibition of his teeth" and "a *whining, piping* strain" in the upper notes of his voice, and wished Lewis would correct "a disgusting method he has got of moving his head in regular motions like the pendulum of a clock, and that fixed stare which sometimes approaches a squint." In his *Dramatic Censor* Dutton found Lewis in every part the same to the point of insipidity but admitted that he possessed an "inimitable style of acting" in parts distinguished by whim and volatile eccentricity—like Goldfinch in *The Road to Ruin*, Pave in *How to Grow Rich*, Rostrum in *Secrets Worth Knowing*, and Gossamer in *Laugh When You Can*.

The testimony to Lewis's superiority in the line of roles which earned him the appellation "Gentleman Lewis" is overwhelming. G. F. Cooke called him "the unrivalled favourite of the comic muse in all that was gay, humorous, whimsical, and at the same time elegant." Leigh Hunt, who considered that "vulgarity seems totally impossible to an actor of his manners,' described Lewis's interpretation of Rover in *Wild Oats*:

Lewis is all heart; all fire; he does not study forms and ceremonies. . . . In the scene where the young rustic expresses his admiration of *Rover's* theatrical talents, and at parting shakes his hand with good-natured familiarity, Elliston in the midst of his reciprocal good humour has too much the air of one who condescends; Lewis gives the bumpkin as hearty a handshake as if it had been his brother and forgets every thing but the honest soul of his new acquaintance. It is in characters like these, full of frankness and vivacity, that Lewis claims an original excellence.

Boaden in his *Memoirs of Mrs Siddons* related Lewis's skill as the Copper Captain in *Rule a Wife and Have a Wife*:

> Where Lewis absolutely exceeded all expectation, even from spirits like his own, was in the first scene of the fifth act, where he meets with Cacafogo, who has been *cozened*, *too*, and by a *woman* also (indeed the same woman); the convulsive joy of his *laugh*, frequently renewed, and invariably compelling the whole audience to a really painful sympathy, was one of the most brilliant exploits of the comedian. . . . Lewis had one peculiarity, which was the richest in effect that could be imagined, and was always an addition to the character springing from himself. It might be called an attempt to take advantage of the lingering sparks of *gallantry* in the aunt, or the mother of sixty, or the ancient maiden whom he had to *win*, to carry the purposes of those for whom he was interested. He seemed to throw the lady by degrees off her guard, until at length his whole artillery of assault was applied to storm the struggling resistance; and the Mattockses and the Davenports of his attentions sometimes complained of the perpetual motion of his chair, which compelled them to a ludicrous retreat, and kept the spectator in a roar of laughter. In short, whether sitting or standing, he was never for a moment at rest—his figure continued to exhibit a series of undulating lines, which indicated a self-complacency that never tired, and the sparkling humour of his countenance was a signal hung out for enjoyment.

The reviewer in the *Monthly Mirror* of December 1798 declared that by his portrayal of Gossamer in *The Road to Ruin* Lewis had created a character "which no actor could play but himself, because no man has that happy freedom and facility, that fashionable playfulness and spirit, so joyous, free, and unrelaxing, which distinguish all his performances of this nature; he is himself the genuine son of mirth."

Genest thought that Lewis had done his best acting in the first half of his career, before he played all the extravagant roles concocted for him by Morton and Reynolds; in these latter characters "he received great applause"—but they could not be compared with his performances of Ranger, Mercutio, and the Copper Captain. The singing-actor Michael Kelly agreed, writing in his *Reminiscences*, "I considered Lewis, in his line, a perfect actor; but candidly speaking, I thought his best days were past before my friend Frederick Reynolds, made him a dramatist [i.e. Vapid in *The Dramatist*]."

Portraits of William Thomas Lewis include:

1. By G. Chinnery. Miniature. Present location unknown. Engraving by W. Ridley. Published as a plate to the *Monthly Mirror*, November 1798. The same plate, with the painter's name "A. Pope" and the address of T. Bellamy, was published July 1798.

2. By George Dance. Crayon drawing in the British Museum. Engraving by W. Daniell, 1810.

3. By Gainsborough Dupont. Exhibited at the Royal Academy, 1795 (No 273), as a "*Portrait of Mr. Lewis*." This portrait has been identified, incorrectly, as the one of Lewis as the Marquis, see below No 28.

4. By Nathaniel Hone. An oil portrait of Lewis by Hone is noted in the art file at the Huntington Library, but the location of the painting is unknown.

5. By Henry Raeburn? A portrait attributed to Raeburn of a sitter tentatively identified as Lewis was offered at Christie's on 2 March 1956.

6. By Martin Archer Shee. Painting in the Garrick Club (No 389). Perhaps the portrait of Lewis by Shee in the Harris sale, 1819.

7. By Gilbert Stuart? Unfinished painting in the Garrick Club (No 436). Presented by John Dawkins, 1835. Listed in the Club's register as by "Stewart" and in the catalogue as by "James Stuart" or "John Stewart." James Stewart, R.S.A. (1791–1863) would have been too young to have painted the portrait. Possibly the artist was Gilbert Stuart, the American working in London between 1782 and 1787.

8. Engraving by J. Corner, after M. Brown. Published by the artists, 1788. Another state was published as a plate to *European Magazine*, 1790. An engraving of the same picture by H. Houston, after Brown, was also issued.

9. Engraving by W. Ridley, after A. Pope. Published as a plate to *Parson's Minor Theatre*, January 1794.

10. As Archer, with Mrs Lessingham as Mrs Sullen, in *The Beaux' Stratagem*. Engraving by Walker, after Barralet. Published as a plate to *New English Theatre*, 1776. This picture usually has been catalogued and reproduced with the male figure identified as W. T. Lewis (the engraved caption identifies only Mrs Lessingham). But if Archer depicts any specific actor, Charles Lee Lewes is a more likely candidate.

11. As Arviragus in *Caractacus*. Study by John Downman. In his sketch books in 1777 the artist recorded that he had made studies of six performers for a picture of a scene in *Caractacus*. Mason's play had opened at Covent Garden on 6 December 1776. The other five performers of whom studies were made by Downman were Hull, Mrs Hartley, Wroughton, Aickin, Leoni, and Reinhold. Present location unknown.

12. As Belcour in *The West Indian*. By unknown engraver. Published as a plate to *Hibernian Magazine*, July 1775.

13. As Castalio in *The Orphan*. By unknown engraver. Published by Wenman, 1777.

14. As Clodio in *Love Makes a Man*. By unknown engraver.

15. As the Copper Captain in *Rule a Wife and Have a Wife*. By Samuel De Wilde. Location unknown. Engravings by: J. Condé, published by J. Bell, 1791; Thornthwaite, published as a plate to *Bell's British Theatre*, 1791; Clayton, published as a plate to Jones's *British Theatre*, 1792; and by unknown engraver, published as a plate to *British Drama*, 1817.

16. As the Copper Captain. Engraving by Alais. Published by J. Roach, 1808.

17. As Crevelt, with Mrs Pope as Charlotte, in *He Would Be a Soldier*. By unknown engraver. Published as a plate to the *Lady's Magazine*, November 1786.

18. As Cyrus in *Cyrus*. By unknown engraver.

19. As Douglas in *Douglas*. Engraving by J. Goldar, after D. Dodd. Published as a plate to *New English Theatre*, 1777.

20. As Douglas. By unknown engraver.

21. As Edgar in *King Lear*. Pencil drawing by T. Stothard, dated 1 September 1781. In the Harry R. Beard Collection, Victoria and Albert Museum. Engraving by unknown engraver, published by Harrison & Co, 1781.

22. As Gingham in *The Rage*. Watercolor by William Loftis. In the Folger Shakespeare Library.

23. As Goldfinch, with John Quick as Silky, in *The Road to Ruin*. By unknown engraver. Published as a plate to *Charlton House Magazine*, 1792.

24. As Sir Harry Wildair in *The Constant Couple*. By unknown engraver. Published by W. Hinton, February 1786.

25. As Hippolitus in *Phaedra and Hippolitus*. Engraving by C. Grignion, after D. Dodd. Published as a plate to *New English Theatre*, 1776.

26. As Hippolitus. By unknown engraver. Published by Wenman as a plate to an edition of the play, 1777.

27. As Hippolitus. On a delftware tile, in the City of Manchester Art Gallery.

28. As the Marquis in *The Midnight Hour*. Painting (95 × 58) by Martin Archer Shee, exhibited at the Royal Academy, 1792 (No 205). This portrait was still in the painter's possession in 1830 but then came into the hands of Thomas Denison Lewis, the sitter's son. In 1849 T. D. Lewis bequeathed this full-length portrait of his father to the National Gallery. Rosa Frances Lewis, W. T. Lewis's daughter, retained the picture during her lifetime and it went to the National Gallery in 1863. A smaller version (28 × 24), incorrectly attributed to Gainsborough, was owned by Sir Charles Tennant in 1896, purchased from a descendant of the Lewis family. An engraving of the large picture was made by J. Jones, 1792; another by H. R. Cook was published as a plate to *Theatrical Inquisitor*, 1812, and *New English Drama*, 1821.

29. As Marplot in *The Busy Body*. By unknown engraver.

30. As Mercutio in *Romeo and Juliet*. Watercolor by Samuel De Wilde. In the Garrick Club (No 68F).

31. As Modern, with Sarah Smith (Mrs Bartley) as Selima, in *Begone Dull Care*. By unknown engraver.

32. As Pharnaces in *Cleonice, Princess of Bithynia*. Painting by Samuel De Wilde. (Once thought to be by Harlow.) In the Garrick Club (No 201). Engraving by P. Audinet, published as a plate to *Bell's British Theatre*, 1795.

33. As the Prince of Wales in *1 Henry IV*. Watercolor by William Loftis. In the Folger Shakespeare Library.

34. As the Prince of Wales. Engraving by Thornthwaite, after E. F. Burney. Published as a plate to *Bell's British Theatre*, 1786. A copy by an unknown engraver was published as a plate to *Hibernian Magazine*, August 1790.

35. As the Prince of Wales. By unknown engraver, after T. Parkinson. Published as a plate to Bell's *Shakespeare*, 1775.

36. As Ranger in *The Suspicious Husband*. By unknown engraver.

37. As Tanjore, with John Quick as Alderman Arable and Joseph Munden as Project, in *Speculation*. By Johann Zoffany. In the Garrick Club (No 104). The picture of Lewis may have been finished by another painter while it was in the Charles Mathews Collection.

38. As Vapid in *The Dramatist*. Engraving by W. Hinton, after W. Naish. Printed by Hinton.

39. As Vapid. Engraving by C. Townley, after W. Naish. Published by Townley, 1792.

40. As Zamor in *Alzira*. Engraving by Thornthwaite, after Roberts. Published as a plate to *Bell's British Theatre*, 1777.

41. Caricature, walking, looking front, hands at back, hat under arm; caption, "A Monstrous Elegant Attitude." Engraving by A. Scratch. Published as a plate to Bentley's *Attic Miscellany*, 1790.

42. Caricature, standing, looking front, right arm extended, hat under left arm. Engraving by S. Springsguth. Published by J. Barker, 1790.

43. Satirical print, by Williams, published 16 January 1802 by S. W. Fores. Lewis, the deputy manager, feeds an enormously fat Mrs Billington a spoonful of guineas. At her side stands R. B. Sheridan. Titled "Theatrical Doctors Recovering Clara's Notes!" See the *Catalogue of Political and Personal Satirical Prints in the British Museum*, (No 9915).

Lewis, Mrs William Thomas, Henrietta Amelia, née Leeson *1751–1826, actress.*

Henrietta Amelia Leeson was born in London in 1751, the daughter of a printer in St John's Square. According to *The Secret History of the Green Room*, her father's inattention to his business and his family made her seek a career on the stage. Charles Macklin accepted her for training, guaranteeing her £60 annually, and soon took her to Dublin. Her articles with Macklin and letters between them are in the Harvard Theatre Collection. She seems not to have been a serious student, being full of alibis for her lack of application and complaints about the shameful state of her wardrobe. Macklin found her mother a shrew. He once wrote to his pupil, "I would visit you, but you know your mother's tongue is not an agreeable instrument to the ear, nor her presence a pleasing object to my eye."

Macklin managed to prepare Miss Leeson for her stage debut at the Crow Street Theatre on 6 December 1771, when she was advertised as "A Young Gentlewoman." The role is not known. After playing the season at Crow Street, Macklin and Miss Leeson went to Limerick, where she made her first appearance outside Dublin on 10 July 1772 as Portia to his Shylock. At Limerick through 12 August she acted Charlotte to his Sir Gilbert Wrangle in *The Refusal*, Desdemona to his Iago in *Othello*, Mrs Diggerty to his Murrough O'Doherty in *The True-Born Irishman*, and Lady Randolpha to his Sir Pertinax Macsycophant in *The True-Born Scotsman*. They moved on to Cork, opening on 19 August in *The Merchant of Venice*. At the Cork Theatre Royal one night Macklin, harboring a secret affection for Miss Leeson and suspicious that she was carrying on with the young and handsome William Thomas Lewis (her Othello), burst into her dressing room and discovered Lewis in the closet. Mrs Leeson's protestations that her daughter had not been conducting herself improperly failed to convince Macklin, who thereafter referred to Lewis as "the man in the closet."

Toward the end of her second season at Crow Street, 1772–73, Miss Leeson played several more times with Macklin and then obtained a release from her articles. No doubt he was relieved to be rid of her. He had written to her on 9 February 1773 to complain that she had for the last three months been making excuses for not rehearsing with him—her clothes had been ruined in the rain; she had come down with a severe cold—which he called "trifling and invidious." He regarded her actions (or lack thereof) "as a breach of your contract as an apprentice." In his letter to her of 30 April 1773 he declared, "You are not to look upon yourself for the future as my apprentice." By that time, it seems, she was living with Lewis, though she did not marry him until about 1780, apparently after the birth of several children. She acted with Lewis at Crow Street in the summer of 1775; later that summer they joined Wilkinson's company at York and Leeds, where she played Portia, Lady Townly, and Juliet.

In the autumn of 1775 she accompanied Lewis to London, where he had been engaged for the past two seasons at Covent Garden Theatre. At that house on 3 November 1775, advertised as "A Young Lady," she appeared as Isabella in *The Man's the Master*, in which Lewis acted Don John. *The Westminster Magazine* identified her as Miss Leeson and wrote that she had "an agreeable pleasing figure, a good face and a marking eye." Her voice was weak, but after she recovered from her stage fright she was "sufficiently articulate." Her second Covent Garden role was Miss Neville in *She Stoops to Conquer* on 8 November, when her name appeared in the bills. On 7 December she played Miss Biddy in *Miss in Her Teens*.

After passing the summer of 1776 at the Liverpool Theatre, where she earned £2 10s. per week, she returned to Covent Garden for her second season, at £2 per week. Her roles in 1776–77 included Miss Biddy, Jacintha in *The Suspicious Husband*, Cynthia in *The Double Dealer*, Clara in the premiere of Woodfall's *Sir Thomas Overbury* on 1 February 1777, and Rose in *The Recruiting Officer*. She returned to Liverpool in the summer of 1777.

Her name continued to appear in the bills as Miss Leeson for two more seasons at Covent Garden. In the summer of 1778 she returned to Crow Street for a brief engagement, and she acted at Birmingham and York in 1779, at Edinburgh in 1780, and at Richmond, Surrey, in 1781.

From 11 October 1779, when she acted Serina in *The Orphan*, the Covent Garden bills called her Mrs Lewis. In 1779–80 her roles there were Lady Anne in *Richard III*, Anne Page in *The Merry Wives of Windsor*, Isabella in *The Wonder*, Miss Neville in *She Stoops to Conquer*, Eleanor in *The Countess of Salisbury*, Belinda in *The Provok'd Wife*, Sylvia in *The Double Gallant*, Necessary in *Woman's a Riddle*, and Cherry in *The Stratagem*. She acted once at Drury Lane Theatre, Lucinda in *The Conscious Lovers* on 19 December 1782, for the benefit of the London Lying-in Hospital.

Mrs Lewis's engagement at Covent Garden lasted through 1790–91, by which time her salary had risen over the 15 years only to £3 per week, reflecting her general lack of importance. *The Secret History of the Green Room* suggested that she continued on the stage because of her large family. At the time, her husband was earning £13 per week for acting and £200 per season as acting manager at Covent Garden. In *The Children of Thespis*, John Williams wrote of her:

> *Like a tremulous hare stealing over the stage,*
> *See neat lovely Lewis illumine Anne Page;*
> *Who fills pretty Godfrey with timid alarms,*
> *And gives Lady Percy—proverbial charms:*
> *But her heart welcomes Ease when the business is ended,*
> *As if Habit and Will in the duty contended.*

Her roles in 1790–91, her last season, were Miss Neville, Emily in *Cross Purposes*, Anne Page, Serina, Myrtilla in *The Provok'd Husband*, and Miss Ogle in *The Belle's Stratagem* (for her last performance on 3 June 1791).

When her husband died, on 13 January 1812, Mrs Lewis inherited a substantial estate which included their house in Westbourne Place, King's Road, Pimlico, and £22,000 in three per cent stocks. By him she had had at least six children, about whom information is given in her husband's notice.

The *Gentleman's Magazine* of December 1826 announced that Henrietta Amelia Lewis, relict of W. T. Lewis, had died on 6 December in Lower Grosvenor Place, at the age of 75. She had made her will on 21 May 1819, when she resided in Sloane Street. All her estate, value unspecified, she divided equally among her children, Thomas Denison Lewis, Rosa Frances Lewis, and Henrietta Lewis. The will was proved at London on 22 May 1827 by her children, the executors.

Lewise, Richard. *See* LEWIS, RICHARD.

Lewiss. *See* LOUIS.

L'Font. *See* LA FONT.

L'Grand, Mr [*fl.* 1777], *performer?*

The Drury Lane accounts contain notes on 20 and 24 May 1777 concerning a Mr L'Grand (or Legrand) whose weekly salary seems to have been £2 2s. 2d. That scale would suggest a performer, but L'Grand is not mentioned in the bills collected in *The London Stage*.

L'Hercule Du Roi. *See* PORTE, LOUIS.

L'Homme, Miss [*fl.* 1732], *actress, dancer.*
Miss L'Homme played Lady Diana in *Henry VII* and performed an entr'acte dance at the Miller-Mills-Oates booth at Bartholomew Fair on 23 August 1732.

Liddel, Mr [*fl.* 1784], *actor.*
Mr Liddel played an unnamed character in *The Reprisal* at the Haymarket Theatre on 23 February 1784.

Liddel, Mrs [*fl.* 1782], *actress.*
Mrs Liddel acted Jezabel in a single performance of *Don Quixote in England* at the Haymarket Theatre on 4 March 1782.

Liddell, Mr [*fl.* 1799–*c.* 1801], *costumer.*
Dresses for the Oriental spectacle *Almoran and Hamet* at the Royal Circus on 25 March 1799 were created by a Mr Liddell and others. He was similarly cited in another bill for a production of *Halloween* about 1801.

Liddle. *See* LIDDELL and LYDALL.

Lidel, Andreas. *See* LIDL, ANDREAS.

Lidgbird, Francis [*fl.* 1794–1815], *horn player.*
Doane's *Musical Directory* of 1794 listed Francis Lidgbird, of Exendon Street, as a horn player who performed for the New Musical Fund and in the Handel concerts at Westminster Abbey. He was a member of the band of the Guards' Third Regiment. Lidgbird was still a subscriber to the New Musical Fund in 1815. His name is so unusual that he was very likely related to the John Lidgbird who witnessed a wedding at St Paul, Covent Garden, in May 1762.

Lidl, Andreas *b. c.* 1740, *baryton player, violinist?*
Andreas Lidl was born in Vienna about 1740 and became one of Europe's greatest performers on the baryton. He increased the number of strings at the back to 27, making the instrument even more difficult to play but extending its possibilities considerably. Lidl (sometimes Lidel; and his first name has erroneously been given as Anton) played in Haydn's orchestra at Esterház and performed all over the Continent before coming to England. A Lidl played a violin solo at the King's Theatre in London on 15 February 1776, and that musician would seem to have been Andreas. In addition, Mee places Lidl at Oxford, playing solos on the baryton at the Oxford Music Room in 1776. Lidl lived in England until his death, which occurred sometime before 1789. The *Catalogue of Printed Music in The British Museum* lists a number of his works for various instruments— violin, viola, violoncello, flute—but his compositions for the baryton were never published. Andreas may have been related to Richard Lidl, a bass singer who appeared at the Oxford Music Room in 1798 and subsequent years.

Liege, John [*fl.* 1734–1735], *boxkeeper.*
John (probably Jean) Liege was the boxkeeper in Francisque Moylin's company of French players that appeared at the Haymarket Theatre from October 1734 to June 1735 and also played twice at Goodman's Fields in May and June 1735. Liege was given two solo benefits, one on 19 March and the other on 18 April 1735.

Ligar. *See* LAGUERRE.

Light, Edward *c.* 1747–*c.* 1832, *singer?, violinist, harpsichordist, organist?, instrument maker.*
The *Dictionary of National Biography* gives Edward Light's birth and death dates as 1747–1832, though the *New Grove* makes each date approximate. Light had a music shop that was destroyed in a fire in King Street, Covent Garden, in 1774, and a benefit was held at the Haymarket Theatre for him on 7 June. Doane's *Musical Directory* of 1794 listed Light as an alto (singer?), violinist, and harpsichordist, a member of the New Musical Fund (he was on the Court of Assistants), and a participant in the Handel concerts at Westminster Abbey. Light's address was given as Kensington. The *Dictionary of National Biography* noted that in 1794 Light was organist of Trinity Chapel (St George, Hanover Square), Conduit Street, though Doane did not list that post.

Edward Light's chief musical concern was with improvements to the harp and guitar. At Kensington in 1794 he was making two instruments which he claimed to have invented, the harp-lute and the Apollo lyre—according to Grove; the *DNB* dates the harp-lute 1798 and does not mention the Apollo lyre. Shortly after that, Grove says, he moved to No 8, Foley Place, Cavendish Square, and was "lyrist to the Princess of Wales." Light's musical inventions were the harp-guitar (c. 1798), the harp-lute (1798), the harp-lyre (1816), the British lute-harp (1816), and the ditel harp (similar to or identical with the lute-harp). Dr Busby found the ditel harp an admirable instrument for accompanying the human voice.

Light also published a number of works, chiefly instructions for playing various instruments and collections of music for the guitar.

Lightfoot, William *c. 1626–1665, painter.*

In his *Decorative Painting in England* Edward Croft-Murray conjectured (correctly) that William Lightfoot was the son of the "Cittizen and Plaisterer of London" William Lightfoot and his wife Elizabeth. We have found Lightfoot's will, which confirms that parentage. William the younger had a brother Edward, who died in 1660. William was apprenticed as a painter-stainer and became a freeman on 13 July 1647, probably when he was just reaching his majority. John Tatham's *London's Triumph*, the Lord Mayor's show presented on 29 October 1659, was painted by Lightfoot and Andrew Dacres; Thomas Whiting was the joiner and Richard Clear the carver on the project; Lightfoot also helped paint the Lord Mayor's pageant in October 1660.

Buckeridge described Lightfoot as "a good English painter in perspective, architecture and landskip," who worked in distemper and oil. For the coronation procession of Charles II in April 1661 Lightfoot and Dacres painted the triumphal arches. Croft-Murray's speculative death date for Lightfoot was 1671, but his will shows that he died in 1665. Lightfoot described himself in his will as a citizen and painter-stainer from the parish of St Leonard, Shoreditch. He wrote the will on 5 August 1665, and it was proved on the fifteenth. Half of his estate he left to his wife Jone. The other half he bequeathed as follows: £10 to his father William, £10 to his mother Elizabeth, 20s. each for rings to John Dyneo (?) and his wife and to Lightfoot's friend Richard Bullock. To his friend and executor John Scott, carpenter, he gave the remainder, asking him to give a percentage to Jone Lightfoot. He also gave Scott first refusal of all his books, papers, manuscripts, and other "things belonging to the arte of paynting that are in my clossett." From the rent from the buildings Lightfoot owned in Moorfields or St Leonard, Shoreditch, he provided an annuity of £12 for his father and mother, with John Scott the residuary legatee. Lightfoot left mourning rings to a number of friends, £5 to his "brother" (-in-law?) John Pervir (?) and his wife Mary, and £4 each to the joiner Whiting and his wife.

Ligney. *See* DELIGNY.

Likes, G. [*fl.* 1787–1788], *violoncellist.*

The accounts for the Academy of Ancient Music in 1787–88 show that the violoncellist G. Likes was paid £6 for the season.

Lilburne, Mrs [*fl.* 1670], *actress.*

Mrs Lilburne (or Lilbourne) played Cydanene in *The Women's Conquest* with the Duke's Company at the Lincoln's Inn Fields playhouse in 1670. Robert Hume suggests September or earlier; *The London Stage* places the performance sometime in November.

Lile. *See* DE LISLE and LISLE

Lilleston, Thomas *d. c. 1673?, actor.*

Thomas Lilleston was a member of the company managed by Rhodes in 1659–60, though no roles are known for him. The *Middlesex County Records* show that on 4 February 1660 Lilleston, Turner, and Rhodes were arrested for performing at the Cockpit. Lilleston was released on £80 bail. He was said to have been one of the mainstays in the troupe and was called a weaver from the parish of St Andrew, Holborn. An investigation of the registers of that church discovered a number of entries which probably concern our subject. Elizabeth, the daughter of Thomas "Lillistone" and his wife Blanch of Rose and Crown Alley, Gray's Inn Lane, was born on 4 July 1657 and christened on the thirteenth. Their daughter Mary was born on 19 May 1659 and baptized ten days later. She may have been the Mary Lillistone, daughter of Thomas of Fisher's Alley, who died in the plague and was buried on 21 July 1665, though the address does not fit. Thomas and Blanch's son Robert was born on 4 December 1660, baptized on the ninth, and buried on 18 March 1661. A Stephen Lilliston, described in the registers as "an antient man" from Angell Alley, Gray's Inn Lane, was buried on 30 October 1664; he may have been Thomas's father on other relative; another man from the same address, Will Lylistone, died in the plague and was buried on 23 August 1665.

When the Duke's Company was formed under the managership of Sir William Davenant, Thomas Lilleston became one of the members. His first known role was Villerius in both parts of *The Siege of Rhodes*, presented at the converted tennis court in Lincoln's Inn Fields on 28 and 29 June 1661. Lilleston is also known to have acted Claudius in *Hamlet* in August of that year, the Duke in *Love and Honour* in October (plus a probable performance on 1 November at the Middle Temple), the Governor in *The Villain* in October 1662 (another work performed at court as well as at the playhouse), Theodorus in *Ignoramus* in November, Suffolk in *Henry VIII* in December 1663, and the Bishop of Canterbury in Boyle's *Henry V* in August 1664 (Downes the prompter, however, lists Lilleston as playing the Duke of Bedford in Boyle's play).

As one of the original actors in Davenant's troupe and a signer on 5 November 1660 of the tripartite agreement that established the company, Lilleston may have been one of the sharers, though just how many shares, or how large a portion of a share, he may have purchased is not known. He, along with the others, posted a £500 bond (a total of £5000) to keep the covenant.

It is not certain when Lilleston left the stage, for the records are scanty for the period. His participation in *Henry V* could have continued through December 1666, when the play was revived after the plague, but from the theatrical records combined with the parish register information, we conclude that Lilleston may well have left London in 1664 or 1665. W. S. Clark in his edition of Boyle's plays stated that Lilleston died in the service sometime before 1674.

Lilley, Mr [*fl.* 1789–1790], *house servant?*

A Mr Lilley was on the Drury Lane paylist in 1789–90 at a salary of 4s. 6d., presumably per week. At that salary he was probably a house servant.

Lillie. See LILLY.

"Lilliputian Burgo-Master." See FERG, MASTER.

"Lilliputian Colombine." See WRIGHT, CHRISTIANA.

"Lilliputian Lucy." See ROGERS, SUSAN.

"Lilliputian Polly." See ROGERS, ELIZABETH.

Lilliston. See LILLESTON.

Lilly, Mrs [*fl.* 1765–1793], *dresser.*

A Drury Lane Company list dated 9 February 1765 has Mrs Lilly down as a women's dresser at 1s. 6d. daily or 9s. weekly. She was still at that salary in 1776–77 and may well have been in 1793, when the account books last mentioned her (but noted her position without mentioning her salary).

Lilly, John *d. 1678, violist, theorbo player, copyist.*

Nicholas Hookes in his *Amanda* (1653) devoted a poem to the violist "Mr. LILLY, Musick-Master in *Cambridge*," one of the most extravagant memorials to a seventeenth-century musician that has survived:

SIR, *I have seen your scip-jack fingers flie,*
As if their motion taugh't Ubiquitie:
I've seen the trembling Cat'lin's *smart and brisk*
Start from the frets, *dance, leap, and nimbly frisk*
In palsie capers, pratling (*a most sweet*
Language of Notes) Curranto's *as they meet*:
I've heard each string *speak in so short a space*
As if all spoke at once; with stately grace
The surley tenour grumble at your touch,
And th'ticklish-maiden treble *laugh as much,*
Which (if your bowe-hand *whip it wantonly,)*
Most pertly chirps and jabbers merrily;

Like frolick Nightingals, *whose narrow throats*
S*uck* Musick *in and out, and gargle notes;*
Each strain makes smooth, and curles the air agen,
Like currents suck't by narrow whirlepits in;
Sometimes they murmur like the shallow springs,
Whose hastie streams forc't into Crystal rings,
And check't by pebbles, *pretty* Musick *make*
I*n* kisses *and such* language *as they speak*
"Tis soft and easie, Heaven *can't out-do't,*
That under Fairie-ground *is nothing to't:*
Who e're that earthly mortal Cherub *be,*
Whose well-tun'd *soul delights in* melodie:
He ventures hard, if for an houre he dares
To your surprizing straines *apply his eares,*
We finde such Magick *in your* Harmony,
As if to hear you were to hear and die.

    Were you a Batchelour, *and bold to trie*
Fortunes, what Lady's she, though ne're so high
And rich by birth, should see the tickling sport
Your finger makes, and would not have you for't;
Beyond those Saints who speak ex tempore,
Your well-spoke viol *scornes* tautologie;
And I in truth had rather hear you teach
O'th' Lyra, *then the rarest* tub-man *preach*:
I*n's holy speeches he may strike my eares*
With more of Heav'n; *you with more o'th' spheres,*
    I've heard your base mumble and mutter too,
Made angry with your cholerick hand, while you
With hastie jirks to vex and anger't more
Correct its stubbornnesse and lash it o're;
I've heard you pawse, *and dwell upon an* aire,
(Then make't i'th'end (as lost to part it were)
I anguish *and melt away so leasurely,)*
As if 'twere pity that its Eccho *die;*
Then snatch up notes, *as if your* viol broke,
And in the breaking every splinter spoke:
I've seen your active hands vault to and fro,
This to give grace, *that to command your* bowe;
As if your fingers *and your* instrument
By conspiration made you eminent.

The poem goes on to name some of the other eminent musicians in England but proclaims Lilly (or Lillie) the glory of Cambridge.

On 9 November 1660 John Lilly (sometimes Lyly) was appointed theorbo player (a large lute with extra bass strings) in the King's Musick. His livery allowance was the standard £16 2s. 6d. annually, though Charles II fell far behind in his payments as the years went on. Lilly's annual salary, which seems to have been paid on time, was £40. The Lord Chamberlain's accounts make frequent mention of Lilly. For example, on 24 March 1663 he was paid £12 for a lute; on 8 November 1666 he was loaned £5 (yet in 1666 his livery allowances for 1661 had not yet been paid); in December 1672 John was in debt to John Turner, a Cambridge merchant, to whom he assigned £32 5s. from livery allowances due him; in September 1673 Lilly took over four children from Pelham Humphrey to teach them the viol and theorbo, for £30 yearly; in the summer of 1674 he attended the King at Windsor; and in February 1675 he played theorbo in the court masque *Calisto*.

In 1664 Lilly, along with John Banister, became one of the Wardens of the Westminster Corporation of Music. He was still a Warden in 1672 and may have served until his death in 1678. Lilly, like some other court musicians, augmented his income with outside work, in his case serving as a music copyist. Typical was his copying of Christopher Simpson's *Months and Seasons* for Edward Lowe, Professor of Music at Oxford: "Thes 4 Bookes," wrote Lowe, "were prickt by Mr John Lillye, who had of me 5£ for the prickinge them 29th of December 1668." Examples of his copy work are now in the British Library and at Christ Church, Oxford.

The Lord Chamberlain's accounts indicate that when in London Lilly was a resident of the parish of St Andrew, Holborn, but he may have owned property in the parish of St Paul, Covent Garden. A map made by Lacy in 1673 shows a parcel of land about 150' by 30' fronting the north side of the Piazza about 150' east of James Street; the plot is marked Mr Lilly. A nearby parcel is marked Mrs Nau, very possibly a member of the musical Nau family.

Roger North wrote about John Lilly:

There was an old soker [i.e. old hand], that lived in Cambridge, and so was his [the Lord Keeper, Francis North's] acquaintance, and had bin frequently with his grandfather for the purposes of his profession. This man, for the sake of places in the King's musik, removed to Lodon; and having a great expensive family, hardly maintained them. And his lordship was so great patron to him, as almost to support his family; onely, to colour giving him pay, he set him to teach me on the theorboe lute, and to write musicke for him and others. He was free of his table as if he were of the house; and his lordship got him his salarys payd him, [and] took a son into a good office. The old man was peice of a droll, but very hearty and honest. He knew his lordship's family well, and particularly the tyranical old lord, his grandfather . . . and old Lilly (so he was called) used to say in his harsh and lowd pronunciation in all places, that he was very sure the 2nd Dudley Lord North's children succeeded all so well in the world, and were blest by God Almighty, for the extraordinary duty of their father, and observance, payd to his father the old Lord North.

John Lilly died on 25 October 1678.

Linacre, Thomas *c. 1640–1719, singer.*

Born about 1640, by 23 April 1685, when James II was crowned, Thomas Linacre (or Linaker) was a clerk and petty canon of the Choir of Westminster. He was sworn a Gentleman of the Chapel Royal on 27 December 1689, but he was not given a salaried post until January 1694. On 1 October 1694 he was sworn Gospeller of the Chapel. He died on 26 August 1719 at the age of 79 and was buried in the west cloister of Westminster Abbey on 28 August. He had written his will on 27 August 1717, leaving 1s. to his son-in-law William Hutchinson, a third of his moveables in trust to his daughter Anne Hutchinson, and everything else equally to his musical son Thomas and his daughter Isabell d'Moulins.

The Westminster Abbey registers contain several references to Thomas Linacre's family. By his first wife, Elizabeth, he had a son John, who died in infancy and was buried on 22 May 1682; a second child, Elizabeth, was buried on 4 September 1683. Mrs Elizabeth Linacre, the wife of Rev Thomas Linacre, was buried on 23 January 1684. Thomas did not wait long to remarry. On 5 August 1684 he and Elizabeth MacKearty were married at the Abbey. Their son Charles was christened on 28 July 1687. Linacre's children Anne, Isabell, and Thomas are not cited in the registers. The second Mrs Linacre was buried on 6 July 1703.

Linacre, Thomas *d. 1721, singer?*

From 1702 to 1720 the younger Thomas Linacre, son of Thomas Linacre (c. 1640–1719) and his second wife, née Elizabeth MacKearty, was named in the Lord Chamberlain's accounts as a court musician, apparently a singer. He attended the Queen at Windsor and Hampton Court in 1702, 1703, and 1706; at Windsor in 1709, 1711, and 1712; at Hampton Court in 1717; and at Kensington in 1720. Linacre was named in his father's will, drawn up on 27 August 1717 and proved on 28 August 1719. But he did not live to enjoy his share of the estate. He was buried at St Margaret, Westminster, on 1 October 1721.

Linam. *See* LYNHAM.

Linco. *See* LINIKE.

Lincoln, Miss [*fl. 1745–1747*], *actress, singer, dancer.*

Miss Lincoln was advertised as making her first appearance in that part when she played Polly in *The Beggar's Opera* at the Goodman's Fields Theatre on 4 February 1745. What other parts she may have performed before then we do not know. During the remainder of the season she appeared as Amphytrite in *The Tempest* and Nell in *The Devil to Pay*. She sang Polly at the New Wells, Clerkenwell, on 30 December 1745 and probably played Nell at her benefit at Hickford's Room on 3 February 1746. At that concert room on 10 March she was Polly once more and shared a benefit with Yeates. In April at Sadler's Wells Miss Lincoln danced and played Liberty in *Britannia Rediviva* and Colombine in *The Fortunate Volunteer*. On 15 September 1746 she held another benefit for herself, this time at the New Wells, London Spa, Clerkenwell, where she was Colombine in *As You Like It; or, Harlequin's Whim*. She sang at Southwark Fair on 14 September 1747 at the Yeates-Lee booth, after which her name disappeared from London bills.

"L'Inconnu, Mlle" [*fl. 1723–1730*], *dancer.*

The dancer masquerading under the stage name of "Mlle L'Inconnu" (or De L'Inconu, L'Inconnue) seems to have been mentioned in London playbills first on 2 November 1723, when she danced, with others, at the Lincoln's Inn Fields Theatre. She appeared there again in December and in October 1724, and she was with the "Italian" troupe at the Haymarket Theatre on 9 May 1726, performing in a new "Chacoon." She danced a *French Peasant* at the Haymarket on 27 June 1730.

Lindar, Miss [fl. 1715–1729], actress, dancer, singer.

Miss Lindar probably acted the Duke of York in *Richard III* at Drury Lane on 6 December 1715, but that casting comes from the edition of 1718 and could concern a later performance. About 1715, however, the song *As Amoret with Phillis sat* from *The Man of Mode* was published, with Miss Lindar named as the singer; that play was performed several times during the 1714–15 and 1715–16 season at Drury Lane, so it is likely that Miss Lindar was active at that playhouse when *Richard III* was given in December 1715. The bills did not mention her again, however, until the spring of 1717, when she spoke two prologues and an epilogue.

Beginning in the fall of 1717 Miss Lindar became a regular attraction at Drury Lane. She played the Page in *The Orphan* on 26 October, and four days later, when she danced a chaconne, minuet, and jig, the playbill stated that she was making her first appearance on any stage as a dancer. Her dancing master, a bill in November stated, was Mr Shirley. During the rest of the 1717–18 season Miss Lindar (once, in *The London Stage*, "Mrs" Lindar) danced between the acts, spoke a prologue and epilogue, was Ariel in *The Tempest*, and appeared in such dances as *Shepherdess*, *Harlequin*, a *Spanish Entry*, and *Greensleeves*. She shared a benefit with Mills's son on 27 May 1718. In 1718–19 she repeated some of her previous assignments and, at her benefit on 12 May 1719, shared with Miss Smith, she spoke an epilogue "in a Harlequin Dress" and danced with a boy who was making his stage debut. Her 1719–20 season was virtually a duplicate of the previous one.

In 1720–21 she added to her small repertoire of little boy parts Falstaff's Boy in *2 Henry IV*, and on 9 August 1721 she made her first public attempt as a singer, offering a song in Italian. Though she remained at Drury Lane, the novelty of her performances must have worn off, for she was cited in the bills—usually as an entr'acte dancer—only occasionally through 1721–22. In January 1723, however, she began appearing more frequently as an actress. On the seventh she played Ariel; then before the end of the month she acted Hymen in *Love in a Forest*, Prue in *Love for Love*, and Lucia in *The Squire of Alsatia*. The following summer she played Dorinda in *The Tempest*, having evidently outgrown Ariel. In August she acted Marilla in *A Wife to Be Let* and Emilia in *The Impertinent Lovers*. As before, she continued offering dances and songs.

From the 1723–24 season to her last notices in the spring of 1729, Miss Lindar was seen at Drury Lane in her old parts plus Sylvia in *The Old Bachelor*, the title role in *The Northern Lass*, a Punch Woman in *The Escapes of Harlequin*, one of the Graces in *The Loves of Mars and Venus*, Busy in *The Man of Mode*, a Countrywoman, Night, and a Shepherdess in *Apollo and Daphne*, Molly in *Love for Money*, Acis and a Nymph in *Acis and Galatea*, Mrs Chat in *The Committee*, Betty in *The Comical Revenge*, Doll in *2 Henry IV*, Fidelia in *The Strollers*, Flora in *Hob*, Dainty Fidget in *The Country Wife*, Dorcas in *The What D'Ye Call It*, Mrs Christian in *The Feign'd Innocence (Sir Martin Marall)*, a Bridesmaid in *Harlequin Happy and Poor Pierrot Married*, Altea in *Rule a Wife and Have a Wife*, Iris in a masque within *Harlequin Doctor Faustus*, an Attendant and an Hour of Sleep in *Perseus and Andromeda*, and Pastora in *Love in a Riddle*. About February 1729 Miss Lindar's name disappeared from the bills.

Lindelheim, Joanna Maria. See "Baroness, The"

Lindley. *See also* Linley.

Lindley, C. [fl. 1790–1794], violist.

C. Lindley was the third and youngest son of the York violinist Shirley Lindley (d. 1792) and his wife Hannah. Advertised as "Master C. Linley," he played a concerto on the viola, with his brother Master Robert on the violoncello, at the Great Auction Room in King Street, Covent Garden, on 4 February 1790. They repeated the performance on 17 February and 17 March. In 1794 C. Lindley was listed in Doane's *Musical Directory* as a violist who played in the Drury Lane oratorios and in the 1793 Oxford Meeting. At that time he was living with his brothers Robert and John in Upper Rathbone Place, London.

An obscure figure in comparison to his older brothers, C. Lindley seems not to have been a member of the Royal Society of Musicians. (It is unlikely that he was the blind organist named Lindley with whom Haydn traveled, around 9 September 1794, described in Haydn's *London Notebook*. He was 25 years old and his bride was 18, and both of them were "stone blind." Having received a dowry of £20,000 from his wife, that Lindley, according to Haydn, had given up playing the organ for a living.)

Lindley, John *b. 1773, violinist, violist.*

John Lindley was baptized on 9 July 1773 at Rothwell in Yorkshire, the eldest son of Shirley Lindley, "from the Glass House," and his wife Hannah. John's father was a musician of York, who died at Gloucester on 14 August 1792 and whose will was proved at London on 29 January 1793.

In 1794, John Lindley was living in Upper Rathbone Place, London, with his two brothers, Robert Lindley, a noted violoncellist, and C. Lindley, an obscure violist. When John was recommended by T. F. Wood on 5 March 1797 for membership in the Royal Society of Musicians, he was described as a single man, 23 years old, a performer on the violin and viola, who played "at most of the Public Concerts" and had several students. He and his brother Robert were unanimously elected to the Society on 4 June 1797, and on 2 July they signed the membership book.

John Lindley was designated as a violinist in the Society's annual May concerts at St Paul's from 1798 to 1800, and in 1802, 1803, and 1806. On 5 July 1801 he was fined for refusing to serve as one of the Society's Governors. The last notice of him in the Society's records occurred on 7 June 1807, when he was ordered to attend the annual meeting because he had sent a deputy to play for him in the recent St Paul's concert without permission.

Lindley, Robert *1776–1855, violoncellist, composer.*

Robert Lindley was born on 4 March and baptized on 12 April 1776 at Rotherham, Yorkshire, the second son of Shirley Lindley and his wife Hannah. His father, a musician of York, died in Gloucester on 14 August 1792, at which time the press described him as "a distinguished performer on the violin," but more eminently known because of the performances of his three sons, one of whom,

National Portrait Gallery
ROBERT LINDLEY
by Davison

Robert, was by then "reckoned among the 1st performers on the violoncello in Europe."

Having been taught the violin and the violoncello at any early age by his father, Robert Lindley came under the instruction of Cervetto, who brought him to southern England at the age of 16. Lindley soon received an engagement at the Brighton Theatre. According to Sainsbury, the Prince of Wales "honoured him with his commands to perform at the pavilion, and expressed himself highly gratified with his playing."

In 1788 and 1789 when Collins gave his musical lecture *The Evening Brush* at the Lyceum in the Strand, Master Robert Lindley occasionally played the violoncello during the interval. Advertised as "Master R. Linley," he and his younger brother "Master C. Linley" played a concerto at performances of *The Evening Brush* at the Great Auction Room in King Street, Covent Garden, on 4 and 17 February and 17 March 1790. In different advertisements for the 1790 concerts Robert was described, incorrectly, as a youth "but Eleven years of age" and "but twelve years old."

Lindley played in the Drury Lane oratorios (at the King's Theatre) in the spring of 1792. On 29 May of that year he performed in a concert at the Crown and Anchor in the Strand. He and his brother John played in the concerts of the Oxford Music Society in the spring of 1793, and Robert was engaged there during Lent in 1794. In 1794 he succeeded Sperati as first violoncello of the King's Theatre, a position he retained for the extraordinary period of 57 years, until his retirement in 1851. Doane's *Musical Directory* of 1794 listed him as a participant in the Concerts of the Academy of Ancient Music, the Professional Concerts, the Oxford Meeting, and the Drury Lane oratorios; his address was Upper Rathbone Place, the same as that of his brothers.

When he was recommended on 5 March 1797 by Dr Arnold for membership in the Royal Society of Musicians, Robert Lindley was described as a single man, 21 years old, with engagements at the King's Theatre, the Opera Concerts, and in the Concerts of Ancient Music. He and his brother John were unanimously elected on 4 June 1797 and signed the membership book on 2 July. Robert's name was on the list to play violoncello in the Society's annual May concerts at St Paul's from 1798 to 1800 and from 1802 (when he sent a deputy) to 1806. On 5 June 1806 he was fined three guineas for declining to serve as a Governor of the Society. As late as 1826, however, he was a member of the Court of Assistants.

During the first half of the nineteenth century Lindley was counted among the greatest violoncellists of his time, appearing in most of the major concerts in London and elsewhere in the kingdom. Upon the establishment of the Royal Academy of Music in 1822, Lindley was appointed professor of violoncello. He often played duets for violoncello and double bass with Dragonetti, a warm and enduring friend with whom he shared his opera desk. In his will of May 1848 Dragonetti left a violoncello to Lindley.

Lindley's first participation in the programs of the Philharmonic Society was on 24 February 1817, when he, Weichsel, Reeve, and Watts played a Haydn quartet. With those and others he also took part in a Beethoven septet. That spring Lindley was heard in seven more concerts. On 19 April 1819 he played a manuscript trio of his own composition, with Eley

National Portrait Gallery
ROBERT LINDLEY
by Chaloner

and Weichsel. With his son William and his friend Dragonetti, he played a sonata by Corelli on 8 May 1820. They played other Corelli sonatas at the Philharmonic Society on 11 March 1822, 2 June 1823, 3 March 1823, 7 April 1826, and 23 March 1835. With the double bass player Howell, Lindley performed Corelli's Sonata, Op 5, No 6, on 23 April 1836, and with other musicians he played more of that composer's music in 1836 and 1841. On 17 April 1826 Lindley played his own concertante for two violoncellos with his son.

Four years after his retirement in 1851, Lindley died at London on 13 June 1855, at the age of 79. His wife Hannah, née Taylor, a singer of Bath whom he had married at Walcot Church in that city on 30 November 1800, had died before Lindley made his will on 26 February 1846, for she was not mentioned in it. Possibly she had been the daughter of the provincial manager William Perkins Taylor (1769–1800) and Hannah Henrietta Taylor, née Pritchard (formerly Mrs Robinson and subsequently Mrs Benjamin Wrench), both of whom were performers on the Bath and Bristol stages.

In his will, which was proved on 6 July 1855, Robert Lindley stated his address (in 1846) as No 39, Perry Street, Rathbone Place, and bequeathed his house at No 22, Perry Street and all within, including all his violoncellos, to his son John Heaviside Lindley. The residue of his estate was placed in trust for the equal benefit of his children William Lindley, John Heaviside Lindley, Mary Mortimer Lindley, Anna Littleton (by 1746 the wife of Charles Wilday), and Eliza Emily Barnett, the wife of the composer John Barnett (1802–1890), whom she had married in 1837.

Our subject's son William Lindley, who had been born on 18 October 1801 and baptized on 1 February 1802 at St Marylebone, was admitted to the Royal Society of Musicians in 1825. Also a violoncellist, he held positions with many London musical organizations, including the band at the opera, but a nervous condition and delicate health prevented him from achieving his great promise as a soloist. He died at Manchester on 12 August 1869, leaving his widow Elizabeth Lindley (then 52) in poverty. At the time of his death the couple had six children, the youngest of whom was 18 years old.

In his *History of the Violoncello*, van der Straeten cites Vidal's assessment of Lindley's playing as "cold, and in technique and style he remained far behind Romberg, Lamarre, Bohrer and Servais." A critic in the *Berliner Musikzeitung* concurred: "Lindley plays the violoncello as beautifully, with perfect intonation and surety of technique, as Hausmann from Berlin, but he has not the fire." According to Grove, however, Lindley's tone on the violoncello was "remarkable for its purity, richness, mellowness, and volume."

As a composer he was less successful. His concertos were judged by a contemporary critic as "peculiar, and suited to every kind of audience." His compositions include about 35 solos and duets for the violoncello, a trio for bassoon, viola, and violoncello or for two violas and violoncello, a "caprice Bohême" for piano, and a handbook for the violoncello, published in 1855.

A portrait by W. Davison of Lindley seated by a table and holding a violoncello is in the National Portrait Gallery. A copy attributed to J. Linnell was bought at Christie's on 19 December 1974 by Rodney Slatford, a London musician. An engraving by J. P. Quilley, after Davison, is in the British Museum. A drawing by A. E. Chaloner of Lindley with his violoncello is in the National Portrait Gallery. In the Harvard Theatre Collection is a process print by an unknown engraver of a half-length portrait of Lindley. An engraving of Lindley and Paolo Spagnoletti, after a picture by Mrs Wigley of Shrewsbury, was published by Sharp in 1836. An engraving by Landseer, published in 1801 and designed by De Loutherbourg from miniature cameos by H. de Janvry, shows Lindley with his good friend Dragonetti, along with 24 other leading musicians of the period.

Lindsey, Mr [*fl.* 1702–1703], *singer.*
Fitzgerald in his *New History* counted Mr Lindsey among the singers at Drury Lane in 1702–3. The document in the Lord Chamberlain's accounts headed "Establishm^t of ye Company," recently re-dated about 1703 by Judy Milhous, lists one Lindsey as a singer at a salary of £20 annually. Mary Lindsey was certainly at Drury Lane in 1702–3, and it is possible that the references to Mr Lindsey are mistakes for her.

Lindsey, Mrs [*fl.* 1730], *actress, singer.*
A Mrs Lindsey had a part in *The Village Opera* beginning on 8 January 1730 at the Haymarket Theatre, but she was replaced on the sixteenth. She played Cleone in *Fatal Love* on 21 January, but her part was omitted on 2 February.

Lindsey, Mary [*fl.* 1697–1715?], *singer, actress.*
Mary Lindsey (or Lyndsay, Lynsey) was first noticed in casts in late June 1697 when she sang in *The World in the Moon* at the Dorset Garden Theatre. One of her songs was Daniel Purcell's "Then come kind Damon." She appeared regularly as a singer in plays and between the acts, usually at Drury Lane, and in June 1698 she acted Fardell in *The Campaigners*. Songs she sang began appearing, sometimes in collections, such as *A Second Book of Songs with a Through Bass* (1699) and *Mercurius Musicus* (periodical). Others were separately printed, like *Tho' over all Mankind* from *Caligula* (1698), *How calm Elesa are these Groves* from

Imposture Defeated (1698), *Great Jove look down* (1698?), *The Jolly, Jolly Swains* from *The Island Princess* (1700), *Where, where's my Pan* from *The Grove* (1700), *Behold the Man that with Gigantick Might*, with Leveridge, from *The Richmond Heiress* (1700?), *Jogging on from yonder Green* (1700?), *Stop, O ye Waves* (1700?), *'Tis Sultry Weather* from the *Four Seasons* (1705?), *Gay, Kind and airy sweet* from *Love's Triumph* (1708), *Can you leave ranging* from *Thomyris* (1710?), and *Plenty Mirth*, with Laroon (1715).

As early as April 1699 Mrs Lindsey began appearing at concert rooms. That month a benefit concert was given for her at York Buildings, and at the same place in July 1702 she sang music by Weldon, possibly including some of his prize music from *The Judgment of Paris* of the previous year. For singing that music at Lincoln's Inn Fields playhouse for the Duke of Bedford, Mrs Lindsey was paid, in 1702, £3 4s. 6d., the highest fee granted.

During the first decade of the eighteenth century London saw the beginnings of what became a rage for opera, especially Italian or in the Italian style. On 16 January 1705 at Drury Lane Mrs Lindsey sang Nerina in *Arsinoe* by Clayton. Her other opera roles during the decade were Tullia in *Camilla*, Grideline in *Rosamond*, Media in *Thomyris*, Serpetta in *Love's Triumph* (at the Queen's Theatre, whence the opera performers had moved in 1708), Leonora in *Clotilda*, Blesa in *Almahide*, and Blesa in *Floro and Blesa*. Among Vice Chamberlain Coke's papers at Harvard are a number of documents relating to the opera performances at the Queen's Theatre. Mrs Lindsey was paid £2 daily for her participation, a salary equal to that of Leveridge but only a third of what Mrs Tofts, the company's leading English singer received. Her season salary was noted in another document as £90, compared to £400 for Mrs Tofts and £100 for Leveridge. In yet another document she was listed at £60, Leveridge at £30, and Mrs Tofts at £500.

It is difficult to determine just how long Mary Lindsey remained active in the London theatres and concert rooms. She had a benefit at York Buildings on 23 March 1711, and she sang Media in *The Loves of Baldo and Media* at the Greenwich Theatre on 19 July 1712—the last specific reference to her performing that we have found. But about 1715 songs were published with Mrs Lindsey cited as the singer: *Now to you yee dry Wooers* from *The Island Princess*, *Plenty Mirth*, and *Tho over all Mankind* from *Caligula*. Those were songs she had sung in earlier years, but their publication about 1715 suggests that she was still an attraction, so she may have been appearing as a singer despite lack of evidence in advertisements. When *Wit and Mirth* was published in 1719 it contained a number of songs from earlier years which Mrs Lindsey had made popular.

Line, Mr [*fl.* 1738–1749], *house servant?*

At Covent Garden Theatre on 21 April 1738 and 25 April 1749 the benefit tickets of a Mr Line were admitted. He may have been one of the house servants.

Ling, Mr [*fl.* 1796], *oboist.*

The *Oracle* on 11 February 1796 reported the first public appearance of a "Lings" Junior, oboist, at a concert at the King's Theatre. Our guess is that the name was misspelled and should have been Ling, since there were two musicians of that name active in London at that time, William and Thomas. The latter was proficient on the oboe, and it is quite possible that the young man making his first appearance in 1796 was Thomas Ling's son.

Ling, Mrs [*fl.* 1775], *house servant?*

At Drury Lane on 8 May 1775 Mrs Ling's benefit tickets were accepted. She may have been one of the house servants.

Ling, Thomas [*fl.* 1784–1805], *violinist, bassoonist, oboist.*

The Mr "Lings" who was listed by Dr Burney as a bassoonist in the Handel Memorial Concerts at Westminster Abbey and the Pantheon in May and June 1784 was probably Thomas Ling. Doane's *Musical Directory* of 1794 listed him as a violinist, bassoonist, and oboist then living in Helmet Court, the Strand (where William Ling lived; they may have been brothers). Doane noted that Ling had played in the Westminster Abbey concerts and that he was also a member of the New Musical Fund and the Academy of Ancient Music. The New Musical Fund records show that he served on the Court of Assistants in 1794 and 1805. On 15 October 1803 at the Royal Circus the band was augmented by Mr Ling on the oboe and Mr Widner on the octave flute.

Ling, William [*fl.* 1794–1805], *organist, flutist, composer.*

Doane's *Musical Directory* of 1794 listed William Ling Junior, of Helmet Court, the Strand, as a composer and organist. Between about 1795 and 1800 several works by Ling were published, including three sonatas for keyboard with a flute obligato and three duets for two German flutes. Their content suggests that the Ling who played several solos on the flute at the Royal Circus on 23 June 1800 was probably William. He was a subscriber to the New Musical Fund in 1805.

Lingham, Mr [*fl.* 1790–1808], *impresario.*

Chancellor in his *Annals of Covent Garden* says that late in 1790 Mr Lingham (a breeches-maker in the Strand, according to Brayley) purchased the old property of the headquarters or Lyceum of The Incorporated Society of Artists. The building had been erected in 1765 by James Paine near Exeter 'Change. Lingham was granted a license for music, dancing, harmonic meetings, and other diversions, and converted the building into a proper theatre. There he offered musical performances by such attractions as Gray, Masters, Mrs Wewitzer, and Mrs Reeve, charging 2s. 6d. for the best seats and 1s. for inferior ones. A portion of the building was occupied by the prize fighter Mendoza, who ran a boxing school and taught members of the nobility self-defense.

In 1794 Lingham leased the Lyceum to Samuel Arnold for musical entertainments; Arnold built another theatre on a plot of ground adjoining the Lyceum—part playhouse and part circus, apparently, but he either could not get a license or was granted one only to have it withdrawn. In any case, the lease went back to Lingham, and in the Public Record Office is a warrant to the effect that Lingham had a lease in 1794 for concerts from 5 February to 1 April, except Wednesdays and Fridays in Lent and Passion Week. In 1795 Handy took over the threatre and presented circus entertainments. The Drury Lane accounts for that year link Lingham and Handy's names in connection with payments for horses, and they may well have worked as partners.

The Lyceum was used by various people in the years that followed, but evidently Lingham kept his interest in it, for the Lord Chamberlain's accounts cited him in connection with licenses for musical entertainments in the springs of 1804, 1806, 1807, and 1808.

"L'Inglesina." See DAVIES, CECILIA.

Lings, Mr [*fl.* 1800], *house servant?*

Benefit tickets for a Mr Lings were accepted at Drury Lane Theatre on 14 June 1800. Possibly he was Thomas or William Ling, but there is insufficient evidence to make an identification.

Lings, Miss [*fl.* 1772–1780], *dancer, actress.*

Miss Lings, probably the daughter of the dancer John Lings, danced a *New Double Hornpipe* with one Master "White" on 5 May. He was very likely the Master "Whitlow" who was Miss Lings's partner on 3 June, when the youngsters were called students of Giorgi. (Whitlow, but not White, appeared in later seasons). The performance of 3 June was a benefit for Mortimer, Tomlinson, and John Lings. Miss Lings may have been among the scholars of Giorgi who danced at the Haymarket Theatre in August, for she was in *The Rehearsal* on the tenth and on 17 September she played Prince Edward in *Richard III*.

Miss Lings performed regularly at Drury Lane in 1772–73 and 1773–74, appearing in an unnamed part in *The Pigmy Revels* and playing Grotilla in *Edgar and Emmeline* and the Page in *The Gamesters*. On 28 May 1773 she and Master Whitlow offered a hornpipe, and those two plus Miss Wilkins were in a *New Wooden Shoe Dance*. All three were mentioned as Giorgi's pupils, and the performance was a shared benefit for Mr Lings and two others. On 14 and 16 June 1773 at the Haymarket with several other Giorgi students Miss Lings danced *The Italian Peasants* and that summer was again in *The Rehearsal* and played Melpomene in *The Register Office*. In May 1774 she danced again with Master Whitlow at Drury Lane.

She left London sometime after the spring of 1774. She danced in the summers of 1775 and 1776 at Birmingham. On 2 May 1778 she returned to the London stage, this time dancing at Covent Garden, where she was a student of Aldridge. For his benefit on that date she was in a new *Comic Dance* with others of his pupils; then she returned, in the 1778–79 season, to dance in *The Norwood Gypsies* and to perform again at a benefit for Aldridge. In 1779–80 at Covent Garden she danced in *The Coquette Quaker, Cupid Recruiting,* a *Triple Hornpipe,* and *The Rakes of Mallow,* and performed a minuet and allemande with Holloway. After that her name disappeared from the London bills.

Lings, John [*fl.* 1764–1776?], *actor.*

John Lings shared a benefit with four others at Drury Lane on 22 May 1764 and was similarly cited at benefit time in 1765. But not until 21 May 1766 was he given a part large enough to warrant mention in the playbills; that night he acted Butler in *The Busy Body* at his shared benefit with three others. No advertised parts came his way in 1766–67. He was in Foote's troupe at the Haymarket Theatre in the summer of 1767 playing Eliot in *Venice Preserv'd,* Crook-fingered Jack in *The Beggar's Opera* (as "Lyngs"), and, presumably, some unadvertised bits and walk-ons.

Lings acted at Drury Lane through 1773–74, spending his summers at the Haymarket. From 13 May 1768 onward he was regularly though not frequently cited in the bills. On that date he acted the Music Master in *Catherine and Petruchio* at Drury Lane, after which he was seen there in such parts as Balthazar in *Romeo and Juliet,* Scentwell in *The Ladies' Frolick,* a Fryar in *The Witches,* a Gentleman to the Duke in *The Chances,* an an unnamed character in *The Pigmy Revels.*

During the summers at the Haymarket from 1768 to 1773 he fared better, playing Thomas in *The School Boy,* Thomas in *The Virgin Unmask'd,* a Countryman in *The What D'Ye Call It,* Hounslow in *The Beaux' Stratagem,* Robin in *The Beggar's Opera,* an Officer and a Senator in *Othello,* Bernardo in *Hamlet,* Lepidus in *Julius Caesar,* a Lieutenant in *Richard III,* a Servant in *The Patron,* a Coachman in *The Devil to Pay,* Bacchus in *Midas,* a Planter in *Oroonoko,* a Servant in *King Lear,* a Watchman in *The Upholsterer,* the Justice in *The Provok'd Wife,* Robert in *The Mock Doctor,* Tricket in *The Register Office,* and a number of unnamed characters in other works. After the spring of 1774 John seems to have left London. He was very likely the Lings who acted at Kilkenny in June 1776. The dancer-actress Miss Lings was probably John Lings's daughter.

Linham. *See* LYNHAM.

Lini, Francesco [*fl.* 1749–1754], *actor, singer.*

Francesco Lini was in the troupe of Italian players under Croza's managership at the Haymarket Theatre from 21 November 1749 to 28 April 1750. He returned to England with Giordani's burletta company in 1753 to perform at Covent Garden Theatre from 17 December to 11 March 1754. He was cited in the bills for three roles: Odoardo in *Lo studente a la moda,* Ormindo in *L'amor costante,* and Odoard in *La cameriera accorta.*

Linike, Mr [*fl.* 1767], *musician.*

A paylist for Covent Garden Theatre, dated 14 September 1767, has a musician named Linike down for 5*s.* daily. That is all that has been discovered about him, but the Mrs Linike and her children who were noted several times in the minutes of the Royal Society of Musicians from 1785 to 1796 were very likely his family. On 3 April 1785 Mrs Linike attended a Society meeting to discuss having her son George Frederick apprenticed. By July she had found a master for him, a watch-movement maker named Thomas Newton, but the Society decided Newton's character was not suitable. They arranged for young Linike to serve at least temporarily under a Mr Cleghorne, watch finisher. By October young Linike decided he did not like working under Cleghorne and asked to be apprenticed instead to William Grakell, a tailor. The Society arranged for the change and paid the £10 fee plus expenses.

On 10 October 1785 Mrs Linike was seized with insanity. In early November the Society arranged for her to be put in the poor house at St Mary, Lambeth, and, by the end of the month, taken to Bedlam. A Mrs Woodcock was paid to take care of Mrs Linike's daughter Louisa. By December 1790 the daughter had reached the age of 14 and wished to be apprenticed to Mrs Tait of Air Street, Piccadilly, a mantua maker. The usual premium of £20 was paid by the Society. Louisa behaved in an exemplary fashion as an apprentice and was given a reward of £5 in 1796.

Linike, D. *d. c. 1725, violist, music copyist.*

D. Linike's surname gave scribes a great deal of trouble during the years he was active in London. He was called Linisce, Leneker, Linigke, Linco, Lenniker, Lumian, Lunican, Lunicour, Liniker, Linoker, and Lunear but usually Linike. Some spellings of his name make it seem likely that he was related to the German violinist and composer Johann George Linigke, who was active during the first 30 years of the eighteenth century and who is said to have come to London after 1713 for a few years.

Linike was cited a number of times in Vice Chamberlain Coke's papers (now at Harvard) relative to his employment at the Queen's Theatre. He evidently asked for £1 nightly to play tenor (viola) in the opera band in the second decade of the century, but the per diem he settled for was 8s. Linike augmented his salary by copying out vocal and instrumental parts, receiving, for example, £26 for his work on the score of *Rinaldo* in 1711. By that time he was earning 10s. daily as a performer in the opera band. References to Linike dwindle after 1713: he served as a copyist in 1716–17, earning £1 12s. for an unspecified amount of work; at Hickford's Music Room on 3 May 1717 he received a solo benefit; he shared a benefit there with Mrs Smith in February 1719; in February 1720, according to the Portland papers at Nottingham, he was in the Academy of Music opera orchestra at a season salary of £40; and on 27 March 1724 he had a benefit at the Haymarket Theatre. Sometime between then and 16 March 1726 D. Linike died, for on the latter date a benefit was held at Hickford's for Widow Linike.

Linley, Elizabeth Ann. *See* SHERIDAN, MRS RICHARD BRINSLEY THE FIRST.

Linley, Maria [*fl.* 1763–1784], *singer.*

Maria Linley was baptized at St James's in Bath on 10 October 1763; she was the eighth child and third daughter of the musician Thomas Linley (1733–1795) and his wife Mary (1729–1820). A pupil of her father, at an early age Maria joined her sister Mary (later Mrs Richard Tickell) in concerts and oratorios at Bath. In 1775 Garrick tried to engage Maria and Mary for the Drury Lane Company, but R. B. Sheridan wrote to his father-in-law

Harvard Theatre Collection

MARIA LINLEY

engraving by Ryder, after Westall

Thomas Linley in the early summer to advise against the engagement, because he feared the girls' reputations would become compromised if they became actresses. According to Sheridan, Garrick was "particularly stimulated by the Reputation of what Maria promises to be," that is, possibly, another singer as talented as Elizabeth Ann Linley, Sheridan's wife. Sheridan advised Linley to keep his younger daughters on the concert circuit. "Maria's Reputation is spreading amazingly," he wrote, "whatever you *did* get by *Betsy*—and what more you *might* have got had you come sooner to town or had I not robbed you of her—you *may* get and if you rely only on yourself, certainly *will* get by Maria."

Evidently her brother-in-law's advice prevented Maria from beginning a theatrical career. She did sing at Drury Lane, however, in the oratorios during the spring of 1776. On 1 March 1776 she and Mary were principal vocalists in *Alexander's Feast*, and her brother Thomas played a violin concerto. The three also performed in the *Messiah* at the Chapel of the Foundling Hospital on 2 April 1776 and in *Ruth* at the Chapel of the Lock Hospital the next night.

On 13 March 1778 it was reported that "The Young Miss Linley improves rapidly, her voice is getting strength, had promises to excel in the *Piano*." Every spring between 1777 and 1783, except perhaps 1779, she sang in the oratorios under the direction of her father at Drury Lane. On 15 February 1782, at a command performance, she sang "Sweet Bird," accompanied on the organ by Stanley, and "Hide me from day's garish eye."

While on a visit with her parents to her grandfather's house in Belmont Row, Bath, she caught a cold after dancing, which led to a violent and rapid fever; she died on Sunday evening, 5 September 1784, in her twentieth year. It was said that in a final paroxysm of the "brain fever" she rose up in bed and sang Handel's "I know that my Redeemer liveth" in a full and clear tone and then expired. She was buried at Walcot on 11 September.

The *Gentleman's Magazine* for September 1784 eulogized that the "union of a sweet voice, correct judgment, extensive compass, and above all beauty of mind and person distinguished the much lamented maid." Elegies appeared in the *Bath Chronicle* that month and a dirge by Charles Leftley, a friend of Maria's brother William, was published in the first volume of *The Cabinet*. An ode to *The Memory of Miss Maria Linley* by a Captain Thompson was published in the *European Magazine* and in *An Asylum for Fugitive Verses*:

> *If wit, if beauty, modesty and sense,*
> *Met earth's applause, or heaven's high recompense;*
> *If e'er an angel left the solar sphere,*
> *To fix in wonder ev'ry eye and ear,*
> *'Twas thee,* Maria—

Verses to Maria written by her sister Elizabeth Sheridan were printed in John Watkins's *Memoirs . . . of Sheridan* (1817).

A portrait of Maria Linley done in pastel by Thomas Lawrence was bequeathed in 1835 to the Dulwich College Picture Gallery. Richard Westall's drawing of her was engraved by T. Ryder and published in 1785; the original drawing was once in the possession of E. H. Ireland's mother, but its present location is unknown.

Linley, Mary, later Mrs Richard Tickell the first *1758–1787, singer, actress.*

Mary (called Polly) Linley, the fourth child and second daughter of the musician Thomas Linley (1733–1795) and his wife Mary, was born at Bath on 4 January 1758 and baptized at St James's, in that city, on 10 February.

Having been trained by her father, Mary—at the age of 11 and advertised as "A Young Gentlewoman who never appeared on any stage"—played Sally in the premiere of Colman's comedy *Man and Wife; or, The Shakespeare Jubilee* at Covent Garden Theatre on 7 October 1769. A James Winston manuscript at the Folger Shakespeare Library identifies the novice as Mary Linley. *Man and Wife*, a popular piece, was offered a number of times that season. Mary also played a principal part in *The Spanish Lady* on 11 December 1769 and several other nights. On 2 June 1770 she was paid a total of £50 for her performances that season.

For the next several years Mary sang in a number of concerts and oratorios, usually with her sister Elizabeth, who married R. B. Sheridan in 1773. In 1771 Mary appeared at the Three Choirs Festival and at the Oxford Music Room; she was also heard at the Music Room in the Commemoration of 14 July 1773. She sang at Bristol in May 1772 and December 1773. In the New Assembly Rooms at Bath Mary performed with Elizabeth in *Acis and Galatea*, *Judas Maccabaeus*, and the *Messiah* in April 1772. At the Chester Musical Festival in June 1772, in the oratorios *Samson*, *Judas Maccabaeus*, and the *Messiah*, "the amazing powers of the two Miss Linleys," reported the *Chester Courant*, "conspired to render the Entertainment so great and excellent as can be expected, or ever was produced from the human voice." Her brother, Thomas Linley the younger, distinguished himself as a violinist during that festival. That year Mary also performed at Gloucester.

In February and March 1773 Mary sang in the Drury Lane oratorios, and on 12 April she participated in a concert at the King's Theatre. The managers of both winter patent houses wished to hire Mary and Maria Linley as singing actresses but in a letter written in May or June 1775 Sheridan dissuaded their father from making any such engagement, warning him of the loss of reputation and respect the girls would eventually suffer and assuring Linley

By permission of the Governors of Dulwich Picture Gallery

ELIZABETH ANN LINLEY SHERIDAN and MARY LINLEY
by Gainsborough

that they would be better off remaining under his own professional care. "Polly is certainly at present considered *here* as the best *Oratorio* Singer there now is," wrote Sheridan, "and tho' her Sister Maria may come to surpass her in some things—She will always be respectable and in the first Line."

In February and March 1776 Mary again sang in the Drury Lane oratorios; the 24 February *Morning Chronicle* reported that in *Acis and Galatea* the previous night Miss Linley "gave every delight that the ear, heart, or understanding could receive from music. . . . Her voice is clear and melodious, and capable of truest expression." Mary sang in the Drury Lane oratorios under the direction of her father and Stanley each spring through 1779.

Though Captain Paumier, Sheridan's friend and sometimes second for duels, hoped to wed Mary Linley, she married instead Richard Tickell (1751–1793) on 26 July 1780 at St Clement Danes. Tickell was described by John Watkins in *Memoirs . . . of Sheridan* (1817) as an "ingenious and good-natured, but thoughtless man," a native of Bath, who had squandered away a small inheritance. He was, it seems, the grandson of Addison's friend, Thomas Tickell, whose wife Clotilda was descended from Eustace Plantagenet, brother of Henry II. Richard Tickell's father was probably John Tickell (d. 1782), who had three sons and two daughters. Though trained in the law Richard Tickell did not follow that profession, preferring to write political pamphlets. His friendship with Brummell, secretary to Lord North, secured him a place in the Stamp Office and a pension of £200 per year. Evidently Tickell broke off an "imprudent connexion" with a woman at the time of his marriage to Mary Linley, but settled a share of his pension upon her and some illegitimate children.

Upon her marriage to Tickell, Mary retired from public singing, and went to Wells, where she lived happily but frugally for a while, until her husband was appointed a Commissioner of the Stamp Office at £500 a year, and they were given rooms at Hampton Court. They also kept a residence in London, at one time in Brook Street, later in Queen Anne Street. They were living at Hampton when she was struck down by tuberculosis. On 20 June 1787 she was taken to Bristol Hot Wells, where she died on 27 July 1787, at the age of 29. She was buried in Wells Cathedral. Verses to her written by her sister Elizabeth Sheridan in the spring of 1788 were printed by Thomas Moore in *Memoirs . . . of Sheridan* (1825). The following verse by an unknown author is taken from a Folger clipping:

> To the Memory of Mrs. TICKELL
> Replete with every charm to win the heart,
> To soothe life's sorrows, or its joys impart,
> Soft—timid—elegant! her beauteous mien
> Bespoke the feeling—gentle mind, within.
> Torn from her Husband's fond adoring arms,
> From Friends who weep her matchless worth and charms,
> By pale disease, which one her Beauties prey'd,
> Her roses blighted and her form decay'd;
> They—like the graces of her virtuous mind—
> Were not for weak mortality design'd!
> Thus the sweet tub'rose, in the thorny shade,
> Whose flow'rets wither, and whose honors fade,
> Till fost'ring dews and sun shine's chearing ray
> Again call forth its beauties into day—
> Thus, 'midst the agonizing tears of woe,
> Truth whispers from the grave—Thus shalt thou blow!
> There is a coming morn, shall bid her rise,
> And in the bloom of Virtue grace you skies.
> Where Truth and Piety shall live sublime.
> And Worth shall find its own congenial clime.
> Then mourn not that THE SAINT, thus undismayed,
> Died—at that dread command—she e'er obey'd!

On 24 August 1789 Richard Tickell was married again, to Sarah Ley, the daughter of Thomas Ley of Gower Street. On 4 November 1793, in a fit of despondency, he killed himself by jumping from the window of his apartment at Hampton Court Palace. His comedy *The Carnival of Venice*, with music by the elder Thomas Linley, had been produced successfully at Drury Lane on 13 December 1781. Tickell's alteration of Ramsay's *The Gentle Shepherd*, which had been played on 29 October 1781, owed its merit to Linley's Scotch airs. Tickell's second wife subsequently married John Cotton Worthington.

Three children are known to have issued from the marriage of Mary Linley and Richard Tickell. The youngest was Samuel Tickell (1785–1817), whose education at Winchester was financed, in part, by R. B. Sheridan. He died in India in 1817, leaving three young children. The middle child, about whom little is known, was Richard Brinsley Tickell, born about 1783; he entered the navy and was killed in action off the coast of Sardinia in 1805. The eldest, Elizabeth Ann Tickell, called Betty, was born about April 1781. In a will dated 17 January 1832 and a codicil dated 6 May 1833, William Linley left his "niece Elizabeth Ann Tickell" substantial bequests, including manuscripts, musical instruments, some family portraits, a leasehold house in Bath, other real estate, £1000 in cash, and his share in Drury Lane Theatre. She raised a monument to her uncle William's memory at St Paul, Covent Garden. Betty Tickell lived for a long time at No 23, Charlotte Street, Bedford Square, where she died, unmarried, in 1860.

An illegitimate daughter of Richard Tickell, by one of his earlier "imprudent connexions," married Ebenezer Roebuck and became the mother of the politician John Arthur Roebuck. Tickell also had an illegitimate son.

A miniature portrait by Richard Cosway, after a sketch by a Bristol artist, of Mary Tickell asleep, shortly before her death, was owned by Dr Lumsden Propert. Another portrait, of Mary full-length, walking on a garden terrace, was painted by Cosway; its present location is unknown, but it was engraved by Condé, 1791. A miniature by Gainsborough, according to *The Dictionary of National Biography*, belonged to C. E. Lees. The famous painting by Gainsborough of Mary and her sister Elizabeth Ann, once owned by Sheridan, was bequeathed by William Linley to the Dulwich College Picture Gallery in 1831. In that will Dulwich was also given a portrait by O. Humphry of Mary when a child. Romney's portrait of Mrs Tickell, sometimes called a portrait of Mary, is actually of the second Mrs Tickell, Sarah Ley.

Linley, Thomas *1733–1795, composer, conductor, music director, singing-master.*

Thomas Linley, progenitor of a large and prominent family of musicians, was born in Badminton on 17 January 1733 and was baptized there on 20 January. He was one of at least three children of William Linley (1704–1792) and his wife Maria (1701–1792). The family, sometimes called Lingley in earlier generations, had roots in Norton, Derbyshire, where William Linley was born. The old home of the Norton line of Linleys was Bole Hill. William Linley was originally a carpenter at Badminton and then at Bath; he was later

By permission of the Governors of Dulwich Picture Gallery

THOMAS LINLEY
by Gainsborough

sometime Clerk of the Works to St Mary's Chapel at Bath. His other known children were Isabella, baptized at Badminton on 9 October 1737, who married the carpenter Richard Philpot at Bath Abbey on 7 October 1764 and probably was the mother of the Bath musician John Philpot, who lived at No 12, Kingsmead Terrace, in 1800, and William Linley, who was baptized at Badminton on 29 July 1744. The elder William Linley and his wife, parents of our subject, both having died in 1792, were buried at Walcot Church, Bath.

Thomas Linley was taught music by Thomas Chilcot, organist of Bath Abbey. It was also said that he studied under Pietro Domenico Paradies at Naples. But in 1746 Paradies came to London for at least five years. There he had many pupils, including Gertrud Schmeling (later Madame Mara) and Cassandra Frederick; so perhaps young Thomas went to London rather than Italy for instruction.

At Batheaston on 11 May 1752, Thomas

Linley married Mary Johnson, several years his senior. Little is known about her. She seems to have been related to a clergyman named E. Johnson who performed marriages at Wells Cathedral. Between 1752 and 1771 Thomas worked hard to establish himself as a singing-master at Bath. At least twelve children were born there during that period. Of the children who survived to maturity, five had notable careers on the London stage.

It was claimed by Parke in his *Musical Memoirs* that as a singing-master Linley was "almost unrivalled in England." He prospered at Bath, moving by 1767 from a modest location in the Abbey Green to an eleven-room house in Orchard Street, near the Bath theatre, and then in 1772 to a fine house in the Crescent.

Linley conducted concerts in the Bath Assembly Rooms and the Long Room at Bristol Hotwells which met with great success. No doubt his children Elizabeth Ann and Thomas had made some appearances at Bath before they were taken to London, when they were 12 and 11, respectively, to perform in Hull's masque, *The Fairy Favour*, at Covent Garden Theatre on 31 January 1767. The father appeared at that theatre on 19 February 1767 to play a violin solo before the royal family. Linley's earliest composition for the London stage was the music for *The Royal Merchant*, a comic opera adapted by Hull from Beaumont and Fletcher that had its premiere at Covent Garden on 14 December 1767. Neville wrote in his diary that "the music may be good, but the piece is trifling and childish." The words and music were published by Welcker in 1768.

By 1770 Linley's daughter Elizabeth Ann (later to become Mrs Richard Brinsley Sheridan) had acquired a reputation at Bath as a great beauty and a fine singer. She sang in *Ruth* at the King's Theatre on 5 April 1769. When Harris and Colman made overtures to engage her for Covent Garden Theatre, Linley wrote to the latter on 11 October 1770 to state that it was contrary to his inclination to have his daughter sing at any London oratorio or theatre where he himself was not a principal in the undertaking, for he believed more money could be gained for his own account than for others. Since he saw no possibility at that time of obtaining a share in a patent on "reasonable terms," he was determined not to allow his daughter to be introduced as an actress, but he did offer her services in an oratorio of her choice for 200 guineas and a clear benefit. Indeed, not until three years later did he again bring Elizabeth Ann to sing in London, and then not at Covent Garden but at Drury Lane. She was a principal in the oratorio *Judas Maccabeus* on 26 February 1773 and again in *Alexander's Feast* on 10 March. Also singing on those nights was Mary Linley, a younger daughter (who became Mrs Richard Tickell). The sisters sang at the King's Theatre on 12 April 1773, in a concert for the benefit of the younger Thomas Linley, who played violin that night. The elder Linley also played violin in those several oratorios and concerts.

In 1774, upon the retirement of J. C. Smith, Linley became associated with the blind organist John Stanley in the conduct of the oratorios at Drury Lane. After Stanley died in 1786 Linley continued in the management of the oratorios with Samuel Arnold. He contributed one song to Dibdin's *The Quaker*, a comic opera that opened at Drury Lane on 3 May 1775. With his son Thomas, he composed and compiled the music for his son-in-law's *The Duenna* (seven songs by the father, six by the son, and 10 by other composers, although only the elder Linley's name appears on the published score). Linley's role in the preparation of the piece evidently was crucial, for on 2 November 1775 his daughter Elizabeth Ann Sheridan wrote to him: "Our music is now all finished and rehearsing, but we are impatient to see *you*. We hold your coming to be *necessary* beyond conception." *The Duenna* opened at Covent Garden on 21 November 1775 and was an immediate and enduring success, playing some 60 nights before the end of the season.

On 19 January 1776 the *Morning Chronicle* made the noteworthy announcement that David Garrick had sold his share of the Drury Lane patent to a quartet composed of Dr James Ford, Simon Ewart, Richard Brinsley Sheridan, and Thomas Linley. The price was £35,000; Sheridan and Linley each paid or promised to pay £10,000. The agreement had been signed by all parties the previous day. In a letter to Garrick (now in the Forster Collection at the Victoria and Albert Museum) written sometime late in 1775, Linley told the great actor-manager that he wanted to purchase his share in order to improve the means of his family, wishing to "remove myself from the place I am in, where

I do not see the least chance of being any other than a Servant to ye (Bath Assembly) Rooms." Linley explained to Garrick how he planned to raise the money:

I should suppose upon a fair calculation that my little Estate in Bath would sell for £6000 i.e. I have a House in the Crescent w^h. is let for £130 p^r: Ann:—that which I live in I paid £1100 for, I have another in Milsom Street w^h: is lett upon a long Lease at £60 p^r Ann: I have a 3^d Share in Margaret Chapel situated in Brock Street, which I may justly value at £1000 and am on ye point of purchasing another Share of one of ye Proprietors who is under a necessity of selling. Thus I have money sufficient to purchase without mortgaging, and with a little Freehold w^h lets for £15 p^r An: & w^h I have reason to think will lett for more when the Lease is out, as I have made considerable improvements on ye Estate [a farm and lands called Oldbury in Didmarton which he mentioned in his will?], this is ye Bulk of my Fortune, which I can either sell, or make over for any sum that may be thought a reasonable security for. . . .

On 3 January 1776 Garrick wrote to John Hoadly his opinion that Linley would be of "great Service" to the new management: "Sing Song is much the Fashion, & his knowledge of Musick & preparing Subjects for the Stage, will be a Strength, that the Proprietors may depend upon, when the Heroines are prankish." A manuscript in the British Library, which is a lawyer's bill in the amount of £23 12s. for perusing Linley's Bath properties and drawing up documents, indicates that on 24 June 1776 it was agreed that for Linley's purchase of two-sevenths part of Garrick's moiety he "should give Bond to Garrick for the Consideration and also a Mortgage on the Theatre & Estates at Bath as further Security."

For his services as director of music at Drury Lane Linley was to receive £500 per year; his wife was appointed wardrobe mistress at £1 10s. per week. The Linleys took a house in Norfolk Street, between the Thames and the Strand, and never returned to live at Bath, though they made visits.

Drury Lane opened under the new management on 21 September 1776. That season Linley wrote additional accompaniments to Locke's music for *Macbeth*, produced under his musical supervision on 25 November. He provided music, adapted from Grétry, for the premiere of Collier's *Selima and Azor*, a romance got up with great scenic splendor by De Loutherbourg on 5 December 1776. He wrote the song "Here's to the maiden" for *The School for Scandal*, the comedy by Sheridan that was a phenomenal success at its premiere on 8 May 1777. His son Thomas, who had become leader of the oratorios under the elder Linley's direction, provided incidental music for *The Tempest* on 4 January 1777.

On 7 November 1779 John Ashbridge recommended Linley for membership in the Royal Society of Musicians, to which he was admitted on 5 March 1780.

During his career at Drury Lane Linley wrote music for the following productions: *The Camp*, a musical entertainment with words attributed to his two sons-in-law, R. B. Sheridan and Richard Tickell, on 15 October 1778; orchestration and accompaniments to the airs for *The Beggar's Opera* on 29 January 1779; music for Sheridan's *Monody on the Death of Garrick* on 11 March 1779; music for the epithalamium in Hodson's *Zoraida* on 13 December 1779; additional songs to Sheridan's revision of Woodward's *Fortunatus* on 3 January 1780; a pastoral interlude to Lewis's *The Generous Impostor* on 22 November 1780; the score for Sheridan's *Robinson Crusoe* on 29 January 1781; a rondo for Andrews's *Dissipation* on 10 March 1781; the score for Tickell's alteration of *The Gentle Shepherd* on 29 October 1781; music for the epithalamium in *The Fair Circassian*, added to the production on 29 November 1781; the score and overture to Tickell's *The Carnival of Venice* on 13 December 1781; vocal and instrumental music to the revival of *Braganza* on 16 March 1782; music both new and partly compiled, for King's *The Triumph of Mirth* on 26 December 1782; the overture, new airs, and accompaniments to Lonsdale's *The Spanish Rivals* on 4 November 1784; additions to the music of Purcell and Arne for an alteration, probably by J. P. Kemble, of Dryden's *King Arthur*, called *Arthur and Emmeline*, on 22 November 1784; music new and compiled for Cobb's *The Strangers at Home* on 8 December 1785. Linley also provided music, compiled and composed, for Cobb and King's *Hurly-Burley; or, The Fairy of the Well* on 26 December 1785; a song "For tenderness form'd," adapted from "Saper bramate" in Paisiello's *Il Barbiere di Siviglia*, introduced by Mrs Crouch in the character of Miss Alton in the premiere of

Burgoyne's *The Heiress* on 14 January 1786, and sung in all subsequent performances; adaptations of Grétry's music for Burgoyne's *Richard Coeur de Lion*, taken from Sedaine, on 24 October 1786; the overture and accompaniments for Cobb's *Love in the East* on 25 February 1788; orchestrations of Kelly's music for Kemble's adaptation of *The Tempest* on 13 October 1789; a song in Cobb's *The Haunted Tower* on 24 November 1789; two songs in *Cymon* on 31 December 1791; a song in *The Mariners* on 10 May 1793; and accompaniments to *Macbeth* on 21 April 1794 (the inaugural production at the new Drury Lane Theatre). Linley also composed a number of specialty songs; these were often introduced in scenes of plays by his pupils, Mrs Crouch, Miss Hagley, Dignum, and others.

In 1789 the Linleys moved from Norfolk Street to a house at No 11, Southampton Street (a house on the east side, pulled down in 1890). Linley passed the last years of his life suffering physical ailments, real and imagined. He traveled about to Bath, Exeter, Brighton, Margate, and other resorts but found few lasting pleasures. He suffered from rheumatism, excruciating headaches, and deep sorrow over the premature deaths of his promising children: Thomas in 1778, Samuel in 1781, Maria in 1784, Mary Tickell in 1787, and Elizabeth Ann Sheridan in 1792. His mind became unsteady in the last days before his death at his Southampton Street house on 19 November 1795. He was buried on 28 November in Wells Cathedral, beside his daughters and his grandchild, Mary Sheridan. A memorial tablet was placed by his son William in the nave but was later transferred to the cloister.

The bequests in his will, drawn on 12 August 1788, deny the rumour that Linley was ruined financially by the necessity to support the extravagance of his son-in-law's management. Bequests of £100 were made to his grandson Thomas Sheridan, his granddaughter Elizabeth Tickell, and his daughter Jane Linley. To his daughter Elizabeth Ann Sheridan he left his harpsichord, musical books and manuscripts; and to his sons Ozias and William he distributed equally the remainder of his musical instruments and materials. To R. B. Sheridan he bequeathed the picture of Elizabeth and of Mary Tickell. He gave all other pictures, plate, linen, glass, china, and household goods that "shall be in my Dwelling House in Town at the time of my Decease unto my Dear Wife Mary Linley." His estate at Didmarton went to Ozias, with provisions for dividing it up should Ozias die before he reached 21. In a complex tangle of legal language he arranged for a provision of £300 per year for his wife and lesser amounts for Elizabeth, Ozias, William, and Jane, and for Richard and Samuel Tickell. (Mrs. Sheridan's portion lapsed, she having died in the lifetime of the testator.) He requested that his Drury Lane shares be kept in the family, or sold only to members of the family, as long as possible. Income from those shares was listed as £500 per year, though the family had difficulties obtaining the money from Sheridan, and consequently were often in distress. Other incomes from rents and stocks were specified. The will was proved at London on 1 April 1796 by R. B. Sheridan, to whom administration was granted, with reservation of the like grant to Mary Linley, who actually possessed herself of the assets and rents.

The baptisms of 12 children of Thomas and Mary Linley were registered at Bath:

George Frederick Linley was baptized at the Abbey on 12 March 1753. He died in infancy.

Elizabeth Ann Linley, born at Bath on 7 September 1754, was baptized at St Michael's on 25 September 1754; she died at Bristol Hotwells on 28 June 1792 and was buried in Wells Cathedral. She is noticed in this dictionary as Mrs Richard B. Sheridan.

Thomas Linley was baptized at St James's on 11 June 1756 and drowned at Grimthorpe on 5 August 1778; he was buried at Edenham. His successful but brief career as a violinist and composer is noticed separately.

Mary Linley, born on 4 January 1758, was baptized at St James's on 10 February 1758. She married the public official and writer Richard Tickell and died on 27 July 1787 at the age of 29. Her musical career is noticed separately under her maiden name.

Thurston Linley was baptized at St James's on 15 May 1759 and was buried there on 13 May 1763.

Samuel Linley was baptized at St James's on 23 June 1760. Though musically talented, he became a midshipman. He died at London in December 1781.

William Carey Linley was brought to St James's on 8 September 1761, after having been privately baptized. He was probably the William Linley who was buried there on 9 October 1762.

Maria Linley was baptized at St James's on 10 October 1763. After a brief singing career at London she died at Bath on 5 September 1784. She is noticed separately.

Ozias Thurston Linley was baptized at the Abbey on 22 August 1765. He became an organist and composer and took holy orders. At the time of his death on 6 March 1831, at the age of 65, he was a fellow and organist of Dulwich College. He seems not to have performed in London.

Jane Nash Linley and Charlotte Linley, twins, were brought to St James's on 17 February 1768, after having been privately baptized. Charlotte died in early womanhood, about 1788. Jane who seems never to have performed in London, married Charles Ward, secretary of Drury Lane Theatre, and died in 1806.

William Linley was baptized at St James's on 27 February 1771. After serving in the East India Company, he became a composer at Drury Lane. He died in London on 6 May 1835. His career is noticed separately.

A list of Linley's published works appears in the *Catalogue of Printed Music in the British Museum*. In addition to his music for productions at Drury Lane, these published compositions include *Elegies for Three Voices, with an Accompaniment for a Harpsichord and Violincello* (c. 1770), *Twelve Ballads* (1780), and a number of songs. *The Posthumous Vocal Works of Mr. Linley and Mr. T. Linley, Consisting of Songs, Duetts, Cantatas, Madrigals and Glees*, in two volumes, were published by Mrs Linley about 1800. Some manuscripts for part-songs by Linley are in the British Library. His music for Sheridan's *Monody* on Garrick's death, never published, was called by Sainsbury "tenderly melodious, and pathetic in the highest degree."

Linley's style of composition, wrote Dr Burney, "seems to have been formed upon the melodies of our best old English masters." Burney described him as "a masterly performer on the harpsichord." Linley's music was distinguished for its simplicity of design and taste. Of his *Twelve Ballads*, Sainsbury wrote that "it is impossible to name any compositions, on so simple a construction, which unite so much pathos, spirit, and originality."

A portrait of Linley by Gainsborough was bequeathed by his son William to Dulwich College in 1835.

Linley, Mrs Thomas, Mary, née Johnson
1729–1820, wardrobe mistress.

Mary Johnson was born in 1729, if the memorial tablet in St Paul, Covent Garden, is correct in recording her age as 91 at the time of her death in 1820. She probably was a native of Wells or environs. It has been suggested that she came of clerical stock and perhaps was related to a clergyman named E. Johnson, who officiated at marriages in Wells Cathedral, but nothing is surely known of her antecedents. She was married on 11 May 1752 at Batheaston to the musician Thomas Linley, whose early activities were associated with Wells. At the time of her marriage she was about 23 years of age, some two years his senior.

While Thomas Linley was struggling to develop a musical career which eventually became very distinguished, Mrs Linley was busy caring for a total of 12 children born to them at Bath between 1753 and 1771. As the family

Yale Center for British Art

MARY LINLEY
by Lawrence

grew and prospered they moved by 1767 from lodgings in the Abbey Green to Orchard Street (near the new theatre built in 1750) and thence in the spring of 1772 to a fine new house in the Crescent.

When Linley acquired a share in Drury Lane Theatre in 1776, they moved to London, where he became director of music at that theatre and she took on the position of wardrobe mistress, with responsibilities for the storekeeping and inspecting of costumes. The Drury Lane account books record various payments to her for materials and services at least through 1800. Her salary seems to have been a constant £1 10*s.* per week during most of that period.

Just when she left active service at Drury Lane is not known, but it was not until some five years after the death of her husband in 1795. By his will Mrs Linley received £300 per year and some assets from property. A manuscript accounting now in the Library of the Society for Theatre Research indicates that she prospered, and in 1811, when the journal breaks off, her worth amounted to £9169. She continued to reside in their house at No 11, Southampton Street (having moved from Norfolk Street about 1789), employing at least two servants. Company was provided by several of her children who occupied the place from time to time. Her custom was to make a long visit to Bath for several months each summer.

Contemporary accounts reported her as "A shrewd worldly woman, and clever enough in her particular way." Despite her comfortable financial circumstances, Mrs Linley persisted in taking in lodgers, causing consternation to her family. She was especially parsimonious, it seems, in her control of the Drury Lane wardrobe. Bannister recalled that "from excess of economy, she had been known to abridge what she thought to be the too flowing robe of a tragic performer, to gain for herself the covering of a footstool, or the materials for a velvet pincushion."

In June 1819, at the age of 90, Mrs Linley wrote to a granddaughter that her eyes were beginning to fail her. She died at her house in Southampton Street on 18 January 1820 and was buried in the graveyard of St Paul, Covent Garden, where a tablet to her memory placed inside the church by her sons Ozias and William Linley gave her age as 91.

A portrait of Mrs Linley drawn in pencil by Thomas Lawrence is in the Yale Center for British Art. A portrait once attributed to Ozias Humphry but now identified as by James Lonsdale is in the Dulwich College Picture Gallery. It was exhibited by Lonsdale at the Royal Academy in 1820, the year of Mrs Linley's death. A portrait of her by James Oliver was listed in the Dulwich catalogue until 1892 but has since disappeared.

Linley, Thomas *1756–1778, violinist, composer.*

Thomas Linley, the third child and second son of the musician Thomas Linley (1733–1795) and his wife Mary, was born at Abbey Green, Bath, in May 1756; 7 May is the birthdate given by Gwilym Beechey in his article on Linley in the *Musical Quarterly* (January 1968), and 5 May is stated by *Grove's Dictionary* and a manuscript account of him in the British Library. He was baptized at St James's, Bath, on 11 June 1756.

By permission of the Governors of Dulwich Picture Gallery

THOMAS LINLEY, the younger

by Gainsborough

At a very early age Thomas showed marked powers on the violin. He exhibited "such early and strong passion for Music," wrote Matthew Cooke in his *Short Account of the Late Mr. Thomas Linley, Junior* (1812), that his father decided to fix him in the profession and he was, "by the tuition of his Parent, perfectly grounded in both Theory and Practice." The *Bath Journal* of 25 July 1763 announced that a concert for the benefit of Mr Linley would be given in Loggan's Room at the Bristol Hot Wells on 29 July, in which Master Linley, age seven, would sing with Linley and Higgins and play a solo concerto on the violin. About that time he was placed under Dr Boyce for five years, until the age of 12. He also seems to have been taught dancing by Aldridge, and on occasion he danced in performances at Bristol.

Young Linley's first London appearance was as Puck in Thomas Hull's masque *The Fairy Favour* at Covent Garden on 29 January 1767, when his sister Elizabeth also made her London debut. *Lloyd's Evening Post* of 3 February could not say enough "of the little boy, who plays the part of Puck; his singing, playing on the violin, and dancing the hornpipe, are all beyond expectation, and discover extraordinary abilities in one, who must be considered a child." The only movement of J. C. Bach's compositions for this masque that survives is the music for Linley's hornpipe, the keyboard arrangement of which was published. On 26 March, for his repeated performances in *The Fairy Favour*, "Mas. Lindley" was paid £20. In May, young Thomas played the violin and Elizabeth sang in a concert at Bath. Their father thanked the public in the *Bath Chronicle* of 14 May for "the great Honour and Encouragement his Children received," and he promised his constant study to promote their improvement. Other concert appearances at Bath followed.

During his apprenticeship to Boyce, Linley wrote music for the violin, including a set of six sonatas composed in 1768, one of which survives in manuscript in the royal collection. When his time with Boyce was over in 1768, he was sent to Florence, where he studied for three years with Nardini. There he met young Mozart in April 1770 and they became warm friends. Burney, who also met Linley in Florence in September 1770, wrote that "The Tommasino," as Linley was called, and Mozart "are talked of all over Italy, as the most promising geniuses of this age." Linley presumably wrote a piece called "La Settima Sonata" while at Leghorn in 1769, but the music has not survived.

Linley returned to England in 1771 to become leader and solo player at his father's concerts in Bath and Bristol. He played first violin and offered a solo in a concert for Fischer's benefit at the Haymarket Theatre in London on 30 March 1772. That April he played for the oratorios at the New Assembly Rooms at Bath, and his sisters Elizabeth and Mary sang. At the Chester Festival in June 1772 Linley distinguished himself, reported the *Chester Courant*, "as one of the greatest masters of the Violin which this nation has produced." He performed at his own benefit concert at the King's Theatre in London on 12 April 1773. At the Three Choirs' Festival in Worcester that September his anthem "Lest God Arise," composed with orchestral accompaniments, was performed with great success. Of this large-scale piece by 17-year-old Linley, Beechey writes:

One of the most remarkable movements of the work is the chorus "Magnify him" which takes the form of a double fugue. . . . Further evidence of Linley's genius is provided in this anthem by the overture with which it begins—a typical French overture with an opening section of remarkable harmonic richness and a fugue very skilfully written where a fairly commonplace subject is worked out with great resource.

By 1775 the younger Thomas Linley had written about 20 concertos for the violin, many of which were performed in the London oratorios "to unbounded applause."

Linley assisted his father with the music for Sheridan's comic opera *The Duenna*, which opened at Covent Garden on 21 November 1775, providing the overture, several airs, a duet, and a trio. Though only the elder Linley's name appeared on the published score, manuscripts of the younger Linley's music for *The Duenna* are in the British Library (Acts I and II) and the Gresham Music Library, London Guildhall (Act III); the overture was published in 1775.

In March 1776 Linley played in the Drury Lane oratorios. On the twentieth of that month his "Lyric Ode On the Witches, Fairies, and Aerial Beings in Shakespeare" (set to a poem

Sterling and Francine Clark Art Institute, Williamstown, Massachusetts

ELIZABETH LINLEY SHERIDAN and THOMAS LINLEY, the younger

by Gainsborough

by "a young Gentleman of Oxford") was sung at Drury Lane by his sisters Mary and Maria under his direction; the ode drew very high praise from the *Morning Chronicle*, especially for his choruses. The aria "Ariel who sees thee now" for soprano solo with oboe obbligato and strings is, according to Beechey, "Linley's best piece of this kind and it is remarkable how in 1776 he was foreshadowing the kind of figurations that Mozart was to use in his oboe quartet of 1781." An autograph score of the *Lyric Ode* is in the Folger Shakespeare Library. Linley was first violinist for a performance of the *Messiah* at the Chapel of the Foundling Hospital on 2 April 1776 and for a performance of *Ruth* next night at the Chapel of the Lock Hospital. On 5 April 1776 Dr Burney wrote to Brigg Price Fontaine to recommend Linley as a violin teacher at Bath: "he is a Charming performer, and of a good School. . . . I therefore Enclose a Letter to him upon a Supposition that he is by this Time returned to Bath, after leading at the oratorio in Drury Lane & at 2 or three Hospitals."

When the elder Linley became a proprietor of Drury Lane with Sheridan in 1776, the family left Bath to settle in London and young Thomas became leader of the oratorios under his father's direction. He provided incidental music for *The Tempest* on 4 January 1777. His comic opera *The Cady of Bagdad*, to a text by Abraham Portal, was first produced on 19 February 1778 (after a postponement from its opening originally announced for 17 February). Manuscript scores of both works are in the British Library, and scores for *The Tempest* are also in The Royal College of Music. Linley's oratorio *The Song of Moses* was sung at Drury Lane to a text by John Hoadley on 12 March 1777 and again on 18 March 1778. The score survives in the royal collection. It was called in the press one of the "finest specimens of the Simple, Affecting, Grand and Sublime styles that ever was produced by the pen of a Musician." Sainsbury reports that Linley also wrote additional parts for the music in *Macbeth*, the score for which was destroyed in the Drury Lane fire of 1809.

Linley, described as single, was recommended by Parke in August 1777 for membership in the Royal Society of Musicians, but surviving records do not indicate whether or not he was admitted. His father had been admitted in March 1780.

Linley's impressive career was terminated by his death in a boating accident on the estate of the Duke of Ancaster at Grimsthorpe, in Lancashire, on 5 August 1778, while he was on a holiday with his sisters and several friends. When their sailboat was capsized by a sudden gust, others in the party saved themselves by clinging to the keel, but Linley foolishly attempted to reach shore. Though a good swimmer, he could not overcome the weight of clothes and boots and so drowned, at the age of 22. He was buried in the Duke's vault at Edenham Parish Church on 11 August 1778.

Linley's father, it is said, never recovered from the shock of his tragic loss. Elegies and tributes were printed in the press, and the *Morning Chronicle* on 11 August lamented the removal from the musical profession "of one of its principal ornaments." At Vienna, Mozart told Michael Kelly that Linley was a "true genius" and his loss to English music would be irreplaceable. An anonymous *Monody (after the manner of Milton's Lycidas) on the Death of Mr Linley* was published that year, and Elizabeth

Sheridan wrote some affecting verses, "On my brother's violin."

"In the masterly manner of his performances of the concertos of Handel and Geminiani," wrote Sainsbury, "no English violin player had ever excelled him, and in the neatness and delicacy of his execution he stood unrivalled." Linley composed in his short life an impressive amount of music of considerable merit. Only one of his violin concertos survives. Many of his miscellaneous pieces were published in *The Posthumous Works* of T. Linley senior and junior, in two volumes, 1800.

A portrait of the younger Thomas Linley painted by Thomas Gainsborough, about 1773 or 1774, was bequeathed by William Linley to Dulwich College in 1835. Another portrait by Gainsborough, about 1777 or 1778, was bought by Sedelmayer in the E. L. Tickell sale 3 May 1884 and was once at Vienna; it is now listed by E. K. Waterhouse as in the Liechtenstein Gallery. Gainsborough's portrait of Thomas and his sister Elizabeth, purchased from the painter by the 3rd Duke of Dorset, was at Knole Park for many years; it was sold to J. Pierpont Morgan, through Agnew's, in 1911; subsequently it was purchased from M. Knoedler and Co on 20 September 1943 by Robert Sterling Clark, and in 1955 it entered the Clark Art Institute in Williamstown, Massachusetts. A portrait of Thomas Linley by John Hoppner was owned by Paul Lebaudy of Paris in 1914; a photograph of it appeared in *The Masterpieces of Hoppner* (1912).

Linley, William 1771–1835, composer, director of music, author.

William Linley, the seventh son and the twelfth and youngest child of the musician Thomas Linley (1733–1795) and his wife Mary, was baptized at St James's, Bath, on 27 February 1771. When his parents moved to London to work at Drury Lane with the Sheridans, six-year-old William was left at Bath in the care of Mr and Mrs John Symmons. Both *Grove's Dictionary* and *The Dictionary of National Biography* state that he was sent for schooling first to St Paul's and then to Harrow. Sainsbury, however, claims that he was first at Harrow and then was removed to St Paul's School in order to benefit from his father's musical instruction in London. In any event, his matriculation at St Paul's occurred in February 1785,

Royal College of Music

WILLIAM LINLEY
after Lawrence

at the age of 14. He was taught singing and harpsichord by his father and counterpoint by Abel.

From childhood, wrote Sainsbury, William had been "distinguished for the accuracy of his ear, the sweetness of his voice, and the facility with which he remembered and played favorite passages of songs and lessons." Linley was an accomplished young singer, and his delivery of a Purcell song was the subject of Coleridge's sonnet, "While my young cheek retains its healthful hues." His precocity prompted his sister Mary (later Mrs Tickell) to predict (erroneously) that he would be the genius of the family.

William seems not originally to have been intended for music. His brother-in-law Richard Brinsley Sheridan assisted in obtaining an appointment for him with the Royal Fusileers under the Duke of Kent at Gibraltar, but Charles Fox offered a better opportunity in the form of a writership with the East India Company. Linley sailed for Madras in the spring of 1790. He was appointed assistant collector at Madura and Dindigal in 1791 and deputy secretary to the military board in 1793. Ill health forced his return to England in the summer of 1796.

In November 1795 his father left William some musical instruments and music rights (which he shared with his brother Ozias) and a one-fourth portion of his share in Drury Lane Theatre. Soon after, Sheridan granted William a proprietor's share valued at £300 and a salary of £7 per week as superintendent of the musical department for the term of three years, during which period he was also to receive two per cent of the net profits. That arrangement was reported by Charles Ward, secretary to the Drury Lane proprietors and husband of William's sister Jane, on a document dated 1 June 1808 (now in the British Library).

While directing the musical department at Drury Lane, Linley brought out three pieces of his own composition. *Harlequin Captive; or, The Magick*, a pantomime with scenery by Greenwood, opened on 18 January 1796 and was performed 37 times that season and four the next, a run which would seem to deny the statement in Grove and *The Dictionary of National Biography* that the piece was unsuccessful. On 22 January 1796 the Drury Lane treasurer paid Linley £25 on account for the music. A manuscript of the full score, without libretto, is in the Gresham Library at London Guildhall. His comic opera *The Honeymoon*, with Michael Kelly in the leading role, opened on 7 January 1797 but failed and was not repeated. Both words and music seem to have been by Linley. The songs in *The Honeymoon* are in the Larpent manuscripts at the Huntington Library and also were published in 1797.

On 16 November 1799 his musical entertainment *The Pavilion* had its premiere and was repeated 18 November. It was announced on 20 November that "The Author of *The Pavilion*, has withdrawn it for the present to make such alterations as he hopes may render it an Entertainment better entitled to their approbation." It was brought back in altered form as *The Ring; or, Love Me for Myself* on 21 January 1800. In his *Dramatic Censor* of that date Dutton claimed the piece was hissed from beginning to end, despite the claque of relatives who were there to support it, and he attacked Linley at length for daring to rewrite, with the addition of two new songs, the previously damned musical. *The Ring* was not repeated.

A manuscript full score of *The Pavilion* is in the British Library. Both versions are in the Larpent collection and both were published, *The Pavilion* in 1799 and *The Ring* in 1800. *The Biographia Dramatica* (1812) thought that as a composer William "possesses much of his father's taste and melody; but as a dramatist he has had no success." Linley also composed incidental music and songs for Ireland's Shakespearean hoax, *Vortigern*, on 2 April 1796 (songs published 1796). One of his airs was introduced in *Hamlet* by Mrs Jordan, as Ophelia, on 29 April 1796. He provided an overture and some new music for Franklin's musical interlude *A Trip to the Nore* on 9 November 1797 (the music was published in 1797).

In 1800 Linley returned to Madras; in 1801 he became provincial paymaster at Vellore and in 1805 sub-treasurer and mint-master at the presidency, Fort St George.

Linley returned from India in 1806 with a financial competency which allowed him to devote himself to composing and writing. He was a member of the Catch Club and Glee Club, the Concentores Sodales, and, from 1809 until his death, the Madrigal Society. On 17 February 1810 he was elected to the Sublime Society of Beefsteaks. That year his name, with his address at Southampton Court, Covent Garden, appeared on the list of the subscribers to the rebuilding of Drury Lane Theatre. His "At the dread hour" won the Glee Club prize in 1821, and his words for a requiem in memory of Samuel Webbe were set to music. Many of Linley's anthems were performed at Bath Abbey and St Margaret's Chapel, Bath; he was a joint proprietor of the latter.

Among his literary efforts were two novels and a biography: *Forbidden Apartments*, 2 vols (1800); *The Adventures of Ralpy Roybridge*, 4 vols (1809); and *Charles Leftley's Life and Writings, together with Poems by W. Linley* (1814). He wrote a rhymed epitaph for the monument to his father and several sisters in Wells Cathedral, the text of which may be found in W. Phelps's *The History of the Antiquities of Somersetshire* (1839), II, 86–87; and his verses on the death of Elizabeth Linley Sheridan were printed in Moore's *Life of . . . Sheridan* (1825). A manuscript address he wrote for Drury Lane Theatre is in the British Library.

Some of Linley's activities during the last 18 months of his life are recorded in his diary, now in the British Theatre Museum. He passed his leisure talking to old friends at the Garrick Club, visiting the theatres, and attending meetings of the Glee Club and the Choral Harmonists. Having survived all his brothers and sisters, he died in his chambers at Furnival's Inn, Holborn, on 6 May 1835, at the age of 64, and was buried at St Paul, Covent Garden. His niece Elizabeth Tickell erected a memorial tablet in that church which reads, in part, "The last of a family endowed with genius. He delighted in cultivating his own/And in rewarding that of others. His religious feelings were humble and sincere."

Evidently William Linley never married, though as a young man he had been "extremely susceptible . . . always in love with some charming lady." In a long will drawn on 17 January 1832, with several codicils, and proved at London on 10 June 1835, he left most of his substantial estate to his nieces Elizabeth Ann Tickell and Mary Esther Ward. The bequests to them included all his musical instruments, books, manuscripts, household goods, the leasehold house at the Fountain Buildings in Bath, his interest in St Margaret's Chapel, and his lands and farm at Didmarton, called Oldbury (which he had inherited from his brother Ozias Linley in 1831, Ozias having received that estate from their father in 1795).

To Elizabeth Ann Tickell, William gave the portrait of himself by Lonsdale, two drawings by her late brother Richard Brinsley Tickell, and a small painting and two pencil drawings of landscapes by Gainsborough, a cash gift of £1000, and his share in Drury Lane Theatre. To Mary Esther Ward he gave a crayon drawing by Thomas Lawrence of her mother Jane Linley Ward and a design for a church executed by her late brother Charles Thurston Ward. He bequeathed to Dulwich College portraits by Gainsborough of his father Thomas Linley and of his brothers Thomas and Samuel, a portrait of his sister Mary Tickell, as a child, painted by Humphry. In a codicil dated 6 May 1833, because of the death of Mary Esther Ward in that year, he gave the property previously bequeathed to her to Elizabeth Ann Tickell. Gifts were left to his young friends Ann (£200), Edward (£100) and William (£100), children of his old and dear late friend, the Reverend Edward Ward of Iver, Buckinghamshire; to young Edward and his wife Sophia Ward he left the crayon drawing by Lawrence of Jane Linley Ward and the two pencil drawings of landscapes by Gainsborough. In another codicil on 3 April 1835, the "Revd Edward Ward" having died, Linley passed his former bequest to him along to "my grandnephew Samuel Richard [Ward?]."

In addition to the compositions mentioned above, Linley published *Flights of Fancy*, a set of six glees (1799?); *Six Canzonets, Duets* (1800); *Eight Songs for Tenor or Soprano* (1809); *A Set of Canzonets* (1812?); *Shakespeare's Dramatic Songs*, 2 vols (1816); *Requiem* (1820); and *Eight Glees* (1830). The British Library holds 40 glees in manuscript, in two volumes. In 1863 B. St J. B. Joule owned some volumes of manuscript anthems by William Linley and his brother Ozias Thurston Linley. Extensive reviews of Linley's *Shakespeare's Dramatic Songs* were printed in 1816 in the *European Magazine*, the *Monthly Review*, and *Ackerman's Repository*.

A portrait of William Linley as a boy, by Thomas Lawrence, was exhibited at the Royal Academy in 1789, and was bequeathed by the sitter to the Dulwich College Picture Gallery. A copy, after Lawrence, is at the Royal College of Music. An engraving of the Lawrence portrait by T. Lupton was published in 1840. A portrait by James Lonsdale of Linley was bequeathed in his will to his niece Elizabeth Ann Tickell. The present location of the original is unknown; it was engraved by Sherlock and published as frontispiece to Linley's *Eight Glees* (1830). A portrait called "W. Linley, Esq." was exhibited by James Oliver at the Royal Academy in 1810 (No 179); that picture may be the one by Oliver now in the Dulwich College Picture Gallery and tentatively called the Reverend Ozias Linley by Peter Murray, author of the latest catalogue. A late eighteenth-century portrait of a boy standing beside a keyboard instrument is reproduced in *Country Life* for 26 May 1960, with the suggestion by the editor that it may be of William Linley. Indeed, the subject bears a resemblance to the young Linley in Lawrence's portrait. According to J. Frye Bourne, of Sidbury, near Sidmouth in Devon, the portrait was owned in 1960 by a mason in the neighborhood.,

Linnert, Claus Westenson [*fl.* 1720], *musician?*

Pepusch, in his list of participants at the Cannons concerts in 1720, included Claus Westenson Linnert at a quarterly salary of £7 10s. Presumably Linnert was a musician.

Linnet, Mr [*fl.* 1734–1760], *actor, manager.*

On 24 August 1734 at the Fielding-Oates booth at Bartholomew Fair Mr Linnet played Bindover in *The Constant Lovers.* In view of his later activity in the provinces, it is likely that between 1734 and his next notices in London in 1740–41 he performed outside of London. With the Goodman's Fields troupe under Henry Giffard, Linnet acted Stanmore in *Oroonoko* on 20 October 1740 for his first appearance. During the rest of the season he appeared as Worthy in *The Recruiting Officer*, Lodovico in *Othello*, Feignwell in *A Bold Stroke for a Wife*, Tattle in *Love for Love*, Tinsel in *The Drummer*, Basset in *The Provok'd Husband*, Clincher Junior in *The Constant Couple*, Jaques in *Love Makes a Man*, Duretête in *The Inconstant*, Sussex in *Lady Jane Gray*, and Story in *The Committee.*

The *Bath Journal* on 27 February 1749 noted that "Mr Linnett's Company of Comedians open'd at Chippenham last Thursday with the Tragedy of Cato, to the general Satisfaction of the Audience, who allow'd the Performance surpass'd their Expectation; and that the Roman Habits were not inferior to those at the Theatres in London." About 1746 (*recte* c. 1750), according to *The Theatric Tourist*, "an itinerant troop, commanded by Mr. LINNETT, performed in a newly erected theatre in *Kingsmead Street* [in Bath]." Sybil Rosenfeld in her *Strolling Players* notes that Colley Cibber's daughter Charlotte Charke was with Linnet's troupe about that time, and in August 1750 Sarah Ward acted with Linnet's players.

Though we know of no specific roles for Linnet, he was doubtless acting regularly, and the benefit bills for the summer of 1750 name his wife as a member of the company. In his *Memoirs* Lee Lewes said that about 1760 he appeared for a benefit with Linnet's troupe at the Cross Keys, a public house in Chelsea. Lewis referred to Linnet at that time as an old man who, while at Hammersmith, had wished to apply to the Justice in Chelsea for permission to perform there. Inadvertently he delivered to the Justice a property letter used in *A Bold Stroke for a Wife*, advising the receiver he was about to be robbed. The Justice was ready to apprehend Linnet but discovered the truth of the matter and gave him permission to perform. Lewes said that among the towns Linnet regularly visited were Burford, Woodstock, and Abington—all near Oxford.

Linnet, Mr [*fl.* 1791–c. 1795], *actor.*

On 24 October 1791 at the Haymarket Theatre was presented a single performance of *Venice Preserv'd* with a Mr "Lennet" playing Renault. In Lysons's *Collectanea* at the Folger Shakespeare Library is a playbill for the Assembly Hall, Kentish Town, undated but placed with bills from September 1795. *The Orphan* was produced, with Mr "Linnett" playing Acasto and Mrs Linnet as Monimia. It is most likely that Linnet was the correct spelling of their name and that they were related to the Linnets who performed in the 1730s.

Linnet, Mrs [*fl.* 1740–1750], *actress.*

Mrs Linnet is known to have played three roles at the Goodman's Fields playhouse in 1740: Abigail in *The Drummer* on 30 October, Mrs Prim in *A Bold Stroke for a Wife* on 1 November, and Teresa in *The Spanish Fryar* on 22 November. Her husband was also in the company, and in the summer of 1750, when Linnet was leading a troupe at the theatre in Kingsmead Street, Bath, Mrs Linnet was with the group and shared a benefit with her husband.

Linnet, Mrs [*fl.* c. 1795], *actress.* See **LINNET, MR** [*fl.* 1791–c. 1795].

Linsey. *See* **LINDSEY**.

Linton. *See also* **LENTON**.

Linton, Mr [*fl.* 1798], *singer.*

A Linton Junior was a European in *Ramah Droog* from 12 to 20 November 1798. He was certainly not William Linton, who played an Indian in that work, and he was probably not John Linton, who was not noticed in any bills that season.

Linton, Master [*fl.* 1800–1815?], *singer, instrumentalist?*

Master Linton sang in the chorus of *Joanna* from 16 January to 7 February 1800 at Covent

LINTON

Garden. The accounts cited him once in March 1803, and the Linton mentioned there in 1803–4 and 1804–5 may have been Master Linton. From the summer of 1808 through the summer of 1810, during the summers only, a Linton played in the band at the Haymarket, but we have no way of knowing if he was our subject. The accounts also show payments of £1 5s. weekly to a Linton from 1811–12 through 1814–15.

Linton, Miss [fl. 1794], *singer*.

Doane's *Musical Directory* of 1794 listed Miss Linton as a singer who participated in the Handel Memorial Concerts at Westminster Abbey. She also sang at Drury Lane, according to the accounts at that playhouse; on 14 April 1794 she was paid £1 1s. for coach hire. She is not listed in *The London Stage*. One assumes she was a member of the Linton family of performers who were active during the late eighteenth century.

Linton, Charles *d. 1784, violinist, harpsichordist*.

Charles Linton played second violin in the Handel Memorial Concerts at Westminster Abbey and the Pantheon in May and June 1784. On 8 July he was set upon by footpads and killed. Linton was buried on 11 July and his widow Mary was granted administration of his estate on 22 July. An unidentified clipping in the Enthoven Collection hand-dated 18 August said,

Yesterday Henry Morgan was committed to Newgate by William Addington, Esq. charged, on his own confession; with feloniously assaulting Charles Linton on the highway, in the parish of St. Martin in the Fields, in the county of Middlesex, and taking from his person a gold watch, two guineas and a half, and one shilling, his property. He also stands further charged, on his own confession, with wilful murder of the said Charles Linton.

At Covent Garden Theatre on 28 September *Zara* was performed for the benefit of Linton's widow and children, and the members of the band, with whom he had played, "were all dressed in mourning, suited to the occasion, and are entitled," said the *Public Advertiser* two days later, "to their share of applause."

In his *Concert Room and Orchestra Anecdotes* in 1825 Thomas Busby reported that Linton's murderers (not just one, according to him) were executed. He then quoted a notice that had been published the day before Widow Linton's benefit:

Theatre Royal, Covent-Garden.
For the Benefit of Mrs. Linton, &c.

"The Widow," said Charity, whispering in my ear, "must have your mite; wait upon her with a guinea, and purchase a box ticket."

"You may have one for five shillings," observed Avarice, pulling me by the elbow.

My hand was in my pocket, and the guinea which was between my fingers, slipped out.

"Yes," said I, "she shall have my five shillings."

"Good heaven!" exclaimed Justice, "what are you about? Five shillings! If you pay but five shillings for going to the theatre, then you get more *value received* for your money."

"And I shall owe him no thanks," added Charity, laying her hand upon my heart and leading me on the way to the widow's house.

Taking the knocker in my left hand, my whole frame trembled. Looking round, I saw Avarice turn the corner of the street, and I found all the money in my pocket grasped in my hand.

"Is your mother at home, my dear?" said I, to a child who conducted me into the parlour.

"Yes," answered the infant, "but my father has not been at home for a great while; that is his harpsichord, and that is his violin. He used to play on them for me."

"Shall I play you a tune, my boy?" said I.

"No, Sir," continued the boy, "my Mother will not let them be touched; for, since my father went abroad, music makes her cry, and then we all cry."

I looked on the violin; it was unstrung. It was out of tune. Had the lyre of Orpheus sounded in mine ears, it could not have insinuated into my frame thrills of sensibility equal to what I felt.

"I hear my mother on the stairs," said the boy. I shook him by the hand, "Give her this," said I, and left the house. It rained; I called a coach, drove to a coffee-house, but, not having a farthing in my pocket, borrowed a shilling at the bar.

All the story needed to make it perfect for that age of "sensibility" was the news that the Widow Linton was pregnant—which she was.

Linton had been a member of the Royal Society of Musicians, and on 2 January 1785 the Governors of the organization were informed that Mrs Linton was delivered of a child on 18 December 1784. The Society allowed her 10s. monthly for the child and gave her a present of half a guinea for expenses during her lying-in. Covent Garden Theatre accepted her benefit tickets each spring from 1786 through 1800. On 2 November 1794 Mrs Linton attended the Royal Society board meeting and stated that her daughter Louisa would be 14 years old that month; she requested the Society's approval (which involved a payment) to apprentice her daughter. Approval was granted. Mrs Linton died near 6 January 1805, when the Society granted £5 to cover her funeral expenses.

Linton, John [*fl. 1786–1815*], *singer.*

In December 1786 Mr (John) Linton sang at the Pantheon. Doane's *Musical Directory* of 1794 listed John Linton as a bass who sang for the Portland Chapel Society and in the oratorios at Drury Lane Theatre and Westminster Abbey. He was also a subscriber to the New Musical Fund in 1794, 1805, and 1815. From at least 6 October 1796 to the end of the 1800–1801 season Linton sang at Covent Garden Theatre, his first mention in the bills citing him as an Irish Peasant in *Bantry Bay*. He was in the choruses of *Italian Villagers*, *Harlequin and Oberon*, *The Village Fete*, and *Joanna*, and was named as a Friar and Muleteer in *Raymond and Agnes*, a Servant in *The Iron Chest*, and an Infernal Spirit in *The Volcano*.

Linton, William *d. c. 1804?, singer, actor.*

William Linton sang bass in the Handel Memorial Concerts at Westminster Abbey and the Pantheon in May and June 1784, and in 1787–88 he was paid £6 6s. for singing that season for the Academy of Ancient Music. He sang in the chorus at the Haymarket Theatre as early as 11 August 1789, when he was in *The Battle of Hexham*. He seems not to have been mentioned in any Covent Garden bills in 1789–90, though his benefit tickets were admitted on 8 June 1790 at that house, so he may have been singing in the chorus. At the Haymarket in July and August 1790 he was in the chorus of Indians in *New Spain*. He repeated the same pattern in 1790–91 — serving in the Covent Garden chorus, apparently, and singing in *The Surrender of Calais* at the Haymarket for a few performances in July and August 1791.

Beginning with the 1791–92 season Linton was regularly cited in the company rosters and bills recorded in *The London Stage* to the end of the century, and he began receiving more specialized assignments in addition to relatively anonymous chorus work. He was seen at Covent Garden as a Shepherd in *A Peep behind the Curtain*, Ralph and Thomas in *The Woodman*, a Shipwright and a Skaiter in *Harlequin's Museum*, a Guide in *The Midnight Wanderers*, Belial in *Harlequin and Faustus*, the Landlord and a Fisherman in *The Travellers in Switzerland*, a Sea Officer in *Arrived at Portsmouth*, Jupiter in *Midas*, Eustace in *Windsor Castle*, Harry Paddington and Mat o' the Mint in *The Beggar's Opera*, a Servant and a Sailor in *Lock and Key*, a Lieutenant in *Harlequin and Oberon*, a Lawyer's Clerk in *Italian Villagers*, a Midshipman in *The Surrender of Trinidad*, a Bailiff in *Abroad and at Home*, a Fisherman, a Huntsman and Moriat in *The Round Tower*, a Chinese Magician in *Harlequin and Quixote*, Catch and a Fisherman in *Harlequin's Return*, Moggy in *Unanimity*, a Recruit in *The Magic Oak*, a Friar and a Muleteer in *Raymond and Agnes*, a Peasant in *The Mouth of the Nile*, a Farmer in *The Turnpike Gate*, a Demon in *The Volcano*, a Soldier and an Indian in *Ramah Droog*, a Sentinel and the Red Cross Knight in *The Social Songsters*.

Within some of the spectacle productions in which Linton participated were songs which were popular enough to be cited in the bills with the names of the singers, such as "To Arms! Britons strike home!" from *The Soldier's Festival*, "Hark! the Lark at Heaven's Gate sings" from *Cymbeline*, "God Save the King," which was added in December 1792 to *Harlequin's Museum*, "We be three poor Mariners" from *The Sailor's Festival*, or "Our Laws, Constitution and King" from *The Rendezvous*, which he sang with Incledon. Most of the time he sang in small groups or in the choruses.

At Covent Garden Linton was also in the oratorios, and Doane's *Musical Directory* of 1794 stated that he sang in the Handelian performances at Westminster Abbey. He also performed for the New Musical Fund, the Concert of the Academy of Ancient Music, the Portland Chapel Society, and in 1793 at the Oxford Meeting. Linton's address in 1794 was No 13, Cleveland Street, Marylebone, and his salary at Covent Garden was £2 weekly; that salary was up to £2 10s. by 1799–1800.

During the 1790s at the Haymarket, William Linton's chores were similar to those at Covent Garden: chorus singing for the most part, with occasional characters to play, among them a Bacchanal in *Comus*, a Robber in *The Battle of Hexham*, a Moor in *The Mountaineers*, a Sailor and a Servant in *Lock and Key*, a Sailor in *Inkle and Yarico*, a "Centinel" in *The Castle of Sorrento*, and a Negro Man in *Obi*. The *Authentic Memoirs of the Green Room* in 1799 said of William Linton: "This gentleman's name appears occasionally in the play-bills, in conjunction with Street, Lyons, Abbot, &c. As an actor he cannot be noticed." The *Thespian Dictionary* of 1805 stated that Linton had "died lately." The Covent Garden accounts listed a Linton in 1803–04 and 1804–5, but he may have been Master Linton.

The Minute Books of the Royal Society of Musicians cited a Mrs Linton as receiving donations at Christmas time from 1827 through 1837, though she may have been the widow of another Linton.

Liny. *See* LING.

Lion. *See* LEONI and LYON.

Liparotti, Mr [*fl.* 1796–1797], *scene painter.*

The scenery for two new ballets, *Flore et Zéphire* and *L'Heureux Naufrage*, presented at the King's Theatre on 7 July 1796, was by Liparotti. On 7 January 1797 the King's playbill noted that the coffee room under the gallery had been newly enlarged and decorated by Mr Liparotti.

Lipmann, Mr [*fl.* 1762], *performer?*

On 8 May 1762 at Drury Lane Mr Lipman and Master Leoni shared a benefit. Lipmann is not otherwise known, but the fact that he shared a benefit with only one other person suggests that he was a fairly important member of the company, presumably a performer.

Lipparini, Agostino [*fl.* 1791–1806?], *singer.*

Agostino Lipparini was the elder of two Lipparinis who sang in London in 1791 and 1792 and was the *primo buffo caricato* in the opera company at the Pantheon and Haymarket. The two men may have been brothers or, less likely, father and son. Agostino was usually cited as Lipparini Senior, but we take him to have been also the Lipparini cited with neither a Junior nor Senior after his name. His earliest notice in London was on 1 March 1791 at the Pantheon as Conte in *La bella pescatrice*. In May he sang Don Rospolone in *La molinarella*, and in December he was Don Polibio in *La pastorella nobile*. At the Haymarket beginning on 14 February 1792 he sang Clicerio in *La trame deluse*; then he was heard as Arsenio in *La locanda* and Don Polibio in *La discordia conjugale*. Perhaps he was the Lipparini who sang at the Hoftheatre in Vienna from 1804 to 1806.

Lipparini, Giuseppe [*fl.* 1791–1792], *singer.*

Giuseppe Lipparini, the younger of two singers of that name in London in the early 1790s, was the second *buffo* in the opera troupe at the Pantheon and the Haymarket Theatres. On 1 March 1791 and subsequent dates he sang Maccabruno in *La bella pescatrice* at the Pantheon; there on 14 May he was Don Luigino in *La molinarella*; and on 17 December 1791 he sang Don Astianatte in *La pastorella nobile*. When the company moved to the Haymarket Giuseppe sang Don Gerundio in *La discordia conjugale*, beginning 31 March 1792.

Lippie. *See* LEPPIE.

Lippington, John [*fl.* 1672–1673], *scenekeeper.*

The London Stage lists John Lippington as a King's Company scenekeeper at their temporary home in Lincoln's Inn Fields in 1672–73. The Lord Chamberlain's accounts cited Lippington on 14 May 1673.

Lipyert, Mr [*fl.* 1757], *hand bell ringer.*

The *Public Advertiser* on 21 September 1757 noted that one could enjoy "the most singular kind of diversion on twelve Hand Bells by Mr. Lipyert" at Sadler's Wells, Islington.

Li Rich. *See* LA RICH.

Lisle. *See also* DE LISLE.

Lisle, Jeremiah *d.* 1681?, *actor.*

Jeremiah Lisle was a member of the Duke's Company at the Lincoln's Inn Fields playhouse in 1669–70 but not a very faithful one. On 26 April 1670 the Lord Chamberlain ordered Lisle to be apprehended for not attending his duties at the theatre. After that Lisle went to Dublin. A Smock Alley Theatre promptbook for *Julius Caesar*, dating sometime between 1670 and 1676, lists Lisle as the Cobler. Clark in *The Early Irish Stage* has Lisle continuing his activity in Dublin until 1688, but Allan Stevenson in *Shakespeare Quarterly* in 1955 cited the registers of St John, Dublin, as showing the burial of Jeremiah Lisle on 14 July (*recte*: June) 1681. That could have been another Jeremiah Lisle, but the church is in the vicinity of the Smock Alley Theatre, and Stevenson thinks it unlikely that two men of that name would have been in the parish. The register entry does not indicate that the burial was a child, though it could have been of an elder Jeremiah Lisle—the actor's father, perhaps.

In any case, the death date needs to be questioned on the grounds of two pieces of evidence that would suggest that Lisle may have been alive and acting in 1684 and 1685. A cropped manuscript cast in a copy of *The Night Walker* seems to have Lisle's name down for the part of Toby; Clark, unaware of the parish register information, accepted the cast as dating 1684–85 in Dublin. Stevenson, accepting Lisle's death date as 1681, determined that the cast had to belong to a period before then. Neither considered the evidence in the 1684 edition of *The Northern Lass*, which has Jeremiah Lisle, fully spelled out, down for the role of Pate. *The London Stage* suggested that the name was an error for James Carlisle, since Lisle was supposed to have been in Dublin in 1684 and Carlisle was with the Drury Lane troupe that revived the play in mid-March 1684; following their lead we have suggested in volume III the possibility of Carlisle's having taken the part. Without more evidence perhaps no final determination can be made.

Lisley, Mrs. *See* BARSANTI, JANE.

Lislie. *See* LESLIE.

Litchfield, John *1774–1858, actor, author, editor.*

John Litchfield, born in 1774, by the 1790s was a clerk to the Privy Council and author of some prologues and epilogues. The Elizabeth Isabella Litchfield of the parish of St Paul, Covent Garden, who married the musician John Sowerby at that church on 22 December 1781, was probably his sister. On 7 September 1793, billed as "A Young Gentleman," Litchfield made his stage debut at Richmond as Richard III, probably as an amateur. That night his friend, the young Charles Mathews, was also making his debut, in the character of Richmond. Several months later, on 23 December 1793, again advertised as a "Gentleman," Litchfield played Richard at the Haymarket Theatre. The *European Magazine* of January 1794 gave his name and identified him as the person who had acted the character recently at Richmond. (The "Notitia Dramatica" erroneously identified Litchfield as the younger Charles Holland, who was at that time acting at Bath and Bristol.)

Evidently Litchfield's main professional interests were in his clerkship and the editorial work he did for various journals, including the *Monthly Mirror*. In the *Dramatic Mirror* Gilliland described him as "a gentleman well known and admired in the literary world, and much esteemed as a private character." At St Martin-in-the-Fields on 14 September 1796 he married the 19-year-old actress Harriett Sylvester Hay, who enjoyed a useful career in London, acting as Mrs Litchfield, until 1807. During all that time the couple lived at No 36, Bedford Street, Covent Garden.

Litchfield made several other attempts on the stage. On 9 February 1797, again advertised as a "Gentleman," he acted King Edward to his wife's Lady Elizabeth Gray (she was billed only as a "Lady") at the Haymarket for Mrs Yates's benefit. The Litchfields were identified in the *Morning Chronicle* of 10 February 1797. That summer he joined his wife in the Richmond company for one night only, 15 September, to act Glenalvon to her Lady Randolph in *Douglas*. He was advertised as making his fifth appearance at Richmond and his sixth on any stage, so several of his performances have gone unrecorded. No stage appearance by him after 15 September 1797 is known to us.

Litchfield and his wife had been married for almost 58 years by the time of her death on 11 January 1854 at the age of 77. Litchfield died at Mountfield House, the home of his son-in-law, in Harrow Road, in May 1858 at the age of 84. His will, for an estate valued under £450, was proved at London on 10 July 1858

LITCHFIELD

by his daughter Harriet Sarah Dibden Abraham, wife of Henry Robert Abraham of Mountfield House. Information on Litchfield's children will be found in his wife's notice.

Litchfield, Mrs John, Harriett, née Sylvester Hay 1777–1854, actress.

Mrs Litchfield, according to her contemporary biographical notices, was born on 4 March 1777. She was the daughter of John Sylvester Hay, the only son of the vicar of Maldon in Essex. Her father was the surgeon of the *Nassau*, East Indiaman, and afterward the chief surgeon of the Royal Hospital, Calcutta, where he died at the age of 37 from a fever. *The Dictionary of National Biography* suggests the possibility that he was the John Hay, proprietor and printer of the *Calcutta Gazette* and proprietor of the Calcutta theatre, who died at Fort William in April 1787. At the time of her father's death, Harriett was about nine years old, and presumably she had already developed her interest in theatricals.

Little is known of her early life and schooling until 15 September 1792, when, advertised as "A Young Lady" (she was 15), she acted Julia in *The Surrender of Calais* at Richmond. Her success and the applause of Mrs Jordan, a spectator that evening, encouraged her to play several other characters that late summer, and she joined Mrs Esten's Edinburgh company early in 1793. Among the roles she performed on the stage of the Theatre Royal, Shakespeare Square, in that northern city were Serina in *The Orphan* and Charlotte in *Love à-la-Mode* on 20 July 1793, at which time she was billed as Miss Sylvester, the family name she adopted for her earliest efforts. During her stay in Scotland, which lasted less than a year, she enjoyed great favor in Glasgow and Dumfries, receiving a letter from Robert Burns on behalf of the people of Dumfries, inviting her to return. Next she joined Francis Aickin's summer company at Liverpool, where the manager, according to the *Monthly Mirror* of November 1802, had "promised to afford her every proper engagement, and her salary was fixed as high as any other performer's in the company." But Aickin, it seems, reneged on his commitment and treated her in a manner "unmanly and unjust." Her only two roles of any consequence were Sophia in *The Road to Ruin* and Edward in *Every One Has His Fault*, opportunities arranged, it seems, by the kindness of Mattocks, the Liverpool theatre's treasurer.

Advertised as "A Young Lady," she made her first appearance at Covent Garden Theatre as Edward in *Every One Has His Fault* on 27 May 1796, for the benefit of Mrs Davenport, with whom she had become acquainted at Liverpool. Harriett was identified by the *Monthly Mirror*:

A young lady, who under the name of Sylvester had played with great *eclat* in the theatres of Richmond, Liverpool, and Scotland, performed the part of Edward. The male habit became her much; her voice possesses uncommon sweetness and flexibility; her action, allowing for the timidity of a stranger, was unembarrassed; her manner playful and

Harvard Theatre Collection

HARRIETT LITCHFIELD, as Susan
by de Wilde

interesting; and her conception of the character just. . . . The audience received her with great applause."

The St Paul, Covent Garden, registers record that "John Litchfield of this Parish, a Bachelor, and Harriet Sylvester Hay, of the same, Spinster," were married at St Martin-in-the-Fields on 14 September 1796 (and not in 1794 as stated by *The Dictionary of National Biography*). One of the witnesses was Sarah Sylvester Hay, who was the bride's mother or sister. John Litchfield was a clerk to the Privy Council and author of some prologues and epilogues, who also acted several times at Richmond and London in the 1790s. The 19-year-old Mrs Litchfield settled with her husband at No 36, Bedford Street, Covent Garden. A child, the first of at least six, was born on 30 September 1796 and christened Thomas Litchfield at St Paul, Covent Garden, on 21 November 1796.

About five months later, for Mrs Yates's benefit, Mrs Litchfield reappeared on the London stage, at the Haymarket Theatre on 9 February 1797, as Lady Elizabeth Gray in *The Earl of Warwick*, with her husband as King Edward. That evening she also played Little Pickle in *The Spoil'd Child*. They were advertised in the bills as a Gentleman and a Lady, but the *Morning Chronicle* of 10 February 1797 identified them as the Litchfields.

Advertised as a young lady making her second appearance on that stage, she again acted Edward on 17 May 1797, for Munden's benefit at Covent Garden. For Mrs Davenport's benefit on 12 June 1797, again billed as a young lady, Mrs Litchfield appeared at Covent Garden as Julia in *The Rivals*. Having obtained an engagement from Harris, the Covent Garden manager, for the ensuing fall, Mrs Litchfield went for seasoning to play in the summer of 1797 with Haymes's company at Richmond, where she enjoyed success, acting Lady Randolph in *Douglas* (while her husband acted Glenalvon) for her benefit on 15 September. Though the company also performed once a week at Kingston, the *Monthly Mirror* of July 1797 reported that "Mrs. Litchfield having made it a part of her agreement, that she should not go out of Richmond to play, does not act on those occasions."

At a salary of £3 per week, Mrs Litchfield made her first appearance as a regular member of the Covent Garden Company as Marianne in *The Dramatist* on 20 September 1797, a role the management seems to have imposed upon her at very short notice. Next she played Catalina in *The Castle of Andalusia* on 29 September, followed in October by Lady Anne in *Richard III*, Dimity in *Three Weeks after Marriage*, and Cubba in *The Irishman in London*. The October 1797 issue of the *Monthly Mirror*, in a very enthusiastic criticism perhaps written by John Litchfield, who was for a time an editor of that journal, reviewed her characters to date and declared that "Mrs Litchfield, if we exclude scientific singing, has more *versatility* than any actress we ever saw." As for her voice, thought the critic, "there are few women so highly favoured," for every gradation of tone "is perfect, combining strength and melody, it is equal to any task which the theatre (large and extensive as it is) can impose. It is suited to the firmness of declamation, of the tenderness of pathos, and the burst of indignant passion." Her other characters that season were

Courtesy of the Garrick Club

HARRIETT LITCHFIELD
by Drummond

LITCHFIELD

Fringe in *The Agreeable Surprise*, Regan in *King Lear*, Ismene in *Mérope*, Dolly in *The Ghost*, Irene in *Barbarossa*, Urganda in *Cymon*, Betty Blackberry in *The Farmer*, and the Marchioness Merida in *The Child of Nature*. For her benefit shared with Hull and Waddy on 30 May 1798, she acted Moggy in *The Highland Reel* and Ascanio in *Disinterested Love*. Tickets could be had of her in James Street, Covent Garden. Her share of the receipts came to £60 17s. Between 4 January and 17 March 1798 she had not acted, for a second child was born on 12 March 1798 and christened Thomas Hill Litchfield at St Paul, Covent Garden, on 8 April 1798; it is likely that the earlier son named Thomas had died soon after his birth in 1796.

In 1798–99, her second season at Covent Garden (and now earning £4 per week), Mrs Litchfield added to her repertoire Miss Vortex in *A Cure for the Heart-Ache*, Emily in *Laugh When You Can*, Trusty in *The Provok'd Husband*, Lucy in *The Recruiting Officer*, Mrs Sneak in *The Mayor of Garratt*, Doll Tricsy in *The Tobacconist*, Lady Flourish in *Home and Abroad*, Parisatis in *Alexander the Great*, Judith in *The Iron Chest*, Winifred in *Where Is She?*, Susan in *Tell Truth and Shame the Devil*, Isabinda in *The Busy Body*, Rose in *Secrets Worth Knowing*, and Mrs Changeable in *The Jew and the Doctor*. For her benefit shared with Miss Mitchell on 31 May 1799, when tickets could be obtained from Mrs Litchfield at No 38, Bedford Street, Covent Garden, and the total gross receipts were £304, 15s. 6d., she performed Sophia in *The Lie of the Day*. On 15 October 1798 she had played Emilia in *Othello*, the role that proved to be her best. According to a report in the *Monthly Mirror* for July 1799, after the season 1798–99, Mrs Litchfield gave birth to a daughter, but we find no registration of baptism at St Paul, Covent Garden, the family's parish church.

Among the roles she added to her repertoire in 1799–1800, when her salary was raised to £5 per week, were Ruth in *The Honest Thieves*, Nottingham in *The Earl of Essex*, and Mary in *The Prisoner at Large*. When Miss Sims replaced her as Marianne in *The Dramatist* on 23 May 1800, Thomas Dutton, in his *Dramatic Censor* (1800), expressed the hope never to see Mrs Litchfield resume the role; and of Mrs Litchfield's playing of Emily in *Laugh When You Can* he observed that he could "discover no other claim she has to the part than that of *preoccupancy*."

In the summer of 1800 Mrs Litchfield played for Macready at Birmingham, enjoying favor in tragic roles. Then she returned to Covent Garden for 1800–1801, again at £5 per week, for a season in which she emerged from relative obscurity by playing with great success Lady Macbeth with Cooke as Macbeth on 5 December 1800. The *Monthly Mirror*, whose critic in the issue of October 1797 had predicted greatness for Mrs Litchfield, was so delighted with her Lady Macbeth that he wrote in November 1802, somewhat enthusiastically:

A more extraordinary occurrence never happened in stage history, than the sudden announcement of an actress for one of the most arduous and important characters in Shakespeare, whose name was scarcely known to the most constant attendants at the theatre. The attempt was bold and hazardous, but her success in the character was complete, and she was immediately elevated to the highest honours of her profession.

That season Mrs Litchfield also distinguished herself as Emilia in *Othello* and respectably played Mrs Haller in *The Stranger* and Queen Elizabeth in *The Earl of Essex*. On April 1801 the sudden illness of Miss Murray left Mrs Litchfield only three hours' preparation time to fill in that night as Portia in *The Merchant of Venice*; that *Monthly Mirror* was delighted with her rescue, "and her execution . . . evinced a memory uncommonly retentive, together with a judgment correct and nervous." Despite some initial anxiety, she played the role "as if she had been matured in it." During the last half of the season she was again pregnant and delivered a daughter, who was christened Emily Mary Litchfield, at St Paul, Covent Garden, on 5 August 1801. The *Monthly Mirror* had reported the birth in June. But the parish baptismal register erroneously gives the date as 14 July 1801. On that night the bills list Mrs Litchfield as acting. It was a busy summer for her, for she was also engaged at Colman's Haymarket Theatre, where she was announced as making her first appearance on 14 July 1801 as Julia in *The Surrender of Calais*, a role she repeated on 18 July and 3 August. She acted Floranthe in *The Mountaineers* on 3 September.

Her success the previous season at Covent Garden won her renewed articles for 1801–2 at an advanced salary of £8 per week, rising to £9 and £10 in the two subsequent seasons. There she remained through 1805–6, her salary in 1804–5 being £10 and in her last season £12. She played few original characters during that period, among them Ottilia in Lewis's *Alfonso* on 15 January 1802 and Mrs Fermont in Morton's *School of Reform* on 15 January 1803. Some of the other roles in her repertoire included Mrs Beverley in *The Gamester*, Millwood in *The London Merchant*, Mrs Oakly in *The Jealous Wife*, the Queen in *Richard III*, Widow Brady in *The Irish Widow*, Andromache in *The Distrest Mother*, Statira in *The Rival Queens*, Zaphira in *Barbarossa*, Arpasia in *Tamerlane*, and Constance in Dr Valpy's adaptation of *King John* (for her benefit on 20 May 1803). In the summer of 1802 she had returned to Birmingham to play Ottilia, Hermione in *The Winter's Tale*, and some other roles, and then went to Cheltenham for ten nights, mostly in comic roles, including Widow Brady in *The Irish Widow*, "with the happiest effect."

A dispute with the management reputedly caused Mrs Litchfield to leave Covent Garden at the conclusion of the 1805–6 season. On 27 May 1806 she played Alicia in *Jane Shore* and spoke a farewell address from that stage. (Cooke was supposed to deliver Garrick's "Ode on Shakespeare" but was inebriated and incapable.) She went to the Haymarket in 1806–7, playing the Queen in *Hamlet*, Lady Caroline in *John Bull*, Susan in *Follies of a Day*, Elvira in *Pizarro*, and Leonora in *Lovers' Quarrels*. The summer of 1807 at the Haymarket was her final full London engagement. She acted at Bath for six nights in May 1810, when she was seen as Lady Clermont in *Adrian and Orilla* and in a one-scene monodrama by Lewis which had originally been written for her and acted once by her at Covent Garden on 22 March 1803. She returned to the Haymarket stage for Terry's benefit on 8 October 1812, when she played Emilia to Elliston's Othello, a performance which seems to have been her last.

Mrs Litchfield and her husband survived for another four decades, into the middle of the nineteenth century. In the Enthoven Collection are several letters from her: one to Ward in 1808 requested an engagement at Drury Lane; another in December 1818 thanked Elliston for free tickets to the Olympic and stated her family consisted of "Mr L, myself, my Daughter, and Miss Baker"; and a third, written in 1822, thanked someone at Drury Lane for putting her and her husband on the free list.

Mrs Litchfield died, probably at London, on 11 January 1854, at the age of 77. Her husband died at the house of his son-in-law, in Harrow Road, on 30 May 1858, at the age of 84. In addition to the four children cited above (Thomas born in 1796, Thomas Hill born in 1798, an unknown daughter born in 1799, and Emilia Mary born in 1801 of whom only the last-named was alive in November 1802, according to the *Monthly Mirror* of that month), the Litchfields had at least three other children: John George Litchfield, born on 15 November 1803 and christened at St Paul, Covent Garden, on 14 September 1804; and Henry Carr Litchfield and Harriet Sarah Dibden Litchfield, twins born on 15 April 1805 and christened at the same church on 5 May 1805. Harriet Sarah later married Henry Robert Abraham of Mountfield House, Harrow Road, and proved her father's will on 10 July 1858. The *Monthly Mirror* in 1802 described Mrs Litchfield as a "cheerful and unaffected" woman who enjoyed "the blessing of domestic happiness." Until her death, the Litchfields had been married for almost 58 years.

Her good judgment and excellent voice compensated for a disadvantageous figure and allowed Mrs Litchfield to be a most respectable, if not distinguished, actress. Her *forte* was tragedy. As Andromache, particularly when pleading before Pyrrhus to save her infant Astyanax, her most powerful performance attracted great applause. Her Emilia was, by Gilliland's testimony, "a very finished piece of acting." She was excellent in "irascible" characters and could play comic roles with success, as she did with Mrs Oakly and was warmly applauded.

Portraits of Mrs Litchfield include:

1. By Samuel Drummond. Probably the portrait the artist exhibited at the Royal Academy in 1799. In the Garrick Club (No 362), presented by John Poole in 1838.

2. Engraved portrait by W. Ridley, after C. Allingham. Plate to the *Monthly Mirror*, 1802.

3. Engraved portrait by W. Say, after G. H. Harlow. Published by the engraver, 1816.

4. As Belvidera in *Venice Preserv'd*. Engraving by Chapman, after Moses. Plate to *British Drama*, 1817.
5. As Imoinda in *Oroonoko*. By unknown engraver. Plate to *British Drama*, 1807.
6. As Ophelia in *Hamlet*. By Samuel De Wilde. Listed in the *Mathews Collection Catalogue* (No 297), but not in the Garrick Club.
7. As Susan in *The Follies of the Day*. Watercolor by Samuel De Wilde. In the Harvard Theatre Collection.
8. As Zara in *The Mourning Bride*. By unknown engraver. Plate to *British Drama*, 1817.

Little, Mr [*fl.* 1731–1737], *gallery boxkeeper.*

Mr Little was a gallery boxkeeper at Drury Lane from at least 17 May 1731, when he was first mentioned for a benefit (shared with one other), and 27 May 1737, when his benefit tickets were accepted. He was named in benefit bills most years, and he had a special benefit at the Haymarket Theatre on 29 July 1736, saying in his bill that he hoped "to have the Honour of his Brethren the Free Masons."

Little, Master [*fl.* 1798–1800], *dancer, singer.*

Master Little danced as a Swabian Peasant in *Albert and Adelaide*, a musical play which opened at Covent Garden Theatre on 11 December 1798 and ran for 18 performances that season. At the same theatre he sang in the chorus of *Joanna* on 16 January 1800 and 13 other times by May. He was no doubt related to Matthew Little, a vocalist in the same pieces, and to James Little, an oratorio performer.

"Little Ben" [*fl.* 1779], *dancer.*

At Jobson's puppet booth at Bartholomew Fair in 1779 "Little Ben" danced a hornpipe, possibly on the puppet stage. Master Jobson also offered a hornpipe at that performance, and one wonders if the two boys were one and the same.

"Little Bird of Paradise." *See* MAHON, MRS GILBERT.

"Little Child." *See* HANDY, MARY ANN.

"Little Devil, The." *See* REDIGÉ, PAULO; SMITH, GEORGE; SULLY, MATTHEW; SUTTON, GILES.

"Little Devil, The Spanish." *See* "SPANISH LITTLE DEVIL, THE."

"Little English Devil, The." *See* SULLY, MATTHEW.

"Little Flying Mercury, The" *b.* 1784?, *equestrian.*

"The Little Flying Mercury" displayed his equestrian abilities in a yard in back of the Angel in Borough Walls, Bristol, on 26 April 1788 and the days that followed. He was then a member of Handy's troupe; when he appeared on 22 March 1790 at the "NEW COVERED IN *RIDING-SCHOOL*" behind the Full Moon in Stoke's Croft, Bristol, he was with Handy and Franklin's company. A benefit was held for the boy on 18 October 1790. At Astley's Amphitheatre in London on 17 July 1792 he performed equestrian exercises with Mr Davis, and on 15 June 1793 he was listed under the nickname "Equestrian Mercury" as a member of Astley's troupe. That list described him as nine years of age, and if he was the lad who rode in Bristol in 1788, he began as quite a tiny mite. Active about the same time was Master Crossman, but he was already performing in 1784. John Crossman was also called the "Equestrian Mercury" in a Bristol advertisement in 1799.

"Little French Boy, The." *See* [MICHEL, MASTER?]

"Little German Man, The" [*fl.* 1726], *conjurer.*

At Sherwin's booth at Bartholomew Fair on 24 August 1726 "The Little German Man" did dexterities.

"Little Girl, The." *See* BRACEGIRDLE, ANNE.

Little, James [*fl.* 1794], *singer.*

In 1794 James Little was listed in Doane's *Musical Directory* as a singer in the Drury Lane oratorios, the Concerts of the Academy of Ancient Music, and St Paul's choir. His address,

No 8, Brown's Buildings, St Mary Axe, was the same as that of Matthew Little, also a singer.

Little, Matthew [*fl.* 1791–1802], *singer, actor.*

In 1794 Matthew Little was listed in Doane's *Musical Directory* as a member of the Choral Fund and an alto singer in the Concerts of the Academy of Ancient Music, the Handelian concerts at Westminster Abbey, and the oratorios and chorus at Covent Garden Theatre. His address, No 8, Brown's Buildings, St Mary Axe, was the same as that of James Little, also a singer.

No doubt Matthew Little was the Mr Little who shared in benefit tickets at Covent Garden on 9 June 1791. His name is in the bills of that theatre for chorus roles between 1792 and 1800 and at the Haymarket Theatre in the summers from 1791 to 1802. Among his assignments at Covent Garden were singing in *Harlequin's Museum* in 1792–93, *The Mysteries of the Castle* in 1794–95 and 1795–96, *Bantry Bay* in 1796–97, and *Ramah Droog*, *The Magic Oak*, and *Raymond and Agnes* in 1798–99. At the Haymarket he sang in the choruses of *The Surrender of Calais* in 1791 and 1792, *The Mountaineers* in 1794, *The Iron Chest* in 1796, *The Italian Monk* in 1797, *The Castle of Sorrento* and *Tars at Torbay* in 1799, and *Obi* and *What a Blunder* in 1800. The Master Little who performed with him at Covent Garden in *Albert and Adelaide* in 1798–99 and *Joanna* in 1799–1800 was probably related.

On 16 September 1802, Matthew Little, named a creditor, was granted administration of the estate of the late musician Thomas Bodley Francis.

"Little John." *See* RAY, JOHN.

Little John, Ann Maria [*fl.* 1739], *actress.*

Mrs Ann Maria Little John (*sic*) made her first appearance on any stage at Drury Lane on 1 February 1739 playing Indiana in *The Conscious Lovers*. On 4 May at her benefit she acted Angelina (as Mrs Littlejohn) in *Love Makes a Man* and told patrons that tickets could be had of her at Mr Wilson's in David Street near Grosvenor Square.

"Little King Oberon." *See* SWINEY, OWEN.

"Little Learned Horse, The." *See* "LEARNED HORSE, THE LITTLE MILITARY."

"Little Napoleon of Wych Street." *See* ELLISTON, ROBERT WILLIAM.

"Little Pickle." *See* JORDAN, DOROTHY.

"Little Polander." *See also* GARMAN, MR.

"Little Polander, The" *b. 1686, dwarf.*

In 1746 at the New Wells, Clerkenwell, was exhibited "The Little Polander," a dwarf two feet, two inches tall, aged 60. He wore his beard after the fashion of his country, the advertisements said.

"Little Polander, The" [*fl.* 1765], *equilibrist.*

A person called "The Little Polander" performed as an equilibrist at Sadler's Wells on 20 June 1765.

"Little Spaniard, The" [*fl.* 1786], *rope vaulter.*

A person called "The Little Spaniard" performed feats of vaulting on the slack rope at Sadler's Wells on 9 October 1786.

"Little Summer General, The." *See* COLMAN, GEORGE [*fl.* 1732–1794].

"Little Swiss, The" *b. c. 1744, dancer.*

Described in the bills as not five years old and a scholar to Mathews, a boy called "The Little Swiss" danced a hornpipe at Drury Lane Theatre on 7 April 1749. Probably he was the same five-year-old scholar to Mathews, unnamed, who had danced in *The Emperor of the Moon* at that theatre on 26 December 1748. "The Little Swiss" offered his hornpipe again on 14 April 1749 and several times in May. The following season he appeared often in his hornpipe and in *The Savoyard Travellers* and on 20 April 1750 performed the dance *The Black Joke*, one of the standbys of his mentor Mathews, with Miss Foulcade. In the summer of 1750 he danced at the Haymarket Theatre on 26 July. He continued as a specialty dancer at

Drury Lane each season through 1756–57, appearing frequently in *The Genii*, a popular entertainment devised by Henry Woodward, which had its first performance on 26 December 1752.

"Little Welchman." *See* HOPKINS, HOPKINS.

"Little Woman From Geneva, The" [stage name of Mrs Anthony Joseph Dugee?] [*fl.* 1751–1753?], *strong woman.*

Latreille copied out an advertisement dated 19 December 1751 for a "concert" at the Haymarket Theatre by "The Little Woman from Geneva" who had just arrived in London:

1st she beats a red hot Iron, that is made crooked, straight with her naked feet. 2nd she puts her head on one chair and her feet on another in an equilibrium and suffers five or six men to stand upon her body, which after some time she flings off. 3rd An anvil is put on her body, on which men strike with large Hammers. 4th A stone of a hundred pounds weight put on her body and beat to pieces with a hammer. 5th she lies down on the ground and suffers a stone of 1500 pound weight to be laid on her Breasts in which posture she speaks to the Audience and drinks a glass of Wine. . . . Lastly she lifts an anvil of 200 pound weight from the ground by her own hair.

That advertisement bears a remarkable resemblance to one dated 17 September 1753 in the New York *Mercury*:

The FEMALE SAMPSON.
Her performances are as follows: I. She lies with her Body extended between two Chairs, and bears an Anvil of 300 *lb.* on her Breast, and will suffer two men to strike on it with Sledge-Hammers. II. She will bear six Men to stand on her Breast, lying in the same position. III. She will lift the above Anvil by the Hair of her Head. IV. She will suffer a Stone of 700 *lb.* to lye on her Breast, and throw it off six Feet from her. V. She bear [*sic*] a bar of Iron to be broken on her Breast.

The woman who performed those feats in America was Mrs Dugee, the wife of Anthony Joseph Dugee. She prefaced her advertisements by saying that she had entertained the Princess Dowager of Wales and the royal family of Great Britain. There is certainly a very good chance that she and the Little Woman from Geneva were the same person.

If Mrs Dugee was the performer at the Haymarket in 1751, then our entry in volume IV for a Monsieur Dugay should be augmented by the information on Anthony Joseph Dugee in the first volume of Odell's *Annals of the New York Stage*.

Littlegood, Master. *See* LITTLETON, MASTER.

Littleton. *See also* TYNCHARE.

Littleton, Mr [*fl.* 1735–1743], *actor.*

At Lincoln's Inn Fields Theatre on 23 July 1735 Mr Littleton played the Wardrobe Keeper in *The Stage Mutineers*. He continued at that house through 5 September, playing the first Bailiff and Glumdalca in *The Tragedy of Tragedies*, the Constable in *Bartholomew Fair*, and the first Mob member in *The Carnival*. He played a Watchman in *A City Ramble* at Covent Garden on 27 March 1736, and at Bartholomew Fair on 23 August Littleton was seen as a Servant in *The Modern Pimp*.

Littleton was back in town in August and September 1739 playing at Covent Garden Bull in *The Relapse*, Robert in *The Mock Doctor*, and Bardolph in *1 Henry IV*; within that engagement he appeared at Bartholomew Fair on 23 August as a Triton and a Sailor in *The Sailor's Wedding*. He returned to Bartholomew Fair in August 1740 to act a Triton in *Neptune's Palace*, and on 4 August 1743—the last notice of him—he was Duke Chartres in *The Glorious Queen of Hungary* at Tottenham Court. Master Littleton, presumably his son, performed in the late 1730s.

Littleton, Master [*fl.* 1735?–1738], *actor, dancer.*

Master Littleton played the Son of Pompeius in *Caius Marius* at Lincoln's Inn Fields on 22 August 1735; on the twenty-ninth he was the Page in *Love Makes a Man*. Possibly he was the Master "Littlegood" who had played Stocks in *The Lottery* the previous 19 May at York Buildings. On 31 March 1736 at Lincoln's Inn Fields "Young Littleton" acted the Prentice in *The Committee*, and on 23 August 1738 at Hallam's Bartholomew Fair booth Master Littleton danced *Two Pierrots* with Miss Wright. He was, one supposes, the son of the actor Littleton who performed in the 1730s and early 1740s.

Littleton, David [*fl. 1729*], *house servant.*

A note in the Lincoln's Inn Fields accounts dated 23 January 1729 reads "M!" Ryan by David Littleton 1." It would seem that Littleton was one of the theatre's office workers, arranging in this instance a complimentary ticket for Ryan.

Littlewood, John [*fl. 1668–1671*], *actor.*

The promptbook of *The Sisters* shows that John Littlewood doubled as Stephanio and the Scholar when the play was revived by the King's Company at the Bridges Street Theatre in 1668–69. That is the first season Littlewood is known to have performed in London, and he was cited in April 1669 in the Lord Chamberlain's accounts as a member of the King's troupe. Littlewood also played Albinus in *Tyrannick Love*, Carbo in *The Roman Empress*, and Ferdinand in both parts of *The Conquest of Granada* (at the theatre and also at court in December 1670 and January 1671). John Littlewood and Richard Hart were sued on 19 January 1671 for unpaid rent by one Zonch Herbert, but that is the only evidence we have discovered of any difficulties with the law. The last production Littlewood is known to have been in was *The Rehearsal*, which played on 7 December 1671, inspiring a ballad (at the Bodleian) in which the poet said ". . . Littlewood's Motion and Dress had much Wit . . ." His role is not known.

Liury. *See* DE LIURY.

Liveridge. *See* LEVERIDGE.

Livesque, Mr [*fl. 1784*], *singer.*

Mr Livesque sang countertenor in the Handel Memorial Concerts at Westminster Abbey and the Pantheon in May and June 1784.

Livier or **Liviez.** *See* LEVIEZ.

"Living Colossus, The." *See* CAJANUS, DANIEL.

Livingmann, Johan Nicolaus [*fl. 1796*], *musician.*

On 1 May 1796 Johan Nicolaus Livingmann was proposed for membership in the Royal Society of Musicians. The following August he was elected unanimously, and on 2 October he attended and signed the book. The minutes contain no further references to him.

Lloyd. *See also* LOYD.

Lloyd, Mr [*fl. 1703*], *actor.*

The 1703 edition of *The Different Widows* lists a Mr Lloyd as Lord Courtall. The work was presented at Lincoln's Inn Fields Theatre about November 1703.

Lloyd, Mr [*fl. 1746–1751*], *house servant?*

A Mr Lloyd, probably a house servant, shared in benefit tickets at Drury Lane on 19 May 1746, 11 May 1747, and 13 May 1751 (when his name was spelled Loyde), 2 May 1752, and 8 May 1754.

Lloyd, Mrs [*fl. 1783–1785*], *housekeeper, servant.*

A Mrs Lloyd's name is listed in Public Record Office documents as a housekeeper and servant at the King's Theatre between 1783 and 1785.

Lloyd, Mrs [*fl. 1784*]. *See* LYON, MISS.

Lloyd, Mrs [*fl. 1788–1802*], *singer, actress.*

A Mrs Lloyd (not to be confused with Mrs Elizabeth Lloyd who became the second wife of the actor Richard Wilson) was a chorus singer and supporting actress at Covent Garden Theatre from 1788–89 through 1801–2. Sometimes her name appeared in the bills as Loyde. She shared in benefit tickets with other minor performers on 27 May 1790, 26 May 1791, and in subsequent years. Her salary in 1793–94 was a modest £1 5s. per week; by 1799–1800 it had been reduced to £1 per week, at which level it remained through 1801–2, the last year her name is found in the accounts. Mrs Lloyd sang and acted numerous chorus roles of country girls, housemaids, prisoners, nuns, attendants, and the like, in such pieces as *The Picture of Paris, Taken in the Year 1790, The Woodman*, and *The Provocation* in 1790–91; *The Crusade* and *Blue-Beard* in 1791–92; *Harlequin and Faustus* in 1793–94; *The Mysteries of* the Castle in 1794–95; *The Magic Oak* and *Ramah Droog* in 1798–99; and *The Death of Captain Cook* and *Raymond and Agnes* in 1799–1800. Among the named characters she performed were Dorcas in *Florizel and Perdita* on 27 November 1790, Eurydice in *Orpheus and Eurydice* in the spring of 1792, and the title role in *Nina* on 28 November 1793.

In the summers of 1800 and 1801 she also performed at the Haymarket Theatre, appearing in the choruses of the very popular *Obi* and *What a Blunder* in the former year. The Master Lloyd who performed at Covent Garden in 1800–1801 and at the Haymarket in 1801 was probably her child.

Lloyd, Miss [*fl.* 1761], *player on musical glasses*.

The *St James's Chronicle* of 3 December 1761 announced that at Thomas Sheridan's lectures on elocution, "Miss Lloyd succeeds Miss Ford in performing on the musical glasses for the amusement of genteel company." In 1759 Sheridan's lectures had been at Cock's Auction Room, Spring Gardens, and at other times at the Coachmakers' Hall, Foster Lane, Cheapside. But where Miss Lloyd played is not known to us.

Lloyd, Edward [*fl.* 1781–1785], *singer*.

Edward Lloyd was an obscure chorus singer at Covent Garden Theatre from as early as 1781–82 through 1784–85. He shared benefit tickets with other minor performers and house personnel on 8 May 1782 and 29 May 1783. A Covent Garden pay sheet, now in the Harvard Theatre Collection, provides his full name and indicates that in 1783–84 he was kept very busy in the chorus, playing 185 nights at a salary of 3s. 4d. per night or £30 16s. for the season. Among his assignments was singing in *Macbeth*, for which his name appeared in the bills on 4 October 1784. No doubt he was the Mr Lloyd, tenor, that Dr Burney listed among the singers in the Handel Memorial Concerts at Westminster Abbey and the Pantheon in May and June 1784.

Lloyd, Edward [*fl.* 1794–1798], *violinist*.

On 3 December 1797 the violinist Edward Lloyd was recommended by William Park for membership in the Royal Society of Musicians. On 4 March 1798 the Governors decided to postpone balloting on his admission until a meeting previous to the general meeting. At last on 3 June 1798, a vote was taken but Lloyd was unanimously rejected. Very likely he was the Lloyd who was a member of the Covent Garden band in 1796–97 and performed in the oratorios directed there by Ashley in March of that year. In 1794 he had been listed in Doane's *Musical Directory* as a violinist living at No 28, Bow Street, who played with the Portland Chapel Society and in the Handel Memorial Concerts at Westminster Abbey and had engagements at Covent Garden Theatre and Vauxhall Gardens.

Lloyd, Elizabeth. See WILSON, MRS RICHARD THE THIRD, ELIZABETH.

Lloyd, Henry [*fl.* 1727], *singer*.

Henry Lloyd, a former Chapel Royal boy whose voice had changed, was granted an allowance by the Lord Chamberlain on 9 June 1727.

Lloyd, John [*fl.* 1669–1670], *actor*.

The London Stage lists John Lloyd as an actor in the Duke's Company at Lincoln's Inn Fields in 1669–70. The Lord Chamberlain's accounts cited Lloyd on 1 February 1670. The name is too common to make a certain identification, but a John Lloyd of the parish of St Paul, Covent Garden, wrote his will on 24 December 1674, leaving his estate to his son John, who was then a minor. The elder John Lloyd died shortly after that. He was buried at his parish church on 24 April 1675, and his will was proved by his son's guardian on 27 April. But there were, it seems, at least two or more John Lloyds in the parish.

Lloyd, Mrs Morrice. See PALMER, MRS JOHN.

Lloyd, R. E. [*fl.* 1789–1806], *exhibitor, lecturer, actor*.

On 1 June 1789 "A Gentleman" made his first, and evidently his only, London stage appearance, at the Haymarket Theatre as Hamlet. The *European Magazine* for that month identified him as Mr Lloyd, "an itinerant lecturer on astronomy." His London debut was also reported in the *Bath Chronicle* on 4 June 1789, where it was stated that Lloyd had "lately delivered lectures in this city."

We find no further record of Lloyd in London, or elsewhere, until February 1798, when the *Monthly Mirror* reported that a Theatre of Astronomy had opened at the Lyceum, in the Strand:

A GENTLEMAN, of the name of Lloyd, has commenced an astronomical lecture on DIOASTRODOXON, or GRAND TRANSPARENT ORRERY, which is a direct imitation of the worst part of Mr. Walker's ingenious lecture on the EIDOURANION. The exhibition throughout is so extremely defective, and the rules of pronunciation so far violated in Mr. Lloyd's explanation of it, as absolutely to impress us with the whimsical idea that Sylvester Daggerwood of the Dunstable company had turned *philosopher*.

In March 1799 Lloyd took his exhibition to Bristol, where he advertised "Lloyd's Astronomical Lectures" to commence at the Merchant Taylors' Hall, Broad Street, on the twentieth, but his model arrived late from London, so the opening of his show was postponed to 28 March. It played five nights, the last exhibition coming on 13 April. Lloyd carted his new Dioastrodoxon to York on 28 and 30 May 1801; there he offered a course of four astronomical lectures, with 40 changes in classic scenery, for a subscription of 10s. 6d., including the price of the syllabus.

A Public Record Office document indicates that in 1806 Mr R. E. Lloyd was granted a license for a lecture at his Theatre of Astronomy in Catherine Street, the Strand, for an unstated period.

Lloyd, T. A. *d. c. 1807?*, actor, playwright, editor.

T. A. Lloyd was an Irish actor who was performing at the Smock Alley Theatre, Dublin, by 1761–62. In 1768 he was a member of Foote's summer company at the Haymarket Theatre, where his first appearance seems to have been as Gruel in *The Commissary* on 13 July 1768. His other roles that season were Benedict in *The School Boy*, Jack in *The Beggar's Opera*, and Old Hob in *Hob in the Well*. He may have been the Lloyd who was with a touring company in Glasgow in March 1770.

Probably our subject was the Lloyd who acted Iago in *Othello* at the Haymarket on 1 October 1770 and then that season appeared in specially-licensed performances there as Sir Jealous Traffick in *The Busy Body* on 5 October, Sir William Wealthy in *The Minor* on 15 October, the Duke in *Venice Preserv'd* on 29 October, Old Philpot in *The Citizen*, and Gloucester in *Jane Shore* on 16 November, Glenalvon in *Douglas* on 21 November, Gonzales in *The Mourning Bride* and the King in *Tom Thumb* on 19 December, Sciolto in *The Fair Penitent* and the Frenchman in *The Register Office* on 28 January 1771, and Hotman in *Oroonoko* and the King in *The King and the Miller* on 4 March 1771.

In the summer of 1772 Lloyd returned to the Haymarket to act roles in *The Maid of Bath*, *The Devil upon Two Sticks*, *The Nabob*, the Bailiff in *The Apprentice*, Decoy in *The Miser*, Stanley in *Richard III*, and Carter in *Love in a Village*. Over the next four years he performed similar service in Foote's summer productions, some of his roles being Robin in *The Author*, Sir William in *The Minor*, Sir Epicure in *The Tobacconist*, Bates in *The Irish Widow*, Baptista in *Catherine and Petruchio*, Fairplay in *The Lame Lover*, Raymond in *The Spanish Fryar*, and Bardolph in *1 Henry IV*. On 7 July 1775 he played an unspecified role in the premier of John Jackson's *Eldred* and had some trouble with his costume. A press clipping in the Folger Shakespeare Library recommends to Foote's wardrobe keeper

to sew a button or two on the tragedy breeches, worn by Mr. Lloyd in the new play of Eldred, in order to save him the trouble of keeping his hands perpetually on the waistband.—For want of such assistance, this graceful performer yesterday resembled Alderman H——y holding up his breeches in the Presence chamber, while squinting Jack was attending his Majesty with the City Petition.

Announced as from the Theatre Royal, Haymarket, Lloyd acted Sir William Modelove in a performance of *A Bold Stroke for a Wife* at China Hall, Rotherhithe, on 30 September 1776, for Massey's benefit. He returned to the Haymarket on 7 October to play Jonathan and deliver the prologue to *The Prejudice of Fashion*, and then was again at China Hall to act Sir William Wealthy in *The Minor* on 8 October and Gonzales in *The Mourning Bride* on 14 October 1776.

This actor seems to have been the Lloyd who appeared several times in specially licensed performances at the Haymarket in the 1780s. He acted a character in *The Spendthrift* on 12 November 1781; that evening Lloyd's adaptation of Bickerstaffe's *Love in a Village*, now renamed *The Romp*, had its London premiere and became a very popular farce. Evidently Lloyd had revised the piece in Dublin for Mrs Jordan. Lloyd's other roles at the Haymarket included Sir Patrick O'Neale in *The Irish Widow* on 14 January 1782, Sir David Watchum in *The Man's Bewitch'd* on 8 March 1784, Dominick in *The Spanish Fryar* on 30 April 1784, Torrington in *The School for Wives* on 16 November 1784, and Captain Dudley in *The West Indian* on 12 March 1787.

Our subject was no doubt the Lloyd described in the *Biographia Dramatica* (1812) as a person of good education, designed for the church, but who preferred the life of a player. "Finally," according to that notice, "he turned book-builder, and figured away as the most genuine, impartial, authentic, general, original, universal writer, for Mr. Cooke, of Paternoster Row; in whose house he died about five years ago [i.e. 1807?]." A notation on a J. P. Kemble manuscript also indicates that the Lloyd who acted at the Haymarket in 1771 became an editor to Cooke, the publisher in Paternoster Row. For Cooke, Lloyd edited a continuation of Hume's *History of England* and his own alteration of *The Romp* (published in 1786 and 1789).

Loader. *See* LODER.

Lochery. *See* LAUCHERY.

Locke, Mr [*fl.* 1795], *performer?*

A Mr Locke, whose name did not appear in any playbills, was cited on the Drury Lane paylist on 25 April 1795 at £1 10s. (presumably per week). He may have been one of the minor performers.

Locke, Matthew *c.* 1622–1677, *singer, violinist, organist, composer.*

Matthew Lock was probably born in Devonshire about 1622, and was a chorister at Exeter Cathedral under Edward Gibbons from 1638 to 1641, as dates he carved and signed on the organ screen there indicate. He may also have studied under William Wake, for whose scholars he later (in 1651) wrote a *Little Consort of Three Parts*. In 1648 "Lock" (as he spelled his name then; he later added the "e") went to visit the Low Countries and copied out some motets by Italian composers. In 1652 he published *Duos for Two Bass Viols*.

Locke's first attempt at theatre music was probably his contribution to the masque *Cupid and Death*, which was performed at the military grounds in Leicester Fields, London, on 26 March 1653 in the presence of the Portuguese Ambassador. Christopher Gibbons shared in the composition of the music. Locke published his *Little Consort* in 1656 and that year composed the music for the fourth act of Davenant's *Siege of Rhodes*, which was presented at Rutland House in September with Locke singing the role of the Admiral. The *New Grove* states that Locke wrote the music for Davenant's ventures of 1658 and 1659, *The Cruelty of the Spaniards in Peru* and *The History of Sir Francis Drake*.

Faculty of Music, Oxford
MATTHEW LOCKE
by Fuller?

Pepys first met Locke on 11 February 1660 and ten days later wrote in his diary,

After dinner [i.e. lunch] I back to Westminster Hall, here I met with Mr. Lock and Pursell [the elder], masters of musique, and with them to the coffee house, into a room next the water by ourselves.—Here we had variety of brave Italian and Spanish songs and a Canon of eight voices which Mr. Lock had lately made on these words, "Domine salvum fac Regem," an admirable thing.

For the progress of Charles II from the Tower to Whitehall on 22 April 1661, the day before his coronation, Locke composed music "for ye king's sagbutts and cornets."

With the reestablishment of the King's Musick in 1660 Locke had been appointed composer for the violins, replacing the deceased John Coperario at a salary of £40 annually. He was also a member of the King's band of violins. In addition to his salary he received the standard livery fee of £16 2s. 6d., though as the years went on the King fell far behind in his payments. Locke, like other court musicians, added to his income when he attended the King on trips out of London, as, for example, when he received 5s. daily for waiting on the King at Windsor from 29 May to 23 August 1662 or from June 1665 to February 1666, when he attended the King at Oxford and Hampton Court.

The Lord Chamberlain's accounts also reveal that beginning in June 1664 lodgings for Locke and his servants at Margaret Pother's were paid for (10s. weekly) by the crown, and by 1668 his salary was £46 10s. 10d. Yet Locke was in financial difficulties as early as December 1665, when he assigned his livery payment, which was in arrears, to Richard Elton. At that time Locke had yet to receive his livery allowances for 1663, 1664, and 1665. In June 1668 he assigned £20 of his salary to James Ogleby, "in course after the assignments already made to Mr. Edward Darling, Mr. Isaack Walton, and Mr. Richards." But he may have had a change of fortune, for that entry in the accounts was at some later date canceled.

He was not out of debt in 1669, however, for the accounts show that he assigned his livery to Henry Cooke and £20 to Venables Stanton. But about 1671, without giving up his position in the King's Musick, Locke became organist of the Catholic Chapel of Queen Catherine in Somerset House. Roger North said that Locke held the Chapel post "as long as he lived, but the Italian masters, that served there, did not approve of his manner of play, but must be attended by more polite hands . . ." The Italians with whom he was associated there were Sebenico and then Draghi. Locke was of the parish of St Martin-in-the-Fields and lived in the Strand.

At court Locke in 1673 was still waiting to receive his livery allowances for 1666, 1667, and 1671, and in July 1676 he was again in financial difficulties. He was owed £174 10s. 7½d. by the King, and he assigned it all to a creditor, Thomas Whitfield. Locke's work at court involved him in composing a number of works for the Chapel Royal and the band of violins. Once, in April 1666, when he tried to be innovative and compose the responses between the commandments in a *Kyrie Elison* to different tunes instead of repeating the same tune, some members of the choir objected and spoiled the performance. So Locke published his composition with a preface: *Modern Church Music; Pre-Accused, Censur'd and Obstructed in its Performance before His Majesty, April 1, 1666, Vindicated by the Author, Matt. Lock, Composer in Ordinary to His Majesty*. Pepys studied Locke's *Kyrie* and liked it.

Locke's hot temper flared again when he read Thomas Salmon's *Essay to the Advancement of Musick, by casting away the Perplexity of different Cliffs*. Salmon hinted that opposition to simplifying musical notation came from teachers who wanted to prolong their students' lessons and thus make more money. Bridge in his *Samuel Pepys* quotes Locke as responding, "Had I been 'purblind,' 'copper-nos'd,' 'sparrow-mouthed,' 'goggle-eyed,' 'hunchbacked' or the like (ornaments which the best of my antagonists are adorned with), what work would they have been with me!" Locke responded to Salmon's essay with some *Observations*; then Salmon came back with *A Vindication*, and Locke ended matters in 1673 with *The Present Practise of Music Vindicated*. Locke also published in 1673 *Melothesia, or Certain General Rules for Playing upon a Continued Bass, with a Choice Collection of Lessons for the Harpsichord or Organ of all sorts*.

In addition to the music Locke wrote for the Chapel Royal, the Chapel at Somerset House, and the court band, he composed theatre music; indeed, his music for plays is among the best of his work. There is still a debate over whether or not Locke wrote some music for Davenant's adaptation of *Macbeth*. Moore in his article "The Music to Macbeth" thought that possibly Locke wrote all the music for the Davenant revival of *Macbeth* in 1663 (*recte*: 5 November 1664 is the earliest date for a revival in *The London Stage*) and that he wrote music for the 1672 revival (*recte*: the play was revived on 18 February 1673 and a new edition was published that year). John Downes, the prompter for Davenant's troupe credited Locke with the music for the songs, but he was writing long after the fact. Rosamond Harding in her *Thematic Catalogue of the Works of Matthew Locke* points out that there is only "one tune relating to *Macbeth* ascribed to Locke"—"A Jigg called Macbeth" in *Musick's Delight* (1666).

Locke wrote some incidental music and the music for the masque in *The Empress of Morocco*, which was performed in July 1673. For the Shadwell version of *The Tempest* which was performed on 30 April 1674 Locke composed some of the instrumental music. On 27 February 1675 Shadwell's *Psyche* was first performed. Shadwell wrote in his preface:

I chalked out the way to the Composer (in all but the Song of *Furies* and *Devils*, in the Fifth Act) having design'd which Line I wou'd have sung by One, which by Two, which by Three, which by four Voices, &c. and what manner of Humour I would have in all the Vocal Musick.

And by his excellent Composition, that long known, able, and approved Master of Musick, *Mr. Lock*, (*Composer* to his Majesty, and Organist to the Queen) has done me a great deal of right; though I believe, the unskilful in Musick will not like the more solemn part of it, as the Musick in the Temple of *Apollo*, and the Song of the *Despairing Lovers*, in the Second Act; both which are proper and admirable in their hands, and are recommended to the judgment of able Musicians; for those who are not so, there are light and airy things to please them.

Draghi composed the instrumental music for the production.

That Locke was popular during his day is evidenced by the large number of his compositions that were included in collections in the 1660s and later, among them: *Courtly Masquing Ayres* (1662), *Musick's Delight* (1666), *Catch That Catch can* (1667), *Apollo's Banquet* (1669), *The Treasury of Musick* (1669), *Cantica Sacra* (1674), and *Choice Ayres* (1676 and subsequent dates).

One of Locke's last musical tasks before his death was to substitute for Nicholas Staggins in assisting the French performers of *Rare en Tout*, which was produced at court on 29 May 1677. Locke died the following August. His close friend and successor to his post as composer at court, Henry Purcell, composed an elegy for Matthew and, in the years that followed, built on the foundations Locke had laid for English theatre music. A portrait of Locke, ascribed to Isaac Fuller, is at the Music School, Oxford.

Lockery. *See* LAUCHERY.

Locket, Mr [fl. 1729], *house servant?*

A note in the Lincoln's Inn Fields accounts dated 21 January 1729 reads: "Mr. Rich by Young Locket 1." We take that to be an instance of a complimentary ticket being arranged for the company manager John Rich by one Locket. Locket may have been an employee in the theatre office, but there is a possibility he was young James Bencraft, who had recently made a name for himself as Lockit in *The Beggar's Opera* at Lincoln's Inn Fields and was later involved in the operation of the company.

Lockhart, Mr [fl. 1771], *actor.*

A Mr Lockhart played Captain Dudley in *The West Indian* on 15 April 1771 at the Haymarket Theatre.

Lockhart, Miss [fl. 1789–1794], *singer, organist.*

Miss Lockhart sang in *The Triumph of Truth* (a selection of sacred works by a number of composers) at Drury Lane Theatre on 27 February 1789. The following month she sang in *Redemption* on the eighteenth and the oratorio selections on 20 and 25 March. Doane's *Musical Directory* of 1794 listed Miss Lockhart as a soprano and an organist and gave her address as No 20, Stangate Street, Lambeth. She was apparently the daughter of Mr and Mrs (Charles?) Lockhart of the same address.

Lockhart, Charles? [fl. 1766?–1795?], *singer, organist, violist?, composer.*

A Mr Lockhart sang in the Handel Memorial Concerts at Westminster Abbey and the Pantheon in May and June 1784. He was listed by Dr Burney as a bass. Doane's *Musical Directory* of 1794 listed a Lockhart who was a composer, organist, and tenor. If "tenor" was meant to indicate Lockhart's singing range, then the two Lockhart references concern different men, but it is likely that Doane meant that Lockhart was a violist. Doane stated that Lockhart was organist at Lambeth and St Katharine Cree and at the Lock and Orange Street Chapel. His address was No 20, Stangate Street, Lambeth; his wife and a Miss Lockhart, presumably his daughter, were both singers.

The Lockhart in question was probably Charles, who composed a number of songs, marches, and other works that were published from 1766 to about 1795. One of his songs, *Hobbinal*, published in 1766, was sung by Keene at Sadler's Wells.

Lockhart, Mrs Charles? [fl. 1794], *singer.*

Doane's *Musical Directory* of 1794 listed Mrs (Charles?) Lockhart, of No 20, Stangate Street, Lambeth, as a singer.

Lockwood, Mr [fl. 1791–1792?], *actor.*

A Mr Lockwood acted at Richmond in 1791 and may have been the performer of that name cited in the *Thespian Magazine* in 1792 as a member of Bigg's troupe at Taunton.

Loder, Andrew [fl. 1784–1826], *instrumentalist, singer?*

At the Assembly Rooms in Bristol on 7 April 1784, J. and A. Loder were scheduled to be among the instrumentalists, but the concert, a benefit for Master Crotch, was postponed until 22 April. J. and A. were John and Andrew Loder, probably brothers.

The "Master Loader" who sang "treble" in the Handel Memorial Concerts at Westminster Abbey and the Pantheon in May and June 1784 could not have been John, who by then was married and had at least one child, but it may well have been Andrew. The Loders performed again at the Hospital concerts advertised in Bristol on 4 April 1791. Doane's *Musical Directory* of 1794 listed Andrew as a bass (singer we would guess), violinist, horn player, clarinetist, and violoncellist who played for the New Musical Fund and participated in the Handelian concerts at Westminster Abbey and in the entertainments at Vauxhall Gardens. He was from Bath and was, from about 1820 to at least 1826, a music seller and publisher at No 4, Orange Grove, Bath—unless that was a son. A Mrs A. Loder, possibly Andrew's wife, died about 24 December 1800, and an A. Loder, according to notes kindly sent us by Kathleen Barker, sang in Bristol concerts in 1823 and 1824. Grove seems to suggest that the Andrew Loder of the 1820s was of a younger generation, the brother of John David Loder, son of John Loder.

Loder, John *d.* 1798?, *violinist, violist, singer, actor?*

The John Loder of this entry was very likely the one who, on 16 February 1784 with his wife Bathsheba, witnessed a marriage at Bath Abbey. Other entries in the Abbey registers noted the baptism of John, son of John and "Barbary" Loder, and of their son Edward and daughter Harriet, all on 14 August 1788. The son John cited there was probably John David who, along with several other Loders from Bath, was active in English musical circles in the nineteenth century. Only John and Andrew Loder performed in London in the eighteenth century so far as can be determined, and they would appear to have been brothers, John being perhaps the elder. Bathsheba or Barbary Loder, wife of John, was born Cantelo, the daughter of the London musician Hezekiah Cantelo.

In addition to the three children who were christened in 1788, John Loder and his wife had several others who are sometimes difficult to identify clearly. A daughter Mary was born in 1782 and died on 10 September 1798; another daughter (possibly Harriet) married a Mr Cunningham on 28 January 1798; and another, Ann, married a Mr Ridgway in 1805. The earliest birth we have found for a child of John and his wife is 1782, and if John married when he reached his majority, perhaps he was born in the late 1750s or early 1760s. If that guess is anywhere near correct, then the Master "Loader" who played in London in 1774–75 at Covent Garden was probably John.

On 19 November 1774 that youth was Cupid (possibly a singing role) in a "New Pastoral

Pantomimical Masque called the DRUIDS," and he continued in that role through 20 April 1775. The *Westminster Magazine* called *The Druids* "a heterogeneous jumble of monstrous absurdities." If the young performer was seen in anything else in London during the rest of the 1770s we have found no record of it. The next notice we have of him comes from Bristol and is a clearer reference to John. At the Assembly Rooms a benefit concert was scheduled for Master Crotch for 7 April 1784 but was postponed until the twenty-second. J. and A. Loder (John and Andrew, probably John's brother) were instrumentalists. The Master "Loader" who sang "treble" in the Handel Memorial Concerts in London in the summer of 1784 could hardly have been John but might have been Andrew. On the other hand, the Loader who played Ireton in *King Charles I* and Ben Budge in *The Beggar's Opera* at the Haymarket in London on 31 January 1785 may well have been John Loder.

At Bath on 26 April 1786 Loder sang at Hezekiah Cantelo's night, and in Bristol at the Hospital concerts in April 1791 John and Andrew Loder performed. John was probably the Loder cited in the published serenata *Look ere you Leap* (1792) as a singer at Vauxhall Gardens (probably Bristol), and he was a performer in a subscription concert at the Plume of Feathers in Wine Street, Bristol, on 13 January 1792. Doane's *Musical Directory* in 1794 listed John Loder as a violinist and violist from Bath who played for the New Musical Fund in London. The Bristol press reported the death at Weymouth of John Loder, musician of Bath, on 9 September 1795. Kathleen Barker thinks that may have been a rumor, for John Loder was seemingly referred to as still alive when his daughter married Mr Cunningham in January 1798; and when Mary Loder died on 2 September of that year, she was cited as the daughter of "the late Mr, John Loder, musician, of Bath." That would place his death in 1798, but the 1795 report may have been correct. In any case, the Bath-Bristol singer Richardson married John Loder's widow in November 1804.

Lodi, Anna [*fl.* 1707–1715], *singer.*

Two letters preserved at the British Library from the singer Anna Lodi, written in January 1708 to Vice Chamberlain Coke, concern her possible appearance at the Queen's Theatre in the Haymarket. The first note was written on 6 January:

If my Last proposition does not please you I shall never agree to no other because I have maid that propositions against my Interest & desire. If they dont think me fit to act I desire not to be put to a tryall and I am ready to deliver the part whenever tis yr Command

Between the time that letter was written and 10 January, when Signora Lodi wrote again, Coke must have replied and a "tryall" may have taken place:

I shall be contented to sing the part of Media in the opera called Thomyris or the Amazon Queen in my own Cloths on the stage for two or three days and after to perform the part of Eurilla in Valentinis opera as often as the said opera shall be performed from the date hereof untill the 13th day of next June if my health will permit. But no other part in any other Opera during the said season except I shall be consenting thereto myself. And before doe perform, act or sing in either of the said operas Mr. Vanbrugh must oblige himselfe by writing to pay me one hundred and fifty pounds by weekly paym^{ts} (vizt) Seven pounds four shillings every week until the said one Hundred and fffifty pounds be paid. If Mr. Vanbrugh will agree to this I shall be ready & willing to perform the parts as above menc̄ond . . .

(The transcription of the second letter comes from a clearer copy in the Broadley Collection at the Westminster Public Library. Our transcription and dating differ slightly from Milhous and Hume's.)

The upshot of all that is not clear. The part of Media in *Thomyris* was sung, according to the 1707 edition, not by Anna Lodi but by Mary Lindsey. The reference to the singer Valentini's opera was, one guesses, to his benefit, but *The London Stage* cites no benefit for him that season. Anna Lodi may have sung; the bills of the time were often vague about casts. Indeed, an interesting note was put in the Queen's Theatre bill for *Thomyris* on 17 February 1708. The bill stated that Mrs Lindsey would perform her own part, Media, the implication being that in some performances before that another singer had replaced her. Perhaps that singer was Anna Lodi.

In Vice Chamberlain Coke's papers at Harvard is a paylist for opera performers dating about late December 1707; a "Mr Lody" (surely an error for Anna) was down for £100. On 24 April 1711 Signora Lodi was given a benefit concert at Home's Dancing School; on 25 March 1713 she and William Corbett shared a benefit at Hickford's Music Room and she entertained with songs; the same pair shared a benefit there a year later, as they did on 26 April 1715, the last mention found of Anna Lodi.

Lodi, Stella [*fl.* 1773–1774], *singer.*

Signora Stella Lodi sang Lucilla in *Lucio Vero* on 20 November 1773 and subsequent dates at the King's Theatre and beginning 7 December had an unnamed role in *Il puntiglio amoroso.* She seems to have performed only through 5 February 1774.

Lodie, Francesco [*fl.* 1686–1702], *lutenist.*

Francesco Lodie (or Lody) was a member of James II's Catholic Chapel in 1686, serving as a lute player. At some later date he became one of the Duke of Bedford's musicians, for on 23 May 1702 he was paid five guineas for performing, probably at Southampton House.

Lodon, Mr [*fl.* 1761], *trumpeter.*

Mr Lodon was paid 5*s*. on 13 November 1761 by Covent Garden Theatre for serving as a trumpeter in the company's staging of *The Coronation.* He seems not to have been a regular member of the band.

Loe. *See also* **LOWE.**

Loe, [R.?] [*fl.* 1699–1705?], *dancing master, impresario, composer?*

The *Post Boy* on 7–9 March 1699 advertised a lottery "at Mr. Loes Dancing School in Wine-Office-Court, Fleetstreet" on 30 March. Loe held a concert at his school on 25 July 1702. Perhaps he was the composer R. Loe who published a song, *Come bring us Wine,* set to the tune of *A Trip to the Jubilee,* about 1705.

Loeillet, Jean Baptiste 1680–1730, *harpsichordist, flutist, oboist, composer.*

Jean Baptiste Loeillet was christened in Ghent on 18 November 1680, the son of J. B. François Loeillet (1653–1684) and his second wife, Barbe Buuys. Jean Baptiste was a member of a sizeable family of Flemish musicians. Unfortunately, his surname was often spelled Lulli, Luly, Lullie, or Lully, making for confusion with Jean Baptiste Lully (1632–1687).

As early as 10 April 1705 Loeillet was playing in London at Drury Lane Theatre, and Grove states that he was then a member of the opera band at the Queen's Theatre. In Vice Chamberlain Coke's papers (now at Harvard) Loeillet was listed as an oboist at 15*s*. nightly; he earned £40 per season. The Portland papers at Nottingham suggest that he may have remained in the opera band as late as 1720, by which time he could command £60 per season. In addition to his theatre work, Loeillet gave weekly concerts at his house in Hart Street, according to Hawkins in his *General History;* gentlemen apparently came to Loeillet's concerts and paid him well for his assistance. Hawkins estimated that the musician made about £16,000 during his lifetime, and *Grove* (fifth edition) notes that in his will he listed bequests of money, plate, harpsichords, violins, "fflutes of all kinds and bass violins" to his relatives.

On 20 April 1724 at Hickford's Music Room there was a "Benefit [for] Baptiste, lately arriv'd from Paris." The reference is probably to our subject. A month later the *Session of Musicians* came out, with its satire on most London musicians who aspired to a laurel from Apollo, but Loeillet was treated most gently:

> *Apollo's piercing Eye just then espy'd*
> *Merry L{oe}i{l}l{e}t stand laughing at one side;*
> *He gently wav'd him to him with his Hand,*
> *Wond'ring he at that Distance chose to stand.*
> *Smiling, he said, I come not here for Fame,*
> *Nor do I to the Bays pretend a Claim;*
> *Few here deserve so well, the God reply'd,*
> *But modesty does always Merit hide;*
> *A supper for some Friends I've just bespoke,*
> *Pray come—and drink your Glass—and crack your Joke.*

An accomplished flutist, oboist, harpsichordist, and composer, Loeillet published in London in the 1720s a number of sonatas, lessons, and suites. The *New Grove* provides a genealogical chart of the complex Loeillet family. Jean Baptist (or, as he called himself once he settled in London, John) Loeillet died at his house in East Street near Red Lion Square on 19 July 1730.

Loffday. *See* **LOVEDAY.**

Loft, Mrs [fl. 1782], *actress*.

Mrs Loft played Flora in a single performance of *The Beaux' Duel* at the Haymarket Theatre on 21 January 1782.

Logan, Miss, later **Mrs Cary** [fl. 1793–1794], *actress, singer*.

On 4 October 1793 an actress announced as "A Gentlewoman" making her first appearance on any stage acted Yarico in *Inkle and Yarico* at the Haymarket theatre. The *Thespian Magazine* identified her as Mrs Cary, sister to the actress Maria Gibbs who performed Patty that evening (and who later became the second wife of the younger George Colman). Mrs Cary, then, was one of the daughters of Mr and Mrs Logan, an Irish theatrical couple who did not, it seems, ever play in London. Another of her sisters was the Miss Logan who acted at Covent Garden Theatre and the Haymarket between 1795 and 1797.

For her second appearance, Mrs Cary again performed Yarico, on 10 October 1793. On 16 November next, advertised as making her third appearance on any stage, she acted Melinda in *The Recruiting Officer*, and her sister Mrs Gibbs played Rose. After acting Yarico once more, on 9 December, Mrs Cary did not appear again at the Haymarket until 15 February 1794, when she replaced Mrs Powell as Charlotte in *Heigho for a Husband!*, a comic afterpiece by F. G. Waldron. On 20 February, however, Mrs Powell resumed her role, and Mrs Cary was not heard of again. (In a cross-index in volume III of this dictionary, Mrs Cary is listed as Miss "J. H." Cary, but those initials are mistakenly attributed to her; they belong rather to a Miss Logan, who, according to a manuscript in the British Library, signed her name thus to a Covent Garden pay receipt in 1808.)

Logan, Miss [fl. 1795–1797], *actress, singer*.

The "Young Gentlewoman" who made her stage debut as Nerissa in *The Merchant of Venice* at the Haymarket Theatre on 3 August 1795 was identified by the *European Magazine* the following month as Miss Logan, a sister of Maria Gibbs. For her second appearance she played Pink in *The Young Quaker*, after which she was engaged at Covent Garden Theatre for the 1795–96 season. For her first appearance at the patent house she acted Myrtilla in *The Provok'd Husband* on 15 October 1795.

Miss Logan performed at Covent Garden through the 1796–97 season, appearing as an English Amazonian in *Lord Mayor's Day*, the First Shepherdess in *Cymon*, Norah in *Love in a Camp*, Miss Clare in *Life's Vagaries*, Agnes in *The Follies of a Day*, a Villager in *The Battle of Hexham*, Nancy in *Three Weeks after Marriage*, a Maid in *Crotchet Lodge*, Laura in *Werter*, Lady Charlotte in *High Life below Stairs*, a Fine Lady in *Live Lumber*, the Second Bacchant in *Comus*, Nancy in *The Poor Sailor*, a Shepherdess in *The Travellers in Switzerland*, the Duchess in *Barataria*, Belinda in *Modern Antiques*, a Lady in *Philaster*, Leonora in *Two Strings to Your Bow*, Cleone in *The Distrest Mother*, an Irish Peasant in *Bantry Bay*, Penelope in *The Romp*, Zorayda in *The Mountaineers*, and Flametta in *A Duke and No Duke*.

Between seasons, in the summer of 1796, Miss Logan returned to the Haymarket to repeat Nerissa in *The Merchant of Venice* and appear as Lady Percy in *Henry IV*, Lady Anne in *The School of Shakespeare*, and some of her earlier parts. She was also a singer, swelling the Covent Garden choruses in *Macbeth*, *Zorinski*, and *Romeo and Juliet*. Her last London appearance seems to have been on 6 May 1797 in *Bantry Bay*.

If the identification of Miss Logan as Maria Gibbs's sister is correct, their parents were the Mr and Mrs Logan who acted in Ireland from as early as 1767 but who seem not to have appeared in London. Maria Gibbs became the second wife of the younger George Colman. Another sister, Mrs Cary, acted several times at the Haymarket Theatre in 1793–94.

Logan, Maria. *See* GIBBS, MARIA.

Logee, Mr [fl. 1792], *puppeteer*.

According to Speaight's *History of the English Puppet Theatre* the puppeteer Logee exhibited at Bartholomew Fair in 1792.

Loggings, John [fl. 1667], *singer*.

On 3 April 1667 Henry Cooke was to receive £30 annually for maintaining two children of the Chapel Royal whose voices had broken; one of the lads was John Loggings (or Loggins). John and another of Cooke's boys,

"Blaew" (surely John Blow), visited Samuel Pepys on 21 August and sang for him. But they could not control their voices, Pepys told his diary; it "would make a man mad, so bad it was."

Loiscan. *See* LOYSCOEAN.

Lolkes, Wybrand *b. 1730, dwarf.*

William Rayner in *Notes and Queries* in September 1882 reported that the dwarf Wybrand Lolkes had been exhibited at Astley's Amphitheatre in 1790. Lolkes was 27″ tall and weighed 56 pounds. An engraving of him by Mequignon was published by J. Caulfield in 1790, with a caption giving his age as 60, apparently as of that year. The print also depicts his wife, aged 50, "by whom he has had three children, One of which a Son, lived to the Age of 23, and was 5 feet 7 inches high." Lolkes was born, the caption said, in Jelst (*recte* Ijlst) in West Friesland in the Netherlands.

Lolli. *See also* LALLI.

By permission of the British Library Board

MYNHEER WYBRAND LOLKES
by Mequignon

Lolli, Mr [*fl. 1778–1781*], *music copyist, violinist, clarinetist.*

A Mr Lolli was a music copyist and member of the band at Drury Lane Theatre between 1778 and 1781. On 4 January 1778 Lolli, Danby, and Bradford were paid a total of £5 18s. for "Music writing." For similar services Lolli received payments of £2 3s. 2d. on 21 March 1778, £2 16s. on 19 December 1778, £1 18s. 6d. on 2 June 1780, and £2 16s. 3d. on 31 December 1781. In 1778–79 the theatre also paid him a salary of £1 10s. per week for playing violin and clarinet in the band.

Lolli, Antonio *c. 1725–1802, violinist, composer.*

The violinist Antonio Lolli was born in Bergamo, probably about 1725. The register at S. Ippolito in Palermo gave his age as 77 at the time of his death in 1802; Guelli's epitaph gave it as 75. Little is known of his early life save that he seems to have been self-taught in music, and by 1755 he was first violinist in the court of the Duke of Württemberg at Stuttgart, where he shared a desk with Nardini, whose superiority stimulated Lolli to take a year's leave for additional study. During his tour of the Netherlands in 1760 he published his first concertos, at Amsterdam. In 1765 he was noted as concertmaster in the Stuttgart royal chapel, a position he probably held until 1774, when financial constraints caused the Duke to dismiss most of his chapel musicians. Lolli and his wife, Nanette Sauveur, a court dancer and sister-in-law of Noverre, earned a total of 4000 thaler per annum before their discharge. During that period in Stuttgart, Antonio's sister, the soprano Brigida Lolli (who married the dancer Joseph Anelli), and his younger brother Gaetano Lolli, a violinist, also were members of the court opera.

During his Stuttgart service various leaves of absence allowed Lolli to tour—Vienna in the early 1760s and Paris in 1764 and 1766. He also played in various German cities. In 1771 he visited Italy, where he made the acquaintance of the Mozarts.

The Lollis' contracts were terminated at the Württemberg court on 29 July 1774. Lolli then went to St Petersburg, where he gained a salary of 4000 rubles per year and the favor of Empress Catherine, who presented him with a bow bearing the inscription: "Archet fait par

Catherine II pour l'incomparable Lolli." His tenure in Russia was interrupted on several occasions by tours to Germany and Scandinavia. He performed in the Concert Spirituel in Paris in 1779 (he had also played there in 1764), enjoying great success, but he was criticized for his showy performances. Subsequently he was at Madrid, where at the theatre he played one concerto and two solos for a nightly salary of 2000 reales. From the Prince of Asturias he received the gift of a golden box filled with 350 ducats. Lolli's peregrinations throughout Europe brought him 10,000 guldens, a fortune he had shown Dittersdorf and which he placed at interest in a European bank.

After some litigation, Lolli managed to leave the Empress's service in 1783, and he toured Hamburg, Stockholm, and Copenhagen. He arrived in London early in 1785, but, according to Burney, "by a caprice in his conduct equal to his performance he was seldom heard." His appearance was advertised for 4 February but the concert was canceled. He made his first appearance on 18 February 1785 at Willis's Rooms, for his own benefit, in a concert directed by Salomon. He played a violin solo at the end of part I of *L'allegro ed il Pensero* at Drury Lane Theatre on 23 February and also performed that date at the Hanover Square Professional Concert. Burney heard him at the former and found his musical talents as erratic as his personality:

so eccentric was his style of composition and execution, that he was regarded as a madman by most of his hearers. Yet I am convinced that in his lucid intervals he was, in a serious style, a very great, expressive, and admirable performer. In his freaks nothing can be imagined so wild, difficult, grotesque, and even ridiculous as his compositions and performance. After playing at the oratorio, and making the grave and ignorant laugh at very serious difficulties upon which he had perhaps but ill bestowed his time, he suddenly left the kingdom, *à la sourdine*; perhaps, at last, to shun difficulties of another kind.

Subsequently Lolli toured about the Continent giving concerts. In 1778 he resided in Italy, styling himself concertmaster to the Empress of Russia. He was at Berlin in 1791 with a young son (Phillipo?) who received from the King a present of 100 Friedrichs d'or "for his ready and correct performance on the violoncello." That year father and son played at Copenhagen and Stockholm. From the latter city he returned with his son to London, and their names are to be found in Haydn's *First London Notebook* of 1792. Lolli's mental instability caused him to totter on the edge of a breakdown when the Prince of Wales asked him to lead a Haydn quartet. Later Lolli toured the Continent, giving concerts: Palermo in 1793, Vienna in 1794, and Naples in 1796 (where he was heard by Romberg and thought a shadow of his former self). After a prolonged illness, he died in Palermo on 10 August 1802; he was buried in S. Ippolito, a church of the Capuchin friars.

By about 1760 Lolli had married at Stuttgart the dancer Nanette Sauveur, a sister-in-law of Noverre, who danced in the court theatre there from 1760 through 1773 or 1774. She seems to have danced in London in 1755 and is noticed in this dictionary as Miss Noverre. They had at least two sons: one was a member of the royal chapel in Stuttgart by 1770; the other, Phillipo, born at Stuttgart in 1773, was a prodigy on the violoncello.

Lolli was described by Dittersdorf as a handsome man of agreeable manners, a great dandy, and a very extravagant gambler. Others thought him conceited and dissolute. He possessed musical virtuosity, and Schubert wrote, "Octaves and tenths he plays with perfect intonation, also double shakes in thirds and sixths. . . . His speed goes to the point of magic. . . . He goes into the most dizzy realms of sound and sometimes finishes a concerto with a note which appears the *non plus ultra* of all tones." According to the Abbé Bertini, however, Lolli could not keep time, could not read music, and could not properly render an *adagio*. When asked to play an *adagio*, so goes one story, Lolli said, "I am a native of Bergamo; we are all born fools at Bergamo—how should I play a serious piece?"

Lolli's method of composition was no less eccentric, and Sainsbury reports that he "never wrote more than the theme, and then desired one of his friends to write the bass or the parts for the different instruments." His works include four books of sonatas and eight concertos. A list of his compositions may be found in the *International Inventory of Musical Sources*. His editions *Ecole de violon* and *XII Variazioni per il violoncello solo e viola* were perhaps written by his son.

Lolli is pictured as one of a large group of

musicians engraved by Luigi Scotti, published at Florence abut 1805. A drawing of Lolli by Hardrich, at the Deutsche Staatsbibliothek in Berlin, is reproduced in the *New Grove Dictionary*, where also may be found additional information on Lolli's continental career.

Lolli, Signora Antonio, Nanette, née Sauveur. *See* NOVERRE, MISS.

Lolli, Giovan Antonio [*fl.* 1678–1679], *actor*.

In the Duke of Modena's troupe of Italian performers who played six times in London between November 1678 and mid-February 1769, the dottore (in the *commedia dell' arte* tradition) was played by Giovan Antonio Lolli. Rasi quotes a letter from Lolli in London to the Duke, telling him of the miserable circumstances of the actors' stay in London. The *Enciclopedia dello spettacolo* notes that Lolli's character name was Dottor Brentino. Also active in the late seventeenth century in commedia troupes, but apparently not in England, were Giovan Battista Angelo Agostino Lolli, also a specialist in the dottore character, and Eustachio Lolli, who was called Fichetto.

Lollo. *See* LOLLI.

Lombardini. *See* SIRMEN.

Londsdell. *See* LONSDALE.

Long. *See also* LENG.

Long, Mr [*fl.* 1714–1720?], *singer*.

Vice Chamberlain Coke's papers at Harvard show that a Mr Long was hired, at £150 for the season, to sing at the King's Theatre in 1714–15. He was probably the Long cited in the published song *When Phaebus* [*sic*] *addrest* about 1720. (Perhaps he was related to the Mrs Long [or Leng] who supplied the opera house with clothes and accessories in 1716–17. Though she may have been a member of the opera troupe, the accounts would suggest that she was an outside supplier of wardrobe goods.)

Long, Mr [*fl.* 1780], *actor*.

A Mr Long acted Sir Harry in *High Life below Stairs* at the Haymarket Theatre on 28 March 1780, in a specially-licensed performance for the benefit of Mrs Lefevre.

Long, Mr [*fl.* 1782–1817], *boxkeeper*.

A Mr Long was a boxkeeper at the King's Theatre between 1782–83 and 1784–85. Probably he was the same Long who was a boxkeeper at Drury Lane from 1791–92 through at least 1816–17. From 1813–14 to 1816–17 his salary ranged between 12*s*. and 18*s*. per week.

Long, Miss [*fl.* 1774], *dancer*.

Miss Long danced a hornpipe in Act III of *The Beggar's Opera* at the Haymarket Theatre on 4 April 1774.

Long, J. [*fl.* 1787], *lecturer, exhibitor*.

J. Long, who advertised himself as from London, offered for 2*s*. 6*d*. an "Astronomical Lecture" at the Coopers' Hall, Bristol, beginning on 5 June 1787. The lecture was illustrated by a machine called the "Astrotheatron, or Transparent Orrery," and interludes on the triple harp were provided by Mr Evans. Long presented his show about 15 times that summer, through 22 August.

Long, Jane [*fl.* 1661–*c.* 1678], *actress*.

The prompter John Downes said in his *Roscius Anglicanus* that Jane Long was one of Sir William Davenant's original actresses. She and other actresses lived at Sir William's house, at least in 1661 when the Duke's Company was beginning its theatrical activity. In the years before the plague closed the theatres, Jane played Laughing Jane the servant in *Cutter of Coleman Street* (on 16 December 1661, the first mention of her at the Lincoln's Inn Fields Theatre), Flora in *The Adventure of Five Hours*, Diacelia in *The Slighted Maid*, Brianella in *The Step Mother*, the Widow in *The Comical Revenge* (and she spoke the epilogue), the Queen of France in Boyle's *Henry V*, Leucippe in *The Rivals*, and Zarma in *Mustapha*. These were mostly small parts, often servants.

Sometimes in 1666–67 she played Dulcino in *The Grateful Servant*, "the first time," Downes noted, that "she appear'd in Man's Habit." After that she occasionally played other breeches parts. From 1667–68 through 1672–73 Jane acted Hypolito in *The Tempest*, Mrs Brittle in

By permission of the Trustees of the British Museum

JANE LONG

engraving by Tompson, after Lely

The Amorous Widow, Mrs Nell in *Mr. Anthony*, the Justice in *The Woman Made a Justice*, Mandana in *Women's Conquest*, Osiris in *Cambyses*, Crispina in *The Six Days Adventure*, Fickle in *The Town Shifts*, Paulina in *Juliana* (and she spoke the epilogue), Betty Rash in *The Morning Ramble*, and Lady Macduff in *Macbeth*.

A map of the parish of St Paul, Covent Garden, shows a parcel of land on the corner of Russell Street and Bridges Street, close to the Bridges Street Theatre, marked "Mr and Mrs Long." The name is common of course, but there is a possibility that the Longs were related to Jane Long—her parents, perhaps. In 1673, however, Jane Long left the stage. She became the mistress of George Porter (1622?–1683), a Gentleman of the Queen's Privy Chamber. On 17 December 1677 Henry Savile in a letter to the Earl of Rochester remarked that Porter "surfeits of everything hee sees but Mrs. Long and his sonn Nobbs . . ." Some sources say she was the mistress of the Duke of Richmond until his death in 1672. An anonymous satire of about 1678 said the

Malicious Witch Long have a damn'd stinking breath
Which to Bastard in Wombe does give sudden death.

Her portrait was painted by Lely and engraved in mezzotint by R. Tompson. A portrait of her was in the Colnaghi *Catalogue* in 1827; perhaps it was the original Lely, the present location of which is unknown.

Long, John [*fl.* 1767–1794], *violinist, violist.*

By 1767–68 John Long, who may have been related to the musician and composer Samuel Long (d. 1770?), was earning 5s. per night as a member of the Covent Garden Theatre band. Dr Burney listed him as one of the second violinists in the Handel Memorial Concerts at Westminster Abbey and the Pantheon in May and June 1784. Mr Long, presumably John, was listed in Doane's *Musical Directory* of 1794 as an "alto" (violist) who played in the Handelian concerts at the Abbey.

At a date unknown to us, John Long married Ann Condell, the daughter of the Covent Garden boxkeeper, John Condell (d. 1779) the elder, by his second and common-law wife Ann Wilson. In her father's will, dated 3 November 1779 and proved that 24 December, Ann Long was named to become a residuary legatee of his estate after the death of her mother. When Ann Long's brother, the musician Henry Condell, made his will on 5 April 1824 (proved on 31 July 1824), both she and her husband were presumably dead, for they received no bequests. But their sons Edward Long of Limehouse and William Long of the Bank of England, were named their uncle Henry Condell's executors, and their daughter Elizabeth Long received valuable property in New James Street and Battersea, in addition to her uncle's manuscripts and instruments. John Long, another child of John and Elizabeth Long, was mentioned in Henry Condell's will as deceased, but his widow Elizabeth and their children were then living in Beaufort Row, Chelsea.

Long, Samuel *d.* 1770?, *organist, harpsichordist, composer.*

Samuel Long was listed in *Mortimer's London Directory*, 1763, as an organist and harpsichord teacher living in Cross Street, Hatton Garden. Grove reports that Long, a "distinguished musician," had been taught by William Savage. Long's published music includes a three-part glee *Where'er you tread* (1764), which won a Catch Club prize; *I told my nymph, I told her true*, sung by Miss Thomas at Ranelagh (1761); *Ye foplings & smarts, Song for the Mall* (1761); *Come my dear nymph* and *Of All my experience*, both sung at the Public Gardens; and several songs published in the *Royal Magazine* (1763) and *Lady's Magazine* (1763). His *Four lessons and two voluntarys for the harpsichord or organ* was published in London by Charles and Samuel Thompson, "for the widow," in 1770, thereby suggesting that year as the year of Samuel Long's death.

Longbottom, Mr [*fl.* 1728–1729], *singer.*

Mr Longbottom sang Telemachus in the opera *Penelope* when the work was presented at the Haymarket Theatre on 8 May 1728. He was Scrip in *The Beggar's Wedding* at the Haymarket on 16 July 1729 but Swab in that work when it was repeated on 16 August. *The London Stage* is in error in listing the 16 July performance as at Drury Lane.

Longchamp. *See* PITEL, HENRI.

Longdale, Mr [*fl.* 1795], *actor.*

A Mr Longdale played the Brother in *Love and Madness* at the Haymarket Theatre on 21 September 1795.

Longino. *See* CONTI, VINCENZO.

"Longinus." *See* SHERIDAN, RICHARD BRINSLEY.

Longley. *See also* CLARKE, MR [*fl.* 1797].

Longley, Mr [*fl.* 1797–1798], *actor.*

On 25 November 1797 "A Gentleman," who was said to be making his initial bow on the stage, acted Falstaff in *1 Henry IV* at Drury Lane Theatre, in the estimable company of John Philip Kemble as Hotspur. The *European Magazine* of December 1797 identified the neophyte as a Mr Longley, but the *Monthly Mirror* of January 1798 called him Mr Clarke.

It was as Mr Clarke [*fl.* 1797] that we noticed this actor in volume III of this dictionary, where we mistakenly reported that he did not reappear in London. As a matter of fact, at Drury Lane on 7 June 1798, for Wathen's benefit, again advertised as a gentleman, he acted Muley in *The Mountaineers*. This time he was identified by the *Monthly Mirror* of June 1798 as Longley. Of his performance of Falstaff, the critic in the *True Briton* on 29 November 1797 wrote that this actor was not "inferior to some Falstaffs we have seen upon the London stage."

Longley, E[**dward?**] *d.* 1799?, *boxkeeper.*

Mr E. Longley was a boxkeeper at Covent Garden Theatre as early as 1770–71 through at least 1792, usually sharing an annual benefit with other minor employees. The *Public Advertiser* of 13 May 1780 provided his first initial. Possibly he was the Edward Longley, aged 76, who was buried at St Paul, Covent Garden, on 20 January 1799. Baptisms of Edward Longley's children, by his wife Alice, also are registered at that church: Emilia Barclay on 31 March 1764 (buried 4 January 1765), Mary Ann on 23 November 1765, William Barclay on 17 November 1767 (buried 16 March 1768), and Edward Jenkins on 24 November 1771. His wife, Alice Longley, was buried on 30 May 1790.

Longsdell. *See* LONSDALE.

Lonsdale, Mr [*fl.* 1779?–1795], *acrobat, equestrian, dancer.*

The Lonsdale who performed a hornpipe at the Haymarket Theatre on 18 October 1779 and danced in Act IV of *Falstaff's Wedding* on the following 27 December was possibly Lonsdale the equestrian and acrobat of the 1780s and 1790s. He performed as an equestrian at Astley's Amphitheatre as early as 24 October 1782; in that program was also Master Lonsdale (or Longsdell, Langsdale, Londsdell), probably his son. On 4 November the elder Lonsdale gave an exhibition of tumbling. He may have performed in the provinces for a few years, for the next notice of him in Astley's bills dates from the summer of 1785. Again, in 1786, he displayed his abilities as equestrian and tumbler. On 13 June Philip Astley advertised that Lonsdale had thrown "a round-all, 8 ft. high, 19 flip-flaps, and 14 somersets, the like never heard of before, and any other performer doing the same as above, may have 100 guineas paid him by me." In July Lonsdale tumbled within a dance called *The Country Wake*. That September he appeared in a spectacle production, *A Sale of English Beauties at Grand Cairo*, and played the first Columbine in *At the Village Sports*. A critical review of the 1786 season stated that "If tumbling and rope dancing can please, Mr. Astley has to boast of the most noted families in all the world, namely Mess. Laurence [i.e. Joseph Lawrence] and Lonsdale." Lonsdale was in Astley's troupe again in 1788, and he may have been the Lonsdale who was at Ennis, Ireland, in 1791. After several years away from London, he participated in "equestrian exercises" and performed "ground and lofty" tumbling at the Royal Circus in April and May 1795.

A second Master "Londsdell" performed at the Royal Circus in 1803 and 1806 and may have been related. Mark Lonsdale, who was a pantomime contriver and manager of Sadler's Wells (among other activities), may also have been a relative of our subject.

Lonsdale, Master [*fl.* 1776–1782], *acrobat, equestrian, rope dancer.*

Master Lonsdale was in Wilkinson's troupe during the fair at Bristol, performing "astonishing Postures on the Slack Rope, in full swing" at Merchant Taylors' Hall, according to the Bristol papers in March 1776. In the summer of 1782 he displayed his tumbling skill at Astley's Amphitheatre (Mr Lonsdale, presumably his father, also performed). The bill of 23 April 1782 said Master Lonsdale on horseback "rides full speed on his head."

Lonsdale, Mark *d. 1815, manager, author.*
Thomas Dibdin in his *Reminiscences* said

Mark Lonsdale was bred a designer for calico-printing at Carlisle, and when very young, wrote for provincial journals and monthly country magazines: he came to London with a letter of recommendation to the Duke of Norfolk, by whose interest he brought out at Drury-Lane Theatre a farce, written in the unsophisticated style of a country lad, called "The Spanish Rivals." . . .

That work was produced on 4 November 1784, with music by Thomas Linley. Lonsdale wrote the lyrics for "Ching chit quaw" (and possibly other songs), the pantomime "*The Mandarine*" at Sadler's Wells, about 1780. Dibdin said that at Sadler's Wells Lonsdale saved two-thirds of his salary to pay off the mortgage on a small family estate, "which, when redeemed, would enable a female relative to marry." A benefit bill for the Wells, dated 10 September 1788, gave his address as Staple Inn Buildings, Holborn. He collaborated with Rayner Tayler on many Sadler's Wells works between 1784 and 1791.

On 6 June 1791 at Covent Garden Lonsdale's *Tippoo Saib* was presented. It was a pantomime, partly new and partly derived from earlier popular pantomimes, especially *The Rival Knights* and *Provocation*, with music by William Reeve. The work was never published. He seems to have brought out a new work in 1793 at Sadler's Wells, where he had been employed since the 1780s as producer of pantomimes, and Dennis Arundell in *The Story of Sadler's Wells* states that Lonsdale contrived *Valentine and Orson* at that house in June 1794. At Covent Garden on 26 December 1794 the afterpiece *Mago and Dago* was performed, described as "Composed, Prepared and directed" by Lonsdale with music, partly new, by Shields, and dances by Byrne.

On 21 December 1795 at Covent Garden the pantomime *Merry Sherwood*, "Invented" by Lonsdale, was given its first performance. The following year, according to Arundell, Lonsdale joined Covent Garden but still served as deputy manager at Sadler's Wells and let Thomas Dibdin take over his post as stage manager. He contributed in 1796 to *The Cabinet Magazine*, a periodical co-edited by the younger Charles Dibdin. In July 1796 at the Wells, Lonsdale's *Venus's Girdle, or, the World Bewitch'd* was performed, and on 7 May 1798 his pantomime *Alfred the Great* was presented there. The June 1798 *Monthly Mirror* stated that Lonsdale was "sole conductor of the Wells this season," having in May stated incorrectly that Thomas Dibdin and Lonsdale were sharing as proprietors.

The *Monthly Mirror* in May 1799 commented on a new piece at the Wells:

Mr. Lonsdale, who has for many seasons conducted the affairs of this elegant summer theatre, has this year added considerably to his reputation, by the production of a serious ballet called Arden of Feversham, founded on a domestic tale recorded in the annals of Kent, A.D. 1550. . . . In Mr. Lonsdale's ballet, the most striking incidents of the narrative are introduced, and the effect of the whole is equal to the best things of the kind.

Lonsdale was still at Sadler's Wells in October 1799, when Tate Wilkinson wrote him from Doncaster, apparently in connection with a planned production of Lonsdale's *Tippoo* (the letter is at the Huntington). But Lonsdale had left the Wells by April 1800, when the *Monthly Mirror* regretted his absence. Lonsdale's pantomime *Puss in Boots* was performed at the Royal Circus on 28 May 1801.

In December 1801 Lonsdale opened a show at the Lyceum. The *Monthly Mirror* reported on his *Ægyptiana*:

> The Ingenious Mr. Lonsdale, to whom the public have been indebted for various amusements, opened the scenic theatre here December 26, with a Divertisement under the above title, chiefly descriptive of ancient and modern Egypt. It is impossible to pourtray the exquisite variety of this entertainment; there is abundant food for the eye and ear.

Richard Altick in his *Shows of London* quotes portions of one of Lonsdale's bills: "This Part of the Evening's Entertainment, intended to give an amusing Turn to Information, and to exhibit Fact in its most picturesque Form, will be relieved by a few Productions of Fancy, uniting the more sportive Efforts of Poetry, Painting and Spectacle." Those included readings from Gothic romances, "Illustrated by Machinery and Painting, in Six Picturesque Changes. . . ." The evening also featured an "Embellished Recitation of Milton's L'Allegro, Including a Scenic View of the Imagery of the Poet. In Ten Successive Pictures, produced by a System of Machinery upon a plan entirely new." The pictures for the Milton reading showed

> the Poet's Study; A Rural Scene, at Daybreak; Sunrise—An Open Landscape; A Rustic Noontide Repast; The Upland Hamlet and Holiday Sports; Evening—The Cottage Fireside; A Splendid Tournament; An Ancient Hall, with a Banquet; a Theatre—Scenes from Johnson [*recte* Jonson] and Shakespeare; A Music Saloon—Opening to a View of the Elysian Fields.

John Britton wrote and read the script for *Ægyptiana* and in his autobiography called Lonsdale's entertainment a "moving panorama." In January 1802 the *Monthly Mirror* reported that the show was crowded night after night.

The novelty soon wore off, however, and to meet the competition from similar shows Lonsdale introduced his *Spectrographia*, which provided spectators with ". . . Supernatural Appearances as described in popular Stories, and credited by Weak Minds . . . produced to the eye of the Spectator by a system of Machinery connected with a series of Experiments . . . forming a varied and amusing picture of TRADITIONARY GHOST WORK!" The specter raisings were accompanied by readings of poetry, much of it from Shakespeare: *Julius Caesar*, *Richard III*, and *Macbeth*, among others.

His Lyceum show failed ultimately, and Lonsdale retired to Ireland. Dibdin said that Lonsdale had been "extremely unsuccessful in several fair and honourable speculations, where others had largely reaped the fruits of his industry, and he had been left to bear the consequences of disappointment." From Greenville, Ireland, on 29 January 1809 Lonsdale wrote to Dibdin:

> From the very centre of Ireland you are addressed by one who now and then recollects with some pleasure the cheerful hours he has spent with Tom Dibdin, and who would fain believe that similar recollections now and then take place on your side of the water: be that as it may, the writer of this ventures to remind you that such a being as Mark Lonsdale is yet in existence, and hopes, ere long, to rejoin his former connexions, and to wind up his account on the scene of his once happier days, with more satisfaction than at one period of his exile he had any reason to expect.
>
> In truth, my friend, I have made but a sorry business of it these six years past, and "could a tale unfold!"—at present, however, and for the last eighteen months, I have been comparatively comfortable, as tutor in a private family, about fifty miles from Dublin, where I teach reading, writing, arithmetic, drawing, French, and English to three very nice young Irish ladies, and six young gentlemen, and live and lodge as well as any man in the kingdom. . . . A situation like this, you will say, is not so bad a thing for a man who has had previous cause to complain of the world's ill usage; but the fact is, I have a heavy account to settle with the world, which, bad as it is, holds me its debtor; and till that debt is put in some train of liquidation, I dare not think myself happy in any situation: my pecuniary resources amount only to thirty Guineas per annum where I am, and I can do nothing for my creditors in London, who,

having kindly accepted a composition (furnished by a feeling and generous sister), leave me at full liberty to live where I can, undisturbed by any further claims; this circumstance binds me the more to a full discharge of every encumbrance I have been so unfortunately laid under, and I shall not cease to try for the means, at all available opportunities.

Having said thus much, I must now inform you, that about a month ago, I sported a letter to Mr. Kemble, enclosing some sketches of a plan for arranging the wardrobe, dressing-rooms, store-rooms, &c. of your new theatre, in a building detached from the stage, understanding from the newspapers that some such plan was in contemplation, and having projected a similar thing for the Crow-street concern, which the eccentricity of Mr. Jones hindered from being carried into full effect. I also made an offer of my personal services to King John, as storekeeper, registrar, and overseer of the works, specifying particularly the duties I thought myself capable of undertaking in that capacity, and the savings which might thereby accrue to the theatre, without my being in any way concerned in furnishing pieces for the stage, or setting my own invention to work: for, in the first place, I think I could find employment enough without it; and, in the next place, I am determined never to hazard my health and reputation in that department again. I have had too much wear and tear as a manager already, and am well convinced that the getting up of a single pantomime would send my shattered frame to *requiescat in pace.*

Respecting the success of my architectural ideas I have strong doubts, as I now understand that some progress had been made in the new building, and it is not likely that any alteration can be made in the plan; but for my other proposal, I am still anxious about its reception. I have had no answer to my letter, and it may possibly be a long time ere I can be favoured with one from the Great Man: would you, my dear sir, so far oblige me as to remind him of it, or to obtain for me some information on the subject, by applying in any way you may think proper?

Dibdin said he had no luck in renewing Kemble's earlier favorable impression of Lonsdale.

At some point Mark wrote to Dibdin again, requesting help; Dibdin said,

I had a letter of the deepest distress from him, requesting I would solicit the company of Drury Lane for subscriptions to realize a pound or two. All the (professed) saints on the face of the earth are not a hundredth part so ready to assist distress as theatrical performers: in twelve hours I raised thirty-two pounds for Lonsdale, and Mr. Arnold desired me to offer him a situation as housekeeper of the Lyceum. This was doing my friend a solid and permanent service, and doubled and trebled the good news I had to send poor Mark of the subscription. He came to town—grateful, but spirit-broken, and, as it eventually turned out, heart-broken.

The Drury Lane accounts show Lonsdale on the company list in 1812, cited as a stage property man at £2 weekly in 1813–14 and mentioned again in that capacity in 1814–15. Dibdin did not date Lonsdale's death precisely, but it came not long after Dibdin's mother died on 10 October 1814. Since the Drury Lane accounts mention Lonsdale in February 1815 as off nearly every week, it is likely he died sometime in the first half of that year.

Wilkinson called Mark Lonsdale "a literary man, well known in the theatrical world for his talents and ingenuity." Thomas Dibdin, of course, thought very highly of him: "that most clever and strictly honest, but unfortunate artist, if I may not say genius. . . ." Dibdin had in his possession a number of letters and other papers of Lonsdale, among which were some notes relating to the management of Sadler's Wells. Dibdin quoted two of them:

No person taking benefits should be allowed to introduce new performers to sing songs, or play particular characters: these chance bargains seldom turn out creditable to the theatre; on the contrary, they often contribute to get the house into disrepute, and disgust a number of visitors, who think them part of the regular company provided for the season.

The experience of every season *must* convince a stage manager that no point whatever is to be gained by giving what is called "individual accomodation" to any performer in the progress of business. It is better to go on with the regular chain of management, under no restraint as to particular wishes of particular performers: in obliging one, either by called rehearsals out of course, or excusing such individual from business, you are certain to disoblige all the rest; for the members of a theatrical company are so much like other people, that, notwithstanding their professions of friendship to the manager, or good fellowship with one another;—the moment a cause of discontent, real or imaginary, presents itself to an individual, a hundred solid benefits and accomodations are forgotten; the managers are spoken of as every thing bad; brother performers are abused as a set of d———d ungenerous, worthless beings; and the hero of the occasion declares himself everywhere to be the most injured man living upon the face of the earth.

If Mark Lonsdale actually carried out his philosophy of fair play in the running of Sadler's Wells, he doubtless encountered resistance from some of his leading performers that would help explain the broken spirit of his last years.

Lonzetti. *See* LANZETTI.

Loosey, Mr [*fl.* 1783], *cheque taker.*

In the Lord Chamberlain's accounts is a warrant noting that a Mr Loosey was the cheque or money taker at the pit front door at the King's Theatre in 1783.

Lopru, Mr [*fl.* 1708], *house servant.*

The Queen's Theatre staff was listed among the papers in Vice Chamberlain Coke's papers at Harvard. Mr Lopru was noted as one of those working in the wardrobe; his salary was 3s. daily. He was not one of the dressers, for they were listed separately at 1s. 6d. per diem.

Lops, Rosa [*fl.* 1791–1792], *singer.*

Rosa Lops was from Munich, a pupil of Mingotti. She came to London in 1791 to join the opera troupe at the King's Theatre, according to Smith's *Italian Opera in London*. A writer in the *Morning Chronicle* in February, who had probably attended a rehearsal, reported that she was "a good and finished singer; she has every accomplishment but youth and beauty." On 26 and 29 May the unlicensed performers at the King's finally managed to avoid the Licensing Act and open their season by presenting selections from operas with the singers in their street clothes. Haydn listed Mme Lops in his *First London Notebook* in 1792 as one of the singers in London. She was apparently to sing in his opera *Orfeo*, but the work was not produced in London.

Lord, John 1769–1850, *instrumentalist, composer.*

John Lord was born 9 May 1769, the son of John and Susanna Lord of Highworth, Wiltshire, according to the records of the Royal Society of Musicians. He performed "on the Piano Forte, harp, & violin" and was "organist of Brunswick Chapel" and a teacher of piano and harp, testified his sponsor William Dance when he was presented to the Society on 2 March 1800.

At that date Lord lived in Fair Street, Manchester Square, was married, and had three children: John, born 22 August 1795, Mary, born 1 March 1797, and William, born 8 October 1798. Sainsbury in 1825 provided entries in his *Dictionary* for the sons John and William. Both were performers and teachers, William principally on the harp and John on the piano. John was said to be "assistant professor to Dr. Crotch" in the Royal Academy of Music.

Lord, Thomas 1760–1815, *violinist, horn player.*

The Minute Books of the Royal Society of Musicians show that Thomas Lord was born in 1760. By the time he was proposed for membership in the Society on 7 December 1783 he had become proficient on the violin and French horn and had an engagement at Covent Garden Theatre. He was, perhaps, a brother of the elder John Lord, who was a performer on the pianoforte, harp, violin, and organ; if so, their parents were John and Susanna Lord of Highworth. (*The London Stage* guessed that the Lord who played horn in the oratorios at Covent Garden may have been John, but Thomas was clearly the Covent Garden musician.)

In May and June 1784 Thomas Lord played horn in the Handel Memorial Concerts at Westminster Abbey and the Pantheon, and on 12 and 14 May 1789 and in several subsequent years he played violin in the Royal Society of Musicians' St Paul's Concerts. On 7 March 1794 he was mentioned in the Covent Garden oratorio bill, and since he had been playing in the theatre band as early as 1783, he very likely participated regularly in the theatre's oratorio seasons. Doane's *Musical Directory* of 1794 cited Thomas Lord but did not provide his address. The Covent Garden account books listed Lord at a salary of 5s. 10d. nightly in 1799–1800. He served in 1804 as a Governor of the Royal Society of Musicians.

The Society minutes show that on 7 February 1808 Lord was granted four guineas to cover medical expenses; he had been "afflicted with a disorder" of some sort. He was receiving an allowance of £26 annually from the Society in 1813. Thomas Lord died in 1815; the Society paid his funeral expenses on 2 April. His widow was granted an allowance at that time, but when she died a year later a request for funds to cover her funeral expenses was denied because her husband had left her property.

There were other musical Lords in the nineteenth century who were probably related to Thomas. John Lord (mentioned above) had two musical sons, John and William, and a Mr I. Lord played bassoon for the Royal Society of Musicians in 1803. Joseph Lord, possibly an ancestor of Thomas, had been a music publisher in the 1730s and 1740s.

"Lord Chief Justice Joker." *See* SPARKS, ISAAC.

"Lord Flame." *See* JOHNSON, SAMUEL *d. 1773.*

"Lord Ogleby." *See* KING, THOMAS.

Lorenzini, Caterina [*fl.* 1780–1784], *singer.*

Signora Caterina Lorenzini made her first appearance in England on 23 December 1780, when she sang Zelmira in *Rinaldo* at the King's Theatre. She was the second woman, singing the serious parts in comic operas at the King's in 1780–81 and 1781–82, among them Lesbia in *Zemira e Azor*, Donna Stella in *La Frascatana*, Ariene in *Euriso*, Onoria in *Ezio*, Isabella in *I viaggiatori felici*, Marzia in *Junius Brutus*, Clarice in *Le contadina in corte*, Fausta in *Quinto Fabio*, Ulanio in *L'eroe cinese*, Clarice in *Il bacio*, and Elisena in *Ifigenia in Aulide*. Her full name was printed in the libretto of *Pizzarro* in Florence in 1784.

Lorenzo, Signor [*fl.* 1792], *dancer.*

Fuchs in his *Lexique* lists a dancer named Lorenzo as a participant in the pantomime ballet *La Foire de Smirne* at the Haymarket Theatre in London on 14 April 1792. *The London Stage* does not include Lorenzo in the cast of the work, though he may well have been one of the minor dancers.

Lorenzo, Vicenzo [*fl.* 1773–1774], *dancer.*

On 23 October 1773 the proprietors of the King's Theatre announced that among the dancers they had engaged for the 1773–74 season was Vicenzo Lorenzo. His name did not appear in any of the bills that season, so he must have been a member of the corps de ballet.

Lort, Mr [*fl.* 1749–1751], *equilibrist.*

On 15 September 1749 at Southwark Fair at Phillips's booth Mr Lort performed equilibres on the slack rope, as he did again on the eighteenth. At the Haymarket Theatre on 30 September Lort tried to persuade Londoners that he was as good as the famous Mahomet Caratta:

The Englishman, Freeman and Citizen of London, Mr. Lort, this day will perform several new and surprising Equilibres on the Slack Rope at the new Theatre in the Haymarket. . . . As several imagine none of our Natives can equal Foreigners, this is to inform the gentry, that there is not one thing the Turk did perform but Mr. Lort will endeavour to convince them he can perform the same on the slack rope.

On 26 March 1751 Lort joined Caratta for a performance at Bristol:

For the Benefit of Mr. LORT.
At the Great Room, under the Guild-hall, in Broad-street.
On Tuesday next the 26th Instant March,
(Being positively the last Week of PERFROMING [*sic*] here)
Will be EXHIBITED
The surprizing Performances of the GRAND TURK, Mahomed Charatha, on a Slack Wire scarcely perceptible. . . . Likewise the Ladder Dance by Mr. Lort; and he will stand upon his Head on the Wire, which was never perform'd in this city before.
The Whole to conclude with several curious Fire Works. . . .

In the Huntington Library is an engraving which shows Lort as a central figure, surrounded by many smaller depictions of his balancing acts. The print, undated, was published for John Ryall at Hogarth's Head in Fleet Street and bears the inscription: "The surprizing Equilibres on the Slack Wire, By M.ʳ Lort an Englishman, which he has perform'd With Universal Applause at the Theatre in the Hay-Markett Old Sadlers Wells, and now in this Town."

Lottini, Antonio [*fl.* 1735–1740], *singer.*

The basso Antonio Lottini was a native of Pistola and sang in Lucca in 1735, according to the *New Grove*. The 1736 edition of *Il giocatore* notes that Lottini sang in that work with Anna Maria Faini. The opera was presented at the King's Theatre on 1 January 1737. Simi-

Henry E. Huntington Library and Art Gallery

MR LORT

artist unknown

larly, the 1737 edition of *Pourceaugnac and Grilleta* listed the same singers; that work was given at the King's on 25 January. He probably sang Nibbio in *The Impresario* on 26 March. Lottini sang Teobaldo in Handel's *Faramondo* at the King's on 3 January 1738. During the rest of the season he sang in *La conquista del vello d'oro* and was Elviro in *Serse*. Lottini's salary was said to have been £500 per season.

Louch, Mrs, formerly Mrs Middlehurst [*fl.* 1742–1743₁], *performer?*

At Covent Garden Theatre on 11 March 1742 tickets for Mrs Louch were admitted. On 16 April 1743 at the same house her benefit tickets were again taken, and the performance of *The Double Gallant* and *Perseus and Andromeda* for the benefit of Destrade and Rheinhold was presented "At the Desire of several Ladies of Quality, [also?] for the Benefit of Mrs Middlehurst, from Cheshire, whose name is now Louch; Tickets at Mrs Louch's, three Doors above St. James Church, Piccadilly." Possibly Mrs Louch was a performer.

Louder. *See* LOWDER.

Louille, Sophie [*fl.* 1774–1782?₁], *dancer.*

Mlle Sophie Louille was first mentioned in London bills on 19 November 1774, when she danced a pas de deux with Asselin at the King's Theatre. She continued at that house through the spring of 1776, sometimes called "Mlle Sophie" in the bills, dancing such entr'acte specialties as an allemande with Henery, a group number entitled *Champêtre comique*, the pantomime ballets *Apollon e Daphne* and *Pigmalion amoureuse de la statue*, *Les Evénemens imprevues*, *Les Deux Soeurs rivales*, *La Générosité de Scipion*, *La Fête du village*, a solo *Une Bergère*, *Astolphe dans l'île de Alcine*, *Le Retour des matelots*, a *Ballet Pastoral*, *Les Maissoneurs distresses*, and *Triomphe de la Magie*.

A dancer called Mlle Sophie was in Brussels from 1778 to 1782; she was probably our subject.

Louis. *See also* **LEWIS.**

Louis, Mr [*fl.* 1785–1815], *dancer, tumbler, singer.*

Mr Louis (sometimes Lewis, Lewiss, or Lewey) was tumbling and dancing at Astley's Amphitheatre near Westminster Bridge by 27 September 1785. He worked there until October 1786, but then he went to Sadler's Wells, where his name was regularly in the bills from 1788 through 1806. Probably he was the Lewis who worked in the chorus at Covent Garden from 1796–97 to at least through 1800–1801, at 5s. per night.

A Mrs Lewis and a Miss Lewis also performed at Sadler's Wells in 1795 and 1796. Probably they were our subject's wife and daughter. About 1804 Louis married the dancer Mme Pierre (formerly Mlle St Amand). They were members of the Drury Lane Company from 1810–11 to 1814–15. About 1815, having cheated her of all her money, he left her. In 1843, when she was about 80, the second Mrs Louis was reduced to serving as a dresser at Sadler's Wells.

Louis, Mrs the first [*fl.* 1795–1796], *dancer.* *See* **LOUIS, MR** [*fl.* 1785–1815].

Louis, Mme the second. *See* **ST AMAND, MLLE** *b. c.* 1763.

Louis, Miss [*fl.* 1796], *dancer.* *See* **LOUIS, MR** [*fl.* 1785–1815].

Loulworth, Ivitt [*fl.* 1784], *singer.*

Mr Ivitt Loulworth of Cambridgeshire sang countertenor in the Handel Memorial Concerts at Westminster Abbey and the Pantheon in May and June 1784.

Loutherbourg. *See* **DE LOUTHERBOURG.**

Louvicini, Signora [*fl.* 1705–1706], *singer.*

Signora Louvicini was advertised as lately arrived when she made her first appearance in England, singing between the acts at the Queen's Theatre on 15 December 1705. She sang a few times more, but on 29 January 1706 she announced in the bills that she was "being to return very speedily out of England" and would perform "for this one day only."

Lovattini, Giovanni [*fl.* 1760–1782], *singer.*

Giovanni Lovattini, a native of Bologna, was a member of the burletta company at the King's Theatre, London, in 1766–67. He made his first appearance on 21 October 1766 in *Gli stravaganti*. On 25 November he sang Conchiglia in the first performance in England of *La buona figliuola*, a comic opera by Piccini with libretto by Goldoni. Lovattini had created the role in the premiere in Rome in 1760.

Burney wrote in his *General History of Music* that Lovattini's voice, "which was a sweet and well-toned tenor, with his taste, humour, and expression, insured him great and constant applause in whatever character he appeared; but the Music of this drama was so admirable . . . that a worse singer than Lovattini, would have been sure of a favourable reception." On 31 January 1767 he appeared in the sequel, *La buona figliuola maritata*. Probably he sang in *Il signor dottore* on 12 March 1767. On 9 April he, Morigi, and others sang in Jomelli's intermezzo *Don Trastullo*.

Lovattini was engaged regularly as the first man in comic opera at the King's Theatre for nine years, through 1774–75. Among the operas in which he sang were *La schiava* in 1767–68, *Le contadine bizzarre*, *L'uccellatrice*, and *Il disertore* in 1769–70, *Le vicende della sorte* and *Le contadina in corte* in 1770–71, and *La marchesa giardiniera* and *I viaggiatori ridicoli* in 1774–75. Lovattini left England in the summer of 1775. He subsequently retired to his native Bologna, where he was visited by Michael Kelly in the fall of 1782.

Burney believed that after Lovattini's departure comic opera in England fell into "a languid and declining state," and singers who followed, like Morelli, were "inadequate to the expectations of those who remember the sweet voice and excellent humour of Lovattini."

Love, Mr [*fl.* 1743], *singer.* See LOWE, THOMAS.

Love, Master. *See* DANCE, WILLIAM.

Love, Charles [*fl.* 1739–1783?], *musician.*

Charles Love was listed as one of the original subscribers, "being musicians," in the Declaration of Trust which established the Royal Society of Musicians on 28 August 1739. He was the Mr Love who performed the "Quaker's Sermon on the Violin" at the Assembly Room, St Augustine's Back, Bristol, on 21 September 1745, in a concert given "By the best Hands in *Bristol*, and from Bath and other Places."

He was, no doubt, the Charles Love, "musician from London," who with his wife went to the American colonies with Lewis Hallam's company in 1752. Love played violin and oboe in Hallam's company and preached his Quaker's sermon on the violin, while his wife was the star soubrette. On 2 July 1753 Love advertised in the New York *Mercury* that he proposed "teaching gentlemen musick" on the "Violin, Hautboy, German and Common Flutes, Bassoon, French Horn, Tenor, and Base Violin." On 24 January 1754 he presented a concert at the New Exchange Ball Room in which he performed "several select pieces on the hautboy" and his wife sang. He seems no longer to have been involved in the theatre at that time, but probably he was teaching. His wife continued to act in New York and Philadelphia until 1759. By 1757 Love was wanted in Virginia for stealing a "small white horse" and a "very good bassoon" from Philip Ludwell Lee. At that time he was described as "a tall, thin Mann, about sixty of age."

In 1759 a "Love, Sr" was at Norwich in England, and Charles Love, presumably the same person, was playing in the Norwich band by 1763, by which time Mrs Love, also back from America, had become a member of the company. On 25 January 1769 the Norwich committee agreed "to retain Mr Love as an Additional & Leading Musician in the Orchestra at the Rate of one Guinea p Week. He undertaking to teach & instruct the company of Comedians in all Music & to attend the rehearsals." (It seems likely that this person was Charles Love, then about 70 and an experienced musician, rather than, as has been suggested in the publication of *The Committee Books of the Theatre Royal Norwich*, William Love [or Dance], son of the actor James Love, who would have been only 14 at the time.) Charles Love, or his son, remained connected with the Norwich band for some years. On 29 December 1775 he was ordered "struck out of the Band," and on 2 August 1779 the Committee "order'd That Mr Love be discharged." Yet once more, on 30 May 1783, the Committee "Ordered that Mr Lambert, Mr Love, Harper and Lacey be discharged from the Band."

Mrs Love seems to have acted at Norwich at least through 1766, but evidently she did not appear on the London stage. She should not be confused with Mrs Love, the wife or mistress of James Love, an actress in the same line, who worked at Drury Lane and Richmond, Surrey, during the period the Norwich actress flourished.

Love, James, stage name of James Dance 1721–1774, *actor, manager, author.*

James Dance was born on 17 March 1721, entering a numerous family of practitioners of several arts. He was the great-grandson of James and Elizabeth Dance of Winchester. His grandfather was Giles Dance (1670–1751), a stonemason of London, whose wife was Sarah Brett of Carshalton. James's father was George Dance (1695–1768), Clerk of the City Works and architect of the Mansion House, and his mother was Elizabeth Gould. Our subject had four younger brothers and a sister. Giles Dance (b. 1733) became a grocer in Gracechurch Street, Cornhill. Nathaniel Dance (1735–1811), a distinguished portrait painter who took the name Holland upon entering Parliament, became Sir Nathaniel Dance-Holland when created a baronet in 1800. William Dance (b. 1736) was apprenticed to John Fenton, a Sheffield apothecary, in 1753. James's youngest brother, George Dance (1741–1825), became the famous architect who designed the second Newgate and other important London buildings. His sister, Hester Dance (1742–1812), married a cousin, Captain Nathaniel Smith of the East India Company and later M.P. for Rochester. (Information on the family pedigree and activities may be found in Dorothy Stroud's *George Dance*; members of the family are also noticed in *The Dictionary of National Biography*.)

In 1732 James Dance entered Merchant Taylors' School and on 1 March 1738 he matriculated at St John's College, Oxford, as the son of George Dance, gentleman, of Cripplegate, London. Though he possessed an excellent mind he never took a degree, preferring to idle away his time. When a poem satirizing Sir Robert Walpole was published with the title *Are These Things So?*, Dance, a Whig supporter, printed a smart poem in reply, *Yes They Are: What Then?* Reportedly Walpole rewarded his supporter with £100 and invitations to some parties. Dance left Oxford in the summer of 1738 with the hope of entering the legal profession. He enrolled at Lincoln's Inn on 28 November of that year. But having "contracted habits of indolence and expense," as Baker put it in *Biographia Dramatica*, Dance soon gave up the law and took to touring with small theatrical companies.

Just when Dance turned to the stage is not clear. Indeed, facts about his life from 1738 to 1745 are sparse. About 1740 he published a long heroic poem about cricket, dedicated to the Earl of Sandwich, in which he exhorted his countrymen "to leave all meaner sports and cultivate cricket only as most adapted to the freedom and hardship of its constitution." (The poem was published again in his *Poems on Several Occasions* in 1754 and 1767 and as *Cricket. An heroic poem: illustrated with the critical observations of Scriblerus Maximus* in 1770.) Dance has also been credited with the authorship of *Pamela*, a comedy adapted from Richardson's novel, which had its premiere at Goodman's Fields Theatre on 9 November 1741. The play, "As it is perform'd, gratis, at the late theatre in Goodman's-Fields," was published by J. Robinson in 1742 without an author stated; the British Library and Folger Shakespeare Library catalogues attribute the play to Dance. But William Sale, Jr, points out in "The First Dramatic Version of Pamela," *Yale University Library Gazette* (1935), that two versions of the play were published in autumn 1741: *Pamela; or, Virtue Triumphant*, "designed to be acted at Drury Lane," and *Pamela*, the one later performed at Goodman's Fields. Additionally, a second edition of the latter also appeared in 1742 and two pirated versions came out, one dated 1741. In a letter to his brother Peter in January 1742 David Garrick stated that the Goodman's Fields *Pamela* was written by Henry Giffard, manager of that theatre. Garrick, who acted Jack Smatter in the play—his third character, after Richard III and Chamont in his debut season—denied the rumor that he had written it, but he acknowledged composing the "French Letter wch was vastly lik'd, & tagging ye Fourth Act." The question of Dance's part in the authorship of the play, in either version, remains obscure.

Nothing is known of Dance's acting career until he turned up in 1744–45 as a member of the Hallam company playing at Goodman's Fields. Announced as "a Gentleman," he acted Bayes and delivered the epilogue to *The Rehearsal* on 7 January 1745. That play was repeated on 8, 10, and 14 January, but it could not be acted on the fifteenth because "of the indisposition of the Gentleman who performs Bays." He recovered sufficiently by 7 February to reappear as Bayes. On 12 March the bills carried the name of "Dance, who acted Bays" for the role of Caled in *The Siege of Damascus*. By "the particular Desire of several Persons of Distinction" the evening was designated a benefit for Dance, from whom tickets were available at his lodgings with Mr Boteler in Fenchurch Street. Dance's other roles that season were the Ghost in *Hamlet* on 23 March 1745 and Falstaff (a character in which he developed a reputation of sorts) in *1 Henry IV* on 26 March and *The Merry Wives of Windsor* on 28 March. His last performance of the season, as Falstaff, was on 17 April 1745.

Though he had no regular engagements in London during the rest of the decade Love appeared occasionally on the stages of the patent houses. At Covent Garden on 2 May 1746 he shared a benefit with Nivelon, for which he acted Bayes. The *Daily Advertiser* two days earlier printed a message to him which emanated from Tom's Coffee House:

Mr Bayes: By the unanimous Desire of a number of your Friends here assembled, who attend to sit in judgment upon you . . . I take upon me to advise you in some Particulars, as to your present Undertaking. Let not any Success you might meet with at one End of the Town where the Audience must be composed of a different Class of People from what you may expect at Covent Garden, tempt you to think of mimicking an Actress whom the Town doats upon; and particularly avoid Puffing; a Scheme long ago worn threadbare, but lately demolish'd by an enterprizing Genius. Not even an Epilogue from the Gods would be of any Service now; and therefore if you have anything that's new, any fiery Flights of Fancy, and all that, let them lie dormant till the Time of action, and then endeavour to elevate and surprize. Value these Hints.

A week later, on 9 May 1746, he acted Falstaff in *1 Henry IV* at Drury Lane. When he played Bayes at Goodman's Fields on 23 March 1747, for some odd reason his name was spelled backwards in the bills. He returned to Covent Garden on 17 October 1748 to play Worcester in *1 Henry IV*, but his name appeared in no other bills that season.

At some time during his strolling, about mid-century, Dance adopted the stage name of Love. The first instance we find of his use of that name was in July 1751 at Dumfries, where he was placed by the *Scots Magazine* of September 1751, but the bills of some other provincial theatre may have carried it earlier.

In the winter of 1751–52 Love was head of a company of strolling players—consisting of Mr and Mrs Tobias Gemea, Mr and Mrs William Lewis, Philip Lewis, and Mr and Mrs Tyrer—which performed at the Vaults in Belfast. Their repertory included *Jane Shore*, *The Virgin Unmask'd*, *The Honest Yorkshireman*, in which Love acted Blunder, and *The Merry Wives of Windsor*, in which he acted Falstaff. Also in the company and playing Arabella and Anne Page in the last two pieces, respectively, was Mrs Love, whose identity presents a dilemma.

On 27 August 1739 the *Daily Advertiser* had announced the marriage, the previous week, of Elizabeth Hooper to James Dance. (The *Political State of Great Britain* for September 1739 also carried the report and identified Dance as of St John's College. At that time, however, the eighteen-year-old Dance was a member of Lincoln's Inn.) Elizabeth was the daughter of James Hooper, a customs official. In his *Random Records*, the younger George Colman circulated the story, initiated in the *Biographia Dramatica*, that Dance's wife's maiden name was De L'Amour, wherefore the actor adopted Love as his stage name.

Dorothy Stroud in her study of George Dance claims that, indeed, James abandoned his legal wife for an actress named Catherine L'Amour, but she cites no better source than the *Biographia Dramatica*. She does, however, state that Dance's parents made themselves responsible for the three children by Elizabeth Hooper whom he had deserted and that they took Nathaniel, the eldest, to live with them. In an account of Nathaniel Dance given in the *Naval Chronicle* for 1804, it was reported that James, shortly after the birth of Nathaniel, having "adopted habits of dissipation, quitted his family altogether and formed an unfortunate connection with Mrs. Love, an inferior actress of that day," and assumed her name. Elizabeth, James's legitimate wife, died in 1783, according to Stroud. The actress Mrs Love performed in London until 1790 and did not die until 1807.

The implication, then, is that the Mrs Love who was with our subject at Belfast in 1751–52 was not Elizabeth but the legendary Catherine L'Amour. But at least one of James Dance's three children was not born until over three years after that time: the younger son William was born on 20 December 1755; the elder son Nathaniel was born in 1748; and the birthdate of a daughter Sarah is unknown.

In 1752 Love was performing with Mrs Ward, West Digges, and Stamper in a wooden booth in the Castle Yard, Glasgow. About that time Love sold his Irish company at Newry to William and Philip Lewis.

Early in 1754, Dance, now regularly called Love, acted in Edinburgh, appearing at the New Canongate Concert Hall in March as Bayes, Siffredi in *Tancred and Sigismunda*, Macheath in *The Beggar's Opera*, and Falstaff in *1 Henry IV*. "Mrs Love," whoever she was, was seen as Miss Biddy in *Miss in Her Teens* on 4 and 9 March. Announced as from Edinburgh the pair acted at Limerick in 1754. They were at the Smock Alley Theatre, Dublin, in 1754–55, where he made his first appearance on 25 October 1754 as Falstaff; another of his characters there was Malvolio in *Twelfth Night*. In the spring of 1756 they acted at Tralee.

That autumn the Loves returned to Edinburgh where they were to settle for six years. Announced as making his first appearance there in two years, Love acted Bayes at the Canongate Concert Hall on 27 September 1756. On 14 December 1756 he played Glenalvon in the first performance of Home's *Douglas*. Among his other roles in the 1756–57 season were Friar Lawrence in *Romeo and Juliet*, Peachum in

The Beggar's Opera, Trinculo in *The Tempest*, Sealand in *The Conscious Lovers*, Pierre in *Venice Preserv'd*, Antonio in *The Merchant of Venice*, Bonniface in *The Beaux' Stratagem*, Dominic in *The Spanish Fryar*, Horatio in *The Fair Penitent*, Claudius in *Hamlet*, and Serjeant Kite in *The Recruiting Officer*.

In the spring of 1758 he acted Cacafogo in *Rule a Wife and Have a Wife*, the King in *The Mourning Bride*, and roles in *Agis* and *The Male Coquette*. That season he was drawn into a dispute between Digges the manager and the band, which had been led out on strike by a musician named Marine. The musicians published accusations against Digges among which was the charge that the Loves had refused to act until they were paid salary arrears, but Love wrote to deny the allegation.

By 1758 Love was acting as manager of David Beatt's theatre at Newcastle. That year Beatt and James Callender wrested the management of the Canongate from Digges and in 1759 installed Love as their stage manager, a position he held for three years. In *A View of the Edinburgh Theatre during the summer season, 1759* (published at London in 1760) the young James Boswell, probably assisted in the writing by Francis Gentleman, gave Love a constant drubbing for his management practices, accusing him of choosing "improper" plays (such as *Amphitryon; or Trick Upon Trick* on 14 July 1759), miscasting, and playing favorites.

Boswell, who credited Love with starting him on his habit of journal-making—when 18 he had set off on an expedition during which he had kept "an exact journal at the particular desire of my friend Mr. Love and sent it to him in sheets every post"—was more generous in his assessment of his acting, though sometimes censorious. Love's Bonniface "was altogether the hearty, old *English* Landlord," his Peachum was well played (though when he tried Macheath he "afforded ample Matter for *Risibility*," as if Sir Tunbelly Clumsy had turned highwayman), and his Mock Doctor was highly commended. His figure, voice, and manner extremely ill-suited him for the dignity of serious drama, but Boswell thought Love had "perhaps, as great Power in forcible comic Action, as any Performer we have seen" and claimed it would be difficult for any one "to succeed better in his Cast of Parts." He extracted cheap laughs as Sofia in *Amphitryon* and as Bayes,

seducing applause by "uncouth Gesticulations." As Falstaff, however, there was "not a Player, at present, in the three Kingdoms, who can do so much Justice to the humorous old Knight." Instead of adopting the melancholy approach taken by many actors, Love

has got a rough, broken, fat Voice, a remarkable Command of Features, and, above all, a sly, roguish, leering Eye, the most essential Requisite for this Character in particular. As there is much redundancy of Wit in it, we greatly approve of Mr. Love's judicious Method of varying his Expression; by means of which we are enabled to relish every Grain of the *Sal Atticum*, with peculiar Poignancy.

It is interesting to note that soon after that summer Love began giving elocution lessons to Boswell.

Some time in the spring or early summer of 1762 David Garrick sent an offer of an engagement at Drury Lane to Love, who replied in a lengthy letter of acceptance on 5 July 1762 and told Garrick he was in the midst of problems with his Edinburgh proprietors. Love was seeking repayment of some sums he had advanced, but the proprietors were insisting they would reimburse him only if he would stay on as an actor. Garrick's offer had come, Love said, as a great relief, because regardless of whatever justice he might receive from the proprietors, he would not refuse Garrick's proposals to come to London.

The letter is full of flattery of Garrick and of Love's assurances that he would strain every nerve in the master's service. Love, furthermore, hoped that Garrick would allow him to appear under his new name (he had been using it for over a decade) because he desired evermore to be called by it. He promised to be in London in about six weeks. In closing he claimed that he had found Edinburgh to be a barren spot, though his company praised his administration and lamented his leaving. He had, despite his problems with the proprietors, done well; late in 1760 he wrote to his brother Nathaniel in Italy that he was comfortably off and clearing about £500 per year in Edinburgh.

Love began his Drury Lane engagement on 25 September 1762, when he acted Falstaff in *1 Henry IV* (and was announced as making his first appearance there, though he had played the same role in his only other appearance on that stage, on 9 May 1746). The author of the *Theatrical Review* (1763) was not so impressed with his Falstaff as Boswell had been:

Mr. Love, in our opinion, was not destitute of those masterly strokes of acting which we have heretofore seen so admirably thrown out in this singular character; but it is nevertheless certain, that he was greatly deficient in that joyous something, which in Quin did so much justice to the inimitable author of the ever wittily-facetious Sir John.—In many places Mr. Love was too sententiously serious; and in a few, too buffoonishly comical: In some, however, (though we could wish indeed they had been more frequent) he displayed the genuineness of humour, the loss of which we have so much deplored ever since the Hero in Falstaff made his final exit from the Theatrical Stage.

Love's second role was Strickland in *The Suspicious Husband* on 30 September 1762; Garrick had acted Ranger and Mrs Pritchard Clarinda. His next roles were Jobson in *The Devil to Pay* on 4 October, Siffredi in *Tancred and Sigismunda* on 12 October, and Bonniface in *The Stratagem* on 13 October. Garrick kept him busy for the rest of the season as Gloster in *Jane Shore*, the title role (for his first time on 29 October) in *Cymbeline*, the King in *The Mourning Bride*, Falstaff in *2 Henry IV*, Dominic in *The Spanish Fryar*, Sir Epicure in *The Alchemist*, Sadi in *Barbarossa*, Cacafogo in *Rule a Wife and Have a Wife*, Cimberton in *The Conscious Lovers*, Peachum in *The Beggar's Opera*, Sir Jealous Traffic in *The Busy Body*, Don Alvarez in the premiere of Mallet's *Elvira* on 19 January 1763, Chaunter in *Phoebe*, a character in *Sketch of a Fine Lady's Return from a Rout*, Major Rakish in *The School Boy*, Lord Medway in *The Discovery*, a Witch in *Macbeth*, Gripe in *The Confederacy*, Butler in *The Drummer*, Thorowgood in *The London Merchant*, and the Doctor in *The Mock Doctor*.

Love served Drury Lane 12 consecutive seasons, developing a repertoire in which the town became accustomed to seeing him. A selection of those roles includes Sir Toby Belch in *Twelfth Night*, Claudius in *Hamlet*, Clytus in *The Rival Queens*, Caliban in *The Tempest*, Major Oldfox in *The Plain Dealer*, Sir Francis Wronghead in *The Provok'd Husband*, Jaques in *As You Like It*, Sir Sampson Legend in *All for Love*, Major Sturgeon in *The Mayor of Garratt*, Obadiah in *The Committee*, and, of course, Falstaff in the respective Shakespearean plays and in Garrick's *The Jubilee* in the autumn of 1769. He acted Major Oakly in *The Jealous Wife* for the first time on 19 September 1767 and Polonius in *Hamlet* for the first time on 2 May 1770. Love was the original Serjeant Flower in Colman and Garrick's *The Clandestine Marriage* on 20 February 1766 but also often acted Sterling in that comedy. In 1766–67 he was earning £1 1s. 8d. per night, or £6 10s. per week, but that amount apparently included modest wages for Mrs Love, who had made her debut at Drury Lane late in 1762–63.

When Love played the Scotchman in *The Register Office* for his benefit on 12 April 1764 he was hissed, though his profits that night amounted to £144 10s. 6d. In 1765 he wrote to Garrick, who was on the Continent, to complain that he was not assigned the role of Sir John Brute in *The Provok'd Wife*, and Garrick replied on 3 March 1765, reminding him that his co-manager Lacy was within his authority in giving the part to Tom King. When Love finally acted the role, for his benefit on 2 April 1770, the prompter Hopkins recorded in his diary: "a fat performance . . . and he wanted breath to blow the Jokes out." His portrayal of Freeport in *The English Merchant* at Richmond in June 1767 irked one reviewer: "While this gentleman continued in the third-rate cast of characters, he was a useful hand at Drury-lane House, but when he attempts capital parts, his very friends must blush for him." Thomas Davies in his *Dramatic Miscellanies* thought Love's Sir Epicure in *The Alchemist* was well drawn in outline and justly conceived, but the characterization was deficient in "glowing and warm tints" and he wanted the power to execute the meaning.

Love was more successful as the Chaplain in *The Orphan* on 15 October 1771, or at least so thought John Potter in *The Theatrical Review* (1772): "The Part of the *Chaplain*, though trifling, is rendered of considerable Importance, as represented by Mr. *Love*, who does great justice to it, and appears with as much advantage to himself, in this, as in any Character he plays." In *The Theatres* (1772), Francis Gentleman wrote:

Love, a soft name, but sadly misapplyd,
When giv'n to paltry petulance and pride . . .

and described him as having a "motionless" face, a "bell-man's hollow voice, a bell-man's drone," with a "porter's gait and action of a bear." The audience sat "with patience" to his Bonniface and Falstaff, but Gentleman thought "the merit's small."

Love, however, did achieve some reputation in Falstaff, as the *Rational Rosciad* (1767) explained:

> Love's want of power prevents his playing well,
> Or his unbounded genius must excell;
> But Falstaff's character he fills with grace,
> And by it claims a second rated place;
> In other parts his merit is but small,
> For Falstaff's an epitome of all.

Sylas Neville saw him play Falstaff on 8 May 1767 and wrote in his diary that Love acted "very well"—he "uses his eyes with great propriety in this and many other characters." When Love became too ill to appear in his usual roles between 31 March and 24 April 1772, Garrick wrote an apology to Lord Hardwicke for not being able to comply with his lordship's command for *2 Henry IV*, as there was not another "Stuff'd Man in ye Company to Supply his Place." Roles like Jaques, Sir Toby Belch, Caliban, Jobson, and Falstaff were suited to his manner, his unwieldy figure, and a voice described by William Hawkins in *Miscellanies in Prose and Verse* (1775) as "somewhat asthmatical, and abounding with many inharmonious tones."

Love also shared responsibilities at Drury Lane for the preparations of pantomime, an assignment that Garrick had asked him to assume when he offered Love articles. But Garrick grew disappointed, it seems, with Love's ineptitude for such things. Love's *The Witches; or, Harlequin Cherokee* was produced successfully enough on 23 November 1762. It was altered and revived on 26 December 1771 as *The Witches; or, A Trip to Naples*, with spectacular scenes of Mount Vesuvius erupting. His *The Rites of Hecate; or, Harlequin from the Moon* opened on 26 December 1763 with an overture and comic tunes by Potter and choruses by Battishill. It drew great applause. (A mechanical elephant was "excellent" and had "a Fine Effect" wrote Hopkins in his diary.) Because of Love's deficiencies, however, in providing "business and incidents to carry on the story from one scene to another," reported Hopkins, the day before Christmas was devoted to rehearsing the new pantomime and they "were obliged to call the good natured Mr Colman, to our aid, as we could get no assistance from the author, Mr Love, who seems not to have the least genius in contriving anything of that kind." On 11 April 1764 Garrick wrote from Rome to thank Colman: "I am sure they wanted help—no more humour than Brickbats—I am affraid that *Love* in humourous matters carries too much Gut to be Spirited—flip flaps, & great changes without meaning may distil from the head, whose Eyes are half asleep."

The Hermit; or Harlequin at Rhodes, another of Love's pantomimes, was first played at Drury Lane on 6 January 1766. It brought several crowded houses because it introduced a wild beast eating a Frenchman, capitalizing on newspaper reports of a French beast who was devouring children. Much of the success of the piece was credited by Hopkins to Garrick, who "made most of the Business to it, which is very good." Love's adaptation of Brome's *The Jovial Crew* was produced as a comic opera called *The Ladies Frolick* on 7 May 1770, with music by Thomas Arne and William Bates.

Love is credited by the *Biographia Dramatica* with adaptation of Fletcher's *Rule a Wife and Have a Wife*, which had been published in 1786 as altered by Garrick, despite the fact that Garrick had always emphatically denied any hand in it. In 1811, some 37 years after Love's death, the play was published "as adapted to the Stage by James Love; revised by J. P. Kemble." The play had been a repertory regular during the years Love was at Drury Lane. Nicoll claims the alteration was the version produced at Drury Lane on 14 February 1776, but the comedy had been performed several times previously that season, the first time being on 11 October 1775, and by that time Love was dead. Perhaps Love, who had been with Drury Lane from 1762 until his death, did contribute in some way to the alteration. Fredrick L. Bergmann and Harry M. Pedicord, editors of Garrick's dramatic works, provide a reasoned case for concluding that it owes the major debt for its existence to Garrick.

According to Walter Baynham's *The Glasgow Stage* (1892), Love and Beatt began a management of a new theatre in Argyle Street, Grahamstown, just outside Glasgow, in the spring of 1764. They engaged Mrs Bellamy to appear on opening night, with Reddish and Aickin, but a Methodist mob set fire to the theatre, destroying the properties and costumes. At the insistence of Mrs Bellamy and the assistance of a hastily assembled crew of carpenters and upholsterers the players went on anyway. Love and Beatt supposedly managed there for four years, but by the time he was reported to have begun his connection with Glasgow, Love was already very busy preparing the scheme for a new theatre at Richmond, Surrey, which would monopolize his attention every summer until his death.

Love's Richmond venture was financed mainly by the loan of about £4000 from Richard Horne, Love's uncle by marriage to Hester Dance, a sister of the elder George Dance. The Hornes' daughter Elizabeth was the first wife of Lt Col James Hubbard, of the Middlesex Militia. The theatre was on a site owned by Hubbard and his father-in-law Horne on Richmond Green, where once had stood a mansion they had divided into tenement rentals.

Advice for the building was offered by Garrick, who seemed a genuine friend, though he had written to his brother George on 20 November 1764 that Love was "politick & wary—the Stage has spoilt him & you may tell him so from Me." On 3 March 1765 Garrick, still abroad, wrote to Love to

most heartily wish you success in y^r great undertaking at Richmond—You cannot have a better Man for y^r Business than Saunderson clear-brain'd to ye skull of him—but I fear, y^r house will be too large—90 p^{ds} for Richmond is a monstrous Sum—!however y^r knowledge & Ability will make it a most comfortable thing, & you may come to Hampton for a little (theatrical) Sense (as the Boys do at school) if you think I have any to spare—I shall be glad to have you so near Me—& shall look upon y^r Academy as a kind of Nursery, to ye Drury Lane Garden—prosper the plough—

Though Love's father and brother may have provided some advice for the design of the new theatre, it was "planned and built" by Saunderson, the Drury Lane machinist so highly endorsed by Garrick. His work was specifically praised by the *St James's Chronicle* in June 1765 and the *Universal Museum, and Complete Magazine* for August 1765. The latter issue provided a detailed description of the simple brick building which stood to the northwest of the Green.

. . . Mr. Sanderson, the machinist of Drury-lane theatre, drew the plan; and in a few months, what the builders call the shell was entirely compleated. In the prosecution of this undertaking every imperfection in either of our royal houses was studiously avoided, and every advantage most sedulously retained. In the embellishment, simplicity and elegance alone had the direction; and it may be said, with the greatest justice, that, for the size, it is by much the best constructed theatre in the British dominions. The boxes form a kind of crescent, which renders them remarkably commodious; because by this means they all have nearly a front view of the stage. They are lined with a crimson worsted damask, and the lobby is to the full as spacious for the entrance of the company, as either of the lobbies at Covent-Garden or Drury-lane. There is but one gallery: this however turns out not a little to the advantage of the audience, as it totally prevents the necessity of having pillars, which so frequently obstruct the view, and hinder a spectator from enjoying many of the most interesting incidents of a play. The pit, if any thing, is too small for the rest of the house; but perhaps it may have been made so on purpose, as the principal part of the spectators usually occupy the boxes and the gallery, there being but few of what may be called the middling station in the neighbourhood. The smallness of the pit has given Mr. Love an opportunity of allowing a handsome space for an orchestra, which he has judiciously taken care to fill with a very good band of music. One particular improvement we cannot upon this occasion avoid to mention, which is, that the ginger-bread stuccoing, which we see round the boxes at the royal theatres, is totally omitted; all the pannels being painted of a dark colour, which gives the stage an additional degree of light when the curtain is drawn up, and makes every thing on it appear with a double advantage. As to the scenes, they are the workmanship of the ingenious Mr. French, the scene-painter of Drury-lane house; and, to the connoisseurs in that science, a farther recommendation is utterly unncessary.

The New Theatre on the Green was opened on 15 June 1765 with a prologue composed by Garrick and delivered by Love, followed by the comic opera *Love in a Village*. Love's leading actors included Packer, Jackson, Mrs Stephens, Mrs Lee, Miss Slack, and Mrs Love, a collection of performers of less than capital credentials. The *Universal Museum* hoped that Love would manage to improve the quality the next summer. The clipping file in the Richmond Library shows that Love took at least two benefits the first summer and lodged at Mr Gabriel's, back of the Old Court.

The Lord Chamberlain had permitted Love

to perform the first summer at Richmond while a proper license was being drawn. In support of Love's petition for the license Garrick wrote to Sir Robert Wilmot, deputy secretary to the Lord Chamberlain, on 24 February 1766. The press announced on 1 July 1766 that the license had finally been issued, making Love "the only Country Manager in England, who is honoured with that distinction."

But in June 1766 the relations between Garrick and Love had become strained. Garrick had proposed that his protegé—and perhaps natural son—Samuel Cautherley should be allowed to act a leading tragic role at Richmond on a Saturday night. Love replied that he could not afford the risk at the box-office: "I do not desire Mr Cautherly to appear till we can do a Comedy he is in, and then he may play first on a Saturday." On 3 June Garrick wrote chillingly that he had never intended Cautherley to be "a Burden to You, and he never shall. Hopkins is my Witness that I read your Extraordinary Letter to him, with astonishment indeed but no anger; I beg with you that the whole Matter may be *drown'd in oblivion*." That summer Cautherley was at Richmond, acting Romeo and Hamlet to Mrs Baddeley's Juliet and Ophelia, but presumably not on Saturday nights. Hopkins, another Drury Lane stalwart, was working as Love's prompter.

Soon after the Cautherley affair, Love received a letter, dated 13 June 1766, from George Garrick advising him that the Drury Lane managers could not possibly raise Mrs Love's salary "from the little use they have made or can possibly make of the lady," but they offered them a contract for three years at the old rate (£6 10s. per week). Five days later Garrick wrote, insisting on knowing Love's determination to "accept or refuse the proposals as he thinks will best suit his Circumstances." Love accepted.

Love continued to act at Drury Lane in the winters and to manage at Richmond in the summers, through 1773. In the Public Record Office is the notation of the renewal of the Richmond license for the summer of 1773. That autumn he played his usual roles at Drury Lane, such as Sir Epicure, Cacafogo, Jaques, and the Scotchman. His last performance was as Bonniface on 15 December 1773.

Love died early in 1774, on 29 January according to a notation in a Winston manuscript at the Folger Library, or on 5 February according to a report in *Notes and Queries* (8, IV, 524). In 1766 he had subscribed £2 2s. to the Drury Lane Theatrical Fund, but he died before the fund began to operate.

Mrs Love continued to perform in a very modest capacity at Drury Lane until 1790. She died in 1807 at an advanced age.

James Love had three children, presumably by his legal wife Elizabeth Hooper, who died in 1783. Nathaniel Dance, born on 20 June 1748, became a naval commander in the service of the East India Company and was knighted for distinction in a battle with the French off Pulo Aor in February 1804. He died in 1827 and is noticed in *The Dictionary of National Biography*.

A second son, William Dance, was born on 20 December 1755 (perhaps to the actress known as Mrs Love) and became a successful musician, composer, and co-founder of the Philharmonic Society. In his notice in volume IV of this dictionary we failed to report the information that as Master Love on 28 December 1763, at the age of eight, he played the organ in the premiere of his father's pantomime *The Rites of Hecate* and was hissed for being out of tune. The next night the organ was eliminated from the pantomime. At Drury Lane he performed concertos on the harpsichord on 25 April 1767, 9 April 1768, and 1 April 1769. William Dance died in 1840 leaving his widow Jane. His children included Henry Dance, a musician, and Charles Dance (1794–1863), the dramatist who is mistakenly called William's cousin in our volume IV.

Love's third child, Sarah, whose birthdate is unknown to us, married Thomas Poynder, a plumber in Cornhill; their son Thomas succeeded in the business, became treasurer of Christ's Hospital in 1824, and obtained a large estate, Hartham Park, near Corsham, Wiltshire.

James Love's other theatrical writings, in addition to those cited above, included a pastoral entertainment called *The Village Wedding; or, The Faithful Country Maid*, which was produced at Richmond on 18 July 1767 and was published that year; *Timon of Athens*, altered from Shakespeare and Shadwell, produced at Richmond in 1768 and published that year and in 1780; and *The City Madam*, a comedy altered from Massinger and played at Richmond in 1771. Annexed to the 1770 edition of Love's mock-heroic poem *Cricket* was the text of the epilogue called *Bucks Have at ye All*, as spoken by Tom King in the character of Ranger in *The Suspicious Husband* at the Theatre Royal, Dublin, in 1754. That text was reprinted in *Lloyd's Evening Post and British Chronicle* on 4–6 March 1771, where Love was acknowledged as author. Different versions of the popular epilogue were published, including one attributed to Garrick which was spoken by Mr Ward at Edinburgh in 1783.

In 1772 Francis Wheatley exhibited at the Society of Artists a painting of a scene from *Twelfth Night* which includes Love as Sir Toby Belch, Francis Waldron as Fabian, Elizabeth Young as Viola, and James William Dodd as Sir Andrew. The painting, now at the City Art Gallery in Manchester, is reproduced in volume IV of this dictionary (p. 435). An engraving of the picture by J. R. Smith was issued in 1774. In a journal entry written in Edinburgh on 7 November 1762, James Boswell wrote of visiting Mrs Love and seeing "the picture of Falstaff." Nothing more about this picture—presumably of James Love in that role—or its artist and whereabouts is known to us.

Love, Mrs James, [Catherine?, née L'Amour?] *c. 1719?–1807, actress, singer.*

In the winter of 1751–52 the actor James Love, whose real name was Dance, was head of a company of strollers at Belfast in which a Mrs Love acted Anne Page in *The Merry Wives of Windsor* and Arabella in *The Honest Yorkshireman*. Evidently Mrs Love was not the woman named Elizabeth Hooper, daughter of James Hooper, whom Dance had married in August 1739 when he was enrolled at Lincoln's Inn. The *Biographia Dramatica* and George Colman in *Random Records* told the colorful story that Dance's wife's maiden name had been L'Amour and that when he went on the stage he therefore adopted the stage name "Love." He had, however, acted as Dance during the 1740s, after his marriage to Elizabeth Hooper. In her study of *George Dance* (James Love's famous brother the architect), Dorothy Stroud states, without documentation, that Dance abandoned his legal wife for an actress named Catherine L'Amour and used her name, and that his three children by his legal wife were cared for by his parents. But at least one of the children, William Dance, was born some three years after a Mrs Love began to act with Love. According to Stroud the legal Mrs Dance died in 1783; whereas, according to James Winston's Fund Book notations, the actress Mrs Love died in 1807.

The actress who used the name Mrs Love performed with Love in many Irish and Scottish towns before they settled in London in 1762. At the New Canongate Concert Hall, Edinburgh, in March 1754 she acted Lucy Lockit in *The Beggar's Opera* and Miss Biddy in *Miss in Her Teens*. She played singing roles at Smock Alley, Dublin, in 1754–55 and at Tralee in the spring of 1755. From 1756 to 1762 she was with the Canongate company in Edinburgh, where Love was acting manager from 1759, and there she played such roles as Altea in *Rule a Wife and Have a Wife*, Ariel in *The Tempest*, Leonora in *The Mourning Bride*, Maria in *Twelfth Night*, Cleone in *The Distrest Mother*, Florella in *The Orphan*, Jessica in *The Merchant of Venice*, Kitty Pry in *The Valet*, Lady Froth in *The Double Dealer*, and Mrs Foresight in *Love for Love*.

In *A View of the Edinburgh Stage During the Summer, 1759*, James Boswell (probably assisted by Francis Gentleman) censured her Lucy in *The Beggar's Opera*, praised her as Jenny in *The Miller of Mansfield*, judged her uneven as Lappet in *The Miser*, and excoriated her as the Nurse in *Romeo and Juliet*. For the last role she was "utterly unfit" and acted "wretchedly"—"we were presented with the Appearance of a little, prating, impudent Hussey, imperfectly drest in old Woman's Cloaths. The squeaking of her Voice, in that Scene where she supposes Juliet to be dead, was execrable beyond bearing."

In 1762–63 the Loves were engaged by Garrick for Drury Lane. Probably she was the "Gentlewoman," advertised as making her first appearance on that stage, who played Dorcas in *Thomas and Sally* on 9 April 1763. On 23 May the same "Gentlewoman" performed Lucy in *The Beggar's Opera*. Her name appeared as Mrs Love for the role of Muslin in *The Way to Keep Him* on 28 May, and on 31 May she was Lappet in *The Miser*.

Mrs Love began her second Drury Lane season on 17 September 1763 as Mrs Peachum in *The Beggar's Opera*, a role which, Hopkins wrote in his prompter's diary, she played "very bad

Her fit seemed a very awkward imitation of Mrs Pritchard in the Jealous Wife." Her main assignment that season was as a character in the many performances of Love's pantomime *The Rites of Hecate*, which opened on 26 December 1763 (and was her first appearance since she had acted Mrs Peachum in September). That spring she appeared as Dorcas, Margery in *The Register Office* (for Love's benefit on 12 April 1764), and Catherine in *Catherine and Petruchio*.

Over the next several seasons Mrs Love was used infrequently at Drury Lane and seems to have been kept on in deference to Love, who had some important supporting roles. There was some strain between Love and Garrick in the summer of 1766 over Mrs Love's salary. On 13 June George Garrick advised Love that the management could not possibly raise Mrs Love's salary "from the little use they have made or can possibly make of the lady," and he offered Love a renewal of their contract at the old terms, £6 10s. per week for both their services, terms which Love finally accepted.

Mrs Love was also a member of Love's company during the summers at Richmond, where he had opened a new theatre on the Green on 15 June 1765. Boswell visited Richmond in September 1769 and thought she "looked very well, though verging on fifty."

She also remained a member of the Drury Lane company for many years after Love died in 1774, playing a number of modest roles in musical comedies and farces and eventually serving, in her older years, as a chorus singer. The new Drury Lane management in 1776–77 kept her busier than Garrick had done, paying her £2 per week. Among her roles over the years were Lucetta in *The Suspicious Husband*, Mrs Sealand in *The Conscious Lovers*, Deborah in *Love in a Village*, the Landlady in *A Trip to Scotland*, Betty in *The Clandestine Marriage*, Lucy in *The West Indian* (in the original performance on 19 January 1771), the original Mrs Macintosh in *The Fashionable Lover* (on 20 January 1772), Ursula in *The Padlock*, Margaret in *The Deserter*, Mrs Nipikin in *The Cobler*, vocal parts in *A Christmas Tale*, *The Wonders of Derbyshire*, and *Harlequin's Invasion*, Miranda in *The Tempest*, Cicely in *The Quaker*, Mause in *The Gentle Shepherd*, and toward the end of her career the Nurse in *Isabella*, Lady Bountiful in *The Stratagem*, and Diana Trapes in *The Beggar's Opera*.

Mrs Love began to act summers at the Haymarket in 1774, first appearing there on 16 May as Dorcas in *The Mad Doctor*. That season there she acted Ursula in *The Padlock*, Curtis in *Catherine and Petruchio*, Nell in *The Devil to Pay*, Dorcas in *Thomas and Sally*, a role in *The Cozeners*, Mrs Peachum in *The Beggar's Opera*, and Lady Bountiful. Her other Haymarket parts over the years included a role in *The Waterman* and the Dutchman's Wife in *The Dutchman* in 1775; Mysis in *Midas* in 1776; Mrs Ducat in *Polly*, the Nurse in *Polly Honeycombe*, the Wife in *The Recruiting Serjeant*, Mrs Candy in *Piety in Patterns*, the Hostess in *1 Henry IV*, and the Landlady in *The Chances* in 1777; the Landlady in *The Female Chevalier*, the Landlady in *Man and Wife*, and Mrs Subtle in *The Englishman in Paris* in 1778; Peg Pennyworth in *A Widow and No Widow* in 1779; a Caller in *The Manager in Distress* and Warner in *The Chapter of Accidents* in 1780; and Mrs Cloggit in *The Confederacy* in 1781. She also was at the Haymarket in summers from 1782 through 1788. In May and June 1784 Mrs Love was a vocalist in the Handel Memorial Concerts at Westminster Abbey and the Pantheon, listed by Burney as one of the "treebles." In April 1777 she lived at Booth's, Brownlow Street, Longacre. Between 1778 and 1780 she resided in Gerrard Street, Soho.

In *The Children of Thespis* (1782), Anthony Pasquin (John Williams) wrote of Mrs Love:

> *Depress'd by stern Time, see poor* Love *make her way,*
> *And, spurning the tyrant, affect to look gay:*
> *In* Dorcas *she still can administer pleasure,*
> *And shines in old women a dramatic treasure;*
> *Besides, as a vet'ran, poor* Love *has a claim*
> *To draw on Compassion, if not upon Fame.*

Mrs Love's last complete season at Drury Lane was 1788–89, when she played such roles as a Lady in *Henry VIII*, Errand's Wife in *The Constant Couple*, Ursula in *The Padlock*, the Nurse in *A Trip to Scarborough*, Mause in *The Gentle Shepherd*, Margaret in *The Deserter*, and Audrey in *As You Like It*. The following season she seems to have performed only once, as Mause on 1 June 1790, and thereafter was not seen again.

According to James Winston's transcriptions of the Drury Lane Fund Book at the Folger Library, Mrs Love subscribed £1 1s. to the fund in 1766, and she "died 1807." Winston did not indicate whether or not she had drawn on the fund. The death year of 1807 for Mrs Love is also specified in several manuscripts in the British Library. If indeed she was about 50 when Boswell saw her at Richmond in 1769, then she died at about the age of 88.

Loveday, Thomas [*fl.* 1635–1671], *actor.*

Thomas Loveday the Restoration actor was probably the Loveday who was a member of the troupe asking permission on 10 March 1635 to perform in Norwich. About that time Clutch in *Money Is an Ass* was acted by "Tho. Loveday," then a boy actor. The Thomas "Loffday" who was with an English company at the Hague in 1644–45 was very probably the same performer, and he may have appeared in Paris in a troupe maintained by Prince Charles until November 1646. The Paris company was probably the one which performed at the Hague, arriving there from Paris on 24 February 1648.

The London Stage lists Loveday as a member of the Duke's Company under Sir William Davenant in 1660–61, but that must be an error, for he was sworn a member of the rival King's Company on 10 October 1660, according to a Lord Chamberlain's warrant, and he was granted livery with that troupe in July 1661 for the period 1660–1662. On 20 December 1661 Loveday and some of his fellow actors in the King's troupe agreed to pay, as a group, £3 10s. each acting day as a rental fee for the Bridges Street playhouse, then in the planning stage. Loveday was not, however, one of the sharers in the building itself.

It is difficult to determine what roles Loveday played in the early 1660s. A manuscript cast in a Folger copy of *Love's Sacrifice* has him down for Petruchio, but his name was lined through, and Mohun's brother may have taken that part instead, leaving the skirts role of Morona for Loveday. The production was mounted sometime between 1661 and 1664 at either the Vere Street or the Bridges Street Theatre. Loveday is known to have left the King's Company briefly in 1662, though he seems to have returned by 29 September, when Alice Verner went to law against him. According to the manuscript prompt book of *The Cheats*, Loveday played Dilligence when the work was presented at Vere Street about 16 March 1663. Thomas was in financial trouble in the summer of that year, for the Lord Chamberlain's accounts show two separate cases against him, one by Alice Fuller and the other by Mathew Harris, both apparently for debts. On 3 November 1663 Loveday played a Friar in *Flora's Vagaries*, according to notes generously given us by John Harold Wilson.

But the notices for Loveday during the 1660s usually concerned his being sued by one person or another: Alice Fuller was given leave on 16 April 1664 to proceed against him; Robert Toplady went against him and his fellow actor Blagden in September of that year; and Symon Ansell went against him in December 1668. Once, in July and September 1666, Loveday sued someone else, in that case Thomas Hawley. The last mention of Loveday that has been found is in a manuscript cast in a British Library copy of *Julius Caesar*; the cast dates about 1670–71, when the King's Company was at the Bridges Street Theatre. Loveday was named for the character of Flavius.

Lovegrove, William 1778–1816, *actor, singer.*

William Lovegrove, according to contemporary biographical notices, was born at Shoreham, Sussex, on 13 January 1778. (But we find no record of his baptism in Shoreham parish registers.) His father, a plumber and engineer, moved his family to London when William was quite young. The lad was apprenticed to his father, whose occupation he seemed to prefer until he became involved in amateur theatricals. Having successfully acted Hamlet and several other characters at the private theatre in Tottenham Court Road, Lovegrove received an engagement in 1799 at the Richmond Theatre, where Winston was summer manager. Lovegrove's debut there occurred sometime in June. On the list of the 1799 company made by Winston (now in the Richmond Reference Library) Lovegrove's London address was given as No 25, Crown Court, Martlett Court, Bow Street.

Subsequently he went to Dublin, making his debut at the Crow Street Theatre as Anhalt in *Lovers' Vows* on 20 November 1799; but after

Courtesy of the Garrick Club
WILLIAM LOVEGROVE, as Lord Ogleby
by De Wilde

a falling out with Hamerton, the acting manager, Lovegrove proceeded to an engagement at Manchester. On the journey a fellow coach passenger's pistol accidentally discharged, lodging two balls and a slug in Lovegrove's left leg. He was attended by an eminent surgeon named Rowlands at Chester, but the wound severely impaired his performance as Douglas when he finally reached Manchester. He succeeded better as Jaques in *As You Like It*. After playing for Hughes at Guernsey, where he became a favorite, he was at Plymouth in the autumn of 1802. The *Monthly Mirror* of November 1802 called him a "most excellent general actor" and cited, among other roles which he had offered at Plymouth, Hamlet, Davy in *Bon Ton*, and Autolycus in *The Winter's Tale*. He played all of them well, the reporter affirmed: "he has not only much rich comedy, but possesses sound judgment in the serious department." But a correspondent to the *Monthly Mirror* in December complained that Lovegrove had proved to be an actor "of a very inferior kind," despite advance publicity which promised much from him, and that he seldom appeared anyway. Lovegrove replied in the January 1803 issue that he had played on 37 nights at Plymouth.

After leaving Plymouth, Lovegrove applied to Dimond, the manager at the Orchard Street Theatre, Bath, and although the manager claimed to have no room in the company for a regular engagement, he did allow Lovegrove to make an appearance for one night only, on 9 November 1802, as Lazarillo in *Two Strings to Your Bow*. The Duchess of York sent a messenger backstage to express her gratification for that performance, so Dimond took him on for the season, in which Lovegrove also acted Gradus in *Who's the Dupe?*, Walter in *The Children in the Wood*, Edgar in *King Lear*, Sir Luke Tremor in *Such Things Are*, and Sir Bashful in *The Way to Keep Him*. He also acted at Bristol in December 1802. The summer of 1803 he spent playing at Margate and Worthing. Lovegrove returned in 1803–4 to Bath, where he remained through 1809–10, also playing regularly at Bristol. The departure of Edwin for Dublin provided some excellent opportunities for Lovegrove, who assumed such characters as Dr Pangloss in *The Heir-at-Law*, Sim in *Wild Oats*, Trappanti in *She Wou'd and She Wou'd Not*, Sir Anthony Absolute in *The Rivals*, Delaval in *Matrimony*, Croaker in *The Good Natur'd Man*, Isaac in *The Duenna*, and Alphonse in *The Pilgrim*.

In the autumn of 1810, Lovegrove joined the Drury Lane company then playing at the Lyceum, their temporary home, making his debut on 3 October as Lord Ogleby in *The Clandestine Marriage*. He remained at the Lyceum in 1811–12 and the following season went to the new Drury Lane with the company. Job Thornberry in *John Bull*, Lopez in *Kiss*, and Old Fathom in *Policy* were among the many roles he played during that period as a principal supporting performer.

Soon after he took up his London engagement, Lovegrove married Julia Weippert, the daughter of the harpist John Erhardt Weippert and his wife Mary. Seventeen months later, in

Harvard Theatre Collection
WILLIAM LOVEGROVE, as Storm
engraving by Ward, after Bird

1812, her death and the death of his six-month-old daughter soon after broke Lovegrove's spirit, and it is said that his hair turned gray overnight. Soon after his benefit at Drury Lane on 15 June 1814, when he acted Wilford in *The Iron Chest* and a role in the farce *Cheating*, Lovegrove ruptured a blood vessel. He recovered sufficiently to make an attempt at resuming his engagement on 21 June 1815 as Sir Peter Teazle, when the audience gave him an overwhelming reception.

The following season he appeared but once, as Realize in *The Will* on 17 October 1815. The theatre generously granted him half-salary during the several months of his retirement at Weston, near Bath, where he was taken by a solicitous sister. There he died of a cerebral hemorrhage on 25 or 26 June 1816 and was buried in Weston churchyard. In a brief will made on 4 June 1816 Lovegrove gave all his estate and effects, including his stocks in the Bank of England, to his spinster sister and executrix, Susanna Lovegrove, who proved the will at London on 1 March 1817.

Lovegrove was characterized as an "excellent" comic by Henry Crabb Robinson in 1811. In his Elia essay, Lamb praised his Aguecheek, claiming that he came nearest to the old actors and made the characterization "sufficiently grotesque." Mathews, also, spoke of him as "an admirable actor, quite in the style of the old school." He was outstanding as Rattan in *The Bee Hive*, Peter Fidget in *The Boarding House*, and Leatherhead in *M. P.*, and similar roles. Lovegrove was a reserved and prudent man who mixed little and had few close friends.

Portraits of William Lovegrove include:

1. By Samuel De Wilde. Present location unknown to us. Engraving by S. Freeman, published in the *Monthly Mirror*, 1810. This is not the portrait of him as Lord Ogleby, as suggested by Sybil Rosenfeld in *Theatre Notebook* (XX, 1965).

2. In character. Watercolor by Samuel De Wilde. In the Garrick Club (No 488).

3. In character. Watercolor by Samuel De Wilde. In the Harvard Theatre Collection.

4. As Captain Rattan in *The Bee Hive*. Engraving by J. Thomson, after De Wilde. Plate to the *Theatrical Inquisitor*, 1816.

5. As Hasem in *Illusion*. By unknown engraver. Published by W. West, 1824.

6. As Lord Ogleby in *The Clandestine Marriage*. Watercolor by Samuel De Wilde, dated October 1810. In the Garrick Club (No 59D). Another watercolor copy (or original?) by De Wilde is owned by Robert Eddison.

7. As Ludovico in *The Peasant Boy*. By unknown engraver. Published by W. West, 1811.

8. As Storm in *Ella Rosenberg*. Engraving by W. Ward, after E. Bird. Published by Colnaghi & Co, 1817.

Lovelace, [William?] [*fl.* 1703–1728], *boxkeeper, pitkeeper.*

Mr Lovelace was first mentioned in existing bills on 14 June 1703, when he shared a benefit with two other boxkeepers, King and White, at Drury Lane. His benefits at Drury Lane were sporadic, though we may simply lack information; he was cited in 1707 and

LOVELACE

Harvard Theatre Collection

Ticket for MR LOVELACE's Benefit

1708 and again in 1710. On 9 May 1711 a benefit concert at Stationers' Hall was presented for Cuthbert (a musician), Lovelace, and White; it is probable that the last two were the Drury Lane boxkeepers of earlier years, especially since we know that Lovelace left Drury Lane at some point and worked for John Rich at the new Lincoln's Inn Fields playhouse from 1714–15 onward, as did White.

Shared benefits for Lovelace were regular at Lincoln's Inn Fields through 1725–26. The accounts in 1726 show two pension payments to him of 3s. 6d. for three days in October and November. The citations are a bit unclear, but it would appear that after Lovelace finished the 1725–26 season he retired or worked for the theatre only on occasion. The last mention of him, in fact, suggests that: on 22 April 1728 Lovelace served as pitkeeper for that date only.

Perhaps Lovelace the boxkeeper was William Lovelace, whose name appears several times in the burial registers of St Paul, Covent Garden, though we cannot be certain: on 8 January 1711 Mary, the wife of William Lovelace was buried; on 11 February 1722 George, the son of William Lovelace was buried; on 8 April 1735 William's (second?) wife Elizabeth was buried; and soon after, on 20 June, William Lovelace was buried.

Lovelace, Mrs [William?, Elizabeth?] [*fl.* 1726], *house servant?*

The Lincoln's Inn Fields accounts show that on 30 September 1726 Mrs Lovelace, presumably the wife of Lovelace the boxkeeper, was paid 5s. for services unspecified. Perhaps she was a house servant. If the burial register references cited in Mr Lovelace's entry do in fact concern the boxkeeper and his wife, then perhaps Mrs Lovelace's Christian name was Elizabeth and her burial was on 8 April 1735.

Lovell, Mrs [*fl.* 1686–1687], *actress.*

A manuscript cast in a University of Pennsylvania copy of *Epsom Wells* shows that Mrs Woodly was played by Mrs Lovell, probably during the 1686–87 season at Drury Lane. She may have been related to Thomas Lovell, who acted in the 1660s.

Lovell, Thomas [*fl.* 1635–1663], *actor.*

Thomas Lovell (or Loval) was a boy actor before the closing of the theatres in 1642. His name was on a list of players who sought permission to perform in Norwich on 10 March 1635, and about that year he was listed for the role of Money in *Money Is an Ass*. Lovell joined the Duke's Company under Sir William Davenant on 5 November 1660 after serving briefly under Rhodes in 1659–60 and probably acting at Salisbury Court. His first known role after the restoration of the monarchy was Polonius in *Hamlet* at the Lincoln's Inn Fields playhouse on 24 August 1661. He played Malvolio in *Twelfth Night* on 11 September, Old Trueman in *Cutter of Coleman Street* on 16 December, and, after a gap in the records, Gracchus in *The Step Mother* in mid-October 1663.

Loveman, Mr [*fl.* 1766–1769], *actor.*

Faulkner's Dublin Journal stated that Mr Loveman, as "A Young Gentleman," made his debut on 1 November 1766 at the Smock Alley Theatre. He performed there during the 1766–67 season and then joined Samuel Foote's troupe at the Haymarket Theatre in London to appear as Dr Catgut in *The Commissary* on 4 June 1767. He was then Tuck in *The Orators*, Clerimont in *The Old Maid*, Durand in *Venice Preserv'd*, Humphreymingos in *The Taylors*, the Fine Gentleman in *Lethe*, Harry Paddington in *The Beggar's Opera*, Thomas in *The Virgin Unmask'd*, and unspecified characters in *The Countess of Salisbury*, *The Royal Captive*, and *Like Master Like Man*.

Loveman was at Smock Alley again in 1767–68 and rejoined Foote in London in the summer of 1768 to play such new roles as Friendly in *The School Boy*, Jemmy Twitcher in *The Beggar's Opera*, Sparkish in *The Country Wife*, and, after the end of the season, Prince Prettyman in *The Rehearsal*. He joined Miller's company at Derby in the winter of 1768–69.

Lovemore, Mr [*fl.* 1751], *actor.*

Mr Lovemore played Pedro in *No Fool Like the Old One* at Phillips's booth at Southwark Fair on 9 September 1751.

Lovett, Mr [*fl.* 1707–1710], *singer.*

In Vice Chamberlain Coke's papers at Harvard is a list of opera performers and their salaries, dating about late December 1707. Mr Lovett, otherwise unknown, was named as one of the singers at the Queen's Theatre at a salary of £40 annually, very low on the scale.

Low, Mr [*fl.* 1739], *house servant?*

The Drury Lane playbill for 30 April 1739 bore the notation "Tickets delivered by Mr. Low will be taken this Night."

Lowder, Mr [*fl.* 1734–1748], *actor.*

Mr Lowder (sometimes Lawder, Louder, or Lowther) acted Mirvan in a performance of *Tamerlane* given in the Great Room of the Ship Tavern on 4 November 1734 "By a Company of Comedians from the Theatres in London." In the summer of 1735 at Lincoln's Inn Fields Theatre, Lowder played Mons Coupee in *The Stage Mutineers* on 23 and 25 July, Squire Caleb in *Politicks on Both Sides* on 30 July, Clodio in *Caius Marius* on 22 August, Sancho in *Love Makes a Man* on 29 August, and Lorenzo in *The Carnival* on 5 September. At the Haymarket Theatre on 17 September he acted Ratcliff in *Jane Shore*. On 11 November 1735 he played Sir Hugh Evans in *The Merry Wives of Windsor* at Goodman's Fields Theatre; curiously, the bills carried the announcement that Lowder was appearing on the stage for the first time, but perhaps "the stage" meant that of Goodman's Fields.

In the spring of 1736 Lowder returned to the Haymarket to act for Henry Fielding as the Drummer in *Pasquin* on 5 March and George in *The Female Rake* on 26 April. When Fielding's *Tumble Down Dick* was introduced on 29 April Lowder played at least two roles and probably three: a Watchman, Pistol, and a Countryman (the edition listed Lowder in the last role though the bills gave the performer's name as "Mons De la Soup Maigre"). On 26 June he acted James in *The Mock Doctor*. At the Haymarket in the spring of 1737 he played Dangle in *The Historical Register* and one of the Actors in *Eurydice Hiss'd*.

Over the next decade Lowder's occasional performances included Setter in *The Old Bachelor* on 21 October and the Welsh Collier in *The Recruiting Officer* on 22 October 1740 at Goodman's Fields, and Taffy in *Thamas Kouli Kan* at Turbutt's booth during Bartholomew Fair in August 1741. Seven years later he appeared again at that fair, playing Owen Gallows in *The Consequences of Industry and Idleness* at Yates's booth from 24 through 27 August 1748.

Lowe. *See also* LOE.

Lowe, Mr [*fl.* 1683–1686], *actor.*

Mr Lowe (or Low) played the Chaplain in *The Jovial Crew* in December 1683 with the United Company at Drury Lane. He remained with the troupe through 1685–86 to appear as Clark in *The Northern Lass*, Rufee, Butler, and Verdon in *The Bloody Brother*, the Boatswain in *The Commonwealth of Women*, Domingo in *The Banditti*, and a Footman in *The Devil of a Wife*.

Lowe, Mr [*fl.* 1761], *fifer.*

On 13 November 1761 a Mr Lowe was paid 5*s.* for playing the fife in the coronation procession at Covent Garden Theatre (13 November 1761 and many nights that season) in celebration of the accession of George III.

Lowe, Mr [*fl.* 1766], *office keeper.*

A Mr Lowe is listed in a British Library manuscript as an office keeper at Covent Garden Theatre in 1766.

Lowe, Miss [*fl.* 1753–1761?], *singer.*

A "Miss Lowe" is entered in the *Catalogue of Printed Music in the British Museum* as having sung at Vauxhall "No longer let whimsical songsters compare," printed in 1761. That assignment may have been in error for "Mr Lowe," for Thomas Lowe was a prominent singer at the pleasure gardens at that time. However, there was a Miss Lowe performing at Bath's Orchard Street Theatre from 1753–54 through 1756–57, and the Vauxhall singer may have been that lady.

Lowe, Edward *c. 1610–1682, organist, singer.*

Edward Lowe was born in the parish of St Thomas, Salisbury, about 1610 and received his musical training from the organist of the cathedral there, John Holmes, and served as a chorister. Lowe became organist of Christ Church, Oxford, about 1631, succeeding Stonard. He married Alice Peyton, daughter of Sir John Peyton of Doddington. When church music was suppressed during the Commonwealth, Lowe, like many other musicians, turned to teaching. One of his students was Barbara Fletcher, to whom he sent some virginal lessons and the following instructional letter on 25 March 1652:

Most vertuous M^ris Barbara.

I humbly beseech you to play thes Lessons in the Order sett downe Constantly once a day, if you have health and leasure. Play not, without turninge the Lesson in your Booke before you & keep your eye (as much as you can) in your Booke. If you Chance to miss goe not from the Lesson, till you have perfected it. Above all, Play not too fast. Thes few rules observed you will gaine your selfe much Honour & some Creditt to your master whose better title is

> Your most humble servant
> Ed: Lowe

At Oxford Lowe also had plenty of opportunities to hear able musicians, one being Thomas Baltzar, who visited Oxford in 1658 and dazzled Lowe and Anthony Wood with his virtuosity on the violin.

In 1660 with the restoration of the monarchy Edward Lowe was appointed one of the organists of the Chapel Royal in London. He could not have spent much time in London, however, for in 1662 he was made Professor of Music at Oxford, and it is significant that the Lord Chamberlain's accunts contain few references to Lowe beyond indicating he was a Gentleman of the Chapel Royal. At Oxford he published *A Short Direction for the Performance of Cathedrall Service* in 1661, and he wrote some music. By his wife Alice he had two daughters and seven sons; after Alice's death, according to Pulver, he remarried and had a daughter by his second wife. Lowe died in Oxford on 11 July 1682.

On 2 June 1682 Edward Lowe (Senior, he called himself) drew up his will. He asked to be buried in the Divinity Chapel in Christ Church, Oxford, near the remains of his first wife and her children, and his wishes were later carried out. To his wife Mary Lowe he bequeathed £6 annually out of £100 then in the hands of the bookseller Richard Davis of Oxford (Lowe held a mortgage on Davis's estate at Haddington). Lowe also left his wife some of the furnishings of his house at Hampton-Gay, Oxfordshire. To his eldest son Edward, a clerk Rector in Shernfold, Sussex, he left a ring, a tankard, and some pictures. To his daughter Elizabeth Burtchall, wife of Thomas Burtchall of London, combmaker, he left his clothes and 5s., having provided for her before. To her children he gave 40s. each, to be paid out of income gained by the sale of the clothes. To his son Charles he left a ring, watch, and a spoon. To his daughter Susanna Stripe he left a dressing box, and to her and her husband John (minister of Low Leyton, Essex) he gave 20s. each for mourning rings. Lowe left his grandchild Edward, son of his son Charles, £5 and a Bible. All of his music books and papers judged fit for public use he left to the archives of the public music school. To his son Edward he left a choice of books and manuscripts, with his son Charles getting second choices. Lowe directed that his manuscripts of "indecent verses Ballads or Prose shall be burnt and destroyed by my Executo^r." He asked that his organ, virginal, other musical instruments, and pictures should be sold and combined with any arrears in salary from the Chapel Royal and the University to cover funeral expenses and pay debts, especially an apothecary's bill—which indicates that Lowe may have had a lengthy and expensive illness.

To his son Edward he also left his nightwatch and other items relating to his first wife, Edward's mother. He also directed that if Edward wanted it he could have the pane of glass in the window of Lowe's house that showed the coats of arms of the Peytons and Lowes. Lowe also set down small bequests to the poor, to whom he had regularly given money. The great Bible he kept in the organ loft he left to his successor at Oxford. He made small bequests of rings, prayer books, and the like to his "sister Downes," his friend Richard Goodson, his godson Edward Wild, his grandchild Edward (son of Charles), and his daughter-in-law Mary (Charles's wife). Charles and Edward Lowe Junior were made executors and residuary legatees and asked to be kind to their sisters, mother, and one another. Lowe asked for a simple funeral but asked that his friends Mrs Yaldon and Mrs Rocks be invited. His will was proved on 28 July 1682.

Lowe, George d. 1664, singer?

George Lowe was possibly a relative of the musician Edward Lowe; at least they were both from Salisbury. George was a member of the Chapel Royal at the time of the coronation of Charles II on 23 April 1661 and was presumably a singer. He resigned from the Chapel on 7 June 1662 to serve as vicar choral at Salisbury, but he was readmitted on 12 March 1664. He died the following 16 May and was buried in the little cloister of Westminster Abbey the following day.

George Lowe's will, written on 15 May 1664 and proved on 11 July, directed that his wife Mabel should have Lowe's house in Salisbury, and after her death the house was to go to their daughter Elinor. To his wife Lowe also left £200 and some furniture; to his daughter Rachell he left £200 ("if there be money enough") at the day of her marriage—and if she did not marry, then the money was to go to Lowe's wife and their other children. The rest of his goods he left to his wife and the rest of his children equally "(except onely my daughter Banister)." To her instead he left £10. Lowe also made bequests to 20 poor widows of Salisbury. He asked Nicholas Johnson of Salisbury and Edward Lowe "of the Temple" to serve as overseer. He did not call Edward Lowe his brother. Finally, to Sir John Lowe of Shaftsbury, Wiltshire, Lowe left three books on heraldry.

Lowe, Halifax 1762–1790, singer, actor.

Halifax Lowe was baptized at St Paul, Covent Garden, on 27 June 1762. He was the son of Thomas Lowe the eminent singing actor and his wife Mary. He followed, rather weakly, in his father's path as a singer, principally at pleasure gardens.

He made his debut at Sadler's Wells on 15 April 1784. Tate Wilkinson wrote that he had come from "the Wells" to Hull when Wilkinson opened the season there on 1 November 1786, putting him down roughly as "very poor indeed as a performer, and, I believe, a poor fellow as a man." He left the York circuit at the close of the York theatre season on 25 May 1787. Information on his movements after that is scanty. He was at Edinburgh's Theatre Royal, Shakespeare Square, in the season of 1789–90, playing these characters in order: Donald in The Highland Reel, Fifer in The Battle of Hexham; Captain Greville in The Flitch of Bacon, some part unspecified in Liberty Triumphant, a Singing Witch in Macbeth, the Ghost in Tom Thumb, and Hounslow in The Beaux' Stratagem. The Mrs Lowe in the company that season was certainly his wife. She had parts unspecified in The Battle of Hexham and Liberty Triumphant in January and played Lady Macbeth once in February. She is not known to have performed in London.

Halifax Lowe died on 25 September 1790, according to Isaac Reed's "Notitia Dramatica" in the British Library. But the European Magazine of October 1790, calling him "of Sadler's Wells," declared his death to have been on 2 October 1790, in his apartment in the Barbican, caused by the bursting of a blood vessel.

Lowe, James [fl. 1739–1769?], instrumental musician.

James Lowe was one of the original subscribers ("being musicians") of the Royal Society of Musicians of Great Britain whose names were set down in the Declaration of Trust dated 28 August 1739. He may have been the James Lowe for whose benefit a morning concert was played at the Haymarket Theatre on 12 March 1752. A Lowe was being paid 5s. per day for service in the band at Covent Garden Theatre as of 14 September 1767, according to a pay-list preserved by Arthur Murphy. At Norwich, Lowe was retained "as an Additional and Leading Musician in the Orchestra at the Rate of one Guinea per week, He undertaking to teach and instruct the Company of Comedians in all Music and to attend Rehearsals" at the Norwich Theatre in 1769. Conceivably he was James.

On 6 March 1785 Mrs Editha Lowe, 75 years old, "widow of James Lowe," petitioned the Board of Governors of the Royal Society of Musicians for temporary financial relief in the

LOWE

amount of five guineas "she being afflicted with a Cancer in her breasts." She was allowed the sum. On 7 August following, she "being in a very bad state of health," applied for more assistance, but the Governors felt they could not with propriety go beyond the usual allowance for widows. Editha Lowe was dead by 6 November when her daughter Louisa Lowe asked the Governors to discharge debts incurred because of the illness whereby she was "reduced to great distress." She was awarded £8 for medicines "and for the attention shewn her mother."

It is likely that the James Lowe who was active as a musician from about 1784 or earlier was a relative, perhaps a son.

Lowe, James [fl. 1784–1816], oboist.

A Mr Lowe was listed by Charles Burney as a second "hautbois" among performers of the Handel Memorial Concerts in London in the spring of 1784. He is not likely to have been the elder James Lowe, who was dead by early 1785 at the latest. Thus, he was either Richard Lowe or the younger James, probably the latter.

The James Lowe of this entry was certainly the James Lowe who was paid £6 6s. for playing "Hautboy" in Concerts of the Academy of Ancient Music in the 1787–88 season. He was retired from active service by 3 July 1808 when he gave thanks to the Royal Society of Music for a benefaction voted him at a general meeting. He wrote thankful letters for similar benefactions every July or August 1809 through 1813 and in January 1816.

Lowe, Margaret [fl. 1729], singer.

Margaret Lowe, a juvenile, played the minor role Mrs Coaxer in *The Beggar's Opera* with the Lilliputian Company on 1 January 1729.

Lowe, Richard [fl. 1785?–1794], oboist.

Richard Lowe, "oboe," of Chandos Street was listed in Doane's *Musical Directory* (1794) as belonging to the Royal Society of Musicians and as having played in the "grand performances" in Westminster Abbey, that is one or more of the Handel commemorations. He was not in the first, in 1784, but could have played in any or all of the revivals, of 1785, 1786, 1787, or 1791.

Lowe, Thomas c. 1719–1783, singer, actor, proprietor, manager.

Thomas Lowe was born about 1719, probably in London, and, according to Thomas Busby, was apprenticed to a weaver in Spitalfields. How, when, and where he began to sing for a living is not known, but it was probably early and in some London tavern. On 27 March 1732 he received a benefit at Hickford's Rooms and on 2 May he sang both Hebdonah and an anonymous Israelite in Handel's oratorio *Esther* at the King's Theatre.

Lowe came to very influential attention when he sang (the first time it was sung in public) Thomas Augustine Arne's "Rule Britannia" in Thomson and Mallet's masque *Alfred*. That was during a *fête* commemorating the accession of the Hanoverians which was given in August 1740 at Cliveden House, the residence of the Prince of Wales. On that occasion he also sang Mercury in Arne's *Judgment of Paris*. On 11 September following, he acted his first role at Drury Lane Theatre, Sir John in *The Devil to Pay*, singing for the first time Galliard's popular "Early Horn," followed in that busy season by Quaver in *The Virgin Unmask'd*, Leander in

Harvard Theatre Collection
THOMAS LOWE
artist unknown

The Mock Doctor, Le Chasseur in The Rural Sports, Valentine in The Intriguing Chambermaid, Macheath in The Beggar's Opera, a Bacchanal in Comus, Amiens in As You Like It, King Henry in Rosamond, Welford in The Blind Beggar of Bethnal Green, Edgar in The Lover's Opera, Buskin in The Strollers, and Joe in The King and the Miller of Mansfield. In addition, he was much employed in specialty songs and entr'acte numbers. He was on the roster at the Bristol Theatre in the summer of 1741.

Lowe remained at Drury Lane in the winters of 1741–42 and 1742–43. (He was with the Arnes in Dublin in the summer of 1742.) From 16 May 1743 he sang mornings in the concerts at Ruckholt House, near Low-Layton, Essex. He was a member of Handel's oratorio company at Covent Garden in the spring of 1743. He sang some roles at Richmond, Surrey, in July. At the beginning of the 1743–44 winter season he, with a number of other players, revolted from the manager Fleetwood, staying away from Drury Lane until December. In the London Daily Post of 8 October Lowe announced that he was leaving for Ireland again, "by Invitation of Several Persons of Distinction" and thanked his public for their patronage. That winter at Smock Alley he sang in the first performances of Arne's oratorio The Death of Abel.

He returned to Drury Lane in 1744–45, after a season at Dublin's Aungier Street Theatre, and remained during the winter seasons through 1747–48. When the great tenor John Beard returned to Drury Lane in the fall of 1748 Lowe moved over to Covent Garden Theatre. And when Beard moved to Covent Garden in 1759 Lowe shared roles with him for a season before returning to Drury Lane in 1760–61 to finish out his career at the London patent theatres. Lowe then began to manage Marylebone Gardens.

Before discussing that considerable part of Lowe's career which concerns the pleasure gardens, we can list, in approximate order, his roles in the more conventional theatres as they were added, by year and house. At Drury Lane in 1742–43 he added Lorenzo in The Merchant of Venice, Ballad in Miss Lucy in Town, and Marcus in Cato. At Aungier Street in 1743–44 he kept fairly busy but added to his repertoire only Cantileno in Miss Lucy in Town, Moore of Moore Hall in The Dragon of Wantley, Trueblue in Nancy, and Damon in Damon and Phillida. Returning to Drury Lane in 1744–45 he added Bully in The Provok'd Wife, Puppibello in the new afterpiece The Temple of Dulness, Heartly in James Miller's new comedy The Picture, and King Pepin in King Pepin's Campaign, a new musical trifle by William Shirley and T. A. Arne; in 1745–46 he added Neptune in The Tempest, Thirsis, a Volunteer, in Harlequin Incendiary, Damon in Damon and Phillida, a new pantomime (music by Arne), and Camillo in Love and Friendship, "a new Pastoral English Opera set to Music by De Fesch." In the summer of 1746 he was at the Richmond and Twickenham theatres. In 1746–47 at Drury Lane he was Friendly in Flora and Rovewell in The Contrivances.

Moving to Covent Garden in 1748–49, Lowe added War in The Muses' Looking Glass and Hunter in Phebe; or, The Beggar's Wedding; and in 1749–50 the Chasseur Royal in Merlin and Perseus in John Rich's Perseus and Andromeda. In the summer of 1751 he was again at Richmond. In 1751–52 at Covent Garden he was Pyramus in Pyramus and Thisbe and Hibernia's Genius in The Triumphs of Hibernia; in 1752–53 Clerimont in The Lover His Own Rival; in 1754–55 Commodore in The Press Gang and Moore in Lady Moore; in 1758–59 Cadwell (Arviragus) in Hawkins's alteration of Cymbeline; in 1759–60 Hilliard in The Jovial Crew; in 1760–61 at Drury Lane, Zoreb in Garrick and Smith's new musical entertainment The Enchanter; and in 1761–62 Balthazar in Much Ado about Nothing.

The number of named speaking and singing roles which Lowe added to his repertoire during that decade was not large, in the context of the times. He established a repertoire rather quickly and expanded it slowly, in some seasons adding nothing at all. That fact does not mean that he was relatively inactive. His audiences liked to see him in the same parts and the same kinds of parts repeatedly—huntsmen, naval officers, rustics both realistic and classically pastoral. His presence, like the efforts of other great songsters of the century, kept many dubious trifles alive. He sang frequently in musical comedy and the masque-like pieces favored by Rich and was not embarrassed by pantomime. But his roles almost invariably involved song, whether or not he was performing in a piece mainly musical.

Perhaps his most characteristic contribution was the solo song lightly integrated into the drama.

Another aspect of Thomas Lowe was the Handelian. Though Handel never wrote for him with the regularity that he did for Beard, Lowe did sing a number of secondary roles. There is dispute about his Handel repertoire, but a fairly trustworthy chronological list can be constructed: Hebdonah in *Esther* in 1742; Israelite Officer and Philistine in *Esther* in 1743; the title role in *Joshua*, some role in *Judas Maccabaeus*, and Jonathan in *Alexander Balus* in 1748; the First Elder in *Susannah*, a role in *Hercules*, and Zadok in *Solomon* in 1749; the Priest and Mordecai in *Esther*, probably the title role in *Belshazzar*, and an Attendant on Pleasure in the "new act" added to *Alexander's Feast* in 1751; and Septimius in *Theodora* in 1760. He also sang songs composed by Handel in 1745 for Lacy's theatrical volunteers and to celebrate Cumberland's victory at Culloden. On 10 May 1749, he, with Guadagni and others, sang the so-called "Foundling Hospital Anthem" as part of a charity benefit program Handel contributed at the Hospital for the Maintenance and Education of Exposed and Deserted Young Children.

Lowe's chief popularity, however, may have sprung from singing at the various public gardens where he served for many years. We have seen that he began, as a boy, as a tavern singer. He was featured, with the trumpeter Valentine Snow and others, at the Castle Tavern in 1741. In 1743 and 1744 he sang oratorio selections at Ruckholt House, Essex. In 1744 also, he sang for Burke Thumoth's benefit at the Swan Tavern in Cornhill. By at latest 1750 he was singing at Spring Gardens, Vauxhall, and he continued a favorite there off and on in the summers for more than 25 years. Also from August 1750, when he sang with Miss Falkner in *Henry and Emma*, he was frequently at Marylebone Gardens. In 1763 he succeeded John Trusler as manager-proprietor at Marylebone, taking the premises at a yearly rental of £170 on a lease of 14 years. Michael Kelly thought that he had had the backing of the elder Stephen Storace and Dr Samuel Arnold. He opened the Gardens in May 1763 with a "Musical Address to the Town," in which he, Miss Smith, and his pupil Ann Catley apologized that Marylebone lacked the sophistication of Ranelagh and Vauxhall: "Yet Nature some blessings has scatter'd around;/ And means to improve may hereafter be found." He himself took a prominent part in the concerts of vocal and instrumental music. For awhile the Gardens prospered ("Owing," thought Kelly, "[to] the Music and Miss Trusler's plumcakes."), but after the wet summer of 1767 Lowe was forced (in a deed of 15 January 1768) to assign to his creditors all the receipts until his debts were discharged. He retired from the management and sold out to Samuel Arnold in 1769.

By then Lowe's voice was declining in power and quality. He was happy to accept an engagement at a humbler establishment, Finch's Grotto Gardens in George Street, St George's Fields. He managed the entertainment at Ottersley Pool, near Watford, Hertfordshire, for a few weeks in 1770. (The *Whitehall Evening Post* of 9 November 1770 carried the news of the death "lately" of his wife at that place.) On 20 April 1772 the generous Drury Lane comedian Tom King, then manager at Sadler's Wells, engaged Lowe. The Wells was his professional home for the 11 years following, until near the time of his death.

Thomas Lowe obviously had a considerable popular following, and composers as eminent as Handel and Arne found a wide variety of uses for his talents. But critical opinion was not always enthusiastic. Charles Burney, for instance, thought well of his gifts but poorly of his training: ". . . with the finest tenor voice I ever heard in my life, for want of diligence and cultivation, he could never be safely trusted with any thing better than a ballad, which he constantly learned by ear."

Not much is known of the private life of Thomas Lowe. On 31 December 1742 he was assaulted and robbed of 11*s*. as he was going down Snow Hill but was not much hurt. There was gossip that he had had a brief affair with Cecilia, the wife of T. A. Arne, when they were all in Ireland. A number of entries in the baptismal registers of St Paul, Covent Garden, relate to him. On 19 December 1759, "Elizabeth & Mary Twinns Da[urs]. of Thomas Lowe by Mary his Wife" were christened; on 2 March 1760 "Jonathan Son of Thomas Lowe by Mary his Wife" was christened. "Lucy Daur of Thomas Lowe by Mary his Wife" took her turn at the font on 23 March 1761, followed by "Halyfax"

Lowe on 27 June 1762. The burial registers show the grim attrition typical of the eighteenth-century family. Betty, daughter of Thomas and Mary Lowe, was buried on 17 March 1754, Mary on 30 December 1758, Elizabeth on 7 January 1759, Jonathan on 26 April 1760, Thomas on 19 September 1763, and Jane Isabella on 12 November 1765. Of all the children, we know only that Halifax survived, till 1790, and had a career as a singer.

Lowe's benefit bills from his years at the patent theatres reveal from time to time where Lowe lived. At spring benefit time in 1741 he lodged in Beaufort Buildings in the Strand, in 1742 "next the Seven Stars" in Bedford Street, Covent Garden, in 1747 "at Mr Venables, Wine Merchant in the Great Piazza," Covent Garden, and in 1750 "the corner of Southampton Street, Covent Garden." In 1765 he lived in Battersea. He died at his lodgings in Aldersgate Street on 1 March 1783.

Well over 100 songs, published "as sung by" Thomas Lowe, are listed in the *Catalogue of Printed Music in the British Museum*.

Thomas Lowe's portrait in huntsman's dress ("with early horn") by an unknown artist was issued as a plate to the *Vocal Magazine*, engraved by J. Bew 1778. In the Folger Shakespeare Library is a drawing of Lowe as Macheath with Mrs Chambers as Polly in *The Beggar's Opera*. The drawing is unsigned but perhaps it is a sketch for the painting by R. E. Pine for the engraving by J. MacArdell published in 1752. That engraving, showing Lowe with Mrs Chambers, is reproduced in volume III of this *Dictionary*, p. 147.

Lowland, Walter [*fl.* 1744], *trumpeter.*
The establishment list for 1744 named Walter Lowland as a trumpeter in the King's Musick.

Lowther. *See also* LOWDER.

Lowther, Master [*fl.* 1784], *singer.*
Master Lowther was listed by Dr Burney as one of the treble singers in the Handel Memorial Concerts at Westminster Abbey and the Pantheon in May and June 1784.

Loyd, Mr [*fl.* 1776–1777], *dresser.*
A manuscript paylist in the Folger Shakespeare Library reveals that a Mr Loyd was paid 9s. per week as a dresser at Drury Lane Theatre in 1776–77.

Loyde. *See also* LLOYD.

Loyde, Mr [*fl.* 1792–1793], *scene painter.*
A British Museum manuscript (Add 29,948) records a payment of £25 6s. 6d. to McQuoid, Imanuel, and Loyde, scene painters at Covent Garden during the 1792–93 season.

Loyscoean, Francis [*fl.* 1687], *trumpeter.*
On 5 October 1687 Francis Loyscoean (or Loiscan) was appointed a trumpeter in the King's Musick replacing Mathias Shore, who had just been promoted to Sergeant-Trumpeter.

L'Pine. *See* DE L'ÉPINE.

L'Post. *See* LE POST.

Lubbe, Mr [*fl.* 1720], *violoncellist?*
In his *History of the Violoncello* van der Straeten states that two German musicians named Lubbe, a father and son, played in the orchestra of "the Royal Opera"—the King's Theatre—in London. The father was active at the theatre as early as 1720 and was a "base" player—probably a violoncellist. The son joined the orchestra in 1758 and supposedly contributed to the abolition of the bass viol by his performance on the violoncello.

Lubbe, Mr [*fl.* 1758], *violoncellist.* See
LUBBE, MR [*fl.* 1720].

Lucas, Mr [*fl.* 1724–1731], *candleman, office keeper?*
The Lincoln's Inn Fields accounts first mentioned Mr Lucas the candleman on 23 September 1724, when he was paid £2 2s. for candles on account. But on 31 January 1729 a note in the books concerning the free list reads "by Mr Lucas," which suggests that he may have risen to the post of office keeper. He may have been the Lucas who received a solo benefit at the Goodman's Fields playhouse on 16 March 1731. *The London Stage*, in its introduction to part 2, states that a Mrs Lucas received 2 Guineas nightly for candles and lighting, but we take

that to be an error for the citations in the theatre accounts dealing with Mr Lucas.

Lucas, Mr [*fl.* 1746–1760], *dancer.*

The Covent Garden Theatre accounts cite a Mr Lucas on 29 May 1746 at a salary of 10*s.* weekly. He was mentioned again in September 1750 and may have been with the troupe in the years between. He was not mentioned in any bills, however, until 15 April 1755, when he and "Lepy" (i.e. Leppie) offered a comic dance as an entr'acte turn. They repeated that dance subsequently and on 6 May danced *Les Charbonières* together. On 30 March 1756 Lucas made his first appearance on the stage of the King's Theatre dancing a new turn with Signora Banti, but he was back at Covent Garden on 22 April in *Les Paisans Iriquois* with Bienfait.

Lucas continued dancing at Covent Garden to the end of the 1758–59 season, appearing in such named dances as *Fingalian Revels* and *The Threshers* and dancing in *Macbeth, Catherine and Petruchio,* and *The Prophetess.* His most important assignment, probably, was the title part in a pantomime ballet called *The Feast of Bacchus,* which was first offered on 16 November 1758. Lucas danced in 1759–60 at the Crow Street Theatre in Dublin.

Lucas, Mr [*fl.* 1775–1779], *actor.*

Mr Lucas played Gobbo in *The Merchant of Venice* at a single performance at the Haymarket Theatre on 23 March 1775. At the same house on 24 March 1778 Lucas was seen as King Henry in *Richard III,* and he returned to play a principal but unnamed character in *The She Gallant* on 13 October 1779. On the latter date Mrs Lucas, presumably his wife, played a Masked Lady in *A Bold Stroke for a Wife.*

Lucas, Mr [*fl.* 1790–1792], *performer?*

The Drury Lane Theatre accounts show payments of £127 2*s.* in 1790–91 and £334 16*s.* in 1791–92 to a Mr Lucas; the sums are described as expenses paid at the end of the season. Lucas may have been a tradesman, but the wording seems to suggest that he was a theatre employee who during the season provided services of some kind for which he was reimbursed. Could he have been the William Lucas of Duke Court, Drury Lane, who witnessed the will of the Drury Lane musician Frederick Fitzgerald on 3 May 1789? There is not enough evidence to make an identification.

Lucas, Mrs [*fl.* 1779], *actress. See* LUCAS, MR [*fl.* 1775–1779].

Lucas, Daniel [*fl.* 1794], *violinist.*

Doane's *Musical Directory* of 1794 listed Daniel Lucas, of No 1, Chues Alley, White Cross Street, as a violinist.

Lucas, Jane [*fl.* 1693–1707], *actress, dancer, singer.*

Jane Lucas danced in *The Rape of Europa* at the Dorset Garden Theatre in the winter of 1693–94 as a member of the United Company under Christopher Rich. When Betterton and many of the older players broke away to form their own company, Mrs Lucas stayed with Rich at Dorset Garden and Drury Lane, and before the end of the century was seen as Lucy Welldon in *Oroonoko,* Amanda's Woman in *Love's Last Shift,* Maukin in *Pausanius,* Sue in *The Cornish Comedy,* a player and dancer in *The Female Wits,* and a singer in *The World in the Moon.* Her part in *The Female Wits* required her to play herself, and the anonymous author poked fun at her coffee-drinking. In one scene the actors are gathered for a rehearsal, but Mrs Lucas has not arrived. A little boy says she is "but drinking a Dish of Coffee, and will come presently." One of the performers says, "She's lean enough without drinking Coffee," to which William Pinkethman replies, "But 'tis good to dry up Humours." Finally Mrs Lucas arrives, claiming she drinks coffee simply because she loves it.

About 1700 Mrs Lucas had Colley Cibber arrested for some reason, and Cibber petitioned the Lord Chamberlain from the Gatehouse where he was being held, claiming that she had had him apprehended without leave from the Lord Chamberlain. He begged that Mrs Lucas, her attorney, and the bailiffs be brought before the Lord Chamberlain to answer their contempt and that Cibber be set free. Just what that contention was all about is not known, but Cibber was fast becoming a great power in the Drury Lane troupe and no one to meddle with. Possibly he had something to do with the fact that when Mrs Lucas was sworn a member of the troupe on 23 February 1702 (certificates were renewed periodically) her warrant was canceled. For some time afterward she is not recorded as having performed, but the records of the early eighteenth century are very incomplete, and she may have been dropped from the roster only briefly.

From shortly after the beginning of the new century Jane Lucas performed with Rich's company, appearing as Lucy in *The Perjured Husband*, Parley in *Sir Harry Wildair*, Mademoiselle in *The Funeral*, Clora in *All for the Better*, Lucy in *Tunbridge Walks*, Flora in *The Fair Example*, Malapert in *Vice Reclaimed*, Lettice in *The Lying Lover*, Mrs Edging in *The Careless Husband*, Jenny in *Farewell Folly*, Mrs Ap Shinken in *Hampstead Heath*, Apliew in *The Basset Table*, and Constance in *The Northern Lass* (in which she sang a song set by William Crofts). She sang within plays and as an entr'acte entertainer, and occasionally she danced, as in February 1703, when she and "Laferry" offered a *Scaramouch Man and Woman*, or in May 1703, when she and Weaver danced *Tollet's Ground*. One song she sang, *Lord! What's come to my Mother* from *The Bath*, was published about 1702, which suggests that she had a role in that work that the bills and cast lists did not indicate. She seems not to have performed after December 1707 and may have disagreed with the union that was effected between the two London companies at the beginning of 1708.

But as late as 1719 in *Wit and Mirth* Jane Lucas was evidently still remembered, for songs she had sung years before were included, with Mrs Lucas named as the singer, and the anthology also reprinted "An EPILOGUE. *For Mrs.* LUCAS."

> Y'HAVE *seen me Dance, and ye have heard me Sing,*
> *But now I'm put upon another thing;*
> *By way of* Epilogue *to make a Speech,*
> *If I can Frame my Mouth for't, I'm a Witch:*
> *Nor that I find there's ought that can Provoke in't,*
> *But should there chance to be a smutty Joke in't,*
> *Any Reflection, or the least word of Bawdy,*
> *That should disgust a Gentleman, or Lady:*
> *What case were I in then, what Desolation?*
> *Would that be to my Virgin Reputation?*
> *A great huge Girl, to blirt out a Paw word,*
> *Nay, tho' twere Privileg'd and on Record:*
> *I would not such a Thing, by me were said,*
> *For fifty Pistoles, as I am a Maid.*
> *Or should the Plaguy Poet in his Rhimes,*
> *Give some unlucky bob upon the Times;*
> *As—Heaven help us, those that use his way,*
> *In this fine World—May have enough to say;*
> *And so to punish me for Faults, are his,*
> *I should be fetch'd to come upon my Knees;*
> *Me—On my Knees! amongst a throng this Weather,*
> *Ivads no—I an't such a Baby neither;*
> *So I'll speak none on't—but say I'm ashamed,*
> *And let him take his Paper—And be Damn'd:*
> *I'm for no Jerking* Epilogues, *not I,*
> *Unless the words are chopt—Like Mince-meat for a Pye,*
> *But stay, since honest* Bourdon *here stands by,*
> *And that I may more handsomely get rid on't,*
> *We'll sing the last new* Dialogue instead on't.*
>   **Sings and* Exit.

Lucca, Maria. *See* GALLIA, MARIA.

"Lucchesina, La." *See* MARCHESINI, MARIA ANTONIA.

"Lucchesino, Il." *See* PACINI, ANDREA.

Lucchini, Antonia Maria. *See* MARCHESINI, MARIA ANTONIA.

Lucchi, Vincenza [*fl.* 1757–1768], dancer.

The Italian dancer Sga Vincenza Lucchi (or Luchi) made her first appearance at Drury Lane Theatre on 4 October 1757 performing with Signor Giorgi in a dance called *The Italian Peasants*, which was presented after Act II of *Macbeth*. That dance was repeated several more times, and then on 20 October Sga Lucchi appeared with others in a *Pastoral Dance* within the masque scene of *The Tempest*. On 26 November she and De Laître performed a new comic dance called *The Market*, which received high praise from the *London Chronicle* of 26–29 November 1757. With De Laître, Giorgi, and Mrs Vernon she danced *The Prussian Camp* on 23 December. At her benefit on 10 April 1758, when tickets could be had at Signora Lucchi's lodgings with a grocer in James Street, Covent Garden, she performed in a new Spanish dance and a new comic dance; gross receipts were £150.

Over the next three seasons, through 1760–61, she was featured in such specialty dances as *The Flemish Feast* in the pantomime *Fortunatus* and in *The Enchanter*, Garrick's musical entertainment which premiered on 13 December 1760. In 1761–62 she went to dance at Smock Alley, Dublin, with a company of burletta players headed by Anthony Minelli. No doubt she was the "Lucci" who received £48 6s. by contract from Minelli. Her first name is provided in the notes of the late William S. Clark. Perhaps after her Dublin season Sga Lucchi returned to the corps de ballet at Drury Lane, but her name is not seen again until 1764–65, when she was entered on a Drury Lane paylist for 5s. per night, or £1 10s. per week. She was still earning that sum in 1766–67. On 30 April 1768 her name was added to the bills as one of the dancers in *The Cotillion*, the last time we notice her.

Luchi. *See* LUCCHI.

Luchino, Mr [*fl.* 1753], *violinist, composer.*

On 20 November 1753 at the King's Theatre Mr Luchino played his own violin concerto.

Luciani, Signor [*fl.* 1768–1771], *singer.*

According to Burney's *General History of Music*, Signor Luciani was among the singers who presented *La schiava*, *La buona figliuola*, and *Arianna e Teseo* in command performances before the King of Denmark at the King's Theatre in August 1768. The following season Luciani was one of the serious singers in comic operas at the King's; cast listings are not available, but among the pieces performed there in 1768–69 were *Arianna e Teseo*, *Gli amanti ridicoli*, *Il viaggiatori tornati*, *La donne vindicati*, *La buona figliuola*, *La schiava*, *Il mercato di Malmantile*, *Il filosofo de campagna*, *Il re alla caccia*, *La moglie fedele*, *Nanette e Lubino*, *Lo speziale*, and *Le serve rivali*.

In Scotland in 1770 and 1771 Signor Luciani sang in numerous concerts of the Edinburgh Musical Society.

Luciet, Miss [*fl.* 1798–1801], *dancer, actress.*

Miss Luciet (or Luciott) was a dancer and supernumerary actress at Drury Lane Theatre from 1798–99 through 1800–1801 and perhaps later. On 6 October 1798 she was a Slave in *Blue-Beard*, and on 14 November she was listed as a dancer in *The Captive of Spilburg*. On the following 6 December she played a Villager in a dance called *The Scotch Ghost*. On 19 January 1799 Miss Luciet was a Vassal in *Feudal Times*, and in February she danced in *Moggy and Jemmy*. Her name was in the account books on 19 October 1799, but her salary was not given. She danced a Slave in *The Egyptian Festival* on 11 March 1800.

Luck, J. C. [*fl.* 1787–1788], *oboist.*

The accounts for the Academy of Ancient Music reveal that for the 1787–88 season J. C. Luck, an oboist, was paid £6 6s.

Luddington, William [*fl.* 1697], *singer.*

According to warrants in the Lord Chamberlain's accounts dated 29 September 1697 William Luddington had been one of the children of the Chapel Royal and, his voice having changed, had been dismissed and his maintenance provided for. It seems very likely that Jane Luddington, "a Musician's Child" who was buried on 19 September 1709 at St Clement Danes, was related to William—his sister, perhaps. If William's father was a professional musician, we have found no record of his performing in public. It is perhaps worth noting that in the will of Dr John Blow, written on 3 January 1708 and proved by the musician's daughters on the following 14 October, a bequest was made to an Elizabeth Luddington, Blow's servant. She was to receive £100 plus £10 for mourning and all of Blow's rings and wearing apparel.

Ludworth, Mr [*fl.* 1784], *singer.*

Mr Ludworth sang bass in the Handel Memorial Concerts at Westminster Abbey and the Pantheon in May and June 1784.

Luff, Mr [*fl.* 1794], *singer?*

Doane's *Musical Directory* of 1794 listed Mr Luff, of Chichester, as a bass (singer?) who performed in the Handel concerts at Westminster Abbey.

Luffingham, Mr [*fl.* 1723], *impresario.*

Mr Luffingham owned a "Great Room at Hampstead Wells" where in July 1723 a group of players from both patent houses headed by Bullock and Lee put on some plays. In August Luffingham's Room was the scene of a concert on the nineteenth.

Luigione. *See* SAGGIONE.

Luind, Mr [fl. 1784–1785], *performer?*
A Mr Luind was paid £80 for the 1784–85 season at the King's Theatre. He may have been a member of the singing or dancing chorus. He is not listed in *The London Stage*.

"Luke, Old Father." *See* "OLD FATHER LUKE."

Lulli, Lullie, Lully, Luly. *See* LILLY, LOEILLET, TULLY.

Lumian. *See* LINIKE.

Lumiere, Mr [fl. 1776], *house servant?*
Mr Lumiere, possibly one of the house servants, was cited in the Drury Lane accounts on 30 November 1776, along with two others, for a payment of £10 8s. 8d. The three were noted as not on the list—presumably the regular paylist.

Lumm, Mrs Charles. *See* FALKNER, ANNA MARIA.

Lumont, Mr [fl. 1799], *performer?*
Mr Lumont (if we have transcribed the name correctly) was paid £1 13s. 4d. for five days at Drury Lane Theatre in September 1799. At that salary he may have been one of the minor performers.

"Lun." *See* RICH, JOHN.

"Lun, Jr." *See* WOODWARD, HENRY.

Lunardi, Vincenzo *1759–1806, aeronaut, exhibitor.*
Born at Lucca, Italy, on 11 January 1759, Vincenzo Lunardi was secretary to Prince Caramanico, the Neapolitan ambassador in London, in the early 1780s. In 1784 he received permission from George Howard, governor of Chelsea Hospital, to make a balloon ascent from the hospital grounds. His prospectus for the ascent, in which he advised the public that he had undertaken the construction of a globe 32 feet in diameter, is in the British Library. More than 20,000 people paid an admission fee to see the completed balloon suspended from the dome of the Lyceum.

By permission of the Trustees of the British Museum
VINCENZO LUNARDI
engraving by Bartolozzi, after Cosway

When the unsuccessful attempt of another aeronaut named Moret caused a riot, permission for Lunardi's launching from the hospital property was revoked. The venture was further threatened when the Lyceum manager locked up the balloon because he wanted royalties on the subscriptions, but the police intervened. After delays created by technical difficulties the balloon, filled with hydrogen by the chemist Dr George Fordyce, lifted Lunardi from the Honourable Artillery Company's ground at Moorfields on 15 September 1784, watched by a crowd of spectators estimated at two hundred thousand. He went up with only a dog and cat because the weight of his intended English accomplice, George Biggin would have made the load too heavy. As the "first aerial traveller in the English atmosphere," Lunardi soared over London "in view of the whole town" including the King, who witnessed the journey through a telescope at St James's. The balloon descended in a field near Ware, in Hertfordshire, and that night Lunardi brought it back to Essex Street "amidst the acclamations of a great mob." The high-flying Lunardi was made

LUNARDI

By permission of the British Library Board
LUNARDI'S balloon at the Pantheon
engraving by Green, after Byron

an honorary member of the Honourable Artillery Company.

Lunardi's 1784 ascent created great excitement. It was reported that "never did a foreigner leave this land with so many prayers for his safe return." When Windham called at Burke's country house on 13 September, he "found them all going to London the next day on the same errand as myself, viz, to see Lunardi ascend." Johnson received "in three letters three histories of the Flying Man" on the eighteenth. That year John Bell published Lunardi's own *Account of the first Aerial Voyage in England, in a series of letters to . . . Chevalier Gherardo Compagni . . . written under the impressions of the various events that affected the undertaking*. A detailed description of the voyage, with a view of the ascent, was provided in the September 1784 issue of the *European Magazine*, and also in 1784 was published *Lunardi's Grand Aerostatic Voyage through the Air*.

Soon after the flight, Lunardi advertised from his house at No 6, Poland Street, that his balloon was on exhibition, admission one shilling, at the Pantheon, "where it is to be seen in the exact state it was in when Mr. Lunardi descended at Collier's Hill, near Ware, in Hertfordshire" (including the cat and dog passengers). Lunardi's Pantheon enterprise was cut short when a skylight broke and punctured the balloon.

On 13 May 1785 Lunardi again ascended from the Artillery ground about one o'clock in the afternoon, but the balloon, "being overcharged with vapour descended in about twenty minutes in the Adam and Eve Gardens." According to the *Morning Herald* of 14 May 1785, the celebrity was "immediately surrounded by great numbers of the populace, and though he proposed re-ascending, they were not to be dissuaded from bearing him in triumph on their shoulders." After ascensions made in Edinburgh and Glasgow in 1786 he published *An Account of Five Aerial Voyages in Scotland*.

By 1788 Lunardi returned to Italy. On 9 July of that year a notice was published at Rome that, since he had not made a promised ascent, all those who paid to witness it would have their money refunded. In October 1789 the *Biographical and Imperial Magazine* carried an account of another of Lunardi's aerial adventures—an ascent from the inner court of the palace at Naples on 13 September to a descent in a village 18 miles away—for which the King of the Sicilies rewarded him with 2000 ducats, a valuable ring, and a gold medal. He made another ascent at Lisbon in August 1794.

In July 1790 the *Biographical and Imperial Magazine* incorrectly reported that Lunardi had died at Genoa. His death did not occur until 31 July 1806, in the convent of Barbadinas in Lisbon. Lunardi was one of the greatest pioneers of ballooning, his first English flight in 1784 having occurred less than a year after Pilatre de Rozier's first flight and only several weeks after John Tytler's ascent from Edinburgh on 27 August 1784. A fashionable bonnet in Scotland named after Lunardi is mentioned in Burn's "To a Louse."

Portraits of Lunardi include:

1. By Richard Cosway. Drawing in the possession of Lord Tweedmouth in 1889, when it was exhibited at the Burlington Fine Arts Club. Engraving by F. Bartolozzi, published as frontispiece to Lunardi's *Account of the first Aerial Voyage in England*, 1784.

2. Engraving by F. Bartolozzi, after J. F. Rigaud, showing Lunardi in the car of his balloon with two other aeronauts, George Biggin and Mrs Sage. Published by Bovi, 1785,

with title "Aerial Travellers." The same plate, with title altered to "The Three Favorite Aerial Travellers," was published by E. Wyatt on 25 June 1785.

3. Engraving by J. Kay, depicting Lunardi standing in the car of his balloon.

4. By unknown engraver, after Duché de Vaney. Profile in hat. Published by Bichner, 1784. A copy was published as frontispiece to *Lunardi's Grand Aerostatic Voyage*, 1784.

5. By unknown engraver. With dog and cat. Published by E. Hedges, 1784.

6. By unknown engraver. Profile in hat. Magazine plate.

7. Engraving by Barlow; pictures the balloon being inflated, with crude sketch of Lunardi in the car.

8. An engraving by Francis Jukes and Valentine Green, after a painting by F. G. Byron, shows Lunardi's balloon on exhibition at the Pantheon, 1784.

9. "The Aerial Traveller and the engaging Mrs R–ss," by an unknown engraver. Published in *Town and Country Magazine*, 1784.

Lund, Thomas *d. 1730?, trumpeter.*

The Lord Chamberlain's accounts show that Thomas Lund replaced Robert Cox in the King's Musick at £40 annually on 3 April 1719. In 1726 he was one of several court musicians paid for attending the installation at Windsor of the Duke of Richmond and Sir Robert Walpole as knights of the Garter. Lund was listed as a trumpeter when he was replaced by James James on 27 December 1730. Two days later John Hudson was also listed as a replacement for Lund. Such replacements were usually made very shortly after the death or retirement of a royal musician.

Lunear. *See* LINIKE.

Lunery, Mr [*fl. 1776*], *housekeeper?*

Mr Lunery was paid £5 5s. by Drury Lane Theatre on 29 November 1776 for new brooms. Though he may have been an outside tradesman, it is possible he was a theatre housekeeper.

Lunican. *See* LINIKE.

"Lun Junior." *See* WOODWARD, HENRY.

Lupino. *See also* LUPPINO.

Lupino, Signora Casanova Carino [*fl. 1726–1727*], *actress, dancer.*

Signora Casanova Carino Lupino is listed by Sybil Rosenfeld in *Foreign Theatrical Companies in Great Britain* (1955) as one of the actors and dancers in a troupe of comedians from Italy that arrived in London on 21 September 1726 and began to perform at the King's Theatre on 28 September. They also played at Lincoln's Inn Fields Theatre for one night on 24 April 1727. Signora Lupino's name is not found in the few cast lists extant for the productions given by this first *commedia dell' arte* company to perform in London in the eighteenth century. On 25 April 1727 the role of Silvio in *La parodia del pastor fido* was danced, according to *The London Stage*, by Signora Casanova, whom we assume to have been Zanetta Casanova, née Farusi, the performer noticed in volume III of this dictionary.

Perhaps Signora Lupino was related to the Luppino family of dancers reported to have been performing in London in the first half of the eighteenth century, but we are unable to document any connection.

Lupo, Andrew *d. 1695, musician.*

Andrew (probably Andrea originally) Lupo was surely descended from the large family of musicians named Lupo who were members of the royal musical establishment in the late sixteenth and early seventeenth century: Ambrose, Horatio, Joseph, Peter, Theophilus, and Thomas. But our only knowledge of Andrew is of his will, dated 3 October 1689 and proved on 15 April 1695. He described himself as of the parish of St Giles without Cripplegate, "Musitioner." He left his estate to his wife Faith, daughter Ann, and daughter-in-law Faith Tompin, equally.

Luppino, George Charles *1683–1725, dancer.*

George Charles Luppino was born in 1683, according to information given in *Who's Who in the Theatre* and the *Enciclopedia dello Spettacolo*. His father was either George William Luppino (1632–1693), a pre-Restoration performer who was buried at St Leonard, Shoreditch, or George Charles Luppino (b. 1662) who married Helena Dorothea Whitfield (b.

LUPPINO

1659) on 1 May 1679. But little of the information about the early English Luppinos provided either in standard references or in the romantic "histories" related by such modern members of the family as Stanley Lupino or Lupino Lane can be verified. For example George Charles Luppino, our subject, is supposed to have become known as "the Motion Master of Long Acre," but we find no confirmation of his performing, in extant bills or advertisements.

On 3 August 1709, according to the genealogical chart in *Who's Who in the Theatre*, Luppino married Charlotte Mary Estcourt (1688–1754), the daughter of the actor Richard Estcourt. Possibly Luppino then performed at the Bumper Tavern, which his father-in-law opened in James Street, Covent Garden, in 1712. George Charles Luppino apparently died in 1725. Luppino's wife also supposedly was a dancer, but again, we find no evidence of her performances in London or elsewhere, under her maiden or married names. Their son, George Richard Estcourt Luppino (1710–1787), is noticed separately. Parker's genealogy credits George and Charlotte with two daughters: Charlotte Rose Luppino, who was born in 1714, and Mary Anne Luppino, who was born at the Vine Tavern, Hertford, in 1718, and married Thomas Lee Little. The Luppino connection with the Little family, however, seems not to have occurred until the early part of the nineteenth century, according to the registers at St John, Hertford.

Luppino, Mrs George Charles, Charlotte Mary, née Estcourt *1688–1754, dancer.* See LUPPINO, GEORGE CHARLES.

Luppino, George Richard Estcourt *1710–1787, dancer, scene designer.*

According to genealogical charts provided in *Who's Who in the Theatre*, George Richard Estcourt Luppino was born in 1710, the son of George Charles Luppino (1683–1725) and his wife Charlotte Mary Estcourt, both reputedly dancers. Supposedly our subject had a long career in the theatre, nothing of which can be verified through London bills or advertisements. Tradition claims that he performed with John Rich in *The Two Harlequins* at Lincoln's Inn Fields Theatre in 1718; that dance was first noticed in the bills on 28 November 1720, though one called *Two Pulchanellos* was performed as early as 7 January 1716.

The *Enciclopedia dello spettacolo* credits him with designing the scenery and costumes for Galuppi's opera *Enrico*, which first was performed at the King's Theatre on 1 January 1743. He then, it is said, was a ballet master in Dublin and Edinburgh.

George Richard Estcourt Luppino married the dancer Rosina Violante, daughter of Italian rope dancers who came to England in the 1720s. Luppino died in 1787 and she in 1789. Both are reported to have been buried at St John, Hertford, but their names do not appear in the burial register. Their son Thomas Frederick Luppino (1749–1845) was a scene designer in London and married the dancer Rosina Simonet. Thomas Luppino, a tailor and costume designer in the London theatres by mid-century, may have been another son.

Luppino, Mrs George Richard Estcourt. See VIOLANTE, ROSINA.

Luppino, Georgina. See NOBLE, MRS HENRY.

Luppino, Thomas [*fl.* 1757–1814?], *tailor, costume designer.*

By 1757, Thomas Luppino was a tailor providing costumes for Covent Garden Theatre. In February 1760 that theatre paid him a total of £39 18s. for dancing dresses; in 1761 he received £12 14s. 11d. for "making Sundry Dancing Dresses." He was still working as Covent Garden tailor in 1768. By 1774–75 his services were employed by Drury Lane; on 25 November 1774 he received £64 14s. 6d. for making dresses, and on 3 February 1775 he received an additional £18 12s. 6d.

On 21 November 1777 Drury Lane paid Luppino £99 6s., probably for the costumes he supplied for *The Double Festival* and *The Triumph of Love*, two new ballets introduced in *The Maid of the Oaks* on 7 November 1776. The first ballet, scheduled to be in the second act, "was obliged to be deferred till the end of the 3rd Act," wrote Hopkins in his prompter's diary, "as Lupini, who made the Dancers Dresses, had not brought them to the House— this put us all into great Confusion." By the beginning of the third act "most of the Dresses were brought, but not all, and some of the

City of Birmingham Art Gallery
Costume designs, possibly for *L'Amour Jardinier*
by THOMAS LUPPINO

Dancers were obliged to put on what Dresses could be got for them."

By 1775–76 the tailor Luppino was also employed by the King's Theatre, where he also was working in 1776–77, and from 1778 through 1784. His name appeared in opera bills for providing costumes for *Il Convito* on 2 November 1782 and *L'Amour et Psyché*, a new ballet by Noverre, on 29 January 1788. Between 1790 and 1792 he worked at the Pantheon. There he executed costumes for the opera *Armida* on 17 February 1791 and for *La Siège de Cythère*, a new ballet by D'Auberval, on 9 May 1791.

In 1794–95 he returned to Covent Garden Theatre. He designed costumes for the premiere on 17 November 1794 of *Hercules and Omphale* a spectacular ballet afterpiece created by James Byrn. His name appeared in the bills as "Lupino Sen," to differentiate him from "Lupino Jun," who designed some of the scenery. With Mr Dick and Mrs Egan, our subject also designed costumes for the premiere of *Windsor Castle* on 6 April 1795, for which the other Luppino designed scenes.

Probably Thomas Luppino was related to the scene designer Thomas Frederick Luppino, with whom he collaborated on several productions at Covent Garden. Though called "Lupino Sen," the tailor seems not to have been the father of the scene designer, who was sometimes billed as "Lupino Jun." Probably they were brothers.

The Mrs Luppino who was paid £2 16s. 6d. by Drury Lane on 11 December 1781 for serving as a dresser for *The Generous Imposter* (a comedy by T. L. O'Beirne that was first performed on 22 November 1780) was probably the tailor's wife. If so, perhaps she was his second spouse, for on 12 May 1774, "Mary Wife of Thomas Luppino" was buried at St Paul, Covent Garden.

Possibly our subject was that Thomas Luppino whose will was proved by his widow at London on 3 June 1814, but we are unable to support the speculation. He had made the will on 30 August 1808, calling himself a gentleman, and had left some property at Brighton, Lewes, and elsewhere to his wife Elizabeth Luppino, his daughter Elizabeth Ann Luppino, and his sister-in-law Mary Boxall.

Costume designs by Thomas Luppino, owned by Michael Archer, Patricia Butler, and the Birmingham Art Gallery, are reproduced by Sybil Rosenfeld in *Theatre Notebook* 30.

Luppino, Mrs Thomas [Elizabeth?] [fl. 1780–1814?], *dresser.* See LUPPINO, THOMAS [fl. 1757–1814?].

Luppino, Thomas Frederick 1749–1845, *scene designer, dancer?*

Thomas Frederick Luppino was born in 1749, the son of the dancers George Richard Estcourt Luppino and his wife Rosina, daughter of rope dancers named Violante. It is said that Thomas Frederick was at one time a dancer in the family tradition, but we find references to him only as a scene designer and decorative painter. He worked under G. Colombo on the decoration of the Temple of Diana at Weston Park about 1770 and helped to paint the ceiling.

Probably Thomas Frederick was the Luppino who was paid £50 by the Drury Lane Theatre treasurer on 15 February 1781 "on Acct of Salary last season," no doubt as a painting assistant. Next season he was paid £20 on 7 December 1782, £40 on 2 January 1783, and £31 10s. on account on 27 March 1783; and he was paid £35 3s. 4d. for his salary in full on 28 April, when it was noted that his agreement had expired.

In 1783 Luppino was appointed assistant to Novosielski at the King's Theatre, where he remained through 1784–85. He signed as T. Luppino in the attestation in the *Case of the Opera House Dispute*, 1784. That year he was also employed to paint some scenery for the Norwich Theatre; the *Norfolk Chronicle* of 18 September 1784 called him "the celebrated scene painter, whose productions have been so much admired at some of the principal places of amusement in London."

Between 4 October 1786 and January 1789 Luppino worked at Covent Garden, earning two guineas per week. On 23 March 1789 at the Manchester Theatre Royal, *Harlequin Mungo* was produced with "the Scenery, Machinery, &c. designed and executed by Mr. LUPPINO." His new scenes included the "Gateway of the Tower," the "Dens of the Wild Beasts," the "Spanish Armada," and the "Horse and Foot Armoury." He also was employed there on *Don Juan*. In the autumn of 1789 Luppino, with Robertson and Blackmore, painted a scene of Plymouth and the docks for a production of *The Naval Review at Plymouth* presented at Astley's Amphitheater, Westminster Bridge, London. He was resident designer and painter for the Richmond Theatre, Surrey, in the summer of 1790; his work there included *Nootka Sound*. He was assistant painter for the opera company at the Pantheon in 1791, when he was sometimes advertised as Luppino junior, to differentiate him from the tailor and costume designer Thomas Luppino, who seems not to have been his father but may have been a brother.

In 1792–93 Luppino returned to Covent Garden, where he remained through 1803–4. The several account books seem contradictory in respect of his wages, but evidently he earned three guineas per week in 1793–94 and four guineas in 1794–95. In 1799–1800 he was paid £3 13s. 6d. per week and in 1800–1801 £4 4s. Luppino painted scenery (usually with Hodgins, Pugh, Malton, Walmsley, and others) for *Harlequin's Museum* in 1792–93; *Harlequin and Faustus* in 1793–94; *Hercules and Omphale*, *Mago and Dago*, and *Windsor Castle* in 1794–95; *Merry Sherwood* in 1795–96; *The Round Tower*, *Harlequin and Quixote*, *The Raft*, *Joan of Arc*, and *Harlequin's Return* in 1797–98; *Ramah Droog*, *Albert and Adelaide*, and *The Magic Oak* in 1798–99; *The Volcano*, *Paul and Virginia*, and *Joanna* in 1799–1800; *Harle-*

quin's Tour and *Perouse* in 1800–1801; *The Brazen Mask* in 1801–2; and *The Tale of Mystery* and *Harlequin Habeas* in 1802–3. Luppino also was employed with Greenwood, Malton, and Demaria on scenes for the premiere of J. P. Kemble's *Lodoiska* at Drury Lane on 9 June 1794.

At the turn of the century it becomes difficult to distinguish Thomas Frederick's career from that of his son Samuel George Luppino. The father worked at Norwich in 1799 and with Pugh at the Lyceum, London, in 1800, and sometimes for Mrs Baker's Kent Company. Both were engaged by Dibdin for the 1805–6 season at the Peter Street Amphitheatre in Dublin, the father at one guinea per day and the son at two and one-half guineas per week (and travel expenses from London for both). One of them worked at the Beaufort Square Theatre, Bath, in November 1806, on *Forty Thieves*. In 1807 the elder Luppino was at Covent Garden and the younger was at Drury Lane, and both worked at Brighton. Probably the elder was the Luppino at Covent Garden in 1809–10. One of them worked at Sadler's Wells in 1813, the Haymarket in 1814, the Surrey in 1816, Drury Lane in 1821, and Covent Garden in 1824 and 1826. In 1818 the elder had expressed an interest in joining Simpson's Company in America but seems not to have been engaged.

Thomas Frederick Luppino died in late April or early May of 1845 and was buried at St John, Hertford; the burial registers (now at All Saints, Hertford, with which St John was amalgamated) describe him as aged 96 and a resident of Fore Street. His wife Rosine, who died before him and with whom he was buried, was a member of the Simonet family of dancers. She seems, however, not to have performed in London; and she should not be confused with the Rosine Simonet, who was the daughter of the London dancers Louis and Adelaide Simonet. The latter Rosine was a child in the 1770s and continued to perform for several decades as Rosine Simonet. The Luppinos' daughter Georgina (or Rosina?) was born in 1778, was dancing at Covent Garden by 1799, and was for many years a performer at Sadler's Wells; she married Henry Noble (or Noblet), a dancer.

The Luppinos' son, Samuel George Luppino (d. 1830) was a scene painter in London during the early decades of the nineteenth century. The conjectured year of his birth, 1766, in *Who's Who in the Theatre* is probably too early, for his father would have been only 17 at the time. On 15 July 1790 Samuel George Luppino married Marianna Bologna, reputed to have been the daughter of the dancer Pietro Bologna. We find no record of her performing in the eighteenth century, though possibly she made appearances with other members of her family, including two brothers and a sister Barbara. Tradition has it that the daughter of Samuel George and Marianna Luppino, also named Marianna, once lived with the young Joe Grimaldi and had a daughter Florence by him; but the dates for such a liaison are impossible if Marianna was not born until after 1790, and we find no documentary confirmation of such a relationship.

Another of Samuel George Luppino's children, and thus the grandchild of our subject Thomas Frederick Luppino, was Thomas William Luppino (1791–1859). He is identified in the genealogy provided in *Who's Who in the Theatre* as a dancer, but we believe him certainly to have been the Thomas William Luppino who was assistant organist of St John, Hertford, between 1803 and 1813 and then organist of St Mary, Ware, for many years. In the biographical letter (now in the Glasgow University Library) which the musician provided Sainsbury in 1823, he made no mention of having been a dancer; nor, for that matter, did he specify his parents. The connection of the Luppinos, however, with Hertfordshire seems clear. Thomas William Luppino married Charlotte Little at St John's on 11 May 1813. The St John's register records the baptisms of two children: George Henekin Luppino on 30 April 1818 and Georgina Luppino on 7 January 1821. Another of their many children may have been George Hook Luppino. (Lupino Lane, in *How to Become a Comedian*, gives George Hook's birthyear as 1820 and places him as a son of Samuel George Luppino; if that assignment is correct then George Hook was the brother of Thomas William Luppino.) From George Hook Luppino's marriage to Rosine Proctor, daughter of the Kent schoolmaster Emanuel Percival Proctor, issued at least ten children, the main line of the numerous nineteenth and twentieth century Lupinos (as the family began to spell the name), who became connected to such theatrical families as the Websters, Glovers, Crawfords, Pooles, and Lanes.

The musician Thomas William Luppino died at Hertford on 19 March 1859 and was buried at St John's on 25 March; the register gave his late address as Fore Street. His wife Charlotte had been buried at the same church on 1 March 1855, aged 65.

Lusini, Caterina $_{[}fl.$ 1781–1784$_{]}$, *singer.*

Caterina Lusini sang at the King's Theatre during the 1783–84 season, appearing first on 29 November 1783 as Giunia in *Silla*. Signora Lusini also sang Arianna in *Il trionfo d'Arianna* and had an unnamed role in *Demofoonte*. Tickets for her solo benefit on 17 June 1784 were available from her at No 232, Piccadilly. An engraved portrait of her by an unknown artist is in the Civica Raccolta delle Stampe Achille Bertarelli, Milan. The catalogue of that collection states "Canto in Genova nel Teatro di Sant'Agostino nel 1781."

Luskin, Mrs $_{[}fl.$ 1746$_{]}$, *dancer.*

Mrs Luskin was a dancer at Sadler's Wells in April 1746.

Lussant, Mlle $_{[}fl.$ 1753–1754$_{]}$, *dancer.*

During the 1753–54 season Mademoiselle Lussant (sometimes cited as Madame) danced at Drury Lane Theatre, her first appearance being on 13 September 1753, when she appeared in a *Rural Dance* in *The Chaplet* with Gerard. Thereafter she was seen in such works as *Harlequin Ranger*, *Queen Mab*, a dance in *The Old Bachelor*, *The Genii*, *L'Entrée de flore*, *The Savoyard Travellers*, and *Fortunatus*. Her last appearance in London seems to have been on 2 July 1754, when she danced at Theophilus Cibber's benefit.

Lussingham. See LUFFINGHAM.

Lutenborgh. See DE LOUTHERBOURG.

Luther, John Christian *d.* 1789, *singer, harpsichordist, composer.*

Born in England of German extraction, according to the *European Magazine*, John Christian Luther studied under Gates and Nares and sang in the Chapel Royal. He was, the periodical said, a "tenor bass." In May and June 1784 he sang tenor in the Handel Memorial Concerts at Westminster Abbey and the Pantheon. The *European Magazine* noted that Luther taught harpsichord and had a very neat touch on that instrument and that the few compositions he had written did him credit. On 14 September 1789 the magazine reported that Luther had died "lately."

Lutherbury and **Lutterbourg.** See DE LOUTHERBOURG.

Lux. See LAX.

Luxmore, Mr $_{[}fl.$ 1786–1791$_{]}$, *house servant?*

Mr Luxmore, probably a house servant, had benefit tickets out at Covent Garden Theatre each spring from 1 June 1786 to 2 June 1791.

Civiche Raccolte d'Arte Applicata ed Incisione, Milan
CATERINA LUSINI
artist unknown

Lydall, Edward [fl. 1655–1677], actor.

Rollins in his "Contributions" in the 1921 *Studies in Philology* quotes a letter from Newcastle-upon-Tyne dated 28 December 1655, saying that a group of "lewd fellows" had acted a comedy and had been apprehended, convicted, and whipped in public for rogues and vagabonds. Among the players was Edward "Lidell of Jesmond, a *Papist*." He was surely the Edward Lydall who acted with the King's Company in the 1660s and 1670s. About 1661–62, according to a manuscript cast at the Folger Library, he played either the Earl of Chester or Lord Lacy in *The Royall King* at the Vere Street playhouse, though that early notice of Lydall is all that has been found, before that of 10 May 1666, when a Lord Chamberlain's warrant cited him as a member of the King's players. On 15 April 1667 he acted either Alberto or Andrugio in *The Change of Crownes* at the Bridges Street Theatre, and on 12 June 1668 he was Don Melchor in *An Evening's Love*.

In the years that followed, until the Bridges Street Theatre burned in 1672, Lydall is recorded as having acted a Servant and Giovanni in *The Sisters*, the Captain of the Guard in *The Island Princess*, Valerius in *Tyrannick Love*, Statilius in *The Roman Empress*, Prince Abdalla, a major role, in both parts of *The Conquest of Granada*, and Cassidoro in *The Generous Enemies*. During that period, on 28 February 1671, four players, among them Lydall, were ordered apprehended for unnamed misdemeanors.

At their temporary home at the Lincoln's Inn Fields playhouse the King's Company operated until their new theatre, Drury Lane, was ready for occupancy in 1674. It is sometimes difficult to tell at what playhouse Lydall may have played some of his parts, but he probably acted at Lincoln's Inn Fields Argaleon in *Marriage à la Mode*, Don Alonza in *The Spanish Rogue*, Collins in *Amboyna*, possibly the Palatine of Trock in *Brennoralt*, the third Witch in the *Macbeth* burlesque, which served as an epilogue to Duffett's *The Empress of Morocco*, Honorio in *The Amorous Old Woman*, and Villandras in *The Maides Revenge*.

His first role at Drury Lane would seem to have been Piso in *Nero* on 16 May 1674. After that, through the 1676–77 season, he was seen as Dorilant in *The Country Wife*, the Duke in *Othello*, Bacurius in *A King and No King*, Lelius in *Sophonisba*, Loredano in *Love in the Dark*, Apollo in *Psyche Debauched*, possibly Pontius in *Lucina's Rape*, Tiberius in *Gloriana*, Sir Oliver Bellingham in *The Country Innocence*, Perdiccas in *The Rival Queens*, and Oroandes in *Wits Led by the Nose*. A curious note in the Lord Chamberlain's accounts on 7 December 1675 indicates that the playwright Edward Panton had given a script to Lydall—perhaps hoping that the actor could convince his fellow players to produce it—and Lydall had kept it, apparently for a considerable time. The Lord Chamberlain ordered Lydall not to withold Panton's play from him. Nothing more is known of the matter. Nothing more after the summer of 1677 is known of Lydall either, though the second quarto of *Sophonisba* lists a cast for a production of that work in Oxford in 1681, and Lydall's name is down for Lelius, a role he had played years before. It does not seem likely that he was still with the company at that late date, however.

Lyddal, Miss. See STERLING, MRS JAMES.

Lyddal, Anna Marcella [Nancy]. See GIFFARD, MRS HENRY.

Lyddal, Sarah. See HAMILTON, SARAH.

Lyddall, Mr. See GARRICK, DAVID.

Lydel, Andreas. See LIDL, ANDREAS.

Lydell, Mrs [fl. 1712], impresario? See LYDELL, CLEOMIRE.

Lydell, Cleomire [fl. 1711–1712?], actress.

At Punch's Theatre in St Martin's Lane on 14 May 1711 *The Fairy Queen* was presented for the benefit of "the little Child that Dances with the Swords." Playing the Queen was Cleomire Lydell; Dorindall Lydell acted King "Obion." These "Lilliputians" were probably sisters. On 4 June 1712 at the same playhouse one of the girls—identified only as Miss Lydell—played Nottingham in *The Unhappy Favorite* with other youngsters. On 11 June she tried Dorinda in *The Stratagem*, and on 18 June she acted Patch in *The Busy Body*, again with other young people. On 9 July *The Recruiting*

Officer was presented for the benefit of Mrs Lydell and Mrs Kent, who may have been the organizers of those children's performances.

Lydell, Dorindall [*fl. 1711–1712?*], *actress.* See LYDELL, CLEOMIRE.

Lylett [*fl. 1720*]. See AYLETT, MRS.

Lylinston. See LILLESTON.

Lylly. See LILLY.

Lymmet, George [*fl. 1668–1670*], *scenekeeper.*
The London Stage lists George Lymmet, a scenekeeper, as a member of the King's Company at the Bridges Street playhouse in 1668–69 and 1669–70. He was cited in the Lord Chamberlain's accounts on 3 July 1669.

Lynam, Mr [*fl. 1732–1738*], *house servant?*
Mr Lynam received a solo benefit at the Lincoln's Inn Fields playhouse on 11 May 1732 and enjoyed a gross profit of £152 10s. He was evidently a house servant, for he was never cited in the bills as a performer, yet his position in the company must have been one of some importance. He received another solo benefit at the troupe's new theatre in Covent Garden on 6 May 1738.

Lynch, Mr [*fl. 1782*], *actor.*
A Mr Lynch played James in *An Adventure in St James's Park* at the Haymarket Theatre on 21 January 1782. The play was not repeated. It seems unlikely that Lynch could have been the Dublin actor John Lynch, who was active at that time at the Smock Alley Theatre, for the performers who turned up for single performances at the Haymarket in the winter usually declared in the bills where they hailed from—if they had had any previous experience worth hailing.

Lyndsay. See LINDSEY.

Lyne, John [*fl. 1739–1749*], *musician.*
A benefit concert was held for John Lyne at some place unstated on 25 April 1739, according to Latreille, but there was no indication on the bill that Lyne performed. He became one of the original subscribers to the Royal Society of Musicians on 28 August 1739, seems to have become a musician extraordinary (without fee) in the King's Musick by 1740, and on 12 March of that year was granted the position previously held by Joseph Abington. On 5 February 1741 Lyne had a benefit concert at Hickford's Great Room, and on 18 November he succeeded Francis Goodsens in the King's Musick (a second post, perhaps, or a shift in positions).

Lyne (or Lyon) was arrested in December 1745 by an attorney of Clifford's Inn named Jackson, perhaps for a debt. On 26 December 1749 Lyne gave his friend James Nicholson his power of attorney to collect money due Lyne from the King. That may have meant that Lyne had fallen into debt (again?). He seems not to have been the Mr "Line" whose benefit tickets were admitted at Covent Garden Theatre on 25 April 1749, but he may well have been related to the Samuel Lyne who was active as a music publisher about 1743 and had a shop at the sign of the Globe in Newgate Street.

Lyngs. See LINGS.

Lynham, Mr [*fl. 1746–1747*], *actor.*
Mr Lynham (or Linham) played Gibbet in *The Stratagem* at Southwark on 16 October 1746 and then joined the Goodman's Fields troupe to act Vernon in *1 Henry IV* on 29 October. He may not have become a member of the troupe, or if he did, he was given parts too small to rate recognition in the bills. In the summer of 1747 he was seen with the troupe at Richmond as the Manager in *Diversions of the Morning* on 3 October, just as the season was ending. Charles Beecher Hogan in *Shakespeare in the Theatre* suggests that Lynham may have been the Mr Lynam who in the 1730s received solo benefits with John Rich's company, but there is no indication that Lynam was a performer and there is every indication that he was a person of more importance in the theatre than Lynham turned out to be.

Lynnet. See LYMMET.

Lynot, John [fl. 1784–1794], *singer.*

John Lynot (or Lynott) sang bass in the Handel Memorial Concerts at Westminster Abbey and the Pantheon in May and June 1784. Doane's *Musical Directory* in 1794 listed Lynot as a member of the New Musical Fund living in Hyde Street, Bloomsbury.

Lynsey. *See* LINDSEY.

Lyon, Mr [fl. 1781–1788], *gallery keeper.*

The Drury Lane Theatre accounts cited a Mr Lyons, gallery keeper, on 10 July 1788. He was, we believe, the Mr Lyon who was named in benefit bills from 12 May 1781 to 6 June 1788. We cannot be certain, however, for the actor John Lyons was also in the company.

Lyon, Miss, later Mrs Gordon [fl. 1781–1784], *actress, singer.*

The "Gentlewoman" who played the Ballad Singer in *The Genius of Nonsense* at the Haymarket Theatre on 30 May 1781 was, as the bill of 11 June revealed, Miss Lyon. On 5 June she sang a song in the first act of *Separate Maintenance*, and on 8 August and subsequent dates to the end of the month she was Mat o'the Mint in *The Beggar's Opera*. She sang "Auld Robin Gray" on 16 October, after which her name disappeared from London bills for three years. When she returned it was as Lady Macbeth at Covent Garden Theatre on 4 October 1784. She was advertised as "A Lady," but the *London Magazine* identified her as the "Mrs Lyons" who had played in *The Genius of Nonsense* "some seasons since." The *European Magazine* said she had performed some roles at the Haymarket but did not have the talent to replace Mrs Yates as Lady Macbeth. The *Gazetteer* called her, in error, "Mrs Lloyd" and said that she was now Mrs Gordon. After that single appearance as Lady Macbeth our subject once again disappeared from the London stage.

Lyon, James [fl. 1794], *organist, singer.*

Doane's *Musical Directory* of 1794 listed James Lyon, of No 29, Princes Square, Radcliffe Highway, as an organist and alto (countertenor). He may have been a cousin of the violinist James Lyon. Both were listed by Doane as subscribers to the New Musical Fund.

Lyon, James [fl. 1794–1805?], *violinist.*

Doane's *Musical Directory* of 1794 listed James Lyon, of No 20, Wells Street, Oxford Street, as a violinist and suscriber to the New Musical Fund. He was probably the James Lyon who was still a subscriber in 1805. Another James Lyon was an organist and singer and perhaps a cousin of our subject. The Wells Street address was given also for the musician William Lyon, who may have been our subject's father.

Lyon, Myer. *See* LEONI, MICHAEL.

Lyon, Samuel Thomas 1776–1850, *instrumentalist, composer.*

The Minute Books of the Royal Society of Musicians show that Samuel Thomas Lyon was born on 28 December 1776, the son of the musician William Lyon and his wife Sarah. Samuel Thomas was christened at St Pancras on 2 February 1777. Lyon later wrote an autobiographical sketch for Sainsbury's dictionary, stating that he studied music under his father and learned theory from Possin. He made his first public appearance at the age of 13, playing the tenor (viola), and attracted the attention of Attwood the composer (the younger Thomas Attwood, presumably), who encouraged Lyon's musical career.

On 4 February 1798 Samuel Thomas Lyon was proposed for membership in the Royal Society of Musicians. He was described then as a single man who was proficient on the violin, viola, violoncello, and pianoforte. He was engaged at Drury Lane Theatre and for the Concerts of the Academy of Ancient Music and was organist of Berwick Street Chapel. He was elected unanimously and in May 1800 played 'cello in the annual St Paul's Concert that the Society sponsored. He married a daughter of the musician John Dressler on 21 March 1801. In 1803 he was scheduled to play viola at the St Paul's Concert, but he requested permission to send a deputy. The same thing happened in 1804, 1805, and 1806.

The younger Charles Dibdin in his *Memoirs* noted that for his Dublin venture at the Amphitheatre in Peter Street in the winter of 1805–6 he "engaged for the Leader of our Band, Mr. Lyon, [later] Brother in law to Mr. Bishop, the Composer, whom I sent off to Dublin immediately with the power to engage the best Band of Musicians he could possibly collect." (Samuel Thomas Lyon's sister Sarah married Henry Rowley Bishop in 1809.)

By 1807 Lyon had become a piano manufacturer with a shop at No 82, Wells Street, not far from where his father lived. After 1810 he was in partnership with a Mr Duncan, first in Wells Street and then, about 1813–14, at No 22, Suffolk Street, and about 1814–15 at No 22, Nassau Street. He ran the business alone at the last address from 1815 to 1840. Lyon published some music, including a few of his own compositions.

Though Lyon regularly sent a deputy to play for him in the St Paul's Concerts in the first decade of the nineteenth century, he gave time to the Royal Society of Musicians by serving, in 1807, as one of the Governors. The Society Minute Books cited S. T. Lyon as having died about 1811, but that was surely an error for his father William. As Lyon stated in his autobiographical sketch, he was elected in 1819 to the Society's Court of Assistants "or perpetual Governors of that institution." In 1824 Lyon was made an Associate of the Philharmonic Society. He was still active as a member of the Court of Assistants of the Royal Society of Music in 1839, but after that year his name dropped from the records, and he probably went into retirement. He died in 1850.

Lyon, Thomas [*fl. 1790–1802*], *violoncellist, double-bass player.*

Thomas Lyon was very likely related to William Lyon and his son Samuel Thomas Lyon, but of Thomas very little is known. He was probably the Lyon who played in the *Messiah* at Covent Garden Theatre on 19 February 1790 and performed in the oratorios again in March 1791 and February 1792. Though the records of his election to the Royal Society of Musicians have not been found, he was certainly a member. He played double bass at the Society's St Paul's Concert in May 1798 and violoncello at the concert in 1799. Though he was scheduled to participate in the concert in 1802 he was allowed to send a deputy.

Smith in *The Italian Opera in London* states that Thomas Lyon was a bassoonist in the opera company band at the Pantheon in 1791, but the bassoonist was probably William Lyon. The *Times* on 15 January 1798 said "Lyon and son" were playing in the oratorios at the Haymarket Theatre; the "Lyon" was, again, probably William and the son Samuel Thomas rather than Thomas, as *The London Stage* has it.

Lyon, William *d. 1748, actor, singer, playwright.*

The Mr Lyon who acted the title role in *Aesop* at the Smock Alley Theatre in Dublin on 6 January 1724 was almost certainly William Lyon who, when he made his debut at the Goodman's Fields playhouse in London on 25 November 1732 as Sir Jealous in *The Busy Body*, was hailed as from Dublin. The rest of the 1732–33 season at Goodman's Fields saw Lyon as Sir Solomon in *The Double Gallant*, a Citizen in *Julius Caesar*, Humphrey in *The Conscious Lovers*, Dalton in *The Lover's Opera*, Nimming Ned in *The Beggar's Opera*, Sir Francis Firebricks in *The Decoy*, Hecate in *Macbeth*, Sir Marvin Maugre in *The Mad Captain*, and Lucius in *Cato*. At Covent Garden Theatre in August 1733 he acted Aboan in *Oroonoko*, Poltroon in *The Fancy'd Queen*, and Quintius in *The Tuscan Treaty*.

Lyon remained at Goodman's Fields under Henry Giffard's management through 1735–36, adding to his repertoire such new roles as Casca in *Julius Caesar*, Gardiner in *Lady Jane Gray*, Wolsey in *Vertue Betray'd*, Periwinkle in *A Bold Stroke for a Wife*, Burleigh in *The Unhappy Favorite*, Gratiano in *Othello*, Sir Thomas in *Flora*, Corydon in *Damon and Phillida*, Gabby in *The Wonder*, Aristander in *The Rival Queens*, Felix in *The Mistake*, Alphonso in *The Spanish Fryar*, Obadiah in *The Committee*, the title part in *Don Quixote*, Antonio in *Love Makes a Man*, Bullock in *The Recruiting Officer*, a Citizen and a Serjeant in *Britannia*, Coupler in *The Relapse*, Macahone in *The Stage Coach*, Sable in *The Funeral*, Smuggler in *The Constant Couple*, Polonius in *Hamlet*, a Carrier in *1 Henry IV*, Sir Roger in *The Fond Husband*, Carbuncle in *The Country Lasses*, Stocks in *The Lottery*, Tiresias in *Oedipus*, Foresight in *Love for Love*, Lucius in *Cato*, Sir Harry in *The Tender Husband*, Sir William in *Love's Last Shift*, Vulture in *Woman's a Riddle*, the Duke in *Venice Preserv'd*, a Courtezan in *Jupiter and Io*, Lockit in *The Beggar's Opera*, Driver in *Oroonoko*, Dervise in *Tamerlane*, The Host in *The Merry Wives of Windsor*, Bonniface in *The Stratagem*, Bluff in *The Old Bachelor*, Kite in *The Recruiting Officer*, York in *Henry V*, the title part in *Sauny the Scot*, Sampson in

The Fatal Marriage, Lovegold in *The Miser*, and Cacafogo in *Rule a Wife and Have a Wife*.

Giffard's troupe moved to the Lincoln's Inn Fields playhouse in 1735–36, where Lyon continued in many of his old roles and added such new ones as Howdyee in *The Wife's Relief*, Moody in *The Provok'd Husband*, Glendower in *1 Henry IV*, Raymond in *The Spanish Fryar*, Pantaloon in *Harlequin Shipwrecked*, Sackbut in *A Bold Stroke for a Wife*, Brumpton in *The Funeral*, and Hellebore in *The Mock Doctor*. He was engaged at Covent Garden Theatre in 1737–38, playing Sable in *The Funeral* for his first appearance on 30 September 1737 and then appearing as a Sailor in *The Fair Quaker of Deal*, Salisbury in *Richard II*, Jamy in *Henry V*, and Metaphrastus in *The Mistake*.

Lyon left London after that. He played from about 1741 or 1742 to 1745 in Thomas Este's company at Taylor's Hall in Edinburgh, and there in April 1745 his alteration of *The Mistake*, called *The Wrangling Lovers*, was produced. He is known during his tenure at Taylors' Hall to have acted the title role in *Tamerlane*, Pierre in *Venice Preserv'd*, and the Grand Turk's Man in *The Amours of Harlequin and Columbine*. At the New Concert Hall in Edinburgh in 1747 and 1748, where he was a manager, Lyon was seen as Cecil in *The Albion Queens*, the First Gravedigger in *Hamlet*, and King Henry in *1 Henry IV*. The *General Advertiser* reported that William Lyon died in Edinburgh on 15 September 1748.

Davies in his *Dramatic Miscellanies* (and several other sources) commended Lyon's Gibby in *The Wonder* and spoke of the actor's remarkable memory. While tippling one evening Lyon wagered a crown bowl of punch that at rehearsal the following morning he could repeat the *Daily Advertiser* from beginning to end after reading it thrice over. He won his bet.

Lyon, William   *d. c. 1811, bassoonist.*

William Lyon played bassoon in the Drury Lane band from as early as the 1776–77 season, when he was first mentioned in the accounts. Though the records are not complete, Lyon continued performing at Drury Lane into the early years of the nineteenth century.

On 4 May 1777 he was recommended for membership in the Royal Society of Musicians. Robert Rawlings, who put his name up for consideration, said Lyon was married and had one child, six months old. That child was Samuel Thomas Lyon, who had been born on 28 December 1776 and baptized at St Pancras. William Lyon's wife was named Sarah, but we know little else about her. Lyon was admitted to the Royal Society of Musicians on 3 August 1777. Perhaps he was the "Lion" who served the King's Theatre as director of scenes in the 1780–81 season, and surely he was the Mr Lion who played bassoon in the Handel Memorial Concerts at Westminster Abbey and the Pantheon in May and June 1784. He was a Governor of the Royal Society of Musicians in 1785, and from 1789 on he played bassoon in the Society's annual concerts at St Paul's.

Smith in *The Italian Opera in London* says that the bassoonist Lyon who played in the King's Theatre opera company at the Pantheon in 1791 was Thomas, but that, we believe, is an error for William. Thomas was probably related to William in some way, as was another Lyon, James, a violinist who lived at No 20, Wells Street, Oxford Street. That address was given for William Lyon also, in Doane's *Musical Directory* in 1794. Perhaps James was William's son. Doane listed William as a bassoonist who played in the Concerts of the Academy of Ancient Music at the opera house, in the oratories at Drury Lane Theatre, and in the Handelian performances at Westminster Abbey.

The "Lyon and son" who performed in the oratories at the Haymarket Theatre in 1798, according to the *Times*, were not Thomas and Samuel Thomas, as *The London Stage* has it, but surely William and Samuel Thomas. The Drury Lane accounts for 1801 show William and "Lyon Jr" as members of the theatre band. William played at the Haymarket in the summers of 1807, 1808, and 1809 and probably other years as well. His salary at Drury Lane as of 16 September 1807 was £3 weekly.

William Lyon was a Governor of the Royal Society of Musicians in 1806 and a member of the Court of Assistants in 1808. By the summer of 1810 he had left the band at the Haymarket Theatre, and our guess is that he was by then well along in years and perhaps ill. The Minute Books of the Royal Society of Musicians contain a note dated 3 February 1811 referring to the death, apparently recently, of Mr Lyon. A note on 3 March 1811 concerning funds for the funeral of Lyon cited him as S. T.—Samuel Thomas, but surely that was an error, for we know that Samuel Thomas Lyon lived on until 1850.

William and Sarah Lyon had a daughter Sarah, born on 4 July 1787, who married the composer and conductor Henry Rowley Bishop at St Martin-in-the-Fields on 30 April 1809 (according to Grove, 5th edition).

Lyons, John *d. 1824, actor, singer.*

The London Stage separately indexes three performers in the 1780s and 1790s: John Lyons, a busy but minor actor, Mr Lyons, a singer active only in 1784–85, and a Mr Lyons, who appeared once at the Haymarket in October 1792. But the singer Lyons was named in choruses from 1784 to 1798 and seems always to have been wherever John Lyons was performing, so we take them to have been the same person. And the isolated Haymarket performance in 1792 fell on a night when John Lyons was not occupied at his regular house, Drury Lane. We believe, therefore, that all the references are to the same person. There were other men named Lyon or Lyons active in the late eighteenth century, but they were musicians and easily distinguishable in the bills.

Perhaps the Mr Lyons who performed in Roger Johnstone's troupe in Brighton in the summer of 1776 was John Lyons. Mrs Lyons, a dancer, was at Brighton, but she seems not to have performed in London. John was surely the Mr Lyons who acted at the Theatre Royal in Shakespeare Square, Edinburgh, from 1778 to 1780, for he was advertised as from Edinburgh when he appeared in London in 1781. His Edinburgh roles included Beau Trippet in *The Lying Valet*, the Brother in *The Ladies' Wish*, Burgundy in *King Lear*, Conrade in *Much Ado about Nothing*, the Cook in *The Devil to Pay*, the Corporal in *The Deserter*, David in *The Lady of the Manor*, Eustace in *Love in a Village*, Francis Bevil in *Cross Purposes*, Hounslow in *The Beaux' Stratagem*, the Jew in *The Norwood Gypsies*, Marcellus in *Hamlet*, Mervin in *The Maid of the Mill*, Passenger in *Summer Amusement*, Ranger's Servant in *The Suspicious Husband*, Rimenes in *Artaxerxes*, the Secretary in *The Devil upon Two Sticks*, Slango in *The Honest Yorkshireman*, Trip in *The School for Scandal*, Woodley in *Three Weeks after Marriage*, and Gadshill in *1 Henry IV*. At Stourbridge Fair in Cambridge in 1780 Lyons acted in the harlequinade *Fortunatus*.

His first London engagement (as "Lyon" from Edinburgh) was at the Haymarket Theatre, where he played Sir Harry Beaumont in *A Wife to Be Let* on 22 January 1781 and Rigadoon in *Love and a Bottle* on 26 March. He returned to play principal but unspecified characters in *The Fashionable Wife* and *The Lawyer Nonsuited* on 6 May 1782 and the Merchant in *Wit Without Money* on 25 November. He was probably the Mr Lyon who acted Harman in *Lionel and Clarissa* at the Richmond Theatre on 6 November 1781. Benefit tickets delivered by a Mr Lyons were admitted at the Haymarket on 23 August 1783, so perhaps John Lyons had been playing bit parts there that summer. On 17 June 1784 Lyons replaced Painter as Anvil in *Gretna Green* at the Haymarket; on 10 August he played the Corporal in *The What D'Ye Call It*; and on 31 August he replaced Barrett in an unspecified role in *The Noble Peasant*, and on 11 September he replaced him in *The Young Quaker*. On 17 September he sang a "Mad Song" in character in *The Apprentice*.

In May 1785 Lyons sang in Bristol at Merchant Taylors' Hall, at Barton's Rooms at the Hotwells, and at the Spring Gardens Bath with the conjuror Breslaw's troupe. After his performances in Bristol Lyons returned to the Haymarket in London for the summer, appearing as Snuffle in *The Mayor of Garratt*, a Fighting Quaker in *Harlequin Teague*, a Waiter in *The Young Quaker*, a Servant in *The Deuce Is in Him*, a Servant in *I'll Tell You What*, the Genius of the Mine in *Here and There and Every Where*, and unspecified characters in *A Beggar on Horseback*, *The Suicide*, and *Gretna Green*.

Since he played a Messenger in *Philaster* at Drury Lane on 1 December 1785, perhaps John Lyons was a member of the company throughout the 1785–86 season, playing parts too small to gain mention in the bills. He was once more at the Haymarket in the summer of 1786 in his usual line of small parts, such as Tweedle in *A Beggar on Horseback*, a Servant in *The Widow's Vow*, a Waiter in *The Suicide*, a Brother in *Comus*, a Messenger in *The Disbanded Officer*, Morosini in *The Siege of Curzola*, John in *The Agreeable Surprise*, Conrade in *Much Ado about Nothing*, and Frank Bevil in *Cross Purposes*. Since he was not mentioned in London playbills in 1786–87 we believe he was the Mr Lyon who was paid £5 16s. 6d. on 29 November 1786 by the Theatre Royal, Liverpool.

From the summer of 1787 through that of 1799 John Lyons appeared at the Haymarket Theatre in London, and from 1787–88 through 1794–95 he was with the Drury Lane Company in the winters. His summers found him very busy, but he was rarely assigned a role of much size, and typically he played servants, waiters, slaves, sailors, members of mobs, and the like. Among the new characters he played which had specific names were Count Louis in *Peeping Tom*, Timothy in *The Divorce*, Derby in *Jane Shore*, Nathaniel and Gregory in *Catherine and Petruchio*, James in *The Basket Maker*, Blunt in *Richard III*, Tom and William in *The Citizen*, Cambridge in *Henry V*, Flimsey in *Britain's Glory*, Leonardo in *The Merchant of Venice*, the Duke of Somerset in *The Battle of Hexham*, Peto in *Henry IV*, Peter in *The Iron Chest*, Sampson in *Romeo and Juliet*, Squire Robert in *The Mock Doctor*, and Harry Paddington in *The Beggar's Opera*.

His parts with the Drury Lane troupe (at the old Drury Lane, the King's Theatre, the Haymarket, and then the new Drury Lane) were not much different. In the winters some of his new roles over the years were Kingston in *High Life below Stairs*, John in *The Jealous Wife*, the Lieutenant of the Tower in *Mary Queen of Scots*, Jaques in *As You Like It*, William in *All the World's a Stage*, Scroop in *Henry V*, Curio in *Twelfth Night*, Gibson in *The Belle's Stratagem*, Lopez in *Don Juan*, Bandage in *The Fairy Favour*, J. Gurney in *King John*, Guzman in *Love Makes a Man*, Lazzaroni in *The Pirates*, Frank in *The First Floor*, Adam in *Catherine and Petruchio*, Ali Beg in *The Mountaineers*, Raesaces in *Alexander the Great*, and his usual run of servants and the like.

Some of Lyons's parts required singing, and he was often found swelling the choruses, summer and winter, in such works as *Romeo and Juliet*, *The Tempest*, *Arthur and Emmeline*, *Richard Coeur de Lion*, *Macbeth*, *Dido Queen of Carthage*, *The Surrender of Calais*, *The Mountaineers*, *Thomas and Sally*, *The Glorious First of June*, *The Roman Father*, *The Italian Monk*, and *The Iron Chest*. He sang with others such patriotic songs as "The British Volunteers" and "God Save the King." On 23 April 1790 when he and others offered "God Save the King" at Drury Lane, Bannister spoke a monologue called "British Loyalty; or, a Squeeze to St. Paul's." The same monologue was delivered by "Lyon" on 15 October 1792 at the Haymarket (on a night when John Lyons was not scheduled to perform at Drury Lane).

For his labors Lyons received from Drury Lane 10s. per week in 1789–90 and in 1790–91 £1. He seems not to have risen above that. The accounts cited him as a tenor and a member of the singing chorus. A Lyons was named in the Drury Lane accounts in 1809 as receiving £15 16s. 4d., but Lyons had not been mentioned in that theatre's bills since 1795. He had, however, been contributing to the theatre's fund since 1787, and he made a claim on the fund in 1803, by which time he was apparently retired. He remained "on the fund" until his death in September 1824.

Lyons was not ignored by the critics. *Authentic Memoirs of the Green Room* in 1799 reported that he was then engaged at Covent Garden Theatre, where he was kept "in his proper sphere [and used] only as a soldier, attendant, &c., but at the Hay-market we have seen him thrust into characters, in which he has disgraced the manager, and rendered himself ridiculous. This gentleman is of a theatrical family, who, if merit were to be consulted, were never born for the stage." The anonymous critic seems not to have remembered Lyons's years of service at Drury Lane and did not reveal who the other theatrical members of Lyons's family were. Perhaps the reference was to the gallery keeper Lyon and the actress Miss Lyon.

Lyons, Myer. *See* LEONI, MICHAEL.

Lysle. *See* LISLE.

Lyster, Mrs. *See* BARSANTI, JANE.

= M =

M'Arthur, Mr [fl. 1800], *instrumentalist*.

Mr M'Arthur was one of the instrumentalists at the Handel concert at Covent Garden on 28 February 1800. Perhaps he was related to the Edinburgh piper John McArthur, who died in 1790, or to the pianist Miss M'Arthur, who played in the oratorios at Covent Garden in 1796 and 1797.

M'Arthur, Miss [fl. 1796–1797], *pianist*.

On 4 and 16 March 1796 at Covent Garden Miss M'Arthur played a *"concerto on the Grand Piano Forte"* between parts of the oratorio. She was doubtless the Miss MacArthur who gave similar performances on the piano at the same house on 5 and 7 April 1797.

Macartney, Alexander [fl. 1775–1800], *actor, singer, manager*.

The late William Smith Clark's *Irish Stage in the County Towns* places the actor-manager Alexander Macartney in Ireland from 1775 to 1795. He managed the theatre at Lisburn in 1775. In November 1780 he took over the playhouse in Kilkenny, redecorated it, and opened with *She Stoops to Conquer* on the twenty-fifth. His company performed only until Christmas, but Macartney was again in Kilkenny in 1781. In July and August 1782 he leased from Daly the theatre in Limerick. His activities for the following ten years are not known, but he purchased an interest in the Kirwan's Lane playhouse in Galway in 1792, refurbished it completely, and opened in the summer with Smithson's strolling company. Macartney was still running the theatre there in 1795, though he had toured to Cork in the winter of 1792–93.

On 14 October 1799 he made his first appearance in London, playing Lysimachus in *The Rival Queens* at Covent Garden Theatre. The *Monthly Mirror* critic was guarded:

He is a fine heroic figure, with an expressive countenance, and a powerful voice. He was received with the most flattering approbation, but we are not at present enabled to form any very favorable judgment of his talents in the tragic department of the drama. He has the reputation, however, of being a singer of considerable humor, and a good representative of Irish characters.

The periodical noted that in the summer of 1799 Macartney had appeared at Margate. There, according to the *Thespian Dictionary* in 1805, "a dispute arose between him and some gentlemen, who took an opportunity of insulting him when on the stage. . . ." Macartney silenced them with a speech.

Thomas Dutton in *The Dramatic Censor* (1800) was greatly impressed with the Irish actor:

Mr. MACARTNEY, in our opinion, possesses one of the finest voices on the stage. His delivery is far superior, as being more distinct, than that of Mr. H[enry Erskine] Johnston. Every word he utters is clearly heard; yet he never fatigues himself, nor puts the audience in pain, after the example of the gentleman just mentioned, by the violence and impetuosity of his enunciation.

During his London engagement Alexander Macartney also played Captain Clifford in *The Irish Mimic*, Cornwall in *King Lear*, Pat in *The Mouth of the Nile*, the Irish Shipbuilder in *The Volcano*, and Captain Arable in *Speculation*. Charles Justin Macartney also performed at Covent Garden that winter, but he seems to have appeared only once. Alexander Macartney was at Covent Garden until 17 May 1800, after which we have not been able to trace him.

Macartney, Charles Justin [fl. 1799–1800], *actor, playwright*.

Charles Justin Macartney, whose initials were sometimes given as C. I., performed at Edinburgh and York before making his first London appearance as Romeo to Mrs Pope's Juliet at Covent Garden Theatre on 9 December 1799. He was not given an engagement for the season, and he apparently appeared only that one time. Another Macartney, Alexander, acted at Covent Garden the full season. The presence of the two Macartneys confused people. The *Monthly Mirror* noted: "Mr. C. J. Macartney,—who appeared at Covent Garden in Romeo, is confounded with the Mr. Macartney who appeared in Lysimachus. . . ."

After leaving London, Charles Justin Macartney acted at Birmingham in the summer of 1800 and there, after a short courtship, married Anne Minton, a girl of fifteen. The *Gentleman's Magazine* in October 1800 reported the marriage and mentioned that Macartney was 40 years old. The *Thespian Dictionary* (1805) report confused C. J. Macartney with Alexander. Upcott's *Biography of Living Authors* in 1816 said Macartney was the author of a comedy titled *The Vow*, published about 1800 in Sheffield. What happened to Macartney after 1800 we know not, but Mrs Macartney was performing at the Royal Circus as late as 1808.

Macartney, Mrs Charles Justin. *See* MINTON, ANNE.

Macawinny. *See* SWINEY.

Macburney, Mrs James. *See* ELLIS, REBECCA.

Macchierini, Giuseppa, later Signora Giovanni Ansani [*fl.* 1782], *singer.*

Giuseppa Macchierini made her English debut at the King's Theatre on 12 January 1782 singing Tullia in *Giunio Bruto*. Though she was hired as the first woman in the opera company, she disappointed everyone so thoroughly that she was evidently not cast in any other roles that were cited in the bills. She became the wife of the singer Giovanni Ansani, who was noted for his temperamental behavior. According to Dr Burney, the couple quarreled constantly. To Burney she was a

peevish, affected, and unfortunate wife; who, if ever she *had* a voice, lost it before her arrival in this country. I never could receive any pleasure from her performance; every note, feeble as it was, she squeezed out with such difficulty, and with a look so cross and miserable, that after her first exhibition I never wished more either to see or hear the *Signora Maccherini*, who was so proper a match for her husband in sweetness of disposition, that in Italy, when employed in the same theatre, if one happened to be applauded more than the other, they have been known *mutually* to employ persons to hiss the successful rival.

She had apparently been a favorite on the Continent at one time, and after her first appearance in Florence had run off with an English nobleman "in her stage dress, before the performance was over."

MacClean. *See also* MACLEAN.

MacClean, Mr [*fl.* 1749–1750]. *See* MCNEIL, GORDON.

McClean, Mr [*fl.* 1765], *dancer.*

A Mr McClean made his only recorded appearance on the stage, dancing at the Haymarket Theatre at a performance of *The Gentle Shepherd* on 16 May 1765.

McClue, Mrs [*fl.* 1774–1775], *dancer.*

Mrs McClue is listed in a document in the Forster Collection at the Victoria and Albert Museum as a dancer at Drury Lane Theatre in 1774–75.

M'Cready. *See* MACREADY.

Macculla, [Thomas?] [*fl.* 1741?–1747], *boxkeeper.*

Mr "Maccula," one of the boxkeepers at Drury Lane, shared benefits on 14 May 1746 and 14 May 1747. Quite possibly he was the Thomas Macculla whose son Charles was buried at St Paul, Covent Garden, on 2 June 1741 and whose wife Alice was buried there on 20 June.

McDonald, Mr [*fl.* 1772–1795?], *singer, actor.*

Mr McDonald (sometimes M'Donald or Macdonald) performed occasionally in specially-licensed productions at the Haymarket Theatre given by players from Scotland between 1772 and 1785. His first advertised appearance was as Patie in *Patie and Roger; or, The Gentle Shepherd* on 21 September 1772. He also sang Patie on 20 February 1775 and 20 November 1775 (when he also offered the song "Terry Woo") on 22 April 1777, 11 January 1779 and 17 January 1780 (when he also played Drover Henpeck in *The Students*), 18 March and 9 April 1782, 9 February 1784, and 24 January 1785. Perhaps he was the McDonald who performed at the Theatre Royal, Edinburgh, in the spring of 1795.

Macdonald, Mr [*fl.* 1778–1812], *doorkeeper, actor.*

Mr Macdonald was a house servant at Drury Lane Theatre by 25 May 1778, when he shared benefit tickets with the boxkeeper Barrett. Macdonald's name continued to be listed in the theatre's account books through the 1811–12 season. His salary in 1796–97 seems to have been £2 2s. per week. By 1801–2 he was identified in the accounts as a doorkeeper. During the 1789–90 season our subject may have temporarily transferred his allegiance to Covent Garden, where on 12 June 1790 a Mr McDonald shared benefit tickets with house personnel and on 16 June a Mr Macdonald acted the Servant in *The Country Girl*.

McDonald, Mr [*fl.* 1793?–1805], *equestrian.*

Mr McDonald was an equestrian performer at the Royal Circus, London, by 17 April 1795. His name appeared in Royal Circus advertisements in July 1797, August 1801, October 1804, and May and June 1805.

Possibly he was the equestrian of that name who performed at the Circus in Greenwich Street, New York, in 1793–94 and 1794–95 and at Rickett's Amphitheatre in Philadelphia from October 1795 to December 1799, but he would have had to make several fast trans-Atlantic trips to accommodate such a schedule. The American McDonald had a wife who sang at New York and Philadelphia in 1798 and 1799. A Mr McDonald, probably not the same person, was a singing actor in New York and Philadelphia between 1798 and 1805 and in Charleston between 1806–7 and 1811–12.

Macdonald, Archibald [*fl.* 1699], *swordsman.*

The *Post Boy* carried an announcement that on 1 April 1699 "at the New Red Theatre in Winchester Street, Southwark, next Door to the Pair of Tongues and Keys, will be perform'd a curious Trial of Skill at Back-sword, Single-Rapier, Quarter-Staff, &c. between Archibald Macdonald, late of Dublin; and Dapper Daniel of Abington, for Fifty Guinea's. . . ." The exhibition also included a wrestling match and some songs and dances (the full bill is in Dapper Daniel's entry).

Macdonald, Duncan [*fl.* 1753], *equilibrist.*

Disher in *The Greatest Show on Earth* says that the Scottish equilibrist Duncan Macdonald performed in the Sadler's Wells Musick House. As the descriptive engraving of 1753 (this page) shows, the Caithness acrobat was quite accomplished.

Macdonald, Samuel [*fl.* 1791–1794], *giant, performer.*

Samuel Macdonald was the Prince of Wales's porter at Carlton House between 1791 and

Harvard Theatre Collection

DUNCAN MACDONALD
engraving after Biotard

Harvard Theatre Collection

SAMUEL MACDONALD, the Prince's Porter, in *Cymon*

artist unknown

1794. He was called "Big Sam" because of his height of six feet, 10 inches. His Highland dress, which consisted of a tartan, sporran with the prince's feathers as a crest, and feathered cap, made him also known as "the Prince's Highlander."

Advertisements published in the spring of 1791 indicated that Macdonald was part of an exhibition at the Lyceum, in the Strand, promoted by G. Pidcock:

to be seen alive . . . The Double-jointed IRISH DWARF, whose strength is beyond conception. He will engage to carry two of the largest men now existing; as he, a few days back, carried Mr. O'Brian, the Irish Giant, and Mr. Samuel M'Donald, the Prince of Wales's porter, both at the same time.

A crude print by an unknown engraver, published by W. Locke on 1 February 1792, depicts "Big Sam" in *Cymon*; he is skirted in military garb and wields a large club against a tiny female figure. The print marks his appearance in a revival of that dramatic romance by the Drury Lane Company at the King's Theatre on 31 December 1791. "The Prince of Wales' Highlander made one of the procession," reported Michael Kelly in his *Reminiscences*, "and entered the lists as a champion, fighting with an enormous club; against him a small female warrior was opposed, by whom he was subdued." *Cymon* was performed 36 times before the end of that season.

An engraving by J. Kay published as a plate to his *Edinburgh Characters* shows Macdonald standing between the dwarf George Cranstoun and a soldier. Macdonald also appears in two scenes described in the *Catalogue of Political and Personal Satires in the British Museum*: Cruikshank's engraving entitled "A Visit to the Farm House" (No 7905), published on 1 October 1791, and Sayers's engraving entitled "Citizen Bardolph Refused Admittance at Prince Hal's" (No 8441), published on 17 March 1794.

MacDougall, Mr [*fl.* 1800], *house servant?*

Mr MacDougall, probably a house servant, had benefit tickets out for the performance at Drury Lane Theatre on 14 June 1800.

M'George. *See* MACGEORGE.

McGeorge, Miss [*fl.* 1774–1790], *actress.*

Miss McGeorge, who was probably the daughter of the provincial players Mr and Mrs Horatio Thomas McGeorge (both occasionally acted at London), was a member of the company at York in 1774 and 1775, and in the latter year she acted at Derby and Cambridge. No doubt she had other engagements in the provinces with her parents. Hired at a salary of £1 10s. per week, she first appeared at Covent Garden Theatre on 21 September 1789, when she sang in Juliet's funeral procession. On 30 September she acted Angelica in *The Constant Couple* and then sang in *Macbeth* on 12 October. After appearing as Mrs D'Arcey in *The Nunnery* on 11 November, she played a Female Milliner in *Harlequin's Chaplet*, James Wild's pantomime which was premiered on 21 December and was performed a total of 45 times before the end of the season.

McGeorge, Horatio Thomas [fl. 1752?–1795?], actor, musician.

Thomas Horatio McGeorge, who had a long but undistinguished career in the provinces, may have been the actor of that surname with the company at Richmond and Twickenham in the summer of 1752. McGeorge's roles during that engagement included a Tradesman in *Aesop*, a Constable in *The Recruiting Officer*, Diana Trapes in *The Beggar's Opera*, Martin in *The Anatomist*, Catesby in *Jane Shore*, Jasper in *Miss in Her Teens*, Sir Charles Freeman in *The Beaux' Stratagem*, Cash in *Everyman in His Humour*, Order in *A New Way to Pay Old Debts*, Alonzo in *The Mourning Bride*, Vernon in *Henry IV*, Mercury in *Lethe*, the Justice in *The Provok'd Wife*, Cimberton in *The Conscious Lovers*, Perriwinkle in *A Bold Stroke for a Wife*, and Beau Tippet in *The Lying Lover*. McGeorge acted at Smock Alley Theatre, Dublin, in 1760–61 and at the New Concert Hall, Edinburgh, in November 1762, when he played Vizard in *The Constant Couple* on the eleventh.

In 1762 McGeorge was at the Haymarket Theatre acting in what was characterized by Philip Lewis as "Foote's company of bladders, which he took particular pains to blow up for the summer season." McGeorge was involved in *The Orators*—Foote's "Oratorical Lectures"—which opened on 1 May 1762 for 36 performances. Subsequently McGeorge returned to the provinces, surfacing first at Edinburgh in 1763 and 1764 (acting Clermont in *The Miser* on 30 June 1764). He was at Derby with Parson's company in September 1765 and with Miller's company in February 1769. Foote brought him back to the Haymarket in the summer of 1766 (now accompanied by Mrs McGeorge), when he played Dick in *The Minor*, Roger in *The Mayor of Garratt*, Dapper in *The Citizen*, and several similar roles. In August he transferred to Barry's company at the King's Theatre to act a Messenger in *Othello*, officers in *Venice Preserv'd* and *King Lear*, Tibalt in *Romeo and Juliet*, Puff in *Miss in Her Teens*, Poundage in *The Provok'd Husband*, a Frenchman in *Lethe*, Rosano in *The Fair Penitent*, and Le Beau in *As You Like It*.

After spending the summer of 1770 at the Haymarket, McGeorge went to play the 1770–71 season at Bath. Soon after, he joined Wilkinson's company on the York circuit. That manager related in his *Wandering Patentee* a tale of McGeorge's impersonation of the younger Charles Fleetwood one night at Beverley in order to fool the bailiff and allow Fleetwood's escape to Kingston-upon-Hull. Wilkinson wrote "it was the best part that *dead* good actor ever performed," adding a footnote that defined "*dead*" as a "theatrical phrase for a very bad actor." Perhaps Wilkinson was also punning and McGeorge was truly dead by 1795, the year of Wilkinson's book.

McGeorge was seen at Derby in September 1775, at Chester in September 1779, and at Edinburgh in 1782. In May 1782 the *Scots Magazine* reported that Horatio Thomas McGeorge, a "musician and comedian," had stood trial for assault. A Mr McGeorge, hailing from the Bath theatre, played at Londonderry in 1794, but that actor may have been the young man, who, as Master McGeorge, had been performing with his family at Derby by November 1771.

Charles Lee Lewes described Horatio Thomas McGeorge as an incorrigible braggart, who was called by all who knew him "the most noble The Marquis of Hatchet, which name he obtained from throwing that metaphorical tool further than most of his competitors in the art of lying, with an unembarrassed countenance." The affected McGeorge carried about "a beautiful scymitar, which, in the rural greenrooms, he would often kiss with the greatest extacy."

McGeorge, Mrs Horatio Thomas [fl. 1765–1796], actress.

Mrs McGeorge, wife of the provincial player Horatio Thomas McGeorge, was performing at Edinburgh in 1765, when in February she headed a company revolt recounted by Tate Wilkinson in his *Memoirs*. In the summer of 1766 she and her husband were members of Foote's company at the Haymarket Theatre; she acted Tag in *Miss in Her Teens* on 18 June and then played Mrs Harlow in *The Old Maid*, Mrs Gadabout in *The Lying Valet*, Maria in *The Citizen*, and Dorinda in *The Beaux' Stratagem*. In August and September she also worked for Spranger Barry at the King's Theatre, appearing as Tag, Grace in *The Provok'd Husband*, Serina in *The Orphan*, Phillis in *The Conscious Lovers*, Celia in *As You Like It*, and Lavinia in *The Fair Penitent*.

After playing at Bath in 1770–71 and Derby

in 1771–72, she joined Wilkinson's Yorkshire company at Leeds in the summer of 1772, making her debut there as the *Countess of Salisbury*; but she "by no means made the usual impression on the audience," reported Wilkinson, as "she had done so often at the head of a little company, in a playhouse only the size of a tap-room." She had a 'well-formed figure, [was] in the prime of life,' and by degrees grew in the audience's esteem during the three years she remained with Wilkinson.

In the fall of 1774 Mrs McGeorge engaged with Whitley's company, playing at Derby that September and at Cambridge in September 1775. By the latter year her daughter was a vocalist in the troupe. Her son, Master McGeorge, had already begun to earn his keep in the Derby company by 1771.

On 22 April 1786 the Newcastle *Chronicle* had announced Mrs McGeorge's death, "lately," at Liverpool, but on 20 May the report was retracted as unfounded. Announced as from the Tunbridge Wells Theatre, Mrs McGeorge acted at Drury Lane Theatre for one night only, 6 December 1786, as Andromache in *The Distrest Mother*, with John Kemble as Orestes and Mrs Siddons as Hermione. After four more years in the provinces, including some time at Norwich in 1789, she returned to London on 16 April 1792 to play the Duchess of York in *Richard III* at the Haymarket. In that performance, for the benefit of the Literary Fund, the male parts were acted chiefly by amateurs and the female parts were acted by professionals.

Mrs McGeorge was at Richmond in 1795 and at Belfast in 1795 and 1796. At Tunbridge Wells on 1 September 1796 she was announced as making her first appearance in four years. That night she offered "a description of the tempers of Spanish, Dutch, French, Italian, and English husbands."

M'Grath, Cornelius 1736–1760, *giant.*

A newspaper obituary at the Huntington Library reported the death on 16 May 1760 of "The Irish Giant":

Dublin, May 20. Friday died, in College-Green, Cornelius M'Grath, the late Irish giant, born in the county of Tipperary, within five miles of the silver mines, in the year 1736. His parents were no way remarkable for their stature, being of the middle-size, and were common country people; nor

By permission of the Trustees of the British Museum
CORNELIUS M'GRATH
artist unknown

were their other children taller than ordinary. In July, 1752, Cornelius was in the city of Cork, being then about 16 years of age, and was followed about by crouds of people, on account of his extraordinary size, for he then measured six feet eight inches and three quarters. The preceding year he was much afflicted with violent pains in his limbs, for which he bathed in the salt water; however, these were no other than growing pains; for he actually grew from little more than five feet to the above-mentioned stature in the space of one year. The good Dr. Berkley, then Bishop of Cloyne, kept him at his house for two or three months, and was very charitable and humane to him, and caused great care to be taken of him until he recovered the use of his limbs. His hand was then as large as a middling shoulder of mutton; and the last of his shoes, which he carried about with him, measured 15 inches. He always eat and drank very moderately; his drink was then chiefly cyder, and that he took only at meals. When he was at Cork he was persuaded to exhibit himself as a show; and he went for that purpose to Bristol, and from thence to London; and an account was given of him in the London Magazine for July 1752. He afterwards went to Paris, and to most of the great cities of Europe. At Florence, one Bianchi, a physician there, wrote a small tract concerning him. About two months ago he returned to his native country, and then measured seven feet eight inches without shoes. When he arrived he was in a very bad state of health, owing as he said, to an intermitting fever that he had been first seized with in Flanders. His complexion was miserably pale and sallow, his pulse very quick at times for a man of his extraordinary heighth, and his legs were swollen. Upon his death, his body was carried to the dissecting-house in the College; where his skeleton, on account of its extraordinary size, will amuse the curious, and fill posterity with wonder.

In the British Museum is an engraving of "Magrath" with a guardsman standing under his outstreatched arm.

Macgregor, John [*fl.* 1791–1794], *piper.*
At Covent Garden Theatre on 18 May 1791 was held "The HIGHLAND COMPETITION PRIZE, exactly as represented annually in the city of Edinburgh" by Maclane, Mactavish, and Macgregor. The last-named was probably John Macgregor, a bagpiper listed in Doane's *Musical Directory* of 1794 as resident at "Mr. Balnearis's, Edradont," meaning at Henry Balneave's in Endradour, a small place near Pitochry, Perthshire.

As William A. Cocks points out in a note to *Music & Letters*, XXX, the Macgregors were a famous piping family who lived at Fortingale, Perthshire. Their instrument was the Great Highland Bagpipe. A John Macgregor was piper to Colonel Campbell of Glen Lyon and at the age of 73 won third prize in the competition held at Falkirk in 1781, when Patrick (or Peter) Macgregor, piper to Balneaves, won first prize. Others named John Macgregor, any one of whom could have been the Covent Garden piper, included first prize winners: of Fortingall, 1784; of Strathtay, 1788; of the Breadalbane Fencibles, 1793; of London, 1806; of the 73rd Regiment, 1808; and of no address, 1811. In 1785 three John Macgregors had competed: John of Fortingall, John of Glen Lyon, and John junior, son of the latter, aged 12.

McGuffock, Mr [*fl.* 1783–1785], *constable.*
Mr McGuffock was a constable at the King's Theatre from 1783 to 1785, according to the Lord Chamberlain's accounts. Perhaps he was related to William Montgomery McGuffolk, who married Mary Taylor at St George, Hanover Square, on 16 March 1800.

MacGuire, Mr [*fl.* 1733], *actor.*
A Mr MacGuire played the Bawd in *The Harlot's Progress* at Mile End Green on 28 September 1733.

MacGuire, Mr [*fl.* 1760–1768?], *actor.*
Mr MacGuire (sometimes Maguire), who had been acting at the Smock Alley Theatre, Dublin, in 1760–61, made his debut at Covent Garden Theatre on 30 September 1761 as Frankly in *The Suspicious Husband.* That season he also appeared as Worthy in *The Recruiting Officer,* Poins in *2 Henry IV,* the Governor in *The Pilgrim,* Charles in *The Jealous Wife* (for a benefit he shared with Tindal on 1 May 1762), and Clerimont in *The Old Maid.* In *The Rosciad of C–v–nt G–rd–n* (1762), MacGuire was described as "dull."

Probably he was the Maguire who acted at Kilkenny in 1767 and 1768 with Mrs Maguire and Master Maguire. His wife played at Drury Lane, Covent Garden, and the Haymarket in 1761–62.

MacGuire, Mrs [*fl.* 1760–1768], *actress.*
Mrs MacGuire, wife of a minor Covent Garden actor, made her first appearance on 2 July 1761 as Miss Harlow in *The Old Maid,* performed at Drury Lane Theatre, which had been rented for that summer by Arthur Murphy and Samuel Foote. On 1 May 1762 she played the same role at Covent Garden Theatre, for her husband's benefit. Next summer she was again under Foote's management, this time at the Haymarket, where on 10 August 1762 she once more was seen as Miss Harlow. The listing in *The London Stage* of "Miss" Maguire for that part is evidently an error. That summer Mrs MacGuire also acted Mrs Honeycomb in *Polly Honeycomb.*

Probably she was the Mrs Maguire who, with husband and son, played at Kilkenny in 1767 and 1768.

McGusty, David [*fl.* 1740], *house servant?*
The Covent Garden accounts show a payment of 5s. 7d. on 20 November 1740 to

David McGusty "in full for his and his wife's wages & all Demands." The following day a correction was made and McGusty received an additional 15s. Perhaps he and his wife were house servants.

McGusty, Mrs David [fl. 1740], house servant? See MCGUSTY, DAVID..

Machen. See also MACHIN.

Machen, [Edward?] [fl. 1729–1749], actor.

Mr Machen (or Machin, Mechin, Meachen) was first noticed as Priuli in *Venice Preserv'd* at the Haymarket Theatre on 11 February 1729. The remainder of the season brought him out as an unnamed character in *The Loyal Captives*, Theorboe in *Hurlothrumbo*, Dervise in *Tamerlane*, Rapp in *The Smugglers*, and Cant in *The Beggar's Wedding*. In August at Bartholomew Fair Machen had roles in *The Beggar's Wedding* and *Damon and Phillida*. He joined the Goodman's Fields troupe for the 1729–30 season and appeared as Whisper in *The Busy Body*, a Bravo in *The Inconstant*, the Duke in *Venice Preserv'd*, Freeman in *A Bold Stroke for a Wife*, Hotman in *Oroonoko*, Raymond in *The Spanish Fryar*, Bardolph in *The Merry Wives of Windsor*, a Sailor in *The Fair Quaker of Deal*, Stephano in *The Rover*, Cornwall in *King Lear*, Brabantio in *Othello*, Drama in *The Fashionable Lady*, and Sir Charles in *The Fair Quaker of Deal*. He finished out the summer of 1730 playing at Tottenham Court and Bartholomew Fair.

Machen remained with Giffard at Goodman's Fields in 1730–31 trying such new roles as the Father in *The Devil of a Wife*, Raleigh in *The Unhappy Favorite*, Gratiano in *Othello*, a Mutineer in *Cato*, and Gonzalo in *The Tempest*. In September 1731 he acted at Fielding's booth at Southwark, after which he may have left London for a time. On 10 May 1732 he turned up at the Haymarket, playing Raymond in *The Spanish Fryar*, and he had a role there in *The Coquet's Surrender* on the fifteenth. The following 29 November at the Haymarket he acted Lord Valerius in *The Miseries of Love*, and then in the spring of 1733 he played there as Bajazet in *Tamerlane*, Old Heedless in *The Farmer's Son*, Sir Charles in *The Beaux' Stratagem*, Hellebore in *The Mock Doctor*, Thorowgood in *The London Merchant*, Father Martin in *The Old Debauchees*, and Kite in *The Recruiting Officer*.

On 19 January 1734 he was seen as Index and Sir John in *The Author's Farce*; then at the Haymarket in April and May he acted a Voter and Sir Thomas Loveland in *Don Quixote in England*, Leathersides in *The Covent Garden Tragedy*, and Blunt in *1 Henry IV*. In August at the same house he played Gibbet in *The Beaux' Stratagem* and Thorowgood in *The London Merchant*.

He next appeared in London at York Buildings in March 1735 with a group of younger players and acted Cassio in *Othello*, Charles in *Love Makes a Man*, and Lovegirlo in *The Covent Garden Tragedy*. In July and August he tried Lincoln's Inn Fields, playing Poundage in *The Provok'd Husband*, the Second Manager in *The Stage Mutineers*, Glumdalca and the first Bailiff in *The Tragedy of Tragedies*, Sulpitius in *Caius Marius*, a Watchman in *Bartholomew Fair*, and a Lawyer in *Love Makes a Man*. On 4 August, in the middle of that engagement, he was at the Haymarket as Chamont in *The Orphan*.

Machen acted mostly at the Haymarket in 1735–36, playing such roles as Gloster in *Jane Shore*, Rodulpho in *The Carnival*, Ballance in *The Recruiting Officer*, Morelove in *The Careless Husband*, Old Mirabel in *The Inconstant*, Sneerwell in *Pasquin*, King Arthur in *The Tragedy of Tragedies*, a Player in *The Beggar's Opera*, and the Duke of Rum in *The Deposing and Death of Queen Gin*. Within that engagement he assisted Charlotte Charke at York Buildings by playing, in late September and early October 1735, Bloodbolt in *The Art of Management* and Thorowgood in *George Barnwell*. In the spring of 1737 he was again at the Haymarket with Fielding's troupe, playing a Patriot and a Politician in *The Historical Register* and a Gentleman and an Actor in *Eurydice Hiss'd*. After that Machen was not mentioned in London advertisements for several years.

At the James Street Theatre on 7 April 1742 Machen appeared as Lusignan in *Zara*, and the following 31 May he acted the title role in *Ulysses*. His next venture was at the same playhouse on 5 January 1743, when he played Dorax in *Don Sebastian*. Then, after a long absence, he appeared at Southwark Fair in September 1748 as Alonso in *The Tempest*. A year later at Bartholomew Fair he played Caliban in the same work. One Edward Machen subscribed in 1746 to the *Works* of Henry Ward, and Charles Beecher Hogan has suggested that perhaps he was the actor.

Machen was given considerable attention in Hill's *The Actor* in 1750. Hill discussed Richard III, which Machen evidently played somewhere at some point:

we have had a proof that even the peculiar bodily imperfection which is mentioned in the play itself as belonging to the heroe of it; and which we even expect the performer shou'd counterfeit to us by bolsters and bandages, yet if he be unhappy enough really to possess it, he offends us in the representation. There is some where about town a person of the name of Machen, who had been long the darling of the theatres at the Blue Boar, the Tennis Court in James-Street, and sometimes of the Bartholomew Booths; and who has of late been honour'd with the title of the lame actor of low comedy in Mr. Foot's drolleries. This person has, from an habitual attendance on the players, and a labour'd imitation of them for perhaps forty years together, acquir'd a knack of speaking something that sounds like tragedy declamation. It is his misfortune to be lame of one leg; which is so much shorter than the other, that the highest heel he can wear is not enough to raise that side of his body to a level with the rest. Tragedy is the darling passion of this player, and he concluded, from this natural imperfection, he was the fittest of all men to perform the character of Richard III, which Shakespeare himself (with how much justice we do not presume to say) has figured to us as lame.

Vast were the expectations of applause with which this man had flatter'd himself, when he should come to that part of the character where this peculiar natural defect, by which he thought himself qualified to perform the part, should come on: But what was the event? The audience, when he hop'd across the stage as he spoke the line,

Dogs bark at me as I halt by them,

instead of the applause he listen'd for, burst out into a loud laugh. They could never reconcile themselves to have an original imposed on them, when they expected or desir'd no more than a copy.

Machin. *See also* **MACHEN**.

Machin, Mr [*fl.* 1774–1784], *singer.*

On 28 November 1774 Mr Machin was paid £6 by Drury Lane Theatre for singing in the chorus for 24 nights. The accounts in the late 1770s indicated that he was probably not a regular member of the company but was hired as an occasional extra singer, usually for 5*s*. nightly. In 1776–77 the accounts described him as a "contra alto." His name was variously spelled: Michim, Meachum, Mitchim, and, in the bill for *Macbeth* on 25 November 1776, Michan. Dr Burney called him Machin when he listed him among the countertenors who sang in the Handel Memorial Concerts at Westminster Abbey and the Pantheon in May and June 1784.

Machin, O'Brien [*fl.* 1778], *actor.*

On 9 February 1778 O'Brien Machin, hailed as from the Crow Street Theatre in Dublin, played Dumont in *Jane Shore* at the Haymarket Theatre in London. He was probably the Machin who acted Shylock in *The Merchant of Venice* at the temporary booth theatre used by the troupe from the China Hall Theatre, Rotherhithe, on 30 August.

Illustrations

MUSIC AND MUSICIANS

From the Collection of Edward A. Langhans

"The Chorus" (1732)
by Hogarth

"The Music Master" (c. 1733)

By permission of the Trustees of the British Museum

A satire on the English admiration for foreign musicians (c. 1730)

Folger Shakespeare Library

A song by Richard Leveridge (1744)

Folger Shakespeare Library

Music by Lampe for *The Dragon of Wantley*

Folger Shakespeare Library

The 1784 Handel Memorial Concert at Westminster Abbey
from Burney's *Account of Musical Performances* (1785)